CW01391466

WELL BEINGS

How the Seventies Lost Its Mind and Taught Us to Find Ourselves

James Riley

ICON

Published in the UK and USA in 2024 by
Icon Books Ltd, Omnibus Business Centre,
39–41 North Road, London N7 9DP
email: info@iconbooks.com
www.iconbooks.com

ISBN: 978-178578-789-8
ebook: 978-178578-790-4

Text copyright © 2024 James Riley

The author has asserted his moral rights.

No part of this book may be reproduced in any form, or by any
means, without prior permission in writing from the publisher.

Typesetting by SJmagic DESIGN SERVICES, India

Printed and bound in the UK

Contents

PART II: THIS FLOATING WORLD

The Voyage In   359

Alan Watts talks about dreams. Cruise ships set off again. Exploring the inner oceans of the post-viral landscape. Dreaming differently. Having the courage to ask the most radical question of all.

The Voyage Out

From the main deck of the *Celebrity Edge*, the entire ocean looks like an infinity pool. Launched in 2018 and costing a cool billion, the *Edge* is the flagship liner of the high-end travel company Celebrity Cruises. As well as a 1,000-strong crew, the *Edge* can accommodate nearly 3,000 guests in an ambience of spacious opulence. There are grand state rooms, multilevel villas, a portfolio of restaurants, the inevitable shopping concourse and the main deck itself: a rooftop plaza of gardened spaces and heated pools resting some fifteen storeys – 128 feet – above sea level. At this height the nuances of the sea recede, and the panorama dominates. Aside from its amenities, the privilege of this view is one of the main luxuries of a trip on the *Edge*. As 'the most refined ship at sea' it places its guests luxuriously *nowhere*: out of time and out of place. The numerous stops on its Atlantic and Mediterranean itineraries are, of course, full of local colour but in between, when the *Edge* glides quietly across the ocean, life on board becomes a pleasing experience of *drift*. Passengers reclining on the roof deck get the full spectacle of this calm movement: a featureless vista where the sea and sky are nothing but two shimmers of blue converging at the horizon.

Celebrity Cruises sell a piece of the celebrity lifestyle. Before the coronavirus pandemic took a massive bite out of the entire cruising industry, they excelled in offering guests aspirational holidays full of peak experiences, prestige service and the trappings of wealth (plus all-day, all-night, all-you-can-eat buffets). To that end the company regularly courted the great and the good to act as product partners and social media cheerleaders. Which is why, in what now seems like the far distant past of early 2019, the *Edge* welcomed a delegation from Gwyneth Paltrow's health and lifestyle brand Goop. Elise Loehnen, Goop's chief of content, and an entourage of Goop staffers came onboard to sample 'the ultimate in modern cruising'. By all accounts it did not disappoint. 'It's not that we were ever afraid of the water', trilled an unattributed write-up on the Goop website sometime after the trip, 'it's just that we've always enjoyed it from the perspective of the shore, with a drink and a book in arm's reach'. Having managed to wrench themselves away from this comfort zone, the Goopers found, unsurprisingly, that the *Edge* was one massive, floating comfort zone. Not only did its poolside plazas offer plenty of places to drink and read, but its elegant Suite-class rooms with their 'wall-to-wall glass [...] fragrant Le Labo personal care products and fluffy Frette robes' (not to mention personal butler service) made the huge ship feel like the 'chicest of penthouses'.

Strolling into the Grand Plaza, the *Edge*'s very own piazza – where you can sip espresso by day and take a martini by night – Loehnen and her party were spoilt for choice. Should they go for a glass of biodynamic wine at Blu, or order a plate of sashimi 'in the buzzy atmosphere of Raw on 5'? Eventually they opted for the virtuous, but no less luxurious, option of a few hours in the ship's gym and spa. Spread over two floors and accessed via a curving white staircase, the spa is a palace of marble and glass that offers a full menu of treatments: facials, acupuncture, reflexology, halotherapy and many more. Entering like souls offered passage to paradise, the Goopers found massage beds filled 'with warm quartz sand' the texture 'of a soft powder beach', subtle lighting precisely calibrated for colour therapy and a cloud of 'rattan pod-style seats suspended from the ceiling in the Float Room'. They each took a pod and were 'lulled to sleep by the gentle swaying'. It is a moment that sums up the excess of the *Edge*: onboard a ship that was gently floating across the sea, they chose a private experience that simulated the feeling of gently floating across the sea. Given that Goop was offered the full-on VIP treatment it's hardly surprising that, quid pro quo, they responded with some utterly uncritical brochure copy. However, beyond the sales pitch, Goop's account of a cruise on the *Edge* carries traces of a much older idea, one that is deeply inscribed into the human imagination: that of the sea voyage as a journey of transformation.[1]

In the mind-bending odysseys of Homer, Apollonius and Virgil, the sea in all its vastness and uncertainty is a space of the impossible. Those who head out into this fluid territory of giant monsters, whirlpools and uncharted islands are deeply affected by their experiences. Their oceans are watched over by the likes Neptune, Poseidon and, as in the case of the sacred Buddhist text the *Mahānipāta Jātaka*, the goddess Manimekhala. These are the deities who rescue sailors, control the weather or otherwise consign the unfavourable to the waves. In these stories, taking to the water is not just a matter of finding safe passage, it is also a rite of passage. The star-led captains who make it to the other side or who gloriously return to port are often not the same as those who began the journey. Somewhere out there, in full fathom, as the water took them or as they reached the peak of enormous waves, they changed, and often for the better.

So too for those aboard Sebastian Brant's *Narrenschiff*, the 'Ship of Fools' that glides through the 'imaginary landscape of the renaissance' in search of lost reason, as Michel Foucault elegantly put it. The same could be said of Samuel Taylor Coleridge's mariner who endures a torturous, albatross-heavy voyage in his journey towards redemption. And so it was for the sea-bound Goop contingent. If they were seeking deep relaxation, the pods and the other spa treatments seemed to do the trick. But later, when trying out the gym with its Peloton bikes and hot yoga, Loehnen and company noticed a subtle but distinct change of mood. Running on the treadmills, facing the glacial sea as if there was no window between, they began to lose their moorings. Their outlines faded: 'We fell quickly into rhythm with the waves.' Sigmund Freud called this sense of unbounded oneness a feeling of the 'oceanic'. For the Goopers it was a revitalising moment of aquatic ease. Having previously been tied to the comforts of the shore, the team found themselves eagerly slipping into this new state: 'We're definitely water people.'²

✱✱✱✱✱

Since it launched online in 2008, Goop has grown into a business empire worth some $250 million and in so doing it has become the market leader in the contemporary wellness industry. This burgeoning commercial sector is driven by 'consumer interest in exercise, healthy eating, self-care, mindfulness, stress reduction, healthy aging, complementary medicine, holistic health' and many other on-trend practices. With an estimated global value of $4.5 trillion the wellness industry is a contemporary success story but neither the word nor the concept is new. The first written record of 'wellness' dates to 1654 and can be found in a diary entry by the Scottish statesman Archibald Johnston, Lord Wariston. Writing with poignant relief, he records that his daughter has recovered from a period of illness and he blesses God for her present *wealnesse*. As James William Miller puts it, Lord Wariston 'meant simply that his daughter was no longer ill'. Here 'wellness' was used as an 'antonym of illness' and this 'continued to be the common meaning of the term until the middle of the twentieth century'. At this point, in the light of the reconstructive politics of the post-1945 period, the word took on a more specialised meaning. In the work of the American physician and biostatistician Halbert L. Dunn, wellness, or 'high-level wellness' as he termed it, described an aspirational rather than a functional state of health. Writing across the 1950s and early 1960s, Dunn advocated for a movement beyond treatment models that, in his view, sought only to alleviate the symptoms of disease. He was not interested in 'patching up', nor did he believe that such a makeshift approach was sufficient for the challenges and opportunities of the post-war world. Instead he wanted to inspire an appetite for the zestful, maximised fulfilment of individual and social potential.[3]

Later, as the countercultural projects of the 1960s began to merge with the New Age beliefs, speculative therapies, and health-focused attitudes of the 1970s, Dunn's ideas were gradually embraced by those seeking an alternative to 'conventional' medicine. Programmes offered by the Wellness Resource Center in California's Marin County, founded by Dr John Travis in 1975, sought to foster this sense of affirmative self-responsibility by teaching clients how to, in his words, 'diagnose common illnesses and, where possible, to treat themselves'. Heavily influenced by Dunn, Travis worked on the principle that 'health is not simply the absence of disease' and, as such, his intention was neither to diagnose nor prescribe but rather to help clients 'discover why they are sick'. To that end he encouraged a thorough examination of their 'whole lifestyle: their diet, work habits and physical activities'. With this holistic approach at its heart, wellness emerged as a lifestyle choice oriented towards 'optimal health' and the achievement of your 'highest potential for well-being'. As Dan Rather put it on the American television show *60 Minutes* in 1979 when he reported on Travis' work, wellness was 'the ultimate in […] self-care'.[4]

At the same time, terms like 'self-care' were generating significant political currency among the period's feminist and civil rights movements. As Aisha Harris puts it, in the 1970s 'women and people of color viewed controlling their health as a corrective to the failures of a white, patriarchal medical system to properly tend to their needs'. For a wide range of activist groups, undoing the link between poverty and ill health was a key target in the overall struggle against inequality. As such, taking on the responsibility of self-care was a way to achieve an autonomous, empowered state of personal and political advancement.[5]

In contrast, the high-net-worth, 21st-century version of wellness appears to have lost much of this radicalism. As Daniela Blei has described, it seems that 'wellness' and 'self-care' have become catch-all terms to describe the rapid rise of 'juice bars, meditation retreats [and] detox diets'. For the pharmaceutical company Pfizer, the emphasis remains on the idea of 'thriving' rather than 'surviving', while the Global Wellness Institute similarly defines wellness as 'the active pursuit of activities, choices and lifestyles that lead to a state of holistic health'. However, the attainment of such optimal gains now seems more like a matter of leisure than health, a recalibration that is very much to the detriment of those most in need of a holistic model of care. For example, Latin America was one of the most buoyant sectors of the wellness market in terms of its pre-lockdown travel opportunities. Its spas, health hotels and glamping sites saw exponential growth in the decades leading up to 2020. At the same time, though, domestic health care funding underwent a significant decline. If you were fortunate enough to be able to travel to Brazil or Colombia for a spiritual detox you would have found a healthy and welcoming market. If, however, you lived there and needed basic care, it is likely that you would have encountered the sharp end of economic inequality: severe privations and a considerable lack of access. The continuing worldwide impact of the pandemic has served only to widen this 'wellness divide'. [6]

Contemporary wellness brands sell an attractive lifestyle that is superficially depoliticised and philosophically diluted. For Goop, wellness is a 'deeply individual' but largely non-specific approach to personal health, in which 'the mind' is never removed from 'a conversation about the body', nor 'the body from a conversation about the mind'. Similar companies like WellCo, Well+Good and Thrive Global, not to mention a wave of bloggers, Instagrammers and influencers, work in the same vein, offering what typically amounts to a combination of self-help, product-focused diets and secularised spirituality. With their spectacles of aspirational health – often made by and for an affluent, white, middle-class demographic – wellness brands typically cherry-pick from a rich history of global food cultures, New Age ideas and religious traditions. The resulting products are lucrative, palatable and often peculiarly anodyne: websites and books which, in Hadley Freeman's words, 'mix recipes with vague nutritional advice and, of course, many, many photos'. In the world of wellness, yoga can be added to your daily routine as easily as goji berries to a smoothie. If that doesn't work, you can just swipe onto the next screen and watch the latest vlogs about crystal therapy or energy cleansing. The idea is that this restless (or in Goop's terms 'curious' and 'open-minded') movement from one product to the next will not just keep you generally healthy but will also open a path to fulfilment. It will help you find your better, truer self.[7]

To its advocates, wellness is a vital toolkit. The word describes a set of techniques that bring moments of calm into the accelerated pace of modern life. It's often said that pursuing wellness helps people realise their potential and achieve their goals, and that in their championing of women's health the likes of Goop and WellCo offer platforms of support that are ever more necessary in the post-#MeToo world. To its detractors, however, not least Sir Simon Stevens, former head of NHS England, contemporary wellness is mere quackery: a confidence trick in which celebrities – with their disappearing jade eggs, their super elixirs and their expensive bags of stones – promise miracles by peddling little more than snake oil.[8]

Goop's detractors and defenders were equally on hand in January 2020 when the company announced, with great fanfare, their latest venture: 'Goop-At-Sea'. Having been suitably impressed with their time on the *Edge*, Goop pressed forwards and pitched a high-profile event to take place aboard her sister ship and Celebrity's flagship liner, the *Apex*. Intending to take full advantage of the *Apex*'s facilities – gourmet cuisine, plunge pools and a crystalarium – 'Goop-At-Sea' promised a grab-bag of 'transformative workshops' led by 'trailblazing healers', talks presented by 'fascinating culture changers' as well as the main event: an intimate Q&A with Paltrow herself. Promoting the cruise on the interview circuit, Paltrow offered a glimpse of the chat guests could expect. 'I love being on the water, I love being by the water, and I love being in the water,' she told *USA Today* with a typical combination of the vague and the obvious. 'I think, energetically, it's very cleansing to be near the sea or in the sea.'

Soon after, the Goop website warned that space would be limited and it encouraged readers to book before the full programme had even been finalised. This limit was not due to the close confines of the ship – like the *Edge*, the *Apex* had capacity for thousands of guests. Space would be limited because Goop's headline-grabbing, widely reported, heavily advertised, social-media-circulated 'ultimate getaway' was, from the outset, intended to be resolutely exclusive. Originally scheduled for August 2020, during Celebrity's eleven-night Mediterranean cruise, 'Goop-At-Sea' was only open to luxury-class passengers: those who were prepared to pay $4,200 for both the 'basic' cruise and a suite at the *Apex*'s onboard spa, 'The Retreat'. It was only then that these high rollers had the privilege of paying a further $750 for the event itself, a single day of 'goopy perks'. Hitting peak Goop at the apex of health, celebrity and cruising culture would thus be a snip at just under $5,000.[9]

Clearly, there is a distinct exceptionalism at play here in which the attractions of leisure and travel elevate the pursuit of wellness beyond the concerns and practicalities of social health. Based on its price tag alone 'Goop-At-Sea' says that in order to access the riches that come with *being well* you already need to have *done well*; you need to be standing high on the pyramid of available time and money. The seafaring modernists of Virginia Woolf's debut novel *The Voyage Out* (1915) come to mind here. Having reached the South American resort of Santa Marina after weeks on board the good ship *Euphrosyne* one of Woolf's ensemble, Mr Flushing, announces that he'd like to push into the further journey of a long life and carry on 'for a hundred years'. 'Think of all the things that are bound to happen!' he says before Mrs Thornbury, one of his fellow travellers, responds with a cheerful echo. With total faith in the progress of history, momentarily ignoring the recent, feverish death of another in their party, she looks forward to 'the changes, the improvements, the inventions—and beauty'. *The Voyage Out* was set in 1905 and those reading it in 1915 as Europe was sinking further into war may have had difficulty sharing Mrs Thornbury's optimism. More than a hundred years later, though, 'Goop-At-Sea' promised nothing but 'improvements' and 'beauty', on board a ship which according to Celebrity Cruises was 'designed to leave the future behind'. At a time when the modern ocean was a theatre of socio-political crisis, a disputed space in which the tragedies of migration, piracy and pollution played on without pause, 'Goop-At-Sea' invited its clients to float above it all; unhindered, unaware. 'A cruise does away with the most annoying aspects of travel,' gushed the sales pitch with all the ease of Mrs Thornbury. 'The details – every destination, reservation and breakfast pancake – are in the expert hands of someone else.'[10]

✲✲✲✲✲

In Alejandro Jodorowsky's film *The Holy Mountain* (1973), there is a scene in which a group of men and women seeking enlightenment embark on a sea voyage. In the company of a grinning alchemist, they try to reach the sacred site of the title. However surprising Elise Loehnen and the Goopers found their transformation into 'water people', this was nothing compared to the experiences of Jodorowsky's travellers. They are made to symbolically divest themselves of all the trappings of their former lives, which have to go overboard like so much excess baggage. It is only when they are free of their names, their clothes and their identities that they are truly ready to climb the mountain. It is a necessary ritual given the nature of their destination. Although they travel miles across the sea, Jodorowsky's characters are really voyaging inside their own heads. They are on their way to inner space. Here the problems of the mind can be encountered, the ego can be unravelled, and the 'self' can be recalibrated.

John Travis had a similar idea in mind when he published *The Wellness Index* (1975) and then later *The Wellness Workbook* (1981). Among other concepts he wrote of the 'Iceberg Model', the idea that in order to ease mental and physical ailments one must *go deep* into the personality to find the underlying root cause. Contemporary wellness, by contrast, appears to have moved very much in the opposite direction. The industry looks outwards towards business models that accumulate economic and cultural capital, that depend upon masthead personalities, that promise lives of resonating health by encouraging feelings of perpetual illness.[11]

That said, with its programme organised around the classic wellness trinity of the 'mind', the 'body' and the 'soul', 'Goop-At-Sea' was still coded as a personal, interior journey. As with the other key players in the wellness industry, Goop invited its guests on a voyage *out* that was equally a voyage *in*. While today's glossy websites are a far cry from the experimental therapy centres of the 1970s, there is a bridge between the pursuit of wellness then and the pursuit of wellness now when it comes to this exploration of an individualised inner space. The two industries also appealed to similar markets. Many of the alternative medicine and New Age retreats of the 1970s may have seemed like the preserve of hippie survivors but they advertised themselves towards the suburbs rather than the underground. They had in mind the type of affluent, comfortable but quietly fragile households who had fondue on the dinner table, Valium in the medicine cabinet and Alex Comfort's *The Joy of Sex* (1972) in the bedroom.

It is simply too easy to see the two versions as utterly polarised. Whenever the latest wellness trend is decried on account of its consumerism, its appeal to a luxury market and its invitation to narcissistic self-indulgence, these criticisms repeat objections levelled at the culture of well-being in the 1970s: the quintessential 'Me' decade. It was the author Tom Wolfe who bestowed this enduring title upon the period, by way of an essay he wrote for *New York* magazine in 1976. Wolfe had in mind the growing popularity of that decade's wellness and alternative health practices and in an argument that could easily apply to Goop and their contemporaries, he claimed they were generating a pervasive cultural solipsism. For Wolfe, health retreats were little more than playgrounds for the rich; holiday sites where navel-gazing white people could go to luxuriate through their mid- – or even quarter- – life crises. Wolfe was one of the main critical voices who helped frame the 'seventies' as a comedown decade, one in which the vibrant radicalism of the 'sixties' dwindled into a period of beige, suburban complacency. In this reading the anxieties of the prior decade remain, particularly those relating to nuclear power, inequality and generational tension, but for writers like Christopher Lasch – the American sociologist who dubbed the 1970s a 'culture of narcissism' – this new decade found the satisfaction of individual material needs taking priority over the fulfilment of a wider social agenda. If the 1960s were all about changing the world, the 1970s were all about changing yourself. It is an enduring story, one that often points to an arc of cultural decline extending out from the decade and reaching its nadir in the current smartphone-obsessed, selfie-fixated online era.[12]

Other versions of the 1970s see it as a time of socio-political and personal crisis, a veritable 'post-trauma' decade. In this telling, a wide range of therapists, writers, artists and practitioners variously responded to the idea of a 'sick' society – one defined by Watergate, international industrial discontent, the exhausting pace of modern life and what President Jimmy Carter termed in 1979 the 'Crisis of Confidence' – by striking out for inner spaces and questioning accepted notions of health, wealth and happiness. While the alleged narcissism of the decade may well have anticipated our own contemporary self-regard, the fifty-year gap between the 1970s and the 2020s also closes when it comes to this matter of crisis, personal and political. We are equally living through a time of trauma with global conflict, climate change, inequality, racism and misogyny standing alongside and feeding into poverty, housing emergencies and economic precarity. Add to this the enormous mortal and psychic implications of COVID-19 and it is clear that health and well-being should, more than ever, be on the agenda.[13]

'Goop-At-Sea' was one of the many, many events cancelled as the virus took hold. As well as the unfeasible logistics, one could easily argue that a celebrity-branded cruise was not what the world needed as the shutters came down. Advances in epidemiology are more of a priority during a semi-apocalyptic pandemic than luxury wellness holidays. However, the unprecedented experiences of lockdown, which sent many of us into our own inner spaces and from which some of us are yet to fully emerge, have since placed mental health at the centre of a web of intersectional support needs. As with other sectors of the health service, provision in this regard is suffering from significant privations. A period of intense anxiety and uncertainty requires a strategic therapeutic response and as we move further into a post-viral period, the work of Ministers for Mental Well-Being, access to online and offline therapy and the practice of robust self-care measures all need to be prioritised. With these imminent conversations in mind, then, it is necessary to reassess and in some cases remember what wellness could and should involve.

This is the focus of *Well Beings*: in charting the birth of modern wellness, it argues that the 1970s can point the way to such a re-examination. There is much that this often misunderstood and maligned decade can teach us – in both a cautionary and an instructive sense – about what it really means to be well. Terms like 'wellness', 'well-being' and 'self-care' have long histories, but they only really took root in the 1970s. These concepts, which seem so very 21st-century, started to gain traction over four decades ago at the meeting point of alternative medicine and the wider health care profession. Promising not just the absence of disease but a better, healthier and more fulfilled life, these methods, projects, diets and even cults offered an antidote to the strains of the modern world.

The 1970s marked the point where a generation of innovators and psychic explorers, borne out of the tumult of the 1960s and facing a new and uncertain world, set off into off into their own equally uncharted waters. These experimental voyages were grand adventures; sometimes perilous, often problematic, but not without potential. Buried within them are maps of our own road to recovery, not least because the world they were responding to was busy rolling out mobile phones, credit cards and the tendrils of the internet, the very engines of alienation that have since come to dominate and in many cases damage the wiring of contemporary life. *Well Beings* is the story of these journeys and, like any number of relaxing cruises, floatation sessions and guided meditation tapes, it starts with the gentle sound of lapping water.

PART I

Bright Horizons

CHAPTER I

The Possibility of an Island
1970–1972

The town of Westport, in Ireland's County Mayo, opens out into the buffeting waves of Clew Bay. Storms come easily here. With the force of the Atlantic feeding it, the bay can quickly turn into a cauldron of cloud and churning water. Fishermen setting out on a quiet Westport day can often be in for a rough ride once they reach the deeper waters. This was the case one morning in September 1970 when a loose group of friends gathered at the harbour. Not long out of summer, the weather was still warm and with blue skies, Westport looked its postcard best. A light breeze carried the sound of gulls as the water gently lapped against the sea wall. The friends were a curious lot: a gaggle of long hair, beards, flowing scarves and rucksacks. 'Hippies' the locals would have called them, with a fair amount of disdain and suspicion. Chatting and excited, they clambered into a few waiting oyster boats and set out to brave the waves. Through waters variously calm and turbulent, the small flotilla made for Dorinish, one of Clew Bay's many rocky, exposed and uninhabited islands. Standing proudly at the fore of the leading boat, with a shock of flame-red hair, was Sid Rawle, a 25-year-old Englishman recently dubbed 'King of the Hippies' by the British press.[1]

Rawle was an enterprising visionary with a background in trade unionism. A passionate believer in the liberative promises of the 1960s counterculture, he had spent the last few years moving through England's network of squats and communes in pursuit of a utopian or, more specifically, *eutopian* agenda. It was the English statesman Thomas More who coined the term 'utopia', a compound of the Greek *ou* for 'not' and *topos* for 'place'. By this he meant a 'no-place' or 'nowhere', because the main hook of More's political fiction *Utopia* (1516) was that his idealised island society does not exist. However, in one of the book's prefatory poems, 'On Utopia', More gave his concept a small, but telling, tweak. He had his poet 'Anemolius' give voice to the book's utopia, and it proceeds to compare itself to Kallipolis, the imagined city of Plato's *Republic*. Where that city has been 'depicted with words', however, More's utopia claims to be more than a fiction having been 'produced / With men and resources and the best laws'. As such, it is keen to be known by another name, not 'Utopia' but 'deservedly, by the name Eutopia'. Replacing *ou* with *eu* – meaning 'happy' – gives rise to 'eutopia', a happy or 'good place'; a concept that is no less idealised than the 'no-place' but, in keeping with the suggestion of the poem, carries with it the teasing sense of a somewhere that does or *could* exist. It is this sense of possibility that would have chimed with Rawle's worldview. He had no desire to hypothesise an impossible, idealised 'no-place'. Instead, he wanted to actually build a 'good place', somewhere amenable to a better life, a place of happiness and fairness, where all would be well.[2]

For Rawle, getting a better life was contingent upon changing the world. If you were unhappy with your lot you had to alter, reorganise and in some cases dispense with the structures that govern how you live, where you live and why you live. For Rawle, the ambitious simplicity of this project 'all [went] back to the land'. He was aghast at the iniquitous history of English land rights that had led to 'some folk owning hundreds of thousands of acres and others owning none'. Determined to go beyond the ebb and flow of stoned conversation, Rawle wanted to realise his good place by revivifying the public claim to common land and establish upon these legal, political and physical grounds a viable alternative community. In the mid-1960s, Rawle had taken his cause to London's Hyde Park, an iconic space that had long struck a delicate balance between private ownership and public use. There, Rawle convened a radical collective called the Hyde Park Diggers, and among the expansive grounds and the libertarian atmosphere of Speakers' Corner he set about extolling the virtues of self-sufficiency. By growing your own food, by living on and with the land, by 'gradually evolve[ing] a new society', as the writer and 'ardent digger' Charlotte Yonge put it, you could break free; you could unshackle yourself from the 'screwed-up' 'straight world'.

The Hyde Park Diggers, later known as Digger Action Movement, were directly inspired by one of Rawle's spiritual forebears, the 17th-century Protestant, activist and land reformer Gerrard Winstanley. Winstanley and his group, the Diggers or 'True Levellers', moved through the uncertain atmosphere of Civil War-era England cultivating vacant tracts and reclaiming land which had been enclosed into private ownership. Anyone who worked with them had equal share in the food they produced. This political project – Winstanley's intervention into the constitutional crisis following the execution of Charles I – came with the added force of mystical vision. It was God who made the earth, preached Winstanley in his pamphlet *The New Law of Righteousness* (1649), it does not belong to landowners whose titles had been 'founded in conquest', and it should thus remain 'a common treasury' for all. Rawle's argument was no less impassioned and similarly infused with a sense of post-war mission as well as an incipient nationalism. If '[w]e can be ordered to fight and die for Queen and Country', he wrote in a later essay, is it 'in peace time [...] too much to ask for just a few square yards of our green and pleasant land to rear our children on'?[3]

There was much talk among the Hyde Park Diggers of starting rural communes and co-operative farms; of spreading out to explore the common ground across the British Isles, but Rawle was also keen to agitate for the means and the right to embark upon this project in the heart of the metropolis itself. An opportunity came in the late summer of 1969 when Rawle and various Diggers joined in with another collective, the London Street Commune. The combined group, which initially numbered about 100 hippies and activists, took up residence at 144 Piccadilly, an empty five-storey mansion and former hotel a stone's throw from Hyde Park's manicured gardens.

After gaining entry in late August they secured water and electrical supplies, barricaded the doors and windows from the inside, installed a makeshift drawbridge to control access from the outside and, finally, with the perimeter secure, cheerfully announced themselves as outlaws by provocatively flying a Hells' Angels flag from the roof. Once word of the squat travelled through the city's alternative scene, the group quickly swelled to about 300 occupiers and attracted the attention of both the tabloid press and the Metropolitan Police. *The People* and *The News of the World* gleefully reported that the building had become a pit of depravity, teeming with such horrors as sex, squalor, drugs and, even worse, 'foul language'. Meanwhile, Rawle's announcement that he wanted the building to be 'a permanent urban guerrilla base for underground activities', got the authorities twitching. The response was inevitable: 'Hippiedilly', as it became known, was raided by the police in mid-September and the squatters were violently removed. There was no way it could have lasted. Aside from the establishmentarian anxiety regarding the so-called 'counterculture' – a wave of left-wing activism, intergenerational tension and social change that reached critical mass in 1969 – Rawle and the London Street Commune were guilty of that other great crime of British manners: the assumption of undue privilege. Staking a largely symbolic claim to public parkland was one thing but taking up residence in one of London's most exclusive enclaves without the prior qualifiers of wealth, property and 'good' social standing was quite another. This was simply not the way things were done in England, particularly in the overheated economy of late-1960s London.[4]

The city was still dominated by the old guard, the English aristocracy. If you looked out from the top of a 1960s tower block then, as now, you would see a city largely in the possession of the Crown, the Church, and the remnants of the landed gentry. Of the latter, the Duke of Westminster's Grosvenor Estate remains one of the wealthiest. Dating back to 1677, shortly after Winstanley agitated against the injustices of landownership, this largely inherited estate has steadily grown, absorbing along the way the most expensive bits of the Monopoly board: around 200 acres of Belgravia and 100 acres of Mayfair. Ducking and diving alongside these empires other territorial claims were being made, based not on ancestral money but on London's post-war enterprise opportunities. In the late 1960s and across the 1970s self-made businessmen like the British club owner and pornographer Paul Raymond, publisher of *King* magazine (1964), bought up large swathes of Soho, one sex shop or massage parlour at a time. The size of Raymond's portfolio was nothing compared to the Grosvenor Estate, but the so-called 'King of Soho' nevertheless shared the Duke of Westminster's attitude to investment. As a speculator, Raymond saw property as an asset, a source of wealth: it was not there for the purpose of living.

This shift towards a post-shelter economy would gain pace across the 1970s, setting the scene for the contemporary housing crisis that has left London all but uninhabitable for most homebuyers, let alone renters. Standing between these holdings, at the nexus of old and new money, 144 Piccadilly was the ideal place for Rawle and the London Street Commune to highlight these problems. As a grand mansion built in the 1790s for Sir Drummond Smith with no expenses spared, it epitomised property privilege. When the squat was forcefully ended, the point was clearly made: this was a charter'd zone in which there was no place for those in need of accommodation. Between the demands of high capital and community action there was no common ground.[5]

Rawle came away from Hippiedilly undaunted but resolved to make good the plans he had previously mooted in Hyde Park. If he was to be excluded from land grabbed by the rich, he would indeed give the Diggers a space *elsewhere*. This would not be a place at loggerheads with the straight world but somewhere beyond it. He began to think seriously about an off-grid, autonomous counterpoint to modern life; an experiment in communal living that could lead the way for others wanting to escape the privacies and privations of this unfair, unsustainable and unhealthy 'society'. And here it was. Little more than a year after leaving the London squat, Rawle was cutting through the waves off the West Coast of Ireland, watching the cliffs of Dorinish loom into view. With a fleet of followers behind him, and a fine prospect in front, Rawle felt that he had finally struck gold. Here, it seemed, was the coastline of a new world, a place where he and his Diggers, now rechristened the 'Tribe of the Sun', could pursue their great eutopian work uninterrupted.

Disembarking on the island's pebble beach, the group got started. The most important thing was to find fresh water. Tommy Cribbons, the Westport boatman, showed Rawle 'where the old water place had been', and after a little bit of digging they soon found 'the stone lips of a well', the opening of a 'vast underground network [...] connected to the shore'. Next a fire was made using driftwood from the beach, and then the tents went up. With dusk falling, Cribbons cast off in his oyster boat and faded from view, effectively severing the link between Rawle, his group and the mainland. Undaunted, they celebrated their good fortune. The island had granted them safe passage, it had welcomed them ashore, and it had provided them with fuel and water. With the smell of food and firewood in the air, an aura of well-being descended on the camp. They gave thanks to Dorinish, toasted each other, and looked forward to the adventures to come. There was also a wave of gratitude towards their benefactor, the actual *owner* of the island who had given them the opportunity to come here in the first place: the writer, artist and – most famously – ex-Beatle, John Lennon.[6]

✻✻✻✻✻

Lennon had bought Dorinish in 1967, paying less than £2,000 for it at an open auction. Buying an island might sound like the most rockstar of rockstar indulgences, not least because Lennon had, by proxy, outbid a group of Westport farmers who had wanted to use Dorinish as grazing land. It was not quite modern-day enclosure, more like a grandiose version of second-house syndrome: the flow of distant capital drowning out local needs. Unlike the speculators of central London, however, Lennon was willing to share his asset. He did not intend to zombify the island and take it out of use, but rather to put it to use in a particular way.[7]

Since the mid-1960s Lennon had, like Rawle, been giving serious thought to another way of life. He wanted to find a space of playfulness and creativity for The Beatles and a select entourage. What Lennon had in mind was not so much a revolution as a retreat, a movement away from the demanding glare of publicity into a more contemplative phase. Spending time with the Maharishi Mahesh Yogi in Wales in 1967, and then again in Rishikesh in India in 1968, had been an attempt at this. Lennon's eventual disillusionment with Transcendental Meditation and the yogi himself, coupled with a set of seismic upheavals in his private life and his 1969 exit from The Beatles, meant that by 1970 he was looking for a very different direction. In part, this came in the form of 'Primal Therapy', a course of radical psychotherapy he and Yoko Ono undertook between April and September 1970 with the method's originator, an intense and iconoclastic psychologist from Los Angeles named Dr Arthur Janov.

Primal Therapy was a supercharged form of psychodrama that eschewed the analysis of psychoanalysis in favour of an intense, non-verbal treatment of neurosis. Janov was not interested in getting into the minds of his patients. Instead, he wanted them to perform a psychic purge by opening their heads and spilling it all out. For Janov, neurosis was ignited by the trauma of birth, developed during early years of unmet emotional and physical needs and fully ingrained by subsequent mistreatment from adult and authority figures. To survive all this 'Pain', argued Janov in *The Primal Scream* (1970), we repress it all. We push it so deep down that we are relived of the need even to express it. The problem, however, is that it stays down there, growing, radiating. 'Pain' in Janov's terms does not return like the repressed fixations and phantasies analysed in Freudian theory. Rather, it spreads out like a canker-blossom, causing illness at a physical and psychological level. Worse still, this dark flower carries on whispering to us, reminding us that repression is the only way to deal with our emotions, our desires and ourselves. Gradually, as the tendrils reach further, we are split in two: the 'real', suffering, pain-saturated 'authentic' being and the unfeeling, neutral 'automaton' who interacts with others. Janov's method sought to unlock this trapped self.

Working out of the LA clinic he opened in 1968, Janov would encourage his patients to relive traumatic memories and thereby express the unprocessed pain associated with them. Typically, a course of therapy would last around seven months and it would begin with a series of open-ended individual sessions with Janov. In a sound-proofed, semi-darkened room he would invite the patient to lie on a couch before starting to probe at their 'tension and problems'. This was an information-gathering exercise. Janov was trying to get a glimpse of the patient's defence systems and any emotional fissures pointing to issues that lay deeper than surface-level headaches and general low moods. From here, he would carefully steer the patient away from the 'personality (or unreal self)' that describes, intellectualises and largely avoids painful memories in order to prompt them into 'feeling': an often overwhelming re-experience of a previously buried, unarticulated emotion. After this first phase the patient would then join an extended series of group sessions in which the same process would take place but with the added support – and intensity – of the other members working through their private dramas at the same time. In each instance the aim was to have patients arrive at the emotional breakthrough of a 'Primal': a volcanic moment of yelling, pillow-thumping, floor-banging catharsis. Janov saw the crying and screaming that often occurred at these turning points as acts of unblocking, a 'methodical emptying out of the tank of Pain'. When the floodgates opened, he argued, the mask of neurosis would shatter, leaving in its place the clear face of the authentically 'feeling' self. Over the course of the whole treatment Janov wanted to leave his patients drained, finally free of their psychic baggage. 'Once the tank is empty,' he wrote, 'I consider the person real, or well.'[8]

The Primal Scream has its origins in the counterculture of the 1960s. Indeed, Janov cites the confrontational, emetic performances of 'destructivist' artist Raphael Montañez Ortiz as the inspiration for the first 'eerie scream' he heard from a patient. For Paul Williams and Brian Edgar, though, Janov was not merely reflecting isolated works but pulling into his therapy room the radical ideology of the decade's New Left politics. As they put it, Primal Therapy mirrored the 'act first, analyse later' anti-intellectualism of Abbie Hoffman, Jerry Rubin and the Youth International Party (the 'Yippies') as well as the idealisation of childhood experience central to the playfulness of Ken Kesey's Merry Pranksters as well as Richard Neville's book *Play Power* (1970). With its emphasis on liberation from inherited patterns, *The Primal Scream* also echoed the general sense of intergenerational tension that characterised the countercultural impetus. This effort to break away from the normative grip of sexual mores, work patterns, drug laws and adult authority was visible across the spectrum from the emergence of 'hippie' enclaves to Rawle's attempt at communal independence. More specifically, when Janov called the 'forceful upheaval' of Primal Therapy 'revolutionary' he was also aligning his work with the self-conscious violence of 1960s radicalism, evident according to Williams and Edgar not just in the provocative art of Ortiz and his contemporaries but also the political extremities of far-left pseudo-terroristic groups like the Weather Underground.

The Weather Underground (or Weathermen) grew out of the nominally non-violent national protest group Students for a Democratic Society. They were a militant splinter cell frustrated with the apparent ineffectuality large-scale marches, preferring to bomb buildings rather than occupy them. Their rhetoric spoke of an assault against 'the system', an aggression that chimed with Janov's own stated attempts to eliminate 'neurosis'. Both had the pernicious effects of modern capitalist society in mind. Janov, however, was not a voice from the activist bunkers mounting a transgressive attack on bourgeois values. In *The Primal Scream* he was trying to highlight and minister to the day-to-day struggles of modern Americans, those shuttling between atomising jobs and nuclear families while quietly disappearing into insomnia, loneliness and depression. As Janov put it, 'hard work takes care of some feelings, yelling at the children helps a little more, cigarettes and alcohol drain off even more' but 'there is still a need for tranquilizers and sleeping pills'. More so than the much-publicised menace of LSD (available under the trade name Delysid from 1947 until 1965), it was the pharmacy-bought contents of the medicine cabinet like Valium, Quaaludes and Sominex – as well as the social rituals feeding their use – that at the turn of the 1970s were giving rise to widespread, high-functioning catatonia.[9]

For all his fiery rhetoric, hip credentials and tendency to set himself apart from rival therapeutic systems, Janov was keeping pace with an increasing public interest in psychology, mental health and the psychodynamics of everyday life. Consciously or not, *The Primal Scream* incorporated ideas from a full spectrum of parallel writers and thinkers ranging from the 'anti-psychiatry' of R. D. Laing's *The Divided Self* (1967) to the poststructuralist interrogations of psychoanalysis that philosophers Gilles Deleuze and Félix Guattari would develop into *Anti-Oedipus* (1970–72). Janov's emphasis on the suffocating weight of the inauthentic, 'public' self also resonated with Eric Berne's *Games People Play* (1964). This bestselling introduction to 'transactional analysis' dissected the adult–child dynamics that extend out from private to public life and back again. We are constantly playing games, argues Berne, and the family structure of 'Parent, Adult, Child' reoccurs in every social aggregation. Partners, teachers, bosses: they are all 'parents', explains Berne; they are all struggling to subjugate the 'child'. He offered *Games People Play* as a rulebook, that his readers might better understand and thereby navigate these power-laden interactions. While Janov would have agreed with Berne's portrait of social conditioning, he was not interested in using therapy to teach the 'rules'. If anything, he was keen for his patients to dispense with the game altogether so they could start to live on their own terms.[10]

In this way, the attempt of Primal Therapy to revive the submerged or hidden self overlapped with another school of thought: the field of 'humanistic psychology'. A broad church made up of varying approaches and methodologies, humanistic psychology made its public presence known in 1961 with the *Journal of Humanistic Psychology*, a publication spearheaded by the academic psychologists Anthony Sutich and Abraham Maslow. Maslow, along with such like-minded correspondents as Carl Rogers, author of *On Becoming a Person* (1961), was frustrated with the then dominant approach to the study of psychology: behaviourism. As David Cohen explains, the 'central tenet of behaviourism is that thoughts, feelings and intentions, mental processes all, do not determine what we do'. Instead, led by empirical evidence and with a focus on experience, behaviourists saw the individual as a conditioned product of their environment. According to this view autonomy is an illusion. We humans are not thinking, feeling, individually wilful agents, but environmentally programmed 'biological machines' who do not consciously act but rather '*react* to stimuli'. For Maslow, this emphasis on conditioning too readily disregarded the value of inner motivations, the variation and potentiality of psychological experience and what he outlined in *Toward a Psychology of Being* (1962) as 'the depths and the heights of human nature'. Maslow was not content to liken cognitive human experience to that of rat in a maze responding only to the next corner, obstacle or puzzle. The mind, he argued, had the ability and the plasticity to take us beyond such reactive limitations. As such, the focus of humanistic psychology was not then on 'sickness, not health even' but 'transcendence', what Maslow called 'self-actualization': the growth of 'full humanness'.

An early definition of self-actualisation appeared in Maslow's paper 'A Theory of Human Motivation' (1943). Drawing on the work of neurologist Kurt Goldstein and his book *The Organism* (1939), Maslow described self-actualisation as 'a desire for self-fulfilment', a tendency that 'might be phrased as the desire to become more and more what one is, to become everything that one is capable of becoming'. For Maslow, self-actualisation was about realising one's own capabilities in excess of the 'warped, repressed or denied' personality conferred by the behaviourist view. It was a goal that depended on the prior satisfaction of other, more basic needs. 'Man', wrote Maslow in 'A Theory of Human Motivation', is a 'perpetually wanting animal' who is constantly driven to satisfy a set of somatic and psychic demands. These range from the immediate physiological needs for food and water to the pursuit of 'safety', the acquisition of material and emotional security. Having satisfied these, Maslow argues, the individual moves ever onwards, seeking out the psychological satisfactions of love and self-esteem. Self-actualisation is the crowning point of what has come to be known as Maslow's 'Hierarchy of Needs'. It is the moment at which we do not merely exist but thrive in the full realisation of what we are 'potentially'; what we are 'fitted for'.

For Maslow, the pursuit of self-actualisation was a human duty. It was a way of avoiding *accidie*, the 'sin of failing to do with one's life all that one knows one could do'. But for all its rewards, self-actualisation remained a rare and glittering prize because, as Maslow explained, a decreasing percentage of satisfaction could be expected as one navigates the hierarchy. The 'average citizen', he surmised, 'is satisfied perhaps 85 per cent in his physiological needs' with the number dropping to 70 'in his safety needs', 50 'in his love needs', 40 'in his self-esteem needs', eventually reaching a mere '10 per cent' when it came to 'his self-actualization needs'. As such, self-actualisation was to be sought through very particular techniques and seized upon when in the throes of very particular states. It could be felt in the elevation of what Maslow termed 'peak experiences': the occasional but ecstatic moments of exhilaration, joy or insight that are powerful enough to take us beyond the mundane limits of the everyday.

For Rogers, meanwhile, the ideal arena for actualisation was the 'encounter group'. Encounter groups were a 'person-centered' form of communal therapy based on corporate feedback models and product-based focus groups. Each participant would try to be open and truthful in the communication of their own feelings and their observations of each other, so that the group could become a sphere of emotional authenticity. They could be spaces of brutal honesty, but the overall aim of an encounter group was to foster trust, intimacy and mutual support. What Janov was offering under the banner of Primal Therapy was, in essence, an extreme synthesis of these models. He was guiding his patients towards a powerful peak experience during which they could encounter themselves. And the scream, when it came, would be the scream of the actualised self.[11]

Janov's ideas also chimed with the gestating work of practitioners yet to publish. In 1970, just as The Primal Scream appeared, a young doctor called John Travis took up an internship at the Public Health Service Hospital in San Francisco. He quickly felt a depressing sense of helplessness when confronted with an enormous number of terminal cancer patients. As Travis puts it, he was instructed not to talk about their pain nor 'the fact they were dying'. All he could do was drug them to oblivion with painkillers that did 'little to mask [their] symptoms'. Elsewhere, Travis found himself prescribing Theodore Rubin's The Angry Book (1969) to patients with high blood pressure. He saw little point in handing out yet more pills.

Like Janov, Travis thought it better to get in touch with the feelings causing this illness rather than repress its symptoms in waves of chemical insulation.[12]

For Janov, Primal Therapy was 'revolutionary' because it liberated the self. It offered freedom from the past, 'who you were' and who you 'thought you were'. It had the potential to be a tool of mass political emancipation but only as an extension of this initial, individually focused recovery of an 'authentic' identity. As Janov argued, 'The transformation of members of society is inevitably the transformation of that society'. Primal Therapy was thus in pursuit of what Maslow would term a 'eupsychic' end. Janov was not interested in establishing a 'benign place' for his patients; he wanted instead to put them in a 'good place' psychologically. It was by focusing on this self-fulfilment and psychological health that the 'good society' – Eupsychia as Maslow called it – could gradually shimmer into being with 'the right order' emerging from the 'enlightenment of individuals'.[13]

When Janov started to work with Lennon and Ono in 1970, first at Tittenhurst Park (their mansion home in Berkshire), and then at the Los Angeles clinic, he found a pair of deeply conflicted individuals. Their lives and feelings were entangled, but for Lennon, his particular psychological landscape was shaped by the stress of fame, the breakup of The Beatles, a set of complicated relationships and a knotted political stance that found him hovering between pacifism and the decade's demands for direct action. It was layer upon layer of neurosis built on a set of difficult, largely unprocessed childhood experiences of parental stress and abandonment. Ono, meanwhile, had been under similar pressures. A clamour of voices, both public and private, all routinely laden with racism and sexism, had long been telling her what she could and could not do as a woman, a mother and an artist. Since meeting Lennon she had also been repeatedly cast as the *other* woman in every sense of the word: the homewrecker, the band-breaker, the weird foreign girlfriend and non-musician who had no right to be in the gang and who really should just shut up and obey the nearest patriarch. Gradually, Janov helped the pair start to drain these pent-up reservoirs of anger, need and upset. For their part Lennon and Ono fed the results into their respective *Plastic Ono Band* albums which they recorded between September and November 1970 and released that December. As if coming straight from the therapy room, the screams heard on tracks like Lennon's 'Mother' and Ono's 'Why?', were not cries of fear but acts of personal exorcism. In Janov's terms Lennon and Ono were healing themselves in the most literal sense: they were making themselves whole by casting out the 'false' self and bringing to the surface the healthy, Primal being. But they did not go far enough. Speaking about Lennon, Janov would later reflect that he broke off the treatment too early. He had opened up, but more work was needed to really process the psychic spill.

Some aspects of Lennon's outlook, however, had clearly shifted by the time he returned to the UK. Dorinish still floated among his assets, and although his desire for island life remained, Lennon resolved to put it to better use. Seeing the demise of Hippiedilly, Lennon was much taken with Rawle, the firebrand de facto leader of the occupation. Rawle embodied the street-level leftism that Lennon had been pilloried for apparently questioning in songs like 'Revolution' (1968) and, as if seeking some kind of political redemption, he was keen to offer support. Summoning Rawle to the Apple offices, Lennon made him an offer he couldn't refuse: an island, far away from everything, there for the taking with no strings attached. In 1967 Dorinish had been a rich man's fantasy but now, three years later, a post-Primal Lennon had changed his mind 'for the common good'. A site of private escape had been given over to a social experiment. It was kind of field test. Lennon was genuinely curious to see if it could be done. Could a gaggle of green-fingered idealists with a handful of tents actually make a go of it? He thought they could. In the event, though, the Tribe of the Sun lasted barely a year.[14]

*****

It started well enough. Arrangements agreed with Lennon, Rawle placed newspaper ads asking for interested parties to join him in the enterprise. Having worked with several hundred at Hippiedilly, he found a core of around twenty-five – a much more manageable number – willing to make the leap to Dorinish. This was the group that gathered at the Westport harbour in the late summer of 1970. The original idea was 'a six-week summer camp on the island'. They would get a feel for the place, see how they fared and then decide if they wanted to extend their stay. Everything looked good, but soon after the balmy evening of their arrival, Rawle and the group found that Dorinish was bleak, its ground was difficult to work, and the island's exposed terrain was open to the full ferocity of Clew Bay's fearsome storms. When they rolled in, these Atlantic winds brought sheets of rain and enough force to dislodge the boulders from the cliffs. There was little that Rawle and the others could do other than collapse the tents, wrap themselves in the canvas and hold on for the night. After one horrendous storm that saw them nearly lose their tents to the gale, Rawle announced that the project was over. They could not endure another punishing night and so he was going to signal for Tommy, the boatman, to sail over. And then they would evacuate.

As they day brightened, though, Rawle started to feel the pang of regret at the idea of leaving, as if he was pulling on a stem that had just taken root. The others, too, had come to see the island, simply and definitively, as their home. 'This is where I live,' said the woman the group knew as 'Princess' as they started to break down the camp. 'This is where I'm going to continue to live.' Rawle paused, suddenly recognising the meaning of Princess' resolve. They had weathered the storm and would have to weather many more: that was the challenge of Dorinish, the one they had all accepted as soon as they stepped off the boat. It was not going to be any other way. Quickly, quietly, with neither argument nor fanfare, Rawle made the decision and turned back to the group: 'Alright lads, let's get the tents back up.'[15]

Alan Sidi captured this commitment at the start of his remarkable short film *Tribe of the Sun* (1972). Sidi was a semi-professional filmmaker from Yorkshire and the chief member of the Mercury Movie Makers, a cine group formed in Leeds in 1959. He got wind of Rawle's projects thanks to his wife, Kay, who was originally from

Westport and had been following all the local news about Beatles, islands and hippies. Visiting Dorinish with his camera the summer after Rawle's arrival, Sidi found a busy, happy and harmonious group. He shows them digging gardens, planting crops and fetching water; in one scene they all muck in to haul a huge driftwood log out of the sea to use as a totem pole. Clearly, the experience of the first stormy weeks had given rise to a communal fortitude. Seen in Sidi's film, the 'Tribe' are a gang of men and women aged from about eighteen to fifty. Via on-camera interviews and voiceovers they variously explain their motivations for joining the group. As travellers and former squatters they were all looking for a way to build an alternative lifestyle away from 'the sterile relationships' of the 'outside world' and its 'big money scene'. With their own money and property held in common, the group appear impressively united in their shared cause. Rawle had made the same point in early 1971 to another film crew, this time reporting for the RTÉ programme *Newsbeat*. Moving to Dorinish, he explained, was a way of dispensing with 'the paraphernalia and claptrap of 20th-century society' in favour of a peaceful and loving community: 'This is the way human beings should live.'

It was a stance neatly summed up in the song that bookends Sidi's film, a folkish ballad that works as a kind of manifesto for the group:

We wanted something better
We needed to be free
Free from the sham of living and life's insanity
[...]
Free from the bloody rat race, we're the Tribe of the Sun.
Running free, living as one.[16]

Clearly the key word here is 'free', and the 'sham of living' from which the Tribe wish to be delivered is that perennial bugbear of creatives, independent thinkers and would-be rebels: the 'rat race'. This now familiar description of the professional grind was originally drawn from aviation training in which an experienced pilot would instruct a novice to follow them into a 'rat race' – to keep up with and copy their manoeuvres exactly. From around 1945 onwards the term was applied to the workplace, particularly the urban, competitive white-collar workplace. Here 'rat race' described the unedifying pursuit of a wage, a process that in Marxist terms exerts a deeply alienating effect upon the worker. Labouring for those who own the means of production, the worker is thus 'estranged' from the final product, that which is typically exchanged elsewhere, through other hands. The commodity 'exists outside' them, independently, as something alien. For Marx, then, labour does not belong to the worker's 'essential being', it contributes nothing to their sense of self, precisely because they do not work for themselves. So too in the post-war rat race. Bound by contract of labour to their employer, the agency of the worker is reduced until their professional life becomes a game of follow-the-leader, or in the most extreme readings of the rat-race metaphor, a life akin to that of a rat in a maze or a mouse on a wheel. 'Freedom' in this context means the assumption of self-determination, self-mastery, self-governance: a state in which one can choose *not* to follow another's lead.[17]

As Marx argued in *The Communist Manifesto* (1848), this autonomy was to be achieved through the development of workers' co-operatives, by gaining collective rather than private ownership over the means of production. It was a call to arms that chimed with the thinking at play in the parallel history of British and American communitarianism. For Gerrard Winstanley's Levellers, true freedom could be attained 'only where every man had an unrestrained opportunity to use the land and gain his livelihood from it'. Anything that blocked this sovereignty – employment on private property, expenditure of labour for another's gain, lack of access to the fruits of one's labour – equated to a state of material and spiritual bondage. So too for religious groups like the Anabaptist Hutterites who established rural farming communities in America from 1847 onwards. With a culture of shared property and a guiding 'principle of separation' from the wider world of non-believers, the Hutterites connected spiritual freedom – the right to practise a particular belief – with the operation of their economically self-sufficient 'colonies'. They kept company with themselves and with God; they were not going to devote their time and energy to another's cause, and certainly not for the sake of a small financial reward.[18]

More than a century later and the link between collective effort and freedom – personal as well as economic – remained central to the counterculture of the 1960s and early 1970s. Operating as part of the same nexus as Rawle's Diggers and the Piccadilly squatters, London-based projects like the Free City Committee offered advice on how to access vital services and resources free of charge. Meanwhile, for a few months in 1968 the Anti-University, nominally 'led' by psychiatrist Joseph Berke from a set of rooms in Shoreditch, offered a diverse range of courses (ranging from 'Dragons' to 'Guerrilla Communications') virtually for free, to all comers, regardless of age, experience or educational background. At the same time Haight-Ashbury, San Francisco's hippie epicentre, was being served by its own group of Diggers. Led by Peter Coyote and Emmett Grogan, two energetic and imaginative activists in their twenties, the San Francisco Diggers were a community-focused network that came to prominence in 1966, just before the Haight gained its moment in the sun during the 'Summer of Love' in 1967. Drawing on the same radical history as Rawle, Coyote and Grogan worked to make the Haight a viable countercultural enclave, a self-sufficient city within a city. As Digger associate Chester Anderson put it, they believed in and practised freedom, which included 'feeding the hungry, clothing the naked, sheltering the homeless, befriending the stranger [...] all for free'. This support, as well as free access to community schemes like legal aid, was offered as an attempt to maintain the Haight's underpowered and often buckling infrastructure.

For all their altruism, these groups were not charities; they were not there solely to fulfil a social need or to plug a gap in the existing governmental provision. Rather, there was a distinct element of subversion at play in their work. By offering so much for free, they were trying to outflank the very idea of privately owned property and the prevailing orthodoxy of financial exchange. Theirs was a gift economy which set out to critique commodity capitalism. As Grogan wrote in a broadside distributed across the Haight in 1967, 'When it is no longer bought with money, the commodity lies open to criticism and modification.

Affluence is by no means natural or human, it is simply an abundance of goods.' This theory was put into practice through the distribution of free food. The Diggers would scour San Francisco's food markets and scoop up any leftover vegetables before adding them, along with other donations, to huge soups and pots of spaghetti. These free dinners took place all round the Haight, but the Diggers became best known for sharing food in Golden Gate Park, a daily ritual that began in autumn 1966. Here, the anti-capitalist agenda was boiled down to its de-alienating, humanitarian essence: the provision of food to those who needed it. There was no poverty shaming, no hoop jumping, nothing expected in return. Their food was a reminder that a sense of genuine commonwealth could exist in a world otherwise defined by vast economic inequality. 'It's free,' the Diggers would say as they handed out another bowl, 'because its yours.'[19]

These groups were not just expressing what Timothy Miller calls the 'beat-hippie disdain for money, material comfort and [regular] work'. Neither the British nor the American Diggers were lotus eaters, languishing in a state of idleness. It took *work* to sustain anything even approaching a state of communal self-sufficiency, as well as an enormous amount of imaginative and emotional labour. Those involved had an occupation, but it was not tied to the fortunes of those who controlled the means of production. Instead, they worked for themselves and for the good of others in pursuit of a social mission. Gene Bernofsky, one of the key members of Drop City, a short-lived artists' commune in Southern Colorado, crystallised this stance when he spoke of the difference between 'employment' and 'gainful employment'. Drop City was always a hive of activity and Bernofsky recognised that it was 'important to be employed' but 'to be gainfully employed', to provide one's labour power in exchange for monetary reward, 'was a sucking of the soul'. He and the other members of the commune saw Drop City as a beacon, a model of co-operative activity that could demonstrate how, in the 'new civilization', the aim 'was to be employed, but not to be gainfully employed, so that each individual would be their own master'. Operating on this basis put the commune in line for another kind of reward, not unlike that sought by Gerrard Winstanley and his followers. As Bernofsky reflected: 'We idealistically believed that if we were true to that principle, that if we did nongainful work [...] the cosmic forces [...] would supply us with the necessities of survival.' This was an idealised form of economic freedom, a fantasy that went beyond financial autonomy to a movement away from monetary exchange altogether: to *be* free by somehow getting it all *for* free.[20]

Back on Dorinish, Rawle and the Tribe were much more pragmatic in their pursuit of the non-gainful life. In such a harsh environment, you simply could not afford to rely on a sense of cosmic grace. As such, they not only worked on their own crops, gardens and shelters, but also explored shell fishing, a potentially viable micro-industry which, according to Rawle, was underdeveloped on the West Coast of Ireland 'because of the great immigration problem amongst young people and work people in particular'. In cultivating this autonomy, Rawle was aiming for 'freedom' but also, as the Tribe's song put it, 'something better'. An alternative lifestyle for Rawle was not a wholesale rejection of or step away from 'Life's insanity', but a sense of freedom that could respond to it, that could ease the effects and undo the detrimental habits of 'the bloody rat race'. As he put it to the RTÉ interviewer, Dorinish was 'simply a case of living, working, eating and enjoying' together but without the contemporary trappings of 'cars and television and families'. Attitudes of corrosive self-interest, the mindset of 'damn you, Jack, I'm alright' were not 'good enough' for Rawle. That was 'not the way human beings should live'. Dorinish, then, was Rawle's ethical line in the sand. For all his apparent eccentricity and rebelliousness, turning away from 'the claptrap of the 20th century' to an experimental island life was his attempt at being 'civilised'.

For Rawle, who later wrote of his project as 'The Vision of Albion', an alternative did exist, but it required a return to the communal systems of Britain's 'tribal' past; a rediscovery that, in his mind, could point the way to a fantastical, egalitarian future, 'a vision of all the people uniting in love and harmony'. In using 'Albion', the ancient name for Britain, Rawle was invoking a dense matrix of national myth. Eclipsed by the name 'Britannia' following the Roman conquest of AD 43, 'Albion' (variously meaning 'world', 'land' or even 'white', an alleged reference to the cliffs at Dover) persisted in the imagination as a British promised land: a mystical, heavily romanticised version of the island formed from a combination of memory, nostalgia and geography. For the poet William Blake, writing in the 18th century, Albion symbolised a complex and esoteric image of a fallen 'mankind', a dormant society that awaited a glorious rebirth in a state of unified harmony. When Rawle used the term, he had in mind a community in 'this green land, living in equity and peace', a 'vision of unity in diversity'. With a nod to Britain's ignoble history of Empire and colonisation, Rawle admits that so many of the 'white man's' dreadful actions and attitudes 'originated here', and by encouraging a lifestyle of autonomous peace and harmony he was advocating for a state of *corrective* freedom.[21]

The optimism of 'The Vision of Albion' is captivating, albeit naïve. There is also something problematic about Rawle's use of 'tribe'. As well as using the word in its anthropological sense to describe a particular group dynamic, Rawle also seems to use 'tribe' to conjure a sense of premodern atavism to which is connected – with little or no substantiation – an implied authenticity. Clearly, Rawle intends for 'tribe' to carry a positive, galvanising emphasis in line with the political thrust of his essay, but with its suggestions of a stereotypical, 'uncivilised' primitivism and noble savagery, the word never fully jettisons its colonial baggage. The trope was common, particularly among Rawle's countercultural contemporaries. Lew Welch, an American poet and associate of the San Francisco Diggers, used similar language in his broadside 'A Moving Target Is Hard to Hit' (1967). Written, duplicated and distributed across Haight-Ashbury in March 1967, the missive was a response to the area's overcrowding, a problem that became acute in the months leading up to that year's Summer of Love. 'Disperse', Welch urged, 'gather into smaller tribes'. Rather than cramming into a single urban base that was already bursting at the seams, he suggests that Haight residents should get out of the city and form into 'communal "families" of five adults ... and the natural number of children thereby made'. These groups should spread out into 'the beautiful public land your state and national governments have already set up for you, free'. He adds that 'most Indians are nomads' as if to suggest that the proposed mobility of the counterculture echoes that of Native American culture. The irony, which Welch fails to recognise, is that many of America's national parks and so-called 'wilderness' sites were native territories renamed and put into public use across the 19th century by treaties (i.e. land grabs) of ambiguous legality. As with Rawle, 'tribe' resonates in Welch's writing with a sense of freedom, but it is a distinctly exclusive sense of freedom: an idealised state of autonomy imagined by *white* America which largely obscures, or otherwise fails to acknowledge, the freedoms historically denied to the country's indigenous peoples.

Beyond the questionable myopia of their language, Welch and Rawle were issuing very similar calls to action. They were asking their readers and potential followers to seize the day, to reject an indentured half-life of alienation and dispossession with its limited horizons and to live 'properly' instead. It was an invitation to exist expansively, in tune with one's own needs and desires as well as those of others. 'The Haight-Ashbury is not where it's at,' counselled Welch. He argued that whatever freedoms the area had come to represent had little to do with the particularities of place and more to do with the attitude, the shared mindset of those who made up the community: 'It's in your head and hands. Take it anywhere.'

Like Rawle as he cast off for Dorinish, Welch was inviting the residents of the Haight to seek out and to fully realise a more nour-ishing and rewarding way of being. Given the pressure placed on the likes of the Haight Ashbury Free Clinic as the area reached critical mass, it is not surprising that Welch and the Diggers would be advocating for such a dispersal. The social ills that the British press feared would emerge from the likes of Hippiedilly – drug addiction, inadequate sanitation, criminality – became endemic in the San Franciscan enclave particularly as the 1960s drew to a close and the media images of 1967 began to lose their lustre.[22]

This turn to new pastures was not just limited to the British and American Diggers. In 1970 the English group the Shrubb Family established themselves as a 'self-actualising commune' on the Norfolk flatlands and attempted to step outside the bindings of capitalism while the crumbling Postlip Hall near Cheltenham became a 'practical commune' focused on 'co-housing'. Over in Vienna, the Austrian performance artist Otto Muehl, a member of the transgressive Vienna Actionists (1960–1971), was taking this communal intent in a much more confrontational direction with the *Aktionsanalytische Organisation* (AAO). Influenced by the writings of psychoanalyst Wilhelm Reich, author of *The Function of the Orgasm* (1942), the AAO aimed to 'liberate society from its psychological dependence on repressive bourgeois norms and consumerism'. By 1972, the dictatorial Muehl had moulded the AAO into the Friedrichshof commune in eastern Austria where his large 'family' – at one point the biggest communal gathering in Europe – 'liberated' themselves through what Mark Lilla calls a 'program [of] free love, let-it-all-hang-out group therapy, and a return to nature'. Soon after, the neo-pagan Oberto Airaudi was in the hills above Turin laying the foundations for Damanhur, a spiritual ecovillage officially established in 1975. In between, the Bolivian mystic and philosopher Óscar Ichazo opened the doors of Arica, his 'mystery school' held in the Chilean city of the same name from 1968 to 1971. There, his adepts would undergo intensive programmes of self-analysis to liberate themselves from the 'quest for false security and status' and the tyranny of 'ego-centered thoughts'. A similar goal was sought by those who, from the mid-1970s onwards, travelled in the other direction to Pune, India, to join the Acharya Rajneesh Ashram, led by the charismatic holy man and teacher Bhagwan Shree Rajneesh. Rajneesh, later known as 'Osho', used deep meditation, ecstatic ritualism and devotional work to teach his followers how to become, in the words of his principal follower Ma Anand Sheela, 'free, free of all limitations, free of all conditioning, and just become an integrated individual, a free being'.[23]

These and many other communal gravitation points dotted the international cultural landscape across the 1970s. Although different in their aims and intentions these communities – secular, spiritual, experimental and intentional – all shared the same basic outlook. Collectively, the appearance of these ashrams, schools, communes and islands announced a subtle but significant shift in the trajectory of period's radical thinking as the 'sixties' became the 'seventies', as the activist politics of the counterculture flowered further into the 'New Age' search for alternative ways and states of being. In the mid- to late 1960s 'freedom' was the primary buzzword. As Peter Fonda famously announced in *The Wild Angels* (1966) – years before he was sampled by the appropriately named Primal Scream – the young rebels of the post-war generation wanted to be set free from the demands of society to 'do what we wanna do'. It was the San Franciscan Diggers who put this message on the street in January 1967 when they announced via a printed broadside that 'the time has come to be free', giving the Haight in the process its enduring motto, 'Do your thing'.

As the 1970s began, though, this libertarian and emancipatory intent morphed into a web of projects which were, to use Theodore Roszak's phrase, 'primarily therapeutic in character'. Roszak was writing in his sociological study *The Making of a Counterculture* (1969) and was commenting on the pathological effects of alienation under capitalism. He was arguing that the 'revolution which will free us from alienation' must not be 'merely institutional'. To be effective, its theorisation must go beyond 'an economic analysis' and focus on matters of 'behaviour', namely the human and psychological effects of alienation, hence the recourse to therapy. Roszak, writing towards the end of the 1960s, was clearly picking up on the various undercurrents flowing through the decade. At that point, whether in response to chronic facilities or in pursuit of a higher, more mystical goal, the therapeutic drive kicked up a gear. The desire to be set *free* from society gave way to an attempt to *recover* from it and practices of self-sufficiency became a means to heal the damage done to the body and the mind by the manifold pressures of the workaday, bourgeois world.

We might remember the 1960s by way of Timothy Leary's 1967 call to 'turn on, tune in and drop out', but 'dropping out' was never really intended as an end in, and of, itself. The idea was to step into another kind of life, another way of being. As the 1970s opened, this sense of a 'new' life increasingly took the form of a better, fitter, healthier life, one in which the 'dropout' could realise their potential, not squander it. The mission, for those who chose it, was not just to find a way of living free, but also a way of living *well*.[24]

CHAPTER II

The Grand Project
1942–1972

The drive to be well is a grand project, possibly *the* grand project, the modern progress of which preceded and fed into the countertrends of the 1960s. While the varied projects of Rawle, Janov, Berne, Maslow and others assumed a broadly revelatory and revolutionary stance, their work was paralleled, if not enabled, by a mainstream political focus on matters of mental and physical health. Specifically 'well-being', the 'state of being healthy, happy, or prosperous' – an enjoyment of 'physical, psychological, or moral welfare' – was a dominant theme of the reconstructive impetus that characterised the global socio-political landscape after 1945. In the case of Britain's political agenda, this was set by the Beveridge Report of 1942, a wholesale review of welfare measures or, as the report's title officially termed it, 'Social Insurance and Allied Services'. Commissioned by the Labour–Conservative coalition government under Winston Churchill, the report, led by Liberal William Beveridge, examined existing provision and looked towards likely social needs in the post-war world. It outlined a model of Britain as a *welfare* state rather than a *warfare* state, one in which central and local governments took on the nation's social problems. Chief among Beveridge's targets were the 'five giants': 'want, sickness, squalor, ignorance and idleness', which, as Arthur Marwick has summarised in less Dickensian terms, equated to social security, medical services, housing, education and the avoidance of unemployment.[1]

At the same time, America was also exiting the war with a battery of federal, state and local welfare policies relating to 'education, health, social security, social services and veterans' programs'. Some of these measures were built on Depression-era New Deal legislation such as the Social Security Act of 1935, which 'laid the basis for a nationwide system of unemployment insurance'. Others, like the National Mental Health Act of 1946, responded to the immediate impact of the war, particularly the high levels of psychological problems reported by returning soldiers. As in the UK, 'welfare' defined a multi-faceted approach to the 'the well-being of individuals and families', which encompassed social, economic and personal factors. Following on from this, President Truman's Commission on the Health Needs of the Nation published its report 'Building America's Health' (1952–53), which focused on the promotion of health rather than the treatment of disease. As James William Miller summarises, the 'so-called Magnuson Report' named after 'the Commission's chairman, Dr. Paul A. Magnuson' was 'unusual in its attention to the social component of health'. Similar to the Beveridge Report, it concluded that 'if a person's social environment involved a lack of security about such basics as food, shelter, or employment, the achievement of positive health was much more difficult than if these were not a source of stress'.

Maslow had made much the same point in 'A Theory of Human Motivation' when discussing 'safety', the basic human need to live in a 'predictable, organized world'. Children and adults alike crave safety, argued Maslow. For the child, safety is conferred by the routine and stability of a supportive situation free of quarrels, violence and angry parental outbursts. Adult security similarly veers towards anchorage in a world of change. At the extremes, notes Maslow, we might seek out safety in the consolations of religion or philosophy. More likely, however, we find it in the type of 'basics' discussed in the respective Magnuson and Beveridge reports, the daily securities which, according to Maslow, keep us afloat materially and economically: 'the common preference for a job with tenure and protection, the desire for a savings account, and for insurance of various kinds (medical, dental, unemployment, disability, old age)'.[2]

Maslow, as well as the policies of the British and American governments, were reflecting a wider, international turn in the understanding of health, one that moved away from a singular, medicalised focus on illness. It was a shift formalised by the United Nations and the World Health Organization who in 1946 moved to ratify their constitutional definition of health to describe 'a state of complete physical, mental and social well-being and not merely the absence of disease and infirmity'.[3]

Despite these commendable aims, the leap from a new theory of health to the practice of it proved to be difficult, particularly in America, where the widespread rollout of a post-war social welfare programme was limited by the country's lack of a universal health care system. Access to medical services then, as now, relied on often unaffordable private health insurance albeit with some provision for public health care coverage. It was not until the 1965 Social Security Amendments signed under Lyndon B. Johnson that the country gained something approximating a general care provision in the form of Medicare and Medicaid. The former programme mainly catered to those over 65 while the latter was rolled out as a means-tested form of health care support for those on low incomes. By contrast, the principles running through the Beveridge Report fed into the formation of the National Health Service, which Clement Attlee's Labour government officially brought into operation in July 1948. Britain's health provision had previously 'depended on a primitively unstable mixture of class prejudice, commercial self-interest, professional altruism, vested interest and demarcation disputes'. The NHS cut through these variances by extending a universal service to every citizen, free of charge. The Beveridge Report argued that post-war social security depended on this foundational level playing field. This was the type of general, all-inclusive provision that could alleviate the deprivation of the pre-war period and as far as Beveridge was concerned, there was no better time to do it. 'A revolutionary moment in the world's history is a time for revolutions,' he argued, 'not for patching.' With a comprehensive approach that offered access to hospital and specialist services, dental care, eye care, maternity services as well as 'medicine, drugs and appliances', the NHS was given the tools to do substantially more than 'patching'.[4]

Beyond the significant social benefits that came with this pioneering model of 'cradle to grave' care, other sectors of Britain's developing welfare state quickly ran into problems. This was particularly the case with housing. The Beveridge Report had decried the 'hideous surroundings' that emerged from the 'disorderly growth of great cities' and the resultant link between 'bad housing and ill health'. It was a clear critique of 'squalor', and one that Beveridge continued in the essay 'Four Stones for Goliath Squalor' (1943), in which he called out:

> the conditions under which so many of our people are forced to live in houses too small and inconvenient and ill-equipped, impossible to keep clean by any reasonable amount of labour, too thick upon the ground and too far from work or country air.

These material deprivations made it almost impossible to satisfy a need for safety not least because, as the essay went onto contend, they leak into physical ailments and psychological problems. Dealing with the 'Goliath' of squalor was thus for Beveridge an essential task for the sake of the nation's overall health. However, a post-war shortage of building materials coupled with continual political tussles over the provision of private *versus* council dwellings meant that ambitious attempts to counter this 'squalor' were slow to get off the ground. Efforts were redoubled during Harold Macmillan's Conservative government of 1957–63, which took on the task of building 300,000 new homes per year, a drive that continued once Labour regained power in 1964 under Harold Wilson. Wilson added a range of measures to control rents and to protect tenants but as with the Macmillan government, there was a push towards home-ownership. This kept in play the widely held Conservative view that a stable society should take the form of a 'property-owning democracy'. Although the housing policies of both prime ministers had essentially egalitarian intentions, this emphasis on ownership created a buoyant market for private dwellings. Health provision may have been nationalised, but housing remained an area where the process of 'levelling up' was economically contingent. Worse still, by the end of the decade many of the new, electorate-pleasing, target-meeting council houses had fallen into disrepair.[5]

This combination of sub-par properties and low-income employment or no employment at all (contrary to the myth of 'full' employment) meant that high levels of poverty remained through-out the 1960s. Full employment was generally understood as a low level of unemployment, no higher than 3 per cent as William Beveridge had explained in 1944. He saw it as a target state in which there was no shortage of jobs, where all those looking for work were able to find it. This goal may well have been achieved in the 1960s when Britain enjoyed an average unemployment rate of 2.1 per cent, but such low figures gave no guarantee that any given job would be able to support a worker and their dependents. Poverty, as the soci-ologist Peter Townsend argued was not just a matter of an income lack – the state of those unfortunate enough to find themselves in the 2.1 percentile. Rather, it described the inability of those on low incomes to actively participate in society.

As the case very much remains today, wage differentials meant it was entirely possible to simultaneously be in work *and* be in poverty. In other words, to enjoy the material benefits that glittered in the white heat of 1960s welfare policies you needed the necessary income to rise above this threshold of 'relative poverty': to partici-pate in what Townsend called the customary 'living conditions and amenities'. He estimated that by 1965 some 7.5 million Britons were nowhere near this level and were thus shut out of 'the societies to which they belong'. Hence the appearance in 1966 of the housing charity Shelter, which by 1969 was lobbying the government to attend to the damp, squalid, overcrowded state of areas like East London's Tower Hamlets and the mental, physical and emotional toll they took. These were the conditions which drove up the numbers of homeless in the metropolitan area and which in turn fuelled the projects of Sid Rawle and the London Street Commune.[6]

In the late 1960s and across the 1970s, squatting became an alternative to the combined problem of income barriers, endless council waiting lists and the emergent unaffordability of property. As Chris Hamnett notes, the early 1970s saw the maturation of the 'post-war baby boom generation, most of whom were entering the housing market for the first time'. As they did so, the number of housing starts and completions underwent a decline, a dip which started in the late 1960s, despite the big construction pushes seen earlier in the decade. With demand outstripping supply, then, prices inevitably started to increase. In 1970 a house could be bought for an average of £5,000, but by 1973 that price had almost doubled. It would be the first of a series of sharp spikes that would continue across the decade. In 1974, at the peak of this first price rise, the poet and playwright Heathcote Williams established the Ruff Tuff Creem Puff Estate Agency, an under-the-radar operation that spread the word about London's vacant properties and advised on how to access them, secure them and make them habitable. 'Office hours were round the clock,' Williams later wrote. 'In most cases we told people where the house was, what its history was as far as we knew, explained the score in law and lent them any available equipment.'

What began as an attempt to offer the 'lushes and werewolves' of the 'Ladbroke Archipelago' somewhere to sleep after weekly rave-ups in a former bingo hall quickly became a semi-official social service. Shelter, the Campaign for the Homeless and Rootless, as well as Harrow Road Police Station, relied on Williams' resourcefulness, and on average he found himself helping fifteen to twenty people a day find somewhere to live. As with Hippiedilly, Williams' project highlighted the availability of vacant properties in the city, the extreme need for such accommodation as well as the barriers in place preventing such a resource from entering public use. You effectively had to housebreak to find a home. Clearly, the giants of 'want' and 'squalor' still dominated the social landscape in a way that demonstrated the complex intersections underpinning welfare provision. Economic poverty overlapped with material poverty, and both had an impact on personal health and well-being. As the wide scope of the Beveridge Report implied, if a welfare state was to function at its best, it was not sufficient to prioritise one vector over another nor attempt to separate the entangled strands of the public's social and material needs.[7]

The necessity of a holistic approach to post-war health was a view shared by Halbert L. Dunn. Between 1935 and 1960, Dunn worked for the US Department of Health, Education and Welfare where he was Chief of the National Office of Vital Statistics. His office was responsible for the collection of data relating to births,

deaths and marriages, information which in the form of volumi-
nous annual reports was cross-referenced with other variables
including place of occurrence and place of residence. Dunn, who
also served as Secretary General of the Inter-American Statistical
Institute (1941–52) and later became Assistant Surgeon General
for Aging (1960–61), was well placed to see ripples and patterns in
this enormous dataset. In collating the reports he could observe the
fortunes of a steadily growing population, chart the growth of the
post-war baby boom, assess the health of seemingly cherished institutions like marriage through analysis of divorce rates, and identify
points of critical mass where location and mortality converged. If
America's social security system was busy building post-war society,
Dunn's metrics offered a view of what it was actually like to live in
this new world.

   As far as Dunn was concerned, the outlook was troubling.
Post-war Americans were enjoying an increased life expectancy due
to high levels of infectious disease control, but the 'chief source of
mortality' now lay with the diseases of 'civilization', such as 'cardiovascular disease and cancer'. In articles published between 1957 and
1959 in the *Journal of the National Medical Association*, the *American
Journal of Public Health* and the *Canadian Journal of Public Health*,
Dunn noted that the population was expanding and ageing, and that
this growth was in turn leading to urban overcrowding alongside an
increasing degree of technological interconnectivity. As such, people
were living closer together, for longer, in cities that ran according to
ever more urgent tempos. In this pressure-cooker context, Dunn
argued that social health should encompass more than a defensive
battle against disease. The emphasis should also be affirmative,
focusing on the maintenance of a high quality of life, one that that
enables the individual to function within society 'as a dynamic unit'
with a 'sense of value and dignity' up to and including their later
years. Dunn believed that the human species, with its intelligence,
its adaptability and its capabilities, can and should strive to be more
than merely 'not ill'. It was possible to step outside of the negative
half-existence of 'unsickness' and live in the positive, 'alive with the
glow of good health'. Dunn defined this resonating, radiating state

as 'wellness' and in using this word he did not have the opposite of illness in mind. Wellness for Dunn was not merely the experience of 'being well or in good health'. Instead, he redefined it to mean a fluid, productive and propulsive condition of change. Dunn saw wellness as an improving process 'in which the individual moves forward, climbing towards a higher potential of functioning'.

Dunn was not selling a miracle cure, nor did he have a simple three-step solution to hand. Rather, he used the article 'What High-Level Wellness Means' (1959) and the resulting book, *High-Level Wellness* (1961), to describe the human being as a 'neuromuscular complex', a processing conduit that takes energy from its surroundings and expends energy into the world. Adding detail to this 'panoramic view', Dunn also argued that the human exceeded the physical structure of the body and its 'organized manifestation'. It encompassed two further interconnected spheres: 'the mind', that which 'transcends the body through the projection and use of the imagination'; and, more ambiguously, 'the spirit', not a 'metaphysical or religious entity' but the 'vitality of the person and their will to do things', their 'aliveness'. These human coordinates have since become the holy trinity of the wellness industry, with 'Mind, Body and Spirit' naming everything from magazines to festivals and entire publishing categories while furnishing any number of boutique websites with a catch-all strapline. Dunn, however, was not interested in wind chimes, chia seeds and crystals. He was using these terms to describe the interrelated faculties that make up the organic, cognitive and sensitive entity that is the human.

Each individual, he argues, is a unique 'total personality' within 'an ever-changing environment and flow of events'. This continuum affects our 'inner and outer worlds' in different ways and we are continually responding to and influencing our environments in relation to these physical, psychological and spiritual capacities. It is not enough, then, to base our survival on our biological needs alone. Food, water, oxygen and heat are all necessary energy sources but beyond this there are other 'basic needs': fellowship, love, balance and a sense of purpose. These are the qualitative interactions that support our lives as thinking and feeling beings. We require these to grow, to fuel our creativity and to give our lives meaning. Without them we wither like the leaves of a plant straining for the light. Dunn implies that the overcrowded, overstimulated modern world puts us in this etiolated position because it so often denies us the 'freedom and space' to really flex and live life to the full. This expansive and energised optimum state is the health goal Dunn defines as 'high-level wellness': an 'integrated method of functioning' which appeals to and activates human totality and is 'oriented towards maximizing the potential of which the individual is capable.'[8]

This theorisation of wellness as an excess of health clearly echoes the ecstasies of self-actualisation described by Maslow in 'A Theory of Human Motivation'. Indeed, Maslow gets a brief citation in *High-Level Wellness* when Dunn speculates on the creative faculties and how to motivate people towards achieving their maximum potential. For the most part, though, Dunn's writing on wellness sees him joining the great tradition of sweeping humanistic statements. In both *High-Level Wellness* and the articles that fed into it, he tells us what we should be doing and what we are capable of, but he provides little in the way of specific, technical details as to how this great goal is to be achieved. He argues that wellness is contingent on satisfying his own list of 'basic needs'; he talks about the importance of balance, rest and leisure; he impresses upon his readers the need to improve 'urban blight' and continually reminds us of the value of mental as well as physical and spiritual health. But, beyond this, the challenge of wellness is left for others to resolve. Dunn notes only that it should be an interdisciplinary, non-partisan goal sought 'both by individuals and society within its various groups, ideologies, races, religions and cultural patterns.'[9]

As he made clear in *High-Level Wellness*, Dunn was following the World Health Organization's constitutional definition of health as a complete state of well-being, and he was also influenced by the Truman Commission's recommendations on immediate and long-term health requirements. These were not merely passing references. Dunn's professional life took him to the heart of health administration. As well as his roles at the Office of Vital Statistics, he also served, from 1951 onwards, on the WHO's Advisory Panel of Experts on Health Statistics. Furthermore, he was keen to draw a distinction between 'good health' and the 'active pursuit' of wellness. As Daniela Blei argues, Dunn regarded good health as an objective matter, 'dictated by the cold, hard truths of modern medicine', while wellness was subjective, based on 'perception' and 'the uniqueness of the individual'. This model, as Anna Kirkland puts it, was 'explicitly hierarchical'. Dunn would not have disagreed with the WHO's policy claim that health was the 'fundamental right of every human being', but he also believed 'there were lower levels of wellness and higher ones'. His aim was to advocate for a personal ascendency, 'to move everyone up from where they started to high-level wellness'. Hence the emphasis on individual as well as social responsibility. Wellness was not going to be conferred upon society, but it was the ongoing responsibility of each individual to pursue it.[10]

In this regard, Dunn's thinking carries with it shades of neoliberalism, the economic theory then being road tested by the scholars and economists of the Swiss think tank the Mont Pelerin Society. As we will see later, neoliberalism became an aggressive, corporatist ideology and the primary discourse of the Western New Right in the later 1970s. In the immediate post-war period, however, neoliberalism entered an 'activist phase' as a non-partisan, economically oriented response to the crisis of totalitarianism. It proposed a worldview in which the operation of the markets superseded that of national governments and freedom is understood in terms of a competitive, propulsive consumerist mentality unhindered by state interference. Similarly, although Dunn does not explicitly stray towards matters of political economy in his writings and lectures, he nonetheless advocates for something of a free-market approach to the achievement of personal health. Specifically, Dunn was not lobbying for a top-down system of welfare but was instead arguing for a liberalised approach to well-being in which individuals should be free to thrive in an unrestricted, self-generated culture of wellness.

Such a target, coupled with this emphasis on self-responsibility, initially suggests that Dunn had a laissez-faire politics of well-being in mind. However, *High-Level Wellness* did not share the aggressively individualistic pursuit of self-interest as proposed by parallel post-war voices like Ayn Rand and her novels *The Fountainhead* (1943) and *Atlas Shrugged* (1957). The apparatus of the state was necessary in Dunn's model, and it had a crucial role to play as part of a multilevel, social, cultural and political approach to the proactive cultivation of personal agency and the pursuit of well-being. As Miller explains, Dunn believed that 'governmental policies, as well as a thick network of supportive social and cultural institutions' were required 'to support the individual in his quest to achieve high-level wellness'. The ideological problems informing this outlook, though, do start to appear when we look to the margins of Dunn's thought. Aside from his professional roles, he was a member of the American Eugenics Society and placed 'great importance on genetics as a way to improve the human condition'. His vision of social well-being thus extended to the question 'of whether society should help nature along in the process of natural selection', in order to 'yield individuals' better able to meet the elevating demands of wellness. As Miller rightly notes, it is difficult to tally this position with the clear line of humanism that otherwise runs through his work.

One way of interpreting, rather than defending, such a provocation is to return to the social mission of *High-Level Wellness*. In addition to conceiving the human as a complex of the body, the mind and the spirit, Dunn spoke of each individual as an active agent in a series of other groups including the family, the community and the wider society. He claimed that the positive pursuit of wellness at a singular level could thus feed into these interconnected networks. The more people focused on this self-improvement at a personal level, the better it would be for the social group as a whole. There is thus an implied sense of duty connected to Dunn's theory of wellness. It emerges as a contemporary version of the Greek virtue of *eudaimonia*, the sense of 'good-spirit', welfare and happiness that Aristotle argued for as the highest good. We should strive for this, Dunn encouraged; we should extend our limits and exceed them not merely as an act of private investment but also for the purposes of social betterment: a release of creative energy for 'the good of all'.[11]

*****

This deeply aspirational but not unproblematic concept echoed ideas offered by other public thinkers at the time, particularly the English polymath and author Aldous Huxley. An Englishman in California, Huxley began his career with biting satires of British manners like *Crome Yellow* (1921) before later delving deep into Buddhism, Hinduism and other branches of 'Eastern' thought. He experimented with mescaline and extolled its mystical virtues in *The Doors of Perception* (1954) and then went on to try LSD, conjuring up in the process the counterculture's very own magic word 'psychedelic'. Like Dunn, Huxley was an advocate for human development or, as he termed it, 'human potentialities'. He too assumed a broad approach focusing not on the practicalities of health care but upon the social, political and evolutionary implications of the theme.

Huxley stated his case most clearly in two lectures, one given at the University of California, San Francisco Medical Centre in 1960 and a second delivered at the Massachusetts Institute of Technology in 1961. The texts were subsequently revised and published as two separate essays, 'Human Potentialities' and 'Education on the Non-Verbal Level'. In each, as Jake Poller explains, Huxley started with the same point, that there has been 'no Darwinian evolution in *Homo sapiens* in the past twenty thousand years'. Great progress had been made in technology – in the tools, the instruments and the equipment that has extended the abilities of the individual – but the meaning, the purpose and the *capabilities* of the human have remained largely within the same parameters.

Why then, in light of these achievements, can we not push further? Affluent, scientifically sophisticated, 20th-century 'man', Huxley argued, sits on a vast reserve of potential: creative, economic and psychological. If the same energy that went into the construction of the modern world could be channelled into human advancement; into the search, for example, for ways of accessing more than 'ten percent of all the neurons in his brain' the species could be poised to make an enormous leap forwards: 'We might be able to produce extraordinary things out of this strange piece of work that a man is.' Dropping the gendered emphasis on 'man' would have been a good start, but instead of taking that *truly* radical step, Huxley sprints on. He calls for a massive injection of research funding to develop education programmes that will cultivate the potential 'for rationality, for affection, for kindliness, for creativity – still lying latent in man'.[12]

Huxley followed his lectures with his last novel, *Island* (1962), which is essentially an extended essay on the human mind, its plasticity and the enduring question of the ideal society. It is set on Pala, a mysterious island community somewhere in the Indian Ocean upon which Will Farnaby, a cynical, world-weary journalist, finds himself conveniently 'stranded'. Farnaby quickly discovers that Pala is a pacifist society, one that has dispensed with the dogma of organised religion and has replaced the 'traditional' family unit with a communal and harmonious sense of group identity. When Sid Rawle spoke to RTÉ about living on Dorinish together, 'peacefully, loving, helping one another', he could easily have been talking about Pala. Except, of course, that Huxley had the good sense to imagine Pala as a tropical paradise, not a damp and desolate rock in the middle of Clew Bay.

As the novel progresses, Palanese culture is revealed to be a hybrid of 'Western empirical science' demonstrated by the 'soil science and planting breeding' of the island's 'Agricultural Experimental Station' and 'Eastern mystical philosophy' that includes yoga, meditation and 'Buddhism shot through with tantra'. It is a syncretic system oriented towards an ideal of 'Good Being', designed to make 'every man woman and child' as 'perfectly free and happy as it's possible to be'. As Farnaby learns from the island's little green book, Old Raja's *Notes on What's What*, Good Being is a state of mindfulness found 'in the knowledge of who in fact one is in relation to all experiences'. Access to this knowledge is gained through Moksha, Pala's psychedelic drug that lies at the heart of a highly ritualised initiation ceremony. Moksha is a 'reality-revealer', the 'truth and beauty-pill'. It is a transformative and liberating substance that frees the user into an enlightened state of symbiosis with the world. In Huxley's better known novel *Brave New World* (1932) the inhabitants of his bleak urban dystopia rely on Soma, a controlling sedative that numbs the mind. Moksha, by contrast, opens it up and launches the initiate – and eventually Farnaby himself – into a blissful, transfigured unity 'with Oneness'.

Islands and altered states were closely connected in Huxley's thinking. In 'Heaven and Hell' (1956), another of his mescaline essays, he spoke of the 'antipodes of everyday consciousness', the territory of 'visionary experience' that one can access via the drug as well as LSD and other forms of psychic augmentation such as hypnosis. Exploring one's inner world was, for Huxley, akin to an epic ocean voyage, a movement 'beyond a dividing sea' from the 'Old World of personal consciousness' to a series of 'New Worlds', the largely unexplored 'far continents of the mind'. According to Huxley, it was necessary to visit these inner extremes – the antipodes – which were further than the 'not too distant Virginias and Carolinas of the personal subconscious' and the 'Far West of the collective unconscious' to fully understand the psyche and the extent of its abilities. With *Island* he was attempting to literalise this elaborate metaphor by bringing into clear relief his prospect of the 'terra incognita'. Pala is offered not just as a place of escape but also as an exemplum, a demonstration of what human culture could achieve in terms of social, psychological and spiritual advancement if the idea of community and communal well-being was courageously rethought. As Huxley put it to *The Paris Review*, *Island* was a 'fantasy [...] about a society in which real efforts are made to realise human potentialities'. In part, *Island* suggests that we all have a Pala somewhere inside our heads, the task is to find the right vehicle – chemical, psychic or otherwise – to travel there, to learn from it and to put such lessons to work in our wider lives. To use Gorman Beauchamp's neat distinction, it was a 'eutopian' essay grounded in 'eupsychic' principles: Pala represents the 'right ordering of society', but it is a society that emerges from and is driven by the shared enlightenment of its population.[13]

This call for evolutionary cultivation very much reflects the attitude and economic culture of Huxley's adopted homeland. The basic argument of 'Human Potentialities', a lecture given by a British-born intellectual steeped in Asian philosophy, is, in essence, Californian. As the coastal goal of America's westward progression, a state formed out of the gold rush, rich in orange groves and luscious farmland, home by 1960 to the appropriately named Richfield oil well (one of the deepest and most profitable in America) and awash with readily available cheap labour, California has always been a capitalist paradise. As America's wealthiest state, California has continually projected an aura of potential, the sense that its resources are not merely plentiful but infinite: there to be exploited and enjoyed by anyone drawn towards its seemingly endless sun. As The Beach Boys put it in 'California Girls' (1965), neatly but nauseatingly eliding abundance, consumption and sexuality, it is a place where there are 'two girls for every boy'. With 'Human Potentialities', Huxley was arguing for a similar free enterprise of the mind, a means of priming the psychic pump to ensure that coming generations would be able to reap the rewards of their genetic inheritance. Like the oil field that bubbles underneath the family plot, we already have the raw material in our grasp. The challenge, Huxley would argue, lies in tapping, extracting and refining this vast source of energy.[14]

Dunn would have agreed with Huxley's basic argument, but he also recognised the need for a systemic as well as individual realisation of human potential. For all his emphasis on self-responsibility, Dunn understood the key role of public institutions like hospitals in shaping attitudes towards health and well-being. Between 1923 and 1935 Dunn had worked as Assistant in Medicine at the Presbyterian Hospital in New York and held a Fellowship in Medicine at Mayo Clinic in the same state before directing the University Hospital at the University of Minnesota. Writing in *High-Level Wellness*, the book he published just as Huxley was touring the campus circuit, Dunn reflected on this phase of his career and recalled a professional culture of doctors whose 'training was oriented towards disease'. They were well equipped to 'fight against sickness' but little time was spent on the other battle, the fight 'for a condition of greater wellness'. This limited approach filtered down to the patients who wanted to be 'well' but only in terms of being 'free from sickness'. Dunn found that once 'cured' in the short term, they were 'rarely interested in becoming more well'. At each level wellness was assumed to be a single state, a neutral plateau which offered neither the debilitation of illness, nor the peak experience that comes when firing on all cylinders; when we are, as he puts it, radiant with 'energy to burn'. So deeply ingrained were these attitudes and procedures that Dunn, like Huxley, believed it would take vision and commitment to define a different approach.[15]

✳✳✳✳✳

One member of Huxley's audience at the University of California was certainly ready to commit. Richard 'Dick' Price was what *Look* magazine would by the mid-1960s be calling a 'seeker': ambitious, spiritually curious, intellectually adventurous, and deeply, deeply frustrated with the expected callings of American middle-class life. Price was twenty-nine in 1960 and by that time he had studied psychology at Stanford and spent an unfulfilling spell in its graduate school. He had served in the Air Force, been married and divorced, had entered and exited the corporate rat race and in between had undergone electroshock treatments in several psychiatric institutions. All the while Price had been immersing himself in the lectures and study circles of San Francisco's North Beach, pursuing an intense, self-directed study of meditation, comparative religion and Zen Buddhism.

This study had been his refuge, but it had also been the source of his unease. Exploring Buddhism had altered Price's sense of self, unhooked him from such binding concepts as 'I' and all the social expectations that came with it, to say nothing of the restrictions of organised religion with its personal, paternalistic, authoritarian god. What could be called Price's 'breakdowns' were symptomatic of this cognitive dissonance. Spiritually and philosophically Price was at odds with the 'normal' world, but it seemed to him that there was little in way of a coherent, alternative framework to step into. Similar existential crises had, in the 1950s, led others to North Beach and the city's nascent 'Beat' scene while later in the 1960s the destination would have been the hippie epicentre of Haight-Ashbury. Price, standing at the start of the 1960s as one subculture waned and another was yet to fully form, was desperate to define his own space of psychic and physical anchorage. After all his difficulties, he was looking for guidance and Huxley's message of spiritual entrepreneurship fired him up with a sense of mission. Price did not so much drop out as jump in.[16]

Within a year, Price, along with his friend and fellow seeker Michael Murphy, had taken over the operation of Slate's Hot Springs. Slate's was a motel resort up on Highway 1, the spectacular coastal road running through the bohemian artists' community of Big Sur. The business was owned by Murphy's grandmother and the land had been in his family since 1910. However, by 1961, the fortunes of the resort (which was little more than a collection of buildings, a bar and a gloomy bathhouse) had faltered. Despite the views, Slate's was just too far-out of town to attract more than a few of rowdy Big Sur locals and occasional gay weekenders looking for a clandestine alternative to San Francisco's saunas. Price and Murphy thought it was perfect: far-out was exactly what they were looking for. Deal done with Murphy's family, the renamed 'Big Sur Hot Springs' opened to the public in September 1962 as an 'experimental center for the exploration of new ideas'.

They invited Huxley to visit and soon after hosted a lecture by the writer and philosopher Alan Watts, the English author of *The Way of Zen* (1967), a book generally credited with bringing the liberative potentials of Zen Buddhism to the Californian counterculture. Then, taking their cue directly from Huxley's lectures, Price and Murphy formalised their programme with 'The Human Potentiality', an inaugural season of lectures and workshops. This initial offering featured academics and writers who were boldly and collaboratively pushing at the boundaries of their disciplines. As Walter Truett Anderson describes, one of the earliest speakers was the Stanford engineer Willis Harman, who offered 'The Expanding Vision', a seminar dealing with what he termed 'the current conceptual revolution in psychology'. Later in 1962 the psychologist Joe K. Adams and the anthropologist Gregory Bateson led a seminar on 'Individual and Cultural Definitions of Reality' while Myron Stolaroff, an electrical engineer and psychedelic researcher, convened 'Drug-Induced Mysticism', a ground-breaking session on LSD. Overall, the programme was built on a principle of 'synthesis:

the flowing together of East and West, the ancient and the modern, science and religion, scholarship and art', all in the confines of a stunning clifftop location complete with the added benefit of mineral-rich, restorative hot-water bathing. The project quickly gained pace and by 1965 Price and Murphy were offering adventurous seminars and provocative group work alongside 'yoga, massage, t'ai chi [and] meditation'. By this point the branding had shifted again with 'Big Sur Hot Springs' giving way to another name that was both more formal and somehow more mysterious. Appropriating the name of the extinct indigenous tribe, variously known as 'Eslen, Eclemach, Excelen [or] Ensen', to whom the land used to be sacred, Price and Murphy renamed their centre the Esalen Institute.[17]

Esalen was Murphy and Price's very own Pala, an island of ideas sitting at the far edge of America where the expansion of the mind and care of the body could be fully and productively integrated. Its founding has become an oft-told classic in the twin histories of modern American health and modern American spirituality, a story that often casts Price and Murphy as the exceptional inheritors of ancient traditions. In his history of the centre, Jeffrey J. Kripal speaks of a 'tantric transmission' that links Esalen to the vast reserves of pan-Asian philosophy. In this telling, these ideas are passed, like a ceremonial torch, to Price and Murphy who appear in the story as two young, unique visionaries able to convert challenging theories into pioneering practice and who, in turn, go on to inspire a wave of alternative health systems.[18]

The reality, as ever, was more complicated and far less linear, mainly because Esalen was not the first of its type. In 1958 the 'holistic medical retreat' Meadowlark opened in Hemet, California, offering its clients a 'composite of medicine and religion, art, psychology, homeopathy and nutrition'. Before that, the British writer and philosopher Gerald Heard established his monastery-like Trabuco College (1942–49) in California's remote Trabuco Canyon as a residential centre for mediation, prayer and the study of comparative religion. Heard was a close friend of Aldous Huxley and a fellow spiritual explorer. It was Huxley who advised Murphy and Price to consult with Heard when they first mooted the idea of an institute, and what became Esalen mirrors much of the Trabuco model. Elsewhere, across the Atlantic, similar projects were emerging independent of Esalen's influence like Centre House in London, founded in 1966 by the businessman turned micro-biologist Christopher Hills. Residents of Centre House studied yoga and meditation and attempted to bridge spiritual and scientific disciplines in pursuit of a 'group consciousness'. Within this growing milieu, Price and Murphy also took a magpie approach to the development of their programme, combining humanistic psychology with spiritual practices to the extent that Hatha yoga, when served up at Esalen, became a secular means of achieving self-actualisation rather than the ecstatic awakening of Kundalini.[19]

With encounter groups also in place, Esalen's remit could be summarised as a syncretic, multifocal approach to the treatment of those who are, in a basic physical sense, already well. Having absorbed the mission of humanistic psychology to develop the potentialities of the 'self-fulfilling human being', the project inevitably came to mirror aspects of Dunn's wellness concept. Both Dunn and the Esalen team wanted to supercharge what *High-Level Wellness* called the creative capacity 'latent within the individual'. They envisaged an idealised human figure who, glowing with the benefits of holistic health, could, in Dunn's words, step confidently into an 'open-ended and ever expanding tomorrow'.[20]

Despite this overlap, however, Dunn's work failed to gain the audience that grew up around Esalen. *High-Level Wellness* certainly had its supporters in the medical sector, like the health policy planner Henrik L. Blum and Lewis Robbins, author of *How to Practice Prospective Medicine* (1970), but the book made no large-scale impact and there was no widespread rollout of its ideas. Part of the problem was exposure. Dunn frequently gave public lectures and appeared on radio, but these were often at a very local level like the series he presented at Arlington Unitarian Church, West Virginia during 1959, which laid the basis for *High-Level Wellness*. The book stayed in print throughout the 1960s but its small publisher, R.W. Beatty, did not have the resources to give it national visibility. So, while Huxley became the patron saint of psychedelia and Esalen absorbed his work as well as that of Maslow and Rogers into the human potential movement, *High-Level Wellness* remained something of a cult text among medical and administrative professionals. Dunn's book lacked a bridge, a point of linkage that could connect its small but enthusiastic readership with the kind of ideas flowing in and out of the Esalen scene. This eventually came in 1971 when John Travis, then a resident doctor in preventative medicine at Johns Hopkins Hospital, 'rediscovered' *High-Level Wellness* via the remainder pile at the university's medical bookshop. 'It changed my life,' he later explained. *Saved* his life might have been a better way of putting it.[21]

Travis was the young physician whose first internship at the Public Health Service Hospital in San Francisco had led him into a severe state of depression. Months of pumping drugs into terminal cancer patients had left him feeling irresponsible and utterly powerless; at one point his despondency became so bad that he even started to contemplate suicide. One day in 1970 he found himself on the hospital's roof, gazing down at the ground below, wondering if the drop was high enough to kill him. Eventually, he decided it wasn't. Travis stepped away from the edge and, still burdened with all his problems, slowly made his way back down to the wards. Back to the treadmill. Travis was 27 years old at the time and he had entered medicine keen to follow in the footsteps of his father, Boyd Travis, a respected country doctor from Ohio. As the frustration and disillusionment of the internship mounted, Travis' crisis was compounded – and likely instigated – by the thought he was not living up to the standards set by this looming presence in his life. The expectation to be just as good, just as *loved*, as his father was almost overwhelming. Reading Eric Berne on the dynamics of the parent–child 'game', Travis realised that a big part of this pressure came from the sheer weight of these expectations: the views and presumptions of other people. Like Richard Price, he felt that he was living out a prewritten script, effectively trying to become his father simply because that is what everyone wanted him to do. A dose of Maslow's *Towards a Psychology of Being* helped Travis to realise his life could be more than a failed copy of someone else's, that there was a 'self' of his own, deep down in there, just waiting to be actualised.

When Travis happened upon Dunn's book less than a year later it proved to be a revelation. It offered similar arguments to Berne and Maslow, but it also reflected Travis' growing dismay with the limited scope and inefficiency of an illness-focused, 'unsickness'-producing health care system. Dunn's advocacy for wellness offered an alternative to this model but in arguing for the possibility of fully realising one's potential – of discovering and drawing on reserves yet untapped – *High-Level Wellness* also spoke irresistibly to Travis' deeper, psychological needs. Here was a book, then, that could address his professional concerns *and* help him step away from the tethering of family expectation. An evening spent at a party with Bob Dylan on the stereo provided the glue to fuse all these disparate ideas together. Listening to 'It's Alright, Ma (I'm Only Bleeding)' (1965), Travis heard the now classic line 'He not busy being born is busy dying' and suddenly realised that he had been dead too long. He was dead even before he reached the hospital roof. There and then, Travis decided it was high time he turned away from the precipice and got on with the task of being born.[22]

Just prior to this, Travis had worked closely with Lewis Robbins on his Health Hazard Appraisal Chart. A forerunner of the Health Risk Assessment, this computerised chart analysed likely obstacles in a patient's health trajectory and suggested ways of avoiding them such as lowering blood cholesterol and blood pressure. It was invaluable experience for Travis. Robbins' methodology clearly highlighted the advantages of taking a programmatic approach to defining health needs. When combined with Dunn's aspirational outlook, Travis felt he had both the theory and the practice upon which to develop his own comprehensive approach to wellness. His first step was to diagrammatise the concept into what he termed the 'Illness-Wellness Continuum' (1972). In *High-Level Wellness* Dunn used the image of dart rising through a trio of intersecting circles to summarise his ideas. This was intended to represent the matrix of mind, body and spirit with the arrow-like dart plotting the individual's intersecting trajectory of purpose as they grow 'in wholeness towards the maturity of self-fulfilment'. Travis' continuum converted this image into a horizontal scale with one arrow pointing left and another pointing right. In the middle was the 'neutral point' marking 'no discernible illness or wellness'. To the left of this was the sphere of the 'treatment model', the preserve of conventional medicine which can bring you to the neutral point through the recognition and alleviation of disease. To the right, by contrast, was the soaring arrow of wellness that moved through the stages of treatment, past the neutral point and further onwards towards the outer territories of 'education', 'growth' and 'self-actualization'. It was a direction of travel towards high-level or, as Travis renamed it, 'full-spectrum wellness'.

'If you are ill, treatment is important,' counselled Travis when later reflecting on his approach to wellness, but the message of the continuum was 'don't stop there'. We should not accept the limitation of merely being at the neutral point, a few stages away from 'premature death'. Being on the verge of a 'progressively worsening state of health' is no life at all, it is just time spent waiting for the end. Instead, argued Travis, we should be going as far beyond this as possible. To pursue wellness, as Travis conceived it, was to take this great step. It was an adventurous movement towards something extra, a life of health *plus*: an 'ongoing, dynamic state of growth'.[23]

❉❉❉❉❉

While Travis was having his epiphany, Sid Rawle and the Tribe of the Sun were falling apart. By 1972 Dorinish was becoming a distinctly unhappy place. Following their arrival at the tail-end of 1970, the group did have some success and across 1971 they fell into a comfortable rhythm, growing vegetables, building up their supplies and regularly hopping over to Westport on Tommy Cribbons' boat. Rawle was also shuttling back and forth to England getting involved in the nascent festival scene. At the same time, though, relations with the Westport locals were souring. Many in the town saw the denizens of 'Beatle Island' as a bad influence with unfounded stories of drug use and other naughtiness making the rounds. But the worst was yet to come. In 1972, strong winds tipped over an oil lamp which ignited the tents and destroyed most of the food stores. Soon after this disaster, discord started to seep through the group and numbers slowly dwindled as, one by one, exhausted Diggers headed back to the mainland. In Kevin Barry's novel *Beatlebone* (2014), a fictional account of John Lennon and Dorinish, Rawle sticks it out until the bitter end. He becomes the last man standing: a solitary figure wandering through a ravaged campsite. Eventually, he is rescued and taken back to Westport, haggard, close to starvation and ranting about heaven and hell. For Barry, the end of the camp was no accident, it was the island's occult forces doing their work. In the novel Dorinish is obliquely described as a crucible of powerful energies that push unwary visitors into states of intense introspection. It is not a paradise but a site of physical and psychic extremity, a place perfect for 'midnight screaming' because 'when you live far out there's no place left to go but deep inside'.[24]

A very different take on the last days of the Dorinish commune can be found in Alan Sidi's *Tribe of the Sun*. Sidi first covers the group's early days *circa* 1970–71 before moving to an extended coda shot in 1972, titled 'One year later'. By this point, there is only one Digger left and it is not Rawle, but a young man called Tom who struggles to survive with only his dog for company. As he collects shellfish among the grey stones, on the grey shore and under a grey sky, it looks as if he is sifting through the absolute ruins of the world. Tom explains that he has been on the island for eighteen months. When he arrived, he found 'fields being dug and chickens on order and houses being built'. This was all fine; the problem was the other people. As Tom puts it, the 'tribe' was actually an unbonded group of loners, a set of 'individuals with their own ideas' who suddenly found themselves having to 'live together like a family. Like the family you grew up in'. The dreaded family: the unit of conformity that the counterculture had spent the best part of the 1960s trying to subvert.

There is something tragic and even slightly comic in the thought of Tom travelling to an isolated island only to find the very structures he tried to leave behind. And true to form, it seems that the old tensions quickly started to emerge when Tom began to butt heads with the island's self-appointed patriarch. Without giving a name he talks about 'one man who seemed to have taken over the whole thing'. This alpha male had no time for compromise: 'Everything that was done was his own idea and he'd drawn up all these plans and didn't want anything changed.'

Sidi provides a glimpse of this dominance in the scenes of the group at work. In these moments, it is noticeable that it is the oldest member – a man blessed, coincidentally, with the loudest voice – who seems to have taken charge. Things may not be as communal or egalitarian as they appear, a point that is given a further nudge when Sidi frames a beautiful, slow motion shot of the younger members dancing across the grassland hand in hand. Watching this sequence, one might be forgiven for thinking that the young have split off from the old. They are hopeful and energetic but clearly very different to Rawle and the older, veteran squatter elsewhere on the island, both of whom toil away caked in mud, struggling to build a shelter.

It's a vignette that suggests the failure of the commune may not have been due to the island's occult forces nor the self-evident difficulty of the project. Rather, the problem lay with the all the psychological baggage the tribe brought with them: the power plays, the squabbling, the infighting, all the mindgames that Eric Berne would tell us families like to play. It takes more than an expedition to a far-off island to get rid of these tendencies. They are bound to us like shadows. Tom makes this clear as he sits alone, contemplating the future: the family structure 'doesn't work, it hasn't worked'.[25]

This downbeat end to *Tribe of the Sun* recalls the denouement of Huxley's *Island*, which sees Pala invaded by oil-seeking military forces from the neighbouring country of Rendang-Lobo. At this point it is heavily implied that Huxley's perfect society is quickly destroyed. Such a terminal end, though, is not a sign of cynicism on

Huxley's part. He has not lost faith in his ideas. Rather, the fall of Pala is his way of saying, 'We are not ready.' Whatever the social and cultural attractions of the island, the human species has, in Huxley's view, not yet realised the potential to achieve something similar. The short-term allure of political and mercantile exploitation continues to hold us back.[26]

So too for the Tribe of the Sun. They had arrived with the intention of living autonomously, away from the rat race of jobs and money, but it was not enough for them to pitch their tents, start tilling the land and expect the new society to simply fall into place. They all could have done with a bout of primal screaming before they set off, and a course of transactional analysis when they arrived. They should have gone deep inside to reset themselves psychically in order to better respond to the personal and communal challenges involved in physically building and living in their good place. Autonomy is not just a matter of breaking free from the hardwired structures of the working world. It is also a matter of thinking free; free from the patterns, norms and expectations that previously governed such an experience. As Muriel James and Dorothy Jongeward put it in *Born to Win* (1971), their primer on transactional analysis, 'Being autonomous means being self-governing, determining one's own destiny, taking responsibility for one's own actions and feelings, and throwing off patterns that are irrelevant and inappropriate.'

In the final moments of *Tribe of the Sun* the solitary Tom offers the hope that a revived Dorinish project might possibly move in this direction. Thinking out loud, he talks about the need for sustainability and the long-term survival prospects of any populated camp that might start again on the island. To make it work, Dorinish would have to bring its community an income, not just the occasional crop yield. Any future group would have to sweat the asset and so, in a moment of entrepreneurial insight, Tom starts talking about attracting paying guests. Dorinish could provide the perfect retreat for stressed-out city workers. They would not need to give up their lives and carve out new ones on the island, but they could spend short, restorative breaks there.

Warming to his idea, Tom looks around his desolate beach. It could be the perfect place for 'therapeutic holidays', he muses. You could get well on Dorinish and really sort your head out. Then, having briefly lived among those trying to do their thing, you would be free to return to the world, refreshed and ready for another crack at the rat race.[27]

CHAPTER III

Where Do I Begin?
1970–1973

In the summer of 1972, many miles away from Dorinish, a 'very shy, weird, nerdy kind of guy' called Glenn Perry was very much in need of a therapeutic holiday. Perry was a 31-year-old programmer at the American technology company Scientific Data Systems, a Santa Monica-based subsidiary of Xerox that specialised in 'time-sharing' computing. Time-sharing allowed multiple users to work on a mainframe simultaneously rather than form a queue of individually scheduled, consecutive tasks as was the case with 'batch-processing': the operating norm for the low-speed, room-size, punch-card computers of the 1950s and early 1960s. A crucial building block in the development of the modern internet, time-sharing opened the way for fully networked computing. When the US Department of Defense approached UCLA and the Stanford Research Institute to explore the possibilities of 'computers talking to each other', it was SDS machines that bridged the gap. In October 1969 they duly made possible some of the informational traffic that would lead, two years later, to Ray Tomlinson's first network 'email', an 'entirely forgettable' bit of self-spamming sent across the ARPANET system sometime in late 1971.

Perry was in the middle of all this, working at his moveable terminal, but while great communicative leaps were taking place across computational synapses, he was beset with chronic shyness. Social interactions were nigh-on impossible. Perry could talk well enough one-to-one but anything more than that – say, sitting with *two* people in the cafeteria – and he would shut down into stony silence. He would crash like a memory-starved computer straining to send the briefest of messages. In the collaborative, team-working atmosphere of SDS, such reticence was not good. It was not doing Perry's social life any favours, either.[1]

Outwardly, he was fit and physically healthy. In the terms of Halbert Dunn and John Travis, however, Perry was not well. He was unhappy, unfulfilled, strangely disconnected from those around him. Were Travis to have placed Perry on the 'Illness-Wellness Continuum', he would have been looking left, from the neutral point on the chart towards a 'progressively worsening state of health'. As the sociologist Robert Weiss would put it, Perry's problem was a matter of 'emotional loneliness'. He was cut off. Unable to express himself, Perry could neither air his feelings nor properly relate to those around him. We need these interactions, explains Travis. They are the vital points of contact that allow us to move towards the blossoming, potential-fulfilling experience of self-actualisation. In transactional analysis they are known as 'strokes'. Stroking, according to Eric Berne, is any act that implies recognition of another's presence. Strokes can be physical, emotional or psychological but in general they are forms of acknowledgement that satisfy 'recognition-hunger', a motivating desire that has its origins in 'infantile-stimulus hunger'.

Berne's point, grounded in the importance of physical closeness in infant development, is that our ongoing well-being (if not survival) depends on this intimacy just as much as it does upon the metabolic demand for food. Problems arise when we are deprived of it, Berne adding the cautionary and colloquial note that 'if you are not stroked, your spinal cord will shrivel up'. So crucial is this need to mammal life that we seek it out even 'after the period of close intimacy with the mother is over'. Strokes appeal to the limbic system, the feeling part of the brain that governs emotions and underpins the motor of our thinking capacity, the neocortex. Strokes anchor us, shoring up our position in the world and fuelling our self-worth. Hugs and handshakes are strokes, as are gestures of approval, as are a catalogue of other signs – positive and negative – that remind us we do exist in the eyes of others. More recently, we might strain to hear strokes at the end of a phone line or listen out for them as returning texts pinging in the night. Strokes have become the red dots and the 'likes' that tell us someone is out there watching our stuff, and all the time and energy that has gone into making that video, writing that tweet and Instagramming that perfect selfie has not been in vain.

As if sounding a future echo of the detrimental psychological effects of the online world, Perry was there at the start, slipping into an internal exile while the global village of the Information Age stared to take shape around him.[2]

The irony, of course, is that Perry was not alone in his isolation. Nor, for all its apparent precognition, was his predicament new. 'Modern man,' argued Erich Fromm, 'is a mass man, he is highly socialized, but he is also very lonely.' This view is echoed by Edward Hopper in his painting *Nighthawks* (1942) as well as by David Riesman in his sociological analysis *The Lonely Crowd* (1950) and Martin Scorsese in his cinematic portrait of urban psychosis, *Taxi Driver* (1976). These and many other examples present post-war America – and modern urban life in general – as an experience of individual isolation within large, densely populated areas. William Beveridge linked 'conurbation', the 'irresistible disorderly growth of great cities', to the rise of 'squalor', one of his five giants, but the point made by Fromm and others relates to the additional, psychological, effects of city life. In the absence of the communal and social support often assumed to exist in smaller towns and villages, cities give rise to crowds in which no one mixes, where relationships are reduced to the most basic of commercial transactions, where commuters stand in virtual silence in packed trains or sit in traffic jams, alone, in cars designed to carry five. The result is a form of social atrophy in which the individual retreats from this unaccommodating environment yet suffers in the absence of this connection. As Fromm puts it, 'modern man is alienated from others and confronted with a dilemma: he is afraid of close contact with another and equally afraid to be alone and have no contact.'[3]

John Travis would later add to this analysis by calling America, with a sly nod to Alexis de Tocqueville, 'the greatest experiment in loneliness'. He was not just adding to the battery of pre-existing examples with this comment, he was also reflecting on his own personal experiences. In April 1972, having endured his time in San Francisco, Travis was part way through a preventative medicine residency in Baltimore. He was living in a commune-like 'intentional community' called Koinonia, having decided it was 'either that or Vietnam'. One night Travis was at home, in bed, with his wife Sally by his side and their two-month-old daughter Hanne asleep next door. On the face of it, this was a scene of domestic contentment: the young family at rest. In reality, things were far from well. Sally was sat up, shouting at Travis, calling out her husband's chronic lack of emotion. Neatly proving her correct, Travis just lay there, staring at the wall and saying nothing, worried about what the neighbours were thinking. He felt hurt to be the target of Sally's anger, but he was simply speechless when he tried to respond and make his feelings known. Suddenly, though, something kicked in. Travis felt a growing sense of pressure welling up inside him and a 'sense of unreality' descended. He sat up, let out a yell and then rammed his head into the plasterboard at the top of the bed. In the silence that followed he sobbed and stared at the dent: a splintered Rorschach. It was a while before he realised Sally was no longer there. She had left the room and, with Hanne in her arms, left the apartment.

In 1978, some six years later, Travis wrote about the incident in his diary. It is a vivid account but one that largely sidelines Sally's distress in favour of emphasising his own feelings of isolation. If anything, the implication is that what Travis calls his 'depressions' were somehow Sally's fault: she was 'spending so much time nurturing Hanne that she hardly had any time for me'. What Travis came to call the headbutting 'Capricorn Incident' did prompt him to seek help, but in 1972 his options within traditional care were limited. According to the American Psychiatric Association's *Diagnostic and Statistical Manual of Mental Disorders (DSM)*, then in its second edition, Travis' issue would have been a matter of 'Marital Maladjustment', a category for those who are 'psychiatrically normal' but experience 'significant conflicts' with their spouses. Perry would similarly have been described as 'occupationally' maladjusted, in tension with or ill at ease at his place of work. As non-specific conditions 'without manifest psychiatric disorder', those consulting the *DSM* would have considered Travis and Perry's problems 'severe enough to warrant examination by a psychiatrist' but their issues would also have fallen short of a clearly 'diagnosable mental disorder'.[4]

This was a crucial point, because although America's Mental Health Act of 1946 and the creation of the National Institute of Mental Health had done much to advance the post-war understanding of psychiatric needs, professional diagnosis remained the gatepost for the receipt of mental health care in the 1970s. It was a similar situation in the UK. A range of legislation and institutional reform including the 1959 Mental Health Act and the 1971 formation of the Royal College of Psychiatrists placed mental health needs firmly on the public agenda. However, as John Turner notes, access to 'specialist mental health services' required a GP referral to either 'a consultant psychiatrist at an out-patients clinic' or direct to a clinical psychologist. It was easy for 'mental disorders' to go unrecognised in this often administratively complex system, or for those in need of support to simply fall through the diagnostic cracks. There was also the additional, definitional issue of what conditions or behaviours came under the umbrella of mental (ill) health. For example, at the time of Travis' crisis the American Psychiatric Association still regarded homosexuality as a disorder. It would be removed from the *DSM* in 1973 only to be replaced with 'sexual orientation disturbance'. UK heath providers held much the same view across the 1970s and beyond. Although 1967 had seen the partial decriminalisation of homosexuality it continued to be thought of as a sickness, a condition to be 'cured' through psychoanalysis, aversion therapy and electroshock treatment.

A further problem was the emphasis on deinstitutionalisation, a policy shift that had been growing on both sides of the Atlantic since the 1950s. This focus on 'community care' had resulted in the closure of dedicated psychiatric hospitals and the ramping up of admissions policies for those who remained. It was a process that suggested living in society was better for mental health than being removed from it. Given the physical state of some institutions by the 1970s, many of which dated to the 19th century, this was arguably true, but for the likes of John Travis 'society' was a big part of the problem. With its crowds of atomised, post-industrial commuters shoving their way to all-consuming, unedifying jobs in isolating, ever-growing conurbations, the modern world was far from healthy.[5]

Thanks to companies like SDS the world was indeed getting smaller, but this shrinkage was based on an accelerating rate of information and communications exchange. The 'global village' that Marshall McLuhan spoke of in 1967 as a 'simultaneous happening' of media networks in which 'time has ceased and space has vanished' was a cacophony of voices: syndicated radio, cable television and electronic data feeds. McLuhan's visionary language also obscured the material shifts involved in this acceleration. International village life was woven out of criss-crossing flight paths alongside rapid commercial developments as well as such key domestic changes as the rise of white- over blue-collar businesses, the interlinked growth of commuter-belt suburbs and the spread of choking traffic flows in between. The 'global' view in the early 1970s also brought with it (televised) images of international conflict and the mission-creep of the Vietnam War into Cambodia and Laos. Meanwhile, this ominous outward view was further darkened by the headline-grabbing forecasts of *The Limits to Growth* (1972). This socio-economic report commissioned by the Club of Rome used computer simulations to argue that unchecked economic and population growth would result in an imminent, unsustainable drain on the planet's finite resources.[6]

As such, when Travis spoke of America as 'the most discon-nected culture on the planet', he was not just talking about the high frequency of people who, like Perry, struggled to make cafeteria small talk, nor the typicality of his own domestic crisis. He had in mind the pressure, anxiety and velocity that characterised modern American life. His and Perry's feelings of isolation reflected the detrimental effects of this overload. In 1970 Alvin Toffler spoke of this as 'future shock', the overstimulated shutdown that occurs when individuals are forced to 'operate' in excess of their 'adaptive range'. Writing at the start of *Please Touch* (1970), her study of the human potential movement, *Life* journalist Jane Howard described the same state as a stifling feeling of stress, exhaustion and *angst*:

I hate inhaling smog, listening to jack-hammers, watching high-rise geometric slabs dominate landscapes [...] I grieve for birds drowned in oil slick, lakes ruined by garbage, and sheep dead of nerve gas, not to say boys dead in Vietnam [...] I think of estimates that by the year 2000 (if such a year comes) there will be 7.4 billion of us – twice as many as we are now, twice as crowded as we are now. And, because crowdedness has been proven to beget alienation, they will be twice as alienated as we are now.

Like Glenn Perry and John Travis, Howard was medically healthy: young, fit, no underlying conditions. What she describes is not the effect of an acquired illness or diagnosable psychosis that places her at odds with the world, but a feeling of deep disquiet generated by a culture that is itself unhealthy. Its rhythms and dynamics are detrimental to Howard's and, by implication, her readers' well-being. While America entered the 1970s with its economy reaching towards capital's bright horizons, its society was ill-equipped to cope with the rate of change. A shift in behaviour and attitude was needed. As Howard put it: 'Shoving and pushing and slaughtering do not suit us; we need trust. Alienation does not suit us; we need intimacy.' Perry and Travis knew things had to change, too. Fed up with their bubbles of isolation, they decided the time had come for radical action. The help that Travis sought after the 'Capricorn Incident' was one-to-one counselling and a self-led study of transactional analysis. Perry meanwhile took an even more drastic step: he went on holiday. As the summer of 1972 came round, he went on vacation to Big Bear, a quiet resort town among the lakes and mountains of Southern California.[7]

✿✿✿✿✿

Holidays and vacations were big business at the start of the 1970s. From camping trips to seaside resorts, package tours to jumbo jets, leisure time – time away from 'necessary occupations' – was increasingly spent *elsewhere*. In the UK, as Leonard J. Lickorish reminds us, four or more nights away from home count as a 'longer' holiday and in 1970, Britons enjoyed around 34.5 million of them. By 1971 some 4 million of these trips were being taken abroad. These numbers would continue to rise over the next two years, with the figures for foreign holidays nearly doubling by 1973. Back home, though, the outlook was not so sunny. While the British 1970s opened with an economy healthy enough for people to afford holidays in droves, the country, as Patrick Wright notes, was reaching the tail-end of its 'long boom', the period of growth and prosperity it had enjoyed since '1950 or so' thanks to a combination of 'centralised planning, industrial policy and the tripartite "corporate state"'. These were the circumstances that greeted the Conservatives when they took power from Labour in 1970.

As Prime Minister, Edward Heath inherited relatively low levels of unemployment and rising real living standards. However, a weak pound and a steadily increasing rate of inflation exacerbated tensions between a government that spoke of buoyant international exports and the ever more entrenched discontent of its domestic trade unions. Such fractiousness was compounded across the early 1970s by the rise in far-left militancy and the continued 'troubles' in Northern Ireland. It was a climate of perceived disorder that yielded the 'declinist' view of the 1970s, a reading that sees only a 'dismal, benighted decade' riven by strikes, urban decay and social discord. To account for the rosier picture of soaring holiday numbers across the same period, the declinist might argue that the country's political strife was so intense that the annual holiday became a getaway in every sense of the word: it satisfied a need for escape as well as rest. Certainly, there was something of an overlap between the work of Britain's policymakers and the preferences of its holidaymakers. The early decade's peak of tourist numbers came in 1973, the summer of the UK's entry into the European Economic Community. This move, intended to slough off the residual financial impact of the Second World War and to avoid political isolation, further intensified debates about sovereignty and the country's economic security. Such political soul-searching, though, did little to dampen the public's appetite for continental travel, with British tourists taking 9 million holidays abroad that year. A sizable percentage of these were spent on the Costa Del Sol, the Spanish simulacrum specifically designed to capture this new, outward-facing wave of tourism: a paradise of white sands, English pubs and unfinished hotels.[8]

The idea of the 'holiday' has its roots in the religious calendar, with 'holy days' traditionally designating points of rest, or at least periods of worship, rather than work. The American 'vacation', by contrast, attempted to carve out a secularised third space between the church and the workplace: a time to get away from it all, to 'vacate the premises and go off on your own'. In the late 19th century business owners began to encourage vacations just as the wider American public started to question 'the Puritan presumption that idle hands were the devil's workshop'. As the cities grew across the first half of the twentieth century, so did the means of getting away from them thanks to the railway and then the freeway. Despite the widespread encouragement to take time away, travelling for health and rest had previously been the preserve of the rich, with captains of industry and those graciously unburdened of the need to work drifting to luxurious European sanatoria for bouts of *lebensreform*. When John D. Rockefeller travelled to Michigan's Battle Creek Sanitarium in 1922, John Harvey Kellogg's famous 'Temple of Health' was charging guests the equivalent of nearly $3,000 for a week of chewing songs, sunbathing and hydrotherapy. As the 20th century gained pace, however, more and more resort hotels began to wait at the end of the railway line and motels started to pepper scenic roadsides, making it relatively easy for exhausted workers – especially exhausted middle-class workers – to seek similar respite and thus stave off 'a complaint of the heart or trouble in the head'.[9]

'We need to intersperse work and leisure,' argued Dunn in *High-Level Wellness*, adding that a 'balanced life is a good life'. A vacation was a key part of this balance, but as a health benefit it could only ever be a temporary tonic. Vacations were controlled forms of freedom bound to, and defined by, the world of work, an entanglement that was wound particularly tight in the 1970s when it came to working-class leisure. While British holidaymakers leafing through Thomas Cook's glossy brochures may have been offered a luxurious lifestyle – akin to the Riviera intrigue of *The Persuaders!* (1971–72), one of the many jet-setting television shows that combined wealth, sex and travel – the reality was often closer to the crushingly bleak outlook of *Holiday on the Buses* (1973). *Holiday* is an utterly joyless serving of beer and skittles, the cinematic equivalent of a fag-end in a urinal. It tries to match the equally limp achievements of rival cheeky comedies like *Carry On Camping* (1969) while unconsciously evoking a mood of desperation akin to the existential angst of Jean-Paul Sartre's play *No Exit* (1944). In this film hell really is other people. It follows Stan and Jack, two unemployed bus drivers, as they are re-employed at a Pontins holiday camp. There they work for the same boss and chase the same 'skirt', while the other campers endure an extended adolescence of exploding toilets, swimming pool mishaps and failed attempts to 'have it off' (it is a *British* comedy, after all).

Despite its lazy stereotyping, Bryan Izzard's film was depressingly true to the spirit of Pontins in the 1970s. Shot on location at Pontins Prestatyn, the site was at that time welcoming thousands of high season guests seeking a cheaper alternative to overseas package deals. Founded in 1939, Prestatyn's modernist architecture 'captured something of the glamour and fantasy of the ocean liner in its clean functional styling'. There was an emphasis on family entertainment, single guests were discouraged and Pontins, like its larger rival Butlin's, aspired to create a healthy, spa-like atmosphere. However, by the mid-1960s and early 1970s, this branding had quietly changed. Brochures still showed families gathered in chalets, but there were also plenty of photos of nightclub scenes, cabarets and revue shows, not to mention waitresses dressed as Playboy Bunnies. Drinking seemed to be going on day and night. Meanwhile, women in bikinis lounged by the pool and sat invitingly on the edge of spraying fountains, always in the foreground as the cameras took their shots.[10]

The Pontins in the seventies, then, was a bit more 'adult', not a 'veritable Beveridge of leisure', as journalist Ray Gosling memorably described Butlin's in Skegness, but something more like a massive singles bar, as some of its invisible literature attests. In a postcard sent on 6 August 1974, from Pontins Broadreeds in West Sussex, a camper called Sue writes to her friend Jackie. 'The weather is lovely', they report, 'we're going swimming later'. The big news, however, is that Sue's 'well away' with one of the Blue Coats, 'an Elvis fan'. If that fizzles, there are loads of other 'dishy fellas' that Sue and their mates can go after: 'I think we've succeeded with a couple,' they add, teasingly. Maybe this happened in 'The Lobsterpot', the pub on the front of Sue's postcard that is full of lounge suits, dimpled glasses and horse brasses. For all the outdoor pursuits on offer at Broadreeds – sailing, horseriding, beachcombing – Sue seems to be enjoying exactly what Stan and Jack hoped to find in *Holiday on the Buses*: a paradise of pools, pints and pulling. When Sue dreamily signs off with 'hope to see you around' it almost sounds as if they might stay there forever. But return they must, and it may well have been with the bump that closes *Holiday*'s terminal cycle. At the end of the film everyone is tried, spent and miserable, having come back to the drudge of families, jobs or, as in the case of Stan and Jack, the dole queue.

It was a bleak but accurate outlook. By the time *Holiday* was released on Boxing Day 1973, the socio-economic fissures that greeted Heath's government had ruptured into a complex loop of intersecting crises. Inflation had continued to rise across the first years of the decade, as had unemployment, leading to the toxicity of a 'stagflating' economy – rising prices but little growth. Soaring oil prices following on from the Saudi Arabian oil embargo added to this, while on the domestic front industrial action by miners and railway workers hit by wage-exceeding inflation rates ushered in a coal shortage and a wave of power cuts and blackouts. Buckling under the pressure and trying to stave off a full-on shutdown, Heath's government curbed energy use and put in place the three-day week. The sweeping measures were announced on 13 December 1973, came into effect on 1 January 1974 and would last for the duration of what became that year's miner's strike. Those sitting in the post-Christmas cinema watching *Holiday* thus faced many more nights in the dark and job security that was just as shaky as Stan and Jack's. When Sue's trip to Broadreeds came round in August 1974, Heath was on his way out, about to cede power to Labour under a resurgent Harold Wilson. Industrial discontent continued but most of the lights had come back on, at least. Meanwhile the tourist industry had taken a substantial hit with those rising fuel prices curbing the quick growth of 1970–73. In 1974 the travel firm Clarksons collapsed amid a price war with its competitors, leaving thousands of travellers stranded across seventy-five different resorts. Back in Broadreeds, what remained for Sue was the familiar grind of the holiday as safety valve; not an escape, but the brief blowout that quickly dumps you back into the very routines the much-desired break was meant to be a release from.[11]

In a more covert manner, the American situation was worse. Despite the profitability of the country's vacation industry, workers were experiencing a steady decline in their leisure hours at the start of the 1970s. Americans were not averse to taking trips, with the 1972 Census of Transportation showing workers taking several per year. But these were not exactly vacations. 'Trips' were journeys of 100 miles or more over the course of at least one day. They were often weekend journeys or, more likely, work-related travel. You might be able to squeeze in a visit to the lake on the way back from that convention, but such furtive junkets were a far cry from the Wake Weeks of Northern England that would see entire factory floors decamp to Blackpool. The early 1970s also found the proletarian tourist clubs of the Soviet Bloc in full force. Where American trips were counted per household, proletarian tourism emphasised 'collectiveness and massiveness', bringing together 'workers, peasants, students and intellectuals' in pursuit of 'education, culture and local knowledge'.

This is not to say that Americans abstained from vacations; far from it. By 1972 Saint-Tropez and Rio de Janeiro were seeing high numbers of American visitors. These, however, were prestige destinations that mostly catered to wealthy travellers. For blue- and white-collar workers, meanwhile, *not* taking a vacation started to become the norm. This was due to a number of factors, not least American labour laws which gave no provision for minimum mandatory vacation time. Companies were not actually required to offer paid vacations, despite the manifold and demonstrable benefits to productivity and morale. 'Up until the late 1960s,' writes macroeconomist Alberto Alesina, 'work hours per employee were about the same in the United States and Europe', with unions in both sectors pushing for more time off. In the aftermath of the 'leftist surges of 1968', however, a gap started to emerge with German, French and Italian unions pursuing a 'policy of work-sharing, demanding a reduction in hours worked as a response to rising unemployment, with slogans like "work less – work all"'. Americans by contrast, trudged on. Whether due to a lack of money, a lack of time or – in a sign of the Uberized, casual labour system to come – a fear of losing work, vacations increasingly came to be seen as a choice rather than a right. Add to this a 'rise in consumerism' and a 'slowdown in economic growth' and you had a generation of Americans drowning in affluence, trying to stay afloat by working 'more hours just to maintain an ill-considered standard of living'. As Jack Dickey put it: 'We had volunteered to exhaust ourselves.'[12]

For Travis and other medical professionals, this was a worrying situation. American employment had become a zone of assumed workaholism, a state in which the anticipated or desired vacation so often stood in for the vacation itself. This work rate may have generated gains in overall productivity, but it had come at the expense of the nation's health. As Travis later reflected, care costs nearly doubled in the five-year period between 1968 and 1973, from $53.7 billion to $95.3 billion. Much of this focused on what he called 'illness-care', the 'diagnosis of disease, the repair of injury and the treatment of symptoms'. While this approach had done much to control the 'infectious killers: T.B., diphtheria and influenza', their place had been taken by 'cancer, heart disease and stroke', conditions Travis linked to the 'excessive strains of sedentary work' common among the white-collar middle class. He reported that mortality rates among this group during mid-life (45–65) were higher than those of the population at large. In response, Travis argued that 'after-the-fact attempts at treatment and care' were not the answer. The problem was the damaging impact of a pummelling, work-fixated lifestyle. Preventative attention needed to be given to the factors feeding into smoking, obesity, depression and anxiety. These were the patterns and behaviours which, according to Travis, were leading to 'cancer, heart disease and stroke'. The situation was thus not a crisis of illness but a crisis of wellness.[13]

In turn, adopting self-care would alleviate the strain on the health sector, whose physicians, Travis argued, were regularly experiencing professional burnout. He speaks of high rates of suicide, drug abuse and heart attacks among doctors wrestling with unmanageable workloads, patching up patients and sending them back to the working lives that caused the problems in the first place. *The Year of the Intern* (1973), a novel by the physician turned author Robin Cook, echoed this view with its portrait of the sleepless, overworked, emotionally drained Dr Peters, who lurches from one crisis to another. Cook's semi-fictional character found its real-world double at the other end of the professional spectrum in the form of cardiologist Dr Robert Eliot. Ambitious, driven and consumed with work, Eliot spent the early 1970s trying to establish a cardiovascular research centre at the University of Nebraska and he succeed in becoming the university's Chief of Cardiology at the grand old age of 43. He did not smoke, he was not overweight, he had neither high blood pressure nor high cholesterol. There were no outward signs of heart disease. He was, however, weighed down with a constant sense of career pressure. Eliot later wrote that an overwhelming feeling of 'disillusionment' and 'invisible entrapment' would descend as he criss-crossed the country providing 'on-the-spot cardiology education', one exhausting seminar, conference or consultation after another. As he described in his book *Is it Worth Dying For?* (1984), life on this 'joyless treadmill' led to the inevitable outcome. In 1973, shortly after his forty-fourth birthday, Eliot suffered a massive heart attack. The tagline from *The Year of the Intern* said it all: the work that makes you a doctor threatens to 'destroy [you] as a human being'.[14]

Something had to give, and as far as Travis was concerned it was not enough to merely decry the demanding rhythms of modern American life. Things were not going to improve on their own. If change was to occur, it had to come from the ground up, led by a widespread, proactive, attitudinal shift towards the toxic status-quo. A big part of the problem was what Erich Fromm had, in the early 1950s, called 'the pathology of normalcy': the fact that such 'sickness-inducing' habits were accepted as normal, and therefore not questioned, precisely because they were so widespread and ingrained into the public character. For Travis, one of the most pernicious of these habits was the deferral of self-care. We expect our services and our surroundings to be maintained but rarely give the same attention to ourselves. To do so, says the cultural norm, is unnecessary, indulgent and even selfish. In 1973, for example, the US Civil Aeronautics Board introduced non-smoking sections on commercial carrier aircraft following passenger complaints and concerns regarding the effects of second-hand smoke on attendants. At the same time, air traffic controllers were subject to a long-standing set of medical and psychological assessments as a condition of their entry into the profession. Meanwhile, America was still producing around 600 billion cigarettes a year, the average smoker was getting through nearly 4,000 of them annually, and the prevalent view of health continued to be short-term, unconcerned with matters of mental well-being and largely reactive: 'You get sick, you go to the doctor, and you get fixed.' Preventative measures and the cultivation of long-term psychological health was not part of this general mindset in the early 1970s. If we demand that air travel be an industry of clean air and its professionals be psychologically robust, why not, Travis would argue, apply the same standards to our own daily lives? It was this self-limiting outlook that needed to be short-circuited in order to achieve lasting, resonating change. Such a shift would need a large measure of self-responsibility and a widespread commitment to a better, healthier life.

Glenn Perry thought the same, and it was precisely the debilitating treadmill of short-term solutions that he wanted to avoid. He was not interested in the quick fix. He was actively seeking a greater sense of well-being and wanted to undergo a profound and lasting process of change. He wanted to change the way he thought, the way he spoke, the way he interacted with people and, in so doing, 'improve the quality of [his] life.' And so, as his colleagues either doubled down at their terminals or else sought out the heaving exclusivity of a sun-drenched beach, Perry went inside.[15]

✳✳✳✳✳

In early 1972, Perry had been given a copy of *The Centre of the Cyclone* (1972), a book by the neurophysiologist John C. Lilly. Lilly was an idiosyncratic researcher who, from the 1950s onwards, moved restlessly between the hinterlands of Cold War science and countercultural experimentation. In 1952, after medical training and stints in wartime academia, Lilly travelled to Maryland and took up a position at the National Institute of Mental Health. As head of the Section of Cortical Integration he was involved in cross-disciplinary 'brain-mapping techniques'. As Charlie Williams has described, Lilly combined 'communications theory, neurophysiology, and psychoanalysis' in an attempt to 'physically locate and manipulate behavioural correlates in the brains of monkeys, cats, humans and later dolphins'. It was a project that attracted the attention of 'US military and intelligence officials' because Lilly argued his experiments could be used to 'modify and control the minds of enemy operatives'. As Williams puts it, the potential applications of Lilly's work extended to 'push-button control over the totality of motivation and consciousness' and 'master-slave controls directly of one brain over another'.[16]

In pursuit of this end Lilly developed invasive implantation techniques using electrodes to provide 'real-time' images of neuroelectric activity in macaque monkeys. Soon after, he started to consider dolphin communication because 'with a brain equal to or greater than man's in size and complexity', they made for the ideal electrostimulation subjects. In parallel, Lilly also focused on sensory isolation. If he was to understand the processes of stimulation and propose forms of modification, it was necessary to investigate how the brain receives and processes information. In *The Centre of the Cyclone* he explains that fellow neurophysiologists including 'Professor Bremer of Brussels and Dr. Horace Magoun of UCLA' had hypothesised that 'the brain stayed in a waking state because of external stimulation coming through the end organs of the body'. In other words, he continues, 'outside stimulation was necessary in order to maintain the brain in an awakened state'. To test this, Lilly experimented with a self-designed 'solitude-isolation-confinement tank', a small, enclosed chamber of salt water housed in a soundproof room, in which Lilly, clad in a latex oxygen mask, 'was able to reach a state of suspended neutral buoyancy just below the surface of the water in the tank'.[17]

At the same time, similar experiments were being conducted by psychologist Donald Hebb at Canada's McGill University. Proposed in 1950 and rolled out in 1952, Hebb had volunteers placed in small cubicles wearing light-cancelling goggles and insulating tubes round their arms. There was no water in these chambers. Hebb's subjects were instead cast adrift on waves of sound from white noise generators. On paper, Hebb was investigating the 'unusual sensory effects' experienced by radar observers and radio monitors whose monotonous routine jobs caused them to see a 'radar pip that isn't there and hear messages that aren't real'. The extreme enclosure expected of manned space travel was also a consideration. However, the actual – and classified – aim of the programme was to experimentally investigate communist indoctrination techniques reportedly in use during the ongoing Korean War of 1950–53. When using his chambers to experimentally recreate these states of suggestibility, Hebb did note the rapid onset of cognitive shifts in his subjects. They lost track of time and felt unable to properly orient themselves in the space. Some quickly fell asleep as if the absence of external stimuli caused them to simply shut down. Others reported that at a more advanced stage in the isolation period they drifted into 'reverie over which they had little control'.

This 'freewheeling' mental activity matched Lilly's experience. Floating in the silence of the tank, enfolded in darkness and weightlessness, he moved into a state of blissful withdrawal. Rather than sensory 'deprivation' and the cut-off of his faculties, Lilly found his mind expanding in a way that bordered on metaphysical extension. He found that the tank offered a way to explore 'dream-like states, trancelike states and mystical states', as if the introspection it induced caused doors to open that normally remained closed under the weight of the external world's constant stimulation. From here, he started to move away from the Cold War agenda of his research, and across the late 1950s and into the 1960s he became increasingly focused on accessing a higher level of consciousness: the state of

'Satori, or Samadhi, or Nirvana' described 'in the Eastern mystical literature'. This involved an immersion in what Williams calls 'a series of esoteric practices involving human-dolphin communication, psychedelic drugs and extra-terrestrial communication'. In 1970 Lilly also spent time in Chile working with Óscar Ichazo at the Arica School, searching for ways of getting into new spaces with the aid of neither the tank nor LSD.[18]

When *The Centre of the Cyclone* appeared, there was little mention of mind control or master-slave dynamics, save for a brief reference to Lilly's study of the 'neurophysiology of the brain' at the National Institute of Mental Health in 1954. Lilly had instead written an 'autobiography of inner space', an often startling account of the 'unusual, unordinary states, spaces, universes, dimensions' he experienced in search of the 'inner realities'. Eclectic and eccentric, the book could easily sit alongside the science fiction of Philip K. Dick were it not for the granite rationality of Lilly's prose. Free of exposition and context, stripped bare of any details not directly relevant to John C. Lilly, the book was not quite fantasy, nor was it an allegory posing as fact in the mode of Carlos Castaneda's story of shamanic initiation, *The Teachings of Don Juan* (1968). Rather, Lilly offered a field report on a set of extraordinary phenomena, the 'field' in this instance being the inside of his own head.

Whether recalling encounters with strange beings in the profound silence of the tank or the death and rebirth experiences he had when attempting some of Ichazo's exhausting exercises, Lilly's unifying theme was that of the 'Human Biocomputer'. As he explained it, consciousness consists of multiple operating levels, each one exceeding the complexity and sophistication of the last. We might feel that our identities are bound by fixed notions of 'I', 'me' and a certain relationship to the world's stimuli, but beyond these parameters lie the largely unexplored 'supraself' and 'supraspecies levels'. These higher states, the points at which we move beyond normal brain activity to the optimum levels of bliss, paranormal ability and cosmic awareness, represent different modes of 'programming'. They describe the various ways in which the combined system of our minds, bodies and spirits can operate and, more importantly for Lilly, can be instructed to operate. Humans *cogitate*: we receive, transform and transmit information. Echoing Aldous Huxley's views on human potentiality, Lilly argued that the success and efficiency of this procedure depends on the extent to which we can access the vast, often untapped reserves of thinking power in the mind. Such access is hampered by lack of insight, ingrained patterns of thought and poor physical health. The road to this high-level functioning, then, lay in getting fit, enhancing your well-being, and pushing your mental and physical capabilities to the limit. By opening yourself to the type of procedures Lilly outlined, particularly the mind-expanding potentialities of isolation, you could experience these higher states *and* map them. Such detailed exploration of the inner landscape was necessary to allow for sustained access to these plateaux rather than having only teasing glimpses of their vistas at the apex of peak experiences.

In *The Centre of the Cyclone*, Lilly used the word 'metaprogramming' to describe this self-generated, self-improving process of rewiring. This was the idea that lit such a fire under Glenn Perry. Not only did *The Centre of the Cyclone* speak his language of computing, but as John Travis found when reading Halbert Dunn for the first time, it also gave voice to Perry's deepest desires. Here was a human operating manual, a computer programmers' guide to self-actualisation, that outlined a scrupulous process of experimentation geared towards seismic personal growth. Best of all, Lilly clearly saw himself as a teacher. Beyond its abstract concepts and intense self-focus, the tone of the book was resolutely practical. Lilly, it seemed, was keen to guide others into their own inner spaces. This was not just a matter of rhetoric. Soon after he read the book, word reached Perry that Lilly himself was running a residential workshop where attendees could try out metaprogramming for themselves. It was to be held among the lakes and mountains of the quiet resort town of Big Bear, California. This was to be Perry's holiday destination.[19]

Once there, Perry found that the workshop was focused on a particular spot in the landscape, 'a large flat-bottomed stone bowl cut from a mountain rock with a shack on top'. The bowl was filled with 'twenty inches of fresh water' and the first morning was spent 'closing all the holes in the shack so that no light would penetrate'. Under Lilly's watchful eye, Perry and the other would-be metaprogrammers were building a makeshift isolation chamber. Once complete, they stepped back and looked at the small, mysterious structure, wondering who would go in first. Perry volunteered. He stepped into the darkness, made it down their handmade ladder and let himself float in the water, working his way through the breathing exercises Lilly had taught him. Perry was not just following the guidance of *The Centre of the Cyclone* when he entered this chamber, he was also stepping into an ancient meditative tradition of isolation and withdrawal integral to shamanic initiation and spiritual contemplation. The Tibetan Buddhist practice of *mun mtshams* or 'dark retreat', for example, suggests that deliberate and intensive sensory deprivation can produce 'profound shifts in perception and cognition'. Perry's experience was no exception. Down in the darkness he felt his sense of time expand, his spatial awareness of the pool began to change, and he quickly started to slip inside his own mind. The real change, however, started as soon as he left the chamber.

'When I came out', Perry later described, 'it was as if the whole earth was a shimmering, shining, scintillating energy system, and time had slowed way down. I was in a totally different, unfamiliar state of consciousness'. Better still, when Perry rejoined his companions for lunch, he found, to his great surprise and delight, that he was able to hold court and speak freely about his experiences. He did not shut down, he did not clam up, he was able to talk at length despite the presence of other people. All the chronic shyness that had so hampered him at SDS had fallen away. 'What a change in my consciousness', Perry reflected, 'if something could make me able to open my mouth in front of a group of people – wow, it must be really incredible!'

Keen to keep this positivity flowing beyond the workshop, Perry resolved 'to build [his] own tank to use, a lot'. He felt confident that with the right design he could also manufacture tanks for sale. He discussed the idea with Lilly and received his enthusiastic blessing before returning to Santa Monica to start work in earnest. For the next six months Perry experimented with temperature gauges, saline densities and sound insulation. At each stage Perry's aim was to recreate the powerful feeling of floatation, not just isolation. The water level had to be right, the temperature had to be adjustable and the whole casing, the tank itself, had to look and feel right. It had to be large enough to facilitate the sense of weightless drift but small enough to fit in a reasonably sized domestic space like a garage. Mountain-hewn pits beneath raised, lightless shacks in spectacular semi-rural environments did not make for easy, daily use.

Finally, Perry had a prototype and soon after, in early 1973, he was on the road again, heading along Highway 1 with the new tank strapped to the roof. He was on his way to a curious place hidden from the road and accessible by reservation only: the Esalen Institute. Lilly was running another workshop there and had invited Perry to help facilitate a 'mass-water tank experiment'. Lilly was well known to Esalen, having been attending talks at the centre since 1968 and running seminars on dolphin communications since 1969. For Perry, though, going to Esalen was a new venture. He was excited and apprehensive. Esalen was secretive, seductive and shrouded in rumour, but he knew enough from Lilly's accounts in *The Centre of the Cyclone* and articles in *Life* magazine for its name to conjure up stories of mind expansion, strange processes and naked bodies luxuriating in healing waters. Getting through this workshop would be another big step outside of his comfort zone. He would also have to ensure that his still experimental tank was up to the job and could meet Lilly's exacting standards. If ever there was to be a test of his recently acquired, floatation-inspired confidence, this would be it.[20]

*****

1973 found Esalen a decade on from its first seminars on 'The Human Potentiality', and in that time it had blossomed into an outwardly successful 'health promotion centre'. In its early years, the centre had stuck close to Huxley's party line, referring in its brochures to vast changes in 'our physical environment' in the space of a 'single lifetime' but 'little corresponding change in how we, as individuals relate to the world and experience reality'. From here, the 'tools and techniques of the human potentiality' were said to be 'generally unknown to the public and to much of the intellectual community'. Not unlike the San Jose chapter of the mystical fraternal order the Rosicrucians, who in 1963 advertised their book of 'personal power' *The Mastery of Life* in the sci-fi magazine *Worlds of Tomorrow*, Esalen initially presented itself as a source of secret knowledge. By the early 1970s, however, thanks in no small part to extensive media coverage (*Look* editor George Leonard joined the Esalen board in 1965), human potentiality had become a high-profile cultural *movement*. It was no longer the preserve of a hidden coterie but was marketed as a lifestyle; one that had grown out from the speculative, evolutionary terms of Huxley's lecture to encompass an inventory of pre-existing therapies, practices and beliefs – from the Alexander Technique to Zen Buddhism – each directed towards positive self-improvement.

Quickly spreading out from Esalen, human potential was a field in which psychology and spirituality blurred together and where the traditional psychiatric emphasis on the single individual gave way to 'a consideration of the individual within [...] small group networks'. Rather than a subject of study, human potential had become a way of being, an experiential practice, one that promised great benefits to the individual and to society at large but which should be pursued *in situ*, in the company of others. As a result, with human potential taking root in the cultural landscape, there came the parallel rise of the residential retreat, the so-called growth centre.[21]

In 1970, *Time* magazine counted 100 growth centres across the United States, Canada, Mexico and Puerto Rico, with the Association for Humanistic Psychology reporting a combined international number of more than 170 by 1972. These figures represented a diverse list of projects ranging from the 'transpersonal' Kairos centre in San Diego to the management-oriented Berkeley Center for Human Interaction. Growth centres also catered to a wide range of clients. When Jane Howard spent a year participating in encounter groups for her book *Please Touch*, she did not sink into a hippie underworld. Of course, she met her share of 'bearded guitarists', but she equally spent time with:

> cattle barons, clinical psychologists, wife-swappers, black militants, associate professors, movie stars, a professional poker player, computer programmers, publishers, insurance adjustors, engineers, dancers, ex-convicts, stockbrokers, the idle rich, the embittered poor.

It is a list that mainly consists of middle-class occupations, suggesting that while Howard met people from all walks of life, the demographic scope of her fellow members was quite narrow, despite her nod to the 'rich' and the 'poor'. In her view, though, there was no 'typical' attendee just as much as *Please Touch* outlines no 'typical' encounter group model. The main function of her list is to suggest the level of stress and overwhelm which led Howard to human potential was felt across the professional and social spectrum. It also tellingly shows that those who would have been considered part of the 'straight' world in the 1960s – the 'insurance adjustors' and 'stockbrokers' – are now, in the 1970s, seeking out experimental forms of self-development. It was a trend that had international reach outside of the growth centre model. As Howard was touring the human potential circuit, the French health sector was seeing a rise in demand for *les médicines parallèles* and homeopathic remedies were experiencing a spike in popularity in their native Germany. While communes like Friedrichshof, the Rajneesh ashram in Pune and the Tribe of the Sun on Dorinish may have carried the countercultural diaspora into the 1970s, it was the decade's *almost* mainstream industry of alternative therapies and growth centres which were rapidly cultivating a wide-ranging, popular appeal.[22]

Within this scene Esalen was frequently cited as the first of the lot, despite its debt of influence to Gerald Heard's Trabuco College as well as other long-standing institutions like the Vedanta Society of Southern California, founded in 1930. In addition to the small and often short-lived nature of its immediate contemporaries, Esalen's location, public profile and diverse programme helped it to cement this foundational status. It certainly had the facilities to stand out.

Although it was spoken of as a 'secular monastery', Esalen was not a closed order with a fixed, hermetic community. At its heart Esalen was a resort: a busy hospitality enterprise that operated accommodation, a kitchen, extensive grounds, teaching spaces as well as the bathhouse. A rotating, fluid work force of up to 50 staff members lived on site and the centre could welcome up to 70 guests, each of whom would pay around $270 (equivalent to $1,171 today) for a week's worth of room, board, and seminars. Quarterly catalogues and a mailing list numbering more than 35,000 meant that those 70 places were often fully booked throughout the year. All this was managed through a delicate leadership balance between Esalen's founders, the thoughtful introvert Richard Price and the ambitious extrovert Michael Murphy. Price handled the centre's day-to-day operations while Murphy refined the programmes and handled publicity as the de facto public face of the project.

In 1965 Esalen offered twenty programmes throughout the year. By 1968 this schedule had expanded to more than 120. As the 1970s opened, catalogues which had initially listed weekend retreats were heavy with details of week-long workshops, extended residential fellowships and the inevitable internship equivalent: the work-scholar programme. In 1967, Esalen had also opened a second outpost in San Francisco focusing on 'education, sports and social change'. This urban centre, which made use of meeting spaces in Berkeley and the city's Grace Cathedral, welcomed upwards of 10,000 attendees in its first few months. Such growth did come at a cost, and behind the scenes things were not looking good. Despite the constant flow of visitors, Esalen's $1 million annual budget barely made ends meet. By 1971 the centre was on the verge of bankruptcy. Its buildings were falling into despair and similar psychic cracks were also appearing between Price and Murphy. Price liked to keep things small, informal; Murphy saw continued expansion as the key to Esalen's future. While they tussled over the centre's direction, its practical operations started to slide.[23]

At the start of the 1970s, then, the success of Esalen was rather more symbolic than it was financial. As a central node in the world of human potential, it was able to attract key speakers and, in turn, establish significant links within an increasingly international network. In March 1970, for example, an Esalen contingent that included Michael Murphy and Alan Watts embarked on a European trip that involved a stay in London. There they connected with the British branch of the Association for Humanistic Psychology and mounted a weekend workshop showcasing Esalen-style therapy sessions. This gave a big boost to groups that were already beginning to form, like Quaesitor (which meant 'seeker'), established by the husband-and-wife team of Patricia and Paul Lowe in 1969. Soon after the Esalen visit the Lowes, along with their colleague Tom Feldberg, were running intensive encounter groups for 'singles, couples, families' from their basement flat in St John's Wood. It was not difficult to find meditation, therapy and spiritual groups in London in the late 1960s and early 1970s, but rather than fall in with the British New Age scene, the Lowes explicitly aligned themselves with Esalen's methods and language. Quaesitor advertised itself as 'a full experimental growth centre for the development of the human potential', a place to 'relax the defences [...] built up against the stresses of modern life, the rush, the noise, the pressures', where 'we can be told how other people see us, and where we can see how other people really are'. July 1970 found another Esalen group travelling to Chile to participate in a gruelling programme offered by Óscar Ichazo of the Arica School. This opportunity arose after the institute had played host to the Chilean psychiatrist Claudio Naranjo between 1967 and 1969. In the latter half of 1969 Naranjo had entered the Arica retreat and when he returned to teach at Big Sur in January 1970, he enthusiastically relayed Ichazo's offer to welcome 'a group of fifty Americans for a ten-month training period'.[24]

Price and Murphy were excellent human potential ambassadors, and their networking skills were second to none. Esalen's real problem, however, lay in that lack of business acumen. In theory, their centre was open to all comers, and it proudly presented itself as non-ideological in terms of the practices it provided. There was no specific 'system', as it were. Instead, Murphy and Price thought of Esalen as a test bed, a space in which guests could explore multiple options and soak up ideas before gravitating towards an individual programme. Like undergraduates auditing lectures, guests often registered for one group but sat in on many more during their stay. A little meditation here, a little bit of the Feldenkrais Method there before a plunge in the baths and some vegetarian food later on. Esalen had no specific monopoly on what was taught nor who taught it. Its instructors were all employed on a semi-freelance basis. This relieved Murphy and Price of the need to attend to such trifles as decent liveable wages, health care benefits and secure contracts. It also meant that in the face of such precarity, their often highly trained specialists plied their trades elsewhere. Despite the success of their showcasing trips and despite pushing forwards with the San Francisco branch, Esalen's ever-revolving door meant that its basic package was always changing. As a result it had little in the way of a specific model upon which to build a franchise. Esalen was a place, an attitude; what it had to offer was an atmosphere rather than a doctrine. Esalen was not a brand. It was, in essence, an experience.[25]

Meanwhile, after completing his work with the Esalen group in April 1971, Óscar Ichazo relocated operations to New York where he opened the Arica Institute, 'a tax-exempt corporation authorised to conduct charitable and education services'. The institute offered programmes featuring Ichazo's methods only. There was no smorgasbord of practices and therapies like at Esalen; it was the Arica approach to the expansion of consciousness and the Arica model alone. The institute also 'trained students to become teachers of its system' in the hope of spreading out operations to a series of affiliated centres. Each of these enterprises were held together by Arica's lifeblood: a set of carefully disseminated and securely copyrighted course materials. At the same time, Werner Erhard, a brash, cocky former encyclopedia salesman, erstwhile scientologist and regular Esalen visitor, was setting up shop in San Francisco and showcasing his own personal development system.

Erhard could have stepped right out of *Mad Men* (2007–15). He's a man from nowhere, a self-invented Don Draper. Born John Paul Rosenberg in 1935, Erhard sold cars in Philadelphia until 1960 when, at the age of 25, he abandoned his wife and his four children and travelled west with his second wife-to-be. It was during this transit that 'Werner Erhard' came into being. Sat on a plane with his old life behind him, Rosenberg glanced through an issue of *Esquire* magazine and found an article on the physicist Werner Heisenberg and another on the German Chancellor, Ludwig Erhard. Things started to fuse together and by the time the plane landed, Rosenberg had disappeared, and it was Erhard who disembarked. The encyclopedias came next before he joined Mind Dynamics (1968–73), a Texan company specialising in business-focused self-motivation courses. With his confidence and his conviction (clearly born from experience) that you could change your life, Erhard quickly become a highly regarded instructor at the company, adept at taking clients through the visualisation and guided meditation exercises developed by its founder, a former trainee minister called Alexander Everett. At one point, Everett considered making Erhard vice president but his protégé had already decided to branch out on his own. In October 1971 he launched Erhard Seminars Training or 'est'. Using many of the techniques he had learnt from Everett, Erhard offered a highly profitable 'power-seminar' format that sought to break down the psychological barriers between attendees and their personal goals. In practice, this amounted to weekends spent in hotel conference rooms being yelled at by a group of 'coaches'. Where Mind Dynamics avoided 'direct confrontation' and the 'personal sharing of experience', est was one long, aggressive encounter session. Over the course of a virtually non-stop 32-hour marathon, participants would be berated into airing their perceived problems in front of the hundred or so other sleep-deprived, caffeine-starved, bathroom-needing participants. A coach would then let rip, telling them and the rest of the nervous group that it was all their fault: that they and they alone were responsible for their failings.

Beneath this bruising model lay Erhard's alignment of 'self-realization' with self-confidence. He was encouraging participants to acknowledge their hesitancy, their reticence in life and their progress-blocking lack of self-esteem before willing them to ecstatically cast it all off. Once purged, exhausted and vulnerable, est would rebuild you by encouraging an attitude of extreme entitlement. You are perfect as you are, ran one of Erhard's central tenets, therefore if you want something, you should go out and get that thing. When the doors finally opened and the bad air wafted forth, you were meant to step out into this new worldview, having finally grasped the mysterious quanta of est: at some point over the weekend, you *got it*. Enlightenment retooled for the Dale Carnegie-reading entrepreneur, est was not about finding your self but about finding your guts. It convinced you that you deserved that raise, that you were going to fight for that promotion or, better still, that you were going to quit your job and, like Erhard, start your own damn company.

Unsurprisingly, given that Erhard put his name to the programme, est was as tightly and as singularly branded as Arica. Despite drawing on as wide a range of spiritual and philosophical influences as Esalen, the message of est was filtered entirely through Erhard's all-consuming presence and persona. Local offices sprung up in other cities and a stream of books and tapes followed, each reiterating what was, in effect, a cult of personality based on Erhard's image of self-made success. The barking coaches who ran the marathon seminars all spoke like Erhard and dressed like Erhard: the same flares, sports jackets and open shirts; the same macho patter of the salesman smashing that month's targets. Signing up to an est seminar meant buying into this hype; it meant embarking on a journey of discovery that was exclusively mapped out by Erhard's distinctive intellectual property. Like Ichazo, Erhard also had no qualms about aggressively protecting this product. In the 1970s and beyond, Arica and est became embroiled in various copyright suits against authors who wrote about their experiences on the programmes as well as ex-students who had, unsanctioned, attempted to teach the methods for themselves.[26]

With the arrival of JP Tarcher in 1973, a publisher specialising in human potential titles, the 'movement' was clearly on its way to becoming a profitable industry. For their part, Esalen had negotiated a publishing deal with Viking in the late 1960s and their catalogues offered much of what could be found at Arica and est, albeit with some of the volume turned down. However, unlike these other enterprises, Esalen never made the leap into a fully fledged franchise. In some ways it was a victim of its own success. Esalen gathered together a range of disparate practices in a business model that could be easily replicated by anyone who had the basic facilities, products and specialists at hand. You did not need a coastal panorama, either. Down in San Francisco growth centres were springing up in shopfronts and hired community halls. As Quaesitor proved, you could even turn your own flat into a growth centre. For some members of the Esalen board, the absence of a string of resorts was a principled refusal, for others it spoke of a failure to capitalise. Either way, while Esalen led the public understanding of human potentiality throughout the 1960s, once the field morphed into a bullish market in the 1970s it lost ground to a new, bustling mix of competitors.[27]

*****

When he arrived at Lilly's Esalen workshop, Glenn Perry was eager to see how his tank would run. He set it up, added a salt-water solution to help with floating, got the filter working and turned on the temperature control system. In addition to the tank being 'lightproof and soundproof', the water had to be, as per Lilly's suggestion, 'at ninety-three to ninety-four degrees' so you 'can't tell where the water ends and your body begins'. Having this constancy was crucial, it meant the difference between the blissful loss of outlines and an hour spent sploshing about in a dark, tepid pool. Heater on and with the workshop underway, Perry thought he could permit himself a little relaxation, so he dropped a tab of LSD and took in the glorious Pacific view. Sometime after he was approached by Lilly who, much perturbed, told him the tanks were cold because the water was not heating up. They needed a quick fix, and Perry – still tripping – suggested driving to the next town to find a replacement heater. Realising that Big Sur probably didn't have a repair shop catering to experimental isolation tanks, Perry and Lilly came up with another idea. They found a hosepipe, ran hot water through it and submerged it in the solution to act as a makeshift radiator. Perry tended to the pipe throughout the weekend and managed to keep the water warm. 'I had survived the ordeal,' he later wrote. The 'old' Glenn Perry would have crumpled if put on the spot to solve such a problem. Now, even under the haze of acid he was able to 'change [his] state and become functional'. The tank was clearly doing its work.[28]

Perry's maintenance skills aside, the 'mass-water tank experiment' was successful because it closely aligned with Esalen's standard offerings. By 1973, as the human potential market diversified, Esalen doubled down and stuck with its stock-in-trade, three therapeutic methods that collectively ministered to the mind, the body and the spirit: gestalt therapy, bodywork and encounter groups. In the main, Esalen's encounter sessions continued to follow Carl Rogers' person-centred approach but under the direction of facilitators like the social psychologist Will Schutz, author of *Joy: Expanding Human Awareness* (1967), they had developed into marathon, free-flowing sessions that could last for days, if not weeks. Groups of around ten to fifteen people would convene and with neither leader nor agenda, they would try to break the social ice, pushing through the layers of hostility and awkwardness until a baseline of trust was achieved. Then, when the emotional flow began and members found themselves sharing the details of their inner lives, the group would variously act as audience, critic and confidant in a spontaneous, self-defined form of communal therapy. The aim, according to Schutz, was to create 'joy': the fulfilment of one's potential, 'fulfilment' being a feeling of confidence and capability. It was the sense that you can respond to the challenges of your environment and express yourself freely.

Schutz shared common ground – and no small amount of rivalry – with another of Esalen's key figures, the gestalt psychologist Fritz Perls. A fixture of the institute from 1964 to 1969, Perls was in his seventies when he began working at Big Sur. By then, he had seen both world wars play out as bookends to his psychoanalytic training in Vienna and Germany, a period that brought him into contact with both Sigmund Freud and Wilhelm Reich. The gravity of this illustrious experience, however, had not given rise to a cerebral, sedate elder statesman. Rather, he descended on Esalen as a puckish and provocative ringleader who fully embodied the confrontational attitude he brought to his gestalt practice. Gestalt – the

up the cogitating human being. Reading Lilly and Perry's accounts of their transformative experiences gives the impression of them crawling into the darkness only to discover a private sea, one that opens out to an 'oceanic feeling': an unalienated, undifferentiated immersion in the unconscious and its creative, fluid potential, free from the regulating agency of the ego. If Esalen was a 'Cape Canaveral for inner space', as it was enduringly labelled in the late 1960s, then Perry's homemade tank was a psychic starship. You could climb aboard and drift off, much like the cosmonaut Kelvin in Andrei Tarkovsky's *Solaris* (1972). Awaiting launch to the sentient planet and its orbiting, afflicted space station, Kelvin sits enclosed in the dark with only his eyes visible. 'When is lift-off?' he asks over the radio to ground control. 'You're already flying,' comes the reply, back into the capsule. Kelvin does not notice his departure because he is, of course, travelling without moving. Despite all the film's talk of far-off destinations, he's not going anywhere. The voyage played out in *Solaris* is a trip to the interior, to the depths of Kelvin's fears and memories. Perry's tank moved in a similar direction. When you turned away from Esalen's grand panorama and closed the door, you were onboard a vessel bound for the vast expanse of the mind.[32]

*****

For those seeking respite from the world and time to rethink its effects, early-1970s Esalen was hard to beat, despite its emerging fissures. 'Sun, sea, sand and sex' may have been the four sacred offerings of modern tourism, but Esalen was able to go one better. It had another 's' on offer, one that was far more vital, personal and important, and which could not be found at the bottom of a piña colada sipped at a beachfront bar. As Richard Atcheson put it in a 1968 article on Esalen written for *Holiday* magazine: 'I got in touch with my body this winter. I made contact with my SELF – and it was the best trip I've ever had.' Other observers, particularly those looking at these Californian goings-on from afar, were not so convinced. Writing in *The Daily Telegraph Magazine* in December 1968, Alexander Frater let rip with a dismissive, hugely condescending review of Gunther's *Sense Relaxation*. 'Review' is, in fact, a generous description of the article. Frater just takes a few quotes out of context and adds his own hilarious versions. For example, Gunther's instructions on 'head-knowing' – 'gently get acquainted with your partner's head, hair, back of neck, ears' – is rewritten by Frater as 'if you're happy with the head then check it for dandruff [...] close your eyes and see with the fingertips, what the head reminds you of – a watermelon?' Frater's weak attempt at satire says much more about the satirist than the satirised. He loudly confirms the British stereotype of a recoiling disdain towards the merest hint of anything 'touchy feely'. Such disregard, though, does not stop *The Daily Telegraph* from running a set of slightly titillating images from Gunther's book, mainly of young semi-nude women enjoying a massage. British readers of the late 1960s may have scoffed at 'anything goes' California with its permissiveness *gone mad*, but they still expected their share of mild kink at the breakfast table.

The feature begins with Frater looking beyond *Sense Relaxation* to the wider human potential scene. With a barely veiled sigh, Esalen is introduced as 'America's latest substitute for the psychoanalyst':

> [...] Its methods centre around group therapy, psychodrama (Stanislavsky for tired businessmen), massage and Oriental philosophy, and its function is explained by a Californian psychiatrist thus: 'It is the concern of psychiatry to adjust people to the social environment. Esalen is concerned rather with those who are too well-adjusted, too tight and too controlled. It attempts to release them for growth and greater integration.'

Esalen would agree with the thrust of this outline, and it would also tally with John Travis' calls for the necessity of a drive towards greater wellness. Society is overwhelming and overwhelmed, they would argue, and so tightly bound are we to the accelerated stresses of the everyday that we need moments of recalibrating, expansive release. Frater's tone, however, points to superfluity, the sense that this is all so unnecessary. The practices offered at Esalen and elsewhere, he suggests, are a means of ministering to the faddish needs of those who have no real problems or indulging those who are just too sensitive. Were it not for the 'tired businessman' reference, you could almost expect Frater to start decrying *snow-flakes* some fifty years early.[33]

Given that Frater's review appeared in an issue filled with adverts for alcohol and cigarettes alongside another article offering a largely uncritical discussion of English nationalism, one could argue that *The Daily Telegraph Magazine* was on shaky ground when it came to criticising experimental attempts to improve physical and mental health. The gist of Frater's argument, though, would find reflection and amplification in the work of other writers and in other quarters across the 1970s. Human potential, growth, alternative therapies, bodywork and similar would be routinely aligned with an apparent shift in Western, and particularly American, culture towards a widespread self-centeredness. In Luke Rhinehart's novel *The Dice Man* (1971), for example, encounter groups and sensitivity training are lumped in with all the other psychotherapies that find the 'prospective rich (the therapists)' providing 'mental first aid' to the 'already rich (the patients)'. *The Dice Man* purports to be the autobiography of a jaded middle-aged psychiatrist who sees life as 'islands of ecstasy in an ocean of ennui'. To get himself away from the sandbars of familiarity he 'lets the die decide', turning his life over to the combination of chance and determinism that comes with a roll of the dice. This uncompromising decisiveness is, for Rhinehart, a much more effective way of altering one's life than giving in to the soft indulgence of the encounter group. As the novel puts it, the only thing to be gained from a $200 weekend at the 'Fire Island Sensitivity Training Headquarters' is a feast of cliché-ridden emotional cushioning. 'Dicelife', by contrast, embraces the challenge that comes with constant change.[34]

These readings conjure an aura of wallowing self-regard that was also evident in the culture at large, particularly such fixtures of the early 1970s as Erich Segal's ubiquitous novel *Love Story* (1970) and Stephen Pearson's mass-marketed, late-psychedelic print *Wings of Love* (1972). Pearson's image of naked figures lounging on an oceanic plaza in the embrace of an auroral swan aligns eroticism with the experience of a dreamlike landscape. It is a softcore fantasy that celebrates sexual intimacy as a pathway into a world that is not just private but is wholly interiorised. While somewhat lacking in spectral swans, Segal's *Love Story* is built on similarly solipsistic foundations. Although not without nuance in its portrait of a relationship, Segal's famous but peculiarly atomised framing of 'love' as an absolution of responsibility ('Love means not ever having to say you're sorry') shifts the focus of the novel from the couple to the individual. *Love Story* is ultimately about the emotional experience of the self-absorbed, self-loathing rich kid Oliver Barrett IV, not his life with or even the life of girlfriend (and then wife) Jennifer Cavilleri. Apart from setting aside her career ambitions for the privilege of marrying Oliver, Jennifer's other role in the novel is to quietly expire with a considerate lack of fuss. This leaves Oliver free to seize the sentimental bragging rights and parental reconciliation he feels entitled to. The covert jeopardy of the book is not will they/won't they live happily ever after, but will he – Oliver – manage to make it back into the wealthy family fold? When the novel was adapted into a film by Arthur Hiller in 1970, it was packaged with Andy Williams' theme song 'Where Do I Begin?' (1970). A hymn to the self, the song goes much further than the novel in placing the 'I' front and centre. 'I know I'll need her till the stars all burn away', croons Williams, in a line that is both maudlin and utterly solar in the intensity of its self-regard. The anonymous 'her' is merely a foil that allows the equally anonymous but dominant 'I' to express the singularity of their own emotions. There is no 'our' here, just an almost apocalyptic level of need that brings with it the ambience of a burnt-out cosmos, not unlike the otherworldly desolation of Pearson's uncanny coastline.[35]

Beyond these terminal beaches, however, there were other visions of personal identity circulating in the popular imagination of the 1970s, ideas that remind us it is far too reductive to read the 'self' as the period's main point of focus, not least because at the start of the decade, the 'I' was simply not what it used to be. Rather than a triumph of marketing, the success of *Love Story* is frequently attributed to its popular appeal. After the traumatic 1960s opened a gulf 'between generations that seemed unbridgeable', argues Francesca Segal, the reconciliation of Oliver and his father 'was the secret hope of fathers and sons across America'. The novel expressed what she calls 'an understanding of and care for the everyman', as if to assume that a collective set of hopes, dreams and desires unified the nation. It is a fine sentiment, but one that belies the deeper rifts of the 1960s that continued to resonate for the emergent 1970s. The 'gulf' that Segal alludes to could more accurately be described as the work of the New Left, which by the turn of the decade had comprehensively re-evaluated the definitions of class, gender, ethnicity and sexuality. In parallel, Roland Barthes, Michel Foucault, Jacques Derrida and other poststructuralist provocateurs were busy unpicking the philosophical and linguistic scaffold upon which these categories were based. Elsewhere, Stewart Brand, editor of *The Whole Earth Catalogue* (1968–72), as well as James Lovelock, Lyn Margulis and other thinkers associated with the growing ecological movement were increasingly questioning the centrality of the human within the networked complexity of the ecosystem. At the same time, quantum mechanics was also pushing at the very fringes of what might be termed 'our' reality with its entangled particles and simultaneous, proliferate worlds. Who were 'we', then, at the start of the 1970s? Could the 'I' even be used with any certainty anymore? Politically, philosophically and scientifically, this once secure pronoun was rapidly losing definition and slipping far away from its familiar moorings. The humanism of *Love Story* provided no insight into this transition. The real cartography was being done by novels like *The Dice Man* with their frontal assaults on anything akin to a singular, unchanging and therefore 'true' self.[36]

Regina Holloman felt this disturbance at an educational and social level just before she undertook her anthropological study at Esalen. In the early 1970s she had returned to teach at Chicago's Roosevelt University after a break of five years and found a difficult, 'post-Berkeley' atmosphere. The campus-based protests and agitation of the late 1960s had generated a critical, activist mood leaving her, for the first time in her career, uncomfortable with students. 'I was often confronted with value positions with which I could not deal adequately', she wrote, and yet 'they seemed to be important to me both as a person and an anthropologist'. Going to Esalen was for Holloman a way of experiencing and exploring some of this 'ferment'. Over in the UK, a similar dissonance was being felt by Jean Clark, who in 1971 joined Leicester Polytechnic as a 'Welfare Officer' with a remit to 'undertake some Student Counselling'. Clark went on to build one of the first dedicated student counselling services in the UK, based largely on Carl Rogers' person-centred approach, the methodology that had been so influential to the development of Esalen's encounter groups. In post across the 1970s, she saw the student population grow and change, bringing with it a spectrum of ever-evolving problems. The 'old' image of white, UK-born students using university as a 'time of freedom and autonomy' was morphing into a diverse, multicultural demographic 'experiencing a clash of cultures' and language problems as well as the disappointments and frustrations of changing educational expectations. As Clark's workload increased, the only point of certainty was that the 'typical' student did not exist.[37]

Faced with such flexible parameters, 'who am I?' became something of a redundant question. There would never be a satisfactory answer because the self coming into view as the 1970s progressed was unmappably multitudinous. For those exploring this territory like Glenn Perry and John Travis, the untethering of the 'I' brought distinct opportunities. It could be remade. As they returned from their holidays and therapeutic hiatuses both were keen to capitalise on their experiences personally and entrepreneurially. Perry, now calmer and more confident than he had ever been, ploughed on with his intention to manufacture and market what he would come to call the 'floatation tank'.

As for Travis, he decided to 'give up doing sick care'. After reflecting on his experience with counselling, transactional analysis and other body therapies, he realised the 'script' of following in his father's footsteps had run its course. He would never be a 'family doctor'. There were other ways to help people and the pursuit of such a project would ease his own, personal sense of crisis. In 1973 he made the commitment to his diary. 'I can make my own script', Travis wrote as he realised his potential, 'and be what and who I want to be.'[38]

CHAPTER IV

The Deep End
1972–1974

Oakland, California, 6 November 1973. It had been a long day. Marcus Foster, Oakland's first African American school superintendent, was leaving a meeting of the Board of Education with his deputy, Robert Blackburn. It was 7pm, night was falling, and as they walked across the parking lot Foster and Blackburn discussed the day's business. As they talked, Blackburn noticed two men idling in the shadows by the side of the education building. It looked as if they were waiting for someone. Thinking little of it, Blackburn continued to his car at the far edge of the parking lot, close to line of bushes. Moving to open the passenger door for Foster, Blackburn stepped in front. As he did so, he saw the men start to approach. They had indeed been waiting – for Blackburn and Foster. With determined poise the men came up close, pulled out handguns and opened fire.

Time slowed. Blackburn heard a strange popping sound fill the air. He saw Foster fall to the ground before more movement caught his attention. He turned to see a third man looming out of the bushes, like a tiger in the night. Had he been there all along, watching? This man carried a shotgun, and he had his eyes fixed on Blackburn. There was another pop, much louder this time, and then a bright flash. Blackburn suddenly felt a great shard of pain spread out across his shoulder before a force heavier than a sledgehammer blow spun him to the ground. Numbed and with ringing ears, Blackburn managed to haul himself up and make for the education building. He did not get far before an explosion went off across his back and the concrete rose to meet him again. He lay there, dimly aware of the popping noises dying away. Seconds later, staff from the education building rushed to the commotion. They found Blackburn at the doorway. He was unconscious, severely wounded but alive. Foster, however, was lying face down at the side of Blackburn's car, dead from multiple close-range gunshots. The three assailants had vanished. It was later found that their bullets had been laced with cyanide.[1]

It was a swift and unforgiving attack. Although the brutality of the incident was shocking, the sound of fatal gunfire on Oakland's streets would, unfortunately, not have been a surprise. Across the late 1960s and early 1970s, the city not only had the highest crime rate in the Bay Area, but also had one of the highest crime rates in the country, regularly sharing the top spot with New York and Miami. Oakland had entered the 20th century as an industrial boomtown with a strong infrastructure and what Chris Rhomburg calls an 'economy built on manufactures of capital goods, construction, coastal trade and the processing of goods from the area's rural hinterland'. However, the post-war period saw a slowdown in industrial output 'creating far fewer job opportunities inside the city'. These changing patterns of work, coupled with rising levels of car ownership and suburb-supporting highway development schemes, meant that Oakland's urban areas experienced significant economic and social decline. Between 1950 and 1970 the city's central zone lost around 10,000 jobs and 23,000 residents. As a result, by the early 1970s Oakland had become a landscape of serious deprivation marked by high levels of drug abuse, robbery and homicide. At the time, it was Los Angeles that Charles Manson and Elton John alike called 'Sick City' thanks to the way it ate up and spat out the unwary, but this dubious honour could easily have applied to 1970s Oakland. All cities have their criminal and anti-social elements but Oakland, a place within a day's drive of Big Sur and which had the seemingly more peaceable San Francisco on its doorstep, appeared to be entirely consumed by them.[2]

The city was not without its sources of alternative health, but even these were depressingly hard edged. The nearest equivalent it had to Esalen was an outpost of Synanon, an alcohol and drug rehabilitation programme founded by a former member of Alcoholics Anonymous called Charles 'Chuck' Dederich. Dederich began the project in January 1958 when he started running support groups from his Santa Monica apartment. By September he had moved operations into a local storefront and was focused on expanding Synanon into a residential therapeutic community. By 1969, he had properties in multiple California cities, including Oakland, and a combined in-house population of over 1,000 with additional outsourced groups, clubs (or 'tribes' as Dederich called them) active across the country. Synanon members would join a 'one-to-two-and-a-half-year program' that would see them live as part of a community. There they would move through several phases, beginning with a period of detoxifying menial work before progressing to a position of community responsibility and then to a job outside the Synanon residence while continuing to live-in. The final stage took two forms: either 'rehabilitation', which meant leaving the community to live and work elsewhere, or an invitation to join Synanon's staff, a process known as 'retention', or, as it was termed more ominously in academic studies of the group, 'absorption'.

According to sociologist Richard Ofshe, it is unclear how many people Synanon successfully rehabilitated because the group appeared to favour and encourage retention. With its rigid, rule-based lifestyle Synanon inevitably gained a reputation as a cult, an image reinforced by its members' willingness to shave off their hair, wear identical white overalls and listen with rapt attention to tape-recorded missives from Dederich. One of the most notorious of Synanon's rules was the necessity of weekly participation in a ferocious encounter group called 'the Game'. The Game was an arena of verbal violence. No actual physical contact was allowed, but the exchanges could be just as bruising as a sucker punch. Each member would be routinely 'given hell': they would be subject to an all-out, unfettered excoriation by the others. Typically this would focus on personal flaws and any perceived failings, especially those relating to their rehabilitative progress or daily work in the community. Alternately, members would be invited to recount their life stories, only to have them mercilessly picked part by the circle, like vultures descending on carrion.

Scores were settled during these sessions and grudges were aired. Synanon explicitly forbade profanity everywhere except in the charged zone of the Game, a neat safety-valve approach that all but ensured the exchanges were delivered with expletive force. It was not all about high-volume confrontation, though. Praise was regularly doled out during the Game, but it would be typically laid on with such heaviness that to be loved by the group could be just as overwhelming as being attacked by them. Disarming and disorientating, the Game now seems less like a therapeutic tool and more like a psychic bludgeon. It may have been offered to help Synanon members come off drugs and alcohol, but in some ways the Game, with its bait-and-switch offerings of love and hate, replicated the debilitating psychological effects of addiction. It was a quick adrenalised fix of emotional intensity, a high point that could easily become the focus of a working week; an event that you start to look forward to and, rapidly, come to feel that you need. When George Lucas chose Oakland as one of the locations for his dystopic first feature *THX1138* (1971), it was Synanon members he called upon to work as extras. Fresh from their Games, shaven-headed and glassy-eyed, they were the perfect population for the narcotic control society he created in the city's transit tunnels.[3]

Within this bleak, post-industrial scene Oakland's civic authorities also presided over an increasingly tense and combative atmosphere of street-level left-wing politics. The San Francisco Bay Area had been a crucible of the New Left throughout the 1960s, and Oakland often saw demonstrations connected with the anti-war and free speech movements of nearby Berkeley. By the early 1970s, these peace protests had given rise to a diverse network of identity politics. Gay rights, Black Power and second-wave feminism formed the city's dominant intersectional concerns. As the decade opened, Oakland played host to the Berkeley-Oakland Women's Union, founded in 1973, and the Women's Press Collective, founded in 1969. The 'Lesbian-Feminist Arts Journal' *Amazon Quarterly* (1972–75) was published in the city and venues like the White Horse Inn became key West Coast hubs of post-Stonewall activism. Most famously, though, Oakland was home to the Black Panther Party for Self-Defense, a group founded in the city in 1966 by Huey P. Newton and Bobby Seale.[4]

The Black Panthers were formed to defend the city's Black neighbourhoods and to counter the grinding, daily effects of institutional racism. In the 1920s there had been a significant base of support in the city for the Ku Klux Klan, with key members entering Oakland's mainstream political landscape on the back of campaigns framing civic issues in what Rhomberg calls 'ethnic and racial terms'. In the 1960s, a resurgent Klan developed a white supremacist power base in rural North Carolina under its long-term leader Bob Jones. By the end of the decade a series of political crackdowns had evaporated its mass-membership support but, as David Cunningham explains, the group splintered into smaller cells and went underground. This dispersal helped to keep in place the political and racial divisions they had fermented. The Panthers were in combat with this legacy as well as a much wider sense of entrenched prejudice that had a contemporary bearing on the material, political and economic life of the Black community.

Membership peaked in the 1970s, after the Panthers extended out from their base in Oakland to establish a network of offices in 68 other cities. Young, educated and militant, the party pursued a far-left ideology that combined civil rights activism and Black nationalism: they were not in search of equality but self-determination. It was a stance equally informed by the economic politics of Marx's *Das Kapital* (1867) as it was by Frantz Fanon's colonial critiques *Black Skin, White Masks* (1952) and *The Wretched of the Earth* (1961). While groups like Synanon entered the 1970s with racial integration as part of their increasingly socially oriented rehabilitative agenda, the Panthers thought the drive for equality was a loser's game. They would have had little time for Synanon's mass wedding festivals, the likes of which they hosted at their Walker Creek Ranch in California in 1972, which saw 75 mainly interracial couples tie the knot. Following Fanon's analysis of colonial psychology in which the colonised are conditioned to absorb and reflect the authority of the coloniser, the Panthers saw integration as a social process that merely reiterated the arbitrary superiority of white culture. Black people 'must respond in our own way, on our own terms, in a manner which fits our temperaments', argued the party's 'honorary prime minister' Stokely Carmichael, in 'Black Power' (1967). 'The definition of ourselves, the road we pursue, the goals we seek are our responsibility.' Newton and Seale crystallised this desire to 'determine our own destiny' in the party's platform statement, the

'Ten-Point Programme' (1966), which called for a resistance to 'the robbery by the capitalists of our black and oppressed communities.'[5]

Such an agenda repeatedly and intentionally placed the Panthers against the city's mainly Republican municipal leadership. In May 1973, Seale narrowly missed out on an election win against Mayor John Redding and the tight margin was a measure of the very real hunger for change in the community. The key areas of contention were health care and policing. Poor, predominantly Black urban areas across Oakland and the Bay Area had long been neglected by municipal support, leading to sanitation problems and what the party's periodical *The Black Panther* called a wave of 'pneumonia and flu viruses'. As Alondra Nelson describes in *Body and Soul* (2011), her study of the Panthers and medical discrimination, these conditions were compounded by a lack of ambulance provision and low-quality medical services. Those able to get over to the likes of San Francisco General, an 'undersupplied, drastically understaffed' public teaching hospital, spoke of 'frustrating, coercive and demeaning' experiences at the hands of 'disrespectful, unprofessional and even authoritarian' physicians. For the Panthers, such discrimination was the direct result of 'robbery by the capitalists' because within the 'medical-industrial complex', the 'drug companies, the doctors, the insurance companies, and the equipment suppliers' could 'take in huge profits from private hospitals' and sideline those struggling, at best, on Medicaid.

If Black communities had little faith in their city's doctors, steadily rising levels of police brutality caused them to trust law enforcement even less. There had been regular, often fatal firefights and raids between Oakland officers and the Panthers since the early days of the party, but this direct attrition took place within a wider context of community-based, racially oriented police violence. These were the conditions that informed the party's 'defensive' stance. The situation reached a crisis point in November 1973 when Tyrone Guyton, an unarmed Black teenager, was shot and killed in central Oakland by undercover police who wrongly suspected him of car theft.[6]

At the other end of the spectrum, Oakland was also the base of operations for the Hells' Angels Motorcycle Club. All-male, all-white and by some accounts 'militantly white', the Angels hovered somewhere between subcultural community and organised crime network. Led by the military veteran Ralph 'Sonny' Barger, the group mythologised themselves as loyal Americans, the defenders of a traditional and authentic outlaw sprit. In practice, this 'loyalty' took the form of a deeply confrontational sense of entitlement in which members would fight, intimidate, drink and generally cause trouble with an attitude of assumed impunity. White privilege on wheels, the Angels demanded respect while giving none back and were no strangers to accusations of racially motivated violence. Their most ignoble moment came while providing 'security' for The Rolling Stones at their disastrous concert at the Altamont Speedway in December 1969. It was here that in full view of the band, members used chains and pool cues to beat to death a young Black man called Meredith Hunter.

By 1973 the core leadership of the Angels had been decimated by long jail terms linked to drugs charges, but they had left behind a legacy of permission and leniency. In 1965, police stood by while the Angels beat up anti-war protestors at the Berkeley city limits; their own, numerous, attacks on local policemen – often when trying to ride en masse into a small town for a rave-up – often went unpunished, and Oakland law enforcement frequently had to deny offering protection to the Angels in exchange for tips on 'caches of weapons, narcotics and explosives'. Meanwhile, it was the Panthers and their constituents who were continually harassed, surveilled and raided by the police while the California Council on Criminal Justice pushed for a rollout of police security across Oakland's predominantly Black school campuses. This, along with the vexed, ongoing issue of identity cards for students, was seen by the Panthers and others as a further erosion of their civil liberties. Keenly aware and critical of South African apartheid, they saw such measures as an attempt to formalise prejudicial attitudes into a similar domestic policy.[7]

It was a depressingly familiar scenario, one repeated across America, and still in force today, in which cycles of discrimination become hardwired into urban spaces, public amenities and the provision of services. While some groups had almost free rein in Oakland others, mainly Black and minority ethnic, were consistently denied it. For these communities, Oakland was an uneasy place where you were monitored and suspected by those in authority, threatened by those who saw you as different and where, at its worst, you could be shot on the street by those who claimed to protect and serve. In such an environment, the Panthers brandished their weapons not only as a constitutional provocation but also as a protective necessity, just as the Women's Press Collective would go on to promote female self-defence and 'gun consciousness raising' via *The Women's Gun Pamphlet: A Primer on Handguns* (1975).[8]

The connected issues of identity cards and police patrols came to Superintendent Marcus Foster's attention midway through 1973, and by October he was hosting public consultations on the matter. Foster considerately fielded the views of students, parents and the Black Panthers. He listened to, and politely declined, the Panthers' proposal to provide security rather than hand the role over to the Oakland Police. For his part, Foster was extremely critical of campus enforcement and gave no support to the measure. He also saw no need for the rollout of expensive ID, having previously cut the project out of his operating budget. He was sensitive, though, to student voices who claimed that having identity cards made aspects of campus life a lot easier. Overall, Foster came to see the issue as a tricky but not unresolvable problem. There was some public criticism and low-level protests at the meetings – the leader of a group called 'Save Our Schools' cutting up cards and the like – but he was experienced enough to handle it. Such turbulence, however, was an indication that tempers were beginning to flare. Conversations continued and by November, as protests surrounding the death of Guyton started to gain pace, it remained a persistent and emotive matter.[9]

When details of the shooting at the Board of Education started to spread, many took the news as a shocking sign that this complex of simmering tensions had spilled over into deadly direct action. Clearly, Foster and Blackburn had not been mugged, nor had they been shot in a carjacking gone wrong; there was nothing opportunistic about the attack. The shooting was premeditated, and Foster's death bore all the hallmarks of an assassination. It was 'so brutal, so morally unjustifiable and so politically incomprehensible', wrote David Horowitz in *Ramparts*, 'that most Bay Area radicals', the Black Panthers included, assumed it to be a terroristic act of racial hatred, the work of some right-wing or even police group that took as its target a high-profile, influential member of the Black community. The speculation did not last long. Three days after the murder, on 9 November, the culprits went public with a spuriously legalistic 'Warrant' issued on behalf of 'The Court of the People'. Dated to the day of the shooting it ordered an attack on the 'Fascist Board of Education [...] through the person of' Foster and Blackburn. As the text hyperbolically and inaccurately put it, they had been found guilty of three 'criminal' acts 'against the life of the children and the people': the intention to form a 'Special Political Police Force', the intention to implement a programme of 'Bio-Dossiers' and the intention to feed student data into an 'Internal Warfare Identification Computer System'.

The missive was entitled 'Communiqué No. 1' and it was attributed to the 'Western Regional Youth Unit' of a little-known leftist group called the Symbionese Liberation Army. Led by Donald DeFreeze, a 29-year-old African American prison escapee who took the name 'Field Marshal Cinque Mtume', the so-called 'Army' 'never numbered more than a dozen or so members'. The group had made itself known in August 1973 via another document, their 'Declaration of Revolutionary War'. Here they explained that 'Symbionese' stood for 'symbiosis', meaning 'a body of dissimilar bodies and organisms living in deep and loving harmony and partnership in the best interests of all within the body'. Under this banner they claimed to represent a 'United Front and Federated Coalition' formed out of the Bay Area's 'Asian, Black, Brown, Indian, White, Woman, Gray and Gay liberation Movements'. Proceeding from this platform of 'black and minority leadership', the SLA stood against 'The Fascist United States of America' in pursuit of 'FREEDOM and SELF-DETERMINATION and INDEPENDENCE'. As with the Black Panthers' call for 'land, bread, housing, education, clothing, justice and peace', the SLA agitated for positive social change within the 'Oakland–Berkeley area'. However, their calls for a 'liberation struggle' masked a position that was not so much radical as untenably extremist.

The SLA viewed 'Amerikkka' as an evil empire of hierarchical aggression. They described a society held in a conflux of racism and capitalism, dominated by the rich who hoarded resources and waged a debilitating covert war against the disadvantaged. In essence, there was nothing new about this argument. Capitalism is undeniably unfair, exploitative and strategically inhumane. In the light of the prejudicial 'law and order' policies of the Nixon administration that continued the intelligence-gathering operations of COINTELPRO (1956–71), the SLA were also accurate in calling out the government as aggressively surveillant and systemically racist. At a basic level their critique shared much common ground with the outlook of the Panthers. However, the language of their communiqués drew a wildly exaggerated view of a hyperreal dictatorship. Like the sci-fi revolutionaries of William Burroughs' *Nova Express* (1964) and Spain Rodriguez's *Trashman* (1968–85), the SLA imagined, and pitched themselves against, a vast network of biometric super-computers. They called this punitive, all-encompassing control mechanism 'the fascist insect'. However prescient this vision may have been as regards the contemporary privacy politics of Google and Facebook, the SLA blunted their critique by clinging onto a naïve and dangerously polarised worldview. Their thinking had elements of post-Situationist sophistication, but its theorisation took the form of a reductive guerrilla fantasy that obscured the complex-ity of their socio-political milieu. As singular heroes fighting against a cadre of faceless villains, theirs was a position of such extremity that a policy of violence was the only practical option.[10]

By contrast, the self-defensive militancy of the Panthers was also an attempt to transform the gun – an historic tool of oppression – into a symbol of autonomous self-determination. This was the type of lib-erative thrust missing from the SLA's paradigm of perpetual warfare. Their offensive strategies fell straight into the conceptual trap Frantz Fanon cautioned against. Although calls to violence crackle through his writing, Fanon ultimately argues for the development of a national culture to resist and circumvent 'imperialist oppression'. It is a revolu-tionary agenda that *The Wretched of the Earth* figures as an overt act of cancellation: the 'destruction of the colonial world [...] the abolition of one zone, its burial in the depths of the earth or its expulsion from the country'. In its place a revived (or newly made) national culture is to be formed to provide the former colony with a dignified, autonomous and sustainable platform. In this regard Fanon defines national culture as 'the whole body of efforts made by a people in the sphere of thought to describe, justify and praise the action through which that people has created itself and keeps itself in existence'. To lose sight of this humanistic, post-revolutionary aim is to build an 'empty shell'; to merely step into the vacuum left by the imperial power, thus 'replicating the conditions' which originally instigated the combat. In proposing to meet violence with violence on equal terms, the SLA were lining themselves up for this type of *coup*, rather than what Fanon would term a structure-altering, culturally productive *revolution*. Whatever the sense of radicalism informing their thinking, the actions of the SLA did nothing to affect the overall system they deemed so problematic. Worse still, their deeply misguided gestures helped to keep it in place. The 'revolutionary' agenda of the SLA essentially boiled down to a single, absolutist policy: the summary execution of anyone they disagreed with. It was a stance just as fascistic as the establishment they claimed to oppose.[11]

Beyond the obvious ethical and legal problems, the SLA's attack on Foster as 'an enemy of the people' was also spectacularly ill-judged. Foster was an enormously respected educator and administrator who had come to public prominence after turning round the fortunes of Simon Gratz High School in Nicetown, Philadelphia. When he took over the role of principal in 1966, he found a failing school with undisciplined and demotivated students who were running rings round an exhausted staff. Simon Gratz had the highest levels of truancy and the most dropouts in the city and only a tiny percentage of those who did graduate went on to higher education. Foster responded to the problems with a combination of control and humility. He reimposed order over the school's daily routine and personally approached those who had left with opportunities to re-enrol. Foster offered an aspirational view of education designed to instil pride and build self-respect. Night schools and skills training programmes were developed with local industries and by 1968 not only had truancy plummeted at Simon Gratz but, in relative terms, the number of graduates taking up college places had skyrocketed.

Although the SLA claimed to be working holistically, for the wider health of the community, it was Foster who actively worked to this end out on the educational frontlines. Indeed, on the day of his death he had spent the day in meetings with Oakland's City Council about keeping school gyms open after hours. As well as promoting fitness, the measure was intended to keep young people occupied. If they had somewhere to go after school, they would stay off the streets and away from the crime that circulated there. Unsurprisingly, then, despite their claims of leading a unified front, the SLA garnered little to no support from Oakland's 'Black, Chicano, Asian and conscious White youth'. In fact, the Panthers stood alongside Mayor Redding in open condemnation of the attack. The consensus view saw Foster as the victim of an ill-informed political group trying to wage a futile war on a public institution. The SLA may have liked to think of themselves as explosive radicals who collapsed the 'traditional' battlelines of left *versus* right, Black *versus* white, protest *versus* direct action, but for many in Oakland, particularly Robert Blackburn, they were revolutionaries in name only. Beyond their agenda of violence there was nothing but rhetoric to support them.[12]

The SLA made their way through California's underground political landscape for more than a year after the attack at the Board of Education. It was a chaotic and deadly journey that peaked in February 1974 with the kidnap of Patty Hearst, heiress to the publishing empire of William Randolph Hearst. In a further display of their skewed ethics, the group held her to ransom, demanding that the Hearst family 'provide every poor person in California with seventy dollars' worth of food'. By April, Patty Hearst issued a statement claiming to have joined the SLA and soon after she appeared to wilfully take part in a San Francisco bank robbery. Such allegiance, though, was very probably a form of Stockholm syndrome conditioned by her traumatic confinement. It was an experience that not only involved her being bombarded with SLA propaganda, but it is highly likely that she was also raped by DeFreeze and other members of the group. Soon after the headline-grabbing robbery, the LPAD cornered the SLA and DeFreeze was killed in the ensuing shootout.[13]

*****

As the SLA's bizarre and disturbing drama unfolded, the private and public mourning for Foster continued. Memorial services were planned, moves were made to establish a charitable foundation in his name and, towards the end of 1973, the trustees at Simon Gratz High School unanimously voted to name its sports fields and swimming pool in his memory. Of all the tributes made, it was the naming of this small swimming pool that arguably carried the most resonance, not least because sports and physical health were crucial elements in Foster's holistic vision of education. He believed that playing in school teams – football, baseball and swimming – were a way of keeping fit but also of building self-respect. When he arrived at Simon Gratz and found its sports facilities underused and dilapidated, he quickly set about reviving the school's teams and a formal programme of physical activities. Sports, he argued, generated discipline, built camaraderie and provided a much-needed outlet for all that classroom tension. A good, harmonious school needed the kind of pride that came with achievements on the field.

Naming Foster's pool was also a powerful gesture in the wider politics of public swimming. In the late 19th and early 20th centuries, American swimming 'baths', as with those in Victorian Britain, fulfilled a need for public hygiene. With crowded urban housing often lacking proper sanitation facilities, bathhouses were popular and necessary spaces in which 'working-class blacks, immigrants, and native-born whites' swam and washed together. Here the division revolved around gender, with the baths being a largely male environment. 'Women of all classes did not swim in public pools', notes Taunya Lovell Banks, 'while affluent and middle-class white Americans swam at private resorts or clubs because they believed that working-class whites, and all blacks, were unclean and bearers of diseases.' This toxic mix of racist, classist and sexist prejudice continued across the 1920s and 1930s as urban baths gradually morphed into European-influenced 'pools'. These 'park-like public spaces', funded by municipal and government spending, were not unlike 'public beaches'. Leisure rather than hygiene became the main function of the pool, with swimming promoted as a way of strengthening 'family and community sociability'. White men and women began to swim together across the classes and as a result, not unlike public beaches, the pools were increasingly segregated along racial lines.[14]

Black bodies, it seemed, posed two threats to the porcelain fragility of white culture: they were not just unclean but also thought of as uncontrollably lascivious. The morality and modesty of white women had to be protected from what Jeff Wiltse calls the 'visual and physical intimacy' of mixed pools. 'Racial segregation,' he suggests, 'enabled communities to restrict white women's choices by limiting their opportunities to meet and form relationships with black men.' Of course, this did not prevent the parallel sexualisation of the female swimmer. While Black swimmers were being excluded based on a spurious and racist morality, newspapers were '[filling] their pages each summer with gratuitous photos' of 'attractive young [white] women in and around the pool'. With bathing costumes offering women greater mobility and yet another opportunity 'to be viewed as sex objects', it appeared that 'family'-oriented pools could happily accommodate the erotic gaze, just as long as it was the heteronormative gaze of the white male. A report from the summer of 2021 circulated by the news outlet *The Black Bay Area* indicates just how ingrained these views remain. In the pool of Sacramento's Kempton Sawyer hotel, a group of white women 'demanded' that a Black woman 'stop kissing her girlfriend' because 'there were children present'. Witnesses to the scene claim that straight, white couples were being similarly affectionate that afternoon, but it was only the young Black woman, Domonique Veasley, who was berated. The gender politics may have been different – this was not men 'defending' the modesty of women – but the combination here of prejudice and homophobia barely concealed by a flimsy appeal to public decency makes it clear that Black bodies, and *gay* Black bodies at that, continue to cause offence at poolside America.[15]

As 'public accommodations', swimming pools were desegregated by the Civil Rights Act of 1964. This measure followed on from the landmark *Brown* v. *the Board of Education* case of 1954 and a range of state-led attempts to end segregation. However, this top-down legal approach failed to have much of an impact on the ground.

Across the country, in both the northern and southern states, segregation was maintained in public pools either through separate hours, 'separate but equal' facilities or by way of more traditional methods like threats, intimidation and affray. As Andre Toran notes when describing the contention that greeted the rollout of integrated swimming: 'Whites threw nails to the bottom of pools in Cincinnati and poured bleach and acid in pools in St. Augustine, Florida.' Aside from this ugly show of force, many municipal authorities got around the terms of the Act by simply taking their pools out of use. They were either filled in or relaunched as fee-charging, members-only clubs. This shift to private facilities was already in effect before 1964. In 1959 the National Swimming Pool Institute listed 10,550 private swimming clubs, a number that would increase to more than 23,000 by 1962.

In between, domestic pools started to appear like giant raindrops in affluent back gardens across suburbia. While the UK spent much of the 1960s and 70s converting its Victorian baths and lidos into multi-usage sports centres, America became the kingdom of the private swimmer. As Ryan Reft notes, this was particularly the case in Southern California, with the *Los Angeles Times* reporting in 1961 that no other region in America boasted more swimming pools. In 1966, 'over 150,000 swimming pools accounted for seven and one-half square miles of the region's real estate', with predictions made the same year that '12,000 to 15,000 more pools' would be added to the amount of land under water. The densest concentration could be found in the celebrity haven of Palm Springs. In 1955 the resort city recorded 900 pools but within a decade, as more and more of Hollywood's elite decamped there, the number had grown to 2,000. This gave Palm Springs the highest rate of pools per capita in America, 'one for every six residents'. Most of these pool-owning residents were white.[16]

While this new domestic market was a welcome boon to pool salesmen who had spent the early 1960s trying to furnish the suburbs with nuclear fallout shelters, it also marked the evaporation of yet another public service from struggling, often predominantly Black, urban areas. Writing in *Sports Illustrated* in 1971, Martin Kane reflected on one measurable cultural impact of this economic deprivation: a distinct lack of diversity in Olympic-level swimming. He notes that track and field events are well represented, with 'the success of Black athletes' accounting 'for all eight Olympic records set by U.S. runners at Mexico City in 1968'. However, because 'environmental factors have a great deal to do with excellence in sport', the same could not be said for swimming, as well as golf, tennis, skiing, sailing and hockey. These are the sports that typically require the combined privileges of time, space, equipment and money. As a result, Kane argues, they tend to be dominated by white athletes. As he glibly but directly puts it: 'There is a marked shortage of country clubs in ghettos'.

Having offered this basic critique, however, Kane goes on to perform a stunningly offensive switchback. He focuses on what he regards as a more significant variable: the racial, apparently physiological, and genetic, reasons why Black athletes make 'bad' swimmers. Pulling together a range of speculative, anecdotal and pseudo-scientific 'evidence', Kane claims that African Americans lack 'buoyancy': they are 'sinkers' because compared to their apparently lithe, torpedo-like white counterparts they have a 'greater density of bone and muscle', different 'fat distribution' and smaller lung capacity. Not content with such outlandish claims, Kane goes even further and attributes these differences to the generational inheritance of slavery. 'Without a doubt, the slaves were brought across the Atlantic under the most inhuman conditions', he states in what has become the controversial article's most objectionable section, and 'only the strongest survived the passage'. Slavery 'weeded out the weak', thus giving rise to descendants built for speed and power, the qualities necessary for survival. To excel at swimming, though, you need strength, which Kane defines as the ability to overcome resistance, a quality which in the prejudicial world of the article is implicitly aligned with dominance not survival – with the white man, not the Black.[17]

For the African American swim coach Jim Ellis, such eugenic claims would have exemplified the systemic racism he encountered throughout his career. At the start of the 1970s Ellis, a former competitive swimmer, was a safety instructor at the Sayre-Morris Recreation Centre in West Philadelphia. Mirroring the approach of Marcus

Foster, he was keen to offer swimming to the local Black community as a 'mental and physical outlet, a way to develop discipline'. To that end he formed the 'PDR (Philadelphia Department of Recreation) Swim Team', a moniker that also stood for 'Pride, Determination and Resilience'. It was the first African American swim team in the US and by 1972 Ellis was soon fielding young, fast, ambitious and dedicated swimmers to national competitions. Just as *Sports Illustrated* was offering its racist analysis, then, Ellis was busy disproving it. For him, the fact there were 'no outstanding black swimmers' in the late 1960s and early 1970s had nothing to do with genetic history. The main reasons were socioeconomic. A lack of facilities, a lack of inner-city investment in the sport and a lack of high-profile role models meant that swimming had little traction in Black culture.

Fred Hampton, chairman of the Illinois chapter of the Black Panthers, had long campaigned on the same issue, from his teenage years with the NAACP (National Association for the Advancement of Colored People) until his death in a police raid of dubious legality in 1969. He lived in Maywood, Illinois, and had to travel five miles away to Brookfield to find a pool 'that allowed Black people to swim'. His local pool was 'whites only'. For Hampton, the drive for an 'unrestricted pool' was a push for equality as well as a matter of public health. Chronic lack of access to public pools meant that large numbers of Black people grew up not knowing how to swim. This, in turn, meant that drowning was disproportionately common in their communities. Fat and bone density? *Nonsense.* The rarity of Black swimmers was due to the lack of opportunities to swim. It was a matter of material inequality maintained and enabled by the type of discriminatory arguments propounded by Kane. His shocking attempt to use slavery as an explanation for the lack of diversity in professional sport ultimately works as an easy defence of the status quo. The article implies there is no need to improve existing facilities nor to extend pool access nor to promote swimming as a viable choice for up-and-coming Black athletes because there is no point. It is a waste of time because 'they' are simply not 'bred' for it.[18]

*****

Meanwhile, far away from this urban deprivation and its associated struggles, all those private pools were forming into what the British writer J.G. Ballard called a 'concealed marine world'. This landscape of gentle ripples and quietly clinking glasses was only really visible from the air. Fly over Beverly Hills, wrote Ballard, and the walls of gated properties will flatten out, revealing 'scores of blue rectangles' cut into the ground. Tightly packed but gracefully arranged, these pools gave the bird's-eye cartography of the busy city the clean serenity of a Cézanne canvas. While Ballard gazed down, proud pool owners were equally looking up. As a marker of middle-class status, the swimming pool was also aspirational: it reached towards an extra sense of wealth and exclusivity, the type of effortless plenty that Terry O'Neill captured in his 1977 photoshoot of a post-Oscars Faye Dunaway. Alone and untroubled in the haze of an after-party morning, the images find Dunaway luxuriating beside one of the most sought-after inlets of the Beverly Hills marina: the unrippled pool of the Beverly Hills Hotel.

However, all was not well beneath these svelte surfaces. Despite its popularity and desirability, the private swimming pool often floated uneasily through the American imagination. Where the public pool became a repository for prejudicial social anxieties, the private pool dutifully took possession of the personal. It frequently appeared in films of the era as both a space of vulnerability, as in the massacre that opens Ted Post's *Magnum Force* (1973), and one of utter horror, as in the pool full of sea snakes in William Girdler's *Asylum of Satan* (1972). A more intimate but equally uncomfortable framing appears in *A Bigger Splash* (1973), Jack Hazan's documentary portrait of painter David Hockney. A post-1960s comedown film charting the end of Hockney's relationship with the artist and model Peter Schlesinger, *A Bigger Splash* takes canvases like 'Portrait of an Artist (Pool with Two Figures)' (1972) and dramatises them into vignettes of isolation. Hazan's pools are just as clean and cool as those of Hockney's paintings *circa* 1967–72, but in their stillness, they uneasily reflect the stasis, if not stagnancy, of the artist's personal life. As the amphibian Schlesinger swims beautifully underwater, the pool becomes an unbridgeable gap that Hockney cannot cross.[19]

Preceding all these films is the best example of such troubled waters, Frank and Eleanor Perry's *The Swimmer* (1968). Based on John Cheever's 1964 short story, *The Swimmer* finds Burt Lancaster playing Ned Merrill, a man, in Cheever's words, 'far from young' but with the 'slenderness of youth'. We first meet Merrill as he lounges by the pool of his friends, the Westerhazys, nursing a weekend hangover. Basking in the glorious sunshine of an early Sunday afternoon, Merrill has a sudden vision as he looks out to the neighbouring properties. He sees a 'string' of private pools, a 'quasi-subterranean stream that curved across the country'. This he names the 'Lucinda River', after his wife, before resolving to swim it, pool by pool, in a compulsive homeward journey. Merrill's quest is an 'essentially fabulous, and foolhardy' challenge typical of Cheever's 'heroic fables'. His characters are often everyday Quixotes, middle-aged 'comfortably-off, white middle-class suburbanites' who attempt to bring fantasy into their ordinary lives. However, with 'The Swimmer', Cheever was offering something substantially darker than a portrait of comfortable ennui punctured by a bout of eccentricity. The surface focus of both the story and the film is not heroism, foolhardy or otherwise, but anxiety and disquiet; the silent, gnawing malaise that grows out of the routines of affluence and flowers into existential angst. At the outset at least, Ned Merrill is comfortable *and* 'harried', superficially satisfied *and* restlessly trapped; with his outward confidence, charisma and hyperactivity he is the type of character who asks, to no one in particular as another weekend of gin drinking passes by, 'Is this it?' And then, before hearing the inevitable reply, he dives under.[20]

With these vignettes of desperation Cheever emerges not as the Homer of the suburbs but the Chekhov: he is the poet laureate of the 'the mid-life crisis'. This uneasy transitional state was first described in 1957 by the psychoanalyst Elliott Jaques. Writing later in 'Death and the Mid-Life Crisis' (1965), a widely cited article published in *The International Journal of Psychoanalysis*, Jaques reflected on his own experiences. He described an extended depressive episode that surfaced in his mid-30s, sparked by the realisation of having reached life's half-way point, 'the crest of the hill'. Death was 'observably present' from this high plateau and Jaques grimly believed it would rapidly approach as soon as he embarked on the 'downward slope' into middle age. Those reaching this turning point, he argued, would either slip further into morbid depression or go the other way and attempt to deny the crisis through 'religious awakenings, promiscuity [...] and "compulsive attempts" to remain young'.[21]

Each of these denials are at play in *The Swimmer* but it is the fight against fading youth that saturates the physicality of Lancaster's brilliant performance. He was a taut and trim 52-year-old when he starred in the film, easily able to take on the athletic challenges of the role, but he gradually nuances each swim to evoke a growing sense of exhaustion. At the start of the film Lancaster is a picture of vitality, suffused with 'energy to burn' as Halbert Dunn would put it, as he leaps with gazelle-like grace and bursts into horsepower sprints. But as the swim continues the seasons change. The waning afternoon stretches into a lifetime and each successive lift out of each successive pool gets tougher as Lancaster's Merrill gradually loses ground to the absolute tragedy of the sagging gut.

By the time *The Swimmer* appeared in cinemas with its analysis-inviting tagline – 'When you talk about *The Swimmer*, will you talk about yourself?' – the mid-life crisis was well on its way to becoming an adult rite of passage, rather than a neurosis. As Pamela Druckerman explains, by the mid-1960s 'the average life expectancy in Western countries had climbed to about 70'. Making a significant life change 'in your 30s or 40s' now made sense 'because you could expect to live long enough to enjoy your new career or your new spouse'. Hovering somewhere between a biological event and a cultural construct, the mid-life crisis fed into the spirit of the revolutionary 'sixties', because 'it was getting easier to change your life'. Women 'were going to work in record numbers, giving them more financial independence', more and more middle-class professionals 'were entering psychotherapy and couples counseling' and people were 'starting to treat marriage not just as a romantic institution, but as the source of their self-actualization', a fluidity aided by loosening divorce rules. With the 'social upheaval' of the 'civil-rights movement and the birth-control pill' forming a backdrop to this personal re-evaluation, 'it wasn't just individuals who had midlife crises'. As Druckerman puts it, 'The whole society seemed to be having one, too.'[22]

Despite the apparent ubiquity of these crises, their stereotypical explorers were mainly white, male and middle class. Writing in *Feminism and Therapy* (1974), Anica Vesel Mander and Anne Kent Rush described married women as the 'most likely candidates for [...] a nervous breakdown and/or suicide'. Unlike married men they experienced the combined social, psychological and economic pressures to 'work at home at no pay without complaining' with 'the added confusion of emotional ties with the exploiter'. Wives were required to work in 'the field-factory-office at minimal wages' and 'to do the *housework* there as well'. In *The Feminine Mystique* (1963), Betty Friedan called this the 'problem that has no name' and in so doing she simultaneously announced both the collective feeling of malaise and the lack of a coherent discourse to conceptualise it. By the time Germaine Greer published *The Female Eunuch* (1970), the argument was more stridently theorised but the problem seemed even more acute. Greer argued that historically, women have been severed from their identities and libidos by their socially constructed roles of wife, mother and homemaker. The pressure that Mander and Rush described stemmed from this erasure. To 'find yourself' against this backdrop meant deviating from generations of cultural norms and confronting the even bigger task of revitalising an identity that had all but disappeared under layers of patriarchal conditioning.

Novels like Thomas Wiseman's *The Romantic Englishwoman* (1971), Jenny Fabian's *A Chemical Romance* (1971) and Erica Jong's *Fear of Flying* (1973) wrestle with this limitation. Although their female characters defiantly step out of various (dis)comfort zones, they either remain tethered to a series of validating men, or otherwise find themselves looping back to the situations they attempted to escape. The liberative intent is loudly acknowledged in these texts, but so is the gravitational pull of the underlying social norm. 'Why don't you stop all this and come home,' says novelist Lewis Fielding to his wife Elizabeth during a tense phone conversation at the start of *The Romantic Englishwoman*. She has left London and is in the

German spa town of Baden-Baden, where 'taking the waters' is known to relieve 'conditions of exhaustion'. Down the line from her hotel room, Elizabeth tells Fielding she becomes 'more myself' when she is away from him. In asking Elizabeth to stop 'all this' in a voice that is 'smug and right', Fielding is not exactly forbidding her to be there, but in questioning the purpose of her being there, he is asserting his authority in a more insidious way. He is refusing to acknowledge the importance of her seeking time and space elsewhere to 'breathe'. Why would Elizabeth want to set off in search of herself, he asks, when the perfectly functional domestic identities of wife and mother are waiting for her back in London?

The weight of this social convention was just as acute for working-class and Black people who, as Druckerman suggests, were meant to accept their lot and 'weren't supposed to self-actualize'. The mid-life crisis, however, dispensed with the sense of pathologised collapse linked to the 'nervous breakdown and/or suicide' and it offered any number of men who were stressed, distressed, exhausted or just plain bored a ready-made narrative that celebrated the importance of having arrived at a personal turning point. If you had the necessary social freedom to capitalise on it, the crisis was almost to be welcomed; it could mark the moment when the newly divorced and ready to mingle, sports-car-driving, drum-kit-playing self could emerge from the depressed shell of the commuting family man.[23]

The Swimmer shows this freedom in full force. Merrill's physical journey is driven by a mindset of white privilege and male entitlement, the self-assured confidence that allows him to glide from property to property, pool to pool, picking up and dispensing with companions as easily as he takes the next drink. By contrast, the women of Merrill's world are fixed firmly in their roles of wives, mothers and girlfriends, the working classes are safely corralled in their overcrowded, overchlorinated public pools and the few Black characters in the film wait deferentially at the margins, ready to refill glasses and drive their employers' cars. However, the liberative thrust of this journey is not without its darker aspects as Merrill's 'project' ultimately brings him to a decidedly bleak conclusion. When he finally reaches the end of the 'Lucinda River' and arrives home, cold, shivering and limping in the twilight, there is no familial welcoming committee waiting to pay homage to the patriarch. Instead, Merrill finds his once opulent house boarded up and semi-derelict. Something awful has happened before the main events of the film, possibly a breakup or maybe a breakdown, the surface symptoms of which have been the eccentric affectations of the mid-life crisis. All the hints and intimations from the other characters make sense at this point, as if Merrill's friends have always known what waits for him at journey's end. He seems, then, to have been in a state of denial so extreme as to induce an amnesiac fugue and rather than a heroic flight for personal freedom, his swim has been a post-traumatic dive into the deep end of his memories, fears and regrets.

A doomy conclusion, certainly, but it is also quietly validating. It is a testament to Merrill's 'spiritual privilege' that he has been able to embark on this physical and psychological odyssey at all. As Marion Goldman explains, 'spiritual privilege' describes 'an individual's ability to devote time and resources to select, combine, and revise [their] personal, religious beliefs and practices over the course of a lifetime'. The white American middle-class male is stereotypically rich in the 'time' and 'resources' that underpin this cultural currency. Merrill's life may be in ruins but just like Don Draper, who 'oms' his way into the 1970s at the end of the Cheever-influenced *Mad Men*, he has the luxury of choosing to take an introspective hiatus. One could well imagine Merrill following Draper's lead by heading from his boarded-up property to the era's private pools par excellence: the mineral baths and, later, floatation tanks at the Esalen Institute. He would also have been a prime candidate for one of Paul Bindrim's marathon weekends of 'nude psychotherapy', hosted in motel swimming pools and rented suburban homes across California from 1967 to 1971. Working on the basis that 'clothing means we don't really trust each other', Bindrim would encourage his clients to step naked into his designated 'womb pool' and 'relate' to each other free of the modern 'fetish about privacy'. It was intended to be a regressive exercise that would take participants away from the 'vexed, harried, over-civilized' world of the intellect and closer to a floating, 'primordial', trust-based 'animal' state. From here, Bindrim argued, we could be more honest with ourselves and each other. If we are unable to relate to our bodies, how can we expect to relate to anyone else?

A similar scene appears in *The Swimmer* in the film's most unsettling moment: Merrill's confrontation with his former mistress, Shirley. He enters her pool unbidden, refuses to leave, and proceeds to rake over the details of their affair while attempting to coerce her into sex. The dialogue seethes with Shirley's anger and such a sense of pressure on Merrill's part that it is hard to sympathise with any of his stated regret. It plays out like an abusive encounter session, full of unequal power balanced in Merrill's favour and dispensed under the auspices of his 'honesty'. Mirroring the format of the self-actualising exchanges occurring at Esalen and elsewhere, the scene suggests that Merrill need not travel far to take a disquieting plunge into his own self. Rather than making the trek to California, he could execute this swan dive perfectly well in the enabling confines of his own social sphere.[24]

*****

'Health', it is often said, is 'wealth'. It is a motivational maxim that reminds us of the intangible value of being well. Built within the phrase, though, is a more literal implication that speaks of the exclusivity of health if not its wealth contingency. Other classic phrases like the Greek *kalos kagathos* and its aphoristic Latin counterpart *mens sana in corpore sano* carry a similar message. Both are routinely translated to refer to a sense of balance, an enjoyment of physical and mental harmony and the cultivation of a 'sound mind in a sound body'. It is easy to see the attractions of such a target, but in their original contexts the pursuit of these virtues was the preserve of a particular class. In the Greek world *kalos kagathos*, 'the beautiful and good' referred to a paragon of character and conduct. We might reach for the term 'gentlemanly' here, particularly as the word was commonly used to describe the Greek aristocracy. Similarly, when the Roman poet Juvenal spoke of sound minds and sound bodies in his *Satires*, he was listing values desirable to Roman citizens, those who enjoyed the legal protections and participatory privileges of *civitas*. In essence this meant freeborn male residents of Rome. The same rights were not extended to slaves, and they varied when applied to women, freedmen and members of the extended empire. It is certainly worth aiming high when it comes to health, but the background to these aspirational phrases reminds us that such a virtue was, historically, aligned with those already occupying the enjoyment of an elevated social position.

Benessere, the Italian for 'well-being' or 'welfare', tightens this link because it also means material affluence, suggesting that being well is connected to, if not dependent on, being wealthy. The gulf between public and private health care would give weight to this overlap with better services and facilities being readily available to those who can afford it. Admission requires both material and social currency. As the Black Panther Party and many others since have pointed out, the lines of deprivation and disadvantage that bar access to this market frequently fall along racial lines. So too for the higher, less quantifiable levels of human potential and wellness. Those heading to Esalen in search of their unalienated selves would, like Ned Merrill, typically have had little to no direct experience of the marginalisation, discrimination and economic alienation felt in the Black communities of 1970s Oakland. It is a division still in place today, with such fixtures of the commercial wellness sector as yoga being dominated by white, middle-class instructors teaching white, middle-class students, those with the necessary time and money to make it a regular practice. Sometime in the 1990s a scrawl of graffiti appeared at the entrance to Esalen that spoke to this division. For the unidentified tagger, the institute was not an outpost of universal humanity but a bubble of privilege that peddled 'Jive shit for rich white folk'.[25]

These issues were neatly and uncomfortably distilled in one of the highest-grossing films of the early 1970s, Guy Hamilton's James Bond vehicle *Diamonds Are Forever* (1971). The film featured Sean Connery in his sixth outing as the British spy and, in keeping with the rest of the series, *Diamonds* captured the zeitgeist by endorsing the very worst attitudes of the surrounding period. Playing out across a typically jet-setting range of locations, the film features gay men who are demonised, ridiculed, stabbed and blown up, Africans who are little more than silent vessels for the white diamond trade, and a parade of women – the most disposable commodity in Bond's world – who are variously mistreated and killed. Drowning seems to be this film's particular fetish, with women dying in canals, falling into the sea and suffering a significant amount of abuse in and around swimming pools. Plenty O'Toole (Lana Wood), one of Bond's casual conquests, is first thrown into hotel pool before being drowned in a suburban pool. Aspiring higher, Bond then goes on to thoroughly humiliate two women in the private pool of a reclusive billionaire. Bambi and Thumper (played by an uncredited Lola Larson and Trina Parks) are the bikini-clad bodyguards of the industrialist Willard Whyte (Jimmy Dean). They patrol his Californian stronghold and give Bond a sound drubbing when he comes looking for their boss. Eventually, after what seems like endless kicks to the face, the fight spills out to the mansion's swimming pool where, predictably, Bond prevails. In a moment that manages to be violent, infantilising *and* disturbingly sexualised, he holds them both underwater like some malevolent swimming teacher terrorising a pool party.

The scene was shot in Palm Springs, the swimming pool capital, at the Elrod House, an elegant modernist mansion built in 1968 by the architect John Lautner. To design the pool Lautner used his signature 'vanishing edge' style, an aesthetically pleasing feat of engineering that allowed excess water to gently drain over the side. The pool thus gained the appearance of having no boundary, of blurring into the horizon. Lautner's much-lauded design laid the basis for the infinity pool, the now obligatory addition to any luxury property, cruise liner or Instagrammable hotel. Making its on-screen debut in *Diamonds*, the film fittingly set the tone for the infinity pool's symbolic life. Built into an opulent house, the pool is a marker of wealth and health, but it is equally suffused with white male power – the economic power of Whyte, who owns it, and the physical power of Bond, who dominates it. Lost in the middle of this whirlpool are two women – one Black, one white – both of whom struggle to keep their heads above the water.[26]

*****

The psychoanalyst and social philosopher Erich Fromm would have read America's underwater empire as a marker of the country's culture of 'having'. Fromm was one of several high-profile left-wing intellectuals associated with the Institute for Social Research, founded in 1923 in Frankfurt am Main. This cadre of consciousness-raising critical theorists revolved around the core group of Theodor Adorno, Max Horkheimer and Herbert Marcuse. Collectively, they combined the thought of Marx and Freud into a diverse and incisive analysis of modern society. Fleeing Hitler's Germany in the 1930s, 'the Frankfurt School' headed to America where they became scholars in exile, offering detailed critiques of fascism while also turning their decoding gazes to the beguiling and alienating mass culture of their adopted homeland. Much of this work would go on to influence the thinking of the New Left of the 1960s, with Marcuse becoming an important figure of the countercultural era. Meanwhile, having taught for Columbia, Yale and New York Universities, Fromm took up academic positions in Mexico until he retired in 1965, at which point he too became involved in political activism. Stepping back from this work soon after the election of Richard Nixon in 1968, Fromm was once again on the move. He took up residence in Locarno, Switzerland where he spent the years 1974 to 1976 trying to diagnose the social shifts he had lived through and the deeply materialistic culture he had left behind. He wrote *To Have or To Be?* (1976) during this time, as well as the chapters later published as *The Art of Being* (1993).

In both, Fromm defined the drive 'to have' as a typical characteristic of a luxuriant, industrialised society. There are 'things', Fromm argues, which are essential for survival and always have been. The ownership of this 'functional property', as Fromm calls it, satisfies an 'actual need' and is required for 'biological existence'. *Homo sapiens* need bodies, shelters, tools, weapons, vessels. 'Nonfunctional property', by contrast, does not serve its owner's skill in the manner of a tool, but instead 'satisfies' a desire for possession. Fromm describes property held as capital, the hoarding of land for example, as nonfunctional because 'it remains valuable even if it is not invested; but if the owner invests it, he does not have to use his skill or make any commensurate effort to bring him profit'. Although different, these categories of property can also overlap. A 'change in function' appears in the property of a growing civilisation, Fromm argues, when the sheer abundance of 'things' exceeds their particular usage. The 'individual may have several suits or dresses […] labor-saving devices, radio and television machines', and within this world of commodified plenty, property 'ceases to be an instrument for greater aliveness and productivity but is transformed into a means for passive-receptive consumption'. 'Having' becomes the dominant socio-cultural mode because although we may *want* all of this stuff, we don't actually *need* it. As long as you are fortunate enough, the modern post-war world meets all of the basic requirements for survival. Once satisfied, that which continues to pour in is the unquenching froth of affluence, an excess that only ever fulfils the need for 'ever-increasing consumption'.[27]

Domestic swimming pools tally perfectly with this analysis. Gloriously non-functional, they stand as monuments to the human control over water and demonstrate how a finite resource can be diverted away from 'basic survival needs' towards the luxury of 'privatized leisure'. As Ryan Reft notes, this is certainly the case with the pools of California that lie tranquil alongside the 'dearth of water in the American West' and their 'proximity to the Pacific Ocean'. There is no actual need for so many pools, the water could better be used elsewhere, you could go swimming elsewhere, and yet they continue to appear thanks to the fuel of status-desire and the alchemical power of wealth.

The same could be said of London's controversial 'Sky Pool', which opened in May 2021 as part of the city's uber-exclusive Embassy Gardens, a property-rich but personality-poor residential and business hub in the Nine Elms regeneration zone of Wandsworth. An aqueduct of privilege, the Sky Pool managed to exceed even the pomposity of the infinity pool. Suspended 115 feet in the air and forming a translucent bridge between two high-rise apartment blocks, the pool is the centrepiece of the development's 'Sky Deck'. This is a leisure space reserved only for the development's wealthiest residents, the members of the perk-filled Eg:le Club. Those living on the site in shared-ownership properties have no access to the pool but many of them can still see it every time they look out of their windows, a particularly galling sight during a sweltering, virtually locked-down London summer. Critics were quick to flag up the ruthlessness of this excess during a metropolitan, national and global crisis of wealth and property inequality. Although private in terms of access, the Sky Pool is clearly intended as a public spectacle, a glacial container of cool, rich bodies that loudly announces their literal and symbolic superiority. It is not there merely to provide exercise but to advertise itself and its users as better than *you*. By all accounts the elite clubbers became somewhat less enamoured of their pool when they realised it was collectively costing them £450 a day to maintain. True to form, the rich made it clear they don't like spending money.[28]

About ten miles east of Nine Elms lie the remains of Robin Hood Gardens, a former housing block in Poplar, part of the borough of Tower Hamlets. Designed by architects Peter and Alison Smithson and completed in 1972, Robin Hood Gardens was a complex of walkways or 'streets in the sky' that looked inward to a communal green space. In theory, the design aimed to foster a self-contained community by blocking out external traffic noise and encouraging interactions between residents as they drifted along their concrete balconies. In practice, though, Robin Hood Gardens soon became a forbidding, isolating unit often likened to a prison in which the dimly lit dead-end corridors became pockets of crime and disorder. Peter Smithson later reflected that 'walking on the walkways is not a pleasure', adding that the fault lay solely with the residents. 'The week it opened,' he claimed, 'people would come in and shit in the lifts, which is an act of social aggression.' Speaking like a true declinist, Smithson was decrying an apparent fall in community values, as if the anti-social miasma emanating from the Post Office bombs of the Angry Brigade and the tabloid 'moral panics' over 'muggers, scroungers, streakers, strikes' had infected his building. However, as J.G. Ballard was at pains to point out in *High Rise* (1975), it is not a spirit of disorder that causes people to revolt against their buildings, but the buildings themselves which exert a psychic effect upon their residents. Ballard would have read the bad behaviour at Robin Hood

Gardens as a direct result of its design, and in this respect the building was doing what it was constructed to do. Consciously or not, the Smithsons had made a disorder machine, one that actively worked against their projected intention of harmonious community networking.[29]

Stokely Carmichael made a similar point in 'Black Power' when describing the ghettoisation of America's Black communities. Confined to inner-city areas away from the income-contingent, predominantly white suburbs, Black people find themselves in under-funded, under-resourced 'internal colonies' where they do not 'control the land, the houses or the stores'. These are generally owned by the suburban whites 'who live outside the community' but who continue to draw on it as a source of 'cheap labour'. It is in the interests of 'white power', argues Carmichael, that these enclaves remain deprived. Keeping the Black population poor maintains the existing social stratification, which explains why 'ghettos' can be found in each American city. Social disempowerment is the intended result of the strategic withdrawal of economic and material agency from the Black community; it is a product, argues Carmichael, of the 'the racist functionings that combine to make society'. This was the argument made by a young Donald DeFreeze around the time of his first probation for carrying firearms in 1967. This was before his 1969 incarceration which led to the formation of the Symbionese Liberation Army. He claims that his anti-social activities – carrying guns, setting fires, dabbling with homemade bombs – were prompted by his failure to make ends meet and provide for his wife and child. They were attempts to 'compensate' for his feelings of economic 'inadequacy and powerlessness', as his probation officer put it. It is a flimsy defence which neither explains nor excuses his offences, particularly those he would go on to commit, but it positions DeFreeze as an extreme example of the pernicious bind Carmichael analyses. Struggling to get by with no discernible avenue for betterment or mobility available, frustration starts to grow into anger, then violence. Before long the police get involved, ready to enforce the law set by 'white power'. At this point the discontent of the troublemaker, rioter, urban guerilla – take your pick – adds to the stereotype of the unruly ghetto, a place in need of order rather than deserving of any kind of 'justice'.[30]

The thrust of these varied arguments is clear: capitalist enterprise and social welfare do not sit easily together. It is entirely possible to commodify 'actual needs' and to control their satisfaction through the diversion of capital. To do so, though, is invariably to the detriment of those nominally in society but not blessed with the arbitrary qualifiers of privilege. Looking in from these margins there can only be one reasonable conclusion. Capitalism makes you ill. Fromm emphasised this in *The Art of Being* when he described the individual and social damage wrought by the culture of having. For Fromm, the drive to have is 'pathogenic' because it destroys 'man's productive development' by depriving him of 'aliveness'. Fromm was writing shortly after the World Economic Forum had, in 1971, instituted itself in the Swiss alpine town of Davos, close to his own base at Locarno.

Davos was the site of Thomas Mann's classic sanatorium novel *The Magic Mountain* (1924) and the World Economic Forum, originally the European Management Forum, intentionally chose the location for their annual meeting to reflect their curative, if not transformative, agenda. Working under the motto 'improving the state of the world', the WEF sought to massage the relationship between markets and politics to align economic and social values. It continues to 'mitigate global risks, promote health for all, improve social welfare' and 'foster environmental sustainability'. For Fromm, the pursuit of this agenda, however laudable, would not offset the pernicious effects of having, because the project overall was tethered to the 'distributive promises of market dynamics'. Such faith in the flow of capital reiterates the necessity of the having mode as it is this impulse that powers the engine of 'market-making and market exchange'. To be individually driven by the desire to 'have' and to engage with the world through consumption does not result in the life-affirming social health that the WEF celebrates. Instead, following Fromm's general argument, you are ultimately transformed into the 'thing' you consume, insofar as the accumulative drive becomes the marker of your identity. It is easy to think of the

Sky Pool swimmers succumbing to this fate as they wave to passing drones, slowly crystallising in their tanks of fluid capital.[31]

To counter these deeply alienating effects, Fromm closed *The Art of Being* with a call for a paradigm shift from 'having' to 'being', an attitudinal movement away from 'I am what I have' to 'I am what I am'. The showstopping, almost Broadway-like tone of Fromm's concluding lines does not find him aligning the pursuit of well-being with a singular, 'spiritual' search for the self. In *The Art of Being* Fromm is keen to distance himself from 'the great sham' of Transcendental Meditation and est. He also would have given short shrift to the residents-only yoga rooms at Embassy Gardens. Fromm saw such processes as placebos that promise 'a deep change in personality' but only ever offer a 'momentary improvement of symptoms [...] and some relaxation'. Fromm argued they were not able to change society, nor improve the social problems for which their clients so often sought help: a 'lack of genuine contact and genuine feeling'. In his model it was not enough to develop and grow the self as an alternative to the 'having orientation', it was instead necessary to analyse, interrogate and change 'the economic realities that produce the having mode'.[32]

Easier said than done. For feminist activists and members of the Black Power movement, the main obstacle involved in achieving such a change was the underlying scaffold of these 'economic realities'. As Mander and Kent Rush put it, the 'sexist-racist-capitalist base' of the Western hemisphere gives hegemonic control to the white male. From the home to the workplace, across the cultural landscape and even into the metaphysical realm, the figure of the power-laden male predominates. Father, breadwinner, boss and God: the material and symbolic authority of these figures is based on the normalised assumption that economic and social power stands in alignment with a specifically gendered, narrowly racial identity. If there was any doubt of this beyond the daily battery of discrimination one only needed to look at the gold-plated plaque attached to the Pioneer 10 and Pioneer 11 space probes launched by NASA in 1972 and 1973. As Jessica Thompson describes, although the probes were tasked with exploring 'Jupiter and the asteroid belt', astronomer

Carl Sagan approached NASA about the possibility of them facilitating an extraterrestrial first contact. So that these aliens would know who sent the probes, 'Sagan, his artist wife Linda Salzman Sagan, and Frank Drake, one of the founders of SETI' designed a plaque featuring a pulsar map of the solar system, directions to Earth as well as an 'image of a naked man and woman'. Sagan claimed these figures were 'panracial' but with their classical stylings redolent of Greek sculpture they appeared distinctly Mediterranean and suggested humanity was 'white, fair and European-coded'. As if to further confuse our space brothers, the 'naked' woman also appeared to lack any genitalia. While the Earth man proudly displays his modest penis, his companion is smooth, blank and oddly cleftless. As an ambassadorial document that hopefully anticipates exchange with other intelligences, the plaque carried a stark message to the cosmos: this is Earth, planet of white men who enjoy the attendant company of women who are utterly alienated from their own sexual identities.[33]

When offering its 'Jive shit for rich white folk', Esalen reiterated this normative view. In 1967 the institute did attempt to engage with racial discrimination and the increasingly visible contingent of Black Power activism in the Bay Area via a series of interracial encounter groups. Mounted by George Leonard and the psychiatrist Price Cobbs, co-author of *Black Rage* (1968), the sessions engineered Black–white conflict as an exploration of the 'inner racist feelings' instilled in the participants by society. Leonard hoped to 'really get down to see what was between the two races' by directly confronting the 'beast of racial prejudice'. Differences aired, the hope was that participants would transcend these feelings and 'encounter each other as individuals'. Frequently involving more white participants than Black, the groups were exhausting, emotionally charged affairs in which each 'side' would more often vent their mutual anger and resentment rather than focus on any kind of resolution. We get a glimpse of these encounters in *Century of the Self* (2002), Adam Curtis' documentary on the commodification of modern identity. The footage shows Black radicals squaring up to white liberals as a thick ambience of distrust fills the room. The Black participants call out the 'phoniness' of the whites while the whites fail to check their own privilege and see only inverted racism coming back their way. Watching the footage, it is clear that any differences 'between the two races' are being further entrenched rather than surmounted.

The problem lay with the idea of 'transcendence', the notion that a group could arrive at a position of post-racial humanity and in so doing resolve the socio-political problem of racism. Not only was this aim impossibly idealistic, but it was also not as 'universal' as it appeared. The implied line of transcendence was from the enmity of racial conflict to a position of neutral, untroubled 'normality'; in other words the position already occupied by the white participants. Despite its good intentions, Esalen was covertly superintending over a generalised 'reality' of whiteness. This was the default identity, and it was the unspoken assumption that all others would stand in reference, if not deference, to it. As Curtis explains, in asking Black radicals to step away from their racial identity to meet the white group members 'equally' as 'individuals', they were being 'liberated' from the 'one marker of their power', their collective radicalism as a Black community.[34]

For groups like the Black Panthers, this collective power was the key to the achievement of self-determination. As a response to the health care problems faced by Black communities, the group developed their own 'activist-run no-cost or low-cost clinics' and 'survival programmes'. In their 'Ten Point Programme', Huey P. Newton and Bobby Seale had called for 'completely free health care for all Black and oppressed people'. They saw it as the government's role to develop 'preventative medical programmes' as well as 'mass education and research' initiatives to give all 'Black and oppressed people access to advanced scientific and medical information'. The Panthers' 'People's Free Medical Clinics' worked to this end, plugging the gap in the government's health provision in addition to offering a platform alternative to the institutions they found to be systemically racist. As Alondra Nelson describes, the clinics 'administered basic preventative care, tested for lead poisoning and hypertension, and helped with housing, employment, and social services'. This care was offered by 'lay and trusted-expert volunteers including nurses, doctors and students in the health professions' who donated their time at the clinics and used 'vans and ambulances' to go 'out into poor communities'. The party also mounted a set of outreach and education initiatives, most notably the 1971 campaign focused on sickle cell anaemia which involved a series of public information events alongside an extensive screening programme. The project extended the party's health care autonomy and carried out a critical function: it 'exposed the racial bias of the medical system that had largely ignored sickle cell anaemia, a disease that predominantly affected people of African American descent'.[35]

In parallel, the Women's Health Movement was directing the energy of feminist politics into the provision of free medical services across America. Between the publication of *Women and their Bodies* (1970) by the Boston Women's Health Book Collective and its high-profile reissue as *Our Bodies, Ourselves* (1973), activist clinics became widespread, offering general health advice and key services, with abortion and contraception being primary points of focus. The UK saw a similar rollout of independent medical support with the appearance of the Well Woman clinics like London's Liverpool Road clinic. First held in 1973, the clinic was 'formed by members of the Essex Road Women's Health Group and prioritised sharing experience and offering support in a group setting, along with expert advice'. These international, ground-level initiatives coincided with *Roe* v. *Wade* (1973), the landmark case that effectively upturned years of state legislation by ruling that a pregnant woman's choice to have an abortion was protected under the constitutional right to privacy.

Each of these projects used collective power and shared resources to undo the prejudicial monopolisation of services that should be open to all. They responded to the gaps left by an evaporating welfare state and helped to foreground the discriminatory basis of public health care provision. Where Esalen's model of human potential aspired to a version of mental, physical, and spiritual well-being that seemed to exceed its social and political surroundings, and the emerging language of wellness encouraged those already thriving towards an excess of health, the Black Panthers and the feminist movement worked at ground level, in opposition to the barriers guarding access to this abundance. That said, their idea of what it means to be well was built on a similarly holistic basis, but with the added charge of overt political commitment. As the Panthers made clear in a three-day 'Black Community Survival Conference' held in Oakland's De Fremery Park in March 1972, their role was to 'Serve the People Body and Soul'. Their 'service programmes' were not solely directed at the alleviation of disease case by case, person by person, but they also sought to improve the material and cultural health of the wider Black community. It was activism that conferred autonomy and dignity upon its stakeholder, the markers of well-being so often denied by existing health providers.[36]

These community programmes were enacting the type of courageous change symbolised by Adrienne Rich in her poem 'Diving into the Wreck' (1972). Rich describes a deep-sea diver encased in an ill-fitting 'body-armor' with a 'grave and awkward mask' who then descends, alone, into the ocean. There in the deep, under pressure and in darkness, they learn how to 'breathe differently'. They survey the wreck and take in 'the damage that was done'. It is a scene that departs from the 'book of myths' that tell the story of the wreck, a 'book in which our names do not appear'. Rich's allegory speaks of a deep dive under the surface of tradition, history and ideology, a difficult exercise but one that holds out the possibility of writing a new set of stories to live by. This was the journey that Jim Ellis embarked on when he started to train Black swimmers as part of the Philadelphia 'Pride, Determination and Resilience' team. As the 1970s progressed and as the Black Panthers and others continued their struggle, he used swimming to push against the tide of discrimination. In 1979 Ellis moved his operations to another facility in the city, the Marcus Foster Pool, part of the Simon Gratz campus in Nicetown. There he pushed on with the mission of its namesake and trained his team to achieve their full potential. It was while based at Marcus Foster that Ellis started fielding swimmers for the US Olympic trials.[37]

CHAPTER V

The Shaping
1973–1975

A young couple stroll down a city street, past a row of cafes and shops. Were it not for the web address posted across one of the windows, you could swear it was the late 1970s. The guy has a tash, a mop of curly hair and looks comfortable in his polyester shirt. The girl has long bangs and is equally at ease in her midi skirt and denim. Pausing, they notice a television set, 1970s vintage of course, that stands in one of the storefronts. It is showing what looks like a public access broadcast. On screen there's a beautiful Indian man with luxurious long hair, festooned in talismans and amulets and draped in a golden cloak. He is also wearing a sweatband and what looks like a leotard. A king in Lycra, he speaks of 'body harmony and wave trance, together, in holy matrimony' and, as if addressing the couple directly, he tells them it is time to 'Shape Up'. The words 'Shape Up' form into a logo on the screen, a jingle starts to play and that's when things begin to get *weird*.

The next thing we see in 'Sleepwalker' (2012), a music video by Hylas Film made for the San Franciscan band Moon Duo, is the couple furtively entering a tawdry community hall. They are now wearing faded fitness gear: leggings, headbands and washed-out spandex. Over in the corner, on a tiny stage, Moon Duo are performing the video's hypnotic title track while the Indian man, the guru of the piece (played by musician King Khan), leads his followers through a snakish dance routine. The couple hesitantly join in. Shape Up, it seems, is a kind of New Age jazzercize, a mix of aerobics and yoga-lite bodywork. As the camera pans over the dancers in loving slow motion, capturing the knowing glances that greet the new arrivals, a faint air of kinkiness descends. The room fills with all the heavy charm and not-quite-rightness of a swingers' party about to begin. Khan's character, though, has another kind of group activity in mind. In a whirl of pot smoke and spookily reversed footage, he approaches the girl, giving her what looks like a psychedelic communion wafer. She eats it and is suddenly glassy-eyed, moving automatically with the rest of the dancers. They form a circle around the guy with the tash and, to his growing horror, start to converge on him like nest of serpents. They claw at him, pulling him to the ground, out of shot. The camera then lingers on the dancers, all now lying in a mandala formation, occasionally twitching. Sated. Meanwhile, back out on the street, the Shape Up video plays on, ready to snare another unsuspecting couple.[1]

Full of cultish vibes and unsettling undertones, 'Sleepwalker' comes across like a strange mix of *Jane Fonda's Workout* (1982) and Dario Argento's ballet-themed horror *Suspiria* (1977). Anchored around Khan's portrayal of the 'bad guru', the video reflects a distinct trend in popular culture that sees covert, malevolent intentions lurking beneath New Age pathways to physical and spiritual health. Jane Campion's *Holy Smoke!* (1999) played with these ideas, at one point aligning the work of the film's Indian teacher, Baba, with the tactics of the Manson Family and the UFO cult Heaven's Gate. More recently Liane Moriarty's novel *Nine Perfect Strangers* (2018) introduced the austere, 'corpse-white' wellness guru Masha Dmitrichenko whose 'East meets West' regime at the remote Tranquillum House includes administering micro-doses of LSD to her guests without their consent. She could learn a thing or two from Jan, the duplicitous, self-serving life coach from the cult vampire sitcom *What We Do in the Shadows* (2021). Jan leads the 'Post-Chiropteran Wellness Center', which offers therapeutic counsel to vampires held in the thrall of immortal ennui. 'Chiropteran' refers to the mammalian order of bats, and Jan's pitch is that through healthy living, yoga and ritualistic bouts of fang extraction, vampires can dispense with their nocturnal, blood-drinking lifestyle and *will* themselves to be human. Where Masha is persuasive enough to get her clients to drink their psychoactive smoothies, Jan takes it up a level; she can convince a squad of vampires to run into the obliterating glare of the sun in the name of good health.[2]

Linked, then, to manipulation, coercion and mind-control, the contemporary 'bad guru' is an updated version of the Svengali character: the seductive villain who dominates through hypnotic charm and sinister charisma. Originally appearing as a Jewish musician in George du Maurier's novel *Trilby* (1894), Svengali also embodied the desires and toxic anxieties of mid-19th century Britain, from music hall aspirations to anti-Semitic prejudice. The modern 'bad guru' trope carries a much broader range of meanings, but the symbolic stakes are similar. In these fictions it is the spectre of perfection, the dream of an improved self, that works as the point of aspiration and its flipside, the loss of identity, that forms the primary anxiety. The fear of the other, however, remains just as strong, with the 'bad guru' often depicted as using a battery of techniques from the 'East' (typically India and China) to threaten ideas of selfhood and spirituality favoured by the 'West' (typically America and Europe).

Running parallel to this remodelling of old stereotypes lies a recent and distressing history of damaging behaviour (from mis-adventure to exploitation) connected to a full spectrum of spiritual teachers, lifestyle coaches and 'self-styled' gurus. In September 2020, the *Toronto Star* ran a story headed 'Gurus Gone Bad', reporting on calls to bring tighter regulation to the self-help and wellness industry. The focus was the case of James Arthur Ray, a former tele-marketer turned motivational speaker 'who was convicted of three counts of negligent homicide in 2011'. As described in the podcast series *Guru: The Dark Side of Enlightenment*, 'three people had died of heat stroke' during one of Ray's Arizona-based 'Spirit Warrior retreats'. Shortly before, the Al Jazeera report 'Gurus Gone Bad in India' described the 2017 sexual assault conviction of Gurmeet Ram Rahim Singh, a 'self-styled saint' who led one of India's wealthiest spiritual organisations and claimed to have 60 million followers worldwide. In between, Netflix launched documentaries like *Wild Wild Country* (2018) about the Indian and American ashrams of Bhagwan Shree Rajneesh and *Bikram: Yogi, Guru, Predator* (2019), an investigation into the abrasive teacher of hot yoga, Bikram Choudhury.[3]

The Rajneesh movement was focused on the Acharya Rajneesh Ashram in Pune, western India. Established in 1974 having previously been based in Mumbai from 1970 onwards, the ashram was led by the charismatic holy man, mystic and teacher Bhagwan Shree Rajneesh. He was born Rajneesh Chandra Mohan in central India in 1931 but took on the names *Bhagwan* (God) and *Shree* (Sir) after settling in Pune. Later, in 1989, he was to drop both titles in favour of *Osho*, a name which, according to Ma Prem Shunyo, one of the first 'Rajneeshees' to write a personal memoir about their time with the guru, was derived from 'a common form of address used in Japan for a Zen master'. The core of this master's practice involved various meditation techniques to achieve a sudden state of enlightenment or 'Buddhahood', as well as a transformative ritual of '*initiation darshan* or "taking sannyas"':

> in which he touched initiates on the 'third eye', endowed them with Sanskrit names, gave each a *mala* (necklace of wooden beads bearing Rajneesh's photograph) and required them to wear orange (later changed to red).

Once renamed, the followers were known as *neo-sannyasins*, after the Hindu tradition of asceticism or *sannyasa*, which typically involved the 'renunciation of much of the world (economic activity, sex, pursuit of comforts)'. However, with the movement's drive towards instant, epiphanic awareness in the here and now, Rajneesh's teaching rejected such privations and encouraged a 'celebratory', approach to the spiritual life. This included his famous tolerance for, if not overt encouragement of, sexual exploration among the members of the ashram.

Rajneesh often spoke in apocalyptic terms about the 'sickness' of the world, an impending 'global suicide' that could be averted with the advent of a 'New Consciousness'. With typical messianic aplomb, he claimed that the *neo-sannyasins* were the harbingers of this 'new human'. The *neo-sannyasins* would not transcend the world, but live in it, liberated from the expectations and codes that governed their former lives while also acting as torch-bearers encouraging others to follow. It was a philosophy of spiritual embodiment that justified Rajneesh's emphasis on sensory pleasures in addition to his own, enthusiastic, 'economic activity'. As well as absorbing the resources of his often wealthy disciples, Rajneesh was supported by private investment and a stream of 'royalties from an international network of schools, centers, hotels, restaurants, stores, and discotheques'. It was an income flow that exploded across the 1970s giving Rajneesh a massive personal fortune that was funnelled into jewellery, property and a fleet of Rolls-Royce cars. Meanwhile, back in the kitchens and workshops of the ashram, the *neo-sannyasins* dutifully carried out their working meditations. Free of such hinderances as a regular wage, they kept all the daily operations smoothly running while patiently awaiting the shock of enlightenment.[4]

In 1971, just as the Rajneesh movement was growing, Bikram Choudhury (or just 'Bikram' as he prefers) arrived in America, claiming to be a part of an esteemed yogic lineage. He taught on the Los Angeles spa circuit for a few years until he set-up shop in Beverly Hills and in 1974 opened the Yoga College of India, down on Wilshire Boulevard. Gathering together a wealthy Hollywood clientele that included Shirley MacLaine, Marge Champion and Alexis Smith, Bikram promoted yoga as 'much more than a system of exercise'. 'Bikram Yoga', as he branded his method, was sold as a 'way of life designed to bring every aspect of living into a harmonious union' and to get the full benefit, he encouraged his clients to take daily classes. Beverly Sassoon, co-author of *A Year of Beauty and Health* (1976), went along to the Yoga College after a recommendation from 'Nancy Dinsmore, the West Coast editor of *Harper's Bazaar*'. Joining a 'beginner's class', Sassoon was introduced to yoga as a 'slow, controlled, graceful' form of exercise that 'gave the heart and the muscles enough of a workout so that the perspiration flows and the oxygen is really coursing throughout the body'. She found that the 'yoga serenity' lasted for hours afterwards and within a month her circulation and complexion had improved, and she felt stronger, more flexible and flush with 'self-control, patience and concentration'. Clearly, for Sassoon, yoga was a 'winning ticket'.

However, it was not for teaching a gentle form of exercise that Bikram became (in)famous. Beyond the beginner's class, Bikram offered his signature brand of hot yoga, an intense, demanding sequence of 26 Hatha poses taught across 90-minute sessions in a mirrored room that sweltered in the funk of its 105-degree heat. Some students revelled in the sheer physical challenge of this class, describing a feeling of near ecstasy as they pushed themselves beyond their physical limits. For others, the muggy studio was a deeply uncomfortable space; an arena of intimidation lorded over by a brash and cocky ringmaster. 'This is my torture chamber,' Bikram would announce as he paraded across the sweat-drenched, bacteria-rich carpets in nothing but a headband and speedos. Frequently spouting misogynistic put downs, Bikram would often physically bend or even stand on top of his predominantly female students to drub them into another spine-stretching *asana*. And with all the money coming in from these daily sessions charged at Beverly Hills prices, Bikram, like Rajneesh, started to buy cars, designer clothes and other luxuries of the material world.

For Rajneesh, such conspicuous excess was, in part, a key aspect of his trickster status. Whether accumulating wealth or celebrating free love, his was a deliberately contradictory stance designed to undercut the very idea of a holy man. He saw both traditional notions of piety and Western fixations on materialism as binding institutions. Celebrating sexuality and accumulating capital to such a degree was thus a way of making these taboos and desires effectively meaningless, thereby freeing oneself from dependence upon them. It was an enormously profitable set of provocations, though. Rajneesh seemed always to be the main beneficiary of that which he declared inessential. It was easy to assume that it was all a confidence trick and that along with the likes of Bikram, Rajneesh was simply in pursuit of his own gratification, material or otherwise.[5]

Seen in this light, both men exemplified the double-edged image of the bad guru trope, that of the tarnished, malevolent 'superstar'. As writer and journalist Arthur Goldwag puts it in his recent study of cult dynamics, the spiritual culture of the late 1960s and early 1970s saw the 'rise to global prominence of a number of Indian spiritual teachers', some of whom acquired 'incredible wealth, fame and power along the way'. Hanif Kureishi sketched out the same trajectory, albeit at a more local level, in his 1970s-set novel *The Buddha of Suburbia* (1990). Paralleling narrator Karim's coming-of-age story is that of his father Haroon, 'a renegade Muslim masquerading as a Buddhist' whose growing public status as a 'guru' teaching 'the Way' allows him to climb London's social ladder. Haroon's story is a narrative of cultural entrepreneurship that plays out to a backdrop of a multicultural, increasingly hybridised experience of British society. What Goldwag focuses on, however, is less the symbolism of the modern guru as the negative accounts of spiritual exploitation connected to certain high-profile figures. In some instances, he argues, their growing influence was put to good use. In others, though, the power appeared to 'corrupt'. In the case of Rajneesh and Bikram, the issue was not just the apparent disconnect between their teachings and their lifestyles but more seriously, as they travelled further along the curve of wealth and fame, they appeared to betray the enormous trust that should lie at the heart of the guru–disciple relationship.[6]

'Guru' is the Sanskrit word for 'venerable'. It has come to generally mean spiritual teacher, but it also refers to a specific type of relationship between an aspirant and their guide. In some Indian traditions, as Goldwag explains,

> The guru is considered the living embodiment of the truth and is venerated as a deity – the student not only grants the guru unconditional devotion but turns over his or her possessions and becomes the guru's servant.

'Surrender is a very important aspect of the guru-devotee relationship', adds the writer Bhavdeep Kang, whom Al Jazeera consulted in their report on Gurmeet Ram Rahim Singh. 'You have to completely surrender yourself to the God-man, which means even when he's wrong, he's right'. Within such a dynamic, the teacher can easily come to dominate and exploit the disciple. This was certainly the case with Bikram and Rajneesh. Variously egotistical and tyrannical, and regarded by many of their followers as beyond reproach, both are alleged to have committed or otherwise enabled widespread psychological and sexual abuse within their organisations. The allegations relating to the Rajneesh Ashram date back to the 1970s, but they only began to formally surface in the 1980s and 1990s, mainly in the aftermath of the group transferring their base of operations to America and 'Rajneeshpuram' ('expression of Rajneesh'), a massive self-sufficient ashram established near the town of Antelope, Oregon in 1981. The release of *Wild Wild Country* gave further exposure to these claims and allowed others to come to the surface. Those made against Bikram are also relatively recent, emerging across the 2000s and gaining significant traction thanks to films like *Yogi, Guru, Predator*. As with the Rajneesh allegations, though, they point to a long-standing pattern of behaviour. Paralleling these accounts are a consistent set of claims made from the 1970s onward against a wide range of spiritual teachers relating to inappropriate contact, sexual harassment and coercion.[7]

One of the earliest came from Baba Ram Dass, formerly Timothy Leary's LSD research colleague Richard Alpert. Writing in the November 1976 issue of *Yoga Journal*, Dass launched a scathing attack on 'Joya' – one Joya Santayana (also known as Ma Jaya), a self-styled guru who lived in Brooklyn 'surrounded by disciples'. Dass was the author of the classic yoga and meditation guide *Be Here Now* (1971). He had learnt much of his practice from the Hindu teacher Neem Karoli Baba, whom he met after travelling to India in 1967. Upon the death of his guru in 1973, Dass found himself in America, 'teaching on a full schedule', getting caught up in 'worldly play' and feeling increasingly 'depressed and hypocritical' as a result. He contemplated returning to India but was quickly steered off the idea when, according to Dass, he had a vision of Neem Karoli Baba and was told to find a new teacher closer to home. Dass dutifully agreed. Following a recommendation from a friend, he sought out Joya in Brooklyn and in late 1974 entered into *sadhana* (daily practice) with her. For the next fifteen months Dass was required to perform *pranayama* (breathing exercises) and other devotional rituals to an extreme degree. In 'Egg on my Beard', his article for *Yoga Journal*, Dass describes how exhaustion came to dominate this intense period of discipleship. *Sadhana* with Joya involved sleep deprivation, psychological battery and an expectation of total, self-sublimating devotion. The main claim, however, was that his new guru neither lived up to nor respected these high spiritual standards. Dass paints a picture of an arch manipulator who deceived her followers and, most damningly, coerced him into a sexual relationship on the auspices of tantric initiation.

At the same time, the writer Tal Brooke was making similar claims in *Lord of the Air* (1976), his portrait of the Indian guru and alleged 'miracle-worker' Sri Sathya Sai Baba. Brooke travelled from America to India in the late 1960s and went on to spend several months in Sai Baba's southern Indian ashram, at one point intending to write a positive, supportive book about his teachings. *Lord of the Air*, however, purports to tell a much more accurate story about what Brooke found there. Like Dass, Brooke describes a closed world of exhausting ritual practices, limited food and frequent sexually abusive encounters with Sai Baba. For Brooke, who later became a committed Christian, Sai Baba was nothing less than the 'modern antichrist', a claim seized upon by those quick to defend their guru. *Lord of the Air*, they argued, was evangelical propaganda, a smear campaign of low blows designed to discredit a growing religious movement and to warn off potential converts. 'Egg on my Beard' was also not without its detractors and it's easy to see why. Overall, the tone of the article is apologetic. It reads like a long *mea culpa*, an act of face-saving rather than whistleblowing in which Dass admits to being 'duped' and bitterly regrets endorsing his former teacher. A cynic might also be tempted to read the piece as Dass' self-serving takedown of a rival spiritual pretender.

Both accounts offered a deeply critical picture of 'alternative' spirituality in the 1970s. They helped to establish a model of accusation in which the guru is seen to intentionally exercise unequal and pernicious power over the follower. This is the distressing reality upon which the 'bad gurus' of later videos like 'Sleepwalker' are based. Such negative views, though, are not entirely the product of 1970s revisionism. A closer look at the decade's understanding of gurus, and Indian religions more generally, indicates that when these teachers appeared in the West, they were greeted with suspicion and scepticism even before the problematic allegations became commonplace. In this sense, the carefully constructed aura of sexuality and horror projected by 'Sleepwalker' is not so much a satirical view of the 1970s formed in the light of what we now know, but rather a distillation of the anxieties already circulating at the time.[8]

★

In 1968, *Life* magazine announced the 'Year of the Guru'. This was mainly in response to the popularity of the Maharishi Mahesh Yogi, who began to spread the good news of Transcendental Meditation to American audiences in 1959. A decade on he was sharing the American stage with other stars like the Hindu teacher of 'integral yoga', Swami Satchidananda. He landed in New York in 1966 and quickly moved through the city's artistic and countercultural scenes. The Maharishi may have held court with The Beatles, but it was Satchidananda who addressed the massive crowd at the Woodstock festival in 1969. By this time he had also gathered thousands of followers and opened a network of yoga institutes across the country. The Himalayan Brahmin Swami Rama followed soon after, quickly gaining fame thanks to his apparent ability to stop his heartbeat. At the same time Yogi Bhajan, the Sikh practitioner of Kundalini yoga, was busy establishing ashrams throughout America's south-west, a number that grew to over 50 between 1969 and 1971.[9]

However, it would be another mid-1960s Indian immigrant who would arguably have the biggest and most enduring spiritual impact on American culture. Arriving virtually penniless in New York's East Village in 1965, the 'seventy-year-old ex-pharmaceuticals salesman' from Calcutta, A.C. Bhaktivedanta Swami Prabhupada gravitated towards Washington Square and began chanting in praise of Krishna, the eighth avatar of Vishnu. Within a year he had established a storefront temple and in October 1966 performed a collective chant or *kirtan* in Tompkins Square Park with the poet Allen Ginsberg, attracting in the process a large crowd and substantial coverage in the *New York Times*. This was the start of ISKCON, the

International Society for Krishna Consciousness, which would soon amass a healthy following of shaven-headed, saffron-robed, deeply devotional Hare Krishnas, all of whom held a sacred duty to convert others to the faith. In this mission they were aided by the celebrity appeal of George Harrison, who recorded 'Hare Krishna Mantra' (1969) with ISKCON's British outpost, the Radha Krishna Temple in London.[10]

While the meteoric rise of these religious figures exemplified the rags-to-riches ideal of the American Dream, their rapid success also recalled its opportunistic flipside. To a public alert to the attractions but wise to the disappointments of get-rich-quick schemes, miracle cures and Charles Atlas seven-day body builds, what the local guru had to offer – easy bliss, drugless highs, spiritual health, a new way of life – seemed too good to be true. Such promises were the preserve of the huckster, not the mystic.

This was certainly the view of the Californian garage band William Penn Fyve who in 1966, nearly two years before John Lennon's takedown of the Maharishi in 'Sexy Sadie' (1968), had a minor hit with 'Swami', a fuzzbox raga about a fraudulent holy man. The song finds its eponymous swami grifting for money from a 'needle bed'; he looks to be in a 'trance' but 'really he's just stoned instead'. The swami offers no insight, imparts no teachings, practices no discernible system, but merely sits by his tent 'fooling people all the time'. As the song ends, the swami has disappeared, and it is heavily implied that the narrator has now assumed his role, thus allowing the hustle to continue. Where parallel bands like The Deep and The Thirteenth Floor Elevators eagerly embraced the inner spaces of psychedelia, the William Penn Fyve remained surprisingly blunt when it came to the possibility of a head trip. The message of 'Swami' was clear: if you put your trust in a spiritual teacher, all you will find is a confidence trick.[11]

At the other end of the spectrum were novels like Martin Thomas' *The Hand of Cain* (1966), Don Pendleton's *The Godmakers* (1970) and later Diana Carter's *Mind-Out* (1973), each of which presented gurus, swamis and other beguiling spiritual teachers as simultaneously attractive and malign. *The Godmakers* is exemplary in this regard. A fast-moving, psychedelic mix of espionage and trash mysticism, Pendleton's book is sensationalistic rather than cynical in its handling of Indian religion. It finds American national security threatened when a government scientist, Curt Wenssler, is sapped of his 'Kundalini', his 'vital life forces', and cast into an astral realm. He is pursued into this 'Ninth Parallax', as Pendleton terms it, by a group of psychically inclined secret agents who use 'libidinal projection' to rend the veil. Thanks to intense bouts of gymnastic sex they can literally orgasm themselves into the beyond. With its supernatural-ism, its conspiracies and its endlessly interchangeable orgies, *The Godmakers* easily stood alongside other works of pop occultism like Philip José Farmer's *The Image of the Beast* (1968) in offering a wholesale assault on the conservative morality of America in the late 1960s and early 1970s.[12]

Following the progressivism of the 1960s, Richard Nixon had entered the White House in 1969 promising to maintain the security of the nuclear family and to shore up the 'traditional moral values' of mainstream religion. It was a domestic policy that tallied with the anti-permissive campaign of the Christian right, exemplified by psychologist James Dobson, author of *Dare to Discipline* (1970), 'a child-rearing manual based on biblical precepts'. Closely mirroring Nixon's 'social issues' party line, Dobson decried the apparent decline of the Bible's social authority, blaming what he saw as the generational rise of 'civil disobedience, vandalism, violence, illegal drugs' on a lack of parental discipline and a diet of immoral popular culture. Books like *The Godmakers* had little time for these Republican 'family values', with Pendleton preferring instead to revel in a provocative, softcore version of what *Dare to Discipline* called 'the altar of overindulgence'. The novel is no Dionysian hymn to the counterculture, though. It pictures student protestors as little more than a chaotic rabble, easily open to the same esoteric forces that beset Wenssler. Neither does Pendleton connect the permissive atmosphere of *The Godmakers* to cracks in the nuclear family, nor to the pernicious influence of the all-American Devil, then lauded by the likes of Anton LaVey, the Church of Satan and other sulphuric subcultures active in the underground networks of San Francisco and Los Angeles. Rather, the orgiastic and pseudo-mystical events of the novel are linked to an outside source: the transformative cultural influence of India. It is to India that Wenssler travels to explore the 'metaphysics of the East'; it is there he meets Hindu adepts who have 'mastered the concept of mind over matter'; and it is from there he returns with the psychic tools that kickstart the intrigue.[13]

Although far from accurate in its portrayal of 'ancient Sanskrit writings' that act as 'Psychic Power Sources', Pendleton's comic-book take on the ideas of 'the East' did reflect some aspects of alternative spirituality in India *circa* 1970, particularly the anti-establishment view of the Rajneesh movement. As Hugh B. Urban describes, Rajneesh was every inch the postmodern guru, an iconoclastic product of post-independence India. His rise to spiritual leadership occurred during a time of 'tremendous religious, social and political turmoil in the fledgling democracy'. India and Pakistan 'had just barely been created [...] and India was struggling to negotiate its role within the complex Cold War landscape dominated by the United States and the Soviet Union'. Rajneesh's plural belief system and calls to overthrow fixed notions of identity in favour of a 'liquid human being' mirrored and exploited this uncertain mood.

It was a stance that paralleled the 'revolutionary' de-individualising impetus of poststructuralism found variously in the work of Gilles Deleuze, Félix Guattari and Michel Foucault. As Foucault wrote when introducing Deleuze and Guattari's *Anti-Oedipus*, between 1965 and 1970, the 'impassioned, jubilant, enigmatic years' defined by Vietnam and New Left activism opened up a 'movement towards political struggles that no longer conformed to the model that the Marxist tradition had prescribed'. Equally, there was a shift towards 'an experience and a technology of desire that were no longer Freudian'. In his own work Foucault had repeatedly charted the cultivation of the individual – the subject – as a 'product of power'. He argued that historically, the 'I' had been conditioned and informed by – subject to – a battery of ideological and systemic forces, including the economic and libidinal precepts of Marx and Freud. With their cultural and intellectual influence waning in the post-1960s period, the stage was set for the likes of the philosopher Deleuze and the (anti)psychiatrist Guattari to speak from the vacuum. 'Sick' of the predetermined, power-laden 'self', they used *Anti-Oedipus* to outline a radically plural political subjectivity, an unfixed, collective modality of 'multiplicities' and 'flows': strategically nomadic and conceptually ungovernable. This militantly fluid schema, what *Anti-Oedipus* termed 'an ongoing process of becoming', had no place for such a symbol of authority as a guru. However, Rajneesh's description of the 'new consciousness' as 'counter to all orthodoxies' nonetheless echoed the liberative thrust of Deleuze and Guattari's thinking. Viewing 'any kind of orthodoxy' as 'a paralysis of the mind', Rajneesh argued that an 'alive person has to be flowing', and 'has to respond to changing situations'.

When considering the popularity of Rajneeshism, it is likely that this fluidity was a key source of the attraction. There is never one singular, fully satisfactory answer as to why people choose to follow leaders or gurus of one sort or another. Or, for that matter, why people decide to join tightly controlled, seemingly dictatorial groups. It is too reductive to say that all such adherents are simply duped, deluded or misguided. Rather, people join because they recognise what's on offer and they want it; because the group, belief system or guru gives them what they believe they need *at that time.* On the surface, what Rajneesh offered was an irreverent form of religiosity that often laid bare the fault lines of mainstream religion and politics. As such, his worldview was attractive to those among India's emergent middle class who were eager for a counterpoint to the restrictions of traditional Hinduism, as well as to travellers seeking an alternative to the social programming of the West after the 'antiwar movement and the student rebellions of the 1960s'. As Urban argues, his basic pitch was a spiritualised version of the philosophical 'postmodern turn' that resonated through *Anti-Oedipus*. Both exhibited what Jean-François Lyotard called an 'incredulity toward metanarratives'.[14]

For the Rajneeshees, this 'dehypnosis' was to be pursued through a close study of his writings, a deliberately eclectic mix of 'Tantric yoga [...], Zen Buddhism, Gnosticism, Pre-Socratic philosophy and therapeutic innovations'. Rajneesh often spoke of his system as a 'religionless religion' but it was also a finely tuned combination of Western countercultural thought and pan-Asian spirituality, much like the offerings of Esalen. A synthesis of the familiar and the attractively unfamiliar, it was a belief system perfectly tailored to those embarking on the hippie trail. An essential element of this teaching was the ecstatic physical practice of 'dynamic meditation'. This cortisol-boosting combination of rapid breathing techniques and cathartic exertion would find followers jumping, dancing and chanting themselves into exhaustion. It was a deliberate attempt to break down the 'false' self – one's familiar movements and physical awareness – and awaken the 'god' inside, the new fluid being. As Rajneesh put it, fully engaging in the practices of the ashram was a statement of 'freedom' and 'individuality', a declaration 'that you will not be any more part of the mob madness, the mob psychology [...] you will not belong to any country, to any church, to any race, to any religion'.[15]

Similar themes were at play in *The Godmakers* with its veil-rending rituals and heightened states of consciousness ultimately revealing the sham of Christian monotheism. The characters have their inner eyes opened to a vast spiritual cosmos and the moralising, restrictive Christian paradigm is seen to be an illusion put in place by a false, tyrannical 'Rogue god'. Pendleton's novel not only contained the kind of 'smut' that the Nixon administration protectively sought to 'eliminate' from 'our national life', but it also distilled the challenge to social tradition then emerging from the likes of the Rajneesh ashram. The 'new' India that gave rise to such figures thus looms in the background of the novel as a storehouse of indistinct but dangerously seductive ideas, fascinating to Pendleton's characters but profoundly disturbing to the rigid, and thereby fragile, belief systems of their Western world.[16]

*****

This double view of India as a symbol of both anxiety and attraction has its origins in America's missionary work of the 19th century. Tracts and periodicals that aimed to garner domestic support for this 'civilising' enterprise promoted a distinctly orientalist view of the subcontinent, framing it as a horrifying place full of naked, contorted holy men using yoga to mortify the body while worshipping the demoniacal goddess Kali. As Rajender Kaur and Anupama Arora put it, caricaturing the 'Hindoos' as savage heathens helped to reiterate for the American public the superiority of Christianity. This, in turn, helped to inscribe a racialised discourse into the 'American imaginary' that 'would later dominate the exclusionary immigration rhetoric levelled against Indian migrants in the late 19th and early 20th centuries'. At the same time, thoughts of 'naked sadhus' and 'unspeakable rites' also appealed to other appetites and formed the stock in trade of Don Pendleton's literary forebears, prurient pulp magazines like *Far East Adventure Stories* (1930–32). As is so often the case in the vexed relationship between the 'Self' and that which it deems 'Other', the identification of difference also carries an undertow of desire. The missionary's eye casts a double gaze. If India was indeed a disturbing crucible of non-Christian activity, then it was equally a kingdom of temptation: a place deliciously free of Christianity's rules, restrictions and moderations.[17]

The mid-20th century saw significant policy-based attempts to modify these attitudes, particularly as regards immigration. In 1965, building on the tide of political will generated by the Civil Rights Movement, President Lyndon Johnson ushered in the Immigration and Nationality Act. This removed the discriminatory barriers previously applied to European and Asian countries and allowed for 'an annual quota of twenty thousand immigrants from all nations of the world to apply to enter the United States'. According to Stefanie Syman, 'In the first year after the bill's passage immigration was up by about 9 percent' and the terms of the bill also positively affected immigrants already in America, with 'twenty-nine thousand more Asians' receiving 'permanent-resident status than had the year before'. One marker of this increase was a rise in traditional medicine and health practices. Acupuncture, herbal remedies and tai chi all flourished in the post-1965 period as new Chinese immigrants established businesses catering to existing ethnic communities and the wider public. Meanwhile, the bill had a much greater impact on Indian immigration, with numbers rising some 2,800 per cent between 1965 and 1972. America had always been a multicultural country, formed out of the social and economic benefits of mass immigration, but this mid-1960s policy saw the country open its doors to new territories. 'For the first time in U.S. history,' notes Amanda Lucia, 'Hindus arrived in significant numbers.' Among these were the new generation of religious teachers who were able to enjoy 'extended stays' in the country and would soon appear in the pages of *Time*.[18]

For the congregations of America's Christian right, like the campus-based InterVarsity Christian Fellowship (founded in 1941) and the think tank the Spiritual Counterfeits Project (founded in 1973), the 'uncomfortably concrete reality' of 'Eastern religions' moving 'fringe fanaticism' into the mainstream was cause for genuine alarm. The likes of ISKCON and Transcendental Meditation were seen as outposts of charming, occultic leaders who 'denied the personal God of the Bible'. While international, Christian-derived new religious movements such as India's Divine Light Mission, Korea's Unification Church and Japan's Church of Perfect Liberty represented heterodox challenges to the authority of Gospel teachings. Here, then, was a test of faith, the appearance of energetic and proliferate rivals in the 'supermarket of religious diversity' from whose pernicious influence the true flock had to be protected. Similarly, although the Hare Krishna Movement sought to engage with Christian teaching, frequently calling Krishna 'the father of Christ' and calling for 'Christ-consciousness', such attempts to define a modern, universal syncretic Hinduism were decried from pulpits as false prophecy, the words of the devil in disguise. As James Bjornstad put it in *Counterfeits at Your Door* (1979), 'unorthodox religious groups [...] reinterpret statements of doctrine and biblical passages' to 'willingly deceive' and to conceal the true nature of 'their whole theology'. Worse still, such groups promoted a doctrine of 'self-worship'.

Christianity is, in theory, a religion of selflessness, humility, service, supplication; to be a Christian means to give oneself over to the paternal authority of the 'Father'. By contrast, according to the preacher and Christian commentator Dave Hunt, the 'cosmic humanism' taught by 'yogis' privileges 'the autonomy, power and inherent divinity of man'. If 'man' is the only God there is, then salvation does not lie in Christ but in the '*Self*, the indulgent cultivation of 'self-confidence, self-potential, self-awareness, self-acceptance, self-love, self-image, self-esteem, self-fulfilment, self-development, self-assertion, self-actualization'. Hunt does not really explain why 'self-confidence' and 'self-esteem' are anti-Christian ideas, a suggestion that is particularly puzzling when considering that most evangelical preachers have an excess of both, but he nevertheless aligned 'Eastern' teaching with a philosophy of *selfishness*. Collapsing Hindu *samadhi* (complete meditative absorption) with Buddhist *satori* (sudden awakening, comprehension and enlightenment) and nodding, for good measure, to the psychologised 'self-actualizing' language of human potential, Hunt castigated meditative practices as unfocused, solipsistic navel-gazing. Where 'Christian meditation' in the form of prayer 'is *contemplation* of God and his written word', he argues, 'Eastern meditation is the opposite: the mind is detached from any objective awareness, and allowed to float passively free, open to influence by demons masquerading as one's higher self'.[19]

At the same time, liberal Christians were busy engaging Hindus in a 'theology of dialogue' for the good of the 'elevation of religion'. Against this backdrop of interfaith conversations, the attempt of the American evangelical church to establish a flimsy philosophical objection to Asian thought comes across as merely intolerant; a fear of 'unfamiliar spiritual technology' and 'non-normative behaviour *vis-à-vis* established religion'. However prejudicial this attitude may seem, it was a view that chimed with the culture at large. For example, a glance at British film and television finds the work of Wilkie Collins and Rudyard Kipling in rude health, with lavish adaptations of *The Moonstone* (1972) and *The Man Who Would Be King* (1975) gaining large audiences. These fantasies of the Raj lament the eclipse of the British Empire while depicting is former colonial subjects as atavistic bearers of 'uncivilised' beliefs. Back in America's drive-ins and grindhouses, audiences could enjoy even less subtle fare such as David Durston's exploitation favourite *I Drink Your Blood* (1970). The film featured Bhaskar Roy Chowdhury as Horace

Bones, the Satan-worshipping, Charles Manson-inspired leader of a violent hippie gang. Chowdhury, better known as 'Bhaskar', was an accomplished dancer from Chennai in India, an expert in the Manipuri dance style. In 1955 he came to America and established the travelling company Bhaskar – Dances of India, which combined traditional styles and contemporary choreography. *I Drink Your Blood* makes good use of Bhaskar's physical presence but has no interest in the subtleties of Indian dance. The film is more concerned with peddling an anxiety-fuelled depiction of the late-1960s counterculture. Further, by making the villain of the piece so clearly 'other' to the white, midwestern townsfolk he terrorises, the film relies on, and further normalises, the old xenophobic trope of the Indian as a figure of 'vice and infamy'. Such stereotyping reaches its peak during the film's ultraviolent climax when a rabid Horace Bones runs riot. Bare-chested, foaming at the mouth and waving a sword, he is equal parts Thug and Nandaka-brandishing Vishnu: a vision of horror worthy of the 19th-century missionary's very worst nightmares.[20]

By the time James Glickenhaus' film *The Astrologer* (1975) was making the rounds, with its malevolent swami posing an apocalyptic threat to the West, Rajneesh was welcoming seekers by the thousand to the Pune ashram. It was a visible trend that seemed to validate the pulpish anxieties of America's grindhouse fare and gave weight to the stories of rapid conversion experiences that caused the curious to disappear from 'normal' life into the hands of ISKCON and the 'Moonies' of the Unification Church. For those left behind this rejection of 'family ties' and the 'impairment of scholastic and professional careers' was often hard to bear and even harder to explain. For many, the disturbing but seemingly logical conclusion was that their friends and relatives had been conditioned to join such peculiar groups. How else could you account for people dispensing with their names, taking up a set of regulation orange robes and declaring obedience to a singular guru whose image they all carried in a locket? These did not seem like free-thinking declarations of 'individuality'. As such, across the 1970s, so-called 'new religious movements' were increasingly rebranded as 'cults' by their detractors. They were seen as authoritarian, self-isolating, worship-based 'little groups' which had broken away from 'the conventional consensus' to 'espouse very different views of the real, the possible and the moral'. According to the physician Dr Eli Shapiro the exclusivity of these closed units meant they were ideally placed to practise 'menticide [...] a dangerous form of mental coercion in which the free mind is attacked.'[21]

It would be 1978 before the threat of the 'cult' became a full-on moral panic in the wake of the Jonestown massacre in Guyana where 900 members of Jim Jones' Peoples Temple died in a massive act of murder-suicide. However, as early as 1971, harried Christian parents were turning to Ted Patrick, a former civil servant and self-appointed 'cult de-programmer', to extricate their children from the clutches of various new religious movements. Patrick practised a confrontational form of intervention in which he would physically rescue (i.e. abduct) his targets, detain them and subject them to an extended process of counterindoctrination. For the most part, this would involve him hurling screeds of verbal abuse at the 'cult believer, his beliefs and cult leader', all the while demonstrating how their group had misinterpreted passages from the Bible. It was an intentionally stressful process designed to shock the alleged cultist out of their conditioning ahead of a return to a life of apparent normality. Families may well have been pleased to have their loved ones restored, but for many of the cult 'victims' against whose wishes Patrick often acted, returning to the fold brought little relief. In some cases, escaping the family had been the main motivation for joining the so-called 'cult' in the first place.

As he described in his book *Let Our Children Go!* (1976), Patrick's own son had been involved in the Californian church the Children of God, which like the Peoples Temple was a home-grown Christian group, influenced more by the evangelical tradition than any Asian belief system. However, the thrust of Patrick's public invective was saved for the Hare Krishnas. They were the type of 'pseudo-religious' group lorded over by 'sinister' gurus that American families should fear. His extreme abreactive tactics were necessary because, according to Patrick, groups like the Hare Krishnas were equally powerful when it came to conditioning their followers. They had the ability to entice your bright and breezy Christian children and turn them virtually overnight into zombified, street-corner-haunting, book-hawking 'flower-pinners'.

Patrick's view of guru figures recalls Charles Render, the 'neuro-participant' therapist from Roger Zelazny's science fiction novel *The Dream Master* (1966). Render can enter the minds of his patients and influence their dreams. He builds visionary landscapes out of their psychic matter as a way of ministering to their anxieties, phobias and neuroses. A 'Sane Hatter', Render can endure the full force of his patients' disturbed psyches. He gets right into their heads, but once there he stands apart, pulling the strings and easing the tension. For Zelazny, Render's abilities give him almost godlike power in the dreamworlds he builds, indicated by the novel's colloquial term for his profession: he is not just a participant, but a 'Shaper'. Much of the novel's jeopardy revolves around Render negotiating this delicate balance between therapy and control. For Ted Patrick, the gurus he lambasts veer towards the latter impulse. They may offer solutions to your problems and welcome you into a world of spiritual well-being but really, they are out to dominate you, to impose their authority over your body and your mind. To combine the language of Moon Duo's 'Sleepwalker' and *The Dream Master*, Patrick was warning that invitations to 'shape up' result in acts of *shaping*. The gurus at the head of new religious movements may have spoken of wisdom, but for Patrick, those who sought it out were more likely to end up brainwashed than enlightened.[22]

✳✳✳✳✳

'Brainwashing' first came to the attention of the American public in September 1950. According to Charlie Williams, it was the journalist Edward Hunter, writing in *Miami News*, who 'claimed that by combining Pavlovian theory with modern technology, Russian and Chinese psychologists had developed powerful techniques for manipulating minds'. Heavy with Cold War paranoia, 'brainwashing' landed like an anxiety bomb lobbed from behind the Iron Curtain.

It conjured the spectre of an automatic method of mind control that could rapidly alter long-held political beliefs. In the McCarthyist boiler room of 1950s America, a place where Reds lurked under the bed and flying saucers filled the sky, this vivid image of thoughts being erased and rewritten quickly gained a foothold in political discourse and the public imagination, particularly in the immediate aftermath of the Korean War. During the conflict China had notched up a flush of symbolic victories involving the apparent conversion of American prisoners to the communist cause. As Williams explains, in 1952 a group of captured Air Force personnel led by Colonel Frank Schwable 'publicly confessed to committing crimes of germ warfare against North Korea', various other captives became 'collaborators' and made 'anti-War and anti-McCarthy broadcasts' while at the tail-end of the hostilities, a group of British and American prisoners 'refused to be repatriated after the war, choosing to relocate to communist China instead'.[23]

Back home, few were convinced that these soldiers had seen the light and willingly gone over to the other side. The consensus was that such a radical shift in loyalty was the result of sustained psychological coercion. As such, in 1955, the US Secretary of Defense's Advisory Committee on Prisoners of War delivered their report 'The Fight Continues After the Battle'. It acknowledged that 'prisoners captured by nations in the Soviet orbit' had been subject to re-education and various forms of conditioning 'to elicit confessions'. In making their recommendations the report showed no hesitation in giving these procedures a blanket definition. They advised 'on how prisoners of war could be trained to resist brainwashing'. Five years after it surfaced in the *Miami News*, then, Edward Hunter's catchy but terrifying buzzword had entered the policymaking arena of national security. The power of 'brainwashing' was that it not only extended the duration of 'the Battle', but also the extent of the battlefield. Once the word entered the lexicon, bolstered by novels like Richard Condon's *The Manchurian Candidate* (1959), war was not just a matter of what happened over there, but a question of what 'our boys' may have been programmed to do upon their return. The paranoic logic of brainwashing suddenly made it possible to think of patriotic friends and neighbours as unconscious fifth columnists, a mere phone call or code word away from attacking the nation from within.

Concerns regarding the 'techniques of rapid political conversion' were also circulating in post-war Britain. Writers like Charlotte Haldane, who had joined the British Communist Party in 1937, came out of the war deeply disillusioned with Stalinism, questioning how she and others had 'failed to detect the falsity of the Russian system for so many years'. Haldane was not alone in her puzzlement. As William Sargant put it in his study of indoctrination, *Battle for the Mind* (1957):

> Many people are also bewildered at the spectacle of an intelligent and hitherto mentally stable person who has been brought up for trial behind the Iron Curtain, and prevailed upon not only to believe but to proclaim sincerely that all his past actions and ideas were criminally wrong. 'How is it done?' they ask.

By the early 1960s psychologist Jack Vernon, author of *Inside the Black Room* (1963), was ready with a single, succinct answer: 'sensory deprivation'. *Inside the Black Room* was, for the most part, an account of the isolation research Vernon conducted from the mid-1950s onwards at Princeton University, but it also covered Donald Hebb's previously classified experiments at McGill. Both projects had received military funding, and although Vernon discusses the standard range of possible applications (spaceflight training, the effects of solitary routine jobs) he makes it clear that as with Hebb's work, 'the problem of brainwashing' was the main point of investigation.[24]

Where Hebb's experiments had involved the limited withdrawal of sensory stimulation, with each of his subjects placed in a 'small *lighted* semi-soundproofed cubicle', Vernon understood sensory deprivation as the 'systematic removal of stimuli' and attempted to investigate what he 'considered as the next phase' on from the McGill experiments. His subjects were placed in an enclosed chamber that was in turn located in a room that admitted neither light nor sound.

Vernon argued that in an indoctrination context such conditions were used to reduce psychological resistance and to increase a subject's susceptibility to ideological material. As he explained, 'U.N. prisoners' of the 'Red Chinese in the Korean War' were often placed in solitary confinement in chambers that admitted low levels of light and sound. Repeated tasks and targeted exposure to propagandistic messages would occasionally punctuate this monotony. Reportedly, the tasks included the instruction to write an autobiography. 'When it was completed', notes Vernon, the captors 'required that it be written again without the benefit of the previous copy'. This would continue 'countless times until the prisoner was extremely bored with the activity'. Ostensibly, the captors were looking for discrepancies in the accounts, likely fissure points that could be prodded during further bouts of re-education. However, Vernon argued that it was also the numbing repetition of this process that made the prisoners susceptible to 'psychological attack'. Starved of stimulus, like plants kept out of the light, subjects would seize upon and absorb new information because it was a relieving point of difference within an otherwise deadening atmosphere. The results of his experiments confirmed this hypothesis, with Vernon reporting high levels of suggestibility among the Princeton test subjects.[25]

The work of Hebb and Vernon was not just a case of them getting to know their enemy, nor was the focus purely defensive. In some quarters the 'problem' of brainwashing was an opportunity to experiment with another, not unconnected process: mind control. As Williams has revealed, this became a research focus of an ambitious neurophysiologist at Maryland's National Institute of Mental Health, one John C. Lilly. It is no coincidence that Lilly was using a 'solitude-isolation-confinement-tank' as the McGill experiments gained pace because Lilly visited Hebb in 1952 and observed his ongoing sensory deprivation studies first-hand. This was just after Lilly's appointment as head of the Section of Cortical Integration, and he was riding the research circuit of overlapping projects and shared funding. Hebb's analysis of isolation and its effects on the susceptibility of his test subjects chimed with Lilly's work on brain mapping and the 'push-button' implications of electrostimulation. As such, once back in Maryland he sought to forge a closer link between these fields of inquiry by diverting a portion of his research budget into the development of his own isolation apparatus, a seawater-filled tank rather than an insulated chamber. Lilly's work, then, was not a meditative mirror-image of Hebb's military-funded brainwashing research which just happened to take place in parallel. It was, instead, an investigation directly inspired by the operation of the McGill programme which not only massively upped the ante in terms of the extremity of the isolation experience but also raised the bar as regards the potential application of the research findings.

According to Williams, Lilly also demonstrated a significant 'willingness to align his work with militaristic aims'. In the late 1950s, Lilly presented a series of research papers to a Pentagon intelligence committee, one of which, 'Special Considerations of Modified Human Agents as Reconnaissance and Intelligence Devices', conceived the human brain as a tool of information storage and retrieval. If it could be reliably conditioned, argued Lilly, then espionage actants could become efficient information carriers and in turn easily accessible data sources. This informatic model of the brain presented implantation and retrieval simply as problems of programming, almost akin to the process of electromagnetic recording, playback and erasure. As described by Williams, the scholar who discovered the archived paper, Lilly argued that isolation was 'the simplest method of modifying the internal processing of human agents'. This point was in line with the susceptibility studies of Hebb and Vernon: Lilly presented the absorption of targeted information allegedly occurring in a context of sense withdrawal as a way of securely implanting the desired data in the brain, particularly if it was augmented with carrier messages and repeated prompts. On the other side of the operation, electrostimulation of certain brain areas could be used in an interrogation to put 'the human agent' in the psychic equivalent of a dentist's chair and yank out the material. By using electrodes to modify behaviour and induce an alarming array of emotional states from panic to pain to intense pleasure, Lilly claimed subjects could be easily influenced and thus 'information probably can be elicited or injected readily in a relatively few hours'.

Lilly was proposing to appropriate the techniques of brainwashing – the previously threatening communist weapon – and redeploy them as tools of covert control that could afford American intelligence a defensive and offensive flexibility across the Cold War's expanding psychological battlefield.[26]

Novels like Len Deighton's *The IPCRESS File* (1962) and James Kennaway's *The Mind Benders* (1963) helped to maintain public anxieties regarding these techniques, certainly in the wake of a 1956 *New York Times* report on Lilly's work, his tanks and the link to brainwashing. Kennaway's book was published the same year as *Inside the Black Room* and where Vernon keeps a tone of scientific detachment throughout, Kennaway's well observed tale of science, suicide and radical behavioural change frames the isolation tank as a black hole of psychological torture. He acknowledged the influence of the McGill experiments 'on the Reduction of Sensation', but it was the type of disclaimer that does little to separate fiction from fact. Once Basil Dearden had adapted the novel for the screen in 1963, shortly after John Frankenheimer delivered his version of *The Manchurian Candidate* (1962) and just before Sidney J. Furie did the same with *The IPCRESS File* (1965), brainwashing was firmly established as an all-purpose signifier of fear and paranoia, perfectly suited to the febrile atmosphere of a post-Kennedy America.

As the Cold War crept into the 1970s, the concept continued to signify involuntary action, political puppetry and ideological ventriloquy, and such ideas frequently remained tethered to the idea of sensory deprivation. Colin Wilson dealt with these themes in *The Black Room* (1971), a novel that features Christopher 'Kit' Butler, a music lecturer and self-identifying 'creative' who is drawn into a set of group experiments using the insulated, soundproofed room of the title. Alongside Wilson's customary discourses on the mind, the primacy of the artist and the power of the intellectual, *The Black Room* offered a digest of the McGill experiments, complete with references to wartime interrogations and radar operators seeing phantom blips. The plot of the novel also hinged upon the same type of ideological conflicts that necessitated the work of both Vernon and Hebb. Wilson's room becomes a chamber of conflict between

British Intelligence and a resurgent fascist force named 'Station K' and equally for Butler, an investigation into the philosophical puzzle of sensory deprivation becomes a struggle against the threat of 'Brain washing'.

Narratively and politically, *The Black Room* was something of a throwback to *The Manchurian Candidate* but the processes it described remained an ongoing concern away from the conventional theatres of war. In 1974 journalist John McGuffin published his critical expose *The Guineapigs*, an account of the treatment of prisoners during the post-1968 Northern Ireland conflict. McGuffin describes how the British forces used interrogation techniques that involved 'the artificial deprivation of the senses — auditory, visual, tactile and kinesthetic'. The intention was to cause severe disorientation to deprive the prisoners' brains of 'oxygen and sugar necessary for normal functioning'. As well as reducing their ability to withstand questioning, these techniques were used as disciplinary measures that allowed the British captors to inflict harm while escaping the consequences involved in the use of direct physical violence. While Wilson's British readers were enjoying a Cold War entertainment and possibly feeling mild horror at what 'they' might do to 'us', 'we' were doing the same to those in Northern Ireland. Nor have we stopped. Western forces have since come to rely on such torturous methods. Much of what McGuffin described in *The Guineapigs* anticipated the 'enhanced interrogations' routinely deployed by American armed forces at Abu Ghraib and which continue at Guantanamo Bay.[27]

✼✼✼✼✼

While the tools of brainwashing became further entangled with covert statecraft, the range of suspicion connected to the process also began to widen. It was not just the shadowy political and martial agents of the post-war world who practised techniques akin to mind control. Such abilities were also believed to be in the hands of the dazzling post-1960s gurus. Ted Patrick was not the only one raising this flag. The sociologist and 'anticult' evangelist Ronald Enroth made his concerns clear in *Youth, Brainwashing and the Extremist Cults* (1977). As the title suggests, it was not a guide to new religious movements but a critical analysis – heavily influenced by Enroth's Christian beliefs – of their public appeal, recruitment methods and internal power dynamics.

Speaking of brainwashing in relation to New Age spirituality might seem a conceptual stretch given the word's connection to contemporary warfare, but as William Sargant was at pains to point out, the techniques of religious conversion have historically relied on the generation of heightened psychological experiences that lead to 'temporary emotional collapse'. In the Greco-Roman 'mystery' religions initiates were routinely isolated and agitated into various states of alarm before undergoing an overwhelming passage from darkness to light, death to rebirth, ignorance to illumination. Brainwashing is thus 'not some new horror invented in the twentieth century', Vernon adds, 'but a technique that has been with us for a long time'. The only thing distinctive about its post-war incarnation, he claims, is the dramatic nature of the 'conversions it has produced'. Similarly, from the perspective of American conservativism, the idea of brainwashing provided a convenient bridge between the spheres of the mystical and the political, insofar as falling in with an alternative religion was considered just as suspect as moving to the extreme far left. Both prospects were as un-American as burning a dollar bill, the conjoined symbol of free enterprise and trust in the Christian God. Who would want to abandon the benefits of this status quo? For writers like Enroth, so keen to defend their national beliefs, the only way to explain the rise of new religious movements was to assume their converts had been in some way coerced, just like the soldiers captured by the Chinese. Surely, no true American patriot would join these groups of their own free will.[28]

To illustrate his claim, Enroth recounts the story of a young man called Jim Ardmore. In early November 1973 Ardmore was working at the Astrodome, a massive sports and events stadium in Houston, Texas. He was on his feet, at a concession stand, using a meat slicer to chop one tomato after another. Everyone around him was busy too. Some were prepping bread; others were slicing cheese. There was little conversation between them, with each person in the production line focused on their own job. There was no time for talk, anyway. Jim and the team knew they had to keep up the pace because, before arriving at the Astrodome, they had been assigned the task of making 20,000 sandwiches. Less than a year earlier Ardmore, then still in his mid-twenties, was a newly divorced social worker in Michigan. He had entered the 1970s after studying at Michigan State University and he started his job still sporting all the trappings of late-1960s campus counterculture: long hair, beard, an interest in mediation and a shelf of books by Ram Dass and Carlos Castaneda. Work stress and a cloud of post-divorce depression led him to take his meditation practice more seriously, and following the recommendation of a friend he became involved with the Divine Light Mission, then recruiting across the US under the leadership of the teenage, Rolls Royce-owning *Satguru* or 'Perfect Master from India', Guru Maharaj Ji.

The Divine Light Mission was officially established in 1960 in Patna, northern India, by Shri Hans Ji Maharaj, known to his followers as Guru Maharaj Ji. He had spent the preceding three decades as a spiritual itinerant, spreading his meditation techniques and message of religious unity throughout India. Starting the Mission was a way of consolidating these teachings and his mass following into a formal organisation. It was a successful restructuring which allowed Ji Maharaj to attract even more adherents across the early 1960s. Only when he died in 1966, however, did things really start to take off. While the Mission was still in an official state of mourning Ji Maharaj's youngest son, then a mercurial eight-year-old called Prem Rawat, assumed his father's mantle of Guru Maharaj Ji and started to push the group in a much more messianic direction. He claimed to be the virtual reincarnation of his father, a king of kings who should be worshipped and obeyed beyond such rival spiritual pretenders as Rama and Krishna. With this miraculous reborn guru at the helm and devoted followers filling the coffers with money and assets, the Mission undertook a rapid international expansion programme. As the 1970s began, Divine Light ashrams appeared across the world and in 1972 an American headquarters was established in Colorado.

Fuelling this growth was the promise of the 'Knowledge', a distillation of Ji Maharaj's original meditation techniques which the new guru spoke of as the ultimate gift, an 'intangible essence of energy which involves a direct experience of god'.

The Knowledge was exactly what the depressed, disillusioned and drifting Ardmore was looking for: a deep and satisfying form of meditation that promised serenity, happiness and a way of realising 'the perfect aim of your life, why you came into this world'. According to Ardmore's friend, learning the Knowledge involved mastering four meditation techniques that collectively governed the senses and the psyche. One was linked to the 'the Divine Light', another was linked to the 'Divine Music', a third helped you taste the 'Nectar' and the fourth allowed you to perceive the 'Holy Word', the 'Holy name of God within yourself'. Best of all, the Knowledge was free – 'all you had to do was ask for it'.

Unsurprisingly, this 'absolute discount' did come with a catch: you had to receive the Knowledge from a *mahatma*, one of Maharaj Ji's appointed disciples. And so Ardmore, having gone to an introductory event about the Mission and then to a local address to find out more, was told that if he wanted to join a 'Knowledge session' he would have to seek out a *mahatma* in another city. After a few false leads, he eventually ended up in Chicago in a darkened room with a handful of other would-be *premies* (devotees). During the initiatory chamber theatre that followed – a series of guided meditations and séance-room atmospherics – the Knowledge was imparted. Or rather, Ardmore and the others were told they had received it. They were then ordered to 'always implicitly obey the commandments of Guru Maharaj Ji' before being sent back to their normal lives, with the instruction to meditate at all times.

After such ecstasies, Ardmore landed with a bump. The demands and routines of the everyday paled in comparison to the possibilities of life with the Knowledge. One brief taste was not enough. He wanted more and it was thus not long before Ardmore left his job, cut his hair, shaved off his beard and moved into a *premie* house, one step away from the full-on commitment of joining an ashram. In the house, the focus of Ardmore's life was narrowed down to a handful of priorities: meditation, listening to spiritual discourses (or *satsang*) and carrying out 'service'. Service meant furthering the aims of the Mission by spreading its word, recruiting new followers and pulling in donations. The organisation's ever-growing infrastructure also needed a lot of work. It was a tightly regulated, zombifying existence in which each moment was accounted for, and Ardmore was relieved of the need to make the simplest of daily decisions.

The magnetised core of this world was the Guru Maharaj Ji, the much longed for but always absent parent, teacher and guide, who was forever in devotees' thoughts but never fully present in their lives. Ardmore, like all the other followers, was pressured to hand over his money and possessions to Maharaj Ji and as a further sign of his devotion he was expected to practise *darshan*, to be within physical sight of the guru. It was this gravitational force that in 1973 drew him to London, where he waited in line for six hours for a chance to bow at his master's feet and receive a blast of energy in return. The same pull took him to Houston, the Astrodome and the concession stand a few months later. The occasion was Millennium '73, an ambitious three-day jamboree spearheaded by Maharaj Ji that featured speeches, music and *satsang*; *mahatmas* everywhere, a clutch of celebrities and the inevitable headlining turn from the guru himself. The whole package was intended to be an era-defining public apotheosis for the Divine Light Mission that promised to kickstart 'a thousand years of peace' after the discord of the 1960s. It turned out to be an expensive, overblown flop. Not that this mattered to the sandwich-making Ardmore. He was eager to join the army of followers charged with running the event, but he would not have had much of a choice if he had decided otherwise. Members of the Mission were expected to be there in full force and behind his smiling, seemingly contented exterior, Ardmore no longer had the will to refuse. By November 1973 the rigours of the Mission's all-consuming lifestyle and constant bouts of meditation had taken their toll. As he later reflected, Ardmore was 'spaced out', exhausted and with his mind turned to 'jelly beans' he had slipped into a state of unthinking passivity: 'I would accept anything my leaders told me since I was not capable of questioning anything'. This is why he barely noticed when, after hours of non-stop chopping at the sandwich stand in the Astrodome, he made a slight fumble and the meat slicer cut off two of his fingertips.

As far as Ron Enroth was concerned, the Divine Light Mission ticked all the cultish boxes. It drew its followers into a closed, hierarchical world on the back of promises too good to be true and forever delayed. Once converted and absorbed they were effectively cut off from friends and family, subservient to and dependent upon their superiors. In this atmosphere 'worship' became a means of control by proxy: the guru stripped his devotees of their material and psychological property and as their sense of self withered, his power increased. For Enroth, the Mission operated a typically exploitative and disorienting process that was clear when observed from the sidelines but difficult to acknowledge from the inside, when you were embedded and invested in a prison with no bars. While potential followers may well have approached the Mission of their own volition, Enroth argues the organisation quickly transforms this curiosity and spiritual autonomy into obedient automatism. Ardmore agrees with this analysis when recalling his time with the group. His assessment is clear and unequivocal: 'I was brainwashed.'

Thankfully, Enroth tells us Ted Patrick was on hand to extricate the physically and psychologically wounded Ardmore from the Mission and put his mind back together. Safely installed in his mother's home, Ardmore was subject to a quick bout of loud evangelical cajoling before Patrick declared the vulnerable, fragile and extremely suggestive Ardmore officially 'deprogrammed'. Ardmore had seen the error of his ways and 'accepted Christ', Enroth tells us with satisfaction. Another soul saved. It is an unsettling and somewhat ironic conclusion to a piece that sets out to expose the workings of a cult. The unfortunate Ardmore, a man with a genuine interest in meditation and with only the most stereotypical of prior links to Christianity (church attendance as a child), ultimately finds himself shuttling from one form of conditioning to another. Enroth doesn't elaborate on the session with Patrick, but there is enough detail to note striking similarities between his methods and those of the Divine Light Mission. Both isolate their subjects, flatten their defences and impose upon them a depersonalising paradigm of obedience. In exchange for receiving the Knowledge, you had to give your life to the guru. Patrick levied a similarly heavy toll. Ardmore was expected to give his life to Christ in exchange for having been 'rescued'. The unconscious message of *Youth, Brainwashing and the Extremists Cults*, then, is somewhat counter to its scaremongering mission. In attempting to castigate the operation of groups outside the American religious mainstream, it inadvertently reveals how actants on both sides of this modern holy war had no aversion to using brainwashing techniques to advance their respective causes.[29]

Other writers of the period like Loren Singer, author of *The Parallax View* (1970), were more explicit when presenting brainwashing as a tool of American political culture rather than a weapon used against it. The novel is a JFK conspiracy thriller that follows a journalist, Malcolm Graham, as he investigates a string of accidental deaths. Each of the deceased, he realises, are linked by the far-too-coincidental detail of them having been witnesses to a spectacular political assassination. As Alex Cox puts it, Singer had in mind the catalogue of material witnesses to the events of November 1963 who had since 'died from heart attacks, car and plane crashes, gun accidents [and] karate chops to the neck'. W. Penn Jones, a newspaper man deeply critical of the Warren Commission's lone gunman theory, had collated these connections in *Forgive My Grief*, a multi-volume book he started publishing in 1966. For Jones, one of the key markers of a cover-up and hence conspiracy surrounding the killing of the President was the unexplained deaths of connected journalists. He wrote at length about Bill Hunter, Jim Koethe and Dorothy Kilgallen, all of whom died mysteriously shortly after investigating – and in Kilgallen's case interviewing – Lee Harvey Oswald's assailant, Jack Ruby.[30]

In *The Parallax View*, Singer's liquidated witnesses and imperilled journalists all come into the orbit of the Parallax Corporation, a 'testing organization' ostensibly interested in social alienation. Parallax is part of a large network of companies connected to a government agency, the Bureau of Social Structure. Singer's conceit is that Parallax uses its profiling techniques to identify disaffected malcontents whom it then recruits, conditions and redeploys as both assassins and patsies. It is an efficient form of outsourcing that provides America's government, or at least its para-government, with a way of eliminating political enemies, crushing dissent and clearing up the collateral. When director Alan J. Pakula and screenwriter Lorenzo Semple Jnr adapted the novel for the screen in 1974, they fleshed out Singer's concept by focusing on the work of the corporation's 'Human Engineering division'. Actor Warren Beatty plays the film's version of Malcolm Graham, an angsty journalist called Joe Frady. He picks up the Parallax trail three years after the Robert Kennedy-esque assassination of Charles Carroll, an independent presidential candidate, and the attendant deaths of numerous key witnesses including his former girlfriend, the film's Kilgallen stand-in, Lee Carter (Paula Prentiss).

The crux of the film comes when Frady enters the corporation's training room and watches a sequence of images while seated in a chair that monitors his biorhythms. In the context of the film the scene is an assessment exercise. The corporation are trying to gauge Frady's responses to see if he fits the profile of a would-be assassin: discontented, alienated and guided by a misplaced patriotism. However, the sequence is so semiotically overdetermined, so shot through with repetitions, juxtapositions and subliminal hints worthy of a William Burroughs cut-up, that it comes to signify an act of brainwashing. It is as if Frady is being conditioned into a worldview of ultra-Americanism. This film-within-a-film begins by establishing a narrative of American idealism anchored around such starkly telegraphed values as 'LOVE', 'MOTHER', 'FATHER', 'HOME' and 'COUNTRY'. These Norman Rockwell-style images of perfect homesteads and archetypal loved ones bathed in the splendour of the golden hour are then countered by signs of encroaching threat: Hitler, Mao and Castro all wait at the gates with their massed and interchangeable forces of fascism, communism and socialism. From here, though, such polarised battlefields become somewhat blurred. The insidious subtlety of the sequence is such that it points to a set of internal enemies: untrustworthy leaders, Black radicals and protestors, all of whom sow division and discord and consign 'ME' – the viewer, the Parallax subject, the assassin-in-waiting – to a life of isolation and poverty while others prosper. Playing further on these ideas of victimhood, the film deploys a subset of images that worry away at the cracks in the fragile edifice of male sexual identity. This combustible mix then gives way to emergent images of individual superheroism. 'ME' flickers in close proximity to 'GOD' as bullets, firearms and occasional images of Marvel's Thor fly by. The cumulative suggestion is not of America under 'foreign' attack, nor does the film offer anti-capitalist propaganda. Rather, it is a sequence that speaks of America in decline, a great country slipping into insecurity, insignificance and impotence. The Parallax subject is thus emboldened to make America great again: to restore the country of God, guns and glorious fields of wheat to its prior potent state of heavenly 'HAPPINESS'.[31]

The Parallax View offered a spectacle of human engineering rather than human potential. It played with the conspiratorial fantasy of conditioned control that Lilly hypothesised in the 1950s. Although high-concept, the film did not present itself as science fiction, nor were its anxieties confined to the cinema. Other analyses of America's corporate culture shared points of overlap with the fictional Parallax, particularly those which examined the intersection of company training with the rigours of the encounter group. In their book *The Pit: A Group Encounter Defiled* (1972), Gene Church and Conrad D. Carnes recounted their experience of a four-day Mind Dynamics leadership course. From its beginnings in 1968 as the provider of motivational training courses that avoided 'direct confrontation', Mind Dynamics mutated into a boot camp for corporate commandos. According to *The Pit*, attendees were subject to bouts of ritual humiliation that played on their perceived weaknesses and insecurities, before being regularly frogmarched across the parking lot of whatever forsaken hotel they had all been corralled into for the duration of the course. The stated aim was to help participants climb the corporate ladder of Holiday Magic, the cosmetics firm of which Mind Dynamics was an affiliate. The programme thus marked the return of the encounter group to its original territory of focus groups and management feedback sessions. For Church and Carnes, though, there was nothing constructive about this noxious combination of Synanon's Game and a nightmare hazing ritual. It did not build confidence as such, but rather instilled an attitude of aggressive competition in which promotion was the reward of survival. The exhausting intensity of the encounter also created a pliant receptivity to authority. The litany of indignities described in *The Pit* – physical and verbal abuse, assault, mock crucifixion – built an image of trainees succumbing to a workplace version of the 'menticide' Eli Shapiro associated with new religious movements. The focus was on obeying the orders given, however extreme.[32]

Mark Brewer provided a similar account of est, the successor to Mind Dynamics, in a 1975 article for *Psychology Today*. Describing the 70-hour course as a 'classic' conversion experience, Brewer recounts the standard patter of the est coach: the course will be filled with all kinds of discomfort but such hardship will eventually act as a psychological purge, a way of throwing out all the belief systems and mental blockages that 'keep you experiencing what is actually happening to you'. 'Such efforts,' notes Brewer, 'are commonly known as brainwashing.' He then specifies the primary technique used during est training: 'abreaction', the reliving and release of a previously repressed emotion. This would occur deep into the second day when attendees would be guided through a long, detailed meditation based on the recall of past problems or failings. It would typically build into a crescendo of sobbing and shouting, not unlike a mass primal scream session in which the repressions of the trainees – as well as the frustrations, the psychological pummelling and the denials of the previous day – would be relieved. The coaches would then be able to announce that the problems of the attendees had been solved in the very act of letting it all out, thus leading many to believe 'they had undergone a mysterious and deeply cleansing ordeal'. As Brewer continues, quoting William Sargant on indoctrination, this seemingly therapeutic technique had been used 'by generations of preachers and demagogues to soften up their listeners' minds'. It was part of the mysterious realisation of 'it' central to the est sales pitch, the type of experience that would lead attendees to more seminars and fire them up enough to leave the conference suite ready to spread the good news to others.

Unlike the Divine Light Mission, the Unification Church and other new religious movements, Mind Dynamics and est were not holding out the promise of a mystical truth. Their attendees were chasing the more graspable but just as easily deferred material success of the American Dream and these lost weekends in stuffy conference rooms appeared to hold the key to such earthly rewards. What connected these varied groups, however, was the shared view that underpins the theory of brainwashing, the notion that the human subject can be shaped and conditioned when placed in certain contexts and under certain stresses. This was the flipside of Deleuze and Guattari's liberative image of a militantly fluid subject. These human engineers set out to program their charges on the assumption that, like the famous motif of 'man' approaching its eclipse that ends Michel Foucault's *The Order of Things* (1966), individual identity could 'be erased, like a face drawn in sand at the edge of the sea'.[33]

✵✵✵✵✵

Back in California, at Big Sur, at the edge of their own sea, Michael Murphy and Dick Price were watching these tides of erasure with some concern. As Esalen entered 1973 it was not only surrounded by ascendent rivals but, like est, its competitors seemed to be morphing into self-contained dictatorships. In Chile, Arica was advising its students to prepare for a coming uprising, while the Psychosynthesis Institute, a relative newcomer on the 1970s Californian scene, was exerting an authoritarian stranglehold over its attendees, graduates or (more accurately) followers. They were cults of personality that first convinced you something was wrong, then waved the carrot of a miracle cure before beating you with the stick every time you reached for it. The threat of failure, the fallacy of sunk cost and the perpetual delay of the much-vaunted transformation was a three-fold lock used to keep those attracted to the promises of these groups in thrall to their confidence-sapping deferrals.

Over in London, the early 1970s also found the Esalen-inspired growth centre Quaesitor accelerating into equally problematic territory. From its beginnings in 1969–70 running workshops on 'music and movement, massage, chanting and meditation', Quaesitor had, by 1972, developed a formidable series of 'intensives': long, aggressively experimental encounter groups that extended over a nine-month period of thrice-weekly meetings, regular weekend sessions and occasional five-day marathons. Links had been established with Synanon's Denny Yuson, who visited across 1973 to run introductory courses on encounter group methods and, under the leadership of Paul Lowe, Quaesitor had gradually dispensed with its therapeutic emphasis in favour of an explicitly challenging credo of 'it is forbidden to forbid'. As early member Tom Feldberg would later reflect, 'two strands' appeared in the group: those who were interested in humanistic psychology and those who wanted to blow their minds and 'experience everything'. Lowe was very much part of the obliviating latter camp and would regularly push people to the extremes, believing that 'if you were afraid of something, you should do it'.[34]

When they first met in San Francisco in 1960, Price and Murphy had bonded over a shared disdain for hierarchical organisations. Price had found Stanford limiting, the military stifling and as for hospitals, he had been nothing less than traumatised by his time under psychiatric care. Likewise for Murphy who had also experienced a bout of anxiety-filled mental ill health after time in the army and an attempt at graduate work. Where Price found himself in a psychiatric ward, however, Murphy had made a break for it. While exploring comparative religion during his brief stint at Stanford, he had become a devotee of the Hindu philosopher Sri Aurobindo and his tome *The Life Divine* (1949), a book that combined Hinduism with contemporary psychology in pursuit of 'the full integration of matter, mind and spirit'. Murphy went on to spend 1956–7 in Pondicherry, India, meditating for eight hours a day (and occasionally playing softball) at the spiritual home of his new guru, the Sri Aurobindo

Ashram. While he was keen to commit to Aurobindo's teaching, Murphy was less enamoured of the ashram's cultish atmosphere. The sight of his fellow *sadhakas* giving themselves over to the authority of 'The Mother' (Mirra Alfassa) – co-founder of the ashram and, following Aurobindo's death in 1950, its de facto leader – did not sit well with his entrenched sense of American individualism.

These discomforts remained at the forefront of both men's minds as they started to plot in San Francisco. As Price enthused to Murphy about Aldous Huxley and as their ideas for a new centre started to come together, they were keen to draw on the influence of 'Eastern' thought, but within the context of a democratic, deliberately pluralist approach. From the outset, the Esalen Institute was intended to be open, egalitarian, eclectic and thus systemically reflective of the aspirational ideas it was trying to promote. No singular view would dominate, hence the early motto: 'No one captures the flag'. However, a decade later, with the horror stories of *The Pit* circulating and groups like Quaesitor testing every boundary, it seemed that the extension of encounter groups and consciousness-raising exercises beyond the Esalen hub had resulted in a dreadful step back to the cultism, hierarchy and exploitation it originally set out to avoid. All around, flags were being captured and replanted in repeated gestures of dominance.

Having said that, in the years leading up to the early 1970s, Esalen had not been immune to its own accusations of cult dynamics. As early as 1968 the *Daily Telegraph Magazine* had described Esalen as 'The New Cult for the Over-Adjusted' while Jane Howard, musing at the end of *Please Touch*, her account of Synanon, Esalen and others, asked: could these groups 'get to be a cult?' 'Get to be?' She replies in answer to her own question, 'Few would deny that they already are.' One of these cautionary voices was the Chilean psychotherapist and frequent Esalen seminar leader Claudio Naranjo. He warned Howard that a 'fanaticism […] could develop around the goodness in this movement. An authoritarian preaching environment could develop around the perfectly defensible enthusiasm.' Hoping to reiterate the 'goodness' of human potential and defend their 'enthusiasm', Murphy, Price and their team decided to tackle these issues of control, authority and autonomy head on. In the time-honoured tradition of all those wishing to change the social agenda and really make a difference, Esalen organised a conference.[35]

'Spiritual and Therapeutic Tyranny: The Willingness to Submit' took place at the institute's San Francisco branch in December 1973, and it was not a success. The event was a fractious and ill-tempered affair full of ego, ad hominem attacks and no small amount of uncomfortable home truths. The 26 panellists included Esalen regulars and insiders like Naranjo, Will Schutz and George Leonard as well as such high-profile competitors as Werner Erhard, whom the conference was effectively accusing of tyranny. Alongside these sat a bank of critics, commentators and fellow travellers as well as a packed, vocal audience. The idea was to conduct a lively, open, extended conversation but most panellists ended up either talking about themselves or firing pre-emptive strikes at each other while variously baiting or playing up to the crowd. Quickly fed up with these internecine squabbles, Peter Marin, a journalist for *Harper's Magazine*, used his spot to express 'his disgust while the whole gathering', letting everyone know he had spent the first night in a pool hall rather than listen to more than a few minutes of their rancour. And so the skirmishes continued.

The one volley that landed with any impact came from the theologian Sam Keen, who had been invited to give the keynote address. He obliged by offering an excoriating analysis of human potential as a veritable system of tyranny. According to Keen, the therapeutic aims of the movement's varied methodologies were a 'game' designed to maintain the unequal power dynamic of the guru–disciple relationship. As if describing Jim Ardmore's experience with the Divine Light Mission, Keen put it that the 'patient/client/disciple' is typically led into a highly structured, rule-based situation in pursuit of a goal 'set so high that nobody can ever get there'. The 'pay-off' for this striving is the 'illusion of power – that we can control life', but the power in question is only ever held by the 'therapist/guru' who sets the rules. Not content with performing this critique of the 'game' before a roomful of players, Keen then got personal. He started to castigate people by name, calling out the hypocrisy and arrogance of their claims to treat, help and improve their clients when they themselves were not without problems. As Will Storr puts it:

> Keen pointed out, devastatingly, that the 'usually male, privileged' leaders of the movement had hardly demonstrated, in their own selves, the efficacy of what they preached. 'The best therapist turns out to have a clay heart. And Fritz was a dirty old man. And Freud couldn't give up cigars. And Bill Schutz doesn't jump for joy.'

Keen also mentioned Ida Rolf in his talk, but unlike Schutz she was not among the speakers. In fact all the panellists were men and bar one they were all white, a point not lost on members of Esalen's Women's Studies Collective, many of whom had been involved in the administrative work of setting up the conference.[36]

The collective had been established in September 1973 by a group of Esalen therapists and bodyworkers that included Anica Vesel Mander and Anne Kent Rush, who would go on to co-author *Feminism as Therapy* (1974). They petitioned for a seat on Esalen's all-white, all-male board and sought to curate an autonomous women's studies programme. This was at a time when second-wave feminism was drawing on the political force of the New Left to radically rethink society's patriarchal norms and the discriminatory practices that dominated everyday life. In addition to the influx of women who had entered the workforce as the 1960s became the 1970s, the decade had by 1973 seen the banning of sex discrimination in federally funded educational institutions, the legalisation of abortion and a groundswell of support for the Equal Rights Amendment. The collective was keen for Esalen to keep pace with this progressive agenda given their liberal image and the high numbers of women attending the institute. However, Mander and the others soon found their requests brick-walled by the board and the clear disregard exhibited by the conference left them disappointed and angry but not surprised. It merely confirmed what they already knew: that Esalen simply 'did not recognize women on an equal footing with men'. They picketed the conference and, in the aftermath, reiterated their requests to the board. They asked for a curatorial role in the next event and requested that all Esalen staff participate in 'political consciousness-raising groups' organised by the collective. The Esalen board responded by firing them.

For Peter Marin, who eventually recovered from his disgust long enough to sit down at a typewriter, the conference was emblematic of a malign contemporary attitude he called 'The New Narcissism'. Writing in *Harper's* in October 1975, Marin argued that the work of Esalen and its contemporaries was based on a fundamental 'denial'. Those who bought into its culture of growth were given licence to reject, in the 'name of higher truth', the 'claims of others upon the self'. It was a mission in which the realisation of one's full potential was prioritised to the exclusion of all other concerns. Adding detail to his analysis, Marin described the 'new' narcissism as 'a kind of soft-fascism' in which 'the deification of the self becomes equal in effect and human cost to what Nietzsche long ago called "the idolatry of the state". As he explained further:

> Just as persons once set aside the possibilities of their own humanity and turned instead to the state for a sense of power and identity no longer theirs, so now we turn to the self, giving to it the power and importance of a god.

There may well be advantages to be gained from the individual cultivation of this confidence but given the shambles of the conference with its warring fiefdoms, Marin was unconvinced that such a wilfully atomising process could be of any social benefit.[37]

The Women's Studies Collective would agree, save for the modification of one detail: that the self prioritised by 'The New Narcissism' was invariably masculine. As Mander described to *The Berkeley Barb* in April 1974, 'due to centuries of living in societal female roles, women have either given away their power to men, to the establishment, to parents and even to their children'. As a result, they have lost 'much of their aliveness'. For an example of this 'establishment', one might look to the arrest policies of the Oakland Police during the 1970s in cases of domestic abuse. Arrest was deemed to be a 'last resort' and officers were directed instead to act as 'mediators and counsellors'. This policy framed domestic abuse as an 'internal domestic dispute' rather than the 'inappropriate perpetration of violence', typically by men against women. Arrest avoidance denied women their 'day in court' because 'without an arrest, women could not file a criminal complaint and a criminal prosecution could not take place'. According to *Scott* v. *Hart*, a 1976 lawsuit filed by four women against the Oakland Police Department, their policy reiterated the idea that a man's home was his castle, that men had the right to physically assault their wives and that a man's ego took priority over 'a woman's battered body'.

These were the conditions and hard-wired prejudices that made women more apt than men to seek therapy 'because of the frustration engendered' by the inferior role 'society forces women to accept'. Women are not 'intrinsically prone to mental disorders', Mander explained to journalist Jessica Thompson, but in the 'present societal environment, these disorders seem to be exacerbated'. Mander was speaking soon after the Women's Studies Collective had broken away from Esalen. After her sacking they had formed Alyssum, a 'feminist growth center' in downtown San Francisco. *The Berkeley Barb* reported on their launch in February 1974 and ran a follow-up story that April. During this time, the newspaper also reported on the kidnapping and captivity of Patty Hearst by the Symbionese Liberation Army. Alongside the Alyssum feature, the April issue also published a long statement from Donald DeFreeze (as Cinque Mtume) and two other members of the SLA, 'Teko' (William Harris) and 'Fahizah' (Nancy Ling Perry) in which they reiterated their claim to speak for and in defence of 'oppressed persons'. If any further evidence was needed of Alyssum's claim that women were objectified, deprioritised and shaped by patriarchal forces, then surely this was it: the contemporary case of a young woman imprisoned against her will, most likely sexually abused by her male captors, and used as collateral to shore up a futile, ideologically problematic socio-political mission.

For Mander and the other Alyssum members, Esalen was part of this establishment and thus part of the problem. Speaking to *The Berkeley Barb*, they claimed the norms prevalent at the institute were power-laden, sexist and predatory. It was a place where 'a male therapist gets laid with a great deal of frequency by his female patients'; where women are routinely ignored 'in anything but a seductive role' and, further, where such inequality was embedded in the institute's hierarchy: 'the only way for a woman to gain status at Esalen is to be a male leader's old lady'. The existing histories of Esalen offer a fair amount of evidence, anecdotal and otherwise, to back up these allegations although such accounts are often directed at the bad behaviour of specific individuals or are more often taken as reflections of a general permissiveness, merely a case of the 'liberal 70s' playing out among the nude baths of the secluded institute. However, in offering their critique, the Alyssum members were making a much more systemic claim. Their argument was that that an authoritarian dynamic fuelled by male superiority was built into the operation of the institute.[38]

There is a glimpse of this power play in John Lilly's *The Centre of the Cyclone*. In the book he recounts how, in March 1969, he moved to Esalen to run a series of workshops having previously held a post at the Maryland Psychiatric Research Centre. He marked his transition from a 'research type of life' to 'the Esalen type of life' by spending his first weekend in an encounter group with 'Bill Schutz and fifty-nine other people'. Recalling the session, Lilly explains that what impressed him the most was not the interpersonal insights generated during the session but the command Schutz exerted over the group. Like Quaesitor's transgressive ringmaster Paul Lowe, Lilly described how Schutz could 'get people to do things they had not dared to do before', like take off their clothes in public. According to Lilly, Schutz instructed the group to undress 'rapidly' to 'realize a greater human freedom'. Everyone complied apart from two women who hesitantly stood apart surrounded by 57 naked strangers, most of them male. 'How can I possibly get my clothes off?' one of them said to Lilly, to which he replied directly and unambiguously: 'Take them off'. He explains that 'the simplicity and quietness' of this instruction 'seemed to release her from her former resistance' and the woman duly obeyed. The other one was not so easily convinced. Lilly reports there was 'quite a fuss' before she eventually caved in and 'got her clothes off'.[39]

It is an uncomfortable vignette, one that passes by in *The Centre of the Cyclone* with no further comment from Lilly. It is not the disrobing *per se* that makes it disturbing. Nudity was not uncommon during an encounter session. Paul Bindrim's nude psychotherapy or 'Nude Sensitivity Training Workshop' made it a requirement of participation, and the spectacle of a group bearing all in the name of honesty, freedom, non-verbal expression and the like has since become an enduring stereotype of the human potential era. No, the problem here is the clear sense of coercion involved. In Lilly's account, the two unnamed women are not presented with a choice. There is no sense of persuasion, no sense of negotiation, no possibility that this exercise might be optional. Instead, we are presented with the spectacle of two men (at least) commanding two women to strip. There is no suggestion of physical violence, but in the telling Lilly's language nonetheless bubbles with authority and force: the women undress when their 'resistance' is broken.

A decade or so earlier Lilly could be found cracking open the craniums of monkeys and dolphins, inserting electrostimulation probes before using the results to outline militarily applicable brainwashing techniques. When he writes in *The Centre of the Cyclone* about taking up a new life at Esalen, it sounds as if he is stepping away from this Cold War past. However, when Lilly describes the session with Schutz and particularly when control of the room seems to uncannily drift between them, it becomes apparent that nothing has changed. Reading between the lines, Lilly still seems to be fascinated by the idea of remote control and the heightened atmosphere of the encounter group allows him to exercise it. No electrostimulation equipment is necessary. By contrast the nervous, vulnerable and embarrassed women are left powerless. They are subject to the forces that shore up Lilly's almost telepathic manipulation, a toxic combination of suggestion, expectation and the pressure of the ritualised, norm-heavy environment of the group: exactly the kind of engine that one might find powering a cult. The women are not liberated by this exercise. They are tyrannised.[40]

Jane Howard describes a similar experience at various points in *Please Touch*. Across her survey of encounter groups, growth laboratories and experimental systems, she repeatedly comes up against the 'circuit riders', the leaders, teachers, guides and practitioners – more often male than not – who frequently operate in the absence of any discernible training save for that conferred by their own self-belief. Her descriptions of these figures crackle with a toughness and ruthlessness. They are never wrong, and they cannot be criticised. If the process is not working, if you have a problem with it, if you find it uncomfortable, then that is your failing. The problem does not lie with the group, it does not lie with the system, and it certainly does not lie with the leader. To use Walter Truett Anderson's description of est, the 'sinuous double-taking salesmanship' of these groups 'convinced' its participants 'that any failure on their part to discover great truths in its teachings was their own shortcoming, but all the breakthroughs and achievements were to be ascribed to the training'. This insidious gaslighting formed the troubling undertow of the introspective focus encouraged by human potential, a point that for Peter Marin was made clear in the rebuttals and pre-emptive strikes aired throughout the 'Spiritual Tyranny' conference. The speakers exhibited a 'tyrannical refusal to acknowledge the existence of a world larger than the self'. 'We are all gods', they argued, a stance that offered ample fuel for self-aggrandisement, but underneath this individual apotheosis one found what Will Storr calls 'the stunning darkness of Esalen's convictions that, as gods, all humans have complete responsibility for everything that happens to them'. If you fail, it is your fault. If you do not take off your clothes, you will not 'realise a greater human freedom'. If you are seduced by your trainer, it is because, consciously or not, you desired it to happen.[41]

When the allegations of sexual abuse started to emerge about the pre-eminent spiritual gurus of the 1970s, this dynamic of subjectification loomed large in the narratives. In 1990 the journalist Katharine Webster published an account of the allegations against Swami Rama in *Yoga Journal*. She outlined a pattern of harassment, coercion, grooming and psychological control that had extended across the 1970s. For the most part the allegations were raised by those who had joined his Pennsylvania-based Himalayan

International Institute of Yoga Science. While Webster gives voice to the physical damage and severe emotional trauma felt by Rama's accusers, she also described their struggle with an acute double bind of disbelief and self-reproach. As she explains, they had suffered abuse at the hands of a teacher who had apparently assumed vows of celibacy, whose 'every deed [was] thought to flow from union with the godhead'. To take it all in meant to recognise the guru as catastrophically human and for the victim to recognise all their prior devotion as disastrously misplaced. With the basis of one's entire, immersed life at stake, Webster suggests that it was easy to slip into denial. There was also the additional institutional pressure to deal with. In 'the mythology of the ashram', Webster notes, 'the guru is the all-powerful, all-knowing father and the disciples are his spiritual children'. Beyond this, the victims know, 'usually without being told', that 'if they break the taboo of silence, they will be blamed for destroying their spiritual families and the "higher" good those families purportedly do in the world'.[42]

At its worst, the guru–disciple relationship generates a form of puppetry, one that realises the fantasies of control harboured by researchers on both sides of the Cold War. It is brainwashing perfected, a process that needs no cumbersome technology, but which causes subjects to comply without question, to act as if everything is okay even when they know something is deeply wrong. Like the young couple who sleepwalk into the trap at Shape Up, the promise of an inner or 'higher' truth can lead the disciple into a powerless corner, a space in which they can participate, often unknowingly, in their own act of conditioning. We might all be our own gods, but we can just as easily become our own gaolers, and while various forms of growth may promise to release us from these shackles, they can also open us to a greater and more totalising form of confinement: the absolute tyranny of the self.

The Hospital Ship

London, 1976. A very strange sea voyage began when Jonathan Cape published *The Hospital Ship*, the debut novel by the British paediatrician Dr Martin Bax. In the slipstream culture of the 1970s, Bax was a fascinating figure who stood in two circles at once. After training and working at Guy's Hospital in London, he became research community paediatrician to the Thomas Coram Research Unit of London University. There he could be found doing his rounds, writing conference papers, preparing journal articles and publishing books like *Your Child's First Five Years* (1974). At the same time he was also running with another, faster, crowd: a group of artists, poets and recovering science fiction writers, all of whom Bax published in the pages of his avant-garde magazine *Ambit* (1959–2023).

Like Michael Moorcock's *New Worlds* (1964–70), *Ambit* pushed at the boundaries of genre and form, regularly publishing new and experimental material that combined literature, science and startling graphic design. Artist Eduardo Paolozzi was a frequent contributor, as was J.G. Ballard, who became the magazine's prose editor in 1967. *Ambit* gave Ballard a platform to develop the 'condensed novels' that later found their way into his cult text *The Atrocity Exhibition* (1970). The magazine's finest hour, however, came in 1968 when it mounted 'Drugs and Creative Writing', a now notorious competition that offered a prize for the best piece written 'under the influence'. A minor scandal thus ensued, with funding bodies reconsidering their support for a magazine that was apparently encouraging writers to rush off and take 'hard drugs'. Meanwhile, as the teacup storm blew itself out, Bax, Ballard and fellow judge Edwin Brock gave the £40 prize to the brilliant novelist Ann Quin, who had written her submission, an extract from her novel-in-progress *Tripticks* (1972), 'under the influence of the contraceptive pill'.[1]

The Hospital Ship, Bax's only novel to date, combined these strands of professional and artistic influence, the intertwined logics of medicine and speculative fiction, and oriented them towards a critique of the contemporary situation. Ballard would have called the book a 'terminal document'. It was a disturbing collage that played out against a near-future backdrop of a world in freefall. The basic plot charts the journey of *The Hopeful*, an atomic-powered sea vessel full of nurses, doctors and therapists, that floats through a post-apocalyptic ocean looking for survivors, those who have either made it to the coastlines of countries in crisis or those who have simply given themselves to the waves in search of anchorage. Once on board, the crew minister to the physical and psychic traumas of their patients and find themselves fascinated by the litany of new syndromes, afflictions and neuroses that have blossomed as society has declined. Often, though, the staff merely ease the exits of their already stricken charges. *The Hopeful*, Bax tells us, is also a floating morgue.

The novel was published in the April of 1976 and as that year's long, hot summer got underway, the reviews started to come in. It quickly became clear that *The Hospital Ship* had given its critics a dose of stimulating but uncomfortable holiday reading. Writing in *The Daily Telegraph*, Martyn Gof celebrated its 'brilliant, shocking' parallels with Albert Camus' *The Plague* (1947) while Michael Mason of the *Times Literary Supplement* praised its bold intertextuality, the ease with which Bax wove into the fabric of the book a range of sources, principally literary and medical. Other readers however were frustrated by the novel's opacity, its refusal to properly sketch out the circumstances surrounding its own version of the end of the world. 'The book would have been more interesting,' wrote Jill Neville in *The Sunday Times*, 'if it had concentrated entirely on this remarkable event'. Instead, she argued, Bax offers 'such a plethora of arbitrary information' that *The Hospital Ship* ends up 'less like a novel than an unsorted out-tray'.[2]

In defence of Bax, he does provide enough detail – just – to sketch out the edges of the novel's 'remarkable event'. It is not a singular unheralded occurrence which gives *The Hospital Ship* its backstory but a 'downward dive' very much in keeping with the mood of the 1970s. Bax alludes to 'the Cambodian adventure', the spread of Nixon-era Indo-Chinese conflicts and a parallel collapse of the global economy. We are told that Wall Street lurches as it is beset by 'anti-war and anti-establishment marches' as well as a virulent tide of patriotic populism. Bax describes crowds of construction workers joining the fray chanting 'USA all the way', as if they see the eclipse of capitalism as the necessary pretext to a state of entrenched isolationism. That said, Bax is not really interested in embellishing the circumstantial details. Reading the novel, you get the sense that the contextual obscurity is all part of his attempt to furnish *The Hospital Ship* with an uncompromisingly horizontal worldview. Characters receive flickers of information about the world beyond their vessel – occasional dispatches, crackling radio reports, disturbing glimpses of chaotic shorelines – but nothing coheres into an overall picture. Neither do the survivors act as reliable witnesses. Traumatised, insulated by psychosis, their occasional gnomic utterances are reminders that Bax allows no one, not even the reader, to occupy a vantage point of panoramic clarity. Those who steer *The Hopeful* are faced with the task of gathering the fragments together, of sifting through the unsorted out-tray in search of a story to tell.[3]

Nearly half a century later, at the tail-end of another blisteringly hot summer, another ship was preparing to weigh anchor. In October 2021 the *Celebrity Summit* left Miami for a six-day cruise that would take in such brochure-ready stop-offs as Mexico's Costa Maya. Health journalist Julia Naftulin was on board, reporting for the online magazine *Insider*. She was not there to review the overall offerings of the cruise, but one of its premium packages, an event which had been launched with a social media fanfare in early 2020 but had since gone under the radar: the luxury floating wellness junket, 'Goop-At-Sea'.

When lockdown descended in 2020, cruise ships across the world's oceans drifted into administrative and virological limbo. With swathes of passengers falling ill, the boats were either quarantined, with disembarkation continually delayed, or else they were prevented from docking altogether and sent back out to sea. Amid all the horror and anxiety of the COVID peak, the plight of the cruise industry generated sympathy, of course, but if we were being truly honest there was more than a little *schadenfreude* in the air. Here were the enormous vessels of a damaging tourist industry, the pirate ships of soft power, suddenly shunned the world over as floating superspreaders. In accordance with COVID guidelines, the industry went into dormancy, tour schedules were erased and, one after another, bespoke events were cancelled. Goop followed suit in June 2020, calling off the previously hyped-up trip before sitting out the rest of the crisis on Instagram. Restrictions aside, people were also spending their time inside reconsidering what 'normal' life meant. Would we want to take cruises again? Spending your holidays in close quarters with hundreds if not thousands of other people, all eating from the same buffet and stewing in the same pool, suddenly seemed like a massive risk, not a luxury.

Later, when things did begin to open, the cruise industry knew it would have to do a lot of wooing to get the wary back on board, so it cranked up the charm offensive. Deals, offers and rebrandings came thick and fast. Goop also surfaced and quietly announced the relaunch of their cruise liner project. 'Goop-At-Sea' would now be a smaller affair, not a maxed-out festival on a single flagship, but a series of events and workshops spread across four separate cruises featuring 'Goop-approved experts'. The show would go on: it seemed that not even a continuing global pandemic could stop Goop. But when Naftulin joined the *Summit* having laid out hundreds of dollars for her stateroom, drinks and food package, she found that, format change notwithstanding, this new 'Goop-At-Sea' was not all it was cracked up to be.[4]

Naftulin had 'expected a yacht of Lululemon-clad ladies and a glamorous Paltrow basking in the salty breeze of the sea'. She even felt a slight tinge of dread at the thought of hurrying up the boarding ramp and encountering 'the inevitable gaggles of pristine, thin women' who would be 'sipping the new smoothie I'd heard Paltrow enthuse over on *The Goop Podcast*'. Naftulin need not have been so anxious. Once checked in, she quickly realised there was a noticeable dearth of Goopies, 'no wellness warriors, and none of the glamourous staffers from Netflix's *The Goop Lab*.' In fact her fellow passengers, all 298 of them, turned out to be 'quintessential cruisers — cargo shorts, leggings, flip-flops — all there for nothing but a good time among slot machines and daiquiris'. The actual offerings had also been scaled down somewhat. In the innocent days of January 2020, 'Goop-At-Sea' had initially promised a packed schedule of events and 'perks'. Come 2021 and the programme seemed just as tired as the rest of us. 'Goop-At-Sea' now consisted of 'a low-impact fitness class' with the trampoline trainer Colette Dong and an 'intuition seminar' given by the 'Goop-approved clairvoyant' Deganit Nuur. It was a quick two-header that barely occupied each afternoon of the trip. No mention was made of the original event's proposed centre-piece, a live Q+A with Paltrow. Goop's CEO did not join any of the 2021 cruises, nor did Goop HQ generate much of a buzz about them. In fact, apart from a couple of cryptic posts leading up to the cruise and some daily perfunctory plugs from the *Summit*'s events team, 'Goop-At-Sea' went pretty much under the radar. The whole thing had the air of a minimum-effort, contract-fulfilling deal. 'Nobody I spoke with *knew* they were aboard a Goop cruise at all,' recalled Naftulin. 'I began to realize I may well have been the only passenger who'd booked a ticket with Goop's offerings in mind.' 'Goop-At-Sea' was going to be exclusive by default.

As the week went on, Naftulin enjoyed her time on board the *Summit*. Sure, the programme was underwhelming and, yes, judging by the photos that appeared in the *Insider* – yoga mats in a function room, drumkit pushed to the side – the ambience was more church hall than bespoke retreat, but that did not prevent the sessions from being affecting. At one point, as Naftulin followed Nuur's guided meditation, she found herself weeping, letting out the pent-up anxiety of the past year, saying goodbye to some difficult memories. She came out 'feeling more whole than I had in months'. A few curious passengers had turned up to the seminar and they too felt relieved, relaxed and keen to know more. All the while, social media dispatches continued to come from Goop HQ, but nothing was said about 'Goop-At-Sea'. Alone in her cabin at night, scrolling through her phone, Naftulin saw posts about upcoming health events, exclusive pop-ups and high-end product launches, but nothing about what was then taking place on the *Summit*. This unofficial embargo was social media doing what it does best: consigning the present to the past and overloading the future with promises yet to be delivered. You never catch up, you always miss out and the weight of this sunk cost – temporal, emotional and often financial – pushes you on. *This must be leading somewhere; what I'm looking for must be at the end of the next link.* The system generates, feeds upon and is fuelled by this restlessness, this anxiety; the feeling in the twisted gut and the too-busy brain that we need to be elsewhere and elsewhen, all the time. For Naftulin, there was an added sting, a sense almost of abandonment. Goop's shiny aura had pulled her to the cruise only to dissolve as soon as she arrived. Meanwhile, her phone was saying the glamour of the brand was about to manifest in another exclusive location. It was as if the Goopers had jumped ship and found a perfect private island just over the horizon, somewhere on the other side of the screen. 'Even as I floated on the Goop cruise,' Naftulin wrote, 'I felt like I was on the outside looking in, via Instagram.'[5]

A cruise on *The Summit* was a lot more comfortable than time spent on a ward of the atomic-powered *Hopeful*. But were the worlds – actual, imagined and somewhere in between – of *The Hospital Ship* and 'Goop-At-Sea' really that different? They certainly sailed through equally troubled waters. By October 2021 confirmed COVID cases stood at 243 million with over 4.9 million deaths recorded since the pandemic began. Such numbers could easily fill in the details of Martin Bax's undefined apocalypse. The global economy, too, was buckling and at the time of writing it has taken an even sharper 'downward dive'. When Bax alluded to the creep of warfare and ill-advised territorial adventures he could have been describing the tensions and conflicts which yielded the Russian invasion of Ukraine in early 2022. His sketch of a divisive, combative atmosphere of protest and populism also rings true for the Trump era and beyond, not least that administration's chaotic final act of 6 January 2021, when crowds of 'patriots' assaulted Washington's Capitol building powered by a conspiracy-rich ideology that purported to prioritise 'USA all the way'.

In stepping out of this world, however briefly, Naftulin was reaching for an experience of guided self-care. In the end, 'Goop-At-Sea' was not 'the spotless pseudoscience festival' she expected, 'but the vacation I needed'. Being away from it all on *The Summit* and having time to reflect seemed to be the main advantage. As for Goop – the company that purported to make people feel special and minister to their well-being – they pretty much left their customer(s) to their own devices. Compare this situation to *The Hospital Ship* and Martin Bax's vision of *The Hopeful*. Given the force of his imagination, we might be tempted to think of Bax as a secret nihilist, a doctor who attends to his patients by day and revels in his dreams of devastation by night. This, however, would be a misreading. *The Hospital Ship* is not a set of private fantasies: its thinking is closely connected to Bax's professional concerns. It is a deeply humanitarian novel, one in which life is precious, hence the focus on care and hence the crew of *The Hopeful* pushing against the tide of trauma.[6]

According to the current news cycle, the world of the still early 21st century is fast returning to that of the 1970s. The air is heavy with decline and discontent. If COVID and its pseudo aftermath was not enough, strikes and stagflation have also returned to the public agenda in full force. Allowing *The Hopeful* and *The Summit* to momentarily dock together brings these historical parallels into focus. It also flags up the differences between the periods by way of noticeable attitudinal shifts when it comes to the notion of care. In essence, the horrors of *The Hospital Ship* serve to amplify the cardinal importance of the novel's simple but radical message: look after each other. Goop, with its commodified approach to wellness, reverses this sentiment. After the point of sale, it tells clients like Naftulin, 'look after yourself'. Maybe, then, we are not actually *returning* to the 1970s after all but simply failing to learn its lessons. Maybe, as that decade's future becomes our present, we are drifting through it without a map.

PART II

This Floating World

CHAPTER VI

The Great Awakening
1975–1977

Mill Valley, California, 1977. It is early evening at the Wellness Resource Center, a medium-sized converted house nestled among the trees of the city's business district. John Travis is sat crossed-legged on the floor of centre's main room, a large-windowed, high-ceilinged lounge decked out in rich, redwood panelling. There is a small gathering around him and despite the comfortable-looking couches, everyone is sharing the floor. Some are sitting upright; others are lying back on cushions. Off to the side there is a full-sized mirror fixed to the wall which adds more light and space to the room. As the relaxed chatter flows, Travis looks round the cosy assembly. Some of his part-time staff are here but the rest are his clients, the people who have signed up to the centre's eight-month programme of weekly meetings and group sessions. As they have learnt about stress, self-responsibility, nutrition, and physical fitness over the past few weeks, he has got to know them well. The parties have helped to break the ice, too. And the hugs. There has been *a lot* of hugging. Clients, then? Actually, they are more like his friends. They are certainly not his *patients*.

Tonight, they have come together for a 'Lifestyle Evolution Group'. It is not a therapy group. No one here has a formal psychological diagnosis, and Travis has no intention of offering one. This is not an evening to dwell on 'problems'. With the clients leading the way rather than receiving the 'physician's intervention', the barriers between group 'leader' and group 'member' are just as blurry as they are in one of Arthur Janov's Primal Clinics. The atmosphere, however, is a lot more benign. There will be no screaming, no crying, no painful expulsions. There will not be any talking cures or gestalt hot seats, nor will the proceedings amp up to the ferocious pitch of an encounter group. Instead, Travis will simply invite his clients to brainstorm; they will exchange ideas and pool insights as to how they can make their lives better and how they can become happier. It will be one conversation among the many facilitated by a programme dedicated to the overall aim of becoming 'more well' rather than 'less sick'.[1]

Travis opened the Wellness Resource Center in 1975. By then he was two years on from his decision to give up professional medicine and three years on from the headbutting 'Capricorn Incident' in Baltimore. The idea was to run a 'quiet little practice' based on the work of Halbert Dunn. Travis wanted to assist clients to 'learn how to be healthy' and empower them to take responsibility for their own ongoing self-improvement. To that end, having used *High-Level Wellness* as the prompt for his 'Illness-Wellness Continuum', Travis continued to design a battery of evaluative and diagnostic tools. He wanted to give a concrete basis to Dunn's hypothesis that a holistic model of health should integrate the mind, body and spirit. As he opened the centre Travis was making extensive use of what he called *The Wellness Index*, a detailed questionnaire designed 'to educate more than to test'. Divided into twelve sections, the index covered a spectrum of topics ranging from 'Self-responsibility and Love' to 'Meaning' and 'Transcending' by way of more measurable subjects like 'Eating' (nutrition), 'Moving' (physical exercise) and 'Breathing' (respiratory health and stress). Incoming clients were asked to respond to statements like 'I use exercise as a metaphor or tool to break through self-imposed limitations' with a score between four and zero, four being 'Yes, always, or usually' and zero being 'No, never or hardly ever'.

The twelve sections contained more than 350 statements which ranged from 'I vote regularly' to 'I remember my dreams'. The idea was to add the numerical average of each section to another document, a graph Travis called 'The Wellness Index Wheel'. This was a pie chart divided into twelve with each segment corresponding to a subject section of the index. Averages were to be marked on the graph by shading each segment outwards, from the centre of the wheel to the circumference. The different scores would thus give the wheel twelve 'spokes' of varying lengths. 'Study the wheel's shape and balance,' Travis advised his clients. A big, long slab in the 'thinking' segment would point to a good level of self-awareness, while a small slither of a spoke in the 'moving' section would suggest that a bumpy ride is expected on the road to wellness, and more physical exercise is needed to balance things out.

The wheel was intended to be instructive, not prescriptive. For Travis, its main purpose was to invite self-reflection by providing the client with a clear, holistic view of their lifestyle priorities. 'What does it tell you?' Travis would ask in a follow-up consultation. 'Are there any surprises in it? How does it feel to you? What don't you like about it? What do you like about it?' From here the client could get a sense of where they stood on their own wellness continuum and, with Travis' advice, they could begin to develop their growth plan. At this point, the physical location of the Wellness Resource Center came into its own. After generating their wheels, clients were invited to attend regular sessions at the centre to learn about relaxation strategies, to work on their nutrition and fitness and to explore the techniques of self-examination, visualisation and creativity practised by the likes of the Lifestyle Evolution Group.[2]

When he started to develop the project in late 1973, Travis gained some interest among his medical colleagues and at one point considered a partnership with a group of doctors in Medford, Oregon. The inevitable issue, however, was funding. To be fair, Travis' proposal was a hard sell: 'Who ever heard of a physician who would not see sick people?' He was not offering courses of treatment or prescriptions but was proposing to work with those who had no physical symptoms, who were broadly healthy but nevertheless 'unwell' in a way that only Travis' questionnaires and graphs seemed able to define. By his own admission the 'Wellness information' he generated was 'subjective and unprovable by current scientific methods'. With this ambiguous data in hand Travis intended to help those whose welfare needs languished in a similarly indistinct grey area. As he later put it, his clients were neither ill enough for the emergency room nor 'crazy enough' for the psychiatrist.

A big part of this branding problem lay with the word 'wellness'. In the early 1970s, it was generally unknown as a health concept. There was a large market for self-help and health-related titles like Adele Davies' *Let's Eat Right to Keep Fit* (1954), Roger J. Williams' *You Are Extraordinary* (1967) and Alan H. Nittler's *A New Breed of Doctor* (1972), but within this field Dunn's own book, *High-Level Wellness*, had gained little traction since its publication in 1961. Beyond the enthusiasm of a small, scattered readership, Dunn had no public profile nor had his writing received much in the way of academic validation. Unsurprisingly, then, when Travis made his pitch to potential backers and insurers, they often thought it hopelessly vague; one to file with all the other airy, New Age 'systems' doing the rounds. There was certainly no recognition that in proposing the centre Travis was carrying the torch of another's work, nor was there much of a ripple felt when Dunn died in 1975.[3]

Tired of spelling out 'w-e-l-l-n-e-s-s' on the phone to another unconvinced investor, Travis decided to use his own savings to get the centre off the ground and set about cultivating a market ready to pay for his services. Hence the move to Mill Valley, a small, vibrant city in Marin County, some fourteen miles north of San Francisco. Until the late 1960s, Mill Valley was a rural, blue-collar area which occasionally played host to writers and artists looking for a Big Sur-like retreat. Travis had lived there at the start of the 1970s during his San Francisco internship and at that time, the city was just beginning to gentrify. As the decade progressed, an influx of new money from the Bay Area's growing business economy and new arrivals from across the country swelled Marin's population to over 200,000, quickly turning Mill Valley into a hot spot for the rich and upwardly mobile. It was just the kind of place you might move to from downtown Oakland if you were fortunate enough to own a profit-making business. By the mid- to late 1970s the city 'still had that real small-town atmosphere', as local author Cyra McFadden put it in her novel *The Serial* (1977), but by that she meant house prices were at a premium. There were other problems too. Cocaine use was common and although the city's fern bars and singles nights gave Mill Valley a bustling social scene, alcoholism was rife among its lawyers, realtors and urban planners. The area achieved something of an 'official' designation in this regard when a 1976 report on 'Drinking Behavior, Attitudes, and Problems' issued by the University of California labelled Marin County a community of 'heavy drinkers.'[4]

For McFadden, this was not just a matter of hedonism. *The Serial*, her satirical account of 'a year in the life of Marin County', is full of disaffection, disquiet and barely masked depression. Ten years after the social upheavals of the late 1960s her white, educated, upper-middle-class characters find themselves comfortable but bewildered, trying to square the prior decade's ideas of sexual and political liberation with the compromises of materialism and middle age. Work and wealth have given rise to a leisured lifestyle but according to the novel it was a sense of freedom measured out by weeknight Tequila Sunrises and five-martini lunches. 'Affluenza', a term that started to circulate in the early 1970s, would be a good label for the unease McFadden describes. Her characters are fortunate enough to have everything they want – money, families, homes, jobs – but are either in restless pursuit of a further (and almost indefinable) sense of fulfilment or are simply bored and demotivated, languishing in a fog of pointlessness precisely because they do not have to try harder. Frequently, the novel suggests that when faced with these first-world problems, the 'only option' is to get 'bombed out of [your] skull.'

It was this change in fortunes and attitude that drew Travis back to Mill Valley. He saw it as a 'wealthy ghetto of people who had discovered money doesn't buy you happiness', reasoning that 'if people have reached material success and they're not happy maybe they'll try something else, and they could afford to pay for it'. A set of sobering statistics backed up Travis' off-hand analysis as well as the emotional undertow of *The Serial*. By the mid-1970s, Marin County had become one of the wealthiest areas in California, and by extension the country, but up to 75 per cent of its marriages were ending in divorce, it had America's highest number of psychiatrists per capita and its suicide rate was twice the national average.[5]

For all his apparent opportunism, Travis was not hovering over Mill Valley's misery like a vulture capitalist in search of a quick buck.

Rather, he was very much in sync with the city and its mood. The year 1975 found Travis separated from his wife, Sally, and they were about to embark on a divorce of their own. A key factor in the split was Travis' discomfort with his medical career and the life it was building for him. The divorce was a turning point that had its origins in the time Travis had previously spent in Mill Valley. Before he discovered Dunn, before he cracked in Baltimore, before he finally gave up medicine, it was while living in the city and working through his depressive internship that Travis' thinking on health care started to change. Coming back was thus a sort of homecoming, a return to the source in terms of his personal and professional crises. Travis believed he could help people dealing with similar problems while continuing to work through his own. By setting up shop and offering his services in Mill Valley, then, Travis was sticking to his cardinal principles: first, that wellness was a dynamic, ongoing process of growth; and second, that its practitioners should 'teach what [they] most need to learn'.

By 1977 the project seemed to be working. Travis was attracting a sizeable clientele, was lecturing on his methods across Marin County and was travelling nationwide giving upwards of 100 presentations a year to doctors and businesses. Out of this came another volume that complemented *The Wellness Index*, *The Wellness Workbook for Health Professionals* (1977). Travis was also networking with other like-minded practitioners including the health promoter and fellow Marinite Donald B. Ardell, the 'wellness physician' Bill Hettler and the health educator Elizabeth Neilson. Like Travis, they had each gravitated towards *High-Level Wellness* having become disenchanted with professional medicine and its focus on disease treatment rather than health promotion. Forming a significant political backdrop to these conversations was the 'Lalonde Report' (1974). Also known as *A New Perspective on the Health of Canadians*, the report was spearheaded by Marc Lalonde, the Canadian Minister of National Health and Welfare. It argued for the consideration of a 'health field' that would approach the individual not just from the perspective of treatment but also in terms of their biology – their physical and mental health – along with their environment and their lifestyle.

The report focused on 'health' rather than the specific practices of 'wellness', but it signalled to Travis and the others, poised at the middle of the decade, that the time was right to attempt an attitudinal shift as regards individual and social well-being.[6]

In 1977, Neilson founded the journal *Health Values*, which was dedicated to Dunn, and which set about bringing his work back into circulation, a publishing drive that included a new edition of *High-Level Wellness*. Hettler, meanwhile, had trained at the University of Cincinnati College of Medicine before becoming involved with the Student Life Division at the University of Wisconsin-Stevens Point. Their 'program devoted to life-style improvement' had been established in 1972 and by 1975, under Hettler's guidance and in accordance with Dunn's ideas, the multi-service programme was focused on improving the intellectual, emotional, physical, social, occupational and spiritual well-being of the student body. Hettler helped to consolidate the status of Stevens Point as the 'rising Wellness Capitol of the country' by using it as the base for the Annual Wellness Conference, which by the time of its third iteration in 1978 had become the National Wellness Conference. As for Ardell, he began his career in the mid-1960s as an urban planner before moving into health-focused roles in various think tanks and city councils. Here he observed the 'dysfunctional nature of the medical system' as well as the 'inability of the planning function to prevent waste' and to 'promote health status'. Upon his appointment as editor of the *American Journal of Health Planning*, Ardell acted on this frustration and moved away from 'trying to co-ordinate medical services'. Instead he started 'issuing reports in the public interest about promoting healthy living'.

Ardell first encountered Dunn's *High-Level Wellness* in early 1975, after receiving a copy from Henrik L. Blum, then head of the health-planning department at the University of California, Berkeley. What he later described as the 'benevolent lightning' of the book pointed a way through all the frustration and Ardell began to seek out those working with similar techniques, which is what led him to John Travis in Mill Valley. Upon learning of Dunn's death in 1975 Ardell also sought out his widow, Phelpsie Dunn, who gave him a library of her husband's papers. With this material in hand and contacts established, Ardell pushed forwards with his own health promotion. He embarked on a programme of wellness-related graduate work and wrote an article for *Prevention* magazine on Travis and the Wellness Resource Center that dubbed him 'the doctor of Well-Being'. The article then became the basis of Ardell's first book, *High Level Wellness: An Alternative to Doctors, Drugs and Disease* (1977), which was specifically intended as a homage to, and extension of, Dunn's volume. Unlike Dunn's original, Ardell's book would go through a number of progressively high-profile editions in the years that followed. It would kickstart his career as a writer and would subsequently be seen as a foundational text of modern wellness.

Such support was a massive boon for Travis. The *Prevention* article appeared in April 1975 and in the months that followed, he received over a thousand letters from potential clients as well as 'nurses wanting to get their Doctors into wellness'. Despite this success, running the Wellness Resource Center was not without its difficulties. It was an all-consuming occupation and with only a small and mainly voluntary staff, Travis shouldered much of the workload himself. It was a responsibility that often left him chasing unrealistic, self-imposed deadlines, the stress of which fired up the old engines of anxiety. Travis was continually berating himself for not being a 'better person'. On the plus side, he was a world away from his life in the medical sector. Back then, Travis was on autopilot. Mired in depression, he looked drawn, pallid and thoroughly vampirised by life. As he put it in his diary: 'I dragged my feet and passively resisted and hurt inside a lot.' But now, in 1977, he was beaming in the glow of the redwood room. He was 34 and having 'the time of [his] life'. As he later put it, 'this was the first time [...] I was doing something I wanted to do'. Travis felt he had stepped away from the scripts of parental and professional expectation and was busy writing his own. Best of all, he was no longer doling out handfuls of drugs with 'awesome side effects' to dull the symptoms of problems he believed had deeper, but easily remediable, lifestyle causes.

If he ever needed a prompt to keep him going, Travis only needed to look up from his place in the redwood room and turn to his left. There he would have seen *All Tied Up*, a large bunch of neckties he had woven together and hung on the wall like a macramé twist. These were the ties he used to wear on the hospital wards, the last vestiges of his former life in professional medicine. Looming there, like some corporate memento mori, *All Tied Up* reminded Travis of just how wound-up and constricted he had felt and how it would be so easy to tangle himself up in knots again. At the same time, *All Tied Up* was a galvanising totem, it symbolised the possibility of transformation, signalling both for Travis and his clients that radical change was in reach. As he brought his attention back to the Lifestyle Evolution Group and the ideas started to flow, Travis felt confident that the road to wellness was open and he was moving in the right direction. It seemed entirely possible to gather up the frayed threads and bind them into something new.[7]

*****

The Wellness Resource Center makes a cameo appearance in *The Serial*. It's where Kate Holroyd, the novel's main character, goes to see a 'Life Goals Consultant' while trying to work through her marriage problems with estranged husband Harvey. Harvey, meanwhile, is enduring the full-blown paranoia and anxiety of a 'nervous breakdown' after claiming that an 'international conspiracy of women' organised 'a hit squad that offed his cat'. *The Serial* first appeared as instalments in 1976 in the Marin County newspaper the *Pacific Sun*. It was intended as Marin's version of Armistead Maupin's *Tales of the City* (1978), an account of intersecting lives and relationships in downtown San Francisco, which had also begun as serial in the *Pacific Sun* in 1974 before transferring to the *San Francisco Chronicle*. After four months, McFadden's project was picked up by the New York publisher Alfred A. Knopf and what she had originally planned as a 'short-lived' sequence of occasional episodes turned into a novel-length 'epic' charting an entire year, week by week, across 52 chapters.

With Tom Cervenak's beautiful, catalogue-like images illustrating McFadden's razor-sharp prose, *The Serial* paints a critical portrait of Marin's 'self' culture during 'the flowering of the human potential movement of the late 70s'. This is the backdrop to the novel's binge-drinking, garrulous dinner parties and restless soul-searching. The Holroyds and their circle leaf through *Prevention* magazine and think about going jogging; they continually brood on 'Life' and then seek solace in 'personal growth' via any number of alternative therapies and awareness groups. It is a repeated cycle that finds them pinballing back and forth from Wallbanger cocktails at Sam's Deck and quarter-pounders at McDonald's to Tuesday morning massages at Moment's Pause and plates of fibrous macrobiotics. The Wellness Resource Center is part of this moveable feast; the name appears among the novel's flooded market of treatments and health programmes that leaves the characters spoilt for choice when attempting to find their 'really authentic' selves.[8]

Although exaggerated, *The Serial* was accurate in framing Marin County as a major hub of the human potential movement. The Arica School and est had outposts in the area and some of Mill Valley's schoolteachers used encounter group methods in the classroom. Michael Murphy lived in Mill Valley as did another Esalen insider, George Leonard, author of the landmark *Look* article 'The Human Potential'. Murphy went on to open an Esalen outreach office in the city while Leonard taught classes in 'Aikido politics' which presented the Japanese martial art as a method of 'personal transformation' and 'social reform' rather than a technique of self-defence. Leonard was one of Donald Ardell's neighbours and became something of a Mill Valley networker when researching *High Level Wellness*. The opening sections of the book read like an unofficial guide to the city's blossoming business of well-being. He interviews Leonard about Esalen, reports on est groups and recounts that his first meeting with John Travis was not at the Wellness Resource Center but another of the city's enterprises, the Wholistic Health and Nutritional Institute. While many Marin locals objected to McFadden's lotus-land portrayal of the area, it was undeniable that the 1970s gentrification of cities like Mill Valley was fuelled by the rise of the alternative health economy documented by Ardell.[9]

This image of Marin as the 'golden ghetto' beside the 'golden gate' was further embellished by *I Want It All Now* (1978), an NBC television special that aired shortly after the publication of *The Serial*. Hosted by the unbearably square NBC newsman Edwin Newman, the film has him wandering around Mill Valley looking completely out of place while he openly castigates its apparently 'loose, swinging lifestyle'. With all the subtlety and understanding of a Mondo movie, Newman mercilessly negs his interviewees, particularly the women, as he prods away at the troubling duality of Marin's affluence and its social problems.

For Newman, the two were very much connected. *I Want It All Now* suggests that the same money and time spent at Marin's yacht clubs and restaurants also bolstered its 'light industry' of alternative therapies, the profit-making services that promised to remake the inner self and point the way to happiness. To give a sense of this range, Newman at one point stands in front of Mill Valley's Center for Designed Change and reels off a list of its most popular, lucrative courses: 'Reichian therapy, postural integration, various kinds of mind control, est seminars, tai chi, aikido, bio-energetics, visualization, guided fantasy, actualization, Rolfing'. 'And that's just a brief list', he scoffs, without dwelling any further on what he meant by 'mind control'. The contention is that this drive for and marketisation of the 'perfection of the self' produces an intense self-absorption. Newman presents Marin as a culture of selfishness, one that has been enabled by the pseudo-philosophical justification of human potential. One image that recurs throughout the film to evidence this view is that of two naked masseurs using peacock feathers to stroke a reclining woman into relaxed oblivion. Newman's voiceover informs us that she has paid $180 for this all-day treatment and, when roused from her stupor to speak to the camera, the woman neatly sums up the thrust of the film. She speaks not about the health benefits of body therapy nor the value of meditative states, but the joy of 'taking': the pleasure to be had in paying for a service that does not require her to 'give' at all. According to the film, it is this attitude which generates

Marin's darker side. The drugs, the alcohol, the divorce and suicide rates are byproducts of this 'tremendous obsession with self'. It is an entitlement that not only seems to permit indulgence but, more seriously, causes inevitable disappointment. The film asks, if you cannot be happy among all the 'advantages and assets' of Marin County, where can you be? *I Want It All Now* paints Marin as both a modern Babylon, a decadent territory that's imploding under the weight of its own pretentions, and the 'end of the rainbow', a toxic, depressing place that promises everything and leaves you with nothing.[10]

For her part, McFadden had no real problem with 'the impulse behind much of the human potential movement'. Rather, as she explained when interviewed by Newman for the film, she objected to the 'smell of sanctimony' that often went with it. *The Serial* is full of therapeutic shopping lists just as varied as those rattled off by Newman, but McFadden's characters also use their pursuit of self-improvement as a virtue-signalling form of social climbing. In the passive-aggressive bear-pit that is the novel's dinner-party circuit, for example, erstwhile host Kate Holroyd is confronted with the 'insensitive' objections of her guest, Ginger Gallagher. She holds forth 'over the beef wellington about *Diet for a Small Planet* and how selfish it was for middle-class WASPs to eat meat instead of soybeans and screw up the entire protein chain'. It's a good point and one which, for the record, comes straight out of the 1971 book by Frances Moore Lappé that McFadden references. In the novel, however, the argument quickly fades as the guests all tuck in. The beef wellington is polished off and it seems that Gallagher was not actually arguing for sustainable eating after all. She was merely point-scoring; bringing up *Diet for a Small Planet* to highlight Holroyd's social *faux pax*, her crime being the decision to serve a dish that was no longer '*au courant*'.

Elsewhere, McFadden's predominantly white, predominantly middle-class est graduates and students of 'polarity balancing manipulation' live according to a credo of determined self-interest. They put '[their] own needs right up in front' and the inevitable result, according to McFadden, is personal chaos: affairs, break-ups, make-ups, impulsive moves to experimental living situations and disruptive re-evaluations of the 'extended family concept'. The novel's main narrative arc, Kate and Harvey Holroyd's separation and reunion, follows this trajectory and McFadden uses it to observe the 'human wreckage' the couple leave in their wake. Over the course of their 'transformative' year, Kate and Harvey's friendships are destroyed, their exploration of human potential drains their finances and, more seriously, they neglect their teenage daughter, Joan. She later finds a substitute family among the 'Moonies' of the Unification Church.[11]

An uncannily similar Mill Valley couple appear in *I Want It All Now*: Bob Gulko and Sandra Robbins. These real-life Holroyds have had what Newman almost splutteringly refers to as a 'happy divorce'. According to Bob, the push to end the marriage came after he attended an est seminar which encouraged him to be totally open with his feelings. Bob took his coaches at their word and duly confessed to Sandra a long history of infidelity. 'Lying got in the way', explains Bob before reflecting on the most valuable lesson he learned from est: it was 'OK to do anything as long as [he was] honest'. In the film, Bob appears completely comfortable with this and is visibly happy, as if a great burden has been lifted. McFadden, however, would point to Bob's stunning lack of contrition. The seminar appears to have encouraged Bob's honesty at the expense of any need for an apology. There is a refreshing openness between the estranged couple, but no sense of responsibility on Bob's part. Erhard's system has given him a way to validate his past actions and valorise his admission. As a result, Bob now sits on a smug pedestal of truth beyond any reproach. Sandra simply cannot be angry in the face of such heroism. According to est it would be unreasonable to vent at Bob. That the family has been split, that she has been humiliated and their children have been upset matters little. As long as Bob's being honest, then everything's okay.[12]

With *The Serial*, McFadden was not making a case for 'traditional' family values, but as with Peter Marin's critique of Esalen and its clientele in 'The New Narcissism', she was questioning the inward, black hole focus of human potential. In his article for

Harper's, Marin had described the 'growing solipsism of a beleaguered class' and an emerging worldview 'centred solely on the self
with individual survival as its sole good'. Similarly, *The Serial* finds
McFadden's characters using the language of growth, self-discovery
and self-development to absolve themselves of any responsibilities
outside of their exalted needs. In her view, this attitude has resulted
in a society of isolated shallowness where characters mutter 'I hear
you' during intimate conversations when really, they are just waiting
for their turn to speak.[13]

✳✳✳✳✳

The residual bleakness of *The Serial* was in sync with two other
era-defining essays that appeared just as the novel was published.
In August 1976 *New York* magazine published Tom Wolfe's cover
story 'The "Me" Decade' followed a month later by 'The Narcissist
Society', an extended review by Christopher Lasch for *The New York
Review of Books*. Wolfe's article, the more famous of the two, moves
far beyond the range of Marin County. It is a long and condescending takedown of est, Esalen, Synanon and other easy targets in which
he dissolves the differences between these groups and focuses on
their common territory, the encounter session. In January 1976, *The
New Yorker* had published a glowing profile of Michael Murphy
by Calvin Tomkins that presented him as a modern-day renaissance man and offered an even-handed analysis of encounter group
culture. It is easy to think that with 'The "Me" Decade' (written for
The New Yorker's upstart rival) Wolfe was trying to cock a snoop
at Tomkins and his subject. He focuses on much of the same
material but with the distinct tone of someone trying to puncture a
bubble of pretension. Where Tomkins talks of encounter groups as
touching 'a highly sensitive nerve in America in the affluent nine-
teen-sixties', Wolfe dismisses them as 'lube jobs for the personality',
the point at which 'Businessmen, businesswomen, housewives –
anyone who could afford it' are encouraged to 'bare their own souls
and to strip away one another's defensive facades' to 'face [their]
own emotions squarely for the first time'. In his article Tomkins

looked into the cultural and historical origins of encounter practices from shamanism to corporate feedback groups, while in 'The "Me" Decade', Wolfe describes them as mere exercises in self-indulgence. In his eyes, the encounter group is a closed circuit, an event at which a captive audience bears witness to the spotlight moment of each successive participant. Tomkins may have suggested the encounter group is a social invention with a wide range of possible applications, but for Wolfe it was a ritual of self-focus purely for its own sake: 'No matter whether you managed to renovate your personality through encounter sessions or not, you had finally focused your attention on the most fascinating subject on earth: *Me.*'

Wolfe goes on to call the 'meditation and psychic frenzy' of the 1970s the 'Third Great Awakening'. In his view it was a cultural shift akin to the 'ecstatic experiences' which previously rippled through American history and inaugurated a series of seismic religious changes. According to Wolfe, the first awakening was the 'holy-rolling pentecostal shout' of the 1740s 'led by preachers of "the New Light" such as Jonathan Edwards, Gilbert Tennent and George Whitefield'. The second was the 'camp-meeting revivalism' of 1825–1850 led by the Shakers, the evangelical Baptists and the Mormons. The first paved the way for 'the American Revolution through its assault on the colonies' religious establishment', the second created an atmosphere of 'Christian asceticism' that swept through the 'West during the nineteenth century and helped make it possible to build communities in the face of great hardship'. And the 'Third Great Awakening', where will that lead? Wolfe responds to his own question with a tone of uncertainty and trepidation:

> [...] who can presume to say? One only knows that the great religious waves have a momentum all their own. Neither arguments, policies nor acts of legislature have been any match for them in the past. And this one has the mightiest, the holiest roll of all, the beat that goes ... Me ... Me ... Me ... Me.

The popularity and intensity of this psychological exhibitionism was for Wolfe one of the 'grand puzzles of the 1970s'. He may not have known where it was leading, but he had a good go at explaining where it came from. He suggests that the present 'wave' has its origins in 'the 30-year boom', the period of spending after 1940 that 'pumped money into every class level of the population on a scale without parallel in any country in history'. Giving the merest mention to those at 'the bottom, the chronically unemployed', and passing over entirely the socio-economic deprivation experienced by America's black and minority ethnic populations, Wolfe's description of an investment into 'every class' is linked solely to the middle class. He argues that post-war affluence filled out this demographic, permitted some upward mobility from a fast-dwindling 'proletariat' and in so doing delivered on the 'much dreamed of' promises of utopian socialism: 'money, free time and personal freedom'. However, rather than these benefits catalysing the formation of a collective political identity, the newly 'liberated working man' simply 'took the money and ran', retreating to the suburbs in station wagons full of brand-new consumer goods. There, according to Wolfe, 'ordinary folks' were free to engage in what had previously been an 'aristocratic luxury', a process of 'remaking, remodelling, elevating, and polishing one's very self'.[14]

Wolfe's analysis may read like an extreme caricature of suburban selfishness, but it was an accurate sounding of the era, at least in economic terms. The year before, in 1975, New York had faced a huge fiscal crisis when financiers stopped underwriting the city government's municipal bonds. For decades, New York's spending had outstripped its income thanks, in part, to its largely unionised workforce and its wide-ranging welfare system. Among other benefits, the city operated public hospitals, day-care centres and provided free tuition at City University of New York. Although laudable, these services were an expense New York could ill afford, particularly in a climate of increasing 'White flight' and northern deindustrialisation. Overspending, though, was not the sole problem. By the 1970s New York's key services were also buckling after a similarly long period of severe underfunding, a situation vividly illustrated by the journalist Robert Caro in his book *The Power Broker* (1974). Published just as the crisis started to form on the horizon, *The Power Broker* was a monumental biography of the super-bureaucrat and master of self-interest Robert Moses. A many-hatted urban planner, Moses had come to dominate the city's development particularly in the 1940s and through to the 1960s via the coordination of multiple road, bridge, tunnel and parkland projects. Moses often claimed to be working for the good of the people, but as Caro repeatedly argued, his planning often favoured the rich – affluent car owners, for example – and frequently came at the cost of, or even actively worked against, the efficient development of mass transit systems. In September 1975, with bankruptcy looming, no federal bail-out in sight, and a nervy Wall Street withholding credit, Moses wrote an op-ed for the *New York Times* decrying the lack of help from Washington and castigating the city's officials for being asleep at the wheel. 'Where were the wisemen of Gotham when our vaunted financial system began visibly to fall apart?' he asked with all the rhetorical thrust of a condemnatory preacher. Read in the light of *The Power Broker*, however, this criticism would have sounded a particularly pompous and ironic note because if anything, Caro had shown that *this* wiseman of Gotham had spent the prior 30 years or so selfishly driving New York into the ground.

The action, when it came, was radical and far reaching. The city authorities were forced to cede their budgetary operations to the Emergency Financial Control Board, a state-run administrative body mainly dominated by bankers. Established just as Moses was passing his public judgement, the EFCB set out to make city governance much less democratic and imposed a swingeing austerity drive to balance the books. Mass lay-offs, cutbacks and service shutdowns followed alongside a fare increase on the subway and the introduction of fees at CUNY. The social effects were predictable and immediate: those hit hardest by the measures were those most in need of welfare support. The logic of this predicament was 'The "Me" Decade' writ large. Those with the money took flight from the city and with them went the sources of tax revenue that had funded a sizeable portion of New York's services. The work of the EFCB proceeded according the same accumulative thinking. They sought not to make good the city's operating deficit, but to stabilise the existing resources in a way that privileged profit over people. It was a reduction in social services and a redirection of spending to private enterprise that set the template for the neoliberal economics of the Reagan years and beyond.[15]

Such self-interest was not just an American phenomenon. In April 1975 the *British Journal of Political Science* published 'The Economic Contradictions of Democracy', a widely cited essay by the economist Samuel Brittan. Reflecting on the 'international crisis caused by the fivefold rise of oil prices at a time of very rapid world inflation', Brittan suggested the UK was 'particularly badly placed to meet such a challenge because of the pre-existing state of its post-war economy'. He refers to the 'low growth rate' and 'rapid rate of inflation', the depreciation of the pound 'two years after it floated in 1972' and the 2.1 per cent unemployment rate in 1973. In Brittan's view these factors fed into the period's strikes and blackouts as well as a growing anxiety that the stability of the UK's 'liberal representative democracy' was under threat. For some this 'threat' was the possibility of social disorder, a fear of what could happen if the lights stayed off. For others, like Colonel David Stirling, founder of the SAS, the threat came from the trade unions. They seemed to be calling the shots as the country ground to a halt. If so, where did that leave the elected government? In imminent danger, claimed Stirling, who spent the mid-1970s corralling together Great Britain '75, a private paramilitary group who were prepared to keep things going should civil unrest and trade union militancy cause the existing political structure to collapse.

Brittan's description of instability, inflation and social anxiety could easily apply to the socio-economic turmoil of the present day, particularly the cost of living crisis and its surrounding interplay of workplace action and establishmentarian calls for order. However, Brittan's argument performs its sharpest incisions and assumes its keenest contemporary relevance when he turns from the specific crises of the 1970s to an analysis of 'liberal democracy itself'. Far from being the will of the people enacted in policy, Brittan understood democracy as an 'institutional arrangement for arriving at political decisions', one in which parties gain 'the power to decide' via a 'competitive struggle for the people's vote'. Within this market-place, the electorate are treated to a carrot-and-stick approach with parties tactically stoking the desires of different social groups. The result is a gap between policy-making and vote-winning in which 'short-run ends, such as keeping the mortgage rate down, prevail over longer-term ends such as producing a sensible housing or credit policy'. At times, Brittan's essay reads like a manifesto for the New Right, a diatribe against the uninformed masses and the oikish demands of trade unions. It could have shored up the ideological stance of the ECFB just as much as it went on to inform Margaret Thatcher's neoliberal moves against unionisation but, down in the detail, the thrust of Brittan's argument is more nuanced than this presumption of a top-down critique would suggest. He has in mind the type of populist and personality-led policy campaigns that have since proved to be both effective and corrosive in the age of Trump, Twitter and talkshow politics.

Specifically, Brittan sees two 'endemic threats' to democracy: the 'generation of excessive expectations' and the 'disruptive effects of the pursuit of group self-interest'. As 'generation' and 'pursuit' indicate, the problem for Brittan lies not with the caprice of the electorate but the way that the present political system panders to this short termism by requiring that politicians continually play to the gallery. They target 'me' and the result, according to Brittan, is a set of crowd-pleasing promises which are rarely realised, and a subsequent process of public judgement based on the perception of performance rather than the appreciation of policy. Brittan cites as an example a 1974 report by the Survey Research Unit of the Social Science Research Council which showed that '67 per cent of respondents felt in 1973 that their standard of living was below the one to which they felt entitled'. The 'average respondent' felt entitled to 'a standard of living 20 per cent more than they actually had'. Following this, although politicians 'called for "sacrifices" on account of the inflation and oil crises', in much the same way that cross-party calls are now being made for decisive action on climate change, they were then (as now) extremely reluctant to take any measures which might reduce consumption. Meanwhile, back in the

1970s, the Labour government pushed forwards with rent freezes for council tenants 'from whom they expected to draw a large vote' just as the Conservatives promised '9½ percent mortgages at a time of rapidly rising prices'. Both were 'actively whipping up expectation among different groups', which in Brittan's view turned the voter into a consumer, someone who browses the political marketplace looking for the deal that best satisfies their own needs. As with the social media scroller of the decades yet to come, the resultant attitude of the 1970s electorate was one of ring-fenced self-interest: anything outside of this individually focused desire for satisfaction was someone else's problem. As Brittan put it, in the 'early spring of 1974', after a general election fought on key issues ranging from 'redistribution' to 'firmness and fairness', a poll indicated 'that only a third of those asked were willing to pay more taxes "to help people who do not earn so much money as yourself"'.[16]

This was the demographic dissected so incisively by director Mike Leigh in his British drama of 1970s manners *Abigail's Party* (1977). An ensemble piece featuring Alison Steadman's career-making turn as the indomitable Beverly, *Abigail's Party* was first staged at London's Hampstead Theatre in April 1977 before appearing on television in November as part of the BBC's *Play for Today* series. It is set in Beverly's front room, a crucible of 1970s suburban chic that is organised around three main components: a leather-look three piece, a well-stocked and frequently visited drinks cabinet and a squabbled-over hi-fi that variously plays host to Beethoven, Donna Summer and Demis Roussos. The play follows Beverly as she (and stressed-out estate agent husband Laurence) host a gathering for their younger, newlywed neighbours Angela and Tony. They also invite Susan, mother of the titular Abigail, who anxiously takes refuge with Beverly away from her daughter's first teenage party. As the silent chorus of Abigail's off-stage party rumbles on into possibly sinister territory, Beverley's 'do' similarly unravels into disaster. Director Leigh, working from extensive improvisations with the cast, orchestrates a typically British catastrophe, one that ripples with violence, leads to an eventual tragedy but otherwise proceeds via the traditional combat methods of the middle class: barbed social niceties, unilateral snobbery and almost unbearable levels of awkwardness. And fags, and booze, and nibbles.

Beverly does not really preside over a 'party' as such. There is no sociability or togetherness here. It is just a room of individuals, each one occupying a different point on the middle-class spectrum, and they are all in some form of competition with each other. Susan tries to cling to her status against a volley of comments about her divorce, Angela artlessly tires to climb the social ladder her new home has opened to her, while Beverly and Laurence embark on various rearguard actions intended to keep her and Tony in their place. As the host, Beverly reminds everyone that it is her house and it is the importance of her stuff, her preferences and her attitudes that they are all required to acknowledge. Laurence meanwhile variously shows off and overcompensates with his high-cultural affectations: his classical music and his unread, leather-bound complete works of Shakespeare. He also has no qualms about calling Beverly's prized print of Stephen Pearson's *Wings of Love* 'cheap pornographic trash', while she responds to his horizontal attacks by regularly puncturing his pretentions, often to a humiliating degree. If she wants to dance with Tony, she will; there is nothing that Laurence, or for that matter Tony and Angela, can do about it. Leigh later described his acerbic characters as an early realisation of Thatcher's generation, but he need not have been so predictive. The fractious gathering perfectly makes manifest Brittan's analysis of a mid-1970s privatism. Laurence, for example, strives for more, like the new car every year, because he thinks he is entitled to it; he expects it as a personal reward for the daily professional struggle he endures and, as a result, he relies on its social capital to give him a sense of superiority over the likes of Tony, the less educated and comparatively less experienced computer operator. As with Beverly, Laurence's discontent gives rise to an aggressive self-interest that adds to the play's atmosphere of relentless one-upmanship. Consumerism fuels this outlook, and the play suggests that accumulation – be that of property or prestige – both satisfies and stokes the characters' psychological needs for a sense of betterment.[17]

In *The Serial*, McFadden makes a similar point about the American version of this market-led development of the self. In her portrait of Mill

Valley, lifestyles can be switched as easy as choosing a new recipe from Julia Child's *Mastering the Art of French Cooking, Volume Two* (1970). More than a decade before Bret Easton Ellis' paeans to Phil Collins in *American Psycho* (1991), *The Serial* finds McFadden nailing the art of satirical superficiality with conversations about 'rolfing and primal screaming' over dinner tables of Childs' *cassoulet* and *saucisson*. Where characters like Beverly use social practices and a parade of possessions in *Abigail's Party* to cover a certain shallowness, those in *The Serial* wilfully gravitate towards restless consumerism as a way of asserting their personalities. No commitment is necessary in this fluid world because the catalogue of human potential offers endless options. If Kate does not have 'absolute, total confidence in the Wellness Resource Center', her friend Naomi explains, she can just go to the 'Center for Designed Change' where Naomi knows a '*beautiful* human being'. It is a buyer's market of disposable identities and the pitch that so troubles McFadden and so attracts her characters is one of seductive simplicity: if you have the time and the money you can develop your inner self again and again, regardless of the consequences.[18]

Christopher Lasch continued this line of critique in 'The Narcissist Society', where he reviews several American books covering much the same ground as Wolfe, chief among them Jerry Rubin's memoir *Growing (Up) at Thirty-Seven* (1976). In the late 1960s Rubin was a provocative left-wing firebrand, deeply immersed in the American New Left, who along with Abbie Hoffman and Paul Krassner founded the Youth International Party in 1967. Rubin was involved in anti-Vietnam activism, was instrumental in organising the 1967 march on the Pentagon and, following the violence between police and protestors at the 1968 Democratic Convention, was rounded up with the 'Chicago Seven' and charged with inciting a riot. However, as Lasch writes, by the turn of the 1970s Rubin found himself in his thirties, 'without a following' and 'forced to confront his fear and anxieties'. Moving from New York to San Francisco, Rubin 'shopped voraciously on an apparently inexhaustible income, in the spiritual supermarkets of the West Coast'. Between 1971 and 1975 he got into health foods, jogging, meditation and tai chi, immersed himself in the practices of est, Esalen and Arica, and worked through the now familiar list of therapies: gestalt, acupuncture and sex therapy. This 'smorgasbord course in New Consciousness' left him feeling energised and after 'years of neglecting his body', Rubin reached 37 feeling 25. Such positive results led Rubin to recalibrate the famous maxim of the New Left regarding the personal and the political. He no longer saw it as a matter of equilibrium but contingency: the personal had to be worked on as a prerequisite to political action. How could you expect to take on revolutionary responsibilities if you couldn't relate to, understand and take care of yourself? Like the narrator of Robert M. Pirsig's bestseller *Zen and the Art of Motorcycle Maintenance* (1974), it was as if Rubin was trying to come to terms with, if not lay to rest, the 'ghost' of his earlier self.

In his review Lasch does not join in with Rubin's self-celebration. He reads *Growing Up* as a document of narcissism rather than a memoir of transformation. 'Narcissistic' might seem an obvious label for Rubin's mansplaining, self-aggrandising account of his 'journey', but Lasch used the word to mean 'more than a metaphorical term for self-absorption'. He draws on the psychoanalytic definition that presents narcissism as a personality type, a way of describing patients 'who "act-out" their conflicts instead of repressing or sublimating them'. The narcissist, Lasch explains, cultivates 'a protective shallowness in emotional relations'. They are defensive, but at the same time 'complain of a sense of inner emptiness'. They often suffer from hypochondria but equally 'entertain fantasies of omnipotence and a strong belief in the right to exploit others and be gratified'. Standing at the borderline between 'neurosis and psychosis', the 'pathological' narcissist is a tightly wound bundle of self-focused contradictions. They are 'ravenous for admiration' but 'contemptuous' of those who provide it; they are 'unappeasably hungry for emotional experiences with which to fill an inner void' but are terrified of acknowledging said void as the inevitable end of mortality.

Having outlined this diagnosis, Lasch turns his attention to narcissism as a cultural phenomenon, a sensibility that in his view has come to 'pervade "normal" everyday life'. Where Wolfe reflected on the social effects of an economic boom, Lasch links the 'collective narcissism' of modern America to a more pessimistic outlook: the failures, rather than the successes, of the post-war world. As a result, 'The Narcissist Society' offers a distinctly declinist view of the still developing 1970s with Lasch finding the period reeling from the body blows of the 1960s while simultaneously failing to live up to the 'soaring heroism' of its predecessor's already celebrated memory.[19]

A moment that summed up the thrust of the essay occurred in August 1974, when a post-Watergate Richard Nixon bowed out from his presidency ahead of a likely impeachment trial, boarded a helicopter on the White House lawn and, as Barbara Keys describes, paused briefly to 'incongruously' flash 'a victory sign'. Prior to this exit, Nixon had presided over an America struggling with a litany of disturbances inherited from the 1960s, including 'the riots, the New Left, the disruptions on college campuses' and the war in Vietnam. When his administration 'officially' brought the Vietnam conflict to an end in 1973, it was widely seen as a colossal waste of money, resources and lives; a war that had ultimately weakened rather than emboldened America's position on the world stage. Job losses, deindustrialisation, the 1973 oil crisis and the start of a debilitating recession had compounded this demoralisation on the domestic front. To cap it all, the reckless adventurism of Watergate had significantly damaged the public perception of political authority. As the middle of the decade came into view, there was little to feel victorious about. Nixon's widely broadcast departure as a 'disgraced' former president thus came to symbolise a mood of individual and social resignation. Fuelled by this disillusionment, Lasch argues, American culture embarked on a compensatory move towards 'purely personal satisfactions'. As Abbie Hoffman later put it, the 1970s became 'one long exhausted inhale'. Given the magnitude of the events that occurred in the decade, we might disagree with him that the 1970s 'didn't happen' and read Hoffman's cultural inhalation more as the prelude to a great sigh of denial. Lots happened during the American 1970s but because much of it was socially and politically traumatic, it was a temptingly easy option to pretend it *wasn't* happening.[20]

Hal Ashby distilled this mood of denial into *Shampoo* (1975), a film released the year after Nixon's departure and set in November 1968, on the night of the election that brought him to power. With a screenplay by Robert Towne and Warren Beatty, *Shampoo* features Beatty as George Roundy, a young, in-demand Beverly Hills hairdresser loosely based on the celebrity stylist Jay Sebring. Roundy draws in plenty of 'heads' to his boss' salon and is keen to strike out on his own, but these ambitions are stymied thanks to Roundy's relentless libido, which causes him to betray the trust of nearly everyone he knows. Mirroring the narcissism Lasch sees in the void-filling pursuits of the 37-year-old Jerry Rubin, the 34-year-old Roundy ultimately admits that his seductions have been one long attempt to 'live forever'. It is a rare moment of self-awareness from a character who otherwise exists in a world of 'protective shallowness'. He is 'great', the women he sleeps with are 'great', everything is 'great', but behind all this inconsequential ease, on unwatched television screens, the election continues. Meanwhile, occasional dispatches from far-off battlefields fade into background noise and the psychic collateral of the film's failed relationships, foreshortened ambitions and gnawing anxieties build up under a thin veneer of coiffured hair and expensive sunglasses.

Shampoo plays out to 'Wouldn't It Be Nice?' (1966) by The Beach Boys, a suitably bittersweet choice given the film's negative, hungover ending. However, if Ashby and company had wanted to use a more contemporaneous track, they could have gone for 'Looking for Space' by John Denver, the lead single from his *Windsong* (1975) album. This countrified power ballad finds Denver 'on the road of experience' trying to find his 'own way', far from all the 'sadness and screams'. Initially, it sounds as if he is yearning for an idealised homeland as in his hymn to West Virginia, 'Take Me Home, Country Roads' (1971), but the territory sought in 'Looking for Space' is not so much a destination as a state of mind. He wants to 'find out who I am', to 'know and understand' and to throw off his 'deep despair' by getting to a point where 'everything's clear'. In *Shampoo* Roundy is on a similar trajectory, but where Denver's song reaches towards a goal of self-discovery, the film's more ironic, if not satirical, lens presents this pursuit as basically selfish. In attempting to realise independence, Roundy gains a superficial freedom that sees him continually attend to his own satisfactions and restlessly extricate himself from anything akin to commitment or responsibility.

When he wrote 'Looking for Space', Denver was heavily involved with est, having taken the training in 1973, just after he turned 30. He would go on to sing Werner Erhard's praises on national television and dedicate *Windsong* to him, claiming that est gave him the 'confidence' to 'search for' and 'completely come to know myself'. 'Looking for Space' is a celebration of this self-regard. It is a song that takes delight in prioritising the 'I' and in so doing departs from the tone of Denver's prior work. His first major label release, *Rhymes and Reasons* (1969), contained some (brief) barbs directed at Nixon and his vice president Spiro Agnew. These 'Ballads' were not exactly the stuff of Bob Dylan, but they pointed, at least, to a modicum of political critique. 'Looking for Space' carries no trace of these contextual markers. It is a vacuum of a song, and its basic message of escapist betterment could apply to anyone, anywhere, which likely accounts for its popularity. However, for all their vagueness, Denver's lyrics do point somewhere: he is looking for *head* space, a private and inward centre that holds 'the sunshine and my dreams'. In the countercultural parlance of the 1960s, 'head space' meant a mindset or worldview, a way of seeing things; to define your head space was a way of telling people how you thought; of answering the question 'where you at?' You would need to enter a particular head space if you were about to join a protest march and potentially stare down a phalanx of police. By the middle 1970s, however, 'head space' had come to describe the fortress of solitude sought by Denver. Head space was the private interior, your inviolable centre of self; the place to which you might retreat for meditation, contemplation or 'me' time.[21]

For Christopher Lasch, this *volte face* signalled 'a growing despair of changing society – or even understanding it'. In contrast to Rubin's self-absorbed optimism, Lasch saw no evolutionary potential in such a shift. The 'inner void' of the narcissistic patient had come to define American society at large and rather than change the world, those who have grown up during a period of 'political turmoil' have turned to the alternative, private pleasure of changing themselves instead. Lasch was not describing an historical anomaly. 'The Narcissist Society' had previously materialised in other circumstances, under other names. It had made itself manifest in Weimar Germany in the 1920s, in *fin-de-siecle* Paris in the 1890s and across the long 18th century of Japan's Edo period, where the decadence of the city of Edo, later to be known as Tokyo, gave rise to the *Ukiyo* or 'floating world'. It was an evocative phrase, popularised by fictions and woodblock images that pulled back the veil on the indulgent, hedonistic culture of Yoshiwara, Edo's main *yukaku* or red-light district. To step into the 'floating world' meant to turn away from the business of the everyday and embrace the luxury of the transient moment. Along with the other pockets of excess that punctuate modernity, the 'floating world' was the preserve of an emergent urban class who reaped the benefits of a surrounding context defined by peace and relative affluence. Readers of *The Serial*, 'The "Me" Decade' and 'The Narcissist Society' could be forgiven for thinking that the floating world of the 1970s was to be found in the hot tubs of Marin County. Their appearance seemed to symbolise a similar slip into cultural languor: a state to which we might wish to gravitate in the short term, but which leads to a long game of ennui that is ultimately difficult to escape.[22]

*****

If hot tubs were one of the markers of Marin County's human potential explosion, then the Wellness Resource Center was a probable ground zero. According to Travis, the centre was the first business in the city to have one installed. It was down in the basement, lined (of course) in luxurious redwood and freely available to staff and clients. Although it is difficult to fully substantiate Travis' claim, an on-site tub was certainly a key part of his all-encompassing programme. It was a way of ministering to the physical needs of his clients who, after attending to their psychological well-being in the group meetings and visualisation sessions, could go down to the basement for some stress-relieving deep relaxation.

In between, Travis would be analysing his clients' lifestyles, their 'work habits', 'physical activities' and particularly their diets. He recommended a broadly vegetarian or pollotarian diet that was low on sugar and full of raw vegetables, fresh fruits and unprocessed foods. Adding bran was good for 'bulk' while 'vitamins B, C, and E' and minerals from natural sources like yeast were key supplements. When developing these nutrition plans, Travis' aim was to increase his clients' energy levels and to help them avoid illness. As with his promotion of physical fitness and aerobic exercise, he had in mind the continuing dangers of a largely sedentary lifestyle and its link to 'the number one cause of death in the U.S.', coronary heart disease. It was a concern that by 1977 stood in sync with government guidance following the publication of the select committee report *Dietary Goals for the United States*. The report detailed rising levels of malnourishment and obesity all wrapped up in an enabling culture saturated with images of fast foods and the joys of immediate gratification. Its sobering statistics included the breakdown of a typical American diet *circa* 1976 which included 125 pounds of fat, 100 pounds of sugar and 295 cans of soda per year. As the Chair of the committee, Senator George McGovern, put it: 'eating patterns of this century represent as critical a public health concern as any now before us'. Echoing Travis' advice, the report recommended an increase in the consumption of poultry, fish and complex carbohydrates (whole grains and pulses) and a reduction in the consumption of fat, saturated fat, cholesterol, sugar and salt.[23]

Travis was not advocating for healthy eating as an end in itself, nor as a means of achieving only short-term weight loss. Rather, he was attempting to foreground the social norms that underpinned this damaging cultural relationship with food. He wanted to help his clients see beyond brand loyalty and really get to grips with the role of different dietary groups and the effects of additives, preservatives and emulsifiers. It was an education drive that also extended to the wider structure of large-scale food production processes. In the 1900s, he argued, 'fruit, vegetables and grain' accounted for 40 per cent of the typical diet. By the mid-1970s this proportion had dropped to a mere 20 per cent. It was a decline that had little to do with scarcity and more do to with a toxic combination of habit and profit margins. America continued to produce vast amounts of grain across the 1970s but, as Travis was keen to point out, 78 per cent of it became cattle feed. It was being added to the cocktail of growth-producing hormones, pesticides and chemical foods used in the beef industry. The result was a pernicious cycle of misdirected resources and overproduction in which the mass consumption of steaks, burgers and processed sausages fed into a nationwide rise in cholesterol, the very health crisis that the country's massive grain mountains could have been used to alleviate.

Individual psychology also played a role in this analysis. Travis would probe his clients' family backgrounds, their work patterns and daily routines to discern any motivations towards overeating or self-denial. Understanding how and why we eat was for Travis just as important as reflecting on what we eat. If a client was buying fast food for convenience and joining the ranks of those helping coffee to dethrone milk as America's number one drink, Travis would zero in on the need for that convenience and caffeinated pep. What was causing this lack of time? Work-related stress? If so, a nutrition plan alone would not be enough to help. The clients' stress triggers would have to be worked on as well. At this point 'biofeedback' would come into play.

'Biofeedback' is a blanket term for the electronic monitoring of body functions previously labelled 'involuntary': 'the brain, the heart, the circulatory system'. Originally developed in 1958 as a way of using an electroencephalogram (EEG) to monitor and maintain alpha brainwaves, biofeedback was purported to offer 'a technological route to self-awareness'. For Travis the value of the technique lay in its application to the preventative treatment of stress, anxiety, tension and migraine headaches. By using the audio-visual outputs from an EEG and an array of other devices including an electromyogram that monitored muscle tension, a thermal trainer than detected changes in skin temperature (a 'function of blood flow') and an electrodermal response censor that observed changes in skin resistance (a function of perspiration), Travis could generate a map of his clients' invisible systems. He would then mark off the peaks of tension from the troughs of relaxation, so as to advise on breathing methods and meditation techniques to help them gain 'voluntary control' over deviations from the body's homeostatic state. In cases involving stress-related eating, biofeedback analysis could thus minister to the physical effects of stress that instigated the psychological pull towards unbalanced and unhealthy diets. Travis saw such issues as clearly interrelated and so, by helping clients to relax, to know their triggers and to ease their experiences of tension, the scene would be set for nutritional improvement. Eating well would then feed back into the ongoing well-being of the entire regulatory system.

Overall, Travis' wellness programme was a comprehensive package that required a significant commitment of time and money. The full eight-month course of assessments, individual sessions and group meetings cost $1,500 (equivalent today to around $6,500), and Travis likened the undertaking to that of a master's degree. The centre could accommodate up to 80 programme members and by 1977 some clients were travelling upwards of 100 miles to attend their weekly meetings. Despite this popularity, Travis did not take on all comers. All potential clients had to go through a rigorous preliminary and pre-programme assessment that typically started with a phone call.

A counsellor would talk through the caller's questions, providing information about the wellness centre, and most of these enquiries would be referred on to other, more specialised treatment-based resources in the community: physicians, psychiatrists and physiotherapists. For those who heard the centre's pitch and thought it was for them, an appointment would be arranged. Those who kept the appointment would then be asked to work through a three-and-a-half-hour evaluation. This included 'the Health Hazard Appraisal, a medical history questionnaire, a life-change index and purpose in life test, a computerized dietary inventory, a vision questionnaire and a nutrition/health/activity profile'. The results of these assessments would be used to plan out a programme of general wellness counselling, biofeedback sessions and lifestyle evaluations. This could involve a series of one-off meetings or a schedule that extended into the full eight-month programme. In each case, Travis was not trying to sell a single package. Rather, he was tailoring his services to the specific needs of the client.

Despite this precision, a course at the centre could easily be seen as a purely self-indulgent pursuit, particularly when the 'Personal Style Consultations' got going in the redwood room. Linked to the Lifestyle Evolution Group, the consultations would involve clients standing in front of the room's full-length mirror and talking through their appearance: their clothes, their hair and their body image. The idea was to raise self-esteem and connect the prospect of a makeover to the goals discussed in the evolution group. You could start to change your life, the consultants suggested, by dressing for success, looking the part and taking control of the image you projected to the world. Although positive and affirmative, the consultation was exactly the kind of exercise that would have confirmed Lasch and Wolfe's account of a culture slipping into self-regard. What clearer evidence could there be of a narcissistic mood than an afternoon of celebratory mirror-gazing down at the Wellness Resource Center? Travis' comparison of his programme to a master's degree struck a similar note. He would play out the analogy in full when his clients 'graduated' from the course and received a 'Grand Certificate' entitling them 'to the degree of Wonderful Person'. The certificate carried no official accreditation, instead it announced the clients as masters of 'me'; it awarded them a diploma in 'yourself'.[24]

✱✱✱✱✱

Parodies came quick, even before *The Serial* gave the Wellness Resource Center a cameo. In 1975 Travis shared a prototype of *The Wellness Index* with staff at the Department of Health Services Research at his old alma mater, the USPHS Hospital in Baltimore. Members of the computer division promptly responded with a spoof of the questionnaire that Travis gamely called 'The Wellness Antidote'. Questions under the headings of 'Productivity, Relaxation and Sleep' and 'creativity, Self-Expression' were rewritten by 'the guys' into such hilarious *bons mots* as 'I enjoy goofing off' and 'I like myself because

I'm so irresistible'. The presumption was that wellness, this message of alternative health arriving in Baltimore from Marin County, was a largely pointless and ineffectual endeavour that sought only to give self-absorption a pseudo-intellectual justification. By her own admission, McFadden built *The Serial* on the same basic 'joke'. Some years after its publication she reflected that while some Marinites gave the novel a frosty reception, her British readers 'received [it] warmly and kept on buying it'. She liked to think this was because the British were 'so discerning, with such sophisticated taste' but in retrospect, she admits, *The Serial* more likely reinforced the British 'suspicion that Californians are all self-obsessed airheads'.

It was a suspicion that had already been aired by the likes of Alexander Frater in *The Sunday Times Magazine* and the British novelist David Lodge, author of the campus satire *Changing Places* (1975). Lodge would later become an enthusiastic reader of *The Serial* and it is easy to see why when we think of one of the main characters of *Changing Places*, Morris Zapp. A literature professor at California's State University of Euphoria, Zapp is the polar opposite of his transatlantic counterpart Philip Swallow, a lecturer at the University of Rummidge, based on Lodge's own academic stomping ground, the University of Birmingham. Where Swallow is a self-deprecating, unremarked-upon generalist with a handful of essays to his name, Zapp is a go-getting, overbearing, unquestionably successful 40-year-old. With 'five fiendishly clever books' published 'by the time he was thirty' and having 'achieved the rank of full professor at the same precocious age', he embodies the all the confidence and self-assurance of the West Coast's 'Euphoric State'. As the novel opens, we are meant to find him insufferable. That said, the satire of *The Serial* as well as Travis' sabotaged questionnaire was not so much anti-Californian as anti-wellness. They each take as their target the idea of a self-led, aspirational approach to well-being that exceeds any discernible physical symptoms.[25]

Although the points of reference were different, this more specific attitude was also detectable in parallel British fictions, as in the case of David Nobbs' comic novel *The Death of Reginald Perrin* (1975). Where Lodge looked west from redbrick Rummidge to sunny

California and back again, and McFadden had her smart professionals go further still, out from San Francisco to Marin County, Nobbs' novel remained firmly within the psychological and geographic landscapes of England. If anything, he had his characters head in the opposite direction to those of *The Serial*, from the pacifying comfort of suburbia deep into London's depressing urban zone of train stations and office blocks. The novel begins with Reginald Iolanthe Perrin, a 46-year-old sales executive at Sunshine Desserts, setting off for work from his Neo-Georgian house in sedate Climthorpe. It's June, the sky is blue, but Reggie feels *rough*: he's got a thunderous headache, his legs feel heavy, and he keeps getting the shivers. It could just be a summer flu, but Reggie suspects something else, something he can't quite put his finger on.

What he does know is that he is miserable. He is unsatisfied, out of sorts and has been for a while. Everyday he lopes anxiously towards the station to catch the 8.16 to London Waterloo which is, invariably, late. Often, Nobbs tells us, when the train finally arrives, Reggie stands on the platform, clutches his briefcase with its embossed initials (R.I.P.) and tries to resist the urge to throw himself under the wheels. When he is at work, Perrin has no energy for the job, he dislikes his colleagues, has no respect for his boss and spends most of the time fantasising about his secretary. Arriving at the office, Perrin goes to see the company physician, Doc Morrissey, who runs through the basics. Reggie's temperature is fine, he has no chest pains, his eyes, tongue and reflexes are all okay. There does not seem to be anything *physically* wrong with him. 'Have you been feeling listless and lazy?' Doc Morrissey asks, gently moving away from the possibility of flu:

Unable to concentrate? Lost your zest for living? Lots of headaches? Falling asleep during *Play for Today*? Can't finish the crossword like you used to? Nasty taste in the mornings? Keep thinking about naked sportswomen?

'Yes, I have. That's exactly how I've been feeling,' says Reggie with relief. 'It's funny. So have I,' replies Doc Morrissey. 'I wonder what it is?' Their conversation peters out. Doc Morrissey gives him two aspirins.[26]

It is a neat joke, one that perfectly encapsulates the combination of sympathy and ridicule that Nobbs generates for Reggie, his middle-class everyman on the brink of a nervous breakdown. Depending on your view, the rest of the novel finds Perrin variously holding off this long-coming crisis or otherwise playing out its logic to the furthest degree. Either way, his meeting with Doc Morrissey is a turning point. Soon after, Reggie engineers a coastal pseudo-cide that allows him to disappear, to dispense with all the drudge and start again on his own terms. So intoxicating is the relief – if not joy – felt by Reggie as he rids himself of one life and steps into another that to 'do a Reggie Perrin' has since become a virtual mantra for all those dreamers, fugitives and errant canoeists contemplating a total reboot. When the novel became the sitcom *The Fall and Rise of Reginald Perrin* (1976) its title sequence showed Leonard Rossiter, the perfect Perrin, throwing everything off on the beach at West Bay, Dorset, as if he was shedding his skin. It is hard to watch this and not think of MP John Stonehouse, who did something similar in Miami in 1974. By contrast, though, Stonehouse had run out of options. He was fleeing spying accusations, a raft of failing businesses and tried to fake his death as a last resort. By contrast Perrin's was the braver, grander and more future-facing project. Although not without self-ishness given the distress it (initially) causes to his family, Nobbs frames the act as a life-affirming flight from the uneasy ordinary in the hope of carving out something better.

For Doc Morrissey, though, there is nothing exceptional or aspirational about Reggie's instigating 'malaise'. Reflecting on his patient, Morrissey later catalogues a familiar set of causes, ones that also underscore his own gnawing disquiet: 'Middle age. Insecurity. Anxiety'. The only difference between the two of them, Morrissey concludes, is that Reggie is less able to deal with it all: he is 'going mad'. John Travis would regard Doc Morrissey as the consummate 'pill fairy'. Deeply wedded to the treatment model, he simply throws painkillers at any and all problems, thereby pathologising Reggie's 'insecurity' as nothing more than a chemical imbalance. Labelling him 'mad' compounds this dismissal. It is an easy, familiar term that obscures far more than it describes. It suggests that Reggie's mental bad weather is the underlying cause of his 'anxiety' rather than a symptom. Such a diagnosis relieves Doc Morrissey of the need to acknowledge the environmental, social, cultural and personal factors that Travis would have considered essential if assessing the health of someone like Perrin. Morrissey focuses on what is wrong with his patient, not – to select just one variable – what is wrong with the workplace that causes him so much dread. It is an attitude indicative of the 'rise of mass-market, prescription-driven psychiatry' that by the time Nobbs was writing had largely relegated the primary theme of his novel, the 'nervous breakdown', to the margins of public health.[27]

The nervous breakdown emerged from the industrial engine-room of America's late 19th century as a way of talking about 'the stress of modern life'. We all have 'a set amount of nerve force', explained George Miller Beard in *American Nervousness* (1881), and this is easily depleted by the acceleration of 'modern civilization'. The 'breakdown' – something of an automotive metaphor at this stage – comes when we can no longer keep up with the pace, when we need respite and time to recharge. In this way, 'the nervous breakdown was not a medical condition but a sociological one'. It served as a bold reaction to the pressure of modernity, not a description of a personal weakness. As the idea gained international currency across the 1920s and 1930s, a breakdown was a signal that life's demands were too much: 'You weren't crazy; the world was.' In this way, the non-specific, ambiguously defined nervous breakdown was an almost heroic slamming on of the brakes, a way of signalling that among all the energy-sapping trials of the everyday, you were 'still functioning' and had within you 'the material for recovery'. However, this all changed with the later-20th-century arrival of specialised, individually focused diagnoses. Diseases like 'major depressive disorder', 'generalised anxiety disorder' and 'obsessive compulsive disorder' replaced the 'catchall' commonality of the nervous breakdown. Such precision was not without benefit to those in receipt of specialised care, but as Jerry Useem describes, the language and methodology of professional psychiatry normalised a medication-oriented focus on 'our personal moods and thoughts'. Gone was the reflective inditement of the surrounding 'economic and social circumstances'. The deficiency now lay with the individual. You were the problem and you needed to be 'fixed', not recharged. Hence Doc Morrissey dismissing Reggie Perrin with a couple of aspirins. Despite all the manifold pressures of life that seem to afflict them both, it is Perrin, the alleged madman, who appears out of step, who seems in need of a panacea and, unlike all the other commuters, office workers and company executives, seems to be singularly unable to cope.[28]

Were Doc Morrissey to look out of the window or pick up a newspaper, however, he would have seen a Britain very much in need of a nervous breakdown. 'Is Everybody Going Mad?' asked the *Daily Mirror* in a headline from December 1973 as the energy crisis took hold, the three-day week came into view and the country seemed on the edge of a socio-political abyss of shortages, strikes and unemployment. As Lawrence Black describes, the period generated an almost 'apocalyptic talk of decline' as politicians and tabloid journalists surveyed the sorry state of Britain 'on the slide'. The anxiety was compounded in 1976, the year that *Reginald Perrin* was first broadcast, when the government went 'cap in hand' to the International Monetary Fund and asked for the largest ever loan, a sum of nearly $4 billion, to deal with the effects of stagflation. As with New York's fiscal bailout the year before, public spending was heavily curtailed under the weight of such a debt. If joining the common market had dented Britain's imaginary sense of global primacy in 1973, going begging to Washington three years later made the humiliation even worse.[29]

For those wanting to pin their pessimism to a single emblematic event, London's ever-reliable Institute of Contemporary Arts was on hand with a ready-made exercise in public outrage. In October 1976 it staged 'Prostitution', an exhibition by COUM Transmissions, a performance group that included the former students, hippies, commune dwellers and now grant-winning artists Genesis P-Orridge and Cosey Fanni Tutti. 'Prostitution' was an exploration of abjection that featured pornography, used tampons and the public debut of COUM Transmissions' next incarnation, the 'anti-music' band Throbbing Gristle. Conservative MP Nicholas Fairbairn did not like it, and he famously launched a castigating broadside questioning the exhibition's receipt of public money during a time of deep recession. In so doing, he gave the miasma of decline its very own culprits. The economic and moral bankruptcy of the country had now been made fully manifest in the bankruptcy of culture, and this dire situation was the fault of people like P-Orridge and company, the so-called 'Wreckers of Civilisation'. All the while the acceleration-ism of work and its exhausting bookend, the commute, rattled on unabated, with Perrins across the country travelling from station to station in thick clouds of dread. Had Nobbs written Perrin as a tube traveller, he may well have traversed the stretch between Ladbroke Grove and Westbourne Park, where a masterpiece of graffiti by the post-situationist collective King Mob appeared sometime in the early 1970s. Plastered across the walls of the siding where the under-ground briefly surfaced, designed to mimic the rhythms of the train itself, the message pulled off that rare feat, a near-telepathic reflec-tion of the mindset occupied by its audience: 'SAME THING DAY AFTER DAY – TUBE – WORK – DINNER – WORK – TUBE – ARMCHAIR – TV – SLEEP – TUBE – WORK – HOW MUCH MORE CAN YOU TAKE – ONE IN TEN GO MAD – ONE IN FIVE CRACKS UP'. Judging by such numbers, Perrin was clearly not the odd one out in this socio-economic pressure cooker. Nor was his the only British sitcom to deal with moments of personal crisis in the 1970s.[30]

In 1975 the BBC launched Bob Larbey and John Esmonde's *The Good Life*, which ran until 1978, virtually in parallel with the *Fall and Rise of Reginald Perrin*. Featuring Richard Briers and Felicity Kendal as Tom and Barbara Good, it focused on their attempts to find 'it' – not the mysterious goal of est, but a way of 'breaking the circle'. Tom is a tired, arrogant, newly 40-year-old draftsman who is stuck in a rut. He has no desire to climb the corporate ladder but is acutely aware that his younger colleagues will soon replace him. Before they do and before, as he puts it, any more nails are hammered into his coffin, Tom wants to really 'accomplish' something. He wants to step away from the circuit of going to work to make money to buy things which inevitably run out, thus requiring him to go to work again to make more money to replace them. As an alternative, he dumps the job and cajoles Barbara into attempting a life of self-sufficiency in their middle-class suburb of Surbiton. They can take such a leap because, despite the vague hints of financial risk in the first episode, they are otherwise free of responsibilities. They have no children, Barbara has no career of her own to give up, and their massive house a mere twenty-minute drive from central London has miraculously long been paid for on the back of Tom's single wage. With this debt-free material safety net in place they can pretty much do what they want. There's no landlord or housemates to tell them they can't buy that goat. It is not *Rising Damp*.

On the surface, *The Good Life* is just that: a cosy comedy that has none of the depression, cynicism or pseudocide of *Reginald Perrin*, just the trials and tribulations of keeping a smallholding while the snooty neighbours look on. But put aside all the jokes about cow dung and pigs in labour and the same stream of discontent starts to bubble to the surface. However much *The Good Life* might appear to be a hymn to the joys of the allotment, it not only radiates with restless despondency but in its framing of the Goods and their project it also reflects much of the diagnosis Doc Morrissey doled out to Perrin. While it is the 'middle-aged blues' that make Tom want to change, once he and Barbara commit themselves to 'the work of life itself' it is as if the crisis blossoms into a stereotypical nervous breakdown. They dance in the goldfish pond at 3am, sell all their possessions, turn their property into something halfway between a farm and a menagerie and generally regress into a semi-feral, semi-childlike existence. In response to such antics, neighbour and company man Jerry calls them 'lunatics', 'mad' and 'totally insane' and the audience is invited to agree. Much of the comedy comes from the well-intentioned folly of the Goods, their lack of money, their pitiful crop yields, their attachment to animals they should at some point be eating: the very fact that they're just not very good at what they're trying to do. Their situation, while not without the occasional victory, is meant to be a comedic aberration from the norm and the message of the show basically boils down to a reiteration of Jerry's jibe: you would have to be mad to do this.

'Mad' is such a generalised term that it does little more than label Tom and Barbara as harmless English eccentrics, but therein lies the problem. As with Morrissey's dismissal of Perrin, the word absolves us of the need to take them seriously. There's a gentleness to *The Good Life* but its affectionate mockery allows us to breezily disregard the importance of contemplating a similar change in our own lives or even reflecting on the reasons why such a change might be necessary. Thanks to its charm, we might fail to realise that there's something disturbingly Ballardian about a man suddenly chucking in his job before taking a heavyweight, smoke-spewing rotary cultivator to his beautifully manicured lawn. Lest we forget the type of problems Perrin and the Goods are trying to avoid, we might also look back to *Abigail's Party*. Part of the *Play for Today* series that Perrin falls asleep to, its characters could easily be found in Climthorpe just as much as Surbiton. They try to keep a lid on the same insecurities too, although Mike Leigh lets none of them try out another way of life. And so, at the end of the play, after the smart social satire has burnt itself out, we're left with a group in disarray, a relationship fractured and the sight of Beverly weeping as the stress of it all finally gets to Laurence, and he dies of a heart attack on the sitting room floor.[31]

It was precisely this kind of foreshortened end that Travis and Ardell argued the wellness lifestyle could help people avoid. Travis unambiguously placed 'premature death' at the far left-hand side of the 'Illness-Wellness Continuum', to signpost that such a termination was the likely outcome of a negative drift away from the positive, gravitational pull of 'growth'. He did not need King Mob to tell him that the social norms of the 1970s that gave rise to lives spent 'moving from bed to table to car to elevator to car to table to TV to bed' hastened this end. When writing *High Level Wellness*, Ardell was also mindful of the difficult socio-economic surroundings affecting him and his American readers: 'high unemployment and runaway inflation, long gas lines, "malaise"'. For both practitioners, wellness was not a way of withdrawing from this fractious world but a means of supporting and improving yourself within it. Travis and

Ardell did not take a declinist view of the 1970s, nor did they deca-dently luxuriate in the self while society imploded. Their outlook was similar to that offered by historians Barbara Keys, Jack Davies and Elliott Bannan, that of the American 1970s as a 'post-traumatic decade'.[32]

According to this reading, the combined impacts of economic shock, governmental crisis and foreign policy disaster gave the 1970s a character 'shaped by a search for recovery after trauma', what Keys *et al.* clarify as a quest for 'a new equilibrium and a revived sense of what America stood for in a changing world'. The presidency of Jimmy Carter was an important public signal of this re-evaluation. He took office in 1976 after a campaign fuelled by promises of honesty and integrity. Carter was the anti-Nixon, someone who could confidently say 'I am not a crook' and have people believe him. As well as restoring faith in the country's leadership, this new admin-istration also faced the massive task of stabilising the nation's energy problems, not just the ongoing oil crisis but also America's depend-ence on international sources of natural gas. Carter's approach to establishing this 'new equilibrium' was to argue for a spirit of restraint and 'individual sacrifice for the common good'. His inaugu-ration speech of January 1977 reminded Americans that 'more is not necessarily "better"', adding that their 'great Nation has its recognised limits'. As such 'we can neither answer all questions nor solve all problems'. These were not the words of a football coach igniting a pregame spark; Carter sounded more like an expectation-managing teacher trying to get a class of boisterous but untalented students to scrape through an exam: 'We cannot afford to do everything [...] we must simply do our best'.[33]

Such conciliatory but low-wattage sentiments would likely have grated with Travis and particularly Ardell. Aside from Halbert Dunn, Ardell's other great intellectual inspiration was the agnostic and orator Robert Green Ingersoll, a dominant figure in America's freethought movement of the mid- to late 19th century. Ingersoll railed against the limiting social conventions of religion with its promises of heaven and the threats of hell. Instead of living a life of constraint in the hope of a reward only at the end of it all, he encouraged his audiences to 'enjoy today, not regretting yesterday, not fearing tomorrow'. His was not a message of hedonism but exuberance, a call to 'suck the orange of life dry', saying to death when it comes 'you are welcome to the peelings, what little there was we have enjoyed'. Almost a century later, Ardell was thinking of 'high level wellness' and 'health' in similar terms. The former was a 'lifestyle-focused approach which you design for the purpose of pursing the highest level of health within your capability', while the latter, the 'dynamic' outcome of such a pursuit, was a matter of physical, mental and emotional 'freedom'. Physical freedom was 'freedom from pain and limiting illness', what Ardell termed 'a state of well-being', while the 'mental aspect of health' was 'freedom from selfishness and aimlessness', a 'state of compassion and purpose'. Each of these states overlapped with 'the emotional component of health', which he defined as 'freedom from disabling stress and excess passion', a mindset of 'serenity and calm' and, in terms most redolent of Ingersoll, the possession of a real 'zest for living'.

Travis echoed this view, describing wellness as dynamic, in the double sense of it being an ongoing process with 'no end point' as well as potentially operating as a socio-cultural dynamo. 'Wellness', he explained, 'is an efficient channelling of energy – energy received from the environment, transformed within you, and sent on to affect the world outside'. Offering wellness as a lifestyle thus held out the possibility of widespread change, not just the personal develop-ment of a singular practising individual. It could act as a catapult of community health, with the interactive dynamism Travis describes spreading the mutually beneficial 'zest' into the rhythms of everyday life. If the 1970s were to move on from its trauma, then 'simply', moderately and austerely doing one's best was not enough. Travis and Ardell would argue there were greater rewards to be had and higher targets to reach via a lifestyle that challenged you to always do 'better'.[34]

To return to Abraham Maslow's language, Travis and Ardell were outlining a distinctly eupsychian perspective in which the trans-formation of the person feeds into the transformation of society. However, neither were advocating 'the deification of the isolated self' that Peter Marin warned against in 'The New Narcissism'. Ardell was aware of these criticisms, citing both Marin's article in *High Level Wellness* as well as Theodore Roszak's comments that the mid-1970s interest in encounter groups and consciousness-raising represented 'the biggest introspective binge any society in history has undergone'. He writes that he is keen to avoid the 'debate' raised by these comments, but elsewhere in the book, Ardell quietly but distinctly distances himself from Esalen and the wider human potential milieu. Esalen is discussed as part of an opening survey of wellness practitioners, but Ardell strikes a somewhat wary, if not sceptical, tone. He calls it an 'educational laboratory and personal growth centre' and quotes their emphasis on 'the potentialities and values of human existence', but despite him noting the impressive roster of international speakers and making the obligatory reference to the spectacular location, he seems to find it all a bit flaky, as if there is no real focus among its manifold offerings. He does not give Esalen a bad review, exactly, but the conclusion to his brief overview is hardly the stuff that ringing endorsements are made of:

> If your interest in wellness tends to emphasise pleasuring, natural beauty, a range of programs from which to choose, and a nonideological program, Esalen might be the kind of place that could be of value in your own evolution.

'If', 'might' and 'could': such conditional language is rare in *High Level Wellness*, a book that otherwise hums with Ardell's confidence and positivity.

In contrast, it is the Wellness Resource Center that gets the gold star precisely because of its discipline 'in encouraging self-responsibility' and its rigour in 'facilitating the client's efforts to comprehend root causes of problems'. As Ardell saw it, Travis would assist clients in becoming 'experts in themselves' by putting the full array of his programme at their disposal. They were not tourists but equal partners in this enterprise. In exchange for their commitment Travis would invest in their development by helping them to relax, to interact with others and to remove personal, psychological, and physical blockages to continuous growth. Among the payoffs for engaging in this circuit of self-care was a 'greater sense of self-worth and self-acceptance' and an ability to 'express your emotions and feeling states'. Where Esalen was, in Ardell's estimation, little more than a holiday spot, Travis' operation was all about 'hard work'.[35]

＊＊＊＊＊

'Your wellness journey has begun,' says the serene counsellor Yao to the beleaguered romance novelist Frances Welty at the start of Liane Moriarty's *Nine Perfect Strangers*. Frances has arrived at Tranquillum House tired and vulnerable, reeling from the double whammy of a personal and professional crisis. She is full of angst and self-loathing, and deeply cynical about the very idea of a wellness 'journey'. It is a view that Moriarty's novel goes on to affirm once the psychotropic smoothies start to flow. But just for a moment, at this early stage of the proceedings, we get a glimpse of a deeply beneficial human encounter. Yao is tending to a papercut on Frances' thumb and as he holds her hand, she finds herself close to tears. There is nothing sexual in the air, it is simply one person taking care of another. Frances' carefully constructed defences begin to ease, and she starts to share her feelings, as much to herself as to Yao: 'I've actually been feeling *very* unwell lately.' Yao's response carries no judgement, no criticism, no disregard. It is an uncomplicated, understanding and thus deeply comforting response: 'I know you have.'[36]

If there is anything narcissistic about this moment of empathy, then it is the type of narcissism that recalls a buried, telling, detail in the version of the myth recounted by the Roman poet Ovid. In his 1st-century opus *Metamorphoses*, Ovid has the young hunter Narcissus flee the non-reciprocal mimicry of the nymph Echo before he catches his reflection in a glistening pool. As he looks down at the reflection, Narcissus thinks he sees someone else. It is certainly a spectacle of self-regard and Narcissus is drawn by a sense of similitude, but at the same time it is self-worship by default. Initially, Narcissus does not see the image as a reflection. He is drawn towards his double out of a desire to connect with another. Where

Lasch, Wolfe and other commentators took this myth and its psychological afterlife to describe a new culture of selfishness, it equally works the other way round, pointing to what was distinctive about wellness as a specific project within this era. The image crystallises the emotional charge that hovers at the margins of ostensibly critical novels like *Nine Perfect Strangers* and which Travis, Ardell and their colleagues placed at the centre of their practice: we are social beings. We need to connect with others. We are drawn to one another and actively seek out contact with one another. No one is an island.[37]

By 1975 groups like Synanon were floating off into their own oceans of separation, having rebranded themselves a 'church for religious purposes' rather than a 'therapeutic community'. Wellness, by contrast, was going inside: not to the black hole of the self, but to calm, companionable yet committed spaces like Travis' Redwood Room, which bore witness to the communality, support and growth of the Wellness Resource Center. If there was a possibility of an island in the 1970s, one that could offer a better life and a healthier way of being, it was more likely to be found in one of these rooms than out to sea or in the solitary depths of the inner ocean. Like the island that bubbles up from the sentient planet at the end of Tarkovsky's *Solaris*, these outcrops, surrounded by the tides of a difficult world, did not promise an escape to an elsewhere. There were other clifftop locales and cults of personality wating to oblige if you wanted such a removal. Rather, these islands of the well returned you to yourself; the self you did not know you had forgotten. In so doing your value to others was reaffirmed and a pathway to even greater gains was laid out.[38]

CHAPTER VII

Body Snatchers
1977–1979

'Dr Janov said he should Scream, and often, and he saw at once an island in his mind.' In his novel *Beatlebone* (2014), Kevin Barry imagines John Lennon attempting a return trip to Dorinish in 1978. Lennon briefly visited the island in 1967 soon after he acquired it, and then again with Yoko Ono in 1968. This was before he offered Dorinish to Sid Rawle, when he was still toying with the idea of somehow making it his home. After that, there is little to no evidence that he ever went again. The Tribe of the Sun bravely stuck it out until 1972, but Lennon never followed through with his idea of putting a Romany caravan on the island or building an elaborate, self-sufficient house there.

Lennon was not feeling himself in 1978. He was in the middle of his 'so-called "househusband period"', having announced his 'retirement' from music and public life in 1976 to focus on his family. He did travel in 1978 but not to Clew Bay. There were trips to Japan and Hawaii, but Lennon spent much of the year in New York, holed up in the Dakota Building with Ono, caring for their son Sean while reading Thaddeus Golas' *The Lazy Man's Guide to Enlightenment* (1971–72). His sixth solo album, *Rock n' Roll*, came out in 1975 along with the compilation *Shaved Fish*, but it would be 1980 before Lennon and Ono had another major label release with *Double Fantasy*. Depending on which biography you read, these five years away from the limelight were either a long overdue domestic respite or a paranoid, agoraphobic hiatus in which Lennon restlessly prowled the Dakota, trying to escape the creative doldrums.

Beatlebone places 'John' between these polarities, with Barry describing his life in New York as a chamber drama of Polanski-esque angst. It is easy to think of a gender-switched *Rosemary's Baby* when he writes that John 'doesn't leave the apartment much' with 'the baby' to look after, the bread to make and a growing interest in the occult to feed. The Dakota provides a 'tidy' life of womb-like security but over the course of a bravura two-page paragraph Barry tactically picks away at the seams. We are told that John makes 'lots of plans', smokes incessantly, starts to drift into nervy insomnia and swerves manically from fizzing levels of energy to a tank-empty 'zero'. He starts to 'have a thing about the elevator' and finds all manner of 'strange thoughts' coming 'unbidden', all the while humming, cooing and burping the baby.[1]

It is a scene of wired exhaustion that any new parent could identify with, but Barry's description also echoes the 'confusion, fatigue, agitation, alternations in mood [and] hyperactivity' associated more specifically with post-partum psychosis. In the 1970s and into the 1980s, post-natal depressive disorders occupied an ambiguous diagnostic position, ranging from the assumption that the 'Baby Blues' were a short-term rite of passage for any new mother, to studies of more extreme, longer-lasting psychotic states. James Hamilton's *Postpartum Psychiatric Problems* (1962) had made a robust case for the condition to be seen as a specific depressive syndrome, a point reflected in the 1968 *Diagnostic and Statistical Manual* which listed 'Psychosis with Childbirth' as a separate clinical entity. By the time of the third edition in 1980, however, the illness had been relegated back under the generalised umbrella of 'manic depression' and its variants. Meanwhile, John Travis, no doubt reflecting further on his own 'Capricorn Incident', was increasingly making a case for what he called 'Male Postpartum Abandonment Syndrome', which he argued was part of the pathology of the nuclear family and a primary cause of the 'epidemic of disappearing dads'.[2]

Despite the resonance of its language, *Beatlebone* does not tarry with the diagnostic politics of the personal experience it describes. Instead, filtered through the biographical lens of Important Man and Musician John Lennon, the domestic situation becomes a tense, if not heroic, struggle between the seemingly opposed axes of fatherhood and creativity. John has everything he wants, and his 'retirement' has brought him everything he intended, but in Barry's telling the overall feeling is one of moribund satisfaction. Stuck in a cloying, insulated bubble of 'Baby spew' and 'sour milk', 'bone dry' in terms of songs, 'John' finds himself so 'happy' that 'he wants to Scream'. Add to this the still-bubbling emotional undertow of his childhood in Liverpool, the expectant public pressure from legions of Beatles fans and 'pressmen', as well as the fast-approaching menace of a 40th year, and the result is a matrix of crisis that appears to pervade John's past, present and future.

Barry is broadly accurate in his portrayal of Lennon's late-1970s state of mind, at least as far as one can judge from the biographies, the interviews and the music. He also captures Lennon's preoccupation with the idea of escaping public attention, a drive that initially fuelled his interest in Dorinish. According to Rawle, when they were discussing the stewardship of the island in 1970, Lennon spoke about the Diggers with no small amount of envy. That Rawle and his friends were able to step away from a media circus like Hippiedilly and go elsewhere with apparent ease was virtually unthinkable for the mega-famous Lennon. 'There's nowhere in the whole of this world where I could go that they can't find me', he ruefully noted. It is not clear who 'they' are in this instance, and it is admittedly hard to sympathise with Lennon's apparent lack of privacy given that he was living in Tittenhurst Park at the time, a palatial Berkshire mansion set in its own extensive grounds. Despite this, Lennon's desire to be both in the world and apart from it persisted. In April 1973, during his attempts to secure permanent residency in America, he and Ono announced the 'birth of a conceptual country, NUTOPIA', a nowhere that had 'no land, no boundaries, no passports, only people'. Designating themselves as Nutopian 'ambassadors', they asked for recognition and 'diplomatic immunity' in the United States. On one level 'Nutopia' reflected the universalising optimism of 'Imagine' (1971). It was a Dada-esque experiment in humanistic thinking that attempted to cut through the divisive ideas of borders and nationalities using blank flags and silent 'International' anthems, as 'heard' on Lennon's album *Mind Games* (1973). On another it was a publicly petulant response on the part of two artists who were so used to hearing 'yes'. When faced with a country and a politicised bureaucracy that said 'no' (Lennon had been denied a Green Card earlier in the year), they simply set about creating a country of their own.[3]

Writing in *Beatlebone*, Barry puts aside Lennon's activist tussles with Nixon-era America and the drugs charges that caused the tension and focuses instead on the very basic urges that make islands so attractive: the need to get away and the pull towards solitude. The novel's conceit is that, faced with his mental log-jam, John does not join the 'epidemic of disappearing dads' but sets out instead for a temporary respite: he heads to Clew Bay in the 'Maytime', the 'hinge' of the year, to spend 'three days alone on his island'. Recalling his time with 'Dr. Janov' in California, he aims to 'scream the days into nights and scream to the stars by night'. He will shake off all the bad moods 'like a dog after rain'. By 1978 Lennon was nearly a decade on from the time he spent with Arthur Janov between June and September 1970. The world had changed, he had changed, as had some public attitudes towards 'alternative' and nominally 'New Age' pursuits. When Irish broadcaster RTÉ covered the Dorinish settlement in 1970, the grainy black-and-white film pictured Rawle as a figure of fear and suspicion for the Westport locals. Fast forward to 1978 and RTÉ was showing *Other Ways*, a series of full-colour, significantly more positive reports on alternative ways of living, including the rise of businesses like the Golden Dawn, a macrobiotic restaurant and whole foods store opened in Dublin in 1976 by Joe Fitzmaurice. The Golden Dawn also doubled as a growth centre teaching forms of 'Eastern self-healing' like shiatsu massage, yoga and tai chi. RTÉ may have presented these 'self-developing activities' as something of a novelty, but unlike the arrival of Rawle and his friends, the appearance of the Golden Dawn was not thrust into Irish living rooms as a threat to the social order.

As the events of *Beatlebone* move through the same period of change, Barry has the 'Scream' remain a potent therapeutic force. Screaming works as a safety valve that uncorks all the built-up pressure and for John it is seen to be just as powerful towards the end of the decade as it was at the start. Travelling to Dorinish, he intends to scream his 'lungs out' so he can get 'at the blood', the deepest matter that's been 'down all the years'. In a daring moment of authorial intrusion, Barry reveals that he too wants to do the same. Writing in 2011, even further away from Lennon's California screams than 'John' of the late 1970s, Barry hears their reverberance loud and clear. He writes in the first person about taking a journey to the island to undergo a psychic purge of his own to 'let out all of the green bile that seeps up in life'. For Barry, screaming is a way of flushing out 'the envy, the jealousy, the madness' and 'especially the hate'. If getting to Dorinish takes Barry and his characters away from the cares of the world, screaming into the storm once they are there dispenses with all the mental baggage they may have brought with them.[4]

*****

Over in San Francisco, 3,000 miles away from the heavy vibes of the Dakota Building and still more from Clew Bay, groups of young American professionals were feeling out of sorts. They were drifting into the summer of 1978 with the uneasy sense that their friends and loved ones had changed. They were just not the same. One city worker, a woman called Elizabeth Driscoll, could not explain it, but she was sure there was something odd about her boyfriend Geoffrey. It had happened almost overnight. One day he was fine, the next he was cold and distant. He looked the same and talked the same, but it was as if there was something missing: 'Emotion, feelings'. It made her 'crazy' to think so, but the best way she could describe it was that Geoffrey was simply no longer the same man. Worried, Elizabeth went to see Matthew Bennell, her friend and colleague at the San Francisco Department of Health. Over dinner she laid it all out: 'On the outside Geoffrey is still Geoffrey, but on the inside, I can tell, there's something different.' She cannot go to Geoffrey's sister because *she* seems different too. As well as being worried about Geoffrey, Elizabeth was also becoming concerned about her own mental health. 'Do you think it's true that if you think you're losing your mind then you're not well?' Matthew, the thoughtful listener, does not try to talk Elizabeth out of her suspicions. He does not think she's 'crazy' but he does think she should go and see his friend, Dr David Kibner, a psychiatrist. Kibner, he explains, could help Elizabeth 'eliminate things [...] all the things that could have happened' to make her feel 'something had changed'. He runs through some of the 'alternatives'. Perhaps Geoffrey has been 'having an affair' or he had 'become gay'. Maybe he had contracted a 'social disease' or, worse still, he might have become 'a Republican'. It turns out that Elizabeth is right. She is not losing her mind: Geoffrey is not the man he used to be. He has changed, or rather, he has been replaced. Elizabeth (Brooke Adams) and Matthew (Donald Sutherland) are talking at the start of Philip Kaufman's complex and provocatively creepy *Invasion of the Body Snatchers* (1978) and in the world of the film, the reality of what has happened to Geoffrey exceeds even the horror of him becoming a Republican.

Kaufman's film is a remake of Don Siegel's *Invasion of the Body Snatchers* (1956), itself adapted from Jack Finney's original 1955 novel *The Body Snatchers*. In Siegel's version, lead actor Kevin McCarthy plays Miles Bennell, a local doctor in the town of Santa Mira, a place of stereotypical white picket fences and happy middle-class families. At the start of the film this façade of contentment starts to crack thanks to a 'strange case of mass hysteria'. One after another, Bennell's patients come to him reporting that their friends and relatives have changed in subtle but disturbing ways. Uncle Ira looks and acts just like Uncle Ira but, like Geoffrey, he is different somehow: emotionless, devoid of any feeling. As Bennell probes deeper, he uncovers a terrifying silent invasion. The people of Santa Mira are being replaced by unearthly imposters, doppelgangers that grow out of monstrous, vegetative pods. In the closing scenes of the film Bennell heads out to the highway, a mob of 'pod-people' in pursuit, and tries to warn passing motorists of the danger that is all around. 'They're already here!' he shouts to everyone, including the audience, 'You're next!' These same lifeforms spread through Kaufman's film. From the primordial cosmic swirls of the opening sequence to the scenes of fully grown, pulsating pods assimilating people in their sleep, *Invasion* shows San Francisco gradually overwhelmed as these interstellar microbes descend, grow and replicate.[5]

According to *Time*, 'Every generation gets the *Body Snatchers* it deserves.' Although Jack Finney claimed not to be making a political point with his novel, it is hard to read Siegel's version as anything other than a Red Scare allegory, either a nightmare vision of communist infiltration or the exact opposite, a critique of the paranoid Americanism that fuelled the anti-sedition drive of Joseph McCarthy and the blacklisting work of the House Committee on Un-American Activities. When Abel Ferrara took a 1990s view of the material in *Body Snatchers* (1993), it became a story of misfits and teenagers trying to escape a pod-infected army base: Generation X against the military industrial complex. More than a decade later the scenario mutated once again into the viral infections, neurological diseases and redeeming vaccinations of Oliver Hirschbiegel's *The Invasion* (2007). This was *Body Snatchers* retooled for the End of History, a post-millennial thriller that owed more the cultural histories of AIDS, Ebola and SARS than the ideological conflicts of the Cold War. After watching *The Invasion* we are meant to fear the all-encompassing horror of a pandemic rather than the subversive influence of a rival political superpower.

The 1978 version of *Invasion* is no exception when it comes to this contextual reflection. In keeping with the atmosphere of the late 1970s, the anxieties of the film are pitched midway between the political paranoia of the 1950s and the viral panic of the 2000s. Screenwriter W.D. Richter has the pod-people emerge into an already uneasy society of pop-psychology, fragile relationships and frayed nerves. His San Francisco is a city of tightly wound poets and suspicious partners, a place where locals argue on the street and spend their evenings in mudbaths reading Immanuel Velikovsky's *Worlds in Collision* (1950). It is a decade on from the city's time in the sun as the hub of the 1960s counterculture and there is no sign of peace and love, just an all-pervasive mood of paranoia and loneliness. The only vestige of flower power is to be found in the enchanting alien blooms that sprout at the start of the film. As critics Karl and Philip French put it, in the 'alienated city' of *Invasion* people 'seem ready for some take-over that would have the effect of putting Prozac in the drinking water.'[6]

Public anxieties were also turning the other way, towards the self, not just an array of apparently external crises. At the time Richter was writing, ideas akin to those discussed in *Invasion* were also being explored in contemporary psychotherapy, albeit with a twist, via the self-alienation of the 'Imposter Phenomenon'.

Between 1973 and 1978 Pauline Rose Clance and Suzanna Ament Imes studied the prevalence of 'an internal experience of intellectual phoniness' among a group of high-achieving women, mainly academics and business professionals. They found that a combination of influences from early family dynamics to the 'introjection of societal sex-role stereotyping' had produced within their subjects an intense, long-lasting sense of inferiority. Those in thrall to 'imposter syndrome', as it became known, believed their own successes to be fraudulent or the result of someone else's misjudgement, a mistake which was perpetually on the verge of being discovered. In essence, the outlook was the reverse of the paranoid logic of *Invasion* and the other classic doppelganger film of the period, *The Stepford Wives* (1975). Clance and Imes' subjects did not think they had been replaced, nor did they fear the arrival of a malevolent double. Instead, they felt *themselves* to be the imposters, the simulators who had slipped into high-functioning roles initially unnoticed. Just like Geoffrey and Uncle Ira, they were not the teachers, authors, lecturers and managers everyone thought they were, nor did they have the competence to back up the paper qualifications. Despite forging stellar careers and excelling in multiple fields, they believed themselves to be the aliens, as it were, the performers struggling to keep up a pretence that was inevitably going to be exposed.[7]

In these fictional and psychotherapeutic contexts, it seemed almost normal to be nervy and restless. What could make you seem 'alien' in the 1970s more than suddenly changing how you vote, who you sleep with and how you live your life was the insistence that nothing was wrong or that you were categorically *not* 'crazy'. For the celebrity psychiatrist David Kibner, however, the distress of his patients was indicative of a deep-rooted social crisis, one that revealed not the anxieties of the imposters walking among us but the pathology of an excessively liberal culture. Played by a charismatic but typically otherworldly Leonard Nimoy, Kibner is less tolerant than his friend Bennell. When Elizabeth starts trying to explain the situation with Geoffrey, he makes no attempt to rationalise a change of character. Instead, he castigates the apparent fluidity of Geoffrey's behaviour and Elizabeth's suspicion. People are 'stepping in and out of relationships too fast', he argues, and as such they convince themselves their partners are 'changing ... Becoming less human' because they 'don't want the responsibility' of long-term commitment. According to Kibner, the mystifying wave of 'hallucinatory flu' that is besetting more and more of his patients is the reason why 'marriages are going to hell'. It is a malaise that has arisen out of a fundamental fracture in the social structure: 'The whole family unit is shot to hell.'

The thrust of Kibner's analysis echoed that conducted on the other side of the screen by Christopher Lasch, whose bestseller *The Culture of Narcissism* was first published in late 1978, shortly before *Invasion* appeared in cinemas. Subtitled 'American Life in An Age of Diminishing Expectations', the book was based on the essays Lasch published between September 1976 and March 1978, particularly 'The Narcissist Society', his September 1976 article for *The New York Review of Books*. This was the piece in which Lasch described narcissism as the 'world-view of the resigned', arguing that the discord of the 1960s and the disappointments of the 1970s had given rise to a 'therapeutic' climate, one marked by a reactive move towards 'psychic self-improvement'. Lasch extended and redoubled this argument in *The Culture of Narcissism*. He continued to see the 'psychological man' of the twentieth century as a figure 'plagued by anxiety, depression, vague discontents' and 'a sense of inner emptiness', adding that what is now sought is neither 'individual self-aggrandisement nor spiritual transcendence' but 'peace of mind'. However, writing in his book towards end of the decade, with a greater degree of distance on both the closure of the 1960s and the post-Watergate 1970s, Lasch was further entrenched in his view that the search for contentment takes place 'under conditions that increasingly mitigate against it'. Finding peace is an uphill struggle because, as Lasch argues, modernity's dominant ideological motors – 'capitalism and the progress of liberalism' – are unable to explain the 'structural and systemic challenges' of the post-war period.

From here, what *The Culture of Narcissism* highlights to a greater extent than 'The Narcissist Society' is the sense of 'social bankruptcy' caused by this loss of confidence in futurity. Coming out of the 1960s with 'no hope of improving their lives in any of the ways that matter', people spent the 1970s ministering to their personal needs – real and suggested – by 'getting in touch with their feelings, eating health food, taking lessons in ballet or belly dancing, immersing themselves in the wisdom of the East, jogging, learning how to "relate", overcoming the "fear of pleasure"'. Although 'harmless in themselves', Lasch argues, the increasingly widespread practice of these pursuits has the effect of weakening social bonds. Such practices encourage you to 'live for the moment' and it is this 'Invasion of the Self' that undermines the family unit, the contemporary health of which was so lamented by David Kibner. The 'prevailing passion', according to Lasch, was to 'live for yourself, not for your predecessors or posterity'.[8]

✳✳✳✳✳

As well as flowing through the narrative of *Invasion*, it is this intent which also powers the narrative of *Beatlebone*. As Barry tells it, the solution to John's problems seems to lie in getting away from his daily circumstances and, quite literally, finding himself in another place. The gravitational pull of Dorinish appeals to these connected desires for escape and solitude. At first glance, *The Primal Scream* would appear to be pushing its readers and practitioners in much the same direction. Janov describes the cry of the 'Primal' as a 'totally engulfing experience', one that renders the patient 'almost unaware' of where they are. The Primal 'seems to crack open the thought-feeling barrier' and causes patients 'to lose track of time'. According to Janov, they enter into a 'conscious coma' and though they 'could come out of them anytime they want they prefer not to do so'. Out of time and almost out of body: Janov suggests that the seismic effect of the Primal is enough to place his patients into a state of extreme insulation and ecstatic isolation.

Specifically, though, the whole point of Primal Therapy is to dismantle 'tension, defense systems and neurosis'. There is nothing escapist about it. Janov does not want his patients to become willing castaways on their own psychological islands. Instead, he wants them to articulate and thereby confront their buried 'pain'. The aim is not to step into a 'new' life, utterly at odds with and detached from the circumstances of the 'old', but to become 'normal'. The 'normal' enjoys a direct contact with their feelings, they are stable and content to be just where they are. The neurotic, by contrast, must often 'invent a superlife or afterlife' where 'real living' is thought to occur. This deferral puts them out of touch with themselves because the satisfaction of their needs, whether that be for love, intimacy, status or success, is always elsewhere and thus always just beyond their reach. Faced with this problem, what Janov hoped to achieve with Primal Therapy was a powerful act of grounding, a shattering of the individual's misleading illusions and a return to the here and now of the fully embodied self.

When Janov writes about a 'normal human being' he has in mind a 'defence free, tensionless, non-struggling person'. What a joy it must be, to be normal. As well as being impossibly aspirational, Janov's model was also problematically normative, an issue that becomes particularly acute when he turns to the matter of sexuality. Elsewhere in *The Primal Scream*, Janov makes it clear that he would not place 'homosexuals' in the category of 'normal'. Janov sees 'homosexuality' as a state of complete sexual denial. A 'truly sexual persona is heterosexual', he argues, while the 'homosexual' is merely working through a form of hysterical bonding, a neurotically eroti-cised need for love from a member of their own sex. His views on 'frigid' women are similarly objectionable. Defining frigidity as an 'inability to achieve full sexual feeling', specifically a 'climax', Janov examines two polarities of behaviour, 'promiscuity' and abstention. For Janov, the frigid woman is either hypersexual – constantly in search of a lost father – or alienated from sex altogether – con-ditioned by the moralising pressure of a puritanical mother. Both positions are linked to a 'suppression of the feeling self' and this nightmare of sublimated libido can only be alleviated by the physical outpouring that comes with a Primal. It is only when the 'body is liberated', adds Janov, that one can start to 'feel'. As with his analysis of homosexuality, however, the same caveat remains: 'One cannot be fully heterosexual with Primal Pain'. Dispensing with the blockages of frigidity thus requires the women of Janov's case studies to embrace a climax-focused erotic life of 'convulsive' orgasms and newly satisfying sex with their husbands. These views not only date

The Primal Scream, but they also blunt the book's much-vaunted 'revolutionary' potential. Despite Janov's repeated pronouncements on the radicalism of being 'yourself', there is little place in his work for anything other than a heteronormative worldview. His thinking clings to a latent intolerance just as inflexible as the didacticism he detects in rival therapeutic methods. It is enough to make him sound like a dinosaur from another age rather than an explorer pointing the way to new therapeutic territories.

Being 'well' for Janov 'means feeling what is happening now'. He sees other therapies, among them psychoanalysis and Transcendental Meditation, as ways of only 'getting well'. By that he means they give you something: they offer either interpretations of neurosis or cushioning worldviews that help you ignore it. Either way, such methods act as psychological crutches akin to LSD, cult membership and religious mania. They are placebos that help to keep the goal of being 'normal' out of reach by intensifying the disconnect between the neurotic and their feelings. Re-establishing this anchorage was crucial because, as Janov saw it, the body was the source of all the blocked-up tension. It needed to be flushed out, not transcended. As he described, it was the stomach 'where nearly all neurotic patients report the focus of their tension'. Taught to 'swallow their words' and choke back their emotions they had tied themselves up in knots emotionally and physically. In Janov's description, the relief of the Primal thus had such a visceral effect because this untying was an exhausting evacuation. It was a process in which feelings were 'jarred loose from their encased abdominal vise' often for the very first time.[9]

This primal shudder ripples through *Beatlebone*, but the novel departs from the gristle of Janov's thinking as soon as John sees 'an island in his mind'. That Dorinish should shimmer into view once he starts to scream, and that Barry should focus the narrative so powerfully on John's attempt to reach the island, tethers the book's therapeutic fantasy to the idea of an 'elsewhere'. This desire for such an escape is another version of the 'superlife' or 'afterlife' that Janov derides. It is not a motif that invokes the windowless consultation rooms of the Primal Clinic, the place where patients would work through intense therapy sessions before going on to report nights of dreamless sleep. Rather,

Barry's recasting of Dorinish as an island of the mind – a place to wish for and drift towards – recalls the calming, transporting work of two other healing voices heard during the late 1970s, the hypnotherapist Barrie Konicov and the entrepreneur Yves Donnars.

In the mid-1970s, Konicov was a former salesman on the lookout for a new angle while Donnars was an ambitious twenty-something economics graduate similarly eager to find a niche for himself. Both came to health and wellness having sensed a lucrative business opportunity. In 1977, after attending a three-day training course on 'Ethical Hypnosis', Konicov set up shop in Grand Rapids, Michigan, as Potentials Unlimited. He ran meditation-focused weight loss and 'stop smoking' seminars before he started to record a long-running series of self-help cassettes with titles like *Psychic Healing* (1978), *Subliminal: Money Prosperity* (1978) and *Self-Confidence* (1978). At the same time, Donnars was busy on the south-western coast of France in the fishing village turned holiday destination Meschers-sur-Gironde. Having spent 1974–75 in America and Canada deeply immersed in the culture of human potential, he saw a gap in the French alternative health market for an Esalen-style enterprise. He returned to Meschers-sur-Gironde and tried to replicate what he had seen and experienced at Big Sur, cannily using some well-placed family connections in the area to acquire a verdant thirteen-hectare site of pine forest, grassland and beach. This became the base for the campsite and growth centre he opened in 1977 under the banner of l'Espace du Possible.

Konicov's tapes were guided meditations that promised everything from better sleep to a better life, all for less than ten dollars. Each cassette began with his soothing voice offering words of welcome before inviting you to imagine 'an exceptionally beautiful day [...] a warm day, a comfortable day'. Filling out the detail, he would prompt the listener to think of a 'meadow', a 'mountaintop', a 'desert' or more typically a 'beach'. Once secure on the shore of this fantasy landscape, Konicov would continue to whisper down the headphones, nudging his singular audience to 'experience the warmth of a gentle breeze' before 'letting go' to sink 'deeper and deeper' into relaxation. Life was easy on this imaginal beach, and anyone could travel there as long as they sat quietly and followed the soothing instructions. For those who could afford more than a supermarket tape, though, l'Espace du Possible offered a real-life equivalent.

Just as Esalen made full use of its spectacular setting, Donnars marketed his campsite as a place of escape, a private bubble 'in the middle of nature, far from everything'. From the outset of the project Donnars offered such growth-centre favourites as gestalt therapy, meditation and bioenergetics but guests could also join theatre groups, art classes, craft workshops and fitness sessions while enjoying evening concerts and salsa dancing long into the night. It was a jolly package that gave l'Espace the distinct feel of an all-inclusive resort, not so much a Cape Canaveral of inner space as a Club Med for well-off hippies. For Donnars, l'Espace was a 'prototype of the 21st century vacation', a place where guests could experiment with synergy by bringing together different pursuits over a small, concentrated period, each of which were angled towards self-development. Rest and relaxation were key factors in the pursuit of this aim, but the overall idea was to feed and foster personal interests. Whether entering an encounter group for the first time or realising a long-held ambition to finally take up a brush and paint, l'Espace was all about finding the real 'you' underneath the layered identities conferred by social norms and cultural expectation. As Donnars put it, l'Espace is 'a place where you are more alive, more oriented in your life, where you get energized, you take charge'.[10]

Despite this philosophy of realised potential, the image of privileged indulgence persisted. More so than Esalen, l'Espace came to be associated with hedonism and the luxury of getting away to an almost fantastical elsewhere. Rather than acting as a continental hub for personal, spiritual and psychological improvement it quickly gained a reputation as a swingers' paradise, a place that elided the pursuit of the human potential project with the loss of one's inhibitions. Konicov's tapes conjured up a similar sense of self-indulgence. At their best, Potentials Unlimited offered the listener a moment of pause and helped to instil a daily practice of undemanding meditation. At their worst, they encouraged a sense of passive entitlement, the idea that all manner of financial, physical and psychological problems could be miraculously solved by simply lying back, listening, and letting the alleged subliminals on the tapes do their work. Overdubbed with their characteristic sounds of the sea, gentle waves breaking on the shore and gulls flying overhead, Konicov's tapes invite the listener into soundscapes that are pleasantly cushioning. The effect is not unlike sinking into a warm bath. Headphones on, you can almost see Meschers-sur-Gironde and feel as delightfully immobile as a guest at l'Espace, one who briefly considers attending a class but then thinks better of it, reaches for the *Ambre Solaire*, and decides instead to stay on the beach.

For writers like Peter Marin, the ambience of escape projected by l'Espace and the escapist tone cultivated by Konicov would exemplify the 'New Narcissism' he described for *Harper's*. As with the Esalen milieu the projects offered a 'retreat'. They encouraged their clients to physically and psychologically 'retreat from the complexities of the world' into a state of self-valorising solipsism. For Marin, the idea of such a withdrawal was neither to be celebrated nor encouraged because it was tantamount to an abdication of social responsibility. In a foreshadowing of Lasch's argument, Marin saw the 'New Narcissism' as an ultimately corrosive social force, one that erodes 'the immense middle ground of human community'. This argument was not solely a deconstruction of human potential and its offshoots. Marin and Lasch were both attempting to critique the overt message of self-focus loudly articulated by the proponents and adherents of a full spectrum of self-improvement systems.[11]

Primal Therapy and its dissemination via John Lennon easily fit this critical frame. Consider, for example, Lennon's song 'God' (1970), a track from *John Lennon/Plastic Ono Band*. Its opening lines, 'God is a concept / By which we measure / Our pain', grew out of in-therapy conversations Lennon had with Janov about the link between religion and fulfilment. As Janov put it to him, 'people in pain usually seek out religion', they latch onto an 'ideational system that [...] reassures, bolsters, supports, makes the person feel not alone, helps him to think that there is a higher power who will help him'. In this way, as Janov later outlined, belief systems 'manufacture a fulfillment that doesn't exist' in order 'to balm the unconscious need'. They work by holding out the promise of fulfilment having first planted the idea that such satisfaction 'is the only thing that can ease a chronic malaise'. In theory, by getting the individual to confront their buried pain, Primal Therapy punctures this false consciousness. It 'restores' the patient's 'self' and severs the bindings that kept them tethered to such reassuring but suffocating ideas like faith, belief and an over-arching 'meaning' of life. 'There is no meaning to life' goes the bleak but (for Janov) liberating message of Primal Therapy. There is 'only meaning to experience, which is life in process'. In other words, you do not need any metaphysical hoists to feel well. You need instead to fully articulate the pain that such defence mechanisms were used to bury. For Janov, there is nothing to be gained from a belief in a higher power, nor 'a belief in a better life somewhere else' or even in the 'hereafter'. Nor is there any value in the modern visionary tradition central to psychedelia in which, as Aldous Huxley put it, hypnotic or chemical means could open a pathway to 'the mind's antipodes'. These deferrals merely cut the individual off from the bedrock of themselves and place both the solution to their problems and the source of their fulfilment beyond an ever-receding horizon. This is the thrust of Lennon's 'God'.

After restating his arresting opening line, his lyrics embark on a wholesale renunciation of the philosophies, politics and influ-ences that populated post-war countercultural thinking. Good and bad, they all go. From the *I Ching* to The Beatles, Lennon sloughs them all off, telling us he doesn't believe in 'Magic', 'Bible', 'Tarot', 'Hitler', 'Jesus', 'Kennedy', 'Buddha', 'Mantra', 'Gita', 'Yoga', 'Kings', 'Elvis', 'Zimmerman'. It is a catalogue just as crowded at the cover of *Sgt. Pepper* (1967) but by the time Lennon gets to the end of it, the stage is bare, and he seems to have called time on the 1960s: 'The dream is over'. In 'Well, Well, Well' (1970), another song from *John Lennon/ Plastic Ono Band*, the lyrics had taken oblique aim at 'two liberals in the sun', talking of 'revolution' and 'women's liberation'. In 'God', the 'we' of this song becomes 'I', a focus on a singular, personal identity that's reiterated as 'me' and elsewhere signalled by 'Yoko and me'. It is this individual 'reality' that takes precedent over the concepts and activist causes that both songs variously reference. 'Revolution', pop-mysticism and post-war politics: they all seem to belong to another decade and another life. In this sense 'God' works as a mission statement for Lennon's new, post-Beatles career in which he dispenses with his former band and their milieu.

As a statement of (non)belief, there's a wilfulness to 'God' that brings with it a wave of relief, as if in cutting his spiritual and cultural ties Lennon has freed himself from a great burden. For Marin and certainly Lasch, however, the divestment of 'God' would emblematise the widespread 'retreat from politics' and the 'repudiation of the recent past' that occurs when the influence of government, elected leaders and public institutions starts to decline. Superficially, Lasch saw this general climate as 'cheerful and forward looking' but also argued its outward show masked a 'culture of competitive idealism'. This mood 'has carried the logic of individualism to the extreme of war against all'. With other aspirations waning, he contends that the 'pursuit of happiness' has been rerouted into 'the dead end of a narcissistic preoccupation with the self'. Accordingly, when all the layers are stripped away in Lennon's 'God', it is indeed the self which remains: the singular identity of 'John'. That said, the lyrics also plot a terminal trajectory towards a conclusion that is more ambivalent than its sense of closure might suggest. On one level, 'God' reflected the goal of Primal Therapy by charting a systematic purge of previously insulating fantasies. 'John' emerges when there's nothing else left. However, on another, Lennon presents a solipsistic descent towards the 'dead-end' of self-regard, insofar as the lyrics end with a final word that obscures all the other reference points in the song: 'me'. While this may be the preferred destination of the egocentric artist, Marin would read this conclusion as marking a break in the 'web of reciprocity and relation'. Lennon may be celebrating the philosophical liberation of the self, but this valorisation of 'me' comes at the cost of 'us'. In Marin's words, it signals a diminution of the world, the point at which 'the felt presence of the other disappears, and with it a part of our own existence'.[12]

*****

Peter Marin, Tom Wolfe and Christopher Lasch collectively paint a picture of the 1970s as a period of political withdrawal. If the 1960s are to be remembered as the time when the personal became political, these writers argued that in the 1970s the former eclipsed the latter: the prioritisation of personal preoccupations superseded the social drive towards political commitment. It has proved to be a persistent analysis, one detectable in such varied reimaginings of the 1970s as Todd Haynes' film *Velvet Goldmine* (1998), Jake Arnott's novel *The Long Firm* (1999) and Peter Flannery's television drama *Our Friends in the North* (1999). In each, life in the decade disappoints the hopes and aspirations of the 1960s. As the baby boomers start to approach middle age, compromise, self-interest and pragmatism take the place of a prior sense of collective idealism and characters who entered the decade full of hope find themselves turning into the very people they previously tried to challenge. Within this sphere pockets of radicalism do remain but particularly in Arnott and Flannery's work it is found only in the detours of criminal enterprise and Angry Brigade-style violence.[13]

The postcolonial critic Edward Said made a similar point in a very different work, *Culture and Imperialism* (1993), his wide-ranging analysis of 'the modern metropolitan West' and 'its overseas territories'. The history of 'resistance' to 'Western dominance' forms a central strand of this study, up to and including the movement towards 20th-century decolonisation, and at one point Said considers the political situation at the end of the 1970s and the start of the 1980s. He offers the now familiar analysis but applies it to a global context, arguing that the movement from one decade to another is defined by a waning of 'support for anti-colonial struggles, in Algeria, Cuba, Vietnam, Palestine, Iran'. For 'many Western intellectuals', Said explains, these causes had represented 'their deepest engagement in the politics and philosophy of anti-imperialist decolonization' but by the late 1970s this energy had given way to 'a moment of exhaustion and disappointment'. As Said puts it, 'One began to hear how futile it was to support revolution, how barbaric were the new regimes that came to power', and in what he calls an 'extreme case', the idea began to circulate that decolonisation had benefitted 'world communism'.

For Said, this evaporation of activist sympathy was reflected in and precipitated by 'an important ideological shift' within the period, a 'dramatic change of emphasis and, quite literally, direction among thinkers noted for their radicalism'. Here, Said has in mind Michel Foucault and Jean-François Lyotard, 'apostles' of 'intellectual insurgency' who emerged from the 1960s charged by the decade's left-wing political ferment. Foucault entered the 1970s on the back of *Madness and Civilization* (1964) and before he published the equally trenchant critique of institutional power *Discipline and Punish* (1975) he had co-founded the Groupe d'Information sur les Prisons, became involved in anti-racist campaigns and joined the left-wing press organisation Agence de Presse-Libération, which established the newspaper *Libération* in 1973. Lyotard's record as an *engagé* was similarly impressive, with a history of support for the Algerian anti-colonial movement while in influential works like *Discourse, Figure* (1971) and *Libidinal Economy* (1974) he combined Freudian, Marxist and poststructuralist thought in a bold decoding of the 'intensities' informing such flashpoints as May '68.

However, Said argues that in the mid- to late 1970s, with the arrival of Foucault's *The History of Sexuality* (1976–78) and Lyotard's decade-exiting *The Postmodern Condition* (1979), their work had come to exhibit 'a striking new lack of faith' in 'the great legitimizing narratives of emancipation and enlightenment'. For Lyotard, the Marxist–Hegelian ideal of a large-scale revolutionary telos was 'no longer adequate for plotting the human trajectory in society' because the 'post-modernist' age was 'concerned only with local issues, not with history but with problems to be solved, not with a grand reality but with games'. Similarly, with his focus on a 'Technology of the Self' Foucault had 'turned his attention away from the oppositional forces in modern society which he had studied for their undeterred resistance to exclusion and confinement – delinquents, poets, outcasts and the like'. As Said puts it, he 'decided that since power was everywhere it was probably better to concentrate on the local micro-physics of power that surround the individual'. Within this sphere of thought the 'self was therefore to be studied, cultivated and if necessary refashioned and constituted'.

With *The History of Sexuality* and *The Postmodern Condition*, Foucault and Lyotard's theoretical engines were, as ever, firing on all cylinders. These projects were not without complexity or necessity but in Said's view they signalled a distinct gear shift in their understanding of power, one that expressed a resounding 'disappointment' in the primary narrative of the 1960s: the 'politics of liberation'. These were not works which fostered a collective, political impetus but in their analyses of grand narratives falling into redundancy and desire rerouted into the construction of the subject there was no sign of a propulsive shift towards a viable alterity. As Said notes, their basic outlook was negative: 'There is nothing to look forward to: we are stuck within our circle'.[14]

Said's geopolitical sweep converges on the political turn of the 1980s, the advent of what he terms 'a new phase of history' marked by a surge to the right, the premiership of Margaret Thatcher and the presidency of Ronald Reagan. His panoramic discussion of the 1970s is thus in the service of this additional narrative, that of the neo-liberal 1980s driven by market forces and characterised by the domestic and international withdrawal of welfare. Although incisive within the specific theoretical context of *Culture and Imperialism*, the broad strokes of this reading obscure the ground-level activist detail of the 1970s particularly as it applies to the West. Rather than the 'exhaustion and disappointment' of the 1970s, one might better speak of an atmosphere of frustration and discontent – a militancy, even – spreading across the social spectrum from far-left violence to the spectacular cultural agitation of punk. In the case of dystopian post-punk albums like Throbbing Gristle's *DOA: The Third and Final Report* (1978), one finds a virtual crystallisation of this febrile atmosphere into its industrial soundscape. As Simon Reynolds described, the album came straight out of London and the 'East London borough of Hackney', one of 'the most deprived inner-city areas in the UK, with bad housing, rising unemployment, terrible street crime and a strong National Front presence'. On both sides of the Atlantic, outposts of second-wave and radical feminism were similarly putting paid to the idea that the only way to register the 'tedium, gloom and despair' of the 1970s was to encounter it with passivity. The 1977 National Women's Conference in Houston, Texas and the 1978 Women's Liberation Conference in Birmingham both demonstrated the maturation of the New Left activism of the 1960s into an organised, agenda-setting social movement. Much the same could be said of the development of gay rights activism, Black Power and other platforms of identity politics across the 1970s. Although the intent of these various collectives eventually dissipated, due in some cases to internal factionalism, they surrounded and influenced some of the decade's key socio-economic legislation and highlighted the strength of what Lynne Segal calls a wave of 'rising excitement, hope and confidence' connected to the linking of 'personal life and political issues'. A *linking*; not a negation.[15]

Any portrait of late-1970s political engagement, however brief and incomplete, also needs to consider the British industrial disputes of the decade's closing years. The so-called 'Winter of Discontent' of 1978–79, a now iconic symbol of declinism, saw an eventual total of 4.6 million workers across the private and public sectors come out on strike. The dispute emerged in response to James Callaghan's Labour coalition government attempting to reduce inflation via the introduction of caps on pay rises. Coinciding with a bout of ferocious winter weather, the initially unofficial strikes undoubtedly brought extreme disruption and hardship to the UK – as strikes are wont to do, hence the efficacy of withholding one's labour. Their status, however, as nails in the coffin of Britain's governability was significantly exaggerated by a hostile tabloid press and a Conservative Party waiting in the wings eager to grasp the reigns of public favour and curb the influence of unionisation. It was easy to stoke fear of a country in collapse with a few well-placed stories of burials at sea due to striking gravediggers and rubbish piled high in the street thanks to binmen who dared ask for a higher wage. Beyond these images of ruination and barely concealed outrage that the country's servants could be so disobedient lay a clear demonstration of the power held by Britain's 13 million-strong trade union, a number that represented 55.9 per cent of the workforce. This was no crisis born of the evaporation of political will, but a realisation of shop-floor political capital.

For economist Samuel Brittan it was this type of activism, not an apathetic malaise, that generated the contemporary crisis that he and others called 'the British disease'. As he described in 'How British Is the British Sickness?' (1978), a widely cited follow-up to his

'Economic Contradictions' essay of 1975, the country had entered a particular and problematic stage in its 'political and economic development'. Where American writers like Lasch considered the social sphere, Brittan deployed a 'political economy framework' that combined an analysis of 'the minutiae of contemporary events' and 'very recent economic data'. As Roger Middleton observes, the prior essay had been written in sight of the miners' strike, while Brittan's diagnosis of the 'sickness' was conceived in 'the interval between the Callaghan government being seen to have surmounted the difficulties of 1975–76' but just ahead of the discontent at the decade's end. However, having observed what he regarded as the detrimental impact of union agitation on government operations and the effects of stagflation on post-war growth and long-term projection, Brittan felt well placed to call out the damaging effects of 'special interest groups' pursuing 'collective action'. In Lasch's analysis America was radiating with a solar selfishness that prioritised the 'immediate gratification of every impulse'; Brittan by contrast saw a crowded political marketplace in which the energy was channelled in the other direction, towards the derailing dominance of 'union power'. The underlying pathology, however, was the same. Whether through activism or introspection, Lasch and Brittan both saw the concern with self-interest as ultimately detrimental to the common good. As Brittan noted in a point that echoed through the following winter and was subsequently seized upon by the theoreticians of Thatcherism, 'special interest groups', principally unions, were holding the country back, 'preventing a reasonably full use being made of our economic resources'.[16]

✳✳✳✳✳

NBC's Edwin Newman had sounded a parallel alarm in *I Want It All Now* in July 1978, some five months before the appearance of *Invasion of the Body Snatchers* and *The Culture of Narcissism*. After all the sly mockery of the programme, he had concluded with an ominous monologue that framed Marin as a bad influence, a test bed for the cultural indulgence others would go onto decry:

Marin County is a trendsetter, a cultural springboard, and what Marin County indicates is that as we Americans get money and free time, we Americans become increasingly self-absorbed which does not remove our problems, it only changes them. So what is happening in Marin County, may soon be happening where you live, unless, that is, it's happening there already.

In 'The Narcissist Society', and *The Culture of Narcissism*, Lasch does echo this warning. In a dovetailing of his social analysis with the economic context briefly highlighted by Newman, he cited human potential (or the 'Awareness Movement') as the source of the problem. This milieu, with its 'rhetoric of authenticity', was the zone to which he saw more and more Americans using their money to retreat in their free time. Were we to pause and imagine a conversation between Lasch and his on-screen counterpart David Kibner, they would likely agree with Newman on the origin of this 'malaise': Marin County. It is from this affluent enclave just as much from the Esalen territory of Big Sur that the spores of human potential emerged before they caught the vapours and started to float over the city like a thick Bay Area fog.[17]

Kaufman's *Invasion* quietly supports this speculative reading thanks to one of the sharpest and most knowing cameos of the 1970s. Early in the film, Matthew Bennell and Elizabeth Driscoll share a car journey through San Francisco's downtown traffic. It is the morning after the evening they spent talking about Geoffrey and they are making their way to work. All is normal until a frantic old man in a battered suit runs into the middle of the street shouting, 'They're coming! They're coming!' Bennell stops the car to avoid hitting him while the man, wild-eyed and ranting, crowds the window. 'Listen to me, listen. You're next, you're in danger.' Driscoll locks the door and neither she nor Bennell move as the man continues to shout: 'Something terrible! You're next! Before they can react, the man looks behind him, starts to panic even more and sets off again, leaving Bennell and Driscoll in their car as he runs around the corner, yelling as he goes: 'They're already here, you're next.' A crowd follows him. Are they the ones chasing him or are they running to help? As he drops out of sight the sound of squealing tyres fills the air. Bennell and Driscoll take the corner slowly and the next time they see the man, he is lying face down in a pool of his own blood with the crowd looking on, silent and emotionless.

The man, played by Kevin McCarthy, is credited only as 'Running Man' but he's not just running into this single scene; he is running out of Don Siegel's *Invasion* and straight into Kaufman's. McCarthy, dressed like a man out of time, is essentially reprising his role as Miles Bennell right down to the lines that closed out the main events of the earlier film. On one level this ranting reappearance is a neat homage. It is a brief encounter between Miles Bennell and his 1970s counterpart, in which the torch is symbolically passed on to another leading man, in this case Donald Sutherland. More covertly, the cameo teasingly hints at a narrative and geographical connection between the two films. When Jack Finney wrote *The Body Snatchers*, he was living in Marin County and he took care to set the novel in familiar surroundings, specifically Marin's affluent city on the up, Mill Valley. When Siegel and producer Walter Wagner started to plan their film, they considered decamping to Mill Valley for a location shoot, but budgetary constraints kept them in Los Angeles. Santa Mira thus emerged as a hybrid of Hollywood sites that most resembled the Marin locations Finney described. While Kaufman's *Invasion* is often seen as a big city remake of Siegel's small-scale sci-fi, the 1978 version is not just departing from a generic image of Anytown USA. Rather, it relocates the action fourteen miles, from Marin County to San Francisco. It is a very particular geographic shift and with his cameo McCarthy effectively strides from one territory to the other. When he bursts onto the screen in 1978, it is as if his character has been on the run for the past two decades, haranguing anyone who will listen as a new wave of invading spores float into the Bay Area. Now, at last, he has escaped Mill Valley and made it across the bridge. But the fact that he is being chased in his final moments suggests something else has also crossed over: the 'terrible' 'danger' that first emerged in Mill Valley has followed him downtown.[18]

In *High-Level Wellness*, Halbert Dunn had warned his early 1960s readership they were living in a 'a sick world', adding that 'it will go on being a sick world so long as we insist on balancing force with force, and bomb with bomb'. For Dunn, the cure for this sickness lay in fostering a sense of mission rather than attrition, the will 'to fight for something instead of just fighting against things, all the time'. Dunn had in mind the collective effort that should emerge in the face of great adversity. As he puts it: 'if we had an invasion from outer space, all the people of the world would probably join in fighting against the invader'. Judging by Kaufman's film, however, the response to this scenario is 'probably not'. The invasion of 1978 plays out in a world devoid of a collective intent. Nearly two decades after Dunn's theorisation of wellness as an individually led form of social improvement, the film suggests that any sense of mission connected to the idea of self-improvement has been absorbed into the black hole of narcissism. *Invasion* amplifies the arguments of its surrounding cultural critics, but there's nothing extreme about its sci-fi allegory. The warning of Edwin Newman is just as doom-laden as that of Miles Bennell. Both speak of a quiet yet pervasive infection that seeps out of areas like Mill Valley into the population at large. In their terms society is staring down an invasion that is easily able to make gains in the atomised environment of the late 1970s. Like a virus, this force is hard to spot, but once it gets into the cells it has the potential to change human culture from within.[19]

*****

Invasion of the Body Snatchers brought to the fore the thinly veiled sense of fear detectable in the work of Lasch *et al.* 'The New Narcissism', 'The "Me" Decade', *I Want it All Now* and *The Culture of Narcissism*: they all spoke in defence of the status quo against the apparent influx of alternative health systems, human potential advocates and experimental, consciousness-raising projects. While they helped embellish the image of the 1970s as a decade in decline, they were equally pushing back against the remains of the 1960s and its revolutionary impetus. Their collective voice was that of middle America filtered through society magazines and semi-highbrow sociology, one that spoke against enterprises which used to be countercultural but now seemed to be gaining consensus-shifting currency in the mainstream.

This was not a marginal view, nor was *Invasion* the only film to play on or otherwise instigate such anxieties.

In 1979 two films appeared, one relatively mainstream and the other virtually underground, that significantly amplified this sense of unease: David Cronenberg's *The Brood* and Wolfgang Dobrowolny's *Ashram in Poona*. *The Brood* was Cronenberg's fourth full-length feature, released by New World Pictures in June 1979, just as *The Culture of Narcissism* was attracting high sales and glowing reviews. Cronenberg had spent the previous decade developing a visceral and clinical style that has come to be known as 'body horror'. In his films the boundary between the physical exterior and the psychic interior is uncomfortably blurred. Early films like *Stereo* (1969) and *Crimes of the Future* (1970) found Cronenberg's characters drifting through strange institutions, opening themselves to the augmenting research programmes they encountered. His commercial debut *Shivers* (1975) and its follow-up *Rabid* (1976) developed this scenario with their focus on dangerous experiments – variously venereal, parasitic and surgical – that go awry, first in a luxury tower block, then across an entire city. Particularly in *Shivers*, Cronenberg had let rip with an attack on 'bourgeois life, and bourgeois ideas of morality and sexuality' in which transgression was heaped upon transgression before the film reached its orgiastic conclusion in that cauldron of middle-class anxieties, the swimming pool. *The Brood*, however, was a 'mature' and comparatively restrained work that combined the institutional focus of *Stereo* and the mutations of *Rabid* with much more personal material. In the years leading up to the film Cronenberg had gone through a fractious divorce and a protracted custody battle. Much of this angst informed the central conflict of the film between Nola Carveth and her estranged husband Frank. As Cronenberg often explained in subsequent interviews: '*The Brood* was my version of *Kramer vs. Kramer* (1979)'.[20]

Ashram in Poona aka *Ashram*, by contrast, was not a genre film but a documentary, a portrait of Shree Bhagwan Rajneesh, his followers and life inside the Acharya Rajneesh Ashram in Pune, India. It was filmed across 1978, released in West Germany in 1979 and went on to gain a limited American release in 1981. Where Cronenberg had the advantage of a mid-range budget and high-profile actors (Oliver Reed, Samantha Eggar and *Invasion* veteran Art Hindle), Dobrowolny had a small crew, handheld cameras, sketchy sound and all the uncertainties that come with trying to capture the multiple spectacles of the ashram: Rajneesh's discourses to rapt audiences, dynamic meditation sessions and, most notoriously, a group of *neo-sannyasins* tearing into each other during an utterly unfiltered encounter session. Although different in form, genre and audience, the two films do share a common focus: bodies. In both, the human body is displayed in graphic detail, falling under the regulation of a highly organised system and as a result it appears to undergo a radical process of transformation.[21]

The Brood focuses on the work of the Somafree Institute, an experimental psychotherapy centre run by the distinctly Janov-esque figure Dr Hal Raglan. Played by a stately Oliver Reed, Raglan is the author of *The Shape of Rage*, an 'Introduction to Psychoplasmics' which like *The Primal Scream* attempts to ease mental illness through a confrontational form of embodied experience. As *The Brood* progresses, these techniques are applied with disastrous, Frankenstein-like results to Nola Carveth, Raglan's star patient. Meanwhile in *Ashram*, although Rajneesh (or 'Bhagwan' as his followers call him with both familiarity and reverence) is a continual point of reference, and although Dobrowolny shows an array of daily activities from work to meditation, significant attention is given to the film's version of Hal Raglan, group leader Swami Ananda Teertha. A tall, severe-looking Englishman whose long hair and beard give him the air of a New Age Rasputin, Teertha joined Rajneesh's inner circle in 1974 when the ashram was still based in Mumbai. Before that, he had another name – Paul Lowe – and he ran the London-based growth centre Quaesitor. Lowe split off from this unit when his boundary-pushing approach to therapy started to clash with the more professional intentions of the other board members. While Lowe's colleagues David Blayden, Tom Feldberg and others had, by 1976, turned Quaesitor into the Institute for the Development of Human Potential, the reborn Teertha was in Pune, digging in, cranking up the transgression having dispensed with the limitations of reputation, ego and commercial interest 'facing all group leaders in the West'.

When we meet him in the film, Teertha speaks with the self-assurance of one whose reputation precedes him. By the late 1970s he was known inside the ashram and out for running the 'toughest, most, extreme' encounter groups. As he quietly but intently expounds upon his philosophy, one hears more than an echo of Raglan and Psychoplasmics. Or rather, Teertha sits easily in the continuum of charismatic, mercurial experimentalists Cronenberg draws upon for his character. Where Raglan argues that the body is the 'dominant' dyadic entity, capable of its 'own means of self-expression', Teertha outlines his attempts to 'contact' a buried reservoir of organic energy, the release of which can cause explosive physical and psychological changes. Where Raglan offers Psychoplasmics as a reversal of the psychosomatic assumptions between physical symptoms and psychological causes and attempts to push beyond the point where 'the mind resists and refuses to act as a go-between', Teertha similarly seeks to access 'energy' that affects the human being 'at a very deep level, beyond the mind, where psychoanalysis attempts to change man'.[22]

The Brood doesn't hold back when demonstrating Psychoplasmics. We are thrown right into the fictional practice in the film's unsettling opening scene, a public therapy session between Raglan and his patient 'Mike', a bearded, 'fairly normal specimen of the middle-aged North American male'. Raglan and Mike sit cross-legged in a ring of spotlight. Wearing matching tunics, they look like judo players about to spar but as the psychic tussle begins it is clear that Raglan has the upper hand. In *Ashram* Teertha is similarly dominant, although he lords over a larger, ecstatic gathering he calls a 'lila group', *lila* or *leela* being the Sanskrit word variously translated as 'play', 'sport' or 'drama'. The aim of the session was to throw off 'seriousness' and to celebrate life as 'god's play'. In practice this meant dancing naked to 'Night Fever' (1977) by The Bee Gees in a small, padded room while the temperature rises, the sweat starts to flow, and the hyperventilation sets in. In this heightened zone, Teertha is seen ministering to each participant, pushing them further towards the tipping point of exhaustion and involuntary movement. Pull away the heavy funk of the stained, padded room and there's the same heady atmosphere one finds in the abreactions of American evangelism and Haitian *voudu* alike: the creation of an altered state via a dizzying combination of physical exertion and sensory overload. For Teertha, the energy of the session is not just about losing inhibitions or being taken by the spirit, it is about opening the wellspring of energy that lies deep down within oneself. As he moves from one convulsing *sannyasin* to another, he does not speak to them but through them, as if addressing the new version being born, that which is surfacing from the inner reservoir. 'Come through, come through, come through,' he repeats to each of his charges as they twitch, oblivious. Back in Raglan's darkened room, his vigil with Mike is solemn but no less extreme. He takes on multiple roles of father, priest and interrogator while Mike struggles to hold off the assault. The roleplay zeroes in on Mike's gender insecurity, the feeling expressed through the projection of parental disapproval that he should have 'been a girl'. Pushing further, alternately addressing Mike as 'Michelle', Raglan manoeuvres his patient into an impasse. Mike finds himself virtually speechless between his conflicting feelings of love and hate for Raglan-the-father. At this point, the body takes over and shows Raglan what Mike is unable to articulate. Convulsing, Mike tears off the tunic and as the audience gasp, he reveals the psychoplasmic emergence: welts, lesions and orifices across his skin. Michelle has 'come through', she has emerged from the psychic reservoir and made herself visible across Mike's body.

In his novelisation of the film, Richard Starks describes Mike shrieking with a 'piercing sound that echoed round the hall'. As the book goes on, Raglan, Nola Carveth and the other characters frequently shout and scream while their bodies are similarly expressive, pulsating with angry swellings and flushed with rage. The volume also goes up in *Ashram* when the lila group plays itself out and a much more confrontational encounter session begins. As Teertha encourages the participants to focus on and release 'some pressure that's harmed you', Dobrowolny's camera lingers over a pile of boxing gloves. Soon, the same sweaty chamber becomes a screeching, riotous arena. There is no music this time, just spumes of profanity as group members beat each other with cushions and fists, gloved and ungloved. Plenty of petty grievances are aired ('I'm sick of you being lazy,' shouts one guy to another) but for the most part, the internal gyroscope of the group veers towards racist and sexist violence, as if instincts of the very worst kind are released as soon as the opportunity arises. The group may well be a safety valve easing the pressure of communal living, group members may well appear calm in later vox pops, the film's voice-over may well offer vague assurances about safety and consent, but it remains difficult to watch a large, bare-chested white man shouting a racial slur at a diminutive Black woman before taking a swing at her. So too for the spectacle of the woman who is stripped and sexually assaulted in the middle of the room while the Bosch-esque scene plays on, unabated.[23]

This is the footage for which *Ashram* has become notorious. Reviewing the film for the *New York Times*, Janet Maslin compared these 'madhouse' scenes to the excesses of a Ken Russell film. She was deeply troubled by the sight of the 'hugely distressed' woman and unconvinced by claims that 'violent therapy has helped her overcome her fear of men'. So too were the anxious residents of Antelope, a small retirement community in Oregon, who watched the film aghast, increasingly concerned as to what was happening in Rajneeshpuram, the ashram on their doorstep. Since taking possession of the property in 1981, Rajneesh's followers had built a self-governing, self-enclosed mini-city which was home to some 5,000 residents and came complete with its own airstrip. It was a hive of activity in which Rajneesh, now ensconced in a vow of silence, came and went in his Rolls-Royce convoy. Daily matters were handled by 'the Queen', Rajneesh's uncompromising second-in-command, Ma Anand Sheela. She not only acted as Rajneesh's representative but also assumed a degree of authoritarian control over the settlement. As the site expanded, tensions with the locals were inevitable, particularly in the light of Sheela's tendency to lock horns with the authorities. Suspicion quickly gave rise to rumour and, in addition to Rajneeshpuram being seen (not entirely unexpectedly) as a den of iniquity, word eventually began to circulate that the group were busy stockpiling weapons. *Ashram* appeared right in the middle of these growing tensions like a smoking gun. For anyone critical of or concerned about Rajneesh and his followers, it was a damning piece of evidence, a virtual snuff movie that in its display of 'beatings, bones being broken and an attempted rape' summed up everything assumed to be wrong about the 'movement'.[24]

Esalen's Richard Price, who was briefly a member of the Pune ashram between 1977 and 1978, severed ties with Rajneesh because of this 'immature' approach to encounter. He too spoke of 'broken bones [...] bruisings and abrasions beyond counting'. For Teertha, the aggression was all part of his long-held maxim that 'it is forbidden to forbid'. He wanted the group members to 'let go', to throw off their fears and to live free of the expectations imposed by others. Teertha saw himself as an appendage of his 'enlightened master' and thus conveniently assumed no responsibility for the actions of the group. Despite this apparent distance, Dobrowolny's footage pictures Teertha right in the fray, where he latches on to any hesitation or hint of reluctance among the participants and tells them it is a blockage to be removed. In a moment of relative calm he focuses on the naked, weeping woman and heaps on the pressure, getting her to articulate what is clearly difficult for her to say. 'It doesn't come out,' she cries, as Teertha continues to push, telling her she's a prisoner of her own fear. 'Words! Come on, make some sound, otherwise you're stuck,' he shouts by way of advice. It is an excruciating sequence that ends with her on the floor, screaming, held in the in grip of a seizure.[25]

Teertha shows no alarm, though, as if this is exactly the result he wanted to achieve: a collapse that is also a release. As in Cronenberg's screaming world, there is no clear distinction between what is verbalised and what the body makes manifest. The central hook of *The Brood* is that Nola Carveth's rages are so intense that they produce a group of ultra-aggressive tulpas; in *Ashram* Teertha's methods blur together psychic disturbance and physical response, resulting in phenomena that is less procreative but just as seismic and revelatory for the individual. In both, it is the scream which signals the intermingling of these inner and outer territories, a distinctly corporeal and emetic representation that also sounds an echo with the language Janov used in *The Primal Scream* and its follow-up *The Primal Revolution* (1972–74). In these books Janov describes sessions with his patients where, just like Raglan and Teertha, he pushes at their long-held neurotic defences. Built out of the pain of unmet needs, these walls initially quicken at the first sign of a possible breach. The patient tenses, their chest gets tight, their throat constricts, their teeth start to grind, but then the dam breaks. As if describing a therapeutic version of the chestburster scene in *Alien* (1979), Janov recalls seeing patients 'quiver' and 'shake' as the Primal arrives. It moves 'up the body and the out of the mouth', bringing with it a wave of overwhelming relief as what needs to be said, however unspeakable, is finally said. Although Janov refers to the process as a 'journey inside', he has no time for meditative leaps into the head. Primal Therapy is intended as a physical jolt that shocks the neurotic system out of its insulating sleep and back into the waking world of 'real' feelings.

In interviews, Janov often played down the 'melodrama' of his therapy sessions, claiming it was 'nonsense' that he 'pulled' the likes of a helpless and weeping John Lennon 'deeper and deeper into the darkest corners of his past'. *The Primal Scream* nonetheless bristles with an intense physicality, particularly in the accounts he includes from former patients. At one point, 'Elizabeth' recalls a group session during which she looked over to another member, 'Steve', only to realise 'Steve's hands' had suddenly become her 'father's hands'. Elsewhere, 'Philip' recounts how during a Primal, his 'body began to move in various uncanny positions that defied any control on [his] part'. As in *The Brood* and *Ashram*, these occurrences are initially framed as if they are curative moments of relief, but they also crystallise the distinct sense of unease if not fear generated by such practices. They worry away at the anxiety of losing physical control. They suggest that our bodies, the most fundamental marker of our autonomy, may not be so secure as they appear. We walk, it seems, on thin ice. With the right amount of stress applied to the right kind of fissure, the fragile structure could easily crumble. Such are the pressures invading our sense of self from within, more so than without. The message overtly and covertly issued by Janov and his cinematic contemporaries Cronenberg and Dobrowolny is that we are continually subject to our own body snatchers. We carry within us forces that we simply cannot resist.[26]

✳✳✳✳✳

Piling up at the end of the decade, the horrors were there for all to see. In the shared arguments and overlapping characters of genre movies, documentaries and sociological analyses the task of self-development was met with criticism, scepticism and more than a little fear. According to these works, playing with the 'Technology of the Self', to use Foucault's phrase, led only to spectacular selfishness and an implosion of eviscerating introspection. It seemed there was more than enough evidence to validate Edward Said's reading of the 1970s as an exhausted detour in the drive towards a politics of liberation. However, when Foucault was analysing this 'technology' over the course of *The History of Sexuality* and particularly in his essay 'Technologies of the Self' (1982) he was doing more than sounding a retreat from the political frontlines. Foucault defined the 'technologies of the self' as those which:

> permit individuals to effect by their own means, or with the help of others, a certain number of operations on their own bodies and souls, thoughts, conduct and way of being, so as to transform themselves in order to attain a certain state of happiness, purity, wisdom, perfection or immortality.

There are echoes here of Lasch describing the retreat of Americans 'to purely personal preoccupations', but in contrast to the 'repudiation of the recent past' that characterises the culture of narcissism, Foucault conducts a much broader historical analysis. He links the technology of the self to two different but 'historically contiguous contexts', the 'Greco-Roman philosophy' of the 'first two centuries A.D. of the early Roman Empire' and the 'Christian Spirituality' and 'monastic principles developed in the fourth and fifth centuries of the late Roman Empire'. He argues that among the Greeks, the 'hermeneutics of the self' took the form of a precept, *epimeleisthai sautou*, which variously means 'to take care of yourself' or 'to take care of the self'. Sourcing the phrase to Plato's 4th-century BCE dialogue *Alcibiades*, Foucault explains that 'to be concerned, to take care of yourself' meant more than 'the simple fact of paying attention'. It was an 'activity and not just an attitude', that could describe 'taking pains with one's holdings and one's health'. 'Care of the self', Foucault tells us, 'is used in reference to the activity of a farmer tending to his fields, his cattle, and his house, or to the job of a king in taking care of his city and citizens or to the worship of ancestors of gods, or as a medical term to signify the act of caring'.[27]

As a precept, 'care of the self' was closely linked to the Delphic principle of 'know yourself', taken to mean 'do not suppose yourself a god'. To deploy this 'technical advice' meant to engage in 'self-examination' as an aid to good social conduct. The Greeks understood the 'self' to mean the 'soul' but in following the injunction to care and thus 'know' oneself, contemplation of the 'divine element' was a means of discovering 'rules to serve as a basis for just behaviour and political action'. Given that Greek identity, particularly when it came to matters of citizenship, was closely linked to the public life of the polis, taking care of the self was thus not a solipsistic procedure. It was 'one of the main principles of cities, one of the main rules for social and personal conduct and for the art of life'. Caring for oneself, coming to know oneself, was the result of living the examined life. Despite its drive for the solitude of the island, it is this type of care that emerges over the course of *Beatlebone*. 'John' ultimately spends precious little time alone on his island. He also gives short shrift to 'Black Atlantis', a sinister encounter group holed up on a neighbouring outcrop. 'It's 1978', he tells them, quickly tired of their well-worn 'open up and bleed' exercises. Considered as an overall character study, Barry's novel is more concerned with John's multifaceted contemplation, the manner in which, once out there at the edge of things, he takes stock of his life, his holdings and his assets before preparing to return to the life he has temporarily departed.[28]

Back in Foucault's analysis, he explains that it was only later, in the Hellenistic and Roman periods, that the pursuit of such care became synonymous with a sense of 'retreat' or *anakhoresis*, a word suggestive of a military retreat, an escape into hiding or a movement from the town to the country. In the 1st and 2nd centuries, explains Foucault, a new experience of self emerged in which 'introspection becomes more and more detailed'. In this context, to be concerned with the self was not a 'preparation for political life' but the pretext to a removal from it. The instruction to 'take care of yourself' was gradually absorbed into the singular focus of 'know yourself', and generating such knowledge was a matter of occupying 'oneself with one's soul'. Foucault describes how the Stoics came to speak of *anakhoresis* in 'spiritualized' terms as a 'retreat into oneself', a way of reflecting to better remember the teachings one has received. In this mode of thought one must 'leave politics in order to take better care of the self'; one must retire, as the Stoics put it, 'into the self and stay there'. For the Christian ascetics of the later Roman Empire, conducting this examination meant turning away from the world and, by extension, the self. As evidence, Foucault cites Gregory of Nyssa's 4th-century treatise *On Virginity* in which he 'renounces the world and marriage', detaches himself 'from the flesh and with virginity of heart and body, recovers the immortality of which [he had] been deprived'. It is a practice of recovery in which the soul is searched for that which God has given but 'the body has tarnished'.

In performing this analysis, Foucault was outlining the historical contingency of the self and associated notions of care. 'Technologies of the Self' is a typically 'archaeological' approach to such familiar phrases as 'know yourself' in which Foucault uncovers the shifting politics informing its usage. As well as indicating the socio-cultural origins of concepts still in circulation, Foucault's examination works as part of a wider, longer project regarding the 'technologies of power', those which 'determine the conduct of individuals and submit them to certain ends or domination'. In mapping the philosophical oscillation between caring for and knowing the self, Foucault was pointing to this 'dominance', he was outlining the way the 'self' has been historically constructed through various practices of contemplation. 'Technologies of the Self', then, is no manifesto for the luxuries of introspection. It is a study of 'governmentality', the way 'technologies of the self' encounter those of 'power', and as such it is just as political and engaged as both *Madness and Civilization* and *Discipline and Punish*.[29]

Place the essay alongside the various analyses summed up by *The Culture of Narcissism* and we begin to see more of Lasch's own underlying viewpoint. It is as if Foucault, writing in 1982, is critiquing this late-1970s discourse just as much as he is examining Greco-Roman philosophy. He reminds us that for Christianity, renouncing 'the self and reality' was the 'condition for salvation'. It was difficult to 'base rigorous morality and austere principles' on the idea of giving 'more care to ourselves than anything else in the world'. Taking care of the self became an immorality, 'a means of escape from all possible rules'. Lasch and his fellow commentators seem to have inherited this tradition. Their unease and that which ripples through the anxiety culture of the 1970s – *Invasion* to *The Brood* and the difficult territory of *Ashram* in between – speaks to the idea that self-development and attempts at transformation equate to an abandonment of a higher mission. For the Christian ascetics 'care of the self' meant turning away from God. For those who surveyed the narcissistic modern world and shook their heads in exasperation and more than a little despair, it meant turning away from social but no less sacred institutions: home life, politics, community and national responsibility. From this perspective *The Brood* presents the horror of the imploding family, *Ashram* shows a community willingly embracing tyranny and *Invasion* vertiginously points to a territory yet unknown. Towards the end of the latter film, Dr David Kibner, now revealed as one of 'them', confronts Matthew Bennell and Elizabeth Driscoll, explaining that they need not be 'trapped by old concepts'. Kibner, along with his fellow pod-people, represents a 'new life form' free of 'anxiety, fear, hate'. In Janov's terms they could almost be 'normal'. The 'untroubled world' they promise, though, is a zombie-like existence, devoid of 'love' and powered only by the need to 'adapt' and 'survive'. It is a world of extreme self-focus, the seeds of which – according to *I Want It All Now* – were already emerging from Marin County in the summer of 1978. Heavy with a sense of moral panic, Edwin Newman closes the documentary with a word of warning, as if a localised trend has started to spread with the velocity of a virus: 'As we say goodbye to Marin County of the 70s, what we might be saying is hello USA of the 80s'.[30]

CHAPTER VIII

The Crisis of Confidence
1979–1981

One person who waved an enthusiastic 'hello' to the 1980s was the computer programmer turned floatation tank designer Glenn Perry. In mid-1979 he was in sunny Beverly Hills, finalising the lease on a former Rolls-Royce repair shop. Working with a small team, he had spent months converting the 'empty two thousand square foot shell' of glass and concrete into the Samadhi Float Center, the first of its kind: a sleek, modern space where you could book the use of a floatation tank for relaxation, contemplation and inner exploration.

Perry had been on a long, strange trip since 1972, the year he met John C. Lilly and had his first blissful experience of floatation in the hewn-out oubliette at Big Bear. After running weekend workshops at Esalen in 1973, he had carried on working at Scientific Data Systems but in 1974 he quit, determined to follow through on the idea of manufacturing tanks for commercial sale. The same year he met Leah (Lee) Leibner, a Los Angeles schoolteacher interested in educational reform and student dynamics. In the hope of managing her classroom stress, she had participated in an isolation tank research programme that used equipment designed by Perry. The two got talking at a post-float party and Glenn Perry, still glowing in his newfound confidence, asked her out on a date. They got on and two years later, in 1976, after an intense meeting of minds, a fair amount of LSD and even more floating, they got married. Lee had left teaching by that point and had joined Glenn in the tank project, a fledgling business they called the Samadhi Tank Company.[1]

It was John C. Lilly who had suggested the name. Straight out of *The Centre of the Cyclone*, *samadhi* was a Sanskrit word meaning a state of union or oneness between the meditator and the focus of the meditation. For Lilly, *samadhi* was the state made available by floating, one of 'total consciousness […] in tune with universal mind'. As a firm believer in the physical, psychological and social value of this experience he was keen to support the Perrys in their enterprise. He certainly thought they were the ones to do it. Lilly later wrote glowingly of their 'expertise and their ingenuity, their skill and aptitude in tank manufacture' as well as their 'integrity and sincerity as researchers'. The time was also right, too. From the middle of the decade onwards, other writers like the activist, networker and educator Marilyn Ferguson were increasingly predicting an imminent paradigm shift. Beginning in 1975, Ferguson published the newsletter *Brain/Mind Bulletin* and she would go on to write a high-profile analysis of 'personal and social transformation', *The Aquarian Conspiracy* (1980). Both reported on what Ferguson termed 'The Movement That Has No Name', a wave of 'new approaches to health, humanistic education, new politics and management'. As evidence of this 'change from the inside out' in which 'personal trans-formation' was begetting 'social transformation', Ferguson cited the results of a 1978 Gallup poll which indicated that around 10 million Americans were 'engaged in some form of Eastern religion'. A 1976 poll had previously shown that some 5 million regularly practised yoga, while Ferguson's own research had also pointed to an 'overwhelming scepticism about organized religion' with high numbers reporting they were 'no longer active in the religion of their childhood'. Elsewhere, other seemingly sacred institutions were feeling the impact of this attitudinal shift. In his study of post-war Britain, Arthur Marwick reported that while football was 'by far the most popular spectator sport' of the mid-1970s its role as a 'participatory activity' had been relegated to the lower leagues of 'squash, cycling and tennis', having lost ground to 'keep fit/yoga'. As if to assure us the world remained sane in the face of such an upset, Marwick reminded his readers that the tra-ditional cultural boundaries remained intact. Football was 'confined to young or youngish males' while the upstart yoga was something of a novelty, a 'growth area, almost exclusively confined to females'.[2]

In her attempt to map the American situation, Ferguson saw no grounds for such condescension nor for such a loaded gender division. In 1977, two years after launching *Brain/Mind Bulletin*, she sent out questionnaires to 'two hundred and ten persons engaged in social transformation'. Of the 185 who responded, '131 were male', '54 were female' and the results indicated high levels of interest across the board in 'spiritual disciplines, growth modalities', 'body therapies' and 'altered states of consciousness'. It was an admittedly small sampling compared to the reach of a Gallup poll, but by focusing on those already in pursuit of what she termed 'psychotechnological' change, Ferguson was able to bring colour and detail to the panoramic image of a culture in transition. Specifically, when describing their 'triggers of transformative experiences' her respondents spoke of the Esalen encounter groups and their 'intense' processes of 'personal and collective change'; the 'forcing through of patterns of recognition' offered by 'Gestalt therapy' and 'the 'consciousness-raising' strategies of various social movements. It is a familiar list that would not look out of place in McFadden's *The Serial*, but the questionnaire also returned indications that a ready market existed for the specific products Samadhi would soon offer. Ferguson's respondents reported an interest in 'sensory isolation and sensory overload' on the grounds that 'sharply altered input causes a shift in consciousness'. Similarly, of the thinkers who influenced her correspondents, 'either through personal contact or through their writings', there was the predictable assembly of 'C.G. Jung, Abraham Maslow, Carl Rogers, Aldous Huxley', but a new, ascendant name also placed high on the list: 'John Lilly'.[3]

In the late 1970s, Lilly was increasingly happy to accept this role of cultural 'influencer'. With books like *The Deep Self* (1977) and his third-person 'autobiography' *The Scientist* (1978), he was emerging as a public proselytiser for the 'isolation tank' and the 'profound relaxation' it offered. Lilly's writing still teemed with the language of metaprogramming but where *The Centre of the Cyclone* had included 'sense withdrawal' as one of several experimental procedures, *The Scientist* brought the tank to the forefront of the discussion. Along with it came a positive, humanistic tone similar to that found in Ferguson's writing, which Lilly used to laud the tank as a 'fertile source of new ideas, new experiences, new integration'. It was confident, evolutionary rhetoric, the type then being heard at large-scale events like the 1976 'World Symposium on Humanity' in Vancouver and the 1978 'Festival for Mind and Body' in London. Sociologist Theodore

Roszak spoke at the Vancouver event on the 'sovereign right to self-discovery' and was later quoted in the *New York Times* celebrating the ability of 'human potentiality to challenge the adequacy of our science, our technics, our politics'. This was an aspirational language that spoke of a sea-change in the culture at large, and with his focus on the isolation tank Lilly offered his readers the tool to enact it.[4]

In parallel, the dramatist and screenwriter Paddy Chayefsky, author of *Network* (1976), published the tank-themed novel *Altered States* (1978), the result of a two-year investigation into the type of fields surveyed by *Brain/Mind Bulletin*: psychophysiology, parapsychology and molecular biology. Despite the depth of this research *Altered States* was essentially an extended film treatment: *Dr Jekyll and Mr Hyde* set on an academic campus. It charts the progress of an East Coast academic, the extremely Lilly-esque Dr Edward Jessup, as he uses isolation tanks to seek out 'a physiological pathway to our earlier consciousness', the 'original self' that is 'somewhere in those hundred-odd billion neural and glial cells in our own minds'. Having established this (pseudo) scientific basis, Chayefsky shifts gear into the more conventional territory of horror, with Jessup effortlessly fulfilling the role of the ill-starred, self-experimenting scientist whose visionary experiences give rise to atavistic regression and post-human transformation. Nearly two decades on from the English brainwashing fantasies of *The Mind Benders*, *Altered States* supercharged the symbolism of the tank, framing it not as a weapon of the Cold War but a product of the 1970s American intersection of psychedelia and academia spearheaded by the likes of Esalen-era Lilly and Stanislav Grof: a terrifying but fascinating vessel loaded with esoteric, if not mystical, power.

Describing the tone of the 'popular bestsellers' of the 1970s, Marwick noted that 'the rage was for works of terror, and, above all, occultism and exorcism', adding that 'almost all the market leaders were American'. William Peter Blatty's *The Exorcist* (1971), David Seltzer's *The Omen* (1976) and Jay Anson's *The Amityville Horror* (1979) all fit this bill, but so too did *Altered States*, with Chayefsky focusing on the efforts of Jessup – his Dr Jekyll – to exorcise himself from the novel's version(s) of Mr Hyde, the externalised visions and devolutions generated by the tank. It was arguably this pulpish sensationalism, rather than any of the novel's 'science', that helped *Altered States* reinstall sensory deprivation as a point of interest in the public imagination.[5]

For Lilly and the Perrys, then, pushing forwards with a dedicated centre was the right way to capitalise on this rising wave of popular cultural and research-based attention. From an experimental perspective, having a base and the possibility of a franchise could also extend the exploratory potential of the isolation tank, the way it afforded what Lilly called 'a new appreciation of the depth within the human mind unfathomed by previous methods of research'. In short, Lilly wanted as many people as possible to float. Glenn and Lee agreed. They needed no convincing of the tank's transformative properties, but unlike Lilly they were not independent researchers spreading the good news of floatation via books and semi-occasional workshops. They were trying to run a full-scale business that had to turn a profit. Making a living meant attending to the bottom line and so they had to build their brand, not just their profile. In short, the Perrys wanted as many people as possible to *pay* to float.

On the surface, then, the brick-and-mortar incarnation of the Samadhi Tank Company may have looked like a stripped-down, single-focus growth centre but it was really a showroom. It was there to provide all the benefits of floating but via a carefully designed customer experience angled towards generating sales, either of hour-long sessions in the centre's tanks or sales of the tanks themselves. To that end, the Perrys installed a friendly reception area and a series of bright corridors that led to changing rooms, shower facilities and five quiet, airy chambers. Each of the five contained a temperature-controlled floatation tank; a *floatation* tank, mind you, not a 'sensory deprivation', 'sense withdrawal' or 'isolation' tank. This Cold War language with its brainwashing vibes had no place at Samadhi. Gone too were the cumbersome tank designs that required you to climb through a hatch in the top and struggle down into hosepipe-heated water. Perry's tanks were not the 'coffinlike bathtub[s]' of aluminium and plywood Chayefsky described in *Altered States*. They were elegant, carefully crafted capsules with light-dimming controls and convenient side-door access. Having set the lights, you could step rather than clamber into them as gentle music was piped into the room to announce the start of your session. Eight feet long, four feet wide and four feet deep, the tanks were made using thin, durable plastic and contained a thick Styrofoam layer of insulation and an inner cavity of smooth, sealed vinyl. This made for a lightweight frame that could keep out the light and the sound and but keep in the ten inches of saline water. It was a design that also meant the tanks could be flat-packed straight off the production line and easily assembled at home.

Decorated with intricate insignia, Samadhi tanks looked more like art objects than finely calibrated meditation tools. Indeed, the centre's bright, minimalist design echoed much of the 'white cube' aesthetic, the default setting for the modern gallery space. According to critic Brian O'Doherty, writing in *Art Monthly* in 1976, this 'unshadowed' and 'limbo-like ambience' typically created a neutral zone, one 'untouched by time and its vicissitudes'. It was the ideal space for the floatation tank given the temporal elongations frequently reported by its users. O'Doherty saw such spaces as odd vacuums in which the presence of the viewer 'seems superfluous, an intrusion'. The Perrys, meanwhile, wanted people to feel welcome. They were trying to combine the atmosphere of a spa with that of hot tub 'retail outlet' and as such they took care to lay out the reception like a lounge. The idea was for clients to arrive and immediately enter a relaxed environment. Samadhi was not one of the dispassionate research zones Jack Vernon described in *Inside the Black Room*, it was more like the type of space Paul Wilson had in mind when he encouraged readers of his *Little Book of Calm* (1996) to try out 'a float tank' and 'weightlessly feel your tensions dissolve'. It was a welcome that continued after the float session had ended. Freshly showered from the tanks, clients were invited to return to the lounge where they could take a cup of tea, mingle, talk and reflect on their experiences. If the insights and the deep relaxation had been to their liking, they might arrange another session or sign up for a discounted package deal. Better still, after leafing through one of the centre's glossy catalogues featuring beautiful models floating luxuriantly, they might take a punt and buy a tank of their own. Everything was for sale.[6]

*****

Over in Mill Valley, John Travis was promoting the Wellness Resource Center in similar terms, but unlike Samadhi he was not selling a product as such, rather a set of services and consultations. The experience he offered *was* the product, and a key part of this package was the centre itself: the actual visitable communal building, which he likened to a modern spa. Spas, he later explained, 'provide the vehicle for replacing the lost village community, the tribe – the extended family'. For Travis, this loss of 'connection' underwrote much of the social and individual 'unwellness' he had been observing since the early 1970s. Both he and Glenn Perry had entered the decade struggling with various forms of emotional 'disconnection' and by the end of it, their personal experiences were resonating with the conclusions of long-term academic studies that focused on the alienating effects of the modern world. 'Social transitions are a fact of life in modern society and so is loneliness,' wrote psychologists Letitia Anne Peplau and Daniel Perlman in 1982, reflecting on the data gained from the UCLA Loneliness Scale. Developed in 1978 as a way of bringing an empirical basis to their study, the scale sought to 'detect variations in everyday life'. Participants were asked to score their responses to statements ranging from the angst of 'I feel left out' to the extremity of 'I cannot tolerate being so alone'. Peplau, along with colleagues Dan Russell and Mary Lund Ferguson, concluded that loneliness was a 'serious mental health problem', one that overlapped with depression and anxiety and was generally subject to a 'disturbing' lack of coherent treatment.

The macro-issues informing this analysis remained consistent with the work of sociologists like Robert Weiss. Weiss, author of *Loneliness: The Experience of Emotional and Social Isolation* (1975), had been mapping American loneliness since the 1950s. For him, its modern prevalence was symptomatic of the primary cultural transformation characterising the 20th century, the transition from an agricultural to an industrial economy and thus a rural to a predominantly urban society. The 'rapid urbanization that followed mass migration out of the countryside', he argued, resulted in 'a breakdown in communication' because people had 'fewer opportunities to participate in communities'. The point was that residents of 'transient communities' – those moving in pursuit of work and, more recently, education – typically 'lacked long-term relationships with friends and neighbours, as well as the benefits of living closer to older generations of their own families'. There was a payoff for such displacement. By the end of the 1970s America was reaping the benefits of this economically oriented movement. Between 1969 and 1979, the period during which the percentage of people living alone started to rise, 'the percentage of people in poverty declined', the number 'who went to college increased', the 'percentage who owned automobiles rose' and 'life expectancy lengthened'. Externally, the country's wage scale also continued to attract 'immigrants from around the world'.[7]

However, from Travis' perspective, what lay underneath the positivity of this panoramic view was an increasingly alienating culture marked by 'unaffordable health care' and a 'lack of social capital'. At ground level, the daily life of the nation was characterised by a panoply of social ills ranging from a growing sense of apathy to various forms of addiction, depression and violence both physical and emotional. Peplau and her colleagues made a similar point in their studies of loneliness, arguing that it was linked to 'a variety of other serious individual and social problems', all of which were on the rise, including 'alcoholism, adolescent delinquency, suicide, physical illness and overutilization of health care services'. Films like Chris Petit's *Radio On* (1979) and George Miller's *Mad Max* (1979) sounded an international echo of this distressing domestic diagnosis. As mirror-image road movies, the two stood at opposite ends of the crisis spectrum Travis outlined. Petit's slow-burning 'cul-de-sac' of a film was a monochromatic embodiment of psychological and cultural burnout. It featured a disaffected, near-silent driver who travels through a washed-out Britain before finding himself stalled at the edge of an English quarry with neither the fuel nor the will for a final plunge. By contrast, the near future Australia of *Mad Max* supercharged this personal breakdown into a barely science-fictional image of societal collapse. Miller's film pushed the logic of the mid-1970s oil crisis from shortage to economic and infrastructural implosion, a decline that pulls down with it the veneer of law and order. *Mad Max* suggests that the next step on from fistfights at fuel pumps is the emergence of outlaw gangs terrorising isolated population pockets, a world of desperate poverty in which a survival-of-the-fittest mentality prevails over any vestige of communality.[8]

The privations and crises of scarcity were not the only factors contributing to the tailspin Travis observed. In the later 1970s, average American household incomes remained in a relatively robust position when compared to their international equivalents. As David Farber describes, households that ranked among the nation's 'bottom 20 per cent' had an 'average income of $15,374, more money than the richest 20 per cent earned in all but a few countries in the world'. This purchasing power was routinely spent on such obligatory consumer durables as the television, a personal *bête noire* for Travis. He claimed that as televisions appeared in more and more households and viewing figures rose across the 1970s, 'things stopped happening' elsewhere: we retreated into our sitting rooms and bathed in the glow of the screen while outside the social bonds withered away. R.D. Laing had made much the same point during his lecture tour of America in 1972. He talked about the incessant interruptions and constant acceleration of the modern world as well as our concomitant 'tendency to distract ourselves'. Arguing for the benefits of meditation, he claimed that Western society was trapped in a cycle of 'doing'. We lacked the opportunity and the capacity to exist in a state of 'being'. It is a contention that continues to have 21st-century relevance. As Adrian Chapman puts it, we would do well to heed Laing's call for a prioritisation of personal rhythms in the neoliberal present in which our minds are never allowed to be at rest. Instead of settling, focusing and filtering out the noise, we give ourselves to it, taking 'dubious refuge' in feedback-led overwork, restless precarity packaged as flexibility and the dopamine fixes that come with social media and online shopping. Against this over-stimulation, Laing argued for the necessity of a 'true' asylum: a place of sanctuary and refuge where people could 'be'. So too for Travis. In making his pitch for the social value of the wellness centre, he saw it as a place that could 'bring people together' to create 'what we are missing the most', the foundational first principles of any functional society: 'community and connection'.[9]

There certainly seemed to be a demand for such a place. By 1979, four years after it opened, the Wellness Resource Center was greeting a healthy stream of clients who were seeking the connection with themselves and with others that Travis promised. In the meantime, he had taken on more staff to keep up with the pace, quickly growing operations from a pair of volunteers to a thirteen-strong team of 'wellness counsellors'. National interest had also continued to grow. By now Travis was regularly criss-crossing the country running weekend seminars for businesses, doctors and psychologists. From the early days of cranking out 50 copies of *The Wellness Index*, the turn of the decade found him printing them by the thousand. Back at Samadhi, Lee and Glenn Perry were also in high demand. In late 1979, four months after their opening, the *LA Times* ran a glowing feature about the centre which extolled the health benefits of floatation. They were soon fully booked and selling five to ten tanks per week. As with other Beverly Hills businesses, they also attracted the celebrity crowd, among them the British film director Ken Russell. In 1979 he was helming the inevitable screen adaptation of *Altered States* after the departure of original director Arthur Penn. Russell's film would turn out to be a dazzling, ultra-psychedelic assault on the turgidity of Chayefsky's prose that plunged lead actor William Hurt into extreme inner landscapes and pulsating cosmic voids. For Russell, though, his visit to Samadhi generated no such fireworks. He was in and out of the tank in ten minutes, claiming that claustrophobia had got the better of him. Apparently, once he entered the tank all Russell could think about was an earlier incident that found him stuck in a lift, in the dark, during a power cut. After this, the Perrys made sure they included in their orientation to all new 'floaters' advice on how to stay calm or, in the event of a panic attack, how to quickly find the door.[10]

In November 1979 it was Travis' turn to bask in the media spotlight when he was the subject of a profile broadcast on *60 Minutes*. Host Dan Rather opened the segment with a breezy tone of discovery: 'Here's a word you don't hear every day: Wellness.' Where Travis previously had to spell out 'wellness' on the phone, he was now being given nationwide exposure, in excess of the conference circuit, as the leader of a 'movement that's catching on all over the country among doctors, nurses and others concerned with medical care'. Rather goes on to describe wellness as a 'positive approach to health', one that 'takes self-care to its farthest point'. Interviewed at the centre, Travis sticks close to the general definition, calling wellness 'an ongoing, dynamic state of growth' rather than 'the absence of disease' before reiterating his antipathy towards the treatment model:

> Just because you aren't sick, you don't have any symptoms and you could go and get a clean bill of health, doesn't mean that you are well. It doesn't mean that you are going to prevent disease further down the line.

Rather next turns his attention turns to some of Travis' clients like Teresa Rose, 'a former nurse who turned to self-care after suffering for years with painful muscle inflammation', and Julio Asposti, 'an executive with a major West Coast firm' who has 'constant headaches and physical pain'. Little detail is given about the nature of Rose's wellness programme but we're led to believe she's a satisfied customer. 'I was just so tied and so fed up being in so much pain,' she explains, before we see her playing squash, running across the court with no hint of discomfort. Much more attention is paid to Asposti's case as we're told his 'illness problems' were solved by 'biofeedback'. Over footage of Travis leading Asposti through the use of a thermal sensor, Rather describes biofeedback as a means of measuring 'the amount of tension or stress in a person's body'. We're told that after 'several sessions Julio learned to not only to relieve his pain but also how to handle stressful situations at work'. Like the now energetic and pain-free Rose, when Asposti started coming to see Travis he was 'getting headaches about three times a week'. He tells Rather that now, thanks to the wellness programme, he's having them only 'about once a month'.

During his own interview for the segment, Travis was keen to present wellness as 'an adjunct to and quite different from the practice of medicine' rather than a 'substitute'. Reiterating the stance that previously caused such difficulties when he tried to gain support for his work in 1975, Travis added, 'We don't treat, diagnose or prescribe'. As ever, the pitch was that the Wellness Resource Center was all about fostering affirmative, client-focused insights: 'Our role is to help the person discover why they are sick.' Despite this specificity, the main angle of the piece was that Rose and Asposti have found an alternative to what Rather calls 'traditional medical care'. Rose is said to have been 'unable to find a cure with regular doctors' and after spending thousands of dollars over nine years seeing 'numerous specialists' she realised she had 'achieved nothing' and 'gave-up conventional medicine'. Similarly, Asposti's doctors 'told him [the illness] was due to stress in his work' but offered no lasting solution, and 'any tests or X-rays doctors administered [...] proved negative'. In the face of this disappointment with 'regular doctors', *60 Minutes* presents wellness as a quick, cost-effective miracle cure. It is 'self-care' in the most literal sense, a way of taking health matters into one's own hands when no one else is up to the job. Between Rose and Asposti, it is Rose the *former* nurse who makes this point most vociferously. Drawing a line in the sand between her work at the Wellness Center and the view of the wider public represented by Rather, she argues that she had 'spent all these years going to *your* credentialed individuals' but it was only when she saw Travis that she 'found someone who was willing to talk it out with me'. According to Rose, Travis listened; he did not 'tell me what was wrong' but helped 'me find out myself'.[11]

✳✳✳✳✳

In the years that followed, Travis would often show clips from 'Wellness', the *60 Minutes* item, when lecturing on his work. While he appreciated the exposure, he maintained that Dan Rather had misread the project. Specifically, he had 'collapsed self-care with wellness'. In Travis' view 'they're really two different things'. The process of self-care, he would often explain, is 'part of the treatment paradigm which is fixing things'. Wellness, however, is a practice of 'learning and growing' which focuses on the interrelationship between mental, emotional, physical and spiritual well-being. Self-care is thus part of this holistic frame but does not entirely define it; it is one technique among many that could be incorporated into a bespoke development programme. Between 1972 and 1977

Travis had adjusted the wording and graphics of his 'Illness-Wellness Continuum' to emphasise this point. The first edition, published in 1972, featured two sectors, divided by the 'neutral point' of 'no discernible illness or wellness'. To the left of this point lay the territory of 'traditional medicine', and to the right lay the stages of 'well medicine'. Within the latter field, the road to 'high-level wellness' consisted of three marker points: 'education', 'growth' and the Abraham Maslow-inspired end point of 'self-actualization'. By 1977, this trio had been adjusted and reordered into a new sequence: 'awareness, education, growth'. It was a slight but significant change. By swapping out 'self-actualization' for 'growth', Travis was untethering his wellness project from the language of humanistic psychology and the aura of Esalen-type human potential. He was also refusing to cap the achievement of 'high-level wellness'. Where 'self-actualization' hinted at an end point, a moment of final realisation, 'growth' was ambiguously dynamic. It helped clarify the idea that the pursuit of wellness was meant to be an ongoing, open-ended movement.[12]

The instant gratification of 'fixing things', though, was a much easier sell than this admittedly nebulous target. It is also not surprising that *60 Minutes* would take this line, given that the empowerment of a do-it-yourself approach held significant currency at the time. From the trenches of punk rock and the good life of suburban allotments to the cosy television interiors of *The Magic of Oil Painting* (1974–82) and *This Old House* (1979–), the DIY ethic extended across the social landscape of the 1970s. By the end of the decade this idea of getting the job done gained an added potency in the face of mounting economic problems, governmental stasis and a seemingly incompetent and unnecessary hierarchy of 'experts'. The chorus of voices emerging from these varied microindustries told you to go ahead and form that band, paint that masterpiece and realise the perfect home. All you needed was a pocket of enthusiasm and a couple of free weekends. Along the way you could also offset any feelings of workplace inadequacy, and with the right 'father-son project' you could even repair some frayed family bonds. With so much to gain by having a go, why should you pause and wait for someone else's permission or approval?[13]

It was President Jimmy Carter who unwittingly crystallised this mood in July 1979 when he gave a televised address on the 'moral and spiritual crisis' befalling the American nation. At his inauguration exactly three years earlier, Carter had stood before a beleaguered public, telling them to struggle on and do their best. Now, in what has come to be known as his 'Crisis of Confidence' speech, Carter focused on the deeper problem foregrounded by the ongoing energy crisis. He continued to call for 'sacrifice', arguing that America must stop relying on oil that 'comes from foreign countries at prices that are going through the roof', but he also drilled down into the national psyche and laid the blame for the situation on domestic attitudes just as much as international tensions. He spoke of a lack of productivity and a 'growing disrespect for government and for churches and for schools, the news media and other institutions'. In part, Carter attributed this unravelling of the social fabric to the post-traumatic overhang of the 1960s and the resonating impact of Watergate. More damningly, though, he also spoke of a pernicious 'self-interest' fragmenting what should be a collective 'spirit'. Born of profligacy and materialism, this was an attitude that worshipped 'self-indulgence and consumption' over 'hard-work, strong-families, close-knit communities and our faith in God'. The implication was that America had wilfully lost its way. People seemed content to pile up material goods to 'fill the emptiness of their lives which have no confidence or purpose' when they could be seizing control of a 'common destiny' and cultivating the country's still potent resources. In Carter's analysis, the energy crisis was a symptom not a cause of this deep disillusionment. It was as if the contemporary unwillingness to rally and to 'save for the future' had prepared the ground for the influx of expensive oil as well as the unemployment and inflation it brought with it.

If the 'Crisis of Confidence' speech carried echoes of *The Culture of Narcissism*, the parallel was not coincidental. According to Richard Cohen, a journalist for *The Washington Post*, the book was one 'you [saw] around the White House' in 1979 and Christopher Lasch, along with the sociologist Daniel Bell and the minister Revd Jesse Jackson, was one of several 'brain trusters' from whom Carter sought counsel as his sense of a systemic crisis deepened. The address was a bold intervention from a thoughtful, committed president who was not content to offer optimistic platitudes, and it was intended to galvanise a weary audience into action. Such home truths, however, had very much the opposite effect upon the pubic. With its downbeat and critical tone, the 'Crisis of Confidence' broadcast dented the image of Carter's executive power. It created an impression of a president beset by problems who looked to those most affected – the voters – for solutions. As Cohen wrote in his column a few days after the speech, there was 'something troubling about the message that we are all in this together [...] that we are all, citizen and president alike, traveling in the same boat down the same stream'. Bluntly, he added: 'It's not that way at all.' If Carter was indeed 'the captain of this boat', then he should be taking the helm, not holding on with everyone else as the vessel drives headlong into the rapids. 'We're waiting for our orders,' Cohen concluded.[14]

A few months later the mood darkened further when, on 4 November, the American embassy in Tehran was overrun by young supporters of the 'Islamic fundamentalist Ayatollah Ruhollah Khomeini'. Khomeini had returned from exile to seize power after the downfall of the liberalising, American-aligned Shah of Iran, Mohammad Reza Pahlavi, who had been given sanctuary in the US that October. The embassy had been the focus of Iranian–American tensions since the start of the Shah's rule in 1953 – the result of a CIA-backed coup – but the flashpoint ignited in 1979 with this decisive change in leadership, the crux of the Iranian Revolution that had extended over much of the previous year. Khomeini wanted to reassert Iranian self-determination and Islamic law. He also claimed to speak for the will of the people when demanding the Shah return to Iran to face trial. To that end, the student-led takeover of the embassy was described as a 'defensive act' to protect the revolution from 'American interference'. It was also a symbolic victory in the 'battle of nerves' between the two countries, a damaging strike against a symbol of America's international influence. Stuck between these gestures were a group of embassy workers, diplomats and marines taken as hostages, 52 of whom would go onto endure 444 days of often hostile captivity. It was a crisis that saw out Carter's first term, arguably cost him a second and was only resolved just as his successor, Ronald Reagan, took office in early 1981. In between, the spectacle of American hostages being used to pressure the US to hand over the Shah compounded the sense of a wholesale crisis pervading American culture. There was trouble at home and trouble abroad and all the governing administration seemed able to do was flounder in its attempts to maintain authority.

When Travis' *60 Minutes* slot aired on 18 November it shared the line-up with 'The Ayatollah', a segment by Mike Wallace in which he interviewed Khomeini, two weeks into the hostage crisis. Although there was no intended connection between the reports, reflecting on the juxtaposition of smiling faces at the Mill Valley Center and that of the uncompromising Ayatollah gives a clue as to the covert appeal of wellness in the late 1970s. Socially, culturally and politically it may have seemed as if things were collapsing, but what Travis was offering was a benign means of re-establishing personal control, do-it-yourself in its clearest and most effective form. 'In wellness, you are the leader', explained one client in response to Dan Rather asking if the 'wellness movement' was a 'middle-class cult'. Continuing, they added: 'You're your own guru and you're the perfect person that is trying to make your life better and more full'. It was a response that, ironically, sounded not unlike a disciple quoting from the texts of a middle-class cult, but beneath the evangelising tone lay a clear emphasis on autonomy and self-determination. As Travis would later write, he did not 'want to be looked on as the expert dictating the one true way'. The 'wellness paradigm', he argued, 'calls for openness, individuality, and choices freely made'. At a time when public confidence in institutions was at an all-time low, when the confidence integral to America's outward-facing identity was withering, here was a rallying reminder that you can and should have confidence in yourself.[15]

The theologian and social critic Ivan Illich had made a similar and more vociferous point three years earlier in his book *Medical Nemesis* (1976). A trenchant critique of modern health care, *Medical Nemesis* appeared at the start of the Carter presidency and coincided with high-profile reports that pointed to a widespread public distrust in the medical profession. As Ferguson describes, one Gallup poll recorded that '44 per cent' did not believe doctors 'to be highly ethical and honest', a point proved in 1976 when 'thirteen of fifteen physicians running for national office [...] lost their elections'. The issue, according to a Senate subcommittee on health, was a growing climate of 'dehumanization' in which medicine, when understood as 'the interface between humanity and technology', prioritised the latter at the expense of the former. Illich echoed this analysis, describing the medical system as a crucible of 'iatrogenic' or 'doctor-induced' illness. Castigating what he saw as the 'expropriation of autonomy' within the doctor–patient relationship, Illich argued that the predominance of drug-based treatment models coupled with the excessive pathologising of human behaviour had created an industrial-scale medical system dedicated to keeping people ill. In a reflection of Travis' theorisation of wellness, Illich saw health as substantially more than the homeostasis of not being ill. Health was a measure of one's 'ability to cope' with the world. In his view, modern medicine neutralised this coping mechanism by generating a two-fold dependency: a dependency on the drugs administered and a dependency on the doctors administering them. Within this illness-care system, patients became the passive consumers of short-term solutions and, according to Illich, were divested of their ability to independently maintain a progressively improving state of health.

Illich was unforgiving in his characterisation of doctors as 'biological accountants' who organised 'disease hunts'. His language, as Ardell noted, 'was overkill to the point of satire'. One can readily agree: at times, *Medical Nemesis* reads like a non-fiction version of Robin Cook's bestseller *Coma* (1977), a thriller about a modern, low-cost treatment facility specialising in comatose patients that doubles as a black-market organ-harvesting operation. Of course, Illich's analysis was as not as fantastical as Cook's speculative fiction, but his descriptions of patient dependency nonetheless echo the image of a hospital consuming and commodifying those it purports to treat. For Illich, though, there were no villains working in the shadows of an otherwise beneficial service. If anything, his analysis was much bleaker. While iatrogenic illness was often taken to mean malpractice, surgical problems, prescription mistakes, unforeseen side effects and other such complications, Illich saw an intentional mendacity flowing through the operation of public health. In his view the medical establishment did not cater to the needs of its patients but instead satisfied the demands of its own 'industrial, technological and basically inhumane system'. He claimed that recommendations for surgery were made to provide an ever-increasing number of newly qualified surgeons with a reliable client base while 'costly therapies of questionable utility' were also rolled out for economic rather than pragmatic reasons. Institutions thus prospered by maintaining low levels of public health either through the induction of dependency or the 'debilitating effects of hospitalization'. 'The miracle of modern medicine', Illich argued, 'is diabolical' because it creates a 'patient population scripted for illness'.[16]

This depressing portrait chimed with Travis' motif of the doctor as 'pill fairy', the purveyor of the short-term fix which distracts from the long-term project of improvement. In *The Aquarian Conspiracy*, Ferguson similarly encouraged practitioners to 'see beyond symptoms to the context of illness: stress, society, family, diet, season', claiming that a 'new level of wellness' could be found if allopathic, analgesic and pharmaceutical remedies were to be supplemented, if not replaced with those attuned to the 'bodymind' such as 'meditation, biofeedback' and other forms of 'autogenic training' that can 'help elicit the body's recovery phase'. In support of her argument Ferguson cited a series of informal working papers issued in 1977 by the National Institute for Mental Health that advocated for 'prevention' rather than 'pathology' and decried the 'too rigid separation of physical and emotional problems' as well as 'the assumption of an asymmetrical relationship between an all-powerful physician and a submissive patient'. They wanted clinicians to look 'for answers in other traditions and techniques' such as 'acupuncture, homeopathy, herbalism [...] psychic healing'. In theory, floatation also worked as part of this array. For the Perrys, time in the tank was not just relaxing, it could also ease chronic pain and help in the relief of insomnia, anxiety and depression.

These practices variously offered an alternative to 'conventional' medicine, one based on what Illich would term 'conviviality', a process of 'mutual self-care' that turned away from a 'neurotic' reliance on professionals and instead attempted to bring 'personal energy under personal control'. In advocating their rollout, Ferguson was sounding a distinctly optimistic note, and over the course of *The Aquarian Conspiracy* she was waving a definite 'hello' to the 1980s. The book radiates with the language of potentiality grounded in an over-idealised image of American identity if not manifest destiny. With the bicentennial celebrations of 1976 forming a potent ideological backdrop, Ferguson largely ignores Carter's moderate, consensus-forming approach and argues in favour of an autarchy, 'government by the self'. She envisages the 'conspirators' of the book, variously active in 'health, humanistic education, new politics, and management' as a leaderless, non-hierarchical network of sole traders, agents of individual change who are not beholden to experts, not receptive to limits nor amenable to sacrifice. Once again, it is a distinctly eupsychian view that recalls Abraham Maslow's contention that the better society will emerge following the cultivation of healthier, happier individuals. Ferguson, however, roots this impetus in the self-determination of 'the founding fathers and of the American transcendentalists of the 1800s'. In her attempt to catalyse 'autonomy, awakening, creativity and reconciliation', then, Ferguson remains tethered to that most attractive and indistinct of national myths, the American Dream.

'There have always been two "bodies" of the American dream,' she explains. 'One, the dream of tangibles', relates to 'material well-being and practical, everyday freedoms'. The other, 'like an etheric body extending from the material dream', pertains to 'psychological liberation' and this is the state Ferguson focuses upon. She also points to the intersection of the two, as well as the economic contingency of her 'elusive' target. Material 'well-being', she suggests, is a prerequisite for 'psychological liberation'. Its 'proponents' have 'nearly always come from the comfortable social classes' because they have the means to pursue this goal. 'Having achieved the first measure of freedom,' Ferguson explains, 'they hunger for the second'. Emerging from affluence, then, this 'hunger' was not, at least in material terms, a response to poverty or privation, it was not indicative of a deficit, but spoke of a desire for *more*. It was an attitude, an appetite, that struck a chord not with the preceding years of the

Carter administration but with the new mainstream political context taking shape at the turn of the decade. By the time *The Aquarian Conspiracy* was published, first in the US in 1980 and then in the UK in 1981, the mainstream political climate had veered towards the right thanks to the arrival of that classic transatlantic double act, Republican President elect Ronald Reagan and Conservative Prime Minister Margaret Thatcher. Their policies privileged an aggressively fiscal version of Ferguson's emphasis on individual development and demonstrated an adherence to an ideology that was fast becoming the dominant form of Western political thought: neoliberalism.[17]

*****

Outlined in its modern form in 1947 by the Swiss-based think tank the Mont Pelerin Society, neoliberalism is a political philosophy of 'anti-bureaucracy' that attempted to recalibrate 'the functions of the state' in a climate of post-war reconstruction. As Germany and Japan rose from the ruins and Soviet Russia extended the reach of communism, neoliberalism attempted to exorcise the ghost of totalitarianism by aligning the idea of a 'free society' with the operation of 'market-oriented economic systems'. Essentially, it prioritised economics over partisanship by equating the 'smooth functioning of the market' with the 'creation of an international order conducive to the safeguarding of peace and liberty'. In this post-war phase, neoliberalism looked forward to a new globalism of 'harmonious international economic relations' in which ideological antagonism was dissolved by the levelling power of capital.

Three decades later, neoliberalism had been retooled into a hegemonic programme of 'pure market logic' which conceived the human subject as a rational economic actor or 'dollar-hunting animal: *homo economicus*'. In Britain, Thatcher, who stepped into power following the Winter of Discontent, put this theory into practice by pursuing a blanket policy of 'entrepreneurship, privatization and de-regulation' that sought to bolster the economy while simultaneously disempowering the trade unions. Over in Washington, Reagan's sunny Hollywood persona similarly fostered a business climate rooted in free market economics. Speaking in 1975, Reagan had predicted the end of communism on the grounds that it was a 'temporary aberration' running counter to 'human nature'. That 'nature' – the acquisitive, competitive, exploitative drive of capitalism – would flourish during his presidency, leading to a culture of materialism and fetishised upward mobility. Where Ferguson hypothesised a government that would incubate 'growth, creativity, co-operation', Thatcher and Reagan variously realised it via a wholesale attempt 'to revive the reputation of capitalism' and to 'liberate those who create wealth'.[18]

In theory, the idea of competitive self-interest as the basis of social and political participation was meant to free the individual from their alleged dependence on government intervention. In practice, however, the 'exposure of the state sector to competition' involved the dissolution of any 'collective structures' or forms of support that might impede the progress of marketisation. It was a politics that ultimately favoured the privileged: a form of liberalism in which opportunity replaced equality in the aggressive pursuit of maximum profit. Upon taking office in 1979, Thatcher set this process in motion by immediately rolling back public spending. One of her government's first white papers claimed that 'public expenditure' was at the 'heart of Britain's present economic difficulties'. By 'public spending', the Conservatives generally meant 'welfare' such as social security and income support. Making these cuts, the party argued, would allow for a growth-producing reduction in the rate of income tax, a policy that would clearly only benefit those fortunate enough to be in a higher income bracket in the first place.

Although the Thatcher government did not fully remove welfare provision, they substantially reorganised it towards a targeted, means-tested form of 'poverty relief' as opposed to the Beveridge-style aims of the post-war Labour government that focused on the 'provision of universal welfare services'. Of course, Labour did not eliminate poverty in the years following 1945 and the Beveridge Report promised more than could be properly enacted in policy. However, there was at least the political will built into the party's ideology to establish a functioning welfare system. Thatcherism, by contrast, dismantled this structure and in the process actively generated a society of 'want'. The entrepreneurial thrust that opened the British 1980s may have promised a future of opportunity for all, but the running of this race inevitably marginalised anyone who lacked the resources to join in. For those stuck in the era's ever-tightening poverty trap at the foot of the enterprise pyramid – a structure that necessarily depended on scarcity and economic inequality – the outlook was bleak. The overriding political message of the time was being broadcast loud and clear: you are on your own.[19]

So too were the aquarian conspirators. According to Ronald Purser, neoliberalism conditions us to think that in 'a market-based society' we are perpetually able to increase 'the value of our human capital and self-worth'. Ferguson thought the same. Writing in *The Aquarian Conspiracy*, as if addressing the nascent yuppies of the emerging 1980s rather than the late hippies of the waning 1970s, she describes 'wellness' as a desirable lifestyle pursued by a growing, but nevertheless limited group who seek 'levels of fulfilment that once seemed impossible'. This is to be achieved not through finding solutions to such questions of social policy as 'how are we going to provide adequate national health insurance', but through the advocacy of individualised strategies of illness avoidance. For Ferguson, 'health' is a concept separate from the realm of 'hospitals, doctors, prescription drugs, technology'. It is to be fostered autonomously through the pursuit of a personal programme of self-development. Similarly, as Purser puts it, the neoliberal agent is required to 'maximize' their 'own welfare, freedom and happiness' in order to 'fully actualize' their 'personal freedom and potential': to remain physically and economically active enough to realise the value of their labour. It is necessary to 'deftly' manage one's own 'internal resources' in this way, because other 'social actors [...] the state, voluntary associations and the like', all those 'obstacles' in the way of free-flowing market logic, have either been removed, repurposed, rationalised or just plain destroyed.

The aspiration of Ferguson's writing neither acknowledges nor laments the loss of this scaffold. She claims to be mapping an emerging network ranging 'across all levels of income and education, from the humblest to the highest', but her outlook carries with it the same undertow of division as that emanating from the marketised orbit of Thatcher and Reagan. *The Aquarian Conspiracy* may have looked for a link between the humblest and the highest, but in the main it focuses on the 'haves' rather than the 'have-nots'. Little consideration is given to matters of class, wealth differentials and relative health-care access that have a bearing on the actual need for 'adequate national health care insurance'. To step away from 'traditional' health care with such adventurous ease was not a shift available to all, nor has it become one. Ferguson may have held out the promise of a 'richness of choice' following on from an exploratory commitment to personal growth, but the pursuit of such independence involved a privileged and risky movement into a zone that had no safety net.

John Travis also saw wellness as 'a choice – a decision you make to move towards optimal health', and therein lay another conceptual problem of self-responsibility in an atmosphere of ambition and individual enterprise. If you can choose to be well, if it is ultimately down to you, then illness is your own responsibility too. Just as Esalen declared us all to be 'gods' and thus 'responsible for everything that happened', some wellness practitioners, particularly towards the end of the 1970s, started to frame illness as a matter of personal fault. At his most cautiously extreme, Don Ardell agreed with Ivan Illich that professional medicine exonerated patients of 'moral accountability' for their illnesses: if your lifestyle is unhealthy, you are the one to blame. According to this argument – as with the thrust of Ferguson's thinking – the solution lies not with the systemic provision of welfare but with individual agency, the adoption of an entrepreneurial approach to well-being. For those suffering under the combined weight of low incomes, low social capital and a lack of access to such opportunities, following through on any decision to be well was much easier said than done.[20]

Despite this attitude, the personal and professional practice of wellness was not enough to keep hardship from the door, however much its ideas reflected those of the dominant ideology. Neoliberalism holds no quarter, as both Travis and the Perrys found out to their cost. As the 1980s opened, the Wellness Resource Center and the Samadhi Tank Company both fell victim to the classic trap facing every fledgling business: overexpansion. By 1979 Travis was struggling to manage day-to-day operations with his thirteen-strong team and he was increasingly playing the role of manager rather than practitioner. He was burnt out, and the image of the 'quiet little practice' in Mill Valley he had established in 1975 had long since vanished in a whirl of consultations, lectures and never-ending administrative tasks. More seriously, despite the workload, the centre was failing to turn a profit. The more it grew, the more unsustainable the whole operation became. Shortly after the PR coup of the *60 Minutes* feature, then, an exhausted Travis was forced to pull the plug. He shut up shop, gathered his resources and considered his next move.

As for the Perrys, it was also a case of too much, too fast, too soon. After the buzz of their first few months running their centre in Beverly Hills, they were keen to extend their client base to 'cultural creatives and influencers', those with the right mix of disposable income and a mindset in sync with the philosophy of floatation. To that end, the Perrys fell in with 'George (not his real name)', a 'satisfied tank owner' who was also 'a very successful and charismatic businessman'. George was keen to franchise the float centre and he raised 'a million dollars from limited partners' to open a '20 tank showroom centre' in downtown San Francisco. Occupying an entire floor of a commercial complex on the city's Van Ness Avenue, the idea was for the centre to sell float sessions, to market tanks from its plush showroom and to train new centre staff in its state-of-the-art auditorium. It was hoped that these new trainees would then take on franchises of their own. Everything looked great on paper and the centre, when it opened, seemed to offer a glimpse into a bright, profitable future.

In the event, though, things quickly went sour. The 'Samadhi Alliance' turned out to be a combustible mix of the Perrys' social agenda – the desire 'to get more people to float' – and George's 'modern values', a quintessentially 1980s outlook of 'personal success and financial gain'. The centre 'ended up a showcase of wealth, comfort and glitz' aimed not at the seekers the Perrys had in mind, but George's fellow high rollers. He had held-out for Van Ness Avenue because it was a twenty-minute taxi ride from San Francisco Airport, and he wanted to capture the lucrative trade of layover pilots and jet-lagged business travellers. It turned out to be a risky bet. George's ideal clientele proved elusive, unwilling to leave their airport hotels just to try a new kind of relaxation. It was much easier to come off the red-eye and stick with the old favourites: the hotel bar and room service. And so, with footfall low and franchises slow to take off, the Samadhi Alliance started to struggle. It soon became clear that the ambitious enterprise could not survive. Bankrupt and owing $750,000, it closed in 1980 after little more than a year. Worse still, not only were the Perrys owed $120,000 for the tanks 'bought' by the alliance, but their Beverly Hills Center was also invested in the partnership. When the Samadhi Alliance went under, so too did their cherished flagship operation. By the end of 1980, the Perrys still had their company name, but they were otherwise 'back at ground zero with no operating capital and no ready outlet for selling tanks'.[21]

In their short lifespans, both the Wellness Resource Center and the Samadhi Tank Company had shown that a ready market existed for wellness practices and alternative approaches to health. They also showed that in the late 1970s, any commercial enterprise had to be able to hit the ground running and turn a healthy profit in an increasingly aggressive economic climate. Whatever the human or social value of a given product, any measure of success was beholden to the ultimate authority of business: the bottom line. If projects of the sort developed by Travis and the Perrys were to flourish in the even more volatile atmosphere of the neoliberal 1980s, they would have to adapt. It was not the time for a new set of ideas. The product was solid. What the emergent wellness sector needed was a new base, a new business plan and a new face. Enter Dr Jon Kabat-Zinn.

*****

On the author photograph that accompanies his book *Full Catastrophe Living* (1990), Jon Kabat-Zinn fixes the camera's gaze with a calm yet confident stare. It is the studied look of the cool doctor, a portrait of a man with responsibility, but who is also at ease with himself. In control. With his tweed sports jacket, his undone top button and his casually loosened tie, he looks like he is taking five after a high-stakes meeting. Or perhaps he is always like this: slightly ruffled, a professional but maybe also bit of a rebel, someone who is slightly at odds with the buttoned-down life, not unlike like Michael Douglas in the film version of *Coma* (1978). His hair is similar, at least – not too short, not too long, but long enough to suggest a vague air of countercultural affectation.

Turn to the book's acknowledgements and you'll find a lot that backs up this impression. As might be expected, Kabat-Zinn thanks his colleagues at the University of Massachusetts Medical Center as well as his former teachers at the Massachusetts Institute of Technology. However, all this cap-doffing is merely a preamble to the impressive list of Buddhists, meditation practitioners, yoga experts and spiritual teachers that follows. He thanks Philip Kapleau, author of *The Three Pillars of Zen* (1967), for 'coming to MIT to conduct meditation retreats among the scientists'; he thanks John Lauder, 'a genius of a yoga teacher, for his wonderfully understated classes in the basement of the church in Harvard Square' and he thanks Ram Dass for *Be Here Now*, a book he reflects, with a slight air of mystery, that he was given 'one day in the desert in New Mexico'. It is a feast of name-dropping that frames Kabat-Zinn as a modern-day mystic, someone who has sought out meetings with remarkable men before returning to the world of professional medicine with their wisdom in hand.[22]

Out of this group, Kabat-Zinn's sincerest thanks are saved for the Vietnamese teacher and proponent of 'engaged Buddhism', Thích Nhất Hạnh, who is praised for his 'gentleness of being, for his unwavering and total commitment to healing the deep psychic wounds of the Vietnam War and those we incur in simply being alive'. Nhất Hạnh – formerly Nguyen Xuan Bao – was born in Hue, Vietnam in 1926. He entered Buddhist training at the age of sixteen and took the name Nhất Hạnh (meaning 'one' and 'action') upon his move to Saigon in 1949. He developed 'engaged Buddhism', the 'kind of Buddhism that responds to what is happening in the here and now', from 1954 onwards, in response to the split and subsequent conflict between Vietnam's communist North and non-communist South. Nhất Hạnh, latterly 'Thay' ('master'), sought to offer the 'confused' country a 'spiritual direction' by advocating for the introduction of

Buddhist thought into everyday social life. As he put it in a 2008 lecture: 'While you brush your teeth, Buddhism should be there. While you drive your car, Buddhism should be there. While you are walking in the supermarket, Buddhism should be there.' Central to this practice was the principle of *satipatthana* or mindfulness, a 'state of maximum awareness of our bodily and mental processes.'[23]

Mindfulness, according to the German-born Buddhist Nyanaponika Mahathera, is 'the heart of Buddhist meditation', a means of achieving the 'highest aim: the mind's own unshakeable deliverance from Greed, Hatred and Delusion'. Pursued through breathing exercises like the *anapanasati*, it is not a matter of turning inside and retreating from the world, but of becoming totally conscious of one's own experience as a living being. To be fully mindful means to be 'wide-awake, aware of reality in its depth and concreteness'. Nhất Hạnh offered this state as a 'direct answer to the war' because it ultimately held out the promise of a 'non-attachment to views, freedom from all ideologies'.

His ostensible message was one of peace and reconciliation, and by the mid-1960s Nhất Hạnh was fêted internationally as an advocate of non-violent protest. Meanwhile, he was being condemned into exile by the South Vietnamese government for refusing to condone the war on communism. Far from being apolitical, though, the meditative approach of engaged Buddhism was grounded in a deeply ethical stance. The process of bringing the mind into the present central to *satipatthana* is also understood more informally within the Buddhist world as *sati*, a living concept and daily practice closely bound up with memory. *Sati*, although generally translated as 'mindfulness', involves 'the use of memory to avoid distraction and cultivate a moralized mastery over the mind'. In this way, *sati* may be used to 'remember past problems to help understand present circumstances', whether that be learning from past mistakes or staving off forgetfulness itself. Either way, the attentiveness of *sati* – not letting the mind wander, recalling 'where one is' and concentrating upon the minutiae of the now – is linked to the practice of a good life because 'it helps you to recollect what one should do [...] to know what is right and what is wrong'. For Nhất Hạnh, bringing

Buddhism into the everyday was not a means of escaping from the problems of the world but a method of discovering the right way to navigate them. At a micro level this could mean knowing 'what to buy and what not to buy' in the supermarket, while at the macro level of the Vietnamese conflict the practice was equally instructive. In this context, Nhất Hạnh was advocating for a 'non-attachment' to partisan concerns, not to ignore the war but to argue for the 'right' way: the avoidance of conflict altogether.[24]

When developing his practice in the late 1970s, Kabat-Zinn stuck close to Nhất Hạnh's definition, calling mindfulness 'the art of conscious living'. He saw it as form of 'moment-to-moment awareness' cultivated 'by purposefully paying attention to things we ordinarily never give a moment's thought to'. This basic definition would appear virtually unchanged throughout Kabat-Zinn's works, with the only substantive adjustment being a later call to pay attention 'non-judgmentally' to the present moment. However, although Kabat-Zinn had been involved in the protest movement of the 1960s and shared his mentor's anti-war stance, his brand of mindfulness – typically deployed as a therapeutic combination of meditation and Hatha yoga – turned its attention away from political activism. Instead, Kabat-Zinn took on the broader target of modern life and its various stresses. Borrowing a line from *Zorba the Greek* (1964), Kabat-Zinn called this pressure the 'full catastrophe': the 'poignant enormity of our life experience'. He had no singular disaster in mind, but rather the multiple happenings 'that cause us distress and pain and that promote in us an underlying sense of fear, insecurity and loss of control'. From the big problems of vulnerability, mortality and 'our collective capacity for cruelty and violence' to the small stuff we can't help but sweat, the 'full catastrophe' was for Kabat-Zinn the measure of the human condition with 'all of its dilemmas, sorrows and tragedies'. Faced with the inevitability of this storm, Kabat-Zinn conceived of mindfulness as a way of weathering the gale. It was not intended as a magic button to solve all of life's problems, but a way of helping clients cope with them.[25]

Kabat-Zinn's mindfulness has become a ubiquitous fixture in the field of modern holistic health, and the word is often taken as a synonym for wellness. It is easy to see why, given that the two practices have similar methodologies, work towards similar aims and share very similar language. Consider, for example, Kabat-Zinn's offer of mindfulness to 'anyone, well or ill who seeks to transcend his or her limitations and move towards greater levels of well-being'. Travis had previously said much the same about wellness, framing his system as a method of 'transcending', a 'never-ending process of moving towards the living of your highest potential'. Both men were also of a similar age, had similar educational backgrounds and having embarked on parallel careers in medicine both greeted their mid-thirties by performing radical shifts in these professional trajectories. They each stepped away from drug-based treatment models towards strategies of 'self-development, self-discovery, learning and healing'. But where Travis had to strike out on his own into the independence and insecurity of the Wellness Resource Center, Kabat-Zinn was able to secure significant institutional support for his project. In 1979, just as Travis was closing down his operation, the 35-year-old Kabat-Zinn established a clinic within the University of Massachusetts Medical Center: the Stress Reduction and Relaxation Program.

The 'stress clinic', as it became known, took on patients referred by their doctors for a catalogue of problems 'ranging from headaches, high blood pressure, and back pain' to heart disease and cancer. It offered an eight-week programme grounded in behavioural medicine

> which believes that mental and emotional factors, the ways in which we think and behave can have a significant effect, for better or for worse, on our physical health and on our capacity to recover from illness and injury.

As with Travis' non-diagnostic, educative approach to wellness, the stress clinic taught patients 'the *how* of taking care of themselves, not as a replacement to their medical treatment, but as a vitally important complement to it'. In essence, Kabat-Zinn offered his 'intensive, self-directed training program' to those who wanted to 'regain control' of their health and 'attain at least some peace of mind'. Having said this, Travis' eight-month master's-level course focused on more than 'peace of mind'. He took his clients through the 'physical, emotional, psychological and spiritual' aspects of well-being, a full spectrum that included detailed advice on nutrition, exercise and work patterns just as much as it encouraged ruminative self-examination. By contrast, the eight weeks offered by Kabat-Zinn were narrower in their teachings but more open-ended in their intended effects. Rather than working with a client to define a personally tailored 'way of life', Kabat-Zinn taught a simple form of meditation that was intended to lay the groundwork for a lifetime of practice.[26]

It would begin with raisins. To introduce the idea of meditation, each patient entering the clinic would be given three raisins with the invitation to eat them one at a time while carefully reflecting on what they were 'actually doing and experiencing from moment to moment'. First, they were asked to feel the texture of raisin number one, and to note any feelings that arose about their food preferences and appetites. Then, Kabat-Zinn would ask them to savour the raisin's aroma and to anticipate its taste, again remaining attuned to any emotional effects. Would it be sweet? Would it be sour? Do they even *like* raisins? After these ruminations would come the quiet instruction to place the raisin in their in their mouths, at which point the slow chewing would begin. After tasting, swallowing and reflecting on being 'one raisin heavier', the process would repeat for raisins two and three. This exercise in 'slowing things down' was designed to illustrate just how 'powerful and uncontrolled many of our impulses are'. According to Kabat-Zinn, although we so often turn to food 'when we feel anxious or depressed', we rarely actually think about what we eat, how we eat or why we eat. The raisin exercise was all about regaining this attention and this control through the cultivation of an intense degree of awareness. Such focus, Kabat-Zinn argues, allows us to see 'more deeply'. We become aware of the 'connectedness between things like food, attitudes and impulses'. By paying attention in this way, 'you literally become more awake' because, as Kabat-Zinn puts it, you realise that the present moment 'is the only time that any of us ever has'.

It was a message reiterated throughout the rest of the course, mainly through the teaching of breathing-based meditation. When we breathe, explained Kabat-Zinn, we enter into a 'rhythmic exchange' with the world around us. Matter and energy 'flow back and forth between our bodies and what we call the environment'. Carbon dioxide is expelled, oxygen is taken in and, as such, we exist in a continual cycle of 'waste disposal and renewal'. Intersecting with this transfer is the flow of oxygen-rich red blood cells around the body, what Kabat-Zinn calls 'the pulse of life', the 'rhythm of the primordial sea internalized'. Recognising and becoming aware of these sensations – the heartbeat pushing the blood, the rising and falling of the chest as the lungs fill up and empty out, the cool breeze of the air that enters the nose and exits the mouth – is the key to mindfulness as 'a formal meditative practice'. By focusing on our breathing, we can relocate our centre of gravity away from the head and its noisy distractions to the slow, regular rhythms of the abdomen. This sets forth a wave of calm that eases the physical and psychological tensions caused by the tightening crank of stress.

To take this anchoring effect further, Kabat-Zinn also taught a technique called the 'body scan'. This involved a 'thorough and minute focus on the body' in which the mind is guided through one physical region after another, pausing at each stage to feel the intricacy of its organic processes. The client was asked to visualise a breath moving from the toes to the feet, the legs to the pelvis, the torso and upwards to the head. The aim was to imagine that one was breathing through the entire body, with the air leaving the crown like spray from the blowhole of a whale. According to Kabat-Zinn, by the time the scan was complete it would feel as if the physical body had dropped away, and disappearing along with it would be all the knotty barnacles of anxiety. From here the unweighted, now translucent body would be free to 'dwell in silence'.

The motif of the whale was not accidental on Kabat-Zinn's part. Oceanic imagery regularly surfaces in *Full Catastrophe Living* to the extent that deep breathing is likened to a descent from 'choppy waters' to an aquatic underneath, a space that is 'calm even when the surface is agitated'. This is the centre of Kabat-Zinn's cyclone and access to it formed the focus of mindfulness training at the stress clinic. Body scans were practised for the first four weeks of the course – daily for two weeks with the help of a tape-recorded programme and then alternated with yoga sessions for the following two weeks. By encouraging his patients to make this routine a habit beyond the end of the course, Kabat-Zinn was emphasising the efficacy of slipping into these personal, private oceans. The difficulties of life will always continue; we will always have a lot on our minds, but by focusing on the diaphragm as one deep breath follows the other, we can sink below the buffeting waves of the next deadline, meeting or crisis to a place that's quiet and still. We all have these depths within us, Kabat-Zinn argued. His job was simply to help his patients travel to them quicky and effectively any time they wished. In terms of wellness practices, this was the ultimate DIY version: meditation without the need for a retreat, stress reduction without the need for a bespoke lifestyle plan, all the physical and psychological benefits of floatation without the need for a tank.[27]

For Ronald Purser, writing in his critical study *McMindfulness* (2018), it is precisely this link between mindfulness and self-regulation that makes the practice problematic. He doesn't doubt the sincerity of Kabat-Zinn and the legions of practitioners who have followed in his wake when they speak of trying to help their clients. Instead Purser points to the overlap between the rise of the 'mindfulness movement' and the 'neoliberal leadership' of Reagan and Thatcher, the point at which, incidentally, the US Department of Health, Education and Welfare became the Department of Health and Human Services. For Purser there was nothing coincidental about this parallel. The two techniques, one therapeutic and the other ideological, were very much in sync. If, as Thatcher put it, 'economics are the method [and] the object is to change the heart and soul', Purser argues that mindfulness goes to work on the latter aim. By asking us to change not the world but ourselves, one slowly chewed raisin at a time, mindfulness acts as a form of human service, rewiring us 'to serve the requirements of neoliberalism'. It allows us to 'navigate the capitalist ocean's tricky currents' by making us robust in the face of its 'inevitable stress' and competition-based anxiety. The need for welfare provision disappears in this climate because rigorous and individually cultivated 'self-care' becomes the norm. In order to be employable, you have to be well enough to deal with the pressure. Corporate culture is never at fault for heaping that pressure upon you.[28]

Bobby Roth's film *Circle of Power* (1981) provides an extreme dramatisation of this expectation. 'Suggested' by Gene Church and Conrad D. Carnes' *The Pit*, the film focuses on the advertising company Mystique, which like Holiday Magic also operates its own version of Mind Dynamics, the distinctly est-sounding EDT or 'Executive Development Training'. Led by the icy CEO Bianca Ray, a corporate tyrant who claims to 'care for every one' of her senior executives, EDT is presented as a leadership and self-actualisation course, an opportunity for her high flyers to 'get in touch with the truth, find out what they really want in life and commit to their goals'. What takes place, however, and what Roth shows with horror-movie glee, is a full gamut of ritual humiliations. As in *The Pit*, the film is full of punishing group exercises, excoriating individual analyses, physical and mental abuse, exhausting conditions, and terrifying mock funerals. EDT is an endurance test as well as a personality-dissolving disciplinary exercise. It is also a virtually Darwinian avenue to promotion. Ray's hopefuls must fight their way through the course to climb the corporate ladder. Under the twin auspices of 'care' and 'development', the programme allows Mystique to constantly raise its bar of productivity and achievement and it is the responsibility of the employees to meet these challenges no matter what indignities are involved. The company constantly moves on. If they want to stay in it, they need to be fit enough and psychologically strong enough to handle it.

Circle of Power offered an exaggerated glimpse into the corporate world that est had been infiltrating for much of the 1970s, but by the time of the film's rerelease in 1984 the sector was being increasingly augmented by mindfulness training. It was an approach that would gain significant traction in the decades that followed, particularly among the tech companies of Silicon Valley. As Purser points out, mindfulness has been eagerly adopted by the likes of Google, Facebook, Twitter, Yahoo and Amazon. In the 2010s, Google had its own 'mindfulness czar' in the form of Chade-Meng Tan, formerly 'employee number 107', who made the leap from Engineering to 'People Operations' when he started to run emotional intelligence courses at the Google Campus. Soon after this, Amazon started installing 'AmaZen' booths in its warehouses, small chambers into which its inevitably stressed and habitually overburdened workers could retire for some quality time. Once inside they could watch a mindfulness video or two and have a small fan blow air in their faces before heading back out into the fray, obviously relaxed, obviously refreshed. Although these booths looked troublingly like packing cases – or, worse, coffins – neither they nor Meng's mindfulness classes subjected their users to the type of overt brutality seen in *Circle of Power*. That said, across these semi-fictional and actual examples, the ideological baseline remains the same. In each case the workplace clearly has an impact upon the well-being of the employees, but it remains the responsibility of the employees themselves to make the necessary changes and, invariably, improve productivity rather than easing the workload that has caused the initial problem. As Purser puts it, echoing the title of Meng's 2014 bestseller, the general order is to 'search inside yourself, for there – not in the corporate culture – lies the source of your problems'.[29]

A vivid example of this dynamic appears part way through *Full Catastrophe Living* when Kabat-Zinn tells us about one of his patients, 'the plant-manager of the largest high-tech manufacturing firm of its kind in the country'. The unnamed manager comes to the clinic experiencing dizzy spells, tailspins of anxiety and sleeplessness, and he's initially concerned that he might have 'a brain tumour or something'. Once he starts to work with Kabat-Zinn, however, these fears are eased as he comes to realise the symptoms are connected to the exhausting pace of his job. The man explains that he was constantly trudging through a chronic work cycle that would hit critical mass at the end of every month 'when the shipments had to go out, the profits had to be made, and the pressure was on'. In response, Kabat-Zinn coaches him through meditation tools and breathing techniques to help him ease the effects of the pressure. Beyond these quick fixes, however, little is done to alter the manager's initial hypothesis: that the problem does indeed lie with him. It is his reaction to stress that's causing the issues. While the conditions and demands of the job are recognised, at no point are they brought into question. Kabat-Zinn gently advises his patient to take a different, quieter commute into work, delegate duties where possible and adopt more of a carefree attitude. *There's no need to take things so seriously, don't worry about it, you're doing the best that you can.* It all comes down to a crisis of confidence. The manager thinks he can't cope and is losing control of the job and so Kabat-Zinn convinces him otherwise. It is a comforting and empowering response, but at no point are the material circumstances of the job brought into question. Taking on an assistant manager never seems to be an option. Nor is there any invitation to question the debilitating normalcy of a business that clearly puts the health of its profits over and above that of its people. The system remains the same, while mindfulness merely retrains the manager to better take the strain.[30]

Compare this to Don Ardell's reflections on the workplace in *High Level Wellness*. He too encourages the pursuit of a destressing commute. He also praises the efforts of large companies like General Motors, Exxon and Mobil to provide gym facilities and incentives for workers who join ongoing fitness programmes, 'all of which make it easy for employees to exert active responsibility for their own well-being'. However, he is no advocate of workaholism and steers away from the idea that being well means being always ready for the office or factory floor. Writing on the 'temptations of job and career', he cites Jimmy Carter's 'contribution to the national well-being' in the form his instruction to staff that they 'safeguard the family space'. Just after his inauguration Carter is reported to have given his team wise counsel: 'You'll be so much more useful to me and to the country if you do have some recreation, get some exercise, see your children and spouses'. For Ardell, the maintenance of this type of balance is essential to his holistic view of wellness. Physical fitness, good nutrition and stress reduction should go hand in hand with 'environmental sensitivity': an awareness of what's healthy for us in our homes, communities and workplaces and what's not. The matter of self-responsibility comes into play when Ardell encourages his readers to make any and all changes in their personal, professional and social spaces to help foster a sense of well-being. As such, he lobbies his readers to ask for longer lunch hours, an 'exercise period in the middle of each day' and the freedom to change the ambience and layout of the workspace to make for a 'healthier setting'. He also pushes employees to ask for *more*. Specifically, more time off: 'one or two wellness days off a year'. Better to be 'too good' to come to work, Ardell reasons, rather than be too ill. Or too bored. Or too stressed. Or just too worn down and wrung out by the pressure of it all.

When pushing for the very highest levels of wellness, Ardell's aim was to alleviate 'negative worseness conditions' in oneself and one's social sphere. He was not content to merely thicken the skin in the face of existing, unyielding difficulties. For him, the full catastrophe of life was not inevitable. It could be modified, improved and smoothed out into something much more liveable. Ardell thought this was possible because his brand of wellness was not just holistic but also outward facing. Wellness for Ardell meant becoming aware of and optimising your interactions in a nest of spheres: not just your body, not just the home, not just the workplace but in the wider community as well. Each of these nodes were connected and good health, he argued, could be gained through the careful nurturing of such an intricate ecology. *High Level Wellness*, as well as the work of colleagues like John Travis, offered a road map to this network. Even when it led to the private darkness of the floatation tank this was never a purely narcissistic project, despite what might be suggested by blanket readings of the 1970s. If anything, the real retreat started at the very end of the decade, in 1979, when the Stress Clinic opened, and harried patients were taught how to close themselves off from the noise of the world. The key lesson of mindfulness as Kabat-Zinn conceived of it is that we all live under the weight of a constant storm. It will never calm down, it will never pass, so all you can do is try to float under and over the crashing waves. Alongside the psychological benefits that come with a daily meditation practice, mindfulness expressed a sense of quiet resignation, the admission that nothing out there can change. The only real option is to accept its irresistible invitation to be still, turn in and 'Come home to your deeper self'.[31]

CHAPTER IX

A Good Place
1980–1982

Marin County, California, 1977. Soon after *The Serial* was published, Cyra McFadden started to dread coming home. More often than not there would be a pile of 'angry, nasty' letters wating for her. Sometimes she would find eggs splattered across her windows. She was still living in Mill Valley at the time 'in an old tract called Sutton Manor', so people knew where to find her. Not everyone, it seemed, had been enamoured with her book.

There had been complaints about *The Serial* since it first appeared in the *Pacific Sun*, and editorials in rival newspapers like the *Marin Independent Journal* had curtly told McFadden to love the place or leave it. When the novel made a splash and thrust her into the limelight, this 'storm of indignation' got worse. Here, they said, was a thinly veiled *roman à clef* that mercilessly tore into local businesses and Marin County's carefully cultivated lifestyle. And all this from a resident, too. There was *some* local support for the book and the reviews in the national press were great, but in a clear demonstration of the fragility that so often underpins an outward show of confidence, lots of Marinites, especially those embedded in its 'alternative' scene, took it all very personally. Local shops and restaurants told McFadden to go elsewhere. Lawsuits were mentioned and back at Sutton Manor the letters piled up. Some days the mailman brought them to her door by the sack-load. On more than one occasion McFadden woke up to find her car tyres had been slashed and, until she unlisted her phone, she regularly had splenetic calls from drunken neighbours in the middle of the night. It was an unpleasant time for McFadden and her family. As a 'new writer', she said later, 'I was totally unprepared'.[1]

While *The Serial* undoubtedly offered a barbed take on the culture of human potential, McFadden saw the book as a 'joke', not an attack. More specifically, she consistently stood by the claim she made in *I Want It All Now*, that the novel was not trying to rubbish the project of exploratory self-improvement. As she put it in a 2016 interview, McFadden was not 'belittling' the likes of Esalen, nor the people who go there to 'look inward' and to 'think deeply about what they want from their lives'. Rather, the target of *The Serial* was the 'ethic' of 'exclusivity' and the attitude of selfishness enabled by the fashionable terminology of growth centres and consciousness-raising seminars. According to McFadden it was a permissive discourse that encouraged you to 'think about your needs' and forget about 'everybody else'. Fundamentally, then, *The Serial* was not a cynical takedown of Marin County, it was a 'book about language'.

McFadden had this intent in mind from the outset. She was not visiting Esalen nor attending a Mill Valley awareness group when the idea for *The Serial* began to take shape. She was actually 'wandering the meat case' at the Red Cart Market, her local neighbourhood supermarket in Mill Valley, and wondering what to cook for dinner. This was 1976, shortly before the offer came to write for the *Pacific Sun*, and at the end of a long teaching day, McFadden couldn't decide what to buy. The butcher, a man 'in his mid-50s, early 60s, a nice, friendly sort of sturdy character', leant over the counter and made some suggestions. With no hint of irony he asked: 'Could you relate to a pork roast?' McFadden was 'dumbfounded'. It was not that she didn't *like* pork nor that she didn't *want* a roast that evening, the problem was that she was simply could not *relate* to one because she had no idea what the question meant. What was her butcher talking about? What had happened to this previously 'plain-spoken man'?[2]

In the parlance of human potential, 'relating' is what should be happening during an encounter group. In theory, they are there to provide face-to-face intimacy and 'social nourishment' for 'those whose lives are for some reason meagre or lacking in intimate social relations'. McFadden's butcher, then, was either so absorbed in the culture of encounter that its language had fully filtered into to his general conversation, or he was merely picking up on, decontextualising and thus misusing a highly specific term that had somehow found its way into the vernacular. Either way, given the emphasis in encounter groups on reciprocal relationships, McFadden would have had a hard time actually relating to a piece of pork. Chances are, it wouldn't have offered much of a response to her empathy. Soon after, she started to hear similarly odd turns of phrase 'all around'. 'My San Francisco State students began pouring it out', she later explained. One told her they were not into 'structure' so they would not be attending classes 'physically' although they would be there 'in spirit', so to discharge her duties as teacher, all McFadden had to do was 'open' herself to the absent student's 'aura'. When McFadden 'flunked' another 'for handing in no work at all for a whole semester', the student complained that she was 'making a value judgement'.

Fascinated by these platitudes, McFadden wrote *The Serial* as a dispatch from this 'crazy house of echoes, where everybody was talking and talking a lot, but nobody was saying anything'. She wanted the novel to show how 'words had ceased to be acquainted with meaning' and how, as a result, 'ordinary experiences took on stranger and stranger forms'. She knew of a friend, for example, who had had a very minor traffic accident. He exchanged details with the other driver only to 'find himself enfolded in a damp hug'. The 'man who'd rear-ended him' was 'moved to tears' because the friend 'had been civil throughout their encounter', and he drove off with the parting words: 'This has been a beautiful experience.' The situations in *The Serial* and much of its humour grew out of the condescension and vacuity of these exchanges. It is not a work of mockery, but an act of satire. McFadden was imitating and amplifying that way that some people in Marin spoke, to argue that this was not the way they should communicate. Those who saw only parodies of themselves failed to grasp, or perhaps did not want to acknowledge, this corrective nuance. It was much easier to label McFadden a 'literary sociopath', and then carry on with the untroubled business of being perfect. And so, when she was once again browsing the pork roasts at the Red Cart Market during the novel's post-publication days of 1977, McFadden would regularly encounter her harshest critics. 'I know you', the 'finger-shaking' strangers would say as they showed no willingness to relate. 'You wrote *The Serial*. What a smear job, you ought to be ashamed.'[3]

✳✳✳✳✳

The ones who failed to get the joke by the widest margin were, ironically, those who likely invested the most time and energy into the book besides McFadden and her publishers, namely Sidney Beckerman and Bill Persky. Beckerman and Persky were the respective producer-and-director team responsible for *Serial* (1980), the novel's ill-conceived and ill-received film adaptation. *Serial* takes the barest bones of McFadden's plot – the separation and eventual reconciliation of Kate and Harvey Holroyd – and turns it into a weak farce that pretends to be a wryly observed commentary on modern relationships. The screenplay, by Rich Eustis and Michael Elias, has elements of Paul Mazursky's *Bob & Carol & Ted & Alice* (1969) and Woody Allen's *Interiors* (1978), and by adding a suicide subplot it is also not without its darker moments, but these echoes of New Hollywood are for the most part drowned out by some misplaced slapstick and lazy stereotyping. Overall, *Serial* ends up standing more in anticipation of the terrible comedies that would come to flood the 1980s like *Police Academy* (1984) and *Bachelor Party* (1984). Essentially, it is a dud of an ensemble piece in which the only real jeopardy relates to the availability of the newly single Harvey (Martin Mull). After having his libido tragically spoilt by years of marriage to Kate (Tuesday Weld), who is 'tired of living with someone who's mind is closed' and has the further temerity to ask for communication 'on an adult level', Harvey steps out into an embarrassment of sexual riches. For much of the film he's torn between the delights of the nineteen-year-old checkout girl Marlene and his new secretary, Stella, with whom he may or may not couple up at the local orgy.

One saving grace is the film's shooting location. Evidently Beckerman had the budget and resources that Walter Wagner lacked when he tried to film *Body Snatchers* in Mill Valley in 1955. There is an impressive sandbox feel to *Serial* as characters go from one

Mill Valley location to another and, if anything, it is this backdrop – all 1970s interiors, outdoor decks and gleaming bar tops – which is the real star of the show. Similarly, the film's stand-out moment is the opening sequence that descends vertiginously from the sky into the rush of a commute from the suburbs, through the city's main strip and then on to the Golden Gate ferry. Don Ardell plotted out much the same route in *High Level Wellness* when he described his daily journey from Mill Valley to his San Francisco office. Rather than taking the 25-minute bus ride, he recommended taking the longer ferry route because of the 'psychic income' to be gained from the 'quality of that commuting', the 'sights, sounds, the cold and clean wind'. As Ardell puts it, so many things about that 'ride on the Bay' contributed to a 'daily celebration of being alive'. For the makers of *Serial*, however, the gallop to the ferry was not a way of making 'all the good things seem richer'. In addition to introducing the characters and the geography of the city, the sequence shows the cyclists pushing to outrun each other while vying for position with motorists. It is simply another version of the rat race, with the convoy clearly telegraphing all the pressures of the white-collar workplace even before they make it downtown.[4]

If Paramount had been serious about the film, they should have been brave, taken a very different stylistic approach and hired someone like Ralph Bakshi to animate Tom Cervenak's illustrations. McFadden has spoken at length about how she and Cervenak were 'in perfect sync' during the writing process. His 'neo-realist' designs 'exactly' matched her impressions of the characters and 'really nailed the period wonderfully'. She attributes much of the book's 'half-life' to the enduring appeal of his artwork. Animating it would have allowed *Serial* to draw deep on the aesthetics of the 1970s while at the same time reflecting the subtle uncanniness of McFadden's Marin County, a place warped by language that refers to mutual transformation, but which keeps its speakers out of touch. In this way, it could easily have been a suburban counterpart to Bakshi's earlier animated feature, the hyperreal inner-city drama *Heavy Traffic* (1973). In the event, what Beckerman and Persky delivered to Paramount was a plodding, miscast and frequently spiteful film that not even the spectacle of Christopher Lee as 'Skull', the leader of a gay biker gang, could liven up.[5]

The main problem with *Serial* was its politics. In the novel, McFadden takes broad aim with her satire and doesn't put herself above 'Marvellous Marin'. Despite what her drive-by critics may have thought, she was fully embedded in the world she described. Mill Valley was her home too; she even based the look, layout and décor of the Holroyd residence on her place, Sutton Manor. As such, there's little in the way of malice expressed towards her characters. It is as if she sits back and listens while they simply talk and let all their anxieties, hypocrisies and self-absorption come spilling out. Not so with the film. Mull's Harvey comes across like an undercover Edwin Newman: an agent of middle America secretly reporting to NBC after sneaking into enemy territory. He is our exasperated guide to the circus of Mill Valley and thanks to his sardonic, withering and wearying asides we're meant to find the whole thing ridiculous. The film's theme song, 'A Changing World' by Lalo Schifrin, Norman Gimbel and Michael Johnson, fixes his mindset from the off. It's 'a changing world', we're told, one that's 'moving fast' and 'spins away', so the only thing someone like Harvey can do is hold on, 'run the race' or else fall off and 'get left behind'. There is no sense of optimism here, this is not a song celebrating the possibility of the future; it is more of a saccharine lament, one that begrudges the very prospect of a change in the order of things, and it is precisely this disturbance in the status quo that Harvey spends the film angrily trying to resist.

McFadden's Harvey is grumpy and equally bewildered by the 'changing world' but he's also vain, neurotic and just as receptive to the latest fads as Kate. As a 40-year-old man who enjoyed being 30 in the late 1960s, part of his discontent comes from the sense he's now shut out of a world in which he once roamed free. By contrast, when watching Mull's Harvey wisecrack and eye-roll his way through the film you get the sense of a character who's utterly dismissive of anything approaching a progressive social agenda. Underneath his conceited calls to common sense there lies a deep conservativ-ism that's not prepared to yield an inch of his social capital. Playing the patronising, self-pitying role of the sane man lost in a world of idiots, he bemoans Kate's health kicks that require him to make such staggering life changes as riding a bike and eating some granola; he complains about having to pay her therapist while forbidding her to have any income of her own and, like any number of contemporary Harveys who rage against the outrageous incursions of 'wokery', he's deeply offended when his friends and families adopt lifestyles different to his own. 'For Chrissake, Kate!' he explodes when she dares to mention 'socialization', 'can't you just speak English!?'

As the film progresses, this fragility spills over into self-appointed acts of often intolerant cultural policing. Miffed at the trappings of alternative spirituality wafting around the memorial service for his friend Sam, Harvey takes it upon himself to disrupt the proceedings, caring little for the distress it causes to Sam's grieving widow. Unhappy with his daughter joining a Hare Krishna-esque group, he invites Skull and his biker friends to smash up their headquarters. Soon after, once reunited with Kate, he wilfully hijacks his own commitment ceremony by reinserting traditional, Christian wedding vows. He throws out all the 'you-ness', 'we-ness', 'pair-bonding' nonsense and bloody-mindedly promises to Kate that he will 'love, honour and cherish' her. Tellingly, the conventional vow to 'obey' is quietly omitted. It is a vulgar display of social power, the revenge of the American asshole. *Serial* is ultimately on the side of big-car-driving, cigar-smoking, unrepentantly red-blooded white middle-class males who have no time for 'lentil loaf' and the 'father-daughter interface', because they're too busy relating to *Johnny Carson* on their 24-inch TVs. Worse still, we're meant to agree with all this *and* find it funny. Every time Mull insults a feminist or trashes another form of self-development you half expect him to turn to the camera and shout, in full expectation of applause, 'Am I right?'

These glaring differences are brought into more nuanced relief when it comes to the language of space. Early in *The Serial* McFadden describes how Harvey returns home from work to find his daughter, Joan, hosting a party. A group of her friends, including boyfriend Spencer – a Ferrari-driving 'high school drop out with no visible means of livelihood' – are dancing in the lounge with an Alice Cooper record playing full blast. 'Where's Joan?' asks Harvey, looking round the room. 'She's in a good space, man,' replies Spencer. Once again, McFadden draws our attention to linguistic elisions, this time the literal sense of space gets mixed up with the word's metaphorical implications as Spencer responds to an obvious question about Joan's location with a comment about her mood, or rather her head space. Later, when Harvey and Kate come to prepare their 'Celebration of Open Commitment', McFadden deploys the joke again. Drawing up their guest list proves to be a problem: 'Nobody, but *nobody* we know is in the same space anymore. My whole address book is totally inoperative.' It is not clear whether the extent of Harvey and Kate's personal journey has caused this phase-out with their social circle or vice versa, but the point is that their friends are not elsewhere, they have not changed their addresses, but somewhere along the line somebody has changed their paradigm. The Holroyds are in a different 'space' because they no longer think in the same way as those listed in the address book.

Serial, the film, bulldozes this subtlety. When the party scene comes round, Spencer hardly gets a line. Harvey simply barges in, breaks up the proceedings and throws everyone out, yelling, 'This is a private home!' When we finally get to the commitment ceremony, Harvey reaches for his sledgehammer of traditional-ism after being asked by the stoned officiator to 'share [his] space with Kate'. In each instance, Harvey is not just expressing an extreme aversion to metaphor, he is defending his own very clear sense of space – his ideological territory. Harvey is a middle-class homeowner whose identity, despite his wanderings, is intimately connected to the values it contains: prosperity, social standing and the proprietary rights assumed to be the preserve of the father and husband. The airy, fluid language of human potential threatens this privilege because – despite its own internal traditionalism – the invitation to change one's head space invariably brings with it an invitation to rethink where you live, how you live and who you live with. As these sands of power start to shift beneath his feet, Harvey's anger comes out in full force. His is the rage of the man who finds himself floundering before performing a rear-guard action to defend his symbolic castle.[6]

Over in the UK, programmes like *The Good Life* and David Nobbs' second Perrin novel, *The Better World of Reginald Perrin* (1978), were poking at the same fears. Where the Goods transform their home into a smallholding, Perrin turns his 'ordinary suburban house in an ordinary suburban street' into a 'community where middle-aged, middle-class people' can 'learn to live in love and faith and trust'. Both are essentially idealistic enterprises oriented towards a sense of social mission – be that self-sufficiency or mutual communal support – but they also up-end the accepted suburban codes of privacy, quietude and a neat compartmentalisation of domestic and social life. These projects realise, on a small scale, the fate that threatens the beleaguered Grantleigh Manor in another of the BBC's timely sitcoms, *To the Manor Born* (1979–81). Facing bankruptcy, the upper-class, socially conservative Audrey fforbes-Hamilton, the latest and possibly last of the illustrious fforbes-Hamilton line, puts the Grantleigh estate up for sale only to find it coming under the vulgar influence of new money and the threat of transformation into an office hub or, worse, a leisure complex. Across the series that follows, the redoubtable fforbes-Hamilton (played by *Good Life* alumna Penelope Keith) kicks against this repurposing in an attempt not just to reclaim her home but to reconstruct the hierarchical order it represents: a world in which everyone has their place, in which serfs live and work in perpetual deference to the manor, in which it is good blood, not good business, that qualifies you for privilege and property.[7]

By putting their homes to work, by using them as tools not assets, Perrin and the Goods short-circuit this system. They carve out zones of independence that exceed the working expectations of their middle-class scripts because their properties no longer act as rewards for doing the job that waits at the other end of the commute. Given this disruption it is no surprise that both projects are short-lived, but they do not fall victim to a NIMBY-like fforbes-Hamilton campaign. Rather, they're destroyed by 'yobbos', the lurking furies of the 1970s who were often vilified in public but relied upon in popular culture – like heavies employed by anxious aristos on a fox hunt – to covertly police social convention. Back in *Serial*, Harvey's response to his own social upset is just as direct as the window-breaking and room-trashing suffered by Perrin and the Goods, although he is careful to leave the physicality of such mischief to Skull and his bikers. He does, however, cut his losses immediately after causing all this upset: at the end of the film he leaves the now inhospitable Mill Valley for a new life in Denver. He bundles Kate and Joan into the station wagon having already sewn up the details of a new job, a new 'place' and a new school. They have no say in the matter, but they also offer no real complaint. As the car speeds on and the camera pulls away, the dislocations of the film are forgotten. Harmony has returned to the family unit and the nuclear three – father, mother, and daughter – are once again in a good space. It is, however, one that has been entirely constructed by, makes the most sense to, and will provide the most advantages for Harvey, the once threatened but now resurgent patriarch.[8]

*****

Todd Rundgren's song 'Utopia Theme' (1974/78) calls the no-place of the title a 'City in my head', a lyric that reminds us just how fine the line is between the utopia and its opposite, the dystopian 'bad' place. Within the speculation, conjecture and projection central to utopian thinking, what differentiates the ideal from this inverse is nothing more than a state of mind. The boundary lines of the eutopian good place are similarly thin. One person's 'happy place' can so often turn out to be another person's nightmare, as Sid Rawle and the Tribe of the Sun found soon after they arrived on Dorinish. According to Rawle, the island was 'heaven and hell', and it needed only a turn in the weather to tip the balance from one to the other. *I Want It All Now* frames Marin County in similarly mutable terms. We're repeatedly told it is an 'earthly paradise' through which flows a great surge of unease, and most of Edwin Newman's interviews find him trying to drill down towards this undertow. He talks with McFadden about the 'physical assets and advantages' of the area but then asks, as if already knowing the answer, 'Is it a sad place?' 'I do find it sad', replies McFadden, adding that the problem lies with the 'searchers' and 'seekers' who bring 'havoc' to their lives, as if their restlessness troubles an otherwise placid atmosphere. Elsewhere Fred Mayer, Mill Valley's no-nonsense pharmacist, thinks the discontent is much more widespread and not just limited to a particular group, however visible. Mental health in the area is generally 'not very good', he opines, and as he dispenses alarming amounts of sleeping pills and tranquilisers, Mayer has no pithily theorised soundbite to offer other than his own puzzlement: 'If we have such a fantastic, good life and if folks are making all this money, why aren't they happy?'[9]

Much of the difficulty in trying to assess Marin County's 'good life' lies with the word 'good' itself. There is no place, no space, nor any thing that is objectively 'good'. This status depends entirely on the subjectivity – the values, the preferences, the politics and the expectations – of those designating it as such. Gary Meer, 'an attorney in private practice in San Francisco', makes this point clear when he is interviewed by Newman for the film. He calls Marin County the 'White person's ideal' and offers little in the way of expansion save that it is 'generally a very attractive place physically' and it is 'free from a lot of the congestion of urban areas'. In other words, it is completely different from somewhere like Oakland, the 'predominantly non-white city of 328,000' a quick 26 miles away from Mill Valley. By the late 1970s, Oakland remained a textbook case of 'urban crisis', beset by 'white flight and black in-migration', high unemployment and a poverty-generating cycle of central deindustrialisation and suburban investment. As one of the busiest ports on the West Coast, Oakland was not without wealth, but much of this was floating capital, money that did not drop anchor in the community, but which instead moved quickly in and out of the city on the tidal flow of trade. As a result, while the fortunes of Oakland declined, those of places like Mill Valley rose because their affluence was post-industrial, and their gentrification was fuelled by the influx of a city-exiting middle class. When Meer speaks of the area as a 'White person's ideal', then, he's indicating that access to the so-called good life is contingent on the possession of considerable social capital. It is a point that raises difficult questions about the function of, and the socio-political ideology informing, those places deemed 'good' as well as the identity of their beneficiaries. That is to say, *who* might the eutopia be good for and *what* might it be good for? Is the eutopia – a 'good place' to be – necessarily exclusive? Is it a place that serves the self-interest and shores up the dominance of only those who institute it?[10]

H.G. Wells, the great 'utopian pessimist', frequently chewed over these questions in novels like *The Time Machine* (1895). As with Aldous Huxley, Wells believed in the enormous potential of humanity but saw only disappointment when he speculated on its development. In *The Time Machine* he imagined one phase of the far future as an arcadian landscape in which the peaceable Eloi live in languor while beneath them toil the subterranean Morlocks. It is a stratification that initially resembles the class divisions of late-Victorian society, but only until Wells reveals that it is the Morlocks who own the means of production. They make possible the material conditions that allow the Eloi to live in passivity and they do so because the Eloi are their food. The Morlocks are not servants to their aristocratic masters, they are cultivators tending to the placidity of their cattle. Wells' good place is thus a site of exploitation at its most visceral, and the stereotypically happy world of the Eloi – a tranquil existence free of work and strife – is little more than a fattening pen.[11]

In the long cultural history of utopian thought, *The Time Machine* is an extreme example of a certain kind of science-fictional extrapolation that reached a peak in the late nineteenth century. The questions it raised, however, remained active in the 1970s in cases where the theorisation of the no-place gave way to practical attempts at constructing functional good places. In 1979, for example, the educators Bryn and Meg Purdy founded the Rowen House School in Derbyshire. It was an educational experiment based on the work of proto-socialist and philanthropist Robert Owen and that of A.S. Neill, headmaster of the pioneering English boarding school Summerhill. Owen's Scottish mill community New Lanark, which he managed from 1800 onwards, was a model of co-operative cohesion between employer and employee. It operated as a 'mini welfare state' which privileged the health and well-being of its workers and placed particular emphasis on the education of their children. Owen saw no contradiction between happiness and productivity, a view that went against the usual capitalistic model in which the demands of the latter frequently cancel out the needs of the former. Similarly, as he explained in *Summerhill: A Radical Approach to Child Rearing* (1960), Neill's educational philosophy was also based on democratic, communal and non-coercive principles. He argued that a school should be built around the needs and proclivities of its pupils; it should not require them to submit to a singular conditioning model. Summerhill, which he established in 1921 and led from its Suffolk base from 1927, was not without rules but it encouraged its students to be self-regulating and independent in the pursuit of their learning. As with Owen's outlook, the happiness of those within the school's community was paramount. So too for the Purdys, who from 1979 onwards welcomed to Rowen House 'troubled' female pupils who had been excluded from other institutions. There they found a 'familial', respect-based dynamic rather than the type of 'schoolteacherly' authoritarianism they had previously resisted. Class attendance was voluntary, there were no specific punishments and chief among the principles of Rowen House was a daily 'Moot', an egalitarian assembly that allowed each child to raise issues and in cases of dispute seek an agreeable resolution.

Prior to this, over in Oakland, the Black Panthers were running a similar educational project, the Oakland Community School. In operation from 1974 to 1982, the school was part of the Panthers' mandate to 'serve the people, body and soul'. As well as opening free medical clinics, the party's 'survival programs' had, from the late 1960s, organised voter drives, breakfast programmes, political education courses and ideologically oriented 'liberation schools'. These initiatives sought to remedy the 'deficits of civil rights "progress"', particularly as regards the 'failure of public schools to adequately prepare Black youth for the life ahead of them'. In 1971 the party formed the semi-residential Intercommunal Youth Institute, which essentially functioned as a boiler room for future militants. It taught a traditional curriculum of 'science, math, English' alongside classes on 'health', all of which came loaded with a significant quotient of party ideology. 'Field work' was also a requirement and, in a reflection of the school's theory sessions, it took the form of party service and saw students 'distributing *The Black Panther* newspaper, visiting prisons, speaking with youth in the neighbourhood, or attending court cases of fellow Panthers'. By the time the institute had developed into the Oakland Community School, its catchment had grown to include 'neighbourhood children' as well as those of party members. The partisan thrust of the teaching had also expanded into a social science-inflected curriculum oriented towards a wide-ranging understanding of Black history. Crucially, though, critical thinking remained a key point of focus. The aim was to create a 'learning environment that fostered collaboration and self/collective accountability, not purely teacher-imposed standards'.

As with Rowen House, this approach was realised by involving students in governance. They had 'the freedom to express their inquiries, fears, concerns and suggestions', and also participated in mediation and correction when dealing with peers whose behaviour 'worked against the collectivist idea of the school family'. At the Oakland Community School, the teachers were not the sole arbiters of truth, nor were they the singular voices of authority. The school was led by the group and the health of that group was paramount. Bryn Purdy later codified the thinking underpinning his anarcho-libertarian approach to education as 'eutopism'. As Purdy put it, eutopism was a matter of practice not theory, a 'how-to' mode of thought that focused on the creation of a 'benign-place-to-be':

We have all – one trusts – experienced happiness, at some time, in some place. We have experienced a 'eutopy' in the middle of a forest, on the top of a mountain, "simply messing about in boats", at a football or cricket match [...] Each of us has known happiness, but happiness was not experienced in a void; it happened there, at a place; it happened then, in time. We associate this inner feeling closely with an outer place: eutopy, 'a-place-where-we-were-happy', personally, uniquely to ourselves.

Purdy's language recalls that of Abraham Maslow and the idea of the peak experience, but rather than describing the ecstasy of a moment spent 'outside of time and space' he grounds this sense of elevated happiness by emphasising the importance of a particular place. The eutopy is rooted *somewhere*, even if it is a location painted from memory. Rowen House aimed to make these feelings manifest in the form of a functional, physical and fully realised happy place. The Black Panthers worked towards a similar end. The Oakland Community School was part of a wider thrust of utopian thinking that intersected with the defensive, strategic project of the survival programme. The various strands of the Panthers' community activism combine into an image of Oakland as a self-determining city for 'the People'.[12]

When we speak now of a 'good place' or 'happy place' we so often mean a mood or a state of mind, rather than an actual location. To be in a good place means to be flush with well-being; it is the headspace we might move into after a period of upset, depression or recovery. A happy place can similarly mean good company, a moment's pause, a treat: a step away from the everyday into a mindset that is comforting and emotionally secure. A favourite spot, the site of a much-cherished visit, may well be your happy place, but it is the charge of memory attached to that location that helps pull you back and later generates this escapist or perhaps compensatory happiness. The ubiquity of these phrases masks their complex history that proceeds from traditional Christian views of heaven as *the* good place to agnostic rejections of this metaphysical belief in the afterlife-as-reward. It was the 'great agnostic' Robert Ingersoll who lived by such a creed of happiness in this world, not the next. 'Happiness is the only good,' he told his late-19th-century audiences, '[and] the time to be happy is now. The place to be happy is here.' For Ingersoll, happiness was not something to be found in the hereafter, by the elect. Rather, it was a virtue that should be realised contemporaneously, by all, through fellowship and mutual accord: 'The way to be happy is to make other people happy.'[13]

Today's good and happy places carry echoes of this secular stance, albeit with the volume turned down on Ingersoll's political provocations and overtures to conviviality. Take 'The Healing Trip', for example, the first episode of the Netflix series *The Goop Lab* (2020). The show looked at the health benefits of psychedelics and found Paltrow and her chief of content Elise Loehnen positioning Goop as the inheritor of 1970s drug research. Claiming that psilo-cybin, a psychoactive substance derived from magic mushrooms, could remedy depression and other mental illnesses, the show set out to demonstrate such remarkable benefits. Following this initial pitch, however, the show largely ignores the existing clinical research regarding anti-depressants, psychotherapy as well as that currently surrounding psychedelic drug trials. Instead, it mainly focused on a bunch of Goop staffers getting high on mushrooms in a retreat resort somewhere in Jamaica. The medical application of psych-edelics seemed not to matter once 'The Healing Trip' became just that: a luxury holiday in search of wellness at its most vague. Most of them seemed to have a great time in pursuit of non-specific 'healing', although photo editor Jenny, who was deep in the throes of bereave-ment, could have clearly done with more help than listening to yet another of Loehnen's laughing soliloquies about 'the bigger universe'.

Despite its generalised references to peak experiences, 'The Healing Trip' ebbs and flows with a free-floating language of indi-vidual contentment. Whatever benefits are to be gained from a holiday in Jamaica, the good places found by most of the Goopers are fleeting, hermetically sealed moments of happiness. Those who get the most out of the trip are those who manage to conjure a haven rather than a heaven; a personal, spiritually indistinct refuge accessed through self-care and superficially ritualised me-time.[14]

Contrary to Ingersoll, 'The Healing Trip' offers a view more in line with the later work of Carl Rogers than 19th-century free thought. Writing in his final book, *A Way of Being* (1980), Rogers reflected on a 'transformed world', the way that developments in modern life – among them informatic, scientific and communicational – had changed the familiar concepts of 'time, space, object, cause, effect'. Holding on to the optimism of humanistic psychology, Rogers argued that those best placed to embrace this world and its 'paradigm shift' are those able to realise their 'hitherto undreamed-of potential'.

According to Rogers, this 'person of tomorrow' strives for a 'wholeness of life, with thought, feeling, physical energy, psychic energy, healing energy, all being integrated into experience'. Specifying, Rogers tells his readers he has found these people 'among those who have experienced encounter groups' who were 'finding a place for feelings as well as thought in their lives'. Immersed in the buffer zones of their psychological good places, these individuals were busy cultivating a 'freer, richer, more self-directed life for themselves'. Rogers applied the same analysis to the 'Blacks and Chicanos and other minority members who are pushing out from generations of passivity to active, positive lives' as well as 'creative school dropouts' who are 'thrusting into higher reaches than their sterile schooling permits'.

Lost in this all-encompassing vision, however, is a sense of the material and social differences separating the groups Rogers describes. The spiritual privilege he invokes may well match that later held by Goop and its clientele, but for the 'minority members' Rogers alludes to, the leap from 'passivity' to activity was not just a matter of such minorities choosing to be positive. If performed at all, such a shift was a matter of groups like the Black Panthers providing the likes of the Oakland Community School as necessary platforms to resist the weight of a prejudicial hegemony. Similarly, for the 'dropout', or as in the case of the Rowen House pupils, those excluded from school, any such 'thrusting' change required a structure alternative to 'sterile schooling' rather than no schooling at all. Rogers may have valorised an attitudinal 'place' as part of his vision for a humanistic future, but what the activist thinking of the mid- to late 1970s made clear was that a physical, functional place – a viable eutopy – was a necessary component in the attempt to enact social change. The problem was, as the 1970s became the 1980s, such a place was becoming difficult to secure for those living across the socio-political spectrum. Popular culture may have fantasised about it, political culture may have hypothesised it, but for many people struggling to get by from one day to the next an actual good place was increasingly moving out of reach.[15]

*****

This is the shadow that hovers over the end of *Serial*, as the Holroyds escape to Denver. The new life that Harvey has arranged will come with challenges and, he warns, they will have to be 'careful' with their finances. In reality, the same would have applied to anyone going the other way and moving to Marin County. New residents would have had to exercise a similar degree of care because by 1980, ten years after McFadden and the fictional Holroyds made Marin their home, the cost of property in the area had gone through the roof. At the start of the 1970s, places like Mill Valley were on the up but still affordable to those chasing a 'sunny blend of affluence, redwoods [and] bohemianism' and who were prepared to take a chance on a decent fixer-upper. McFadden and her husband bought Sutton Manor for $25,000, which was a stretch at the start of the 1970s, but nothing compared to the price hikes to come. By 1978 a similar 'regular'-sized home in Marin would cost you around $91,000, a sum 60 per cent higher than the national average. By the late 1970s there were plenty of properties in the above-average price range too, with houses in Marin's more sought-after neighbourhoods exceeding the $100,000 mark, going up to $250,000 in some cases. Marin was a hot market at the start of the 1980s and the days of local realtors trying to talk up houses they couldn't shift that had sagging foundations, ancient plumbing and foot-sized holes in the kitchen floor were well and truly over. Those were the kind of properties that had given a foothold to quirky start-ups like the Wellness Resource Center. By the turn of the decade, however, Mill Valley's business district was sweating its assets, meaning that for new and existing enterprises, clinging on became an uphill struggle. Like the Holroyds, John Travis had also decided to cut and run. After shutting down the centre, he greeted 1980 by leaving Mill Valley for a life of 'minimalism' among the Monteverde Quakers of Costa Rica.[16]

The fortunes of the Marin microcosm masked a more distressing national picture, one brought into relief by the US 'Misery Index'. Developed by the economist Arthur Okun, an advisor to President Lyndon Johnson, the index combined the rates of inflation and unemployment to offer a snapshot of the nation's fiscal health. Essentially, it tried to 'summarize how the average citizen is doing, economically', and by 1980, the prognosis was bad. The years of the Carter presidency saw the index jump from 12.6 per cent in 1978 to a record high of 21.98 per cent in 1980. There had been a previous spike in 1976, but what had accumulated by 1980 was the hangover of the fraught economic conditions that dominated the decade: recession and stagflation.[17]

It was during this time that charismatic practitioners of positive thought like Louise Hay started to come to public prominence. Hay, a former workshop leader at the First Church of Religious Science who also had a background in Transcendental Meditation, claimed that positive thought and the power of spoken 'affirmations' could enact a beneficial change in the state of your physical, emotional or even economic health. According to Hay, illness – or, as she hyphenated it, 'dis-ease' – was grounded in what she termed 'metaphysical' causes: improper thinking, trapped guilt, repressed anger and other psychological blockages. As she explained in her pamphlet *Heal Your Body* (1976), both 'the good in our lives' and 'the dis-ease' are the results 'of mental thought patterns which form our experiences'. In Hay's view there was a clear connection between thoughts, the parts of the body and physical problems. Once you realised this, she argued, it was possible to alleviate all manner of ailments simply by dispensing with 'negative thought patterns that produce uncomfortable, unrewarding experiences' and prioritising instead those which 'produce good, positive experiences'. To demonstrate the potency of her method, Hay would often speak candidly about her own experience of childhood abuse and adult cancer. In her telling the two were connected, with the psychic and physical impact of the first leading to the growth of the second. Hay claimed that her recovery had little to do with medication and invasive surgery but had resulted from a combination of 'mental and physical cleansing'. She had healed herself by embarking on a detoxifying nutritional regime while also working on the deep resentment she held towards her childhood experiences. Tapped resentment, argued Hay, 'literally eats away at the body', so by releasing these thoughts she was also clearing the 'mental pattern that created the condition called cancer'.

For Hay, then, being healthy was simply a matter of willpower and self-responsibility coupled with a willingness to accept one's own role in a system of cause and effect. As well as taking on the threat of cancer, the method could equally be applied to lower-level complaints like a 'stiff neck'. In Hay's terms such an ache was a marker of inflexible thinking and thus all you had to do was be more open to other people's opinions and the muscles would miraculously relax. The same thinking could also generate the material conditions necessary for happy, fulfilled lives. Hay ends *Heal Your Body* with an affirmation designed to foster self-worth that takes the form of an open-armed acceptance of a home, a job and the comforting security they bring with them:

> I love myself therefore I provide for myself a comfortable home, one that fills all my needs and is a pleasure to be in. I fill the rooms with the vibration of love so that all who enter, myself included, will feel this love and be nourished by it. I love myself, therefore I work at a job that I truly enjoy doing, one that uses my creative talents and abilities, working with and for people that I love and that love me and earning a good income.

Hay's brand of self-help has since been criticised, not only for linking illness and personal failings to an almost karmic degree but also for peddling false hope to readers suffering from chronic if not terminal conditions. Despite the positivity of Hay's message it could easily be read as a medicalised form of victim-blaming. Not only are you the cause of your own 'dis-ease' – be that cancer, coma, coronary thrombosis, or any other 'problem' on the long, alphabetised, largely non-differentiated list in *Heal Your Body* – but, argues Hay, if you fail to recover it is simply because you haven't looked deep enough into your own foibles and affirmed yourself out of their psychosomatic influence. There is also the disarming simplicity of the affirmation above which suggests desire alone is enough to bring about significant material change, that if you want a house and you love yourself enough and harangue the universe enough you will *therefore* receive it.

Heal Your Body paved the way for Hay's full-length bestseller *You Can Heal Your Life* (1984). Before that, from 1976 onwards, the pamphlet went through multiple printings and reached a peak of availability in the early 1980s. Its offer of an easy antidote to a litany of physical and psychological miseries thus paralleled the rise of economic misery charted by Okun's index. His figures spoke of a damaging slowdown in economic growth in which the combination of high unemployment and high inflation equated to a reduction of individual spending power. As such, then, at precisely the point where, for many, purchasing a house became less of a possibility, Hay's mantras of wish fulfilment arrived and transformed such material concerns into virtual fantasies. In this way, *Heal Your Body* was not so much an empowering alternative to its difficult social surroundings, but a covert reflection of them. For those most affected by the economic situation at the close of the 1970s, houses and jobs had become the stuff of dreams. They were objects of desire that took up residence in the imagination once the tangible means to acquire them started to evaporate.[18]

A similarly seismic pattern of inflation was also affecting the British housing market. In 1981, average house prices stood at £24,503, which equated to an eye-watering increase of some 390 per cent when compared to the going rate for property in the 'pre-inflationary eden' of 1970. In such accelerated circumstances, the very idea of home ownership started to change, and over the course of the 1970s into the 1980s, an attitude of speculation quickly filtered into the market as a whole. Buying a house became a wise investment, not just a means of securing shelter. In Britain and America alike, ownership 'came to be viewed not merely as a *store* of wealth and a hedge against inflation but as a *source* of wealth through capital gains'. As the urban planner George Sternlieb put it in reference to the American situation of the early 1970s, 'a house is not only a home', increasingly it is 'purchased to be sold, not lived in'.

Economists writing across the 1970s debated on the long-term implications of this shift and one recurrent argument described how 'property ownership could be seen as the basis for the formation of a political force'. This was a new intervention into the division between the haves and the have nots. It spoke of a widening gap between different forms of occupancy, with the 'capital gains derived from housing' working to the benefit of 'one whole class in society at the expense of another'. The argument foresaw the appearance of an ideological difference between the owner-occupier and the renter, the council and the private sectors, with the additional potential for property inheritance leading 'to the growth of an almost hereditary owner-occupying caste'.[19]

In October 1980, the Conservative government took a step towards the normalisation of this stratification when they rolled out one of the core policies of Thatcherism, 'Right to Buy'. This gave tenants of local authority houses the statutory right to purchase their homes at substantially discounted rates, 'as much as 50 per cent for those who had been resident for 20 years or more'. 'Right to Buy' was popular from the outset and by 1996 some 2.2 million properties had been transferred into private hands. For the Conservative party, this quick uptake validated their view that property ownership was 'the cornerstone of a stable, democratic society of liberated individuals'. Not only was there a 'natural' appetite for ownership, they argued, but the expansion of owner-occupancy was also good for the moral fibre of the nation. It satisfied consumer demand and fostered self-determination, social status and pride in one's possessions. To its critics, however, particularly those of the opposition Labour Party, 'Right to Buy' represented a further corrosion of the welfare state. It also reframed the way the remaining properties and their inhabitants were represented in the public imagination. In films like *Rita, Sue and Bob Too* (1987), based on Andrea Dunbar's 1982 play, the council estates routinely appeared as squalid, crime-ridden enclaves that housed an underclass economically and morally detached from society at large – 'Thatcher's England with her knickers down', to quote *Rita*'s condemnatory tagline. With ownership becoming increasingly normalised, the stereotypically decrepit, deprived and depressing council house emerged as 'the last resort' for those at the bottom of the pile: low-quality housing for the low-quality poor.[20]

On the surface, 'Right to Buy' offered a leg up to a generation of ambitious Arthur Seatons, those who had entered council properties straight out of the working-class terraces of Alan Sillitoe's *Saturday Night and Sunday Morning* (1958). However, the scheme was part of a much bigger project of economic deregulation in which welfare was scaled back to prioritise the private sector. In the longer term, then, it was of more benefit to property developers like Harold Shand, the gangster turned businessman in John Mackenzie's *The Long Good Friday* (1980). They were the ones who stood to gain the greatest rewards from Thatcher's economic – rather than socially – oriented policies. 'Our country's not an island anymore,' announces Shand early in the film as he surveys the development-ready docklands of the emergent 'New London' from the deck of a cruising ship on the Thames. Played by an incendiary Bob Hoskins, Shand is the archetypal Thatcherite: a drum-beating entrepreneurial steersman intent on realising Britain's potential as the 'Leading European state' who is prepared to work with any investor and cross any line and to achieve this end. Labour may have laid out plans for a post-war good place of community centres and social support, but by the time the 1980s arrived this future had been substantially rewritten. Opportunity was the order of the day and inequality was the underlying outcome. Shand's overwhelming will to buy crystallised this attitude. There is no sense of altruism in his enterprising outlook, nor any sense of social vision. His investment into Britain's competitive future is led by the purely capitalistic intent to do well: the desire to acquire an overabundance of economic health, a prize available only to those aggressive enough to pursue it.[21]

One pushback against this complex of attitudes came in the form of a government report called *Inequalities in Health* (1980). Also known as the Black Report after the chairman of its working group, Sir Douglas Black (President of the Royal College of Physicians), *Inequalities in Health* was essentially a review of the 1942 Beveridge Report. Commissioned by Labour in 1977, it set out to assess the contemporary efficacy of the NHS and its key mission: the delivery of 'the greatest health improvements to the most disadvantaged people'. The thrust of Black's conclusions was that by the start of the 1980s, this challenge had not been met. Such improvements were simply not happening, society remained in a state of extreme want and, further, a clear link remained between 'poverty and ill-health'.

Typical among the report's differentials was the fact that 'unskilled manual workers and their wives' were 'two and a half times' more likely to die before retirement than 'professional men and their wives'. Lifestyle, education, health funding and, crucially, housing were all highlighted as contributory factors to this disparity. For Black, the persistence of chronic overcrowding and the lack of adequate social housing had a clear bearing on working-class 'mortality and morbidity'. He also emphasised the psychological damage that comes with short-term tenancies and the threat of eviction. Cumulatively, Black's data pointed to a widening gap between the haves and the have-nots and the associated emergence of a social landscape in which the possession of material assets influences one's physical and mental well-being. In all, it was a deeply critical take on the state of the nation. As Pearce Wright explains, the report 'showed that while the health and lifespan of the wealthy in the UK continued to improve, that of the most deprived groups had fallen for the first time since the Victorian era'.

'Poverty remains the chief cause of disease, and it is a factor which is beyond the immediate control of medicine,' wrote Black in his introduction, quoting medical historian Henry E. Sigerist. It was a call to bring socio-economic policymaking in line with the provision of health care; a call which ultimately went unheeded once the report finally appeared during the first year of Thatcher's government. 'Appeared' is perhaps too strong a word: the Conservatives buried it like an inconvenient corpse. Rushed out over a bank holiday weekend with only a handful of copies being available to the media, it came complete with a condescending foreword by the then Secretary of State for Social Services Patrick Jenkin, who declared the whole project as unaffordable. Among other requirements, Black wanted more spending on community and primary care, a tax-sapping ban on smoking, an increase in child benefit, agreement with unions on minimum working conditions and greater provision of council houses. Clearly, then, the issue was not just affordability. For the Conservative privateers, the Black Report was ideologically untenable given that 'Redistribution, increased public expenditure and taxation and unashamed socialism [were] flaunted on almost every page'. Satisfying the basic needs of health, security and shelter – the fundamentals of a 'good society' – was not a priority for Thatcherism.[22]

*****

At a more implicit level, one could say the same of wellness at the start of the 1980s. In 1981 John Travis published *The Wellness Workbook*, written with his colleague Regina Sara Ryan. It was an accessible, practical guide to the main teachings of the Wellness Resource Center that incorporated the text of *The Wellness Index* and much of the material first circulated in *The Wellness Workbook for Health Professionals*. At this point, Travis was still based in Costa Rica and his life among the Monteverde Quakers was not unlike the time he spent in Baltimore in the early 1970s as part of the 'intentional community' Koinonia, the site of his 'Capricorn Incident'. However, although Travis draws on his personal experiences throughout *The Wellness Workbook* – his family background, his attitude to medicine, the breakdown of his marriage – there is scant reference to this nomadism and preference for experimental living. Travis certainly emphasises the importance of cultivating a healthy 'living space' with good environmental conditions – low noise, low light pollution, a clean and clear atmosphere – but he otherwise writes as if his readers have already achieved a degree of property security.

The issue is not whether they have a home or not, it is a matter of how they are going to fine-tune these homes to maximise their ambient benefits. So too for Jon Kabat-Zinn. Throughout *Full Catastrophe Living*, readers are encouraged to use their domestic spaces to practise the all-important body scan. Kabat-Zinn recommends that his clients, most of whom are in the 30–50 age range, designate 'a special place' in their homes for this purpose, one free of external distractions. Elsewhere he describes how one patient, a woman he calls 'Jackie', returns home from an all-day stress-reduction class at his clinic to find a note from her husband saying he's 'gone off overnight to take care of things in their summer home'. With her husband at house number two, Jackie is suddenly free to enjoy house number one, 'all alone for the first time in her adult life'. Resisting the urge to call a friend over for dinner, she instead wanders around the house 'with a feeling of joy that lasted all evening'. Jackie then opens all the windows and moves her mattress to another room so as get the best view of the Sunday morning sunrise. Shadowing this and other such anecdotes are Kabat-Zinn's references to everyday occurrences that can act as crucibles for mindful practice. Invariably they are activities associated with the home: cleaning out the garage, mowing the lawn, relaxing in the backyard, sitting at the table with the family. It is as if Kabat-Zinn's default setting for typicality is the secure nuclear family unit, peopled by those who do not merely inhabit a domestic space but who are well rooted in the possession of one.[23]

In assuming this focus Travis and Kabat-Zinn were making clear their emphasis on self-actualisation. They were not offering models of social welfare but were trying to cultivate in their readers an enhanced sense of well-being. If we accept Maslow's hierarchical model of development, then this is a zone of fulfilment that must be thought of as standing on the shoulders of other, previously satisfied needs. At the same time, however, in assuming that this need for safety has been fulfilled, books like *The Wellness Workbook* and *Full Catastrophe Living* effectively ringfence their goal. The possession of a good place becomes the prerequisite for a shot at self-actualisation, not a realisation of it. Further, no substantive comment is made in either about the link between housing and well-being, particularly the impact of property precarity upon mental health. Given the connection between 'healing' and the projection of a 'comfortable home' in the work of Louise Hay, it is easy to see just how finely balanced health and homes were in the late 1970s and early 1980s, the point at which ownership started to become a matter of aspiration not practicality.

This intersection has become ever more acute in the decades since the 1970s, with house prices on both sides of the Atlantic rising to almost impossible levels and the associated pressures of scarcity, affordability and insecurity generating an equally high peak of psychological crises. *Health and Wellbeing in Homes*, a 2016 report by the UK Green Building Council, made this point clear when it presented the home as a potential generator of good mental health. Reminding us of the World Health Organization's post-war definition of health as 'a state of complete physical, mental and social wellbeing', the report connected this foundational tenet of wellness to the very architecture of the house and the importance of secure occupation. 'Peace of mind, contentment, confidence and social connection': according to the report these are not qualities to seek out once in situ, they are the intangible benefits that lie inside, a few steps across the welcome mat. They are received when the threshold is crossed, occupancy begins, and the bricks and mortar of the house are actualised by living use into the four walls of a home. Back in the late 1970s, this basic understanding of what a home meant and how it should function beyond its role as a commodity was not particularly well defined. In some cases it had slipped between the lines of texts that otherwise sought to foster lives of well-being.[24]

It is a sense of covert exclusivity that recalls Jeffrey Eugenides' novel of the American 1970s, *The Virgin Suicides* (1993). The tragedy of the title – the unexplained suicide of the five teenage Lisbon sisters of Grosse Point, Michigan – leaves the family home an empty shell; a shunned house, one that fails to sell and quickly falls into disrepair. In the mind of the novel's reflective narrator(s) these events augured Detroit's industrial implosion and the future 'decline of the neighbourhood'. However, towards the end of the novel, we're told that after falling into disrepair, the Lisbon house is eventually bought by a 'young couple' from Boston. These new homeowners bring with them signs of a new economy as they quickly turn the house into 'a sleek empty space for meditation and serenity'. It appears that the 'young couple from Boston' are wellness entrepreneurs and, like Travis setting up shop in a converted Mill Valley home, they have come to Detroit in search of a physical base of operations. Eugenides leaves it to the reader to decide whether this conversion is a green shoot of recovery or a further marker of the neighbourhood's fall into hard times. Either way, the implied gentrification represents the evacuation of a family home. There is no mention of children accompanying the 'young couple' nor any intention to build the type of life the Lisbons once had. To get the right kind of emptiness the couple have chucked out all the trappings of their predecessors' crowded suburban domesticity. To become a source of well-being, the Lisbon house has been taken out of service as a site of shelter.[25]

This is precisely the kind of asset stripping that a character like Harvey Holroyd and a book like *The Serial* fears the most. Beyond all her jokes at the expense of human potential, McFadden wrote one of the classic real estate novels. Closely entangled with the changing economic and material landscape of Marin County, a place that rehearsed the gentrification and speculation that would soon take place elsewhere, *The Serial* offers a portrait of the restlessness that causes people to move and the effects that different properties have upon their occupants. From tract house to apartment to commune and back again, the lurking anxiety of the novel is not that we might fail to communicate. McFadden also issues no apologia for the nuclear family (unlike the film). Instead, the novel is really concerned that we might ultimately fail to find a space of our own. More so than some of the other practitioners at the time, McFadden really understood this basic material need and the way it feeds into a resonating sense of well-being. According to the novel good places can be found at the end of self-actualising rainbows but they should also be lining every street. We might have the keys to fulfilment inside us, but they should also be right there, in our possession, jangling in our pockets. We all have a right to live, which has nothing to do with a relative right to buy. Were more of us, particularly policymakers, to relate to that message, we would all find ourselves well on the way to a better place.

CHAPTER X

The New Age of Enlightenment
1982–1984

In the summer of 1983, maybe a little later, an unemployed French agricultural engineer called Michel Thomas left his home in Paris and paid a visit to l'Espace du Possible. Thin, wiry and intense, Thomas was in his mid-twenties, he was well educated, he was married, and he had a young son. He was also recovering from a nervous breakdown. Studying at the Institut National Agronomique of Paris-Grignon had led him to expect an easy step into the comforts of French middle-class life, but after graduation, when this pathway failed to materialise, a cloud of depression descended upon him. It was a spate of bad mental weather not eased by a sudden sense of indifference towards his hard-won degree. Who needs a 'Specialty in Development of the Natural Environment and Ecology', anyway? Another course of study followed, this time photography at École nationale supérieure Louis-Lumière, but Thomas left before completing. Nothing seemed to work. The depression really took hold in about 1981 and as its second year came into view Thomas, flushed with a mix of despondency and entitlement, decided to invest in himself. Like many before him he set off, alone, for the sun and self-development of the campsite at Meschers-sur-Gironde. Yves Donnars could not have asked for a more suitable guest.[1]

Meanwhile, over on Vancouver Island, 1983 was proving to be a pivotal year for a nine-year-old future filmmaker called Panos Cosmatos. It was the year he made his first visit to the local rental store, Video Attic. There he saw one garish cover after another adorning all the films he wasn't old enough to see, David Cronenberg's *The Brood* among them. Prior to this, Cosmatos had watched Super-8 highlight reels of Disney classics while his father, George P. Cosmatos, was busy taping films off cable TV. This was part of the job for the elder Cosmatos. He was a director known for genre movies like *Of Unknown Origin* (1983) and was building up to the breakthrough hit *Rambo: First Blood Part II* (1985). One night, soon after his visit to the Attic, Cosmatos Jnr snuck down to the sitting room when he should have been sleeping. There he found his parents enjoying a tape of *Alien* and he secretly watched the film as it was reflected on a framed print that hung behind the sofa. This stolen viewing lingered like a fever-dream and gradually started to fuse with his memories of all the video boxes back at the store. Catalysed by this home life steeped in pop culture, Cosmatos started to imagine his own versions of the films he couldn't see. While his father pushed on into a world of blood, sweat and popcorn, Cosmatos slowly evolved his own private form of hypnagogic cinema; psychic fuel for days yet to come.[2]

Back in Meschers-sur-Gironde, Michel Thomas was also getting into gear and enthusiastically embracing the creative, entrepreneurial spirit of l'Espace. With no credentials, save for a handful of unpublished poems and a stint editing a student magazine called *Karamazov*, he put on a series of creative writing workshops. They were well received and in return, l'Espace started to work its strange magic. Thomas returned to mount more workshops and would continue to do so until the late 1990s. All the while, back in the real world, his life started to change. Thomas forged a new career as a computer engineer, then started to work for the National Assembly and in between he focused on the literary ambitions that had first prompted the writing workshops. Thomas published his first poems in 1985 then moved on to non-fiction before making a splash as a novelist. By this time he was no longer Michel Thomas, IT worker, but had metamorphosed into Michel Houellebecq, generation Mitterrand's very own caustic Sartre. His first novel, *Extension du domaine de la lutte* (1994), drew on his own working life and his vicious ruminations on the modern West to give voice to every young, depressed cubicle worker who ever reached for the feasts promised by the Dionysian 1960s, only to have the neoliberal 1990s serve them up yet another meal for one. In 1998 Houellebecq returned to Meschers-sur-Gironde for the fifth time, a few days before his second novel was published. This, he told Donnars, was partly inspired by his time at l'Espace.[3]

As for Cosmatos, the late 1990s proved to be a difficult time. The death of his mother, the Swedish artist Birgitta Ljungberg-Cosmatos, in 1997 hit him hard. The death of his father in the early 2000s would make things even worse. He was able to keep working, and in the middle of all of this he threw himself into a series of creative pursuits: writing, Super-8 filmmaking, graphic design and a proposed store-front installation 'for an institute that doesn't exist', complete with a real pamphlet campaign detailing its imaginary programmes. Gradually, the installation took on a life of its own and blossomed into his directorial debut, *Beyond the Black Rainbow* (2010), a haunted film about strange goings-on in Arboria, an experimental therapy institute straight out of the late 1960s.

In the oversaturated promo reel that begins the film we are told that Arboria is 'a state of mind, a way of being', a place that promises a 'new age of enlightenment' via a 'unique blend of benign pharmacology, sensory therapy and energy sculpting'. With its enigmatic name and patter of human perfection, it is hard not to get heavy Esalen vibes when the Arboria logo fills the screen. It has its own amazing panorama in the form of 'award-winning gardens' and there's also a visionary tag-team in charge with the institute's founder, Dr Mercurio Arboria, and his protégé, Dr Barry Nyle, acting as weird stand-ins for Michael Murphy and Richard Price. The atmosphere of Arboria, however, is substantially darker and more sinister than that of Esalen. Cosmatos sets his film not in the 1960s nor the 1970s but in the Reagan-era of the early 1980s – 1983 to be precise – a time of designer drugs, strange new epidemics, heavy metal and television announcements of the Iran–Contra affair, all of which find their way into the film's lush fabric. In this new decade Arboria is an institution in crisis, presided over by the scarily intense Barry Nyle. He glides through its secret rooms and examination chambers, trying to keep a lid on Arboria's litany of failed human experiments, his own included. A nightmarish flashback scene shows us that in 1966, Nyle barely survived a mind-frying lysergic trip in the dark void of a floatation tank.

Arboria's oppressive atmosphere brings to mind the Academy of Erotic Enquiry and the House of Skin, the troubled research centres in Cronenberg's antiseptic early features *Stereo* (1969) and *Crimes of the*

Future (1970). For all its horrors, though, the world of *Beyond the Black Rainbow* was a comforting emotional crucible for Cosmatos. 1983 was *his* year, ground zero in terms of his imaginative ignition. Making the film was a way of realising the secret cinema he'd conjured behind the sofa, and by giving in to the luxuries of this nostalgia Cosmatos was also grieving, albeit obliquely, the loss of his parents. 'My mother and father haunt every frame of this film,' he would later explain, 'absolutely and completely.' It was as if the near decade-long journey from installation to feature film had been a protracted form of therapy.[4]

Donnars may well have thought the same about Houellebecq's writing. Here, it seemed, was the ultimate validation of his project: a loyal Espacian turning his transformation into art – into *literature*, no less. However, any pride Donnars may have felt soon withered when he read the book. *Les Particules élémentaires* (1998), known in English as *Atomised* (2000), was an uncompromising essay on the dog days of modernity that focused on Bruno and Michel Djerzinski, two half-brothers who move through their teens during the 1970s, the precise moment when, thanks to films like *Emmanuelle* (1974), the sexual liberation of the 1960s went public and hit the receptors of an eager audience. As Houellebecq describes, the brothers' parents had been utterly absorbed by the cultural shifts of that prior decade, and as with the others who 'made their fortunes in the 1960s', they spent the 1970s abandoning their familial responsibilities in favour of socio-political causes and varied business interests. In the case of their mother Janine Ceccaldi, she set out for a life among the squalid communes of the Riviera, which, according to Houellebecq, took their cue from the radical happenings at 'Esalen, near Big Sur'. At one point we are told that Janine falls in with one Francesco di Meola, an Italian American who 'had met Ginsberg and Aldous Huxley and was one of the founding members of the Esalen commune'. Pushed to the margins of this self-exploration, Bruno and Michel grow up lonely and isolated, out of step with the 'leisure society' of the 1970s and emotionally unprepared for the transactional intimacy of the 1980s. When the novel opens, we meet them as two middle-aged men, lost and languishing at the edge of the century. Bruno is hedonistic and rootless, an ex-teacher and sometime writer, while Michel is a biologist, similarly disconnected but harbouring a set of ideas that will have radical consequences for post-millennial human society. Both are typical Houellebecq protagonists, if not alter-egos: they are depressive, prone to caustic bouts of social analysis and chronically aware that they exist as subjects of a hostile, inhuman world. In short, Bruno and Michel personify what Houellebecq terms, almost in passing, 'the suicide of the West'.[5]

Unflinching and often spectacularly misanthropic, *Atomised* became a genuine *succès de scandale*, proof that French literature still had the power to provoke and philosophise in equal measure. To some readers it was a distressingly nihilistic tract, to others it was a bold critique of a dehumanised world. Both camps tended to agree that it was one of the last great novels of the 20th century. Donnars was not among them. He was horrified. His problem lay with the book's second part, 'Strange Moments', that begins in the late 1990s with a 42-year-old Bruno visiting l'Espace, a place Houellebecq identified by name in the text of the first edition. Although he outlines a fairly accurate backstory (formed in the mid-1970s with the intention of creating 'synergies'), and although he gets the general layout correct (a campsite on an estate 'scattered with pine forests'), the overall picture is that of a tawdry sex resort. L'Espace is, in Houellebecq's telling, a place to 'get your rocks off'; it's a 'New Age Purgatory' full of forty-somethings who lament the loss of their once promised futures while bitterly decrying the freedoms of their sons and daughters' generation, a tormenting demographic represented in the novel by the few teenagers who pepper the campsite. Sure enough, a few paragraphs after his arrival, Bruno finds himself mortified and aroused as he steps into the communal shower only to find a group of naked girls, 'all between 15 and 17', frolicking in the spray. Soon after he pairs off with Christiane, a 40-year-old single mother who obligingly becomes the typical Houellebecquian heroine: a cerebral and sensitive emotional crutch who's also quite partial to heavy bouts of group sex.[6]

Atomised brought back the salacious reputation Donnars had spent years trying to downplay. Worse, Houellebecq was also warping it into an orgy zone that came complete with nigh-on paedophilic opportunities. Underpinning it all was a corrosive mood of cultural resignation in which l'Espace was part of the problem, not the solution. Rather than fostering aspirational self-development, l'Espace as seen via *Atomised* became instead the perfect destination for a morose class of swingers who are either clinging on to a dream of youth or who have not yet realised the party's over. Arboria in *Beyond the Black Rainbow* is similarly infused with a sense of decline, but Cosmatos cranks up the hangover to an almost overwhelming degree. At one point in the film, Barry Nyle descends into the depths of the institute to see his mentor. Mercurio Arboria is discovered in a private chamber, old, infirm and decrepit. He sits alone, breathing heavily, slipping in and out of consciousness watching worn-out promo videos and thinking back to 'simpler days'. If Esalen had taught us that all men are gods, then Cosmatos shows us the god that failed. The scene dramatises the virtual collapse of the human potential project in the 1980s, an unforgiving world of needles, caked blood and impacted veins, all of which connect the dying Arboria with a deeply emblematic sense of affliction. What Houellebecq achieves in *Atomised* with eviscerating deprecation, Cosmatos conveys with a clear and unflinching scene of abject unwellness. Writer and filmmaker both agree that whatever the practitioners of the 1970s were trying to achieve in terms of human development, their projects had utterly imploded come 1983.[7]

*****

Although elaborate, the critical thrust of these contemporary works did reflect the attitude of the 1980s. At that time, the language of self-development and human potential seemed to be rapidly losing its potency. It was as if the dreamy metaphors of the 1970s were wearing out in the harsh, strip-lit glare of the new decade. Calling Esalen a 'Cape Canaveral for inner space', for example, sounded great in the 1960s and very early 1970s. It captured the idea of inner space as a new frontier and aligned self-discovery with the adventurous grandeur of the moon-landing. Come the 1980s, however, and the Apollo programme was long gone. The moon had been walked for the last time in 1972.

For writers like J.G. Ballard, Cape Canaveral became a symbol of failed transcendence, a place where the visionary intent of space travel and moonwalking withered into a melancholy reality of ruined launch pads, rootless scientists and evaporated futures. The stories he wrote between 1968 and 1988 and published as *Memories of the Space Age* (1988) were not the soaring, evolutionary parables of Arthur C. Clarke but chamber dramas for dead and grounded astronauts.[8]

It was a downbeat approach to science fiction, typical of Ballard's oeuvre, but it was also reflective of the material circumstances surrounding 'the Cape' and its workforce. Robert Eliot made this point in 1984, in his book *Is It Worth Dying For?*, when he described how heart attacks were rife among 'young aerospace workers, some as young as twenty-nine'. In the 1970s Cape Canaveral was giving Marin County a run for its money as regards its levels of drinking, drug-taking and divorce. The reason, as Eliot put it, was that NASA specialised in 'the firing of people' as well as the 'firing of rockets'. With the American government deprioritising the space programme across the late 1960s and early 1970s, it meant that each time there was a successful launch '15 percent of the workers who made it happen were fired'. By 1973 the workforce stood at 14,000, less than half of its pre-moon landing number of 30,000 in 1965. When he went there as a cardiovascular consultant in the late 1960s, Eliot found a group of highly trained professionals working sixteen-hour days in jobs that were highly pressurised but also highly paid. The next month, however, they were out of work with no transferrable skills, having to make a living as TV repairmen, shelf stackers or 'ticket-takers at Disney World'. Writing as part of his investigation into stress, heart disease and the circumstances of his own heart attack, Eliot's portrait was just as eerie as Ballard's, but in charting the slide from NASA to Disney he was not decrying the cosmic hubris of the space programme. Instead, Cape Canaveral appeared in his book as a symbol of extreme precarity: a workplace that subjected its employees to 'the acute stress of knowing that at any moment they could lose their work, income, status and identity as skilled professionals'. It was not a representation conducive to glorious inner space exploration.[9]

The Space Race of the 1960s had always been a piece of Cold War theatre between America and Russia. What lay behind claims of scientific endeavour and the humanistic attempt to step beyond the bounds of the Earth was the desire of both superpowers to indulge in the spectacle of heavy-duty missile launches. By the mid-1980s, this political power play had been amplified and once again filtered into the public sphere with the arrival – or rather proposal – of Ronald Reagan's Strategic Defense Initiative, or as it became known the 'Star Wars programme'. Reagan's idea (and it was very much *his* idea: a mix of Hollywood fantasy, right-wing theology and arms race politics) was to launch a battery of 'space-borne laser and particle beam weapons with the potential to provide a reliable defense for the entire United States'. As Frances Fitzgerald explains, the Strategic Defense Initiative was first announced during a 'routine defense speech' in March 1983, and from the outset it relied upon the promise of impossible technology. Even when Congress was asked to approve a five-year budget of $26 billion, thoughts of laser-firing satellites remained hopelessly futuristic.[10]

Reagan's vision amounted to an overt militarisation of outer space. The Strategic Defense Initiative unapologetically recast the final frontier as a zone of conflict, a territory to be protected and fought over rather than explored. Correspondingly, as if receiving the trickle-down of this aggressive rhetoric, the cultural idea of inner space underwent a similar weaponisation. Films like Douglas Trumbull's *Brainstorm* (1983) and Joseph Ruben's *Dreamscape* (1984) presented psychic abilities, lucid dreaming and the recording of psychological phenomena as potential tools of the military-industrial complex. *Dreamscape* was originally intended as an adaptation of Roger Zelazny's *The Dream Master*, but the adventure scenario that emerged – featuring psychic operatives entering other people's dreams to combat their nightmares – eventually bore more resemblance to Don Pendleton's pulp epic *The Godmakers* than Zelazny's science fictional take on psychiatric ethics. In the film, the dream world becomes a battle zone as psychics are eventually pushed to act as assassins, killing key targets in their sleep, all of which plays out against a distinctly Reagan-esque backdrop of international nuclear tension. *Brainstorm* is similar with its psychotropic technology initially being used to explore shared emotional, psychological and even mystical experiences (not unlike *Altered States*) before the shadowy military get wind of it and try to use the equipment as an interrogation and brainwashing device.

Both films draw deep on the rich stream of material then available on 1970s paranormal research, be that Andrija Puharich's work with Uri Geller or the remote viewing experiments described by Sheila Ostrander and Lynn Schroeder in *Psychic Discoveries Behind the Iron Curtain* (1970). Hints of Esalen and the human potential scene can also be detected in the mix. Director Trumbull took his cast to the institute while preparing *Brainstorm*, while *Dreamscape* offered a glancing but still pronounced nod when an office conversation in the film's own research building takes place with books by Abraham Maslow clearly visible in the background. During this time Esalen was making its own steps into the geopolitical zone when it launched its Soviet-American Exchange Program. This began in 1980 and as Jeffrey Kripal explains, it ran for sixteen years, eventually changing its name to 'the Russian-American Center'. The exchange programme was there to foster 'cross-cultural dialogue' between spheres of corresponding interest. Esalen wanted to connect with like-minded researchers and practitioners in Russia and find some common spiritual ground in the shadow of their uneasy political rivalry. Reportedly, the project's use value as a diplomatic channel did not go unnoticed by both governments. However, no psychic battles took place between the symposia and the ambassadorial receptions.

Meanwhile, back in *Dreamscape*, its 'dreamlinked' warriors were transforming into terrifying snake-men and attacking their enemies. It was B-movie stylings all the way, but not without a certain echo of 'serpent-power' or Kundalini. In this film, the powerful base chakra energy raised by the postures, internal cleansing practices and breathing exercises of yoga was turned into a weaponised version of the id. It was a startling special effect clearly at home in a popcorn movie but one that covertly said more about the public perception of human potential in the 1980s than Esalen's international handshakes. According to *Dreamscape*, self-development, the realisation of one's potential, meant the manifestation of latent superpowers and such abilities were tallied with an aggressive form of psychic violence. The central drama of *Beyond the Black Rainbow* pushes in the same direction with psychedelic voyages and attempts to cultivate human perfection leading, in the Reagan era, to Barry Nyle's experiments on a young girl who harbours enormous, potentially destructive, psychic abilities. Collectively, these films argue that it's not a 'real' self we have buried within us, but some kind of coiled super-soldier that waits, seething and ready to strike.[11]

*****

Such representations did not go unchallenged. Yves Donnars, for one, responded to *Atomised* by suing Houellebecq's publisher Flammarion. He called for the book to be pulped and requested substantial damages. Eventually, though, Donnars agreed on a settlement with Flammarion that the offending passages of 'Strange Moments' would be altered, not removed. And so, in subsequent editions and in the English translation, l'Espace du Possible in Meschers-sur-Gironde was transplanted to Cholet in the Loire Valley and became Lieu de Changement, 'place of change', a name which, given the general sense of stagnancy suffusing the novel, seems less like an attempt to placate Donnars and more like an ironic choice on Houellebecq's part. It was not unlike Cyra McFadden calling one of her Esalen substitutes 'Moment's Pause', precisely because it *doesn't* offer such a respite. All in all, it was hardly a resounding victory for Donnars. Rather than repairing the good name of his business, the outcome of the case did the opposite: it brought more attention to l'Espace as the now infamous site of the *affair d'Houellebecq*.[12]

However cutting his portrait of l'Espace, Houellebecq was not just trying to embarrass Donnars. To read 'Strange Moments' as merely a satire of the *soixante-huitards* at middle age would obscure Houellebecq's much more seismic detonation of the whole 1960s project. Take the unsettling shower scenes involving Bruno and the teenage Espacians, for example. On one level, this is classic Houellebecq toxicity: underneath Bruno's self-deprecating anhedonia lies a rampant and frequently fulfilled fantasy life. His is the attitude of the lackadaisical sex tourist, a man who simply can't be bothered with the thirteen-hour flight to Bangkok but who none-theless expects his desires to be realised. More tactically, however, the scene reflects some of the stories circulating across the 1990s about Otto Muehl's Friedrichshof commune, particularly those that emerged after his arrest and imprisonment for child abuse in 1991.

When Friedrichshof was founded in 1972 at Zurndorf in Austria's sparsely populated Burgenland region, it was an ambitious DIY project. Muehl had previously operated a commune in Vienna's Praterstrasse district under the auspices of the Aktionsanalytische Organisation, but Friedrichshof took things even further. It was self-contained zone far away from the city where the psychodrama could be played out in full, undisturbed. Muehl and about a dozen or so fellow travellers spent much of 1972 fixing up a farmhouse to make things (barely) habitable and over the next year, a steadily growing group took up permanent residence on site. By this point Muehl had declared a central principle of total sexual freedom. In practice, this assault on bourgeois values forbade commune members from forming long-term attachments nor were they allowed to show anything akin to affection during sex. Muehl's diktat was enforced by connecting the rotation of sexual partners to the rhythm of commune's living arrangements. As Jonathan Margolis describes it, emphasising both the heteronormativity and the reality of punishment in a seemingly free enclave: 'If a man failed to find a woman to sleep with on a particular night, he didn't have a bed.' Inevitably 'gonorrhea, lice, cystitis and diarrhea' spread through the group and before long a gaggle of bewildered children had been born 'having no idea who their father was'.

Friedrichshof was meant to be a creative, therapeutic space of economic communism, defiantly anti-capitalist in its commitment to shared property and shared labour. The deconstruction of the nuclear family was part of this ethic. Everyone 'worked together, bore children together, educated them together, and spent their evenings entertain-ing each other'. No one had the right to impose any proprietorial or emotional claim on anyone else. Except, of course, for Otto Muehl. As the commune grew, a strict sexual hierarchy grew up around Muehl who became an increasingly dictatorial alpha male. He would select favourites from his followers and would eventually claim a wife, his

'First Lady' Claudia Steiger. Meanwhile 'lower'-status members would be left to battle it out for his attention. Far from dispensing with the family structure, this system intensified it into a patriarchal cult of personality that radiated with the force of Muehl's inexhaustible libido.

As described in *Slaves in Paradise* (1999), a documentary released the year after *Atomised* was published, things got even darker in the 1980s, when Muehl's attentions turned to the younger members of the commune. Those born during Friedrichshof's early days were entering their teens in the mid-1980s, and after years living in the eye of the partner-swapping storm, they had been conditioned to regard sex with Muehl as a privilege. It was an aura of superiority he did little to dissuade. He would boast in interviews about the 'fourteen-year-olds' who would 'swarm' around him in the showers. As repellent as this braggadocio was, it paled in comparison to the thrust of the allegations that emerged from 1989 onwards when several commune members described a how newly adolescent girls were taken to him for 'sexual initiation' while the boys would go to Steiger. Both were arrested in 1991 and Muehl received a seven-year prison sentence.[13]

In *Atomised*, Bruno carries none of Muehl's authority nor is the atmosphere of Lieu de Changement as tyrannical as Friedrichshof. However, he still simmers with sexual entitlement equal to any of Muehl's communards. Houellebecq provides enough of an insight into Bruno's desires to suggest that a sexual rota would probably appeal. To use Houellebecq's substitute for the word 'happy', it would make Bruno, the pornography-browsing, partner-seeking consumer, 'almost content'. The shower vignette nods to this. It alludes to the uncomfortably sordid history of communes like Friedrichshof and validates Houellebecq's provocation that 'desire is preoccupied with youth'. It also places Bruno in a zone of constant sexual possibility. Whether feeling attraction or repulsion, Bruno's encounters with women – young and 'old' – are filtered through this lens of presumed availability. In a further echo of the Friedrichshof episode, there's also the shadow of Bruno's mother Janine and her life in the communes operated by the novel's Esalen veteran Francesco di Meola. We are told that Bruno almost commits incest with Janine while visiting her in the summer of 1974. After this, Houellebecq describes Janine's earlier sexual encounters with di Meola's teenage son David in 1963. Such acts are given the same pseudo-justification as those allegedly performed by Muehl and Steiger at Friedrichshof. They amount to an 'initiation' which 'opens the world up to the adolescent'.

Beyond these glancing but troubling asides, Houellebecq eventually grants Muehl a walk-on part in *Atomised*. He is name-checked alongside his Vienna Actionist comrades Hermann Nitsch and Rudolph Schwarzkögler as part of the 'Macmillan hypothesis', one of Bruno's long discourses that Christiane is required to listen to when they reunite for a late-night dinner in Paris after their time at Lieu de Changement. It is a shout-out that puts Muehl alongside the other dark stars of the 1960s: Anton LaVey, The Process Church of the Final Judgement and Charles Manson. Over rollmop herrings, Bruno explains that the Macmillan hypothesis is outlined in *From Lust to Murder: A Generation* a book by David Macmillan, a Vincent Bugliosi-esque district attorney. Like Bugliosi's Manson tome *Helter Skelter* (1974), Houellebecq's grisly book-within-a-book recounts a 1983 homicide case involving kidnap, torture and snuff movies all focused on the now adult David di Meola.

The arrival of coffee gives Bruno time to place di Meola's crimes on a continuum of cruelty, one that extends from the Marquis de Sade to Manson and the Actionists. We are told that Manson and his ilk were not some 'monstrous aberration' but rather the 'logical conclusion' of the hippie movement, if not the entire enlightenment project. In essence, the argument of *From Lust to Murder* is an extreme form of that found in *The Culture of Narcissism*. Christopher Lasch's idea of a solipsistic retreat from politics is amplified by Houellebecq into a much more corrosive diagnosis that describes the 'destruction of moral values' in the 1960s followed by a widespread turn towards the pursuit of individual freedom. Once the possibilities for 'sexual pleasure' had been exhausted and individuals found themselves liberated from 'the constraints of ordinary morality', it was a predictably easy step towards further transgressions. In this sense, argue both Bruno and Macmillan, 'serial killers of the 1990s were the spiritual children of the hippies'. Both luxuriated in a 'cult of power', a rejection of 'the secular rules slowly built up in the name of justice and morality'. They share a purely libertarian creed in which the right of the individual is asserted against social norms and 'the hypocrisy of morality, sentiment, judgment and pity'.[14]

Bruno's Macmillan monologue comes late in the novel. Houellebecq uses it to inject a shot of theoretical fuel into the accumulating theme of *Atomised*: the decline of Western modernity. Earlier on, however, during an equally awkward dinner sequence – this time between Bruno and Michel – the Djerzinskis had rehearsed the gist of the Macmillan hypothesis via a discussion of another set of brothers, Aldous and Julian Huxley. Sat in Michel's Paris apartment with drink in hand, Bruno kicks off with *Brave New World* (1932), arguing that the book is not the 'totalitarian nightmare' that it appears to be. Rather, it offers 'our idea of heaven': social improvement through genetic manipulation, liberated sexual behaviour and war against the ravages of age. In Bruno's telling, *Brave New World*, with its emphasis on 'instant gratification', promises everything Lieu de Changement aspired to but could not deliver. In short, he sees in Huxley's seemingly dystopian future the modern ideal: a fully formed 'leisure society'. After another glass of wine, Michel chimes in and reminds Bruno that most of Aldous Huxley's ideas came from his eugenics-advocating older brother Julian, and his discourse on the improvement of the species, *What Dare I Think?* (1931). Further, he claims that such ideas found their way into hippie culture thanks to Aldous Huxley's influence on 'the founding members of Esalen' and the blossoming 'New Age' scene. That his ideas stretched so far is for Michel proof of Aldous Huxley's cardinal importance. Summoning up the energy for an almost celebratory moment, he and Bruno then head out for a cheap meal at a Chinese restaurant.

Their spark of enthusiasm is short-lived. As they pick away at a set meal for two, Bruno and Michel are faced only with a sense of impossibility when it comes to the prospect of Huxley's 'Utopian Solution' finding form in the late 20th century. While pushing his prawn around a plate of chilli sauce, Michel adds to the mood of futility by bringing up Huxley's *Island*. Although *Island* was integral to Huxley's influence, particularly as regards the early days of Esalen, it also captures Michel's pessimism with its perfect human zone destroyed by humanity's own competitive and accumulative nature.

However, according to Michel, it is not just the parable-like nature of *Island* that communicates a sense of failure. Rather he argues that the very project of the novel is flawed because it suggests – as in *Brave New World* – that to ease the 'suffering, pain and hatred' that comes with desire one must satisfy it immediately. Michel, speaking as someone miserably corralled in the 'sex-and-shopping' society of the late 20th century, claims that the 'opposite is true'. Society needs competition, he argues. Society cannot function in the absence of desire and so, with capitalism helpfully obliging, we find that desire is 'endlessly marshalled and organised and blown out of all proportion'. Further on in *Atomised*, Houellebecq will contrive a provocative conclusion that essentially calls time on this excessive human instinct. But as he pictures Michel and Bruno sitting in the restaurant, neither brother is fully aware of the events to come. Michel in particular feels only that humanity has reached a terminal point. Rampant individualism, given full vent by decades of emphasis on the value of freedom, has resulted in a societal overstuffing. People want to have 'more and more until it fills their lives and finally devours them', says an exhausted Michel as the evening winds down. He leaves the restaurant having barely touched his food.[15]

*****

The tethering of capitalism and desire had been extensively theorised prior to *Atomised*, most notably by Guy Debord, Deleuze and Guattari, and other thinkers working in the poststructuralist laboratories where Marx and Freud were repeatedly mixed into ever more explosive combinations. For Deleuze and Guattari, writing in *Anti-Oedipus* and its follow-up *A Thousand Plateaus* (1980), desire was a transformative flow that circulated within and without us like a vibrating soundwave from the unconscious. As Adam Shatz describes, they saw the unconscious not in terms of Freud's Oedipal theatre, nor as Jacques Lacan's ghostly linguistic structure, but as a radically productive 'factory' constantly producing 'new and transgressive combinations of desires'. Deleuze and Guattari were not existentialists mulling over the angst-ridden human condition; they were not interested in the plight of 'man'. They were handymen, engineers, 'functionalists', as Guattari put it, interested in how things *worked* not what they *meant*. As such, they focused on desire's crackling currents and attempted to map out all the conduits and mechanisms that variously harnessed and suppressed this potentially revolutionary force. To that end, Deleuze and Guattari relied on the concept of the 'machine', famously clarifying in *Anti-Oedipus* that they were concerned with 'real machines, not imaginary ones'. By this, they meant that each individual subject was a vessel for desire. It animates us and we are thus 'desiring-machines', units propelled not by personality, nor by politics but by the intent to seek out couplings, connections and reconnections in a seemingly limitless cycle of exchange. As Deleuze and Guattari describe, we are organ-machines 'plugged into an energy source machine', whether that be understood as bodily functions – the ins and outs of food, water and air – or our sensory faculties that draw various forms of stimuli from the word around us.

Within this schema, capitalism emerges as an exemplary machine. It is the massive factory which dominates the landscape and shadows the town beneath. Capitalism is a producing machine, a disruptive system that works to reproduce itself, but despite is powerful effects (that range from, as Shatz puts it, 'uprooting people from the land to overturning the systems of belief to which they have been anchored') it also seeks to contain flows of desire to ensure its own smooth functioning. According to Deleuze and Guattari, capitalism thus stokes and then funnels these energies into the process of production. Workers invest their time and energy into the generation of surplus value and this, in turn, is driven back into the machine, like a shot of nitro into the heart of an engine. The generation of such excess does not ease the need to work – in the capitalist world the job is never done – rather, it perpetuates the system, creates more growth which then requires more and more labour to sustain it. And so on. As consumers, we are installed into the same machine via a further recalibration of desire, one that sees the buzzing, erupting force that Deleuze and Guattari celebrate funnelled into the fetishised 'missing object' of psychoanalysis. Capitalism tells us what we want, not what we need, and as each want is satisfied, its systems simply direct the flow of our desire towards the next shiny thing, and the cycle begins again. We are perpetually driven on in pursuit of what these objects – these commodities – promise, rather than what they do. Use value comes second to the glittering halos of exchange value, which confers an irresistible aura onto a conveyor belt of products, from food to clothes to cars and any number of objects in between. Invariably we are taught that upon buying these items, we are not just acquiring an object but a key to something more. A better experience; better health, perhaps. Maybe even a better life.[16]

This interplay between desire and deferral is the 'sex and shopping' dynamic that *Atomised* diagnoses so mordantly. Like Deleuze and Guattari, Houellebecq had in mind the general state of late-stage capitalism, but by focusing his attention so specifically on the likes of l'Espace, however thinly disguised, he was analysing the theme from a very particular perspective, that of the increasingly pervasive commodification of 'humanist therapy' and its effects. Houellebecq tells us that in 1984 (around the time he started visiting l'Espace) Lieu de Changement changed focus to keep up with the decade's emergent market demands. Its package of expertise in 'Gestalt, rebirth, walking on hot coals, transactional analysis [and] sex meditation' was rebranded as a toolkit for 'human resources directors in multinational companies'. The Lieu 'ceased to be an association' and 'became a public limited company' offering residential courses aimed at the corporate sector. Hence Bruno hearing about it from 'a secretary'. Houellebecq describes how at that point, the priorities of Lieu de Changement shifted from the 1970s intent to create an 'authentic utopia' to an outlook more in line with the contemporary mood. It worked on the basis that 'business was the leisure industry of the 1980s'.[17]

The latter quote is one of the many snappy, caustic lines that echo through *Atomised*. The novel is a storehouse of aphorisms that could easily fill up *The Little Book of Modern Dread* or some such. But in sketching out this internal shift to 'business', Houellebecq was also speaking with a degree of contextual accuracy. Between the late 1970s and early 1980s, mainly as a means of economic survival, several growth centres, communes and self-development projects started to embrace a more corporate client base and, in some cases, a more explicitly capitalist business model. Having struggled to keep the Wellness Resource Center afloat for four years, for example, John Travis dealt with the cashflow problem by adopting a more free-floating consultancy-based approach. In 1979, shortly before leaving for Costa Rica, he reorganised his operations as Wellness Associates, 'a nonprofit educational organization'. By the time Travis published *The Wellness Workbook*, he was describing his new enterprise as the 'successor' to the Wellness Resource Center. There was no intention to re-establish a singular base of operations to which clients would have to travel. Under the banner of Wellness Associates, Travis delivered his services direct and offered seminars to 'professionals' that focused on 'personal integrity, authenticity and partnership'.[18]

Cashflow was never a problem in the high-profile, ever-confident and ever-confrontational world of est, but by the mid-1980s Werner Erhard was also pushing forwards with a similar rebranding process. So too were est offshoots like the British-based self-development group Exegesis, founded in 1976 by the former actor Robert D'Aubigny. Exegesis mounted seminars on transformation, self-confidence and 'self-disclosure', and although its gatherings were often intentionally smaller than est's mass training marathons, D'Aubigny worked from the same playbook: stuffy hotels, extended encounter sessions and fear-facing rituals. Musician Mike Oldfield of *Tubular Bells* (1973) fame joined the group in the late 1970s and by his own account had a transformative rebirthing experience during an Exegesis seminar that saw him emerge screaming and weeping from a pile of cushions. The main difference between est and Exegesis, though, was the presence of D'Aubigny himself. Born Robert Fuller in 1933, he was just as much a shapeshifter as Erhard, but his urbane persona relieved the group of the need to endure the football coach-style barking of the macho est trainers. Exegesis attendees were instead treated to the spectacle of a pseudo-aristocratic Englishman hamming his way through the seminar material like a Shakespearean luvvie having a go at David Mamet's *Glengarry Glen Ross* (1984). As the group's profile grew, Exegesis claimed to have taken thousands of members though its training but as 1984 came into view a round of bad press caused it to be increasingly castigated as a 'therapy cult'. The allegations were much the same as those still being levelled at est: it was an arena of humiliation that promised lots, delivered little and brainwashed its clients into taking one expensive round of seminars after another.

For Erhard it was time for a change. In late 1984 he mounted his last seminars under the est banner before re-emerging in January 1985 as 'the Forum', ostensibly a 'kinder, gentler iteration of the training that was more success-oriented'. The Forum marked Erhard's return to the corporate training model of Mind Dynamics. It had a more specific remit than est, focusing less on the open-ended personal development of human potential and more upon employee-based productivity enhancement and management-focused leadership techniques. Around the same time, D'Aubigny folded Exegesis and reappeared at the helm of Programmes Ltd, a telesales firm stuffed with Exegesis graduates. Programmes Ltd was a hyperactive selling machine that saw rooms full of chanting, handclapping operatives throw themselves at the phones each morning before spending the rest of the day whoopingly racking up order after order. Gone were the intensive bouts of self-examination. It was as if the adrenalised pursuit of profit had become the new way to find yourself.[19]

Neither est nor Exegesis had ever held back from promising their members business success. It was the ideal carrot: financial riches were within reach, all you had to do was commit to more and more training. Presiding over such assurances were the exemplary possessors of 'it', Erhard and D'Aubigny, those for whom the enterprises had clearly been so lucrative. Travis' work was completely different in terms of its attitude and character, but even when operating the Wellness Resource Center, he had always engaged closely with the professional sector. Neither of these projects underwent a complete turn from the realm of 'leisure' to 'business' in the 1980s; nor would they have classified their work as belonging to the world of 'leisure' in the first place. What was distinctive about their gearshifts, however, was the workplace focus. They were helping clients navigate the corporate ladder rather than the rocky road of life. This was particularly apparent with Exegesis. Once it became Programmes Ltd, members of the seminar group who had previously sat in conference rooms pushing towards a breakthrough suddenly found themselves transformed into a workforce sweating in an office pushing towards a daily sales target.

One of the period's most radical shifts towards a business outlook, however, took place at Friedrichshof. The anti-capitalist Muehl eventually undertook what Margolis calls 'one of those 180-degree ethical turns ideologues are prone to'. This began in 1977 at a formal congress of the Aktionsanalytische Organisation, when it was agreed to reintroduce private property to the commune infrastructure. Common assets, as scholar Martin Göessl explains, 'had not been enough to keep things going'. There was also a need for a large source of regular income. To secure this, Muehl simply began to capitalise upon the commune's economic potential. He started sending squads of commune members back into the world tasked with finding work in the European financial sector. Muehl had previously dominated their minds and bodies, so what was to stop him from now exploiting their labour power? Chief among these new economic animals were Jenny Simanowitz, a graduate of the Department of Peace Studies at Bradford University. She joined Friedrichshof in 1980, but soon after found herself on the move again. Having realised her value, Muehl had placed her with a group of 35 other members whose mission was to join an Amsterdam stockbroking firm. Once there, Simanowitz more than held her own. She quickly moved through the ranks and became one of Muehl's top earners, eventually making millions. 'I was one of the richest women in Europe,' Simanowitz later admitted, 'and I gave it all to the commune and didn't give a damn.' While his workers were off making a killing, Muehl was busy consolidating his resources. By 1983 the original Friedrichshof group had expanded to some 600 members spread over 25 communal outposts, but Muehl was not interested in simply fostering growth for its own sake. He wanted each node of the extended Friedrichshof network to be as profitable as possible and was thus not averse to liquidating economically unproductive units and merging them with other, more successful ones. It seemed that the tyrant of the 1970s had morphed into its 1980s equivalent: the efficient human resources manager.[20]

*****

If, as Houellebecq contends, 'Business was the leisure industry of the 1980s', one could argue that the reverse was also true, that leisure was among the decade's primary businesses. As ever, time away from work was being squeezed during the 1980s, but the range of things to spend that time on was increasing. Jogging, aerobics, cycling and other recreational sports all saw an upsurge across the decade which meant, of course, an increase in sales of all the necessary gear. The era of the stereotypical yuppie or 'young urban professional' might instantly conjure images of pinstripe suits and Rolex watches but look at the cover of the semi-satirical *The Yuppie Handbook* (1984) and you'll see a squash racquet and a pair of running shoes alongside the more familiar Gucci briefcase. They are all status symbols: possession of a squash racquet does not automatically mean that it gets *used*. However, its cultural capital signifies more than the possession of disposable income. It points to a concern for health, a desire for fitness and probably a competitive willingness to blur together the sports court and the office (see Oliver Stone's *Wall Street* (1987), for example). It is the type of commodity that says something about the personality of the owner. It says these things because squash racquets along with all manner of paraphernalia, the very *stuff* of leisure, were sold in the 1980s using a new approach to commercialisation: 'lifestyle marketing'.[21]

'Lifestyle marketing' was spearheaded by the Stanford Research Institute (SRI) in California, a research and development organisation founded in 1946 and which continues to work in partnership with government and industry to 'create and deliver world-changing solutions for a safer, healthier, and more sustainable future'. It was SRI technicians who collaborated with the Department of Defense and Glenn Perry's former company Scientific Data Systems to get 'computers talking to each other' in the early days of the ARPANET. Mainly, though, SRI worked by firing up the desiring-machines. They figure out what people want and then help businesses tailor their products to those needs. Starting in 1978, the institute rolled out a programme of research into what they termed 'psychological values'. The project worked on the assumption that after a decade in which 'the self' had been variously celebrated, consumers would be moving into the 1980s with a different set of priorities. They had become savvy to the machinations of Madison Avenue, they were generally satisfied with the fulfilment of their basic needs, and they were eager to place themselves – symbolically at least – above the cycles of 'mere' materialism. Using a detailed, questionnaire-based approach to market research, the institute found that this group favoured personal satisfaction over status and money. Or rather, 'personal satisfaction' was what their 'status and money' was being used to buy.

The Values and Lifestyles programme (VALS) was directed by Jay Ogilvy, who joined SRI after several years as an academic teaching philosophy at Yale. The year before the programme began, Ogilvy had published *Many Dimensional Man* (1977), a book that argued for the movement away from such grand narratives as monotheism in favour of a multi-disciplinary approach to social progress. Ogilvy applied much the same thinking to the VALS project, claiming that traditional identifiers like social class no longer sufficed as a way of categorising consumers. As Adam Curtis explains in *Century of the Self*, he argued by way of VALS that companies needed to appeal instead to the public's 'individuated wants, whims and desires'. As an intellectual back-up Ogilvy and the VALS team brought a big gun of humanistic psychology back into play: Abraham Maslow. They incorporated his ideas into the expanding customer profile and argued that the modern consumer actively sought to move up the hierarchy of needs towards the apex of the pyramid: self-actualisation. According to Ogilvy, consumers were striving to be 'inner-directed'. They wanted to be defined not by their places in society, nor by their ability to keep up with the Joneses, but by the choices they make, particularly those relating to self-expression. As the SRI team outlined in a 1983 'Values and Lifestyles' promotional video, Maslow's language and the programme's research could be used to map out these different 'lifestyles' and with this knowledge to hand, commercial products could be accurately marketed as 'powerful emblems' of individual desires.[22]

Speaking in 1985, the singer Joni Mitchell reflected on the psychic atmosphere of the prior decade, saying that from the 'vantage point of the 70s', the world had become 'so mysterious'. All the familiar structures seemed to have gone, and many had been swept away by the turmoil of the 1960s: 'the disillusionment, the killing of the president, the strain of the Vietnam War'. In response, she argues, it became 'a natural thing for people to look inside themselves'. From the vantage point of the 1980s, however, when business was leisure and leisure business, seeking the consolations of this introspection was a much harder prospect. The shifts described by Houellebecq in *Atomised*, in which alternative therapy groups turned to the corporate world and commercial companies harnessed desire by looking the other way, back to the resources of human potential, seemed to have pulled the 'inside' out of the head before putting it in a shop window. If the challenge of 1960s had been to politicise the self, that of the 1970s being to change the self, then the 1980s issued a very different call to action. This was a decade in which the self went public. Wrapped up, ready to be personally delivered, it was up for sale, free to anyone who could meet the asking price.[23]

*****

Money could buy you anything. Except happiness, of course, and a secure sense of well-being. It was ever thus but certainly so in the 1980s, because however well the decade was doing financially, there was a distinct sense of threat hanging like a cloud over all that wealth and lifestyle branding. America's mood of optimism was led, as ever, by the likes of Reagan, the well-rehearsed actor who was always looking forward to the next scene. When he won a second presidential term in November 1984 with a landslide victory, he told his supporters that 'America's best days lie ahead'. Such joyful anticipation was unlikely to have been shared by the 751 Oregonians who were at that time recovering from salmonella poisoning, the results of the first mass bioterror attack on American soil. November 1984 also found 7,000 other Americans suffering from a much more serious condition. This was not food poisoning but a little under-stood blood-borne retrovirus, one that had been given an acronym only two years prior, had no cure, and which attacked the immune system with such aggression that some observers thought it almost otherworldly.

The first of the salmonella cases emerged in September 1984 in and around The Dalles, the largest city in Oregon's Wasco County. The numbers would increase across October, and it was not long before a point of connection became clear. All those falling ill had eaten in the same group of restaurants. Someone, it seemed, had poisoned the salad bars. Investigators picked up the trail and contrary to some initial suspicions, it did not lead back to Russia, nor had a long-dormant sleeper cell been activated. The conspirators were found much closer to home, in Antelope, a few miles on from The Dalles. They were all members of the controversial spiritual set- tlement and virtual mini-city Rajneeshpuram. It turned out that the attack had been orchestrated by Rajneesh's second-in-command, Ma Anand Sheela. As a cascade of allegations started to stack up against her, from illegal wiretapping to plans for bigger acts of bio- terrorism and even assassination plots, it transpired that Sheela and a cadre of Rajneeshees had used the salmonella payload to influence the outcome of local elections. They had been trying to incapacitate potential voters.[24]

By contrast, there was no villainous mastermind responsible for the rapidly spreading virus which the Centers for Disease Control had, in July 1982, named as AIDS: 'acquired immunodeficiency syndrome'. AIDS would later be designated as an advanced stage of another disease, HIV: 'human immunodeficiency virus'. HIV targets white blood cells, weakening the immune system thus making the body vulnerable to other diseases like 'tuberculosis, infections and some cancers'. It is spread through bodily fluids, including blood and semen, and for the infection to be carried it must pass into the bloodstream from one person to another. American cases that would eventually contribute to this profile started to be analysed in 1980. Among those affected were haemophiliacs and 'intravenous drug users'. A critical mass of cases were also linked to the East and West Coast gay communities. As James Miller explains, the virus could be carried in blood droplets on anything that pierced the skin like surgical equipment and shared needles as well as blood and blood products from hospitals and blood banks. Unprotected sex, particularly anal intercourse, could also deliver the virus to the bloodstream.

The emerging picture attracted the inevitable response. Conservative America saw a virus that seemed to attack a particular lifestyle, and an 'undesirable' one at that. In some quarters, talk increasingly turned to AIDS as a 'gay cancer', God's revenge on the perpetrators of acts immoral and unnatural. After the blossoming of the sexual revolution across the 1960s, the rise of New Left identity politics and the dawn of the 'Me' Decade, here, it seemed, was an apocalyptic reckoning, a rear-guard action against a narcissistic, hedonistic and pleasure-focused culture. Rajneesh was among those who saw AIDS in these millenarian terms, and he predicted that it would become 'the next great plague of mankind'. In this scenario Rajneeshism would act as a 'Noah's Ark of consciousness', guiding the survivors (his followers, mainly) into the new world. However, despite echoing the more extreme ends of conservative Christian discourse, Rajneesh was subject to the same moralising rhetoric from an anxious and critical public. There was aways a fair amount of xenophobia and intolerance built into the local and national objections to Rajneesh, but when the trail of poisoned food led back to the boundary of Rajneeshpuram, there was a distinct sense of vindication mixed in with the outrage. Both 'events', then, the bioterror attack and the development of the AIDS crisis, issued a stark warning to 1980s America: be vigilant, threats are all around. Should there have ever been any doubt, new religious movements are a danger to the public, gurus are not to be trusted and any talk of modifying, improving or even perfecting the human will always be destructive. As for the public thinking surrounding AIDS, the point was even more blunt. As Stefanie Syman put it, it seemed that in the 1980s 'even sex could kill you'.[25]

These attitudes had a drastic impact on what remained of the alternative and human potential projects of the 1970s. Although the end of Rajneeshpuram did not bring the Western culture of spiritual exploration to a close, it did set the stage for the American authorities to assume a more forthright scepticism of any group that could possibly be considered as a 'cult'. As Arthur Goldwag suggests, for an indication of how the Rajneesh chapter could have played out in Oregon, one only needs to look ahead to the fate of the Branch Davidians at the Waco siege of 1993. Meanwhile the growth of the AIDS epidemic had a more immediate, material effect on the fortunes of once promising enterprises: float centres, for example. Despite their own bad experience with the Samadhi Alliance, Glenn and Lee Perry were able to continue into the 1980s as tank manufacturers, supplying equipment to the growing number of American float centres. It was an expanding and potentially lucrative market. Other supply companies were operating alongside Samadhi like Float to Relax, Ova, Floatarium and Oasis, and by 1983 the emergent industry had given itself a further marker of professional prestige with the establishment of the Floatation Tank Association (FTA). All was going well until, over the course of 1983 and 1984, several of San Francisco's gay bathhouses started to close in response to the rising numbers of AIDS cases and what was then known about its transmission. Float centres were not bathhouses, but these decisions nonetheless had had an impact upon their business. As Glenn Perry explains, a widespread ignorance about AIDS led people to 'avoid public water facilities', not just bathhouses but any space that carried the spectral, groundless threat of water-based infection. As a result, Perry saw a sharp decline in sales over the course of 1985 which continued across the years that followed. At the start of the decade a flourishing of interest in floatation had led to more than 100 centres opening their doors. By 1989 more than half of that number had closed.[26]

Nevertheless, as Randy Shilts reports, 1984 saw many in San Francisco's Castro district respond to the threat of AIDS by privately turning to 'mysticism' and other forms of alternative health. Shilts was a journalist at the *San Francisco Chronicle*, and he would later write *And the Band Played On* (1987), a forensic but problematic account of the AIDS crisis. In Shilts' view such spiritual seeking was merely an act of 'denial and bargaining', a misplaced investment in the type of pseudo-solutions then vying for space alongside reports of other crackpot 'cures of the week'. For some, Shilts argued, the pervasive mood of anxiety and vulnerability also provided an opportunity to make a quick buck. Health food stores, he wrote, 'did a booming business in tapes by such healers as Louise Hay, who guided listeners on meditations geared to visualising good health'. Elsewhere, he writes about people diagnosed with AIDS going off to Mexico and the Philippines in search of 'holistic healers' and 'psychic surgeons', convinced that injections of amino acids would bring to a halt the symptoms which were clearly marching on, unabated.

Shilts' cynicism was indicative of a broader, more pervasive sense of futility in the face of such an overpowering disease. What had self-help experts, motivational speakers or self-styled gurus to offer in such circumstances? What was to be gained by doing yoga, meditating or bodywork when the body itself was under such attack? Growth centres, encounter groups, self-development programmes and the health *plus* of wellness arguably counted for little when the AIDS crisis really needed substantial government support, efficient virological research and a wholesale change in social attitudes towards gay culture. Unfortunately, President Reagan was more content to fantasise about space battles using technology as imaginary as that in *Brainstorm* and *Dreamscape* rather than deal with the public health crisis back on Earth. It would take the loss of such high-profile figures as actor Rock Hudson in 1985 before public opinion slowly started to change and AIDS became a national, rather than a private, concern. The death of Michel Foucault in June 1984 eventually had a similarly catalysing, although not uncontroversial, effect on the public discussion of AIDS in France and beyond. Point being, AIDS was not purely an American experience. It was, and remains, a pandemic.[27]

✳✳✳✳✳

In reality, wellness and alternative health projects did continue into the 1980s and they did offer a response to the challenges of the decade. When he wasn't coaching the 1984 Olympic team through the basics of mindfulness, Jon Kabat-Zinn was hosting AIDS referrals at the Stress Clinic. Louise Hay also stepped into the spotlight with what became known as her 'Hay Rides'. Growing out of the spiritual counselling sessions she ran after moving to Los Angeles in 1980, the Hay Rides were public support events catering to gay men diagnosed with AIDS and their loved ones. Part counselling group and part church service, the sessions ran in halls and gymnasia across Hollywood and focused on Hay's affirmation-led approach to personal therapy. They grew quickly, because the events offered the kind of engagement that other institutions were simply not offering. 'Who else was going to do it?' she asked journalist Mark Oppenheimer in 2008. 'Religions wouldn't touch them.' Hay would go on to preside at many of the men's funerals.

It would be hard to question the sincerity bound up with this offer of emotional care. Hay was not just cashing in, nor was she trying to flog a few tapes. The problem, however, lay with the implications of the therapeutic ideology underwriting her thinking on AIDS. In 1982 Hay republished *Heal Your Body*, shortly before turning it into the bestselling book *You Can Heal Your Life* published two years later. The new edition of the pamphlet added the recently codified 'A.I.D.S' to its list of 'dis-eases' and according to Hay, the 'probable cause' was 'Denial of the self. Sexual guilt. A strong belief in not being good enough.' In response, she suggested a 'new thought pattern'. Those with AIDS should indulge in a magnificent expression of life and 'rejoice' in their sexuality. Although compassionate and empower-ing, the logic of this advice was merely the reverse of those voices who sought to castigate the supposed culture of the self. If Hay was saying to her readers 'love yourself *more*', there were plenty of critics sharing the stance later mimed by Houellebecq in *Atomised*, that the problems of the 1980s arose because people had exited the 1960s and moved through the 1970s loving themselves *too much*. The call to love yourself also had an obvious and troubling flipside. If a celebra-tion of the self was to be used as a therapy against AIDS, then once again the responsibility for the success of this method lay with those suffering from the condition. If the affirmations failed, it was your fault, not Hay's. You succumbed to the 'dis-ease' because you didn't love yourself *enough*.[28]

Too much love or too little: in the 1980s it was this type of impasse, rather than a lack of intent or technique, that caused the aspirational project of human potential – the grand drive to be well – to spiral into the static inertia depicted so succinctly and chillingly in films like *Beyond the Black Rainbow*. Cosmatos' hypnagogic version of 1983 shows an intersection of 1960s idealism and 1980s corporatisation, all wrapped up in an aesthetic that's pitched somewhere between an SRI lifestyle video and a horror movie version of Esalen. The experiments of the film all fixate on the self and speak of 'serenity through technology', but the new age of enlightenment that emerges from its bad trips, failed projects and psychic interrogations is a black hole of human development. The affirmative desire to transform gives way to a process of ruthless reason in which the 'self' is cultivated in excess of the 'I'. Who you are at Arboria does not matter, it is who you can become that does – as long as that process plays out according to a preset programme. Towards the end of *Atomised*, Houellebecq takes this negative view of human perfectibility even further. In a stunning valedictory epilogue, Houellebecq looks some seventy years ahead and describes how Michel's work in molecular biology paves the way for paradigm-changing developments in cloning. Those who prove his experiments eventually succeed in creating a new, asexual and immortal species which outgrows 'individuality, individuation and progress'. A careful hijacking of 'New Age Thinking' and a rebranding of Huxley-esque human potential later allows the vestiges of human society to face their impending obsolescence with meekness, resignation and 'perhaps even relief'. The novel's futurological thrust thus confronts the reader with an unflinchingly posthuman conclusion: the drive for perfectibility will ultimately produce something different to the human; something better, a separate species free of 'egotism, cruelty and anger'. Human potential will be realised but, argues the novel, it will not be to *our* benefit. Instead, it will mark our end. It will be a threat to the very idea of the human and its potential.[29]

Was there a way forward from this? Looking at the contemporary incarnation of wellness it seems that the commercial thrust has continued to develop in full force. Is there any sense of an alternative, then? Are we doomed to this outcome, or can a reverse view reveal another version of the future we now have? Two further exchanges from 1984, both of which went by largely under the radar, hint at a possibility, or at least a potential direction to follow. The first took place between Don Ardell and John Travis. In 1984 Ardell took up a post as adjunct professor at the University of Central Florida. There he would run the campus wellness centre until 1996. Just before he moved, he passed on to Travis his library of papers from Halbert Dunn. Ardell had received these from Dunn's widow Phelpsie during his homage-paying visit to her home in 1975. Travis was at that point running Wellness Associates with various corporate partners. The gesture was an act of resource-sharing, but it could also be read as a symbolic reminder of a key principle within Dunn's wider thinking on wellness: the idea that it was interdynamic. For Dunn, being well meant thriving in society for the collective good of that society. In 1984 Ardell and Travis were redirecting their careers towards this socially oriented direction. Ardell was applying his practice to the outward-facing microcosm of a university community, while Travis was working in various professional settings where he sought to counter the 'existing cultural norms of domination, submission and competition'. They were both turning to the health of the self in relation to the group, not just the self as a singular, sovereign entity.

Over in Westport in Ireland's County Mayo, the town that opens out to the buffeting waves of Clew Bay, the second exchange took place. By 1984 the desolate island of Dorinish had stood largely unused and uninhabited since Sid Rawle, the Tribe of the Sun and the lonely, forsaken Tom had departed. Throughout that time, 'Beatle Island' had remained an asset of John Lennon's estate and now Yoko Ono, his widow, was keen to let it go. Once again, Dorinish went up for sale and this time no rockstar swooped in. There would be no attempt to build a eutopian settlement. Instead, it was bought by a local man, Michael Gavin, who along with other Westport farmers used it as grazing land for sheep until 2012. Ono did well out of the deal. Reports vary of the exact amount involved, but it was a five-figure sum, substantially higher than the amount paid by Lennon in 1967. She then put the money to good use: all the proceeds from the sale were donated to an Irish orphanage. It was a gesture that had little to do with the 'I'. The pronoun had changed. Dorinish was being used to the benefit of an 'us'.[30]

The Voyage In

'L et's suppose that you were able, every night, to dream any dream you wanted to dream.' In 1960 Alan Watts, then deep into his personal exploration of Buddhism, gave a series of seminars on his houseboat in Sausalito, California. One of these talks, a two-part session called 'The Nature of Consciousness', spoke directly from this period of study. It was a long, often exhilarating address on identity, God and the bliss that is to be found in '*What* exists – reality itself'. The talks were recorded, as were many of the other lectures that Esalen regular Watts would give across the 1960s, and for that we should be thankful.

Upon listening to 'The Nature of Consciousness', you quickly realise that the power of the seminar comes not only from the ambition and scope of its subject, but from the sonority of Watts' voice. He is an excellent speaker: clear, sharp, measured and blessed with the ability to modulate his speed and tone as if conducting music. The distinctive Englishness of Watts' accent also brings with it a curious mix of authority and informality. As he outlines 'this adventure of dreams', telling us that we would 'naturally' fulfil all our wishes given the power of such lucidity, it is as if Watts speaks with knowledge, from experience. Deep reading radiates from this voice but also an eagerness to communicate, hence the warmth, the sense that although Watts is easily able to hold the attention of a crowd, he can also make it sound as if he is speaking to *you* and to you alone.[1]

Over the course of 2022, Watts ended up speaking to a much bigger audience from the deck of a very different boat when a version of the dream riff from 'The Nature of Consciousness' found its way on to a glossy advert for the cruise liner Cunard. Playing in cinemas, on television and across the internet, the clip – called 'Dreams', directed by Giles Smith for the ad agency Alpha Century – pulled out all the stops to connect Cunard with an experience of luxurious escapism. 'I wonder, I wonder, what you would do if you had the power to dream any dream you wanted to dream', asks the sampled Watts as images of private swimming pools and glorious oceanic views float by. 'You would, I suppose, start out by fulfilling all your wishes,' he answers while dolphins play in the surf and a beautiful couple dance into each other's arms. Adding detail to the idea of these long-held wishes, Watts speaks of 'love affairs, banquets, wonderful journeys' and, thanks to the magic of editing, this array is utterly in sync with all the delights a Cunard cruise has to offer. From here the ship sails on into the night and its ideal couple slip into contented sleep, leaving Watts free to deliver the punchline. After time spent among such perfection, 'you'd forget that you were dreaming.'[2]

The crux of the ad is clear: a Cunard holiday is a dream come true. Rolled out in the nominally post-COVID period, when all manner of businesses were trying to entice us back, 'Dreams' plays on all our pent-up, locked-down desires. It offers us space, openness, travel, the vastness of the sea and a beautiful elsewhere of stunning privacy. Mixing HD images with flashes of aesthetically pleasing filmstock, the ad also manages to manufacture a keen sense of nostalgia: it hints that we're watching fragments of a long-lost home movie shot during the best trip we've never had. Watts' lecture gives the whole package the necessary intellectual gravitas as if he is propounding a veritable philosophy of travel, telling us why we *need* to do this. It is the perfect mix of voice and brand. Perfect, were it not for the fact that the gist of 'Dreams' is utterly at odds with the original thrust of Watts' argument.

In 'The Nature of Consciousness' Watts' dream motif continues much further than the snippet used by Cunard. He pushes the idea, adding that given enough time spent in reverie, having explored your deepest desires as far as they will go, you would not just 'forget' that you were dreaming, you would, finally, 'dream where you are now'. You would not drift off into an otherworld, you would instead come full circle and 'dream the dream of living the life that you are actually living today'. Watts' point was that 'everybody is fundamentally the ultimate reality'. It is not necessary to transcend into a heavenly realm with all its royal company, nor for that matter to float into the fantastical sovereignty of a perfect holiday, because such an elevated experience is ours for the taking, right here, right now, in the 'gorgeous [...] fullness of total joy' that is life itself. You won't find this on the cruise of the gods.[3]

*****

Speaking in 2014 at the Global Wellness Summit in Morocco, John Travis reflected on his career and offered to sum it up in six words. 'The currency of wellness is connection,' he stated, adding, 'the lack thereof leads to illness.' He was reiterating to this contemporary audience the key principles he had maintained since the 1970s: the importance of social bonds, the need to think of oneself as part of a wider ecology, as well as the way his own practices of analysing the lives of his clients – from diet to exercise to personal goals – had sought to foster an awareness of this interconnectedness. It was an admirably clear crystallisation of Travis' ongoing project and it is one that also sheds light on what's problematic about the absorption of such self-affirming language into ads like 'Dreams', misappropriation of Watts notwithstanding.

In turning the 'Joy' that Watts celebrates into the stuff of dreams, the ad effectively severs us from what Travis considers as the essential glue of wellness, which is a sense of connection. It offers a spectacular display of happiness and well-being but then hides it away, somewhere on the other side of the screen. We're then left to gaze in longingly, occasionally getting a look at the array of delights beyond thanks to a 30-second glimpse during a commercial break or when the algorithm deigns to interrupt us with a pop-up. In this sense, the ad is symptomatic of a much wider operation of contemporary society, one bound up with the digital economy, the cult of wealth and a climate of aggressive competition. It is the idea that we can only be happy if we can achieve that which is always already unobtainable: the impossible realisation of our dreams.

The radicalism of wellness in the 1970s, along with that of the human potential movement, the politics of self-care and consciousness-raising, the work of growth centres and encounter groups, the catharsis of primal screaming, the inner journeys of floatation and so on, was that they comprehensively refused this logic of perpetual deferral. Some of the specific projects that existed under these banners were short-lived, some have survived; some were exploitative and deeply flawed while others were exemplary in their exercise of human care. All, however, were powered by an intoxicating and catalysing core idea: the notion that you could live your dreams, first by accepting their possibility and, second, by then exploring their plasticity. They put this theory into practice by foregrounding the ingrained patterns of stress, of anxiety, of depression; the limiting categories of social expectation and the foreshortened sense of potentiality that had been collectively and chronically normalised in the emergent neoliberal landscape. This was a challenge to the cultural parameters of the possible and as a result it was an invitation to engage in that second process, a reinvention, as Slavoj Žižek puts it, 'of the very modes of dreaming'.[4]

'[If] we change reality only in order to realize our dreams, without changing these dreams themselves,' argues Žižek by way of Herbert Marcuse, 'then sooner or later we will regress to the former reality.' The self-focused projects of the experimental 1970s had no interest in such a regression. They were dedicated to dreaming differently because the contemporary reality they were attempting to change already had such a stranglehold on the inner and the outer life, the way people thought, felt, behaved and imagined. The very limits of their dreams. For these travellers, then, undertaking the voyage in was not a retreat from the world but an interior examination conducted in the hope that it could go on towards making a better one.

Our current socio-political climate owes much to the 1970s. Presently, we live among strikes, strife, shortages as well as a panoply of intersecting global crises that range from the economic to the ecological. In addition to the technology that made the infinite stress-machine of the internet possible, the 1970s also gifted us with assumed presenteeism, strategic precarity and a financial climate that rewards the rich, punishes the poor and favours, if not relies upon, rendering such essentials as housing as increasingly unaffordable. We also have plenty of problems which are uniquely our own, among them COVID and its aftereffects, global war, buckling mental health services, political divisions so intense that they have blossomed into hitherto unknown forms of psychosis, and workplace stress so chronic that corporate mindfulness sessions have become the new lunchbreak that no one has time to take.

It is high time that we started to dream differently.

To do this, we need to re-establish the connections – material, emotional and synaptic – that have too long been frayed under the pressure of contemporary acceleration. No one can do this alone, precisely because this process involves the wholesale revivification of our links with each other. For some this dreaming started during lockdown when all the familiar routines came to a halt and the volume was turned up on the stuff that mattered, that *really* mattered – contact, conviviality and support. For others, the different dreaming is yet to start because there doesn't seem to be a problem (which is, of course, part of the problem). Either way, the first step has already been sketched out by the voyagers of the 1970s and their tools are still lying there like the scatterings of a roadside picnic waiting for us to use them anew. It all begins with a question, one that's easy to ask but hard to answer. It takes courage to ask this question. It also takes commitment to shut up and listen, properly, patiently and productively to what comes back. Sometimes the importance of this question gets obscured because it is so often co-opted into media powerplays of simulated sincerity. But ask it we must – if we want to get things moving. If you're with us, then, this book closes by gifting you the task of this question. If you are up for it, if you think you can handle it, if you are really ready for a different way of dreaming, then your challenge is to ask of someone – now, today – in all seriousness, without irony and without cynicism, the most radical question of all: 'How are you?'[5]

Notes

The Voyage Out

1. The information and quotations in this section are from the respective websites for Goop and Celebrity Cruises, *circa* 2019/2020. They have since been updated in the wake of the COVID-19 pandemic. The current versions of the webpages can be found at: www.goop. com/travel/experiences/apex-ship-celebrity-cruises/ and www.celebritycruises.com/things-to-do-onboard/health-and-wellness. Details of the ships in the Celebrity Cruises fleet, including the *Edge* and the *Apex*, can be found at: www.celebritycruises.com/cruise-ships/.

2. See Homer, *The Odyssey*, trans. E.V. Rieu (Harmondsworth: Penguin, 2003); Apollonius of Rhodes, *The Voyage of Argo: The Argonautica*, trans. E.V. Rieu (Harmondsworth: Penguin, 2006); Virgil, *The Aeneid*, trans. W.F. Jackson Knight (Harmondsworth: Penguin, 1988) and *The Ten Great Birth Stories of the Buddha: The Mahanipata of the Jatakatthavanonoana*, trans. Naomi Appleton and Sarah Shaw (USA: University of Washington Press, 2016). The reference to Sebastian Brant is taken from Michel Foucault, *Madness and Civilization: A History of Insanity in the Age of Reason*, trans. Richard Howard [1961] (London: Routledge, 2001), p. 5. Malcolm Guite's *Mariner: A Voyage With Samuel Taylor Coleridge* (London: Hodder and Stoughton, 2017) is an excellent guide to the redemptive qualities of Coleridge's poem. For a detailed discussion of oceanic states in Freud and others, see Matthew Ingram, *Retreat: How the Counterculture Invented Wellness* (London: Repeater, 2020), 93–6. The quotes on Goop are from www. goop.com.

3. Marina Hyde, 'Gwyneth's Ark: Sailing towards wellness but never quite getting there', *Guardian* (30 April 2021). The general definition of the wellness industry cited here along with its estimated global value (*circa* 2017–18) is discussed in Ophelia Yeung and Katherine Johnston, *The Global Wellness Industry and its Implications for Asia's Development* (Philippines: ADB, 2018), p. 10. For the historical origins of the term 'wellness', see James William Miller, 'Wellness: The History and Development of a Concept', *Spektrum Freizeit*, 27.1 (2005), 84–107: p. 85. See also John Travis, Donald Ardell and Peter Greenberg, 'A Keynote Interview with Jack Travis and Don Ardell' (2014). Online

at: https://www.youtube.com/watch?v=Q1SqpFnoRtw. For the back-ground to 'high-level wellness' see Halbert Dunn, 'What High-Level Wellness Means', *Canadian Journal of Public Health*, 50.11 (1959), 447–457.

4. The quotes used here come from two sources: Dan Rather's com-mentary and John Travis' interview from the *60 Minutes* segment 'Wellness', and the opening section from John Travis and Regina Sara Ryan's *The Wellness Workbook* [1981] (Berkeley: Ten Speed Press, 1988), p. xiv. 'Wellness' was broadcast on American television on 18 November 1979. The clip is viewable online here: www.youtube.com/watch?v=LAorj2U7PR4.

5. Aisha Harris, 'The History of Self-Care', *Slate* (April 2017). Online at: www.slate.com/articles/arts/culturebox/2017/04/the_history_of_self_care.html?via=gdpr-consent. See also Alondra Nelson, *Body and Soul: The Black Panther Party and the Fight Against Medical Discrimination* (USA: University of Minnesota Press, 2011).

6. Daniela Blei, 'The False Promises of Wellness Culture', *JSTOR Daily* (January 2017). Online at: www.daily.jstor.org/the-false-promises-of-wellness-culture/. For the Pfizer definition of wellness, see: www.pfizer.com/health-wellness/wellness/what-is-wellness. The Global Wellness Institute provides their definition at: www.globalwellnessin-stitute.org/what-is-wellness/. For an overview of global inequalities, see their recent report *The Global Wellness Institute: Looking Beyond COVID* (Miami: GWI, 2021) and Thierry Malleret, 'The "Wellness Divide" between Low and High-Income Countries Will Further Sharpen' (June 2022). Online at: www.globalwellnessinstitute.org/global-wellness-institute-blog/2022/06/14/the-wellness-divide-between-low-and-high-income-countries-will-further-sharpen/.

7. The Goop quotes used here are from www.goop.com. Details of the other companies mentioned can be found at their respective websites: www.wellco.co.uk, www.wellandgood.com and www.thriveglobal.com. Hadley Freeman, 'Green is the new black: the unstoppable rise of the healthy-eating guru', *Guardian* (27 June 2015).

8. Simon Stevens quoted in Sarah Boseley, 'Gwyneth Paltrow's Goop wellness products condemned by NHS chief', *Guardian* (30 January 2020).

9. Helen Coffey, 'Goop Launched Wellness Cruise Experience', *The Independent* (13 January 2020). Paltrow's interview with *USA Today* is quoted in Julia Naftulin, 'Goop threw a cruise and no Goopies came', *The Insider* (November 2021). Online at: www.insider.com/goop-at-sea-gwyneth-paltrow-first-cruise-2021-11.

10. Virginia Woolf, *The Voyage Out* [1915] (New York: Dover, 2006), p. 311. The 'Goop-At-Sea' quotes are taken from www.goop.com.

11. *The Holy Mountain* (Alejandro Jodorowsky, Mexico/US, 1973). *The Wellness Index* is a detailed questionnaire which was part of the assessment process for those wanting to undertake a course at the Wellness Resource Center. In 1975 Travis published it under his own auspices as a three-ring binder. He continued to produce ever-larger print runs across the remainder of the decade. The *Index* was later absorbed into each edition of *The Wellness Workbook*, but it continued to be available as a separate text from Ten Speed Press. 'The Iceberg Model' is outlined in Travis and Ryan, p. xix. For a critical take on modern wellness and feelings of perpetual illness, see Ema Hegberg, 'The Myth of Wellness', *Medium* (April 2019). Online at: https://medium.com/@emahegberg/the-myth-of-wellness-4eb60b43c5e2.

12. Tom Wolfe, 'The "Me" Decade and the Third Great Awakening', *New York* (August 1976). Viewable online at: www.nymag.com/news/features/45938/. Christopher Lasch, *The Culture of Narcissism: American Life in an Age of Diminishing Expectations* (New York: W.W. Norton and Company, 1979).

13. Barbara Keys, Jack Davis and Elliott Bannan, 'The Post-Traumatic Decade: New Histories of the 1970s', *Australasian Journal of American Studies*, 33.1 (July 2014), 1–17. Jimmy Carter, 'The "Crisis of Confidence" Speech: President Carter's Address to the Nation (1979)', *A History of Our Time: Readings on Postwar America*, ed. William H. Chafe *et al.* (Oxford: Oxford University Press, 2007), 325–30.

Chapter I: The Possibility of an Island

1. The information pertaining to Sid Rawle's life and work came from several sources: John May, 'Sid Rawle Obituary', *Guardian* (15 September 2010); Sid Rawle, Rick Mayes and Jeremy Sandford, *King of the Hippies: Notes for an Alternative History of Britain, 1960–2000* (unpublished) and Andy Worthington's online essay, 'RIP Sid Rawle, Land Reformer, Free Festival Pioneer, Stonehenge Stalwart' (September 2010). Non-paginated sections from *King of the Hippies* are viewable online at: www.jeremysandford.org.uk/jsarchive/sid-intro.html. Worthington's text is online at: www.andyworthington.co.uk/2010/09/08/rip-sid-rawle-land-reformer-free-festival-pioneer-stonehenge-stalwart/. In addition, Kevin Barry's novel *Beatlebone* (Great Britain: Canongate, 2015) was a useful background source on Rawle. The novel is a fictional account of John Lennon's purchase and use of Dorinish and the references to Rawle occur part way through, 188–191.

2. See May for a brief overview of Rawle's background. Thomas More, *Utopia and Selected Epigrams*, trans. by Gerald Malsbary (CTMS Publishers: University of Dallas, 2020), p. 7.

3. Rawle's views on land use are detailed in 'The Vision of Albion', an essay that works as a prologue to *King of the Hippies*. As with the rest of the extant text it is viewable online at: www.jeremysandford.org.uk/jsarchive/sid-intro.html. Hereafter it will be cited as 'The Vision of Albion' to differentiate it from *King of the Hippies*. Worthington alludes to the longer history of Hyde Park in 'RIP Sid Rawle'. Charlotte Yonge, 'To Whom it May Concern', *International Times*, 1.28 (April 5–18, 1968), p. 13. Yonge describes herself as an 'ardent digger and supporter of the underground'. Gerrard Winstanley, 'The New Law of Righteousness', *The Complete Works of Gerrard Winstanley* vol. 1, ed. by Thomas S. Corns, *et al.* (Oxford: Oxford University Press, 2009), 472–600: p. 478. For a more detailed overview of Winstanley's thinking, see Walter F. Murphy, 'The Political Philosophy of Gerrard Winstanley', *The Review of Politics*, 19.2 (1957), 214–238.

4. Rob Baker, 'Extraordinary Pictures of "Hippiedilly" on Hyde Park Corner, 1969' (2019). Online at: www.flashbak.com/the-rise-and-fall-of-hippie-dilly-in-1969-9044/. For a longer analysis of the countercultural scene *circa* 1969, see my book *The Bad Trip: New Worlds, Dark Omens and the End of the Sixties* (London: Icon, 2019).

5. See: www.whoownsengland.org/2017/10/28/who-owns-central-london/. For details of Paul Raymond and his Soho holdings, see Paul Willetts, *Members Only: The Life and Times of Paul Raymond* (London: Serpent's Tail, 2010). The idea of a 'post-shelter' economy is discussed in Chris Hamnett, 'Regional Variations in House Prices and House Price Inflation 1969–81', *Area*, 15.2 (1983), 97–109: p. 98. The link between Hippiedilly and Sir Drummond Smith is discussed by Baker. With 'charter'd zone', I am nodding to William Blake's poem, 'London' (1794). See William Blake, *The Complete Poems*, ed. by Alicia Ostriker (Harmondsworth: Penguin, 1977), p. 128.

6. Rawle, *King of the Hippies*.

7. For details of the Dorinish auction see: www.dorinish.com/dorinish. In *Beatlebone*, Barry provides an account of the sale indicating that the advertised price was £1,700 and it was purchased for £1,550. See, 176–180.

8. Ian MacDonald, *Revolution in the Head: The Beatles' Records and the Sixties* (London: Fourth Estate, 1994), 17; 265. Arthur Janov, *The Primal Scream* [1970] (London: Abacus, 1973), 38–43; 79–115. See also the book's 'Appendix B: instructions for New Primal Patients', 422–423.

9. Janov, 9–10; 270. For an interview with Janov and Ortiz, see: www.youtube.com/watch?v=BoU37pia7xw. Paul Williams and Brian Edgar, 'Up Against the Wall: Primal Therapy and "The Sixties"', *European Journal of American Studies*, 3.2 (2008), 1–24: 5–7. Richard Neville, *Play Power* (London: Jonathan Cape, 1970). For details on The Weather Underground see Karin Ashley *et al.*, 'You Don't Need a Weatherman to Know Which Way the Wind Blows' [1969], in Chafe *et al.*, 283–86. A useful micro-bio of the group appears in Arthur Goldwag, *Cults, Conspiracies and Secret Societies* (New York: Vintage, 2009), 225–28. LSD as Delysid discussed in Martin A. Lee and Bruce Shlain, *Acid Dreams: The Complete Social History of LSD, the CIA, the Sixties and Beyond* (London: Pan, 2001), p. 26.

10. R.D. Laing, *The Divided Self* (Harmondsworth: Penguin, 1967). Gilles Deleuze and Félix Guattari, *Anti-Oedipus: Capitalism and Schizophrenia* [1972], trans. by Robert Hurley, Mark Seem and Helen R. Lane (USA: University of Minnesota Press, 1983). Eric Berne, *Games People Play: The Psychology of Human Relationships* [1964] (Harmondsworth: Penguin, 1967).

11. On humanistic psychology see Walter Truett Anderson, *The Upstart Spring. Esalen and The Human Potential Movement: The First Twenty Years* [1983] (Lincoln: iUniverse, 2004), 183–88; Nevill Drury, *Human Potential* (Dorset: Element Books, 1989), 32–37 and Matthew Ingram, *Retreat: How the Counterculture Invented Wellness* (London: Repeater, 2020), p. 126. David Cohen, 'Behaviourism', *The Oxford Companion to the Mind*, ed. by Richard L. Gregory (Oxford: Oxford University Press, 1987), 71–74: p. 74. Abraham Maslow, *Toward a Psychology of Being* (New York: D. Van Nostrand, 1962), viii; 5; vi; 71–115. On the transcendent aspect of humanist psychology, see Jane Howard, *Please Touch: A Guided Tour of the Human Potential Movement* (New York: Dell, 1970), p. 16. Maslow, 'A Theory of Human Motivation', *Psychological Review* 50 (1943), 370–396: 382; 387. Kurt Goldstein, *The Organism* (New York: American Book company, 1939). Carl Rogers, *On Becoming a Person: A Therapist's View of Psychotherapy* (Boston: Houghton Mifflin, 1961). For more on encounter groups see Drury, 40–51 and Linda Sargent Wood, 'Contact, Encounter, and Exchange at Esalen: A Window onto Late Twentieth-Century American Spirituality', *Pacific Historical Review*, 77.3 (August 2008), 453–487.

12. John Travis has described this experience in several sources, all of which have been drawn upon in this section and subsequent chapters. A brief account appears in Travis and Ryan, during the longer section 'Wellness, Self-Responsibility and Love', 2–23: p. 8.

Travis went into more detail in his lecture 'How Has the Perception of Health and Wellness Changed?' given in 2017 at Masaryk University, Czech Republic. Online at: www.youtube.com/watch?v=KXAPgz_OdRo. In 2020, he took a much more personal approach in a talk given to the Marin Valley Mobile Country Club. See: 'Marin Valley Biography Night: Jack Travis'. Online at: www.youtube.com/watch?v=v4Puj2azDCE. See also Theodore Rubin, *The Angry Book* (New York: Collier, 1969).

13. Janov, *The Primal Revolution* [1974] (London: Abacus, 1975), 245–6. This line is discussed in detail in Williams and Edgar in relation to the political thought of Antonio Gramsci, p. 11. Maslow, 'Eupsychia: The Good Society', *Journal of Humanistic Psychology*, 1.2 (1961), 1–11: p. 2. Maslow speaks here about the need to cultivate 'a psychologically healthy culture – rather than just another materially-based Utopia'. See also Maslow, *Eupsychian Management: A Journal* (USA: Irwin-Dorsey, 1965). The quotes regarding the 'right order' come from Gorman Beauchamp who applies Maslow's terminology to his analysis of Aldous Huxley's *Island* (1962). See Gorman Beauchamp, 'Aldous Huxley's Psychedelic Utopia', *Utopian Studies*, 1.1 (1990), 59–72: p. 63.

14. Janov discussed his work with Lennon in an interview with John Harris for *Mojo Magazine* (Winter 2000). This text, along with a sequence of other relevant extracts from Lennon and Janov's works are viewable under the collective title 'About John Lennon' on the Primal Therapy Center website. See: www.primaltherapy.net/primal-therapy-and-john-lennon/. An account of Lennon ceasing his work with Janov can also be found in Ingram, 123–25. For details of Yoko Ono and the role of the scream in her work, see Shelina Brown, 'Scream from the Heart: Yoko Ono's Rock and Roll Revolution, *Volume!*, 9.2 (2012), 107–123. In 2007 Rawle discussed his meeting with Lennon and the circumstances of him being given stewardship of Dorinish. See: 'Interview with Sid Rawle (Part Three): Sid, John Lennon and Revolution'. Online at: www.youtube.com/watch?v=azZm1P2FQ9E. Barry discusses Lennon's work with Janov in *Beatlebone*, 21–2; 180–81. He also provides a brief account of Lennon offering Rawle 'custodianship' of the island: 'He wanted to find out if a battalion of freaks could thrive cut off from the mainstream and mainstream values', p. 189. The songs mentioned here, 'Mother', 'Why?' and 'Revolution' can be heard on *John Lennon/Plastic Ono Band* (Apple, 1970), *Yoko Ono/Plastic Ono Band* (Apple, 1970) and 'Hey Jude' [B-side] (Apple, 1968).

15. Rawle, *King of the Hippies*. The quote 'six-week summer camp' is from Barry, p. 189.

16. The *Tribe of the Sun* (Alan Sidi, UK, 1972). It is viewable via the Yorkshire Film Archive which also contains a set of commentary notes on Sidi, the film and its background. See: www.yfanefa.com/record/11500#:~:text=This%20Alan%20Sidi%20production%20is,the%20Hippies%27%2C%20in%201970. The *Newsbeat* film for RTÉ is currently online under the title, 'Westport Residents Reject Hippie Way of Life'. It can be viewed here: www.rte.ie/archives/2016/0107/758290-hippies-in-county-mayo/. The film was broadcast on 7 January 1971 and featured a voiceover and commentary by the reporter Michael Ryan.

17. This definition is from the *Oxford English Dictionary*. Hereafter it will be cited as *OED*. Karl Marx, *Economic and Philosophic Manuscripts of 1844*, trans. by Martin Milligan (New York: Prometheus Books, 2009), 81–2.

18. Karl Marx and Friedrich Engels, *The Communist Manifesto* [1848], Milligan, 203–43. Murphy, p. 226. Karl Peter *et al.*, 'The Dynamics of Religious Defection among Hutterites', *Journal for the Scientific Study of Religion*, 21.4 (1982), 327–37.

19. On the London Free City Committee and others see Riley, 'Terminal Data: J.G. Ballard, Michael Moorcock and the Fiction of the Decade's End', *The 1960s: A Decade of Modern British Fiction*, ed. by Philip Tew *et al.* (London: Bloomsbury, 2018), 257–285: p. 270. 'Anti-University Announces Courses', *International Times* 24 (19 January–1 February 1968), p. 3. The text refers to 'small fees'. For an overview of the Diggers, see Danny Goldberg, *In Search of the Lost Chord: 1967 and the Hippie Idea* (London: Icon, 2017), 17–18; 22–3. Emmett Grogan, 'Term Paper: The Relationship Between Poetry and Revolution Has Lost its Ambiguity' [handbill] (San Francisco: Communications Company, 1967). Anon., 'Spaghetti Dinner – Free' [handbill] (San Francisco: Communications Company, 1967). Chester Anderson, 'if you're not a digger' (San Francisco: Communications Company, 1967). Anon., 'Zucchini Feast Eat Free' (San Francisco: SF Communication Company, 1967).

20. Timothy Miller, 'The Roots of the 1960s Communal Revival', *American Studies*, 33. 2 (1992), 73–93: 86–90.

21. Rawle quoted in 'Westport Residents Reject Hippie Way of Life'. Rawle, 'The Vision of Albion'. Eilert Ekwall, 'Early Names of Britain', *Antiquity*, 4.14 (June 1930), 149–156. On Albion and its mythology, see William Blake, 'Jerusalem: The Emanation of the Giant Albion', Ostriker, 635–848; 993–6.

22. Rawle, 'The Vision of Albion'. Lew Welch, 'A Moving Target is Hard to Hit' (San Francisco: SF Communication Company, 1967). In *Retreat*, Ingram

provides a detailed account of the Haight Ashbury Free Clinic and its work, p. 349. For an account of National Park creation and the racial politics therein, see Isaac Kantor, 'Ethnic Cleansing and America's Creation of National Parks', *Public Land & Resources Law Review*, 28 (2007), 42–64.

23. Andrew Rigby, *Communes in Britain* (London: Routledge and Kegan Paul, 1974), p. 76. Mark Lilla, 'The Tyrant of the Commune', *The New York Review of Books* (7 August 2013). There are various spellings of 'Otto Muehl'. The most common alternative is 'Otto Mühl'. Throughout, I use 'Muehl' which is the spelling used by his estate and archive. See: www.archivesmuehl.org. For more of Airaudi, see Massimo Introvigne, 'Damanhur: A Magical Community in Italy', *New Religious Movements: Challenge and Response*, ed. by Bryan Wilson and Jamie Cresswell (London: Routledge, 2002), 240–252. The reference to Óscar Ichazo is from Nevill Drury, 83–4. Drury also quotes Ma Anand Sheela, p. 109.

24. Defining the 'New Age' is as fraught as defining 'counterculture'. It is variously understood chronologically as a phase of history that begins at a certain time, or philosophically as an umbrella term for a collection of connected, overlapping ideas. In general, though, one could see 'New Age' or at least 'New Age thinking' to signify a strand of cultural thought which gained traction and popularity from the early 1970s onwards and which also extended the countercultural impetus of the prior decade into a more metaphysical direction. In other words, if the 1960s were in part defined by an anticipation of the coming 'Age of Aquarius', speaking of the 'New Age' in the 1970s could indicate the assumption that such a seismic paradigm shift has occurred, and one is now living through the early days of a different era. For more on the Age of Aquarius, see Riley, 20–5. Drury offers a more helpful and succinct definition of the 'New Age' in *Human Potential*. He calls it 'a blend of applied psychology coupled with a diverse assortment of metaphysical and mystical belief systems', p. 14. *The Wild Angels* (Roger Corman, US, 1966). 'Loaded' can be heard on the Primal Scream album *Screamadelica* (Creation Records, 1991). The Diggers first used the phrase 'Do your thing' in their handbill of January 1967, 'The Time Has Come to Be Free' (San Francisco: Communications Company, 1967). Theodore Roszak, *The Making of a Counterculture: Reflections on the Technocratic Society and its Youthful Opposition* (New York: Anchor, 1969), p. 97. Timothy Leary made this famous proclamation at San Francisco's Golden Gate Park, during the 'Human Be-In' of January 1967. For a description of the event, see Goldberg, 27–37. For an alternative view on the stereotype of the hippie as 'drop-out', see Robert Jones, 'Hippie: The Philosophy of a Subculture', *Time* (July 1967).

II The Grand Project

1. *OED*. William Beveridge, *Social Insurance and Allied Services* (London: H.M. Stationery Office, 1942), p. 6. Arthur Marwick, *British Society Since 1945* [1982] (Harmondsworth: Penguin, 1990). p. 46.

2. Ida C. Merriam, 'Social Welfare in the United States, 1934–1954', *Social Security Bulletin*, 51.6 (June 1988), 21–33: p. 22. Miller, p. 90. Maslow, 'A Theory of Human Motivation', p. 389.

3. The Constitution of the World Health Organization can be found here: www.who.int/about/governance/constitution. As the site states, it 'was adopted by the International Health Conference held in New York from 19 June to 22 July 1946, signed on 22 July 1946 by the representatives of 61 States and entered into force on 7 April 1948'. The Constitution's first point reads: 'Health is a state of complete physical, mental and social well-being and not merely the absence of disease or infirmity.'

4. For the background to Medicare and Medicaid via the Social Security Act, see: www.archives.gov/milestone-documents/medicare-and-medicaid-act. The quote regarding 'class prejudice' is from Marwick, p. 49. Beveridge, p. 6. The NHS came into being via the white paper, *A National Health Service* (1944) and then the National Health Service Bill (1946). For this policy background and details of NHS provision cited in this section, see Tony Delamothe, 'Founding Principles', *British Medical Journal*, 336 (May 2008), 1216–1218. The list of services is taken from a NHS leaflet, *circa* 1948. Visible online at: www.history.blog.gov.uk/2023/07/13/the-founding-of-the-nhs-75-years-on.

5. Beveridge, 'Four Stones for Goliath Squalor', *Pillars of Security and Other War-Time Essays and Addresses* [1943] (London: Routledge, 2014), 167–75: p. 167. On post-war housing policy see Marwick, 52–58 and Andrew Gimson, 'How Macmillan built 300,000 Houses a Year', *ConservativeHome* (17 October 2013). Online at: www.conservativehome.com/how-macmillan-built-300000-houses-a-year/.

6. Beveridge, *Full Employment in a Free Society: A Report* [1944] (London: Routledge, 2014), p. 124. Timothy J. Hatton and George R. Boyer, 'Unemployment and the UK Labour Market Before, During and After the Golden Age', *European Review of Economic History*, 9.1 (April 2005), 35–60: p. 37. Peter Townsend, *Poverty in the United Kingdom* (Berkeley: University of California Press, 1979), p. 31. See also Joanna Mack and Stewart Lansley, *Poor Britain* (London: George Allen and Unwin, 1985), p. 204. Dave Williams and Ron Bailey, 'Open Letter to the Underground from the London Street Commune', *International Times* (10 October 1969), p. 10.

7. Hamnett, 97–8. Heathcote Williams, 'The Inside Story of Ruff Tuff Creem Puff, The Only Estate Agency for Squatters' (1978). Online at: www.//pasttense.co.uk/2021/02/23/the-squatters-estate-agency-ruff-tuff-creem-puff/.

8. In this section I have drawn on all of Dunn's published works between 1957 and 1961. He provides a biographical sketch of his career in *High-Level Wellness* (Virginia: R.W. Beatty, 1961), 243–44. Similar details are also recounted in Miller, p. 89. The general approach to wellness in the immediate post-war period is discussed in Dunn, 'Points of Attack for Raising the Levels of Wellness', *Journal of the National Medical Association*, 49.4 (July 1957), 225–35: 229–30. It is in this article that he speaks about the 'dynamic unit'. The same circumstances are covered in more detail in Dunn, 'High-Level Wellness for Man and Society', *American Journal of Public Health*, 49.6 (1959) 786–792. The idea of being 'alive with the glow of good health', the 'panoramic view' and the reflections on 'mind, body and spirit' are from *High-Level Wellness*, iv; 2; 8; 144. The additional quotes here are from Dunn, 'What High-Level Wellness Really Means', 451; 448; 447.

9. Dunn, *High-Level Wellness*, 123; 163; 206. Dunn, 'What High-Level Wellness Really Means', p. 457.

10. Dunn, *High-Level Wellness*, 1–2. Miller discusses Dunn's adherence to the WHO constitution, p. 90. Blei, 'The False Promises of Wellness Culture'. Anna Kirkland, 'What Is Wellness Now?', *Journal of Health Politics, Policy and Law*, 39.5 (October 2014), 957–970: 959–60.

11. Michael A. Peters, 'Neoliberalism, Education and the Crisis of Western Capitalism', *Policy Futures in Education*, 10. 2 (2012) 134–141: 136. Ayn Rand, *The Fountainhead* (Indiana: Bobs-Merrill, 1943). Rand, *Atlas Shrugged* (New York: Random House, 1957). Miller, p. 90–1. Hartley Dean, 'Eudaimonia and 'Species Being': A Marxist Perspective', *Handbook of Eudaimonic Well-Being*, ed. by Joar Vittersø. Dunn, *High-Level Wellness*, p. 124.

12. Aldous Huxley, *Crome Yellow* (London: Chatto and Windus, 1921). Huxley, 'The Doors of Perception', in *The Doors of Perception and Heaven and Hell* [1956] (London, Granada: 1977), 1–69. Jake Poller's excellent analysis of Huxley and the Esalen context can be found in his *Aldous Huxley and Alternative Spirituality* (Leiden: Brill, 2019), 261–317. Huxley, 'Human Potentialities', in *The Humanist Frame*, ed. by Julian Huxley (New York: Harper, 1961), 417–427. Huxley, 'Education on the Non-Verbal Level', *Daedalus*, 91.2 (Spring 1962), 418–36. Anderson provides a brief overview of Huxley's lectures, 10–13.

13. Huxley, *Island* [1962] (London: Vintage, 2002), 40–44; 136. Rawle quoted in 'Westport Residents Reject Hippie Way of Life'. Poller

provides a detailed and insightful analysis of the issues raised here in 'Fully Human Being: Aldous Huxley's Island, Tantra, and Human Potential', *International Journal for the Study of New Religions*, 10.1 (2019), 25–47. Huxley, *Brave New World* (London: Chatto and Windus, 1932). Huxley, 'Heaven and Hell', in *The Doors of Perception and Heaven and Hell*, 69–111: 70–71. Beauchamp, p. 63. Beauchamp also cites Huxley's interview in *The Paris Review*, p. 64.

14. For the history of the Richfield oil well, see: www.aoghs.org/richfield-union-petroleum-company/. 'California Girls' can be heard on The Beach Boys, *Summer Days (And Summer Nights!!)* (Capitol, 1965).

15. Dunn, *High-Level Wellness*, 2–4.

16. Anderson, 33–34. Jeffrey J. Kripal, *Esalen: America and the Religion of No Religion* (Chicago: University of Chicago Press, 2007), p. 80. See also, Barclay James Erickson, 'The Only Way Out is In: The Life of Richard Price', in *On the Edge of the Future: Esalen and the Evolution of American Culture*, ed. by Jeffrey J. Kripal and Glenn W. Shuck (Bloomington: Indiana University Press, 2005), 132–165.

17. Kripal, 99–100; Anderson, 18; 68–70, Drury provides a good, succinct account of the Esalen founding, 40–51. Robert C. Fuller's essay 'Esalen and the Cultural Boundaries of Metalanguage' is also a useful analysis of the institute's main influences and early period. See Kripal and Shuck, 197–224. The founding of Esalen is also outlined in Calvin Tomkins, 'Profile: New Paradigms', *The New Yorker* (5 January 1976).

18. Kripal, p. 18. See also his essay 'Reading Aurobindo From Stanford to Pondicherry: Michael Murphy and the Tantric Transmission', in Kripal and Shuck, 99–132.

19. For details of Meadowlark see E.G. Loomis, 'Meadowlark: A Healing and Growth Experience', *Reflections: Narratives of Professional Helping*, 3.1 (Winter 1997), 45–54. Donald Ardell also offers a useful overview in *High Level Wellness: An Alternative to Doctors, Drugs and Disease* (USA: Rodale Press, 1977), 20–24. His book deliberately shares its title with that of Dunn (although it does not retain the hyphen in 'high-level'). When necessary, for the purposes of clarity, Ardell's text will subsequently be cited with publication date added. On Trabuco, see Anderson, p. 12 and Timothy Miller, 'Notes on the Prehistory of the Human Potential Movement', in Kripal and Shuck, 80–99. For details of Centre House see the entry in *The Aquarian Guide to Occult, Mystical, Religious, Magical London and Around*, ed. by Françoise Strachan (London: The Aquarian Press, 1970), p. 10. See also Christopher Hills, *Nuclear Evolution* (London: Centre Community Publications, 1968). Stefanie Syman discusses Esalen and the secularisation of yoga in

The Subtle Body: The Story of Yoga in America (New York: Farrar, Straus and Giroux, 2010), p. 264.

20. Dunn, *High-Level Wellness*, 120–24; p. 11. When describing the 'capacity latent within the individual', Dunn talks in terms of 'human potential'.

21. A useful overview of Henrik L. Blum's work can be found in Joan M. Altekruse, 'Interview: Henrik L. Blum, MD, MPH', *Family & Community Health*, 8.4 (1986), 76–83. Lewis C. Robbins, *How to Practice Prospective Medicine* (Indiana: Methodist Hospital of Indiana, 1970). Ardell describes the circumstance of Dunn giving public talks in Paul E. Terry and Donald Ardell, 'An Interview with Donald Ardell', *The Art of Health Promotion* (November/December 2015), 2–8: p. 4. Travis vividly recounts his discovery of Dunn's book in Travis, Ardell and Greenberg, 'A Keynote Interview with Jack Travis and Don Ardell'. The idea that *High-Level Wellness* 'saved' his life comes from the interview between Travis and Camille Rowe featured in the documentary *What on Earth is Wellness?* (Posy Dixon, UK, 2016). Online here: www.youtube.com/watch?v=-ZkaE8nq54w.

22. Travis talks specifically about his suicidal thoughts in 'Marin Valley Biography Night: Jack Travis'. The description of Maslow and Dylan as twin influences after the discovery of Dunn is from 'How Has the Perception of Health and Wellness Changed?'. The lyric from Dylan is used as an epigraph in Travis and Ryan, p. xv.

23. Travis described his work with Robbins in 'How Has the Perception of Health and Wellness Changed?'. Ardell also provided a brief overview of this influence in *High-Level Wellness* (1977), p. 12. For details of the Health Hazard Appraisal, see Robbins and H.N. Colburn and P. M. Baker, 'Health Hazard Appraisal: A Possible Tool in Health Protection and Promotion', *Canadian Journal of Public Health*, 64.5 (1973), 490–92. The 'Illness-Wellness Continuum' is described in Travis and Ryan, p. xvi. It has gone through several versions since 1972, which Travis outlines in 'How Has the Perception of Health and Wellness Changed?'. The 1972 version described here can be seen in Ardell, p. 10. Dunn's image can be seen in *High-Level Wellness*, p. vi. Travis outlines 'full-spectrum wellness' in 'How Has the Perception of Health and Wellness Changed?'. His words of advice on illness and the need for treatment are in Travis and Ryan, p. xvi. Wellness as a 'dynamic, ongoing state of growth' is from Travis' *60 Minutes* interview with Rather.

24. Rawle, *King of the Hippies*. Worthington mentions a fire caused by a lamp igniting the tents in 'RIP Sid Rawle', as do the Yorkshire Film Archive in their notes to *The Tribe of the Sun*. Barry, 183; 191. Barry also refers to a 'fire of mysterious origin', p. 190.

25. *The Tribe of the Sun.*

26. Huxley, *Island*, 352–354.

27. *The Tribe of the Sun.* Muriel James and Dorothy Jongeward, *Born to Win* (USA: Addison-Wesley, 1971), p. 263.

III Where Do I Begin?

1. Lee and Glenn Perry, *Floating in Quiet Darkness: How the Float Tank Has Changed Our Lives and is Changing the World* (Nevada: Gateways Books and Tapes, 2020), p. 15. Details and images pertaining to SDS can be found here: www.computerhistory.org/brochures/q-s/scientific-data-systems-sds/. For a description of time-sharing and Ray Tomlinson's first email, see Katie Hafner and Matthew Lyon, *Where Wizards Stay Up Late: The Origins of the Internet* (New York: Simon and Schuster, 1996), 26; 191–2. Lee and Glenn Perry's lecture 'In Pursuit of Nothing' delivered at the 2012 Portland Float Conference is a very useful supplement to their book. Online at: www.youtube.com/watch?v=VdNjPZR2Edw.

2. Perry, 15–17. Travis and Ryan, xvi; 111. Robert Weiss, *Loneliness* (Cambridge: MIT Press, 1975), quoted in Jo Griffin, *The Lonely Society?* (London: The Mental Health Foundation, 2010), p. 14. Berne, p. 14.

3. Erich Fromm, *The Art of Being* (London: Constable, 1993), p. 22. Fromm mentions Riesman's *The Lonely Crowd* (1961). Edward Hopper, *Nighthawks* (1942). See: www.artic.edu/artworks/111628/nighthawks. *Taxi Driver* (Martin Scorsese, US, 1976). The Beveridge quote is from 'The Five Giants: Extract from notes from the advisory panel on Home Affairs on Reconstruction Problems: the Five Giants on the Road, 25 June 1942'. Viewable online via the National Archives: www.nationalarchives.gov.uk/education/resources/attlees-britain/five-giants/.

4. Travis, Ardell and Greenberg, 'A Keynote Interview with Jack Travis and Don Ardell'. 'The Capricorn Incident' is described in Travis and Ryan, p. 118. The American Psychiatric Association, *DSM II: Diagnostic and Statistical Manual of Mental Disorders* (Washington: American Psychiatric Association, 1968), 51–2.

5. Alina Surís, 'The Evolution of the Classification of Psychiatric Disorders', *Behavioural Science*, 6.1: 5 (January 2016). John Turner *et al.*, 'The History of Mental Health Services in Modern England: Practitioner Memories and the Direction of Future Research', *Medical History*, 59.4 (2015), 599–624: p. 608. For homosexuality and the *DSM II*, see Jack Drescher, 'Out of DSM: Depathologizing Homosexuality', *Behavioral Sciences*, 5.4 (December 2015), 565–575. Glenn Smith *et al.*, 'Treatments of Homosexuality in Britain since the 1950s – An Oral History: The

Experience of Patients', *The British Medical Journal*, 328.7437: 429 (21 February 2004). Helen Killaspy, 'From the Asylum to Community Care: Learning from Experience', *British Medical Bulletin*, 79–80.1 (June 2006), 245–258.

6. Marshall McLuhan and Quentin Fiore, *The Medium is the Massage: An Inventory of Effects* (Harmondsworth: Penguin, 1967), p. 63. McLuhan had used the phrase 'global village' in his earlier work, *The Gutenberg Galaxy* (Canada: University of Toronto Press, 1962). On Vietnam, see: Gregory A. Daddis, *Withdrawal: Assessing America's Final Years in Vietnam* (Oxford: Oxford University Press, 2017), 45–76. Donella H. Meadows *et al.*, *The Limits to Growth* (USA: Potomac Associates, 1972).

7. Travis, Ardell and Greenberg, 'A Keynote Interview with Jack Travis and Don Ardell'. Alvin Toffler, *Future Shock* (Great Britain: The Bodley Head, 1970), p. 306. Howard, 1–2. Travis and Ryan, p. 118. Perry, p. 30.

8. *OED*. Leonard Lickorish and Victor T.C. Middleton, *British Tourism: The Remarkable Story of Growth* (Oxford: Elsevier: 2005), p. 29. Stephen Page, *Tourism Management* (London: Routledge, 2000), 70–72. Dominic Sandbrook, *State of Emergency. The Way We Were: Britain 1970–74* (Harmondsworth: Penguin, 2011), p. 64. Patrick Wright, *The Sea View Has Me Again: Uwe Johnson in Sheerness* (London: Repeater, 2020), p. 81. Lawrence Black and Hugh Pemberton, 'The benighted decade? Reassessing the 1970s', *Reassessing 1970s Britain*, ed. by Lawrence Black, Hugh Pemberton and Pat Thane (Manchester: Manchester University Press, 2013), 1–25: 3–4. Marwick, p. 248.

9. *OED*. Jack Dickey, 'Save the American Vacation', *Time* (May 2015). The references to John Harvey Kellogg are from Jerry Useem, 'Bring Back the Nervous Breakdown', *The Atlantic* (March 2021).

10. Dunn, *High-Level Wellness* (1961), p. 141. *The Persuaders!* (Basil Dearden, UK, 1971). *Holiday on the Buses* (Bryan Izzard, UK, 1973). On Pontins Prestatyn, see John Urry, *The Tourist Gaze* (London: Sage, 2002), p. 34. Numerous internet sites host vintage Pontins brochures. For the 1972 example described here, see: www.voicesofeastanglia.com/2012/02/all-your-want-ins-at-pontins-1972-brochure.html.

11. Ray Gosling quoted in Urry, p. 33. Broadreeds postcard: author's collection. This is a genuine postcard, sent in 1974. However, with 'Sue' and 'Jackie' I have taken the liberty of changing the names involved. For a reflection of the three-day week, see Black and Pemberton, 3–4. For the collapse of Clarksons, see Page, p. 71.

12. For a brief overview of Saint-Tropez and tourism, see Philippe Mioche, 'Tourism on the French Riviera', in *Europe at the Seaside: The Economic*

History of Mass Tourism in the Mediterranean, ed. by Luciano Segreto *et al.* (New York: Berghan, 2009), 196–206: p. 198. *1972 Census of Transportation: National Travel Survey* (USA: U.S. Government Printing Office, 1974), p. 121. Odeta Rudling, 'The Cult of the Balts: Mythological Impulses and Neo-Pagan Practices in the Touristic Clubs of the Lithuanian SSR of the 1960s and 1970s', *Region*, 6.1 (2017), 87–108. Alberto Alesina *et al.*, 'Work and Leisure in the United States and Europe: Why So Different?', *NBER Macroeconomics Annual*, 20 (2005), 1–64: 1–4. Jack Dickey, 'Save the American Vacation'.

13. Travis and Ryan, 4–5.

14. Robin Cook, *Year of the Intern* (New York: Harcourt Brace, 1973). Robert Eliot and Dennis L. Breo, *Is It Worth Dying For? How to Make Stress Work For You Not Against You* (New York: Bantam, 1984), 1–9.

15. Fromm, *The Pathology of Normalcy* (New York: Lantern Books, 2011). This book is based on a series of lectures Fromm gave in 1953. On smoking see: Institute of Medicine, *Secondhand Smoke Exposure and Cardiovascular Effects: Making Sense of the Evidence* (Washington: The National Academies Press, 2010) and National Cancer Institute, *Changes in Cigarette Related Disease Risks and Their Implications for Prevention and Control* (USA: U.S. Department of Health and Human Services, 1997), 13–22. On airline smoking, see: James Repace, 'Flying the Smoky Skies: Secondhand Smoke Exposure of Flight Attendants', *Tobacco Control*, 13 (2004), 8–19. On air traffic control assessments, see: Raymond E. King *et al.*, *Use of Personality Assessment Measures in the Selection of Air Traffic Control Specialists* (Washington: Office of Aerospace Medicine, 2003). Travis and Ryan, 6–7; Perry, p. 16.

16. John C. Lilly, *The Centre of the Cyclone: An Autobiography of Inner Space* [1972] (Great Britain: Paladin, 1972), p. 51. Charlie Williams, 'On "Modified Human Agents": John Lilly and the Paranoid Style in American Neuroscience', *History of the Human Sciences*, 32.5 (2019), 84–107: 85. See also D. Graham Burnett, 'Adult Swim: How John C. Lilly Got Groovy (And Took the Dolphin with Him), 1958–1968', in *Groovy Science: Knowledge, Innovation and American Counterculture* ed. by David Kaiser and W. Patrick McCray (Chicago: Chicago University Press, 2016), 13–50.

17. Lilly, 51–2; Williams, p. 85.

18. For details of Donald Hebb's McGill experiments, see: Jack A. Vernon, *Inside the Black Room: Studies of Sensory Deprivation* [1963] (Harmondsworth: Penguin, 1966), 15–17; 21–3; 31. Lilly; 16, 142–8. Williams, p. 86.

19. Lilly, 50; 130–5. Perry, p. 16.

20. Perry, 30–1; 20. 31. J.R. Lindahl *et al.*, 'A Phenomenology of Meditation-Induced Light Experiences: Traditional Buddhist and Neurobiological Perspectives', *Frontiers in Psychology*, 4. 973 (2014), 1–16: p. 10. Lilly, 98–111.

21. Ardell, p. 47. Anderson, p. 117. For The Rosicrucians of San Jose, California, and their 'unpublished facts of life', see *Worlds of Tomorrow*, 1.3 August 1963, p. 5. Regina E. Holloman, 'Ritual Opening and Individual Transformation: Rites of Passage at Esalen', *American Anthropologist* 76 (1974), 265–280: p. 267.

22. The information on growth centres comes from Stratton F. Caldwell, 'The Human Potential Movement: Body/Movement/Non-Verbal Experiencing' (1975). This is the text of a paper presented at the Conference of the California Association for Health, Physical Education and Recreation, April 1973. It is online at: www.files.eric.ed.gov/fulltext/ED110423.pdf. Howard, p. 28. Matthew Ramsay, 'Alternative Medicine in Modern France', *Medical History*, 43 (1999), 286–322: p. 288.

23. Miller in Kripal and Shuck, p. 84. Esalen is described as a 'secular monastery' in the July 1987 issue of *New Realities Magazine*, p. 12. On the expenses involved in a stay at Esalen, see Ardell, 46–47. On the working partnership between Murphy and Price, see Marion Goldman, *The American Soul Rush: Esalen and the Rise of Spiritual Privilege* (New York: New York University Press, 2012), p. 55–57. On the expansion to San Francisco, see Anderson, 147–60.

24. Tom Feldberg and David Jones, 'Quaesitor: How Humanistic Therapy Got Going in Britain', *Self & Society*, 24.4 (1996), 36–40: p. 36. Tom Feldberg, David Jones and David Kalisch, 'The Story of Quaesitor: How Humanistic Psychology Started in Europe and How it Might End!', *Self & Society*, 40.4 (2013), 58–63: p. 59. Anderson provides a brief account of the London visit and the link to Quaesitor, 220; 301. Description of Quaesitor from the entry in Strachan, p. 125. Lilly, p. 123.

25. Goldman, p. 61. Anderson, p. 194.

26. Walter Effross, 'Owning Enlightenment: Proprietary Spirituality in the "New Age" Marketplace', *Buffalo Law Review*, 51.3 (2003), 484–677: 484–589. Peter Haldeman, 'The Return of Werner Erhard, Father of Self-Help', *The New York Times* (29 November 2015). The link between est and Mind Dynamics is outlined in Espy M. Navarro and Robert Navarro, *Self-Realization: The Est and Forum Phenomena in America* (US: Xlibris, 2002), p. 54. This book also describes the 'non-confrontational' nature of the latter. For an account of a typical est session, see Mark Brewer, 'We're Gonna Tear You Down and Put You Back Together', *Psychology Today* (August 1975). Online at: www.

culteducation.com/group/908-est/6150-were-gonna-tear-you-down-and-put-you-back-tpgether.html.

27. Goldman, p. 159. Anderson, p. 191.

28. Perry, 20–1.

29. In 1973 the artist Carolee Schneemann attended a 'mass water-tank experiment' at Esalen with Lilly. See *Correspondence Course: An Epistolary History of Carolee Schneemann and her Circle*, ed. by Kristine Stiles (USA: Duke University Press, 2010), p. 211. My account of Perls and Schutz at Esalen is informed by Drury, 41–51 and Anderson, 85–100. Anderson refers to 'the three basic components of the Esalen inventory: encounter, gestalt therapy and body work', p. 79. In this study, I have opted to use the more common compound version of 'bodywork', which is indicative of a distinct set of practices as opposed to non-specific work done to the body.

30. On gestalt and Rolf, see Anderson, 128–32 and Kripal, 201–5.

31. Holloman, p. 265. Lilly, p. 47.

32. Lilly, p. 130. For an overview of the 'oceanic', see Ingram, 93–6. There are various versions of the 'Cape Canaveral' comparison in circulation. The point of reference cited here is Art Harris, 'Esalen: From 60s Outpost To the Me Generation', *Washington Post* (24 September 1978). The quote reads: 'Esalen became all things to all seekers: a playground for promiscuity, a Cape Canaveral for inner space, a fat farm for pudgy egos, a refuge.' *Solaris* (Andrei Tarkovsky, Russia, 1972).

33. Richard Atcheson quoted in Anderson, p.281. Atcheson's article is 'Big Sur: Coming to My Senses', *Holiday* (March 1968). Alexander Frater, 'New Cult for the Over-Adjusted', *The Daily Telegraph Magazine* 220 (December 1968), 14–19; 15–16. Frater was commenting on Bernie Gunther, *Sense Relaxation* (London: Macdonald, 1969).

34. Among its myriad alcohol and cigarette adverts (most of which suggest giving cigarettes as Christmas presents), one finds Stan Gebler Davies, 'For St. George … and Mr. Halliwell!', *The Daily Telegraph Magazine*, p. 7. Luke Rhinehart, *The Dice Man* [1971] (London: Granada, 1981), p. 315. Luke Rhinehart is the pseudonym of George Cockcroft. Cockcroft, as Rhinehart, would go on to write a book about Werner Erhard, *The Book of est* (New York: Holt, Rinehart and Winston, 1976).

35. Erich Segal, *Love Story* [1970] (London: Hodder and Stoughton, 2013), p. 133. For an image of *Wings of Love* and a discussion of its appeal, see Miranda Sawyer, 'A Temple to Athena', *Guardian* (15 November 2009). Andy Williams, '(Where Do I Begin?) Love Story' (Columbia Records, 1970).

36. Francesca Segal, 'Introduction', *Love Story*, vii–x: viii–ix. Francesca Segal is Erich Segal's daughter and her introduction was written for the novel's 50th anniversary. Representative works by the theorists mentioned here would include Roland Barthes, 'The Death of the Author' (1967), Jacques Derrida, *Of Grammatology* (1967) and Michel Foucault, 'What Is an Author?' (1969). They can be found in *The Norton Anthology of Theory and Criticism* ed. by Vincent B. Leitch *et al.*, 1466–70, 1822–30 and 1622–36. For a brief but insightful overview of their thought, I would recommend the relevant entries in *Postmodern Thought*, ed. by Stuart Sim (Cambridge: Icon, 1998). This also includes a section on quantum mechanics, p. 345. For an insight into eco-logical thinking see James Lovelock, *Gaia: A New Look at Life on Earth* (Oxford: Oxford University Press, 2000) and *The Whole Earth Catalogue: Access to Tools*, ed. by Stewart Brand (Fall 1968). One of the opening epigraphs to *The Dice Man* is 'Anybody can be anybody'. It is, appropriately, attributed to 'The Dice Man' with no other explanation or reference. At the very start of the novel, Rhinehart questions the use of the 'I' in what purports to be this 'autobiography': 'What to do if there is no single man?', 7–8.
37. Holloman, p. 268. Jean Clark, 'In at the Start: Early Experiences of the Emerging Counselling Profession in the 1970s', *Self & Society*, 43.3 (2015), 256–263: p. 258.
38. Perry, p. 18. Travis and Ryan, p. 8. In *Floating in Quiet Darkness*, Perry uses 'floatation' rather than the variant spelling 'flotation'. The latter is increasingly used in the wellness industry to make a distinction between *floating* in the sea or a swimming pool 'where you need to contribute physically to staying afloat' and a *flotation* treatment in a pod, tank or similar 'that allows you complete weightless relaxation'. See: www.goodspaguide.co.uk/features/flotation. I have opted to use 'floatation' throughout this text to reflect Perry's usage.

IV The Deep End

1. John Palmer Spencer, *In the Crossfire: Marcus Foster and the Troubled History of American School Reform* (Philadelphia: University of Pennsylvania Press, 2012), 1–2; 220–221. Other key sources on the Symbionese Liberation Army and Foster are: Les Payne and Tim Findley, *The Life and Death of the SLA* (New York: Ballantine, 1976) and Vin McLellan and Paul Avery, *The Voices of the Guns* (New York: G.P. Putnam's, 1977). I would also recommend Gregory Garth Cumming's unpublished doctoral dissertation, *The End of an Era: The Rise of the Symbionese Liberation Army and Fall of the New Left*

(California: UC Riverside, 2010). Online here: www.escholarship.org/uc/item/8tw2935x.

2. For details of Oakland's crime rates and economy, see: www.oakland-planninghistory.weebly.com/the-changing-face-of-oakland.html. For an analysis of its earlier economic and political history, see Chris Rhomburg, 'White Nativism and Urban Politics: The 1920s Ku Klux Klan in Oakland, California', *Journal of American Ethnic History*, 17.2 (Winter, 1998), 39–55: 40–1. Elton John's 'Sick City' was the B-side to 'Don't Let the Sun Go Down On Me' (MCA Records, 1974). Charles Manson's 'Sick City' can be heard on *LIE: The Love and Terror Cult* (Awareness Records, 1970).

3. George Pendle, 'Shaved Heads, Snipped Tubes, Imperial Marines and Dope Fiends: The Fall and Rise and Fall of Chuck Dederich and Synanon', *Cabinet* 48 (Winter 2012–13). Online at: www.cabinetmaga-zine.org/issues/48/pendle.php. Howard describes Synanon, the Game and in the process of being given 'hell' in *Please Touch*, 62–74; 118–19. See in particular, 63–66. Richard Ofshe, 'The Social Development of the Synanon Cult: The Managerial Strategy of Organizational Transformation', *Sociological Analysis*, 41.2 (Summer, 1980), 109–127: 109–12. *THX1138* (George Lucas, US, 1971). The use of Synanon extras has been widely reported in accounts of the film. For a recent example, see Tyler Maxin, '*Children of Synanon + The Child of the Future: How Might He Learn*' (19 April 2022). Online at: www.screenslate.com/articles/children-synanon-child-future-how-might-he-learn.

4. The Berkeley-Oakland Women's Union, 'The Berkeley-Oakland Woman's Union Statement: Principles of Unity', *Socialist Revolution*, 4.1 (January–March 1974). For a bibliography of the Women's Press Collective, see www.lesbianpoetryarchive.org/node/82. *Amazon Quarterly* 1.1 (September 1972). On the White Horse Inn, see Rachel Brahinsky and Alexander Tarr, *A People's Guide to the San Francisco Bay Area* (Berkeley: University of California Press, 2020), p. 60.

5. Rhomberg, p. 44. David Cunningham, *Klansville, U.S.A: The Rise and Fall of the Civil Rights-Era Ku Klux Klan* (Oxford: Oxford University Press, 2013), p. 59. On Synanon and racial integration, see Carina Ray, 'A Troubled Experiment's Forgotten Lesson in Racial Integration, *Point Reyes Light* (15 March, 2012). For an analysis of the growth of the Black Panther Party, see Arianne Hermida, 'Mapping the Black Panther Party in Key Cities', part of the Mapping American Social Movements Project at the University of Washington. Online at: www.depts.washington.edu/moves/BPP_map-cities.shtml. Karl Marx, *Capital: A Critique of Political Economy*, vol. 1 [1867] trans. by Ben Fowkes (London: New Left

Review, 1976). Frantz Fanon, *Black Skin, White Masks* [1952], trans. by Charles Lam Markmann (London: Pluto, 1986). Fanon, *The Wretched of the Earth* [1961], trans. by Constance Farrington (New York: Grove, 1968). Stokely Carmichael, 'Black Power', *The Dialectics of Liberation*, ed. by David Cooper (Harmondsworth: Penguin, 1968), 150–175: p. 170. The full text of 'The Ten Point Program' can be read here: www.marxists.org/history/usa/workers/black-panthers/1966/10/15.htm.

6. Bobby Seale, 'You Can't Drop Out of the System', *Ann Arbor Sun* (23 April 1973). Nelson, 18–20. For details of the Guyton case see: Dan Siegel, 'Justice for Tyrone Guyton', *Crime and Social Justice*, 2 (Fall–Winter 1974), 61–63.

7. Wallace Turner, 'Jail Terms Deplete Ranks of Hell's Angels', *The New York Times* (18 March 1973). For details of Altamont see Riley, 211–243. Mary T. Bassett, 'Beyond Berets: The Black Panthers as Health Activists', *American Journal of Public Health*, 106.10 (October 2016), 1741–1743: p. 1741.

8. On the Black Panthers and guns, see Nikhil Pal Singh, 'The Black Panthers and the "Undeveloped Country" of the Left', *The Black Panther Party Reconsidered*, ed. Charles E. Jones (Baltimore: Black Classic Press, 1998), 57–109. 'By and for women', *The Women's Gun Pamphlet: A Primer on Handguns* (Oakland: Women's Press Collective, 1975).

9. Spencer, p. 219.

10. David Horowitz quoted in Cummings, p. 59. On the SLA and their membership see Goldwag, p. 314. 'Symbionese Liberation Army Communiqué No. 1' and 'The Symbionese Federation and the Symbionese Liberation Army Declaration of Revolutionary War and the Symbionese Program' can both be found online at: www.freedomarchive.org. COINTELPRO was the FBI's counterintelligence programme. See Winston A. Grady-Willis, 'The Black Panther Party: State Repression and Political Prisoners', in Jones, 326–391. William Burroughs, *Nova Express* (New York: Grove, 1964). Spain Rodriguez, *Trashman Lives!* (USA: Fantagraphics, 1985).

11. Fanon, *The Wretched of the Earth*, 41; 233.

12. Foster's achievements at Simon Gratz are covered by Spencer, 135–185. Robert Blackburn's comments are from an interview with Michael Taylor, 'Forgotten Footnote: Before Hearst, SLA Killed Educator', *San Francisco Chronicle* (14 November 2002).

13. Goldwag, p. 316. See also Jeffrey Toobin, *American Heiress: The Kidnapping, Crimes and Trial of Patty Hearst* (New York: Doubleday, 2017) and Caitlin Flanagan, 'Girl, Interrupted', *The Atlantic* (September 2008).

14. Spencer, p. 233. See also Keshler Thibert, 'Remembering Marcus Foster: Role Model and Mentor to Philly's Broken Schools', *Hidden City* (23 June 2023). Online at: www.hiddencityphila.org/2023/06/ remembering-marcus-foster-role-modle-and-mentor-to-phillys-broken-schools/. Taunya Lovell Banks, 'Still Drowning in Segregation: Limits of Law in Post-Civil Rights America', *Minnesota Journal of Law and Inequality*, 32.2 (December 2014), 215–255: p. 221.

15. Jeff Wiltse, *Contested Waters: A Social History of Swimming Pools in America* (Chapel Hill: University of North Carolina Press, 2007), p. 117. See also 'The Racial History of American Swimming Pools', *NPR* (6 May 2008). Online at: www.npr.org/2008/05/06/90213675/racial-history-of-american-swimming-pools. Another useful source is Liz Rohan, 'The Dolphins and the Bodily Arts: Swimming as a feminist rhetoric and pedagogy at the Detroit, Michigan Women's City Club Pool, 1924 to 1975', *Journal of International Women's Studies*, 21.6 (2020), 265–280. Joshua Bote, 'Women in Sacramento hotel pool video obtain lawyer, allege they saw "sexual activity"', *SFGate* (4 June 2021). Online at: www. sfgate.com/bayarea/article/Oakland-woman-escorted-out-of-hotel-pool-after-16219365.php.

16. Victoria W. Wolcott, 'The Forgotten History of Segregated Swimming Pools and Amusement Parks', *The Conversation* (9 July 2019). Online at: www.theconversation.com/the-forgotten-history-of-segregated-swimming-pools-and-amusement-parks-119586. Andre Toran, 'Unwelcome Waters: Segregated Public Pools and the Lasting Effect They Have on the Black Community', *USA Today* (23 February 2021). Online at: www.eu.usatoday.com/story/sports/2021/02/23/segregated-public-pools-has-lasting-effect-black-america/4539339001/. For a history of British leisure centres see Martin Polley, *Moving the Goalposts: A History of Sport and Society in Britain since 1945* (London: Routledge, 1998). Ryan Reft, 'A Dive into the Deep End: The Importance of Swimming Pools in Southern California', *Tropics of Meta* (June 2014). Online at: www.tropicsofmeta.com/2014/06/30/a-dive-into-the-deep-end-the-importance-of-the-swimming-pool-in-southern-california/. Nicolette Wenzell, 'City of Swimming Pools', *Palm Springs Life* (November 2014). Online at: www.palmspringslife.com/ explore-palm-springs-city-of-swimming-pools/.

17. For details of the overlap between swimming pools and fallout shelters, see Patt Morrison, 'Cold War LA could have been a nuclear target. One response: the fallout shelter', *Los Angeles Times* (8 March 2022). Martin Kane, 'An Assessment of "Black is Best"', *Sports Illustrated* (January 1971).

18. On Jim Ellis, see Michael Klein, 'Making Waves', *The Philadelphia Inquirer* (18 March 2007). For details of the Fred Hampton Pool in Maywood Illinois, see www.atlasobscura.com/places/fred-hampton-family-aquatic-center#:~:text=He%20organized%20youth%20trips%20to,for%20the%20youth%20of%20Maywood. Kane, 'An Assessment of "Black is Best"'.

19. J.G. Ballard, 'Note to Five Hundred Feet High', *The Atrocity Exhibition* [1970] (London: Harper, 2006), 138–9. Terry O'Neill, 'Faye Dunaway' (1977). O'Neill calls the image 'The Morning After'. See: www.npg.org.uk/collections/search/portrait/mw69550/Faye-Dunaway. *Magnum Force* (Ted Post, US, 1973). *Asylum of Satan* (William Girdler, US, 1972). *A Bigger Splash* (Jack Hazan, US, 1973). Hockney's paintings are discussed in Reft, 'A Dive into the Deep End'.

20. *The Swimmer* (Fred and Eleanor Perry, US, 1968). John Cheever, 'The Swimmer' [1964], *The Norton Anthology of American Literature: Literature Since 1945* ed. Nina Baym *et al.* (New York: W.W. Norton and Company, 2003), 2043–51: 2043–45. I have also quoted here from 'John Cheever', the critical note which accompanies 'The Swimmer' in the *Norton*, 2041–2043; 2042. 'The Swimmer' was originally published in *The New Yorker* (10 July 1964).

21. 'John Cheever', pp. 2041–42. The work of Elliott Jaques is discussed in Pamela Druckerman, 'How the Mid-Life Crisis Came to Be', *The Atlantic* (29 May 2018). Online at: www.theatlantic.com/family/archive/2018/05/the-invention-of-the-midlife-crisis/561203/.

22. *The Swimmer*. Druckerman, 'How the Mid-Life Crisis Came to Be'.

23. Anica Vesel Mander and Anne Kent Rush, *Feminism as Therapy* (New York: Random House, 1974), 19–20. Betty Friedan, *The Feminine Mystique* [1963] (Harmondsworth: Penguin, 2010). Her first chapter is entitled 'The Problem That Has No Name'. Germaine Greer, *The Female Eunuch* [1971] (London: Harper, 2006). Thomas Wiseman, *The Romantic Englishwoman* [1971] (Great Britain: Granada, 1973), 18–19. Jenny Fabian, *A Chemical Romance* [1971] (London: Do Not Press, 1998). Erica Jong, *Fear of Flying* (New York: Holt, Rinehart and Winston, 1973). Druckerman, 'How the Mid-Life Crisis Came to Be'.

24. *The Swimmer*. Goldman, p. 2. An Esalen-esque coastal retreat appears in the series finale of *Mad Men*, 'Person to Person' (Matthew Weiner, US, 2015). For an account of Paul Bindrim's techniques, see Aileen Goodson, *Experiment in Nude Psychotherapy: Confrontation with Group Nudity* (Los Angeles: Elysium, 1967) and Ian Nicholson, 'Bearing the Soul: Paul Bindrim, Abraham Maslow and "Nude Psychotherapy"', *Journal of the History of the Behavioural Sciences*, 43.4 (2007), 337–59.

Howard provides a detailed account of a weekend session spent with Bindrim in *Please Touch*, 75–87. A critical, thinly veiled portrait forms the basis of Gwen Davis' novel *Touching* (London: W.H. Allen, 1971).

25. Andrew Cresse, 'Health is Wealth, but Also Wealth is Health', *World Health* (November-December 1992), 4–6. The quote is from Ralph Waldo Emerson, 'The first wealth is health'. Emerson, 'The Conduct of Life' [1860], *The Complete Works of Ralph Waldo Emerson* vol VI, ed. by Edward Waldo Emerson (New York: Houghton Mifflin, 1904), 1–307: p. 56. On *kalos kagathos* see Debra Hawhee, *Bodily Arts: Rhetoric and Athletics in Ancient Greece* (Austin: University of Texas Press, 2004), p. 19. On the history of the Latin phrase and its overlap with the Greek, see David C. Young, '*Mens Sana in Corpore Sano*? Body and Mind in Ancient Greece', *The International Journal of the History of Sport*, 22.1 (January 2005), 22–41. Noelle J. Mole, *Labor Disorders in Neoliberal Italy: Mobbing, Well-Being and the Workplace* (Indiana: Indiana University Press, 2012), p. 150. For a description of the Esalen graffiti, see: Kripal, p. 401.

26. *Diamonds Are Forever* (Guy Hamilton, US, 1971). For images of the Elrod House, see: www.johnlautner.org/wp/?p=1859. See also Daisy Alioto, 'Infinity Jest: How the Infinity Pool Became a Social Media Status Symbol', *The Outline* (24 March 2018). Online at: www.theout-line.com/post/3872/infinity-pools?utm_source=contributor_pages.

27. Neil McLaughlin, 'Origin Myths in the Social Sciences: Fromm, the Frankfurt School and the Emergence of Critical Theory', *The Canadian Journal of Sociology*, 24.1 (1999), 109–39: 111–12. Fromm, *The Art of Being*, 100–6. I am also quoting here from Rainer Funk's 'Editor's Foreword' to *The Art of Being*, viii–xi: p. vii.

28. Reft, 'A Dive into the Deep End'. For a glimpse of the high-rise horror that is the Sky Pool, see Ben Cost, 'Scary, transparent Sky Pool gets a big "No" from detractors', *New York Post* (2 June 2021), Lauryn Berry, 'The residents of the Sky Pool's complex are paying a fortune to heat it over winter', *Time Out* (4 January 2022) and Kriston Capps, 'This Swimming Pool in the Sky is the Ultimate Symbol of London's Affordability Crisis', *Bloomberg News* (25 November 2020).

29. For details of Robin Hood Gardens and the Smithsons, see Philip Tew, James Riley and Melanie Seddon, 'Surfing the Sixties', Tew *et al.*, 1–27: 12–13. For a brief discussion of the Angry Brigade, see Riley, p. 210. J.G. Ballard, *High Rise* [1975] (London: Harper, 2003). As an incidental note, the magazine *Rapid Eye* (1979–94) was instigated at Robin Hood Gardens by its editor, Simon Dwyer. See Simon Dwyer, *Rapid Eye Movement* (London: Creation, 1999), p. 4.

30. Carmichael, 'Black Power', 160–61. Extracts from DeFreeze's probation report and early arrest history are variously available online. The quotes here are from an oft-cited Associated Press source, 'Patty Hearst's Chief Captor Emerges as a Man Capable of Love and Violence', *The Danville Register* (14 April 1974).

31. Fromm, p. 115. Thomas Mann, *The Magic Mountain* [1924] (New York: Knopf, 1927). Christina Garsten and Adrienne Sörbom, 'Magical Formulae for Market Futures: Tales from the World Economic Forum Meeting in Davos', *Anthropology Today*, 32.6 (December 2016), 18–22: 18–19.

32. Fromm, 120; 110–120. Funk, p. vii.

33. Mander and Kent Rush, p. 17. Jessica Thompson, 'The Vagina Missing from Space', *Era Magazine* (December 2020). Online at: www.era-magazine.com/2020/12/21/the-vagina-missing-from-space/.

34. Anderson, 160–65. The work of Price Cobbs is discussed also in Tomkins, p. 46. See William H. Grier and Price Cobbs, *Black Rage* (New York: Basic Books, 1968). My point of reference for this section is *Century of the Self Part 3: There is a Policeman Inside All Our Heads, He Must Be Destroyed* (Adam Curtis, UK, 2002).

35. Nelson, 21; 3; 10. On sickle cell anaemia, see Nelson's fourth chapter, 'Spin Doctors', 95–126.

36. Zoe Strimpel, '*Spare Rib*, The British Women's Health Movement and the Empowerment of Misery', *Social History of Medicine*, 35.1 (February 2022), 217–236. Boston Women's Health Book Collective, *Our Bodies, Ourselves* (New York: Simon and Schuster, 1973). For an account of *Roe v. Wade*, see Chafe *et al.*, 197–201. Nelson, 8–10.

37. Adrienne Rich, 'Diving into the Wreck' [1972], *Norton*, 2949–2951: 2951. Klein, 'Making Waves'.

V The Shaping

1. 'Sleepwalker' can be heard on Moon Duo's album *Circles* (Sacred Bones Records, 2012). The video by Hylas Film can be seen here: www.youtube.com/watch?v=zgqTh6uoenc.

2. *Jane Fonda's Workout* (Sid Galanty, US, 1982). *Suspiria* (Dario Argento, Italy, 1977). *Holy Smoke!* (Jane Campion, Australia-US, 1999). *Nine Perfect Strangers* (Jonathan Levine, US, 2021). 'The Wellness Center', *What We Do in the Shadows* (Yana Gorskaya, US, 2021).

3. George du Maurier, *Trilby* (London: Osgood, McIlvaine and Company, 1895). Christine Sismondo, 'Gurus Gone Bad: Is it time for reform in the self-help and wellness industry?', *Toronto Star* (21 September 2020). Matt Stroud, *Guru: The Dark Side of Enlightenment* (US: Wondery,

2020). Karishma Vyas, 'Gurus Gone Bad in India', *Al Jazeera* (27 August 2018). Online at: www.aljazeera.com/features/2018/8/27/gurus-gone-bad-in-india. *Wild Wild Country* (Maclain Way, Chapman Way, US, 2018). *Bikram: Yogi, Guru, Predator* (Eva Orner, US, 2019).

4. Ma Prem Shunyo, *Diamond Days with Osho* (India: Rebel Publishing, 1992), p. 171. Susan Palmer describes 'taking sannyas' in 'Charisma and Abdication: A Study of the Leadership of Bhagwan Shree Rajneesh', *Sociological Analysis*, 49.2 (Summer 1988), 119–135: p. 124. The emphasis on renunciation, the 'new consciousness' and the economic activity of Rajneesh is analysed Lewis F. Carter, 'The "New Renunciates" of the Bhagwan Shree Rajneesh: Observations and Identification of Problems of Interpreting New Religious Movements', *Journal for the Scientific Study of Religion*, 26.2(June 1987), 148–172: 148; 152; 149. The idea of a 'sickness' and an impending 'suicide' is quoted in Eckart Floether and Eric Pement, 'Bhagwan Shree Rajneesh', *A Guide to Cults and New Religions*, ed. by Ronald Enroth (USA: Intervarsity Press, 1983), 43–59. 119–135. I am grateful to Douglas Field for his comments on this section of the chapter.

5. My account of Bikram and Bikram Yoga is taken from Syman, 268–275 and *Bikram: Yogi, Guru, Predator*. The Sassoon material is from Beverly and Vidal Sassoon, *A Year of Beauty and Health* (Harmondsworth: Penguin, 1977), 96–8. That Rajneesh was merely in pursuit of gratification is the thrust of stories such as that by Myles Bonnar and Steve Brocklehurst, 'The Scot Who Was the Sex Guru's Bodyguard', *BBC Scotland* (4 June 2018).

6. Goldwag, 43–44. Hanif Kureishi, *The Buddha of Suburbia* (London: Faber and Faber, 1990), p. 23.

7. Goldwag, p. 42. Kang quoted in Vyas, 'Gurus Gone Bad in India'. For critical accounts of the Rajneesh group see Win McCormack, 'Outside the Limits of the Human Imagination', *The New Republic* (27 March 2018), 10–40. See also Floether and Pement, in Enroth. This essay has the advantage of being written by a former member, but it has the disadvantage of a being something of a conversion narrative, Floether's assessments are also very much informed by what was, at the time of his writing, a newly found Christian perspective. Enroth's publisher, Intervarsity Press, is part of the American Inter-Varsity Christian Fellowship. *Wild Wild Country. Yogi, Guru, Predator*.

8. Ram Dass, 'Egg on My Beard', *Yoga Journal*, 11 (November-December 1976), 6–12. For a response, see Colette Dowling, 'Confessions of an American Guru', *The New York Times* (4 December 1977). Tal Brooke, *Lord of the Air: Tales of a Modern Antichrist* (Oxford: Lion Publishing,

1976). Brooke is the founder of the Spiritual Counterfeits Project. Some sources see him as a whistleblower regarding Sai Baba, while other see him as a mudslinger. For an example of the latter, see: www. sathyasaibaba.wordpress.com/2008/05/24/tal-brooke-and-his-tall-tales-about-sri-sathya-sai-baba. See also Goldwag, p. 46.

9. Howard, 'Year of the Guru', *Life* (9 February 1968). Syman, 239–40. Brief biographies of those mentioned in this section can also be found in Goldwag, 42–46. See also Ingram, p. 264.

10. Kasper Van Laarhoven, 'How the Hare Krishna Movement Started 51 Years Ago in the East Village', *Bedford+Bowery* (17 June 2017). Online at: www.bedfordandbowery.com/2017/06/how-the-hare-krishna-movement-started-51-years-ago-in-the-east-village/. See also Howard, 'Year of the Guru' and Goldwag, 48–49.

11. David Flint, 'Dynamic Tension: The Charles Atlas Story', *The Reprobate* (18 June 2018). Online at: www.reprobatepress.com/2018/06/18/dynamic-tension-the-charles-atlas-story/. 'Sexy Sadie' can be heard on *The Beatles* (Apple, 1968). William Penn Fyve, 'Swami' (Thunderbird, 1966).

12. Martin Thomas, *The Hand of Cain* (New York: Magnum, 1966). Diana Carter, *Mind-Out* (New York: Pinnacle, 1973). Don Pendleton, *The Godmakers* (New York: Pinnacle, 1970). Philip José Farmer, *The Image of the Beast. An Exorcism: Ritual One* [1968] (London: Quartet, 1975).

13. Matthew D. Lassiter, 'Inventing Family Values', in *Rightward Bound: Making America Conservative in the 1970s*, ed. by Bruce J. Schulman and Julian E. Zelizer (Cambridge: Harvard University Press, 2008), 13–29: p. 13. James C. Dobson is discussed in Paul Boyer, 'The Evangelical Resurgence in 1970s American Protestantism', in Schulman and Zelizer, 29–52: 35; 40. Nat Freeland, *The Occult Explosion* (New York: Berkley Books, 1972). Pendleton, p. 38.

14. Pendleton, p. 40. Hugh B. Urban, *Zorba the Buddha: Sex, Spirituality and Capitalism in the Global Osho Movement* (Berkeley: University of California Press, 2016), p. 26. Urban discusses Rajneesh from a post-modern and poststructuralist perspective with reference to Deleuze and Guattari, p. 48. Michel Foucault, 'Preface', in Deleuze and Guattari, xi–xiv: xi–ii. Mark Seem, 'Introduction', in Deleuze and Guattari, xv–xxiv: p. xxi. Lyotard, *The Postmodern Condition*, p. xxiv. Urban speaks about the middle-class and Western appeal of Rajneesh, p. 42.

15. Urban, p. 35. Goldwag, p. 43. Palmer, p. 130. Carter, p. 158. Vikas Seth *et al.*, 'Osho Dynamic Meditation's Effect on Serum Cortisol Level, *Journal of Clinical and Diagnostic Research*, 10.11 (November 2016), 1–10: p. 5. Rajneesh on being free from 'mob madness' is cited in Goldwag, p. 46.

16. Pendleton, p. 88. Nixon's views on 'our national life' are from Boyer, in Schulman and Zelizer, p. 32. Urban, p. 26.

17. Rajender Kaur and Anupama Arora, 'India in the American Imaginary, 1780s–1880s', *India in the American Imaginary, 1780s–1880s*, ed. by Rajender Kaur and Anupama Arora (London: Palgrave Macmillan, 2017), 3–41: p. 11. *Far East Adventure Stories* was published by Fiction Publishers and ran for twelve issues from 1930 to 1932. A brief overview can be found online: www.thepulp.net/pulpsuperfan/2022/10/17/the-stinging-nting-and-other-stories/.

18. Syman, p. 239. Amanda Lucia, 'Hinduism in America', *Oxford Research Encyclopedia of Religion* (2017). Online at: www.oxfordre.com/religion/view/10.1093/acrefore/9780199340378.001.0001/acrefore-9780199340378-e-436.

19. Brooks Alexander, a researcher for the Spiritual Counterfeits Project, quoted in Dave Hunt, *The Cult Explosion: An Expose of Today's Cults and Why they Prosper* (Oregon: Harvest House, 1980), p. 67. This is part of a longer discussion of false prophets and the denial of the 'personal God', 67–84. James Bjornstad, quoted in Enroth, 'What is a Cult?', *A Guide to Cults*, 10–20: p. 15. The discussion of the 'Self' and Christianity is from Hunt, p. 71. Hunt, like Enroth, is writing from a clear Christian perspective.

20. David L. Gosling, 'Christian Response within Hinduism', *Religious Studies*, 10.4 (December 1974), 433–439. *The Moonstone* (Paddy Russell, UK, 1972). *The Man Who Would be King* (John Huston, US/UK, 1975). *I Drink Your Blood* (David Durston, US, 1970). For Details of Bhaskar Roy Chowdhury see his archives at the New York Public Library: www.archives-nypl.org/dan/18470.

21. *The Astrologer* (James Glickenhaus, US, 1975), Enroth, 'What is a Cult?', p. 14. Shapiro quoted in Thomas Robbins and Dick Anthony, 'Deprogramming, Brainwashing and the Medicalization of Deviant Religious Groups', *Social Problems*, 29.3 (February 1982), 283–297: p. 290.

22. For the definitive account of the Jonestown incident, see Tim Reiterman, *Raven: The Untold Story of the Rev. Jim Jones and his People* [1982] (New York: Tarcher Penguin, 2008). Ted Patrick, *Let Our Children Go!* (New York: E.P. Dutton, 1976). Patrick's background and methods are discussed in Syman, 252–53 and Robbins and Anthony, 286–87. Syman also briefly discusses Jim Jones, p. 260. The 'flower-pinner' comment is from Enroth, 'What is a Cult?', p. 10. Roger Zelazny, *The Dream Master* [1966] (London: Panther, 1968), p. 16.

23. Williams, p. 88. Williams is referencing Hunter's article, '"Brain-Washing" Tactics Force Chinese into Ranks of Communist Party',

Miami Daily News (24 September 1950). As ever, the origins of brain-washing and Hunter's use of the word are more complicated than they appear. For a careful discussion, Williams recommends Marcia Holmes, 'Edward Hunter and the Origins of Brainwashing', *Hidden Persuaders* (26 May 2017). Online at: www.bbk.ac.uk/hiddenpersuaders/blog/hunter-origins-of-brainwashing/.

24. William Sargant, *Battle for the Mind: A Physiology of Conversion and Brain-Washing* [1957] (London: Pan, 1961), 13–14. Sargant is quoting from the Secretary of Defense's Advisory Committee on Prisoners of War, *The Fight Continues After the Battle* (Washington: U.S. Government Printing Office, 1955). Richard Condon, *The Manchurian Candidate* (New York: McGraw Hill, 1962). Vernon, p. 17.

25. Vernon, 22; 41.

26. Lilly, p. 51. Williams, 91–93.

27. Len Deighton, *The IPCRESS File* (London: Hodder and Stoughton, 1962). James Kennaway, *The Mind Benders: A Novel of Suspense* (London: Longmans, 1963). The reference to 'Reduction of Sensation' experiments at 'McGill University of Canada', appears as part of a 'Publisher's Note' reiterating the book as fiction, p. 5. *The New York Times* report, 'Tank Test Linked to Brainwashing', is discussed in Williams, p. 93. *The Mind Benders* (Basil Dearden, UK, 1963). *The Manchurian Candidate* (John Frankenheimer, US, 1962). *The Ipcress File* (Sidney J. Furie, UK, 1963). Colin Wilson, *The Black Room* (London: Weidenfeld & Nicholson, 1971), 6–26: 14–25. John McGuffin, *The Guineapigs* (Harmondsworth: Penguin, 1974), p. 36. On 'enhanced interrogation', see: Senate Select Committee on Intelligence, *The Senate Intelligence Committee Report on Torture* (New York: Melville House, 2014).

28. Ronald Enroth, *Youth, Brainwashing and the Extremist Cults* (Michigan: Zondervan, 1977). Sargant's *Battle for the Mind* includes a chapter by Robert Graves called 'Brain-washing in ancient times', 156–165. Vernon, p. 38.

29. This account of Jim Ardmore, the Divine Light Mission and Ted Patrick is from Enroth, 133–46. For alternative studies of the Divine Light Mission, see Maeve Price, 'The Divine Light Mission as a Social Organization', *The Sociological Review*, 27.2 (1979) and 'The Divine Light Mission', *Encyclopedia of Hinduism*, ed. by Denise Cush *et al.* (London: Routledge, 2008), 204–205.

30. Loren Singer, *The Parallax View* (New York: Doubleday, 1970). Alex Cox was speaking in his introduction to *The Parallax View* (1974), broadcast on *Moviedrome* (November 1993). Online here: www.

youtube.com/watch?v=xDsTpYGIGmQ. W. Penn Jones, *Forgive My Grief: A Critical Review of the Warren Commission Report on the Assassination* (Midlothian: Midlothian Mirror, 1966).

31. Singer, p. 54. *The Parallax View* (Alan J. Pakula, US, 1974).

32. Gene Church and Conrad D. Carnes, *The Pit: A Group Encounter Defiled* (New York: Outerbridge and Lazard, 1972).

33. Brewer, 'We're Gonna Tear You Down and Put You Back Together'. Michel Foucault, *The Order of Things: An Archaeology of the Human Sciences* [1966], trans. Alan Sheridan (London: Tavistock Publications, 1970), p. 385.

34. Anderson, 220–22; 262. See also, Roberto Assagioli, 'Psychosynthesis', in *The Penguin Book of New Age and Holistic Writing*, ed. by William Bloom (Harmondsworth: Penguin, 2001), 64–70. Feldberg describes the arrival of Denny Yuson in 'The Story of Quaesitor', p. 59. A 1973 calendar of events for Quaesitor published in *Self & Society* lists the presence of Denny and Leida Yuson. See 'Growth Centres: Calendar of Events', *Self & Society* 1.1 (March 1973), p. 31. Paul Lowe is named as Teertha in this material. For the wider context, see Edgar and Williams, 'American Healing: Primal therapy, Rebirthing, and Cathartic Encounters in 1970s London (and beyond)', *Journal of Transatlantic Studies* 19.1 (April 2021), 238–260: 250–1.

35. Anderson, 30–31. Kripal, p. 9. Howard, p. 207.

36. My account of the 'Spiritual Tyranny' conference is taken from Anderson, 263–269. For Peter Marin's 'disgust', see, p. 264. The other key account used here is by Will Storr, 'The Birth of the Narcissism Revolution', *Quillette* (16 June 2018). Online at: www.quillette.com/2018/06/16/the-birth-of-the-narcissism-revolution/.

37. *Feminism as Therapy* was published shortly after the conference. Anderson, 263–269. Storr, 'The Birth of the Narcissism Revolution'. For general context on second-wave feminism see, Jane Sherron De Hart, 'The Creation of a Feminist Consciousness', Chafe *et al.*, 166–173 and Marlene Dixon, 'The Rise and Demise of Women's Liberation: A Class Analysis', *Synthesis*, 2.1/2 (Summer–Fall 1977), 21–38. Gloria Steinem's 'After Black Power, Women's Liberation', *New York* (April 1969) is a useful, early account. Jennifer Thompson, 'Reveal Esalen Sexism', *Berkeley Barb*, 19.3 (Feb 1–7 1974), 1; 7. Peter Marin, 'The New Narcissism', *Harper's* 251 (October 1975), 44–56: p. 48.

38. Thompson, 'Eves Drop In: Out of Despair', *Berkeley Barb* 19.13 (April 12–18 1974), p. 8. For details of *Scott v. Hart*, see Pauline Gee, 'Ensuring Police Protection for Battered Women: The *Scott* v. *Hart* Suit', *Signs* 8.3

(1983), 554–67. For the SLA articles, see 'Sgt. Pepper', 'SLA's Fahizah Just Naïve', *Berkeley Barb*, 19.3 (Feb 1–7 1974), p. 2 and 'Toko, Fahizah, Cinque Speak', *Berkeley Barb* 19.3 (April 12–18 1974), p. 8. This article names 'Toko' when the SLA member William Harris used 'Teko'. As an additional point on the sexual politics of the *Berkeley Barb*, it is worth noting that each issue contains nearly twenty pages of ads for Berkeley-based massage parlors.

39. Lilly, 99–100.

40. Lilly, 99–100. For a description of Lilly's work with dolphin brain matter see Burnett, 17–18. See Howard on Bindrim, 75–86.

41. Howard, p.30; 33–32. This image of power is also key theme of Davis' *Touching*. Anderson, p. 262. Marin, p. 48. Storr, 'The Birth of the Narcissism Revolution'. The phrase 'realise a greater human freedom' is from Lilly, 99–100.

42. Katharine Webster, 'The Case Against Swami Rama of the Himalayas', *Yoga Journal* (November/December 1990), 59–94: 60.

The Hospital Ship

1. Martin Bax, *The Hospital Ship* [1976] (London: Picador, 1977). Martin Bax and Judy Bernal, *Your Child's First Five Years* (London: Butterworth-Heinemann, 1974). For details of the *Ambit* episode, see Ann Quin *et al.*, '*Ambit* Drugs and Creative Writing Competition', *Ambit* 35 (1968), 41–48.

2. Ballard described the essays that made up Adam Parfrey's collection *Apocalypse Culture* (USA: Feral House, 1987) as 'the terminal documents of the twentieth century'. I speculatively apply this quote to *The Hospital Ship* due to the thematic similarity with Parfrey's book but also because of the novel's form: the chapters read like a series of documents or reports. For the record, Ballard was full of praise for *The Hospital Ship*, calling it 'the most exciting, stimulating and brilliantly conceived book I have read since [William] Burroughs' novels'. This quote can be found on the back of the Picador edition cited here. Extracts from the reviews by Gof, Mason and Neville came from M.A. Orthofer's review digest, '*The Hospital Ship* by Martin Bax'. Online at: www.complete-review.com/reviews/gbx/baxm.htm.

3. Bax, 25–6. Indeed, from the outset, Bax explicitly refuses to sketch out an overall picture: 'The patients they picked up [...] were unable to give a coherent account of the way things were in the world', p. 14.

4. The quotes from Naftulin come from her account for *The Insider*, 'Goop threw a cruise and no Goopies came'. The cancellation of 'Goop-At-Sea' was announced via various media outlets, such as Kathryn

Hopkins, 'Goop Cruise is Cancelled Due to the Coronavirus', *WWD* (June 24 2020). Online at: www.wwd.com/feature/goop-cruise-is-canceled-due-to-the-coronavirus-1203659759/. The attitude towards the cruise industry, *circa* 2020, is perhaps best summed up by Slavoj Žižek: 'One of the lasting symbols of the epidemic is passengers trapped in quarantine on large cruise ships. Good riddance to the obscenity of such ships say I.' See Žižek, *Pandemic!: COVID-19 Shakes the World* (Cambridge: Polity, 2020), p. 45.

5. Natfulin, 'Goop threw a Cruise'. The images mentioned can be viewed online: www.insider.com/goop-at-sea-gwyneth-paltrow-first-cruise-2021-11.

6. The COVID numbers cited here were taken from the World Health Organization's weekly epidemiological update. Online at: www.who. int/publications/m/item/weekly-epidemiological-update-on-covid-19---26-october-2021. The quotes from Naftulin come from *The Insider. The Hospital Ship* is by no means a sentimental novel, but its violence is meant to be distressing. It does not celebrate the horrors it describes, however excessive the content becomes. The ship's psychiatrist, Kline, functions as something of a barometer in this regard. Reflecting on the analysis he conducts with his patient, Coma, Bax clearly describes him feeling the strain: 'Kline found the material deeply disturbing, and his own training did not provide him with the reserves he needed to meet the situation', p. 60.

VI The Great Awakening

1. Travis, 'How Has the Prevention of Health and Wellness Changed?' Travis and Rowe, in *What on Earth is Wellness?*

2. Travis, Ardell and Greenberg, 'A Keynote Lecture with Jack Travis and Don Ardell'. *The Wellness Index* and details of 'The Wellness Index Wheel' appear as a non-paginated supplement in Travis and Ryan.

3. Travis, 'How Has the Perception of Health and Wellness Changed?'. Travis, 'Marin Valley Biography Night: Jack Travis'. Travis, Ardell and Greenberg, 'A Keynote Lecture with Jack Travis and Don Ardell'. See also Adele Davies, *Let's Eat Right to Keep Fit* (New York: Harcourt Brace, 1954); Roger J. Williams, *You Are Extraordinary* (New York: Random House, 1967) and Alan H. Nittler, *A New Breed of Doctor* (New York: Pyramid House, 1972). The books by Davies and Williams both had successful republications in 1970 and 1971. Ardell includes these and others in his 'Wellness Resource Guide', see *High Level Wellness* (1977), 215–94. Williams is cited in Travis and Ryan, p. 90.

4. Travis, 'How Has the Perception of Health and Wellness Changed?'; Ardell and Greenberg, 'A Keynote Lecture with Jack Travis and Don

Ardell', Travis and Rowe, in *What on Earth is Wellness?* Cyra McFadden, *The Serial: A Year in the Life of Marin County* [1977] (London: Prion, 2000), p. 13. Don Cahalan and Beatrice Treiman, *Drinking Behavior, Attitudes and Problems in Marin County* (Emeryville: Alcohol Research Group, 1976), p. 3.

5. See John de Graaf *et al.*, *Affluenza: The All-Consuming Epidemic* (New York: McGraw-Hill, 2002). McFadden, 21; 146. *I Want It All Now* (Joseph DeCola, US, 1978). Travis, Ardell and Greenberg, 'A Keynote Interview with Jack Travis and Don Ardell'. Travis and Rowe in *What on Earth is Wellness*?

6. Travis, 'How Has the Perception of Health and Wellness Changed?'. Travis, *The Wellness Workbook for Health Professionals* (Marin County: Wellness Resource Center, 1977). Marc Lalonde, *A New Perspective on the Health of Canadians* (Ottawa: Health Canada, 1974). Ardell discusses the 'Lalonde Report' in *High Level Wellness* (1977), 233–237.

7. For details of Elizabeth Neilson see Sharon Elayne Fair, *Wellness and Physical Therapy* (Massachusetts: Jones and Bartlett, 2011), p. 40. Bill Hettler describes his work and the background to the National Wellness Conference in 'The Past of Wellness' (1998). Online at www.hettler.com//History/hettler.htm. See also Brandan Hardie, 'The Past, Present, and Future of the Wellness Movement: An Interview with Dr. Bill Hettler', *The Art of Health Promotion*, 29.5 (May–June 2015), 2–3. Ardell discusses his professional background in *High Level Wellness* (1977), 4–6. See also Terry and Ardell, p. 4. For the article on Travis, see Ardell, 'Meet John Travis, Doctor of Well-Being', *Prevention* (April 1975), 62–69. Travis describes the impact of the article in 'How Has the Perception of Health and Wellness Changed?'. Travis' self-reflections are recorded in Travis and Ryan, p. 8. Travis discusses 'All Tied Up' in 'Marin Valley Biography Night: Jack Travis'.

8. McFadden, 207; 241–2; 233. McFadden described the circumstances of her novel's publication in a 2016 interview with Debra Schwartz for the Mill Valley Oral History Programme. A transcript can be found here: www.millvalley.pastperfectonline.com/archive/1DDF3E40-ADCC-46FE-990F-711023561201. McFadden speaks about the 'flowering of the human potential movement' in her 'Preface' to the Prion edition of *The Serial*, xi–xiii: p. xi.

9. Anderson, 279; 288. Ardell, 6–26; 47.

10. *I Want It All Now.*

11. McFadden quoted in *I Want It All Now. The Serial*, 56; 74–78; 79. See also Frances Moore Lappé, *Diet for a Small Planet* (New York: Ballantine, 1971).

12. *I Want It All Now.*
13. Marin, p. 46. McFadden, p. 19.
14. Wolfe, 'The "Me" Decade'. Lasch, 'The Narcissist Society', *The New York Review of Books* (September 30 1976). Online at: www.nybooks.com/ articles/1976/09/30/the-narcissist-society/. Tomkins, 42; 31.
15. The definitive account of this period is Kim Phillips-Fein, *Fear City: New York's Fiscal Crisis and the Rise of Austerity Politics* (New York: Henry Holt, 2017). Robert Caro, *The Power Broker: Robert Moses and the Fall of New York* (New York: Knopf, 1974). I am grateful to Connor Stait for his insights on *The Power Broker.* Oliver Burkeman provides a useful analysis of Caro's project in his 2015 review of the book for the *Guardian* (23 October 2015). Robert Moses, 'Asleep at the Fiscal Crisis', *New York Times* (16 September 1975). Jake Offenhartz, 'How Bankers & Technocrats Used the 1975 Fiscal Crisis to Permanently Reshape NYC', *Gothamist* (21 April 2017). Online at: www.gothamist.com/ arts-entertainment/how-bankers-technocrats-used-the-1975-fiscal-crisis-to-permanently-reshape-nyc. James Parrott, 'Fiscal Purgatory in New York', *The American Prospect* (9 August 2017). Online at: www. prospect.org/labor/fiscal-purgatory-new-york/.
16. Samuel Brittan, 'The Economic Contradictions of Democracy', *British Journal of Political Science* 5.2 (April 1975), 129–159: 131–32; 134; 139–42. Brittan mentions the 'growth of private armies' as a possible public anxiety. The reference to David Stirling is from Patrick Marnham, *Trail of Havoc: In the Steps of Lord Lucan* (New York: Viking, 1987), p. 115.
17. *Abigail's Party* (Mike Leigh, UK, 1977). Mike Leigh, 'Mike Leigh on *Abigail's Party* at 40', *Guardian* (24 February 2017).
18. McFadden, 11; 240–244. Bret Easton Ellis, *American Psycho* (New York: Vintage, 1991), p. 131.
19. Lasch, 'The Narcissist Society'. Jerry Rubin, *Growing (Up) at Thirty-Seven* (New York: M. Evans and Co, 1976). Robert M. Pirsig, *Zen and the Art of Motorcycle Maintenance: An Inquiry into Values* [1974] (London: Vintage, 1999).
20. Keys *et al.*, p. 5.
21. *Shampoo* (Hal Ashby, US, 1975). 'Wouldn't It Be Nice' can be heard on The Beach Boys, *Pet Sounds* (Capitol, 1966). 'Looking for Space' can be heard on *Windsong* (RCA, 1975). 'Take me Home, Country Roads' is featured on *Poems, Prayers & Promises* (RCA, 1971). The two 'Ballads' can be heard on *Rhymes & Reasons* (RCA, 1969) The link between Denver and est is briefly outlined here: www.erhardseminarstraining. com/influence-2/. The definition of 'head space' is taken from the *OED* which also indicates that by the 1990s, 'head space' had morphed into

its more familiar, contemporary form of 'headspace'. In charting the history of this colloquial usage, the *OED* offers examples which reflect the point made here. The first is from 1972 and it refers to a change of state – an audience sharing the 'head space' with a band on stage. The next example, from 1977, refers to a professional motorcyclist and their emotional state prior to a race. The earlier usage is thus about a collective altered state, the second is about a singular set of personal feelings, in this instance a 'bad head space'.

22. Lasch, 'The Narcissist Society'. For more on 'Floating World', see: John Reeve, *Floating World: Japan in the Edo Period* (London: British Museum Press, 2006).

23. Travis, 'How Has the Perception of Health and Wellness Changed?'. Dietary matters are covered in Travis and Ryan, 64–90. This section discusses *Dietary Goals for the United States*, 64; 75.

24. Travis and Ryan, 69; 76. For 'biofeedback' see Travis and Ryan, p. 32 as well as Travis' *60 Minutes* interview with Rather. For a more detailed overview, see: Raymond Gaeta *et al.*, 'Biofeedback', *The Cambridge Handbook of Psychology, Health and Medicine* ed. by Susan Ayers *et al.* (Cambridge: Cambridge University Press, 2007), 335–340. Ardell discusses the costs involved in and the application process to The Wellness Resource Center in *High Level Wellness* (1977), 11–16. See also Travis, 'How Has the Perception of Health and Wellness Changed?'. For a reproduction of the 'Grand Certificate', see Travis and Ryan, p. 244.

25. For the 'Wellness Antidote', see Travis and Ryan, 162–3. McFadden, 'Preface', p. xiii. David Lodge, *Changing Places: A Tale of Two Campuses* (London: Secker and Warburg, 1975), p. 10. An endorsement from Lodge, calling *The Serial* 'a comic classic', can be found on the back cover of the Prion edition.

26. David Nobbs, 'The Death of Reginald Perrin' [1975], in *The Reginald Perrin Omnibus* (London: Arrow, 1999), 3–287: 10–11. The novel was later published as *The Fall and Rise of Reginald Perrin*.

27. Nobbs, p. 134. *The Fall and Rise of Reginald Perrin* (Gareth Gwenlan, UK, 1976). David Randall, 'Faking It: How to do a Reggie Perrin and get away with it', *The Independent* (20 July 2008). *The Spy Who Died Twice* (Keely Winstone, UK, 2022). Travis and Ryan, p. 7. Useem, 'Bring Back the Nervous Breakdown'.

28. George Miller Beard quoted in Useem, 'Bring Back the Nervous Breakdown'.

29. Black and Pemberton, p. 4.

30. Simon Reynolds, *Rip It Up and Start Again: Postpunk, 1978–1984* (London: Faber, 2005), 228–229. See also Simon Ford, *Wreckers of*

Civilization: The Story of COUM Transmissions and Throbbing Gristle (London: Black Dog, 1999). According to Greil Marcus, the 'SAME THING ...' message appeared in the 'early 1970s'. It was reproduced in the fanzine *London's Outrage* 2 (February 1977). See Marcus, *Lipstick Traces: A Secret History of the Twentieth Century* [1989] (London: Faber and Faber, 2011), p. 135.

31. *The Good Life* (John Howard Davies, UK, 1975–78). *Abigail's Party*.
32. Travis and Ryan, xvi–xvii; p. 157. Terry and Ardell, p. 5. Keys *et al.*, p. 2.
33. Keys *et al.*, p. 2. Carter, 'Inaugural Address: Thursday January 20, 1977', *Inaugural Addresses of the Presidents of the United States*, vol. 2 (USA: Applewood Books, 2001), 145–47. Farber in Chafe *et al.*, p. 323.
34. Travis, Ardell and Greenberg, 'A Keynote Interview with Jack Travis and Don Ardell'. Ardell is quoting from Robert Green Ingersoll, 'Lotos Club Dinner, Twentieth Anniversary. New York, March 22, 1890', *The Works of Robert Green Ingersoll* vol. 12 [1900] (New York: Cosimo, Incorporated), 113–17: p. 114. Travis and Ryan, xxii–xxix.
35. Ardell, *High Level Wellness* (1977), 105; 42–46.
36. Liane Moriarty, *Nine Perfect Strangers* [2018] (Great Britain: Penguin, 2019), p. 60.
37. Ovid, *Metamorphoses*, trans. by A.D. Melville (Oxford: Oxford University Press, 1987). Echo and Narcissus appear in Book III, 51–74. John Donne, 'Meditation XVII ("Now This Bell Tolling Softly For Another, Says to Me: Thou Must Die")', *Dedications Upon Emergent Occasions and Death's Duel* (London: Vintage, 1999), 102–108: p. 103. *Dedications* was originally published in 1624. Ferguson offers a brief reflection on Donne, p. 280.
38. Ofshe, p. 133: 'In August, 1974, Synanon's Board of Directors adopted a resolution proclaiming the Synanon Religion [...]. In September, 1975, the Board also amended Synanon's articles of incorporation to state that one of the primary purposes of the organization was to operate a church for religious purposes [...]. The corporation took the position that Synanon had been a church at least since 1969, but it had continued to use the alternative society metaphor until making these religious declarations. Having redefined the organization, Synanon adopted a new religious rhetoric and attempted to secure church organization status from the Internal Revenue Service (IRS).'

VII Body Snatchers

1. Barry, 22; 101–3. It should be noted here that for the most part, *Beatlebone* refers only to 'John'. However, in the essayistic sixth part, 'Eleven Eleven Eleven – Dakota' (173–202), in which Barry discusses the composition

of the novel, he shifts to 'John Lennon'. Worthington gives 1972 as the end date for the Dorinish commune in 'RIP Sid Rawle', as do the Yorkshire Film Archive in their notes to *Tribe of the Sun*. On Lennon's 'house-husband period', see: John Blaney, *John Lennon: Listen to this Book* (Guilford: The Paper Jukebox, 2005), p. 285; William Ruhlmann, *John Lennon* (New York: Smithmark, 1993), p. 82 and Fred Seaman, *The Last Days of John Lennon: A Personal Memoir* (New York: Random House, 1992).

2. Lynne Murray, *et al.*, 'The Impact of Postnatal Depression and Associated Adversity on Early Mother-Infant Interactions and Later Infant Outcome', *Child Development*, 67.5 (1996), 2512–2526. James Hamilton, *Postpartum Psychiatric Problems* (St. Louis: The C.V. Mosby Company, 1962). *DSM II*, p. 31. Travis discusses the 'epidemic of disappearing dads' in 'How Has the Perception of Health and Wellness Changed?'.

3. Barry, 101–3. Rawle described his contact with Lennon in 'Interview with Sid Rawle (Part 3): Sid, John Lennon and Revolution'. On Nutopia, see Yoko Ono and Hans Ulrich Obrist, *Yoko Ono* (Köln: Buchhandlung Walther König, 2009), 22–24. 'Nutopian International Anthem' is listed on *Mind Games* (Apple, 1973).

4. Barry, 6–8; 192. *Other Ways* aired on RTÉ2 across November and December 1978. The item on The Golden Dawn was shown on 14 November. The clip, titled 'Golden Dawn Healthy Restaurant 1978' is online at: www.rte.ie/archives/2013/1114/486606-alternative-eating-habits-1978/.

5. *Invasion of the Body Snatchers* (Philip Kaufman, US, 1978), hereafter *Invasion* (1978). *Invasion of the Body Snatchers* (Don Siegel, US, 1956). Jack Finney, *The Body Snatchers* (New York: Dell, 1955).

6. Lev Grossman, 'Invasion of the Body Snatchers Snatchers', *Time* (14 June 2007). *Body Snatchers* (Abel Ferrara, US, 1993). *The Invasion* (Oliver Hirschbiegel, US, 2007). Immanuel Velikovsky, *Worlds in Collision* (New York: Macmillan, 1950). *Invasion* (1978). Karl and Philip French, *Cult Movies* (Great Britain: Pavilion Books, 1999), 118–19.

7. Pauline Rose Clance and Suzanne Imes, 'The Imposter Phenomenon in High Achieving Women: Dynamics and Therapeutic Intervention', *Psychotherapy Theory, Research and Practice* 15.3 (Fall 1978), 1–8: p. 2. For Clance's more recent reflections on the term in the age of imposter syndrome, see: www.paulineroseclance.com/impostor_phenomenon.html. *The Stepford Wives* (Bryan Forbes, US, 1975).

8. *Invasion* (1978). Lasch, *The Culture of Narcissism*, 13;3;5.

9. Barry, p. 6. Janov, 136–150; 281–311; 102; 56.

10. Barry, p. 22. For details of Barrie Konicov see www.potentialsunlimited. com/. For an example of the type of criticism his work often received, see Blaine Harden, 'Verdict Mixed on "Sleep Tapes", But Supplier is Getting Rich', *The Washington Post* (27 December 1979). The quotes used here are from the tape *Psychic Healing* (Potentials Unlimited, 1978). For details of Yves Donnars, see Hervé Aubron, 'The Capture of Houellebecq', *Libération* (14 August 1999); Thibaud Cécile, 'Le camping new age, le maire et l'écrivain', *L'Express* (10 September 1998) and Pascale Senk, 'A l'Espace du possible: vacances en group avec soi-même', *Psychologies* (5 February 2009).

11. Aubron, 'The Capture of Houellebecq'. *Psychic Healing*. Marin, p. 48.

12. 'God' and 'Well, Well, Well' can be heard on *John Lennon/Plastic Ono Band*. Janov's comments on belief systems are from his interview with Harris for *Mojo*. Janov's views on religion are also discussed in John Rowan, *The Transpersonal: Spirituality in Psychotherapy and Counselling* (London: Routledge, 1993) p. 269. Janov, *The Primal Revolution*, 152–56. Lasch, *The Culture of Narcissism*, 4: p. xviii. Marin, p. 48.

13. *Velvet Goldmine* (Todd Haynes, USA, 1998). Jake Arnott, *The Long Firm* (London: Hodder and Stoughton, 1999). *Our Friends in the North* (Simon Cellan Jones, Pedr James, Stuart Urban, UK, 1996).

14. Edward Said, *Culture and Imperialism* (London: Vintage, 1993), 29–30. Foucault's activism is outlined in Mike Gane and Terry Johnson, 'The Project of Michel Foucault', *Foucault's New Domains*, ed. by Mike Gane and Terry Johnson (London: Routledge, 2013), 1–10: p. 5. For Lyotard's politics, see Sim, 308–9. See also Foucault, *The History of Sexuality: An Introduction* [1976], trans. Robert Hurley (Harmondsworth: Penguin, 1987); Lyotard, *Libidinal Economy* [1974], trans. Ian Hamilton Grant (Bloomington: University of Indiana Press, 1993) and Lyotard, *The Postmodern Condition: A Report on Knowledge* [1979], trans. Geoffrey Bennington and Brian Massumi (Manchester: Manchester University Press, 1984).

15. Said, p. 30. Reynolds, 230–1. Lynn Segal, 'Jam Today: Feminist Impacts and Transformations in the 1970s', Lawrence and Pemberton, 149–166: 151; 163–4.

16. Marwick, 270–76. Black and Pemberton, 1–4. Brittan, 'How British is the British Sickness?', *Il Politico*, 44.4 (December 1979), 650–664: 660–61. Roger Middleton, 'Brittan on Britain: Decline, Declinism and the "Traumas of the 1970s"', Black and Pemberton, 69–95: 69. Lasch, p. 10.

17. *Invasion* (1978). *I Want It All Now*. Lasch, *The Culture of Narcissism*, p. 5.

18. *Invasion* (1978). For an insight into Finney and Mill Valley, see David Streitfeld, 'The Invisible Man', *The Washington Post* (13 February 1994).

19. Dunn, *High-Level Wellness* (1961), p. 193. *Invasion* (1978). *I Want It All Now*.

20. *Stereo* (David Cronenberg, Canada, 1969). *Crimes of the Future* (David Cronenberg, Canada, 1970). *Shivers* (David Cronenberg, Canada, 1975). *Rabid* (David Cronenberg, US-Canada, 1976). *The Brood* (David Cronenberg, Canada, 1979). For a detailed overview of Cronenberg's career and his film-making philosophy, including his description of *The Brood* as version of *Kramer vs. Kramer*, see *Cronenberg on Cronenberg* ed. by Chris Rodley (London: Faber, 1993), 50; 56–8; 76.

21. *Ashram* (Wolfgang Dobrowolny, West Germany, 1979). The film is also known as *Ashram in Poona*.

22. *Ashram*. Anderson mentions the link between Teertha and Quaesitor, p. 302. Feldberg describes Paul Lowe becoming Teertha by way of the 'Rajneesh cult' in 'The Story of Quaesitor', p. 60. *The Brood*.

23. *Ashram*; *The Brood*. Richard Starks, *David Cronenberg's The Brood* (London: Granada, 1979), p. 17.

24. Janet Maslin, 'Life at an Ashram, Search for Inner Peace', *New York Times* (November 13, 1981). *Ashram* is described by Floether and Pement, Enroth, p. 49. See also *Wild Wild Country* (Part 2). McCormack's description of the experiences of German actress Eva Renzi is similar to the scene in *Ashram*, p. 10.

25. Price quoted in Anderson, p. 302. *Ashram*.

26. *The Brood*, Janov's reflection on the 'melodrama' of his sessions is from his interview with Harris for *Mojo*. Janov, *The Primal Scream*, 269; 259; 315.

27. Foucault, 'Technologies of the Self', *Ethics: Essential Works of Foucault, 1954–1984, Volume 1*, ed. Paul Rabinow (Harmondsworth: Penguin, 1997), 222–251: 225–6; 230–1. Foucault's essay has gained a certain traction in readings of the period, alongside that of Lasch and other commentators. Williams, for example, uses the essay in his discussion of the Lilly and floatation tank, p. 84.

28. Foucault, 'Technologies of the Self', 226–7. Barry, p. 147.

29. Foucault, 'Technologies of the Self', 238–9; 227; 225.

30. Foucault, p. 228. *The Brood. Ashram. Invasion. I Want It All Now.*

VIII The Crisis of Confidence

1. Perry, 89–92; 37.

2. Lilly, p. 48. Lily's endorsement of Lee and Glenn Perry comes from his foreword to *Floating in Quiet Darkness*, xiii–xiv: p. xiv. Marilyn Ferguson,

The Aquarian Conspiracy: Personal and Social Transformation in the 1980s [1980] (Great Britain: Granada, 1982), 17–18; 26–7; 400; 461. The numbers regarding yoga are from Syman, p. 256. Marwick, p. 371.

3. Ferguson, 330; 460–3.

4. Lilly, *The Scientist: A Novel Autobiography* (Lippincott: Philadelphia, 1978), p. 107. Ferguson, 36–42. Roszak quoted in Kenneth A. Briggs, 'New Religious Movements Considered Likely to Last', *New York Times* (22 June 1977).

5. Paddy Chayefsky, *Altered States* [1978] (London: Corgi, 1980), p. 51. The link between *Altered States* and *Dr Jekyll and Mr Hyde* is noted in various reviews. For example, see Kevin Lyons, 'Altered States (1980)', *The EOFFTV Review* (September 2019). Online at: www.eofftvreview.wordpress.com/2019/09/08/altered-states-1980/. For the overlap between John Lilly and Stanislav Grof at Esalen, see Drury, p. 78. Marwick, p. 258. William Peter Blatty, *The Exorcist* (New York: Harper and Row, 1971). David Seltzer, *The Omen* (New York: Signet, 1976). Jay Anson, *The Amityville Horror* (New York: Prentice Hall, 1979).

6. The description of the float centre is in Perry, 70–75. Lee and Glenn Perry offer an overview of the floatation tank and its associated language on their website, see: www.samadhitank.com/sensorydep.html. Brian O'Doherty, *Inside the White Cube: The Ideology of the Gallery Space* (San Francisco: Lapis Press, 1986), p. 7. Paul Wilson, *The Little Book of Calm* (Harmondsworth: Penguin, 1996), n.p.

7. Travis, Ardell and Greenberg, 'A Keynote Lecture with Jack Travis and Don Ardell'. Travis, 'Dr. Jack Travis on Wellness' (2014). Online at: www.youtube.com/watch?v=7fTHygqEAeI. Letitia Anne Peplau and Daniel Perlman, 'Perspectives on Loneliness', *Loneliness: A Sourcebook of Current Theory, Research and Therapy* (New York: Wiley, 1982), 1–18: 1; 10. Weiss quoted in Griffin, p. 12. Farber in Chafe *et al.*, p. 319.

8. Travis, 'How Has the Perception of Health and Wellness Changed?'. Peplau and Perlman, p. 15. *Radio On* (Chris Petit, UK/Germany, 1979). *Mad Max* (George Miller, Australia, 1979).

9. Farber in Chafe *et al.*, p. 319. Travis, 'How Has the Perception of Health and Wellness Changed?'. Adrian Chapman, 'R. D. Laing in the USA: His Message to the Smartphone-Obsessed 21st Century' (November 2019), blog post viewable online at: www.universityofglasgowlibrary. wordpress.com/2019/11/08/r-d-laing-in-the-usa-1972-and-his-message-to-the-smartphone-obsessed-21st-century/. Travis, Ardell and Greenberg, 'A Keynote Interview with Jack Travis and Don Ardell'. In support of Travis' critique of television, we might return to the numbers offered by Syman on the popularity of yoga. While the 1976 Gallup poll

had shown some five million adherents among the American public, this paled in comparison to the recorded readership of *TV Guide*. In 1976 it was America's top-selling magazine and had 'a weekly circulation of more than 20 million'. See Syman, p. 256.

10. Ardell, *High Level Wellness* (1977), p. 19; Travis, 'Marin Valley Biography Night: Jack Travis'. Perry, p. 79.

11. Travis quoted in Rather, 'Wellness'.

12. Travis, Ardell and Greenberg, 'A Keynote Interview with Jack Travis and Don Ardell'. The 'self-actualization' version of the continuum is visible in Ardell, *High Level Wellness* (1977), p. 10. The adjusted version is visible in Travis and Ryan, p. xvi. Travis discusses these changes in 'How Has the Perception of Health and Wellness Changed?'

13. *The Magic of Oil Painting* (Harry Ratner, US, 1974–82). *This Old House* (Russell Morash, 1979). American comic books of the 1970s regularly ran ads for Monogram model kits which were frequently presented as 'father-son' projects.

14. Carter, in Chafe *et al.*, 325, 328. Richard Cohen, 'Carter's New Theme No Sudden Inspiration', *The Washington Post* (19 July 1979).

15. Mike Wallace, 'The Ayatollah', *60 Minutes* (18 November 1979). Farber in Chafe *et al.*, p. 313–14. Frances Fitzgerald, *Way Out There in the Blue: Reagan, Star Wars and the End of the Cold War* (New York: Simon and Schuster, 2000), 111; 181. Travis quoted in Rather, 'Wellness'. Travis and Ryan, p. xviii.

16. Ivan Illich, *Medical Nemesis* (New York: Pantheon Books, 1976), 5–6. The quotes used here are cited in Ardell's analysis of the text in *High Level Wellness* (1977), 231–33. Ferguson, 268–9. Ardell, p. 232. Cook, *Coma* (New York: Little, Brown and Company, 1977). Travis and Ryan include *Medical Nemesis* as one of their sources in *The Wellness Wellbook*. His ideas are reflected in the general tone of the chapter 'Wellness, Self-Responsibility and Love' which contains Travis' critique of the 'Illness-Care' system, 4–6.

17. Travis and Ryan, p. 7; Ferguson, 288–90. Her discussion of the 'American Dream' forms the entirety of her fifth chapter, 'The American Matrix for Transformation', 128–55. The health benefits of floating are outlined in Perry, 162–3.

18. Peters, 134–36. John Lewis Gaddis, *The Cold War* (Harmondsworth: Penguin, 2005), 216–17. Ronald Purser, *McMindfulness: How Mindfulness Became the New Capitalist Spirituality* (London: Repeater, 2018), 19–21.

19. Pierre Bourdieu links neoliberalism to the destruction of 'collective structures'. He is quoted in Purser, p. 19. John Hills, 'Thatcherism,

New Labour and the Welfare State', Centre for the Analysis of Social Exclusion [CASE], CASE Paper / 13 (August 1998), 1–40: 2–4.

20. Purser, p. 20–1. Ferguson, 23–9; 264–306. Travis and Ryan, p. xiv. Ardell, p. 233.

21. Travis, 'How Has the Perception of Health and Wellness Changed?'; Perry, 114–19.

22. *Coma* (Michael Crichton, USA, 1978). Jon Kabat-Zinn, *Full Catastrophe Living: Using the Wisdom of Your Body and Mind to Face Stress, Pain and Illness* (New York: Delta, 1990), xix–xxii: xxi–ii. In writing this section, I was greatly aided by Yvonne Salmon and her knowledge of mindfulness.

23. Kabat-Zinn, p. xxi. Thích Nhất Hạnh provides *Full Catastrophe Living* with a brief preface, p. xiii. Nhất Hạnh, 'History of Engaged Buddhism', *Mindfulness Bell*, 49 (October 2008). Online at: www.parallax.org/mindfulnessbell/article/dharma-talk-history-of-engaged-buddhism/.

24. Nyanaponika Mahathera quoted in Fromm, 49–52. Nhất Hạnh, 'Engaged Buddhism'. Julia Cassaniti, 'Memory, Ghosts and the Good Life: *Sati* in Theravada Cultural Contexts', *Anthropology Today*, 38.2 (April 2022), 4–8: p. 6.

25. Kabat-Zinn, 1–3; 5–6. Joanna Cook, 'Mindfulness and Culture: An Introduction', *Anthropology Today*, 38.2 (April 2022), 1–3: p. 1.

26. Kabat-Zinn, 1–5. Ardell, 8–13; Travis, 'How Has the Perception of Health and Wellness Changed?'.

27. Kabat-Zinn, 27–29; 47–58; 75–94.

28. Purser, 19–22.

29. *Circle of Power* (Bobby Roth, US, 1981). Purser, p. 20. See Chade-Meng Tan, *Search Inside Yourself: The Secret to Unbreakable Concentration, Complete Relaxation and Effortless Self-Control* (London: Harper Collins, 2013). For details of the 'AmaZen' booths see Josh Marcus, 'Amazon's new "AmaZen" booths are a spiritually dark solution for late capitalism', *The Independent* (27 May 2021).

30. Kabat-Zinn, 390–92. Kabat-Zinn refers to Robert Eliot and *Is It Worth Dying For?* during his main discussion of stress, 235–242.

31. Ardell, 173–77; 185–88. Kabat-Zinn, p. 57.

IX A Good Place

1. McFadden in conversation with Schwartz. McFadden, 'Preface', p. xii.

2. *Ibid.*

3. Joseph D. Anderson, 'Human Relations Training and Group Work', *Social Work*, 20.3 (May 1975), 195–199: 195–6. McFadden in conversation with Schwartz. McFadden, 'Preface', xi–xii.

4. *Serial* (Bill Persky, US, 1980). *Bob & Carol & Ted & Alice* (Paul Mazursky, US, 1969). *Interiors* (Woody Allen, US, 1978). *Police Academy* (Hugh Wilson, US, 1984). *Bachelor Party* (Neal Israel, US, 1984). Ardell, *High Level Wellness* (1977), p. 168–9. Mazursky attended a session at Esalen, and the film features locations modelled on the institute.

5. McFadden describes being 'in-sync' with Cervenak in her conversation with Schwartz. *Heavy Traffic* (Ralph Bakshi, US, 1973). *Serial.*

6. *Serial.* McFadden, p. 34.

7. Nobbs, 'The Better World of Reginald Perrin', in *The Reginald Perrin Omnibus*, 575–885: p. 587. *To the Manor Born* (Gareth Gwenlan, UK, 1979–81).

8. See, for example, the New English Library titles published from 1970s onwards and attributed to Richard Allen and Mick Norman as well as the weekly comic *Action* (1976–77). *Serial.*

9. Todd Rundgren's 'Utopia Theme', originally called 'Utopia', can be heard on *Todd Rundgren's Utopia* (Bearsville, 1974). Rawle's 'Heaven and Hell' line appears in Worthington, 'RIP Sid Rawle' and Barry, p. 191. *I Want It All Now.*

10. *I Want It All Now.* 'Oakland, California, Impact of Antirecession Assistance On 52 Governments: An Update' (USA: US General Accounting Office, 1978), 96–100. William H. Frey, 'Black In-Migration, White Flight, and the Changing Economic Base of the Central City', *American Journal of Sociology*, 85.6 (1980), 1396–1417. See also: www.oaklandplanninghistory. weebly.com/the-changing-face-of-oakland.html.

11. H.G. Wells, *The Time Machine: An Invention* (New York: Henry Holt, 1895). See also Adam Kirsch, 'Utopian Pessimist', *The New Yorker* (October 10, 2011). Online at: www.newyorker.com/magazine/2011/10/17/utopian-pessimist.

12. The quotes from Bryn and Meg Purdy on Rowen House and eutopism come from www.eutopism.co.uk. For details of New Lanark and Robert Owen, see: www.newlanark.org. A.S. Neill, *Summerhill: A Radical Approach to Child Rearing* (New York: Hart, 1960). Robert P. Robinson, 'Until the Revolution: Analyzing the Politics, Pedagogy, and Curriculum of the Oakland Community School', *Espacio, Tiempo y Educación*, 7.1 (2020), 181–203: 187–89. Connie H. Choi, 'Educate to Liberate: Black Panther Liberation Schools', *The Studio Museum in Harlem*. Online at: www.studiomuseum.org/article/educate-liberate-black-panther-liberation-schools. Nelson, p. 55. In the writings associated with the Black Panther Party, 'The People' appears frequently as a term of group address which indicates both the idea of a community and the party's left-wing perspective. See, The Dr Huey P. Newton Foundation, *The*

Black Panther Party: Service to the People Programs, ed. by David Hillard (Albuquerque: University of New Mexico Press, 2008).

13. Ingersoll regarded this statement as his 'creed'. It can be found in Ingersoll, 'The Tendency of Modern Thought', *The Works of Robert Green Ingersoll*, vol. 8 (New York: Dresden Publishing Company, 1900), 480–90. My use of 'headspace' here is intended to reflect the post-1990s usage rather than the 1970s form of 'head space'. In addition to the current colloquial use, I have in mind the name of the meditation app, headspace, see: www.headspace.com.

14. *The Goop Lab: The Healing Trip* (Yamit Shimonovitz, US, 2020). See also Victoria Turk, 'Goop on Psychedelics isn't bad, it's just boring', *Wired* (January 2020). Viewable online: www.wired.co.uk/article/goop-lab-netflix-psychedelics.

15. Carl Rogers, *A Way of Being* (New York: Houghton Mifflin, 1980). A useful excerpt and set of commentaries on 'The Human of Tomorrow' can be found in Bloom, 59–63: p. 61.

16. McFadden in conversation with Schwartz. McFadden, *The Serial*, 1–5. *I Want It All Now*. The unaffordability of property in Marin County continues to be an issue. See Bernard Meisler, *There's Never Been a Better Time to Die* (USA: Sensitive Skin Books, 2019). Meisler describes the novel as 'a neo noir meta satire of late-stage capitalism in Marin County'. Travis, 'Marin Valley Biography Night: Jack Travis'.

17. Chafe *et al.*, p. 331. See also: John Phelan, 'The Return of the Misery Index', *American Experiment* (January 2022). Online at: www.americanexperiment.org/the-return-of-the-misery-index/.

18. Louise Hay, *Heal Your Body: The Mental Causes for Physical Illness and the Metaphysical Way to Overcome Them* [1976] (London: Heaven on Earth Books, 1985), 1–5; 31; 35–6. For an overview, commentary and reflection on Hay's work see Mark Oppenheimer, 'Queen of the New Age', *The New York Times Magazine* (4 May 2008). Online at: www.nytimes.com/2008/05/04/magazine/04Hay-t.html. See also 'Affirmations', in Bloom, 179–82. Hay, *You Can Heal Your Life* (Santa Monica: Hay House, 1984). I am grateful to Yvonne Salmon for bringing Hay's *Heal Your Body* to my attention.

19. The information in this section and the quote from George Sternlieb come from Hamnet, 97–98.

20. Aled Davies, '"Right to Buy": The Development of a Conservative Housing Policy, 1945 – 1980', *Contemporary British History*, 27.4 (2013), 421–444: p. 422. For an analysis of Dunbar and the representation of the council estate see, Katie Beswick, *Social Housing in Performance: The English Council Estate On and Off Stage* (London: Bloomsbury, 2020), p. 81.

21. Alan Sillitoe, *Saturday Night and Sunday Morning* (London: W.H. Allen, 1958). *The Long Good Friday* (John Mackenzie, UK, 1980).

22. The full text of the Black Report – *Inequalities in Health* – along with some useful commentary which I have drawn upon for this section, can be found online via the Socialist Health Association: www.scohealth.co.uk/national-health-service/pubic-health-and-wellbeing/poverty-and-inequality/the-black-report-1980/. Pearce Wright, 'Sir Douglas Black', *The Lancet*, 360.9339 (5 October 2002), p. 1103.

23. The details of Travis' living circumstances are from Travis, 'Marin Valley Biography Night: Jack Travis'. Matters of domestic environment are discussed in Travis and Ryan, 41–63; Kabat-Zinn, 43; 122; 132–35.

24. Hay, *Heal Your Body*, 35–6. UK Green Building Council, *Health and Wellbeing in Homes* (London: UK Green Building Council, 2016), p. 4.

25. Jeffrey Eugenides, *The Virgin Suicides* [1993] (London: Bloomsbury, 2002), p. 237.

X The New Age of Enlightenment

1. The information in this section comes from Tim King, 'Gaulish Horrors', *Prospect* (20 December 2001), Theo Tait, 'Gorilla with a Mobile Phone', *London Review of Books*, 29.3 (9 February 2006) and Aubron, 'The Capture of Houellebecq'.

2. The information used here is from two interviews with Panos Cosmatos. Phil Brown, 'Interview: *Beyond the Black Rainbow* Director Panos Cosmatos', *That Shelf* (June 2012) and Amber Wilkinson, 'Retro Rainbow', *Eye For Film* (May 2011). They are online at: www.thatshelf.com/interview-beyond-the-black-rainbow-director-panos-cosmatos/ and www.eyeforfilm.co.uk/feature/2011-05-11-panos-cosmatos-talks-about-beyond-the-black-rainbow-feature-story-by-amber-wilkinson.

3. Tait, 'Gorilla With a Mobile Phone'.

4. Brown and Wilkinson. *Beyond the Black Rainbow* (Panos Cosmatos, US, 2010). At the time of the film's release, various reviewers and interviewers, Brown and Wilkinson among them, mentioned David Cronenberg's early works as a possible influence.

5. Michel Houellebecq, *Atomised*, trans. by Frank Wynne (London: William Heinemann, 2000), 55; 79; 31; 80; 284.

6. Aubron, 'The Capture of Houellebecq'. Aubron describes l'Espace as a 'New Age Purgatory'. Houellebecq, 122–23.

7. *Beyond the Black Rainbow*.

8. For Esalen as 'Cape Canaveral', see Harris, 'Esalen: From 60s Outpost to the Me Generation'. J.G. Ballard, *Memories of the Space Age* (Wisconsin: Arkham House, 1988).

9. Eliot and Breo, 14–17.

10. Fitzgerald, 19–20.

11. *Dreamscape* (Joseph Ruben, US, 1984). *Brainstorm* (Douglas Trumbull, US, 1983). Andrija Puharich, *Uri: A Journal of the Mystery of Uri Geller* (New York: Doubleday, 1974). Sheila Ostrander and Lynn Schroeder, *Psychic Discoveries Behind the Iron Curtain* (New York: Prentice-Hall, 1970). Kripal, p. 316.

12. Aubron, 'The Capture of Houellebecq'.

13. In *Atomised*, the second chapter of 'Strange Moments' is titled 'The Thirteen Hour Flight'. It concludes with a typically acerbic barb about Bangkok, 119–124. Martin J. Göessl, 'The Otto Mühl Commune: Self-Expression, Common Property and Free Sexuality'. This was a paper given at the 2015 conference of the Social Science History Association. Jonathan Margolis, 'The Price of Free Love', *Guardian* (7 October 1999). *Slaves in Paradise* (Madonna Benjamin, UK, 1999).

14. Houellebecq, 118; 125; 80–83; 241–254.

15. Houellebecq, 185–192.

16. Deleuze and Guattari, *Anti-Oedipus*, 1–8. Adam Shatz, 'Desire Was Everywhere', *London Review of Books*, 32.24 (16 December 2010). Online at: www.lrb.co.uk/the-paper/v32/n24.

17. Houellebecq, 119–20.

18. Travis provides an overview of Wellness Associates in Travis and Ryan, 239–41.

19. For the end of est and the start of The Forum, see Haldeman, 'The Return of Werner Erhard'. On Exegesis and Programmes Ltd, see George D. Chryssides, *Historical Dictionary of New Religious Movements* (US: Scarecrow Press, 2012), p. 129. Mike Oldfield, *Changeling: The Autobiography* (London: Virgin, 2007), 1–6. Terry Kirby, 'Caplin "recruited" for therapy cult investigated by police', *The Independent* (12 December 2002).

20. Göessl, 'The Otto Mühl Commune'. Margolis, 'The Price of Free Love'.

21. Marissa Piesman and Marilee Hartley, *The Yuppie Handbook: The State-of-the-Art Handbook for Young Urban Professionals* (New York: Pocket Books, 1984). *Wall Street* (Oliver Stone, US, 1987).

22. For details of the Stanford Research Institute (now SRI International), see: www.sri.com. James Ogilvy, *Many Dimensional Man: Decentralizing Self, Society and the Sacred* (Oxford: Oxford University Press, 1977). Ogilvy sat on the Esalen Board of Trustees until 2018. Curtis, *The Century of the Self Part 3*.

23. Joni Mitchell quoted in Barney Hoskyns, *Hotel California: Singer-Songwriters and Cocaine Cowboys in the LA Canyons, 1967–1976* (London: Harper, 2006), p. 107.

24. Randy Shilts, *And the Band Played On: Politics, People and the AIDS Epidemic* [1987] (London: Souvenir Press, 2011), p. 495. For the idea of AIDS being seen as otherworldly see James Miller, *The Passion of Michel Foucault* [1993] (London: Flamingo, 1993), p. 21. He is citing an early book on the epidemic that refers to a 'strange virus from beyond'. The end of Rajneeshpuram is described in most accounts of Rajneesh, post-1984. The event forms the main focus of *Wild Wild Country*. Palmer provides a useful account (131–32), as does Carter, 160–63. McCormack's *New Republic* article cited earlier is indicative of the Oregonian perspective.

25. Miller, 21–22. Shilts, p. 171. For Rajneesh's view on AIDS, see Palmer, p. 129. The 'Noah's Ark of consciousness' is discussed in Carter, p. 167. Syman, p. 266. I am grateful to Yvonne Salmon for her comments on this section and the opportunity to discuss with her the lecture on AIDS, literary culture and Tony Kushner's *Angels in America* (1991–92) which she delivered at the ADC Theatre Cambridge, in 2013.

26. Goldwag, p. 45; Perry, 131–34.

27. Since its publication *And the Band Played On* has attracted controversy over several issues including its naming of Gaétan Dugas as a potential 'Patient Zero', as well as Shilts' description of some San Franciscan bathhouses being slow to close or otherwise unresponsive in the early period of the epidemic. See Richard A. McKay, 'Patient Zero: The Absence of a Patient's View of the Early North American AIDS Epidemic', *Bulletin of the History of Medicine*, 88.1 (2014), 161–94. For the issues surrounding the public reporting of Foucault's death and AIDS, see Miller, 13–36.

28. Kabat-Zinn, 17; 309–10. Oppenheimer, 'Queen of the New Age'. Hay, *Heal Your Body*, p. 6.

29. *Beyond the Black Rainbow*. Houellebecq, 373; 371; 378–9.

30. Terry and Ardell, p. 4; Travis and Ryan, p. 238. For details of Yoko Ono's sale of Dorinish, see www.dorinish.com/dorinish. In 2007 Rawle offered a brief overview of the (then) contemporary status of Dorinish in his online interview, 'Interview with Sid Rawle (Part 3): Sid, John Lennon and Revolution'.

The Voyage In

1. There are various versions of this material in circulation because Watts delivered this and many other lectures on numerous occasions. The

lecture in question is generally cited as 'The Nature of Consciousness (Part 2)'. *Out of Your Mind: Essential Listening from the Alan Watts Audio Archives* (Sounds True, 2004) contains a very good recording. See also Alan Watts, *Out of Your Mind: Tricksters, Interdependence and the Cosmic Game of Hide-and-Seek* (USA: Souvenir Press, 2018). The recording and transcript cited here can be found at: www.organism. earth/library/document/out-of-your-mind-2.

2. 'Dreams' can be viewed online here: www.bubbletv.co.uk/cunard-dreams. For a brief commentary on the ad and its link to Watts' thought, see Gus Carter, 'The Paradox of Alan Watts', *The Spectator* (8 January 2023).

3. Watts, 'The Nature of Consciousness (Part 2)'.

4. Travis and Ardell, 'A Keynote Interview with Jack Travis and Don Ardell'. Žižek, *Living in the End Times* (London: Verso, 2011), 78–9. Žižek is discussing John Frankenheimer's film *Seconds* (1966) in the context of a much wider analysis of contemporary left-wing politics and the concept of 'revolution'.

5. Examples of insincere and disingenuous versions of this question abound in the media and online. They are simply too numerous to mention. At the time of writing, however, the one that sticks in the mind is Holly Willoughby's 'Firstly, are you ok?' speech on that bastion of benevolence, ITV's *This Morning* (5 June 2023). For a digest of the many responses it generated, see: www.independent.co.uk/arts-entertainment/tv/news/holly-willoughby-this-morning-speech-reaction-b2352084.htm.

Bibliography

I. Books and Articles

Anon., 'Anti-University Announces Courses', *International Times* 24 (19 January – 1 February 1968)

_____, 'IF YOU'RE NOT A DIGGER YOU'RE PROPERTY' (San Francisco: Communication Company, 1967)

_____, 'The Time Has Come to Be Fee' (San Francisco: Communications Company, 1967)

_____, 'Patty Hearst's Chief Captor Emerges as a Man Capable of Love and Violence', *The Danville Register* (14 April 1974)

_____, 'Spaghetti Dinner – Free' (San Francisco: Communications Company, 1967)

_____, 'Zucchini Feast Eat Free' (San Francisco: SF Communication Company, 1967)

Alesina, Alberto, *et al.*, 'Work and Leisure in the United States and Europe: Why So Different?', *NBER Macroeconomics Annual* 20 (2005)

Altekruse, Joan M., 'Interview: Henrik L. Blum, MD, MPH', *Family & Community Health* 8.4 (1986)

American Psychiatric Association, The, *DSM II: Diagnostic and Statistical Manual of Mental Disorders* (Washington: American Psychiatric Association, 1968)

Andersen, Kurt, 'How America Lost its Mind', *The Atlantic* (September 2017)

Anderson, Chester, 'if you're not a digger' (San Francisco: Communications Company, 1967)

Anderson, Joseph, D., 'Human Relations Training and Group Work', *Social Work* 20. 3 (May 1975)

Anderson, Walter Truett, *The Upstart Spring. Esalen and the Human Potential Movement: The First Twenty Years* [1983] (Lincoln: iUniverse, 2004)

Anson, Jay, *The Amityville Horror* (New York: Prentice Hall, 1979)

Apollonius of Rhodes, *The Voyage of Argo: The Argonautica*, trans. by E.V. Rieu (Harmondsworth: Penguin, 2006)

Ardell, Donald, B., 'Meet John Travis, Doctor of Well-Being', *Prevention* (April 1975)

_____, *High Level Wellness: An Alternative to Doctors, Drugs and Disease* (USA: Rodale Press, 1977)

Arnott, Jake, *The Long Firm* (London: Hodder and Stoughton, 1999)

Aubron, Hervé, 'Capture of Houellebecq', *Libération* (August 14, 1999)

Ayers, Susan, *et al.* (eds.), *The Cambridge Handbook of Psychology, Health and Medicine* (Cambridge: Cambridge University Press, 2007)

Ballard, J.G., *The Terminal Beach* (Great Britain: Gollancz, 1964)

_____, *Memories of the Space Age* (USA: Arkham House, 1988)

_____, *The Atrocity Exhibition* [1970] (London: HarperPerennial, 2006)

_____, *High Rise* [1975] (London: Flamingo, 2003)

Barry, Kevin, *Beatlebone* (Great Britain: Canongate, 2015)

Bassett, Mary T., 'Beyond Berets: The Black Panthers as Health Activists', *American Journal of Public Health* 106.10 (October 2016)

Battan, Jesse, F., 'The "New Narcissism" in 20th-Century America: The Shadow and Substance of Social Change', *Journal of Social History* 17.2 (Winter, 1983)

Baudrillard, Jean, *Simulacra and Simulation* [1994] trans. by Sheila Faria Glaser (USA: University of Michigan Press, 1994)

_____, *The Transparency of Evil: Essays on Extreme Phenomena* [1990] trans. by James Benedict (London: Verso, 1993)

Bax, Martin, *The Hospital Ship* [1976] (London: Picador, 1977)

Bax, Martin, and Judy Bernal, *Your Child's First Five Years* (London: Butterworth-Heinemann, 1974)

Baym, Nina *et al.*, (eds.), *The Norton Anthology of American Literature: Literature Since 1945* (New York: W.W. Norton and Company, 2003)

Bean, Orson, 'Growing (Up) at Thirty-Seven', *New York Times* (15 February 1976)

Beauchamp, Gorman, 'Aldous Huxley's Psychedelic Utopia', *Utopian Studies* 1.1 (1990)

Berne, Eric, *Games People Play: The Psychology of Human Relationships* [1964] (Harmondsworth: Penguin, 1967)

Berke, Joseph, *Counterculture: The Creation of an Alternative Society* (London: Fire, 1969)

Berkeley-Oakland Woman's Union, The, 'The Berkeley-Oakland Women's Union Statement: Principals of Unity', *Socialist Revolution* 4.1 (January-March 1974)

Bernstein, Carl and Bob Woodward, *All The President's Men* (London: Quartet, 1974)

Berry, Lauryn, 'The residents of the Sky Pool's complex are paying a fortune to heat it over winter', *Time Out* (4 January 2022)

Beswick, Katie, *Social Housing in Performance: The English Council Estate On and Off Stage* (London: Bloomsbury, 2020)

Beveridge, William, *Social Insurance and Allied Services* (London: H.M. Stationary Office, 1942)

_____, *Pillars of Security and Other War-Time Essays and Addresses* [1943] (London: Routledge, 2014)

_____, *Full Employment in a Free Society: A Report* [1944] (London: Routledge, 2014)

Black, Lawrence, *et al.* (eds.), *Reassessing 1970s Britain* (Manchester: Manchester University Press, 2013)

Blake, William, *The Complete Poems*, ed. by Alicia Ostriker (Harmondsworth: Penguin, 1977)

Blaney, John, *John Lennon: Listen to this Book* (Guilford: The Paper Jukebox, 2005)

Blatty, William Peter, *The Exorcist* (New York: Harper and Row, 1971)

Bloom, William (ed.), *The Penguin Book of New Age and Holistic Writing* (Harmondsworth: Penguin, 2000)

Boseley, Sarah, 'Gwyneth Paltrow's Goop wellness products condemned by NHS chief', *Guardian* (30 January 2020)

Brahinsky, Rachel and Alexander Tarr, *A People's Guide to the San Francisco Bay Area* (Berkeley: University of California Press, 2020)

Brand, Stewart (ed.), *The Whole Earth Catalogue: Access to Tools* (Fall 1968)

Brann, Les R., and Sally A. Guzvica, 'Comparison of Hypnosis with Conventional Relaxation for Antenatal and Intrapartum Use: A Feasibility Study in General Practice', *Journal of the Royal College of General Practitioners* 37 (1987)

Breen, Benjamin, 'In the Mystic', *Aeon* (April 2015)

Brewer, Mark, 'We're Gonna Tear You Down and Put You Back Together', *Psychology Today* (August 1975)

Briggs, Kenneth A., 'New Religious Movements Considered Likely to Last', *New York Times* (22 June 1977)

Brittan, Samuel, 'The Economic Contradictions of Democracy', *British Journal of Political Science* 5.2 (April 1975)

_____, 'How English is the English Sickness?', *Il Politico* 44.4 (December 1979)

Bromberg, Joan Lisa, *NASA and the Space Industry* (USA: Johns Hopkins University Press, 2000)

Brooke, Tal, *Lord of the Air: Tales of a Modern Antichrist* (Oxford: Lion Publishing, 1976)

Brown, David Jay and Rebecca McClen Novick, *Mavericks of the Mind* [1993] (USA: MAPS, 2010)

Brown, Phil, 'Interview: *Beyond the Black Rainbow* Director Panos Cosmatos', *That Shelf* (June 2012)

Brown, Shelina, 'Scream from the Heart: Yoko Ono's Rock and Roll Revolution, *Volume!* 9.2 (2012)

Bugliosi, Vincent and Curt Gentry, *Helter Skelter* (New York: W.W. Norton, 1974)

Burkeman, Oliver, 'Review: *The Power Broker*', *Guardian* (23 October 2015)

Burroughs, William, *Nova Express* (New York: Grove, 1964)

Carmichael, Stokely and Charles V. Hamilton, *Black Power: The Politics of Liberation* (New York: Random House, 1967)

Carr, Gordon, *The Angry Brigade* (Oakland: PM Press, 2010)

Carpenter, Ele and Graham Gussin, *Nothing* (Great Britain: Northern Gallery for Contemporary Arts, 2001)

Carter, Diana, *Mind-Out* (New York: Pinnacle, 1973)

Carter, Lewis, F., 'The "New Renunciates" of the Bhagwan Shree Rajneesh: Observations and Identification of Problems of Interpreting New Religious Movements', *Journal for the Scientific Study of Religion* 26. 2 (June 1987)

Carter, Gus, 'The Paradox of Alan Watts', *The Spectator* (8 January 2023)

Carter, Jimmy, 'Inaugural Address: Thursday January 20, 1977', *Inaugural Addresses of the Presidents of the United States*, vol. 2 (USA: Applewood Books, 2001)

Cahalan, Don and Beatrice Treiman, Drinking Behavior, *Attitudes and Problems in Marin County* (Emeryville: Alcohol Research Group, 1976)

Capps, Kriston, 'This Swimming Pool in the Sky is the Ultimate Symbol of London's Affordability Crisis', *Bloomberg News* (25 November 2020)

Caro, Robert, *The Power Broker: Robert Moses and the Fall of New York* (New York: Knopf, 1974)

Julia Cassaniti, 'Memory, Ghosts and the Good Life: Sati in Theravada Cultural Contexts', *Anthropology Today* 38.2 (April 2022)

Cécile, Thibaud, 'Le camping new age, le maire et l'écrivain', *L'Express* (10 September 1998)

Chayefsky, Paddy, *Altered States* [1978] (Great Britain: Corgi, 1978)

Chafe, William (ed.), *A History of Our Time: Readings on Postwar America* (Oxford: Oxford University Press, 2008)

Chryssides, George D., *Historical Dictionary of New Religious Movements* (US: Scarecrow Press, 2012)

Church, Gene and Conrad D. Carnes, *The Pit: A Group Encounter Defiled* (New York: Outerbridge and Lazard, Inc., 1972)

Clance, Pauline Rose and Suzanne Imes, 'The Imposter Phenomenon in High Achieving Women: Dynamics and Therapeutic Intervention', *Psychotherapy Theory, Research and Practice* 15. 3 (Fall 1978)

Clark, Jean, 'In at the Start: Early Experiences of the Emerging
Counselling Profession in the 1970s', *Self & Society* 43.3 (2015)

Cohen, Richard, 'Carter's New Theme No Sudden Inspiration', *The
Washington Post* (19 July 1979)

Colburn, H.N., and P. M. Baker, 'Health Hazard Appraisal: A Possible
Tool in Health Protection and Promotion', *Canadian Journal of Public
Health* 64.5 (1973)

Coleman, Ray, *Lennon: The Definitive Biography* (New York: Harper
Perennial, 1999)

Coffey, Helen, 'Goop Launched Wellness Cruise Experience', *The
Independent* (13 January 2020)

Comfort, Alex, *The Joy of Sex* (New York: Crown, 1972)

Condon, Richard, *The Manchurian Candidate* (New York: McGraw Hill,
1962)

Cook, Joanna, 'Mindfulness and Culture: An Introduction', *Anthropology
Today* 38.2 (April 2022)

Cook, Robin, *Year of the Intern* (New York: Harcourt Brace, 1973)

_____, *Coma* (New York: Little, Brown and Company, 1977)

Cooper, David (ed.), *The Dialectics of Liberation* (Harmondsworth:
Penguin, 1968)

Cost, Ben, 'Scary, transparent Sky Pool gets a big "No" from detractors',
New York Post (2 June 2021)

Corns, Thomas N., *et al.*, (eds.), *The Complete Works of Gerrard
Winstanley* (Oxford: Oxford University Press, 2009)

Cresse, Andrew, 'Health is Wealth, but Also Wealth is Health', *World
Health* (November-December 1992)

Cush, Denise, *et al.* (eds.), *Encyclopedia of Hinduism* (London: Routledge,
2008)

Cunningham, David, *Klansville, U.S.A: The Rise and Fall of the Civil
Rights-Era Ku Klux Klan* (Oxford: Oxford University Press, 2013)

Dass, Ram, *Be Here Now* (New Mexico: Lama Foundation, 1971)

_____, 'Egg on My Beard', *Yoga Journal* 11 (November-December 1976)

Daddis, Gregory A., *Withdrawal: Assessing America's Final Years in
Vietnam* (Oxford: Oxford University Press, 2017)

Davis, A.R., '"Right to Buy": The Development of a Conservative Housing
Policy, 1945 – 1980', *Contemporary British History* 27.4 (2013)

Davies, Adele, *Let's Eat Right to Keep Fit* (New York: Harcourt Brace,
1954)

Davis, Erik, *High Weirdness: Drugs, Esoterica and Visionary Experience in
the Seventies* (London: Strange Attractor, 2019)

Davis, Gwen, *Touching* (London: WH Allen, 1971)

De Graaf, John, *et al.*, *Affluenza: The All-Consuming Epidemic* (New York: McGraw-Hill, 2002)

Deighton, Len, *The IPCRESS File* (London: Hodder & Stoughton, 1962)

Delamothe, Tony, 'Founding Principles', *British Medical Journal* 336 (May 2008)

Deleuze, Gilles and Félix Guattari, *Anti-Oedipus: Capitalism and Schizophrenia Part I* [1972] trans. by Robert Hurley *et al.* (USA: University of Minnesota Press, 1983)

_____, *A Thousand Plateaus: Capitalism and Schizophrenia Part 2*, [1980] trans. by Brian Massumi (London: Continuum, 2004)

Dickey, Jack, 'Save the American Vacation', *Time* (May 2015)

Dixon, Marlene, 'The Rise and Demise of Women's Liberation: A Class Analysis', *Synthesis* 2.1/2 (Summer-Fall 1977)

O'Doherty, Brian, *Inside the White Cube: The Ideology of the Gallery Space* (San Francisco: Lapis Press, 1986)

Doggett, Peter, *The Art and Music of John Lennon* (London: Omnibus Press, 2009)

Donne, John, *Dedications Upon Emergent Occasions and Death's Duel* (London: Vintage, 1999)

Dowling, Colette, 'Confessions of an American Guru', *The New York Times* (4 December 1977)

Drescher, Jack, 'Out of DSM: Depathologizing Homosexuality', *Behavioral Sciences* 5.4 (December 2015)

Druckerman, Pamela, 'How the Mid-Life Crisis Came to Be', *The Atlantic* (May 2018)

Drury, Nevill, *Shamanism* (Dorset: Element Books, 1989)

_____, *Human Potential* (Dorset: Element Books, 1989)

Du Maurier, George, *Trilby* (London: Osgood, McIlvaine and Company, 1895)

Dunn, Halbert L., 'Points of Attack for Raising the Levels of Wellness', *Journal of the National Medical Association* 49.4 (July 1957)

_____, 'High-Level Wellness for Man and Society', *American Journal of Public Health* 49.6 (1959)

_____, 'What High-Level Wellness Means', *Canadian Journal of Public Health* 50.11 (1959)

_____, *High-Level Wellness* (Arlington, Virginia: E.W. Beatty, 1961)

Dwyer, Simon, *Rapid Eye Movement* (London: Creation, 1999)

Edgar, Brian and Paul Williams, 'American Healing: Primal therapy, Rebirthing, and Cathartic Encounters in 1970s London (and beyond)', *Journal of Transatlantic Studies* 19.1 (April 2021)

_____, 'Up Against the Wall: Primal Therapy and 'The Sixties'', *European Journal of American Studies* 3.2 (2008)

Effross, Walter, 'Owning Enlightenment: Proprietary Spirituality in the "New Age" Marketplace', *Buffalo Law Review* 51.3 (2003)

Ekwall, Eilert, 'Early Names of Britain', *Antiquity* 4.14 (June 1930)

Ellis, Bret Easton, *Less Than Zero* (London: Picador, 2011)

_____, *American Psycho* (New York: Vintage, 1991)

Eliot, Robert and Dennis L. Breo, *Is It Worth Dying For? How to Make Stress Work For You Not Against You* (New York: Bantam, 1984)

Emerson, Edward Waldo, *The Complete Works of Ralph Waldo Emerson* (New York: Houghton Mifflin, 1904)

Enroth, Ronald, *Youth, Brainwashing and the Extremist Cults* (Michigan: Zondervan, 1977)

Enroth, Ronald (ed.), *A Guide to Cults and New Religions* (Illinois: Inter-Varsity Press, 1983)

Eugenides, Jeffrey, *The Virgin Suicides* [1993] (London: Bloomsbury, 2002)

Fanon, Frantz, *Black Skin, White Masks* [1956] trans. by Charles Lam Markmann (London: Pluto Press, 1986)

_____, *The Wretched of the Earth* [1961] trans. by Constance Farrington (New York: Grove Press, 1963)

Fabian, Jenny, *A Chemical Romance* [1971] (London: Do Not Press, 1998)

Fair, Sharon Elayne, *Wellness and Physical Therapy* (Massachusetts, Jones and Bartlett, 2011)

Farmer, Philip José, *The Image of the Beast. An Exorcism: Ritual One* [1968] (London: Quartet, 1975)

Feldberg, Tom, 'Quaesitor — How Humanistic Therapy Got Going in Britain. Tom Feldberg interviewed by David Jones', *Self & Society* 24.4 (September 1996)

_____, 'How Humanistic Psychology Started in Europe...and How It Might End!: The Story of Quaesitor', *Self & Society* 40.4 (Summer 2013)

Ferguson, Marilyn, *The Aquarian Conspiracy: Personal and Social Transformation in the 1980s* (Great Britain: Routledge & Kegan Paul)

Finney, Jack, *Invasion of the Body Snatchers* (New York: Dell, 1955)

Fitzgerald, Frances, *Way Out There in the Blue: Reagan, Star Wars and the End of the Cold War* (New York: Simon & Schuster, 2000)

Flanagan, Caitlin, 'Girl, Interrupted', *The Atlantic* (September 2008)

Ford, Simon, *Wreckers of Civilization: The Story of Coum Transmissions and Throbbing Gristle* (London: Black Dog, 1999)

Foster, Roger, 'The Therapeutic Spirit of Neoliberalism', *Political Theory* 44.1 (February 2016)

Foucault, Michel, *Madness and Civilization* [1961] trans. by Richard Howard (London: Routledge, 1989)

_____, *The Birth of the Clinic: An Archaeology of Medical Perception* [1963] trans. by Alan Sheridan (London: Routledge, 1989)

_____, *The Order of Things: An Archaeology of the Human Sciences* [1966] trans. by Alan Sheridan (London: Tavistock Publications, 1970)

_____, *The History of Sexuality Volume 1: An Introduction* [1976] trans. by Robert Hurley (Harmondsworth: Penguin, 1978)

_____, *The History of Sexuality Volume 3: Care of the Self* [1984] trans. by Robert Hurley (New York: Vintage, 1988)

_____, *Remarks on Marx: Conversations with Duccio Trombadori* trans. by R. James Goldstein and James Cascaito (New York: SEMIOTEXT(E), 1981)

Foucault, Michel and Richard Sennett, 'Sexuality and Solitude', *London Review of Books* 3.9 (May 1981)

Frater, Alexander, 'New Cult for the Over-Adjusted', *The Daily Telegraph Magazine* 220 (December 1968)

Freedland, Nat, *The Occult Explosion in America* (London: Michael Joseph, 1972)

Freeman, Hadley, 'Green is the new black: the unstoppable rise of the healthy-eating guru', *Guardian* (27 June 2015).

French, Karl and Philip French, *Cult Movies* (Great Britain: Pavilion Books, 1999)

Frey, William H., 'Black In-Migration, White Flight, and the Changing Economic Base of the Central City', *American Journal of Sociology* 85.6 (1980)

Friedan, Betty, *The Feminine Mystique* [1963] (Harmondsworth: Penguin, 2010)

Fromm, Erich, *The Pathology of Normalcy* (New York: Lantern Books, 2011)

_____, *The Art of Being* (London: Constable, 1993)

Gaddis, John Lewis, *The Cold War* (Great Britain: Penguin, 2005)

Gaddis, Vincent, 'The New Science of Space Speech', *Worlds of Tomorrow* 1.3 (August 1963)

Galante, Julieta, *et al.*, 'A mindfulness-based intervention to increase resilience to stress in university students (the Mindful Student Study): a pragmatic randomised controlled trial', *Lancet Public Health* 3 (2018)

Gane, Mike and Terry Johnson (eds.), *Foucault's New Domains* (London: Routledge, 2013)

Garsten, Christina and Adrienne Sörbom, 'The Magic of Davos', *Anthropology Today: Capitalism & Magic* 32.6 (2016)

Gee, Pauline, 'Ensuring Police Protection for Battered Women: The *Scott v. Hart* Suit', *Signs* 8.3 (1983)

Germaine Greer, *The Female Eunuch* [1971] (London: Harper, 2006)

Glass, Andrew, 'Congress bans airing cigarette ads, April 1, 1970', *Politico* (January 2018)

Global Wellness Institute, The, *The Global Wellness Institute: Looking Beyond COVID* (Miami: GWI, 2021)

Goldberg, Danny, *In Search of the Lost Chord: 1967 and the Hippie Idea* (London: Icon, 2017)

Goldman, Marion, *The American Soul Rush: Esalen and the Rise of Spiritual Priveledge* (New York: New York University Press, 2012)

Goldstein, Kurt, *The Organism* (New York: American Book Company, 1939)

Goldwag, Arthur, *Cults, Conspiracies & Secret Societies* (USA: Vintage, 2009)

Goodson, Aileen, *Experiment in Nude Psychotherapy: Confrontation with Group Nudity* (Los Angeles: Elysium, 1967)

Gosling, David L., 'Christian Response within Hinduism', *Religious Studies* 10. 4 (December 1974)

Gough, Ian, 'Thatcherism and the Welfare State: Britain is experiencing the most far-reaching experiment in "new right" politics in the western world', *Marxism Today* (July 1980)

Green, Malcolm (ed.), *Writings of the Vienna Actionists* (London: Atlas Press, 1999)

Gregory, Richard L., (ed.) *The Oxford Companion to the Mind* (Oxford: Oxford University Press, 1987)

Grier, William H., and Price Cobbs, *Black Rage* (New York: Basic Books, 1968)

Griffin, Jo, *The Lonely Society?* (London: Mental Health Foundation, 2010)

Griffiths, Robert and Paula Baker (eds.), *Major Problems in American History Since 1945* (Boston: Houghton Mifflin, 2001)

Grogan, Emmett, 'Term Paper: The Relationship Between Poetry and Revolution Has Lost its Ambiguity' (San Francisco: Communication Company, 1967)

Grossman, Lev, 'Invasion of the Body Snatchers Snatchers', *Time* (14 June 2007)

Guite, Malcolm, *Mariner: A Voyage with Samuel Taylor Coleridge* (London: Hodder and Stoughton, 2017)

Gunther, Bernie, *Sense Relaxation* (London: Macdonald, 1969)

Haas, Charlie, 'Goodbye to the Seventies', *New West* 4. 3 (January 1979)

Hafner, Katie and Matthew Lyon, *Where Wizards Stay Up Late: The Origins of the Internet* (New York, Simon and Schuster, 1996)

Haldeman, Peter, 'The Return of Werner Erhard, Father of Self-Help', *The New York Times* (29 November 2015)

Hamilton, James, *Postpartum Psychiatric Problems* (St. Louis: The C.V. Mosby Company, 1962)

Hamnett, Chris, 'Regional Variations in House Prices and House Price Inflation 1969-81', *Area* 15.2 (1983)

Harden, Blaine, 'Verdict Mixed on "Sleep Tapes", But Supplier is Getting Rich', *The Washington Post* (27 December 1979)

Hardie, Brandan, 'The Past, Present, and Future of the Wellness Movement: An Interview with Dr. Bill Hettler', *The Art of Health Promotion* (May – June 2015)

Harris, Art, 'Esalen: From 60s Outpost to the Me Generation', *Washington Post* (24 September 1978)

Hatton, Timothy J., and George R. Boyer, 'Unemployment and the UK Labour Market Before, During and After the Golden Age', *European Review of Economic History* 9.1 (April 2005)

Hawhee, Debra, *Bodily Arts: Rhetoric and Athletics in Ancient Greece* (Austin: University of Texas Press, 2004)

Hay, Louise, *Heal Your Body: The Mental Causes for Physical Illness and the Metaphysical Way to Overcome Them* [1976] (London: Heaven on Earth Books, 1985)

_____, *You Can Heal Your Life* (Santa Monica: Hay House, 1984)

Heron, John, 'Holism and Collegiality', *Self and Society* 29.2 (June-July 2001)

_____, 'My Early Engagement with Humanistic Psychology', *Self & Society* 40.1 (Autumn 2012)

Hettler, Bill, *et al.*, 'Wellness Promotion on a University Campus', *Family and Community Health* 3.1 (May 1980)

Hewison, Robert, *Too Much: Art and Society in the Sixties, 1960-1975* (Oxford: Oxford University Press, 1987)

Hilliard, David (ed.), *The Black Panther Party: Service to the People Programs* (Albuquerque: University of New Mexico Press, 2008)

Hills, Christopher, *Nuclear Evolution* (London: Centre Community Publications, 1968)

Hills, John, 'Thatcherism, New Labour and the Welfare State', *Centre for the Analysis of Social Exclusion* CASE Paper 13 (August 1998)

Holloman, Regina E., 'Ritual Opening and Individual Transformation: Rites of Passage at Esalen', *American Anthropologist* 76 (1974)

Howard, Jane, 'Year of the Guru', *Life* (9 February 1968)

_____, *Please Touch: A Guided Tour of the Human Potential Movement* (New York: Dell, 1970)

Home, Stewart, *The Assault on Culture: Utopian Currents from Lettrisme to Class War* (Stirling: AK Press, 1991)

Homer, *The Odyssey*, trans. by E.V. Rieu (Harmondsworth: Penguin, 2003)

Horovitz, Michael (ed.), *Children of Albion: Poetry of the Underground in Britain* (Harmondsworth: Penguin, 1969)

Hoskyns, Barney, *Waiting for the Sun: Strange Days, Weird Scenes and the Sound of Los Angeles* (USA: St. Martin's Press, 1996)

_____, *Hotel California: Singer-Songwriters and Cocaine Cowboys in the LA Canyons, 1967-1976* (London: Fourth Estate, 2005)

Houellebecq, Michel, *Atomised* [1998] trans. by Frank Wynne (London: Heinemann, 2000)

Hunt, Dave, *The Cult Explosion: An Overview of Today's Cults and Why They Prosper* (Oregon: Harvest House, 1980)

Huxley, Aldous, *Brave New World* [1932] (London: Vintage, 2007)

_____, *The Doors of Perception and Heaven and Hell* [1956] (London: Granada, 1977)

_____, *Island* [1962] (London: Vintage, 2008)

Hyde, Marina, 'Gwyneth's Ark: Sailing towards wellness but never quite getting there' *Guardian* (30 April 2021)

Illich, Ivan, *Medical Nemesis* (New York: Pantheon Books, 1976)

Ingersoll, Robert Green, *The Works of Robert Green Ingersoll* [1901] (New York: Cosimo Incorporated, 2009)

Ingram, Matthew, *Retreat: How the Counterculture Invented Wellness* (London: Repeater, 2020)

Institute of Medicine, *Secondhand Smoke Exposure and Cardiovascular Effects: Making Sense of the Evidence* (Washington: The National Academies Press, 2010)

Jahrmarkt, Billy, *et al.*, *Free City News* (San Francisco: Free City Collective, 1967)

James, Muriel and Dorothy Jongeward, *Born to Win* (USA: Addison-Wesley, 1971)

Janov, Arthur, *The Primal Scream* [1970] (London: Abacus, 1973)

_____, *The Primal Revolution* [1972] (London: Abacus, 1975)

Jones, Michael Owen, 'Herbs and Saints in the City of Angels: Researching Botánicas, Healing, and Power in Southern California', *The Journal of American Folklore* 133. 527 (Winter 2020)

Jones, Charles E., (ed.), *The Black Panther Party Reconsidered* (Baltimore: Black Classic Press, 1998)

Jones, Robert, 'Hippie: The Philosophy of a Subculture', *Time* (July 1967)

Jones, W. Penn, *Forgive My Grief: A Critical Review of the Warren Commission Report on the Assassination* (Midlothian: Midlothian Mirror, 1966)

Jong, Erica, *Fear of Flying* (New York: Holt, Rinehart and Winston, 1973)

Jung, C.G., *Dreams* [1974] trans. by R.F.C. Hull (Routledge: London, 2002)

Kabat-Zinn, Jon, *Full Catastrophe Living: Using the Wisdom of Your Body and Mind to Face Stress, Pain and Illness* (New York: Delta, 1990)

Kaiser, David and W. Patrick McCray (eds.), *Groovy Scientists: Knowledge, Innovation and the American Counterculture* (Chicago: Chicago University Press, 2016)

Kaur, Rajender and Anupama Arora (eds.), *India in the American Imaginary, 1780s-1880s* (London: Palgrave Macmillan, 2017)

Kane, Martin, 'An Assessment of "Black is Best"', *Sports Illustrated* (January 1971)

Kantor, Isaac, 'Ethnic Cleansing and America's Creation of National Parks', *Public Land and Resources Law Review* 28.41 (2007)

Kennaway, James, *The Mind Benders: A Novel of Suspense* (London: Longmans, 1963)

Kerr, Gordon, *A Short History of the Vietnam War* (Harpenden: Oldcastle, 2015)

Keys, Barbara, *et al.*, 'The Post-Traumatic Decade: New Histories of the 1970s', *Australasian Journal of American Studies* 33.1 (July 2014)

Killaspy, Helen, 'From the Asylum to Community Care: Learning from Experience', *British Medical Bulletin* 79-80.1 (June 2006)

King, Raymond E., *et al*, *Use of Personality Assessment Measures in the Selection of Air Traffic Control Specialists* (Washington: Office of Aerospace Medicine, 2003)

King, Tim, 'Gaulish Horrors', *Prospect* (20 December 2001)

Kirby, Terry, 'Caplin "recruited" for therapy cult investigated by police', *The Independent* (12 December 2002)

Kirkland, Anna, 'What Is Wellness Now?', *Journal of Health Politics, Policy and Law* 39.5 (October 2014)

Kirkpatrick, Betty (ed.), *Brewer's Concise Dictionary of Phrase and Fable* (London: Cassell, 1992)

Kirsch, Adam, 'Utopian Pessimist', *The New Yorker* (October 10, 2011)

Klein, Michael, 'Making Waves', *The Philadelphia Inquirer* (18 March 2007)

Kripal, Jeffrey, J., *Esalen: American and the Religion of No Religion* (USA: University of Chicago Press, 2007)

Kripal, Jeffrey J., and Glenn W. Shuck, *On the Edge of the Future: Esalen and the Evolution of American Culture* (Bloomington: Indiana University Press, 2005)

Kureishi, Hanif, *The Buddha of Suburbia* (London: Faber and Faber, 1990)

Laing, R. D., *The Divided Self* (Harmondsworth: Penguin, 1967)

_____, *The Politics of Experience and the Bird of Paradise* (Harmondsworth: Penguin, 1967)

Lappé, Frances Moore, *Diet for a Small Planet* (New York: Ballantine, 1971)

Lalonde, Marc, *A New Perspective on the Health of Canadians* (Ottawa: Health Canada, 1974)

Lasch, 'The Narcissist Society', *The New York Review of Books* (30 September 1976)

_____, *The Culture of Narcissism: American Life in an Age of Diminishing Expectations* (New York: W.W. Norton and Company, 1979)

Lee, Choonib, 'Women's Liberation and Sixties Armed Resistance', *Journal for the Study of Radicalism* 11. 1 (2017)

Lee, Martin A., and Bruce Shlain, *Acid Dreams: The Complete Social History of LSD, the CIA, the Sixties and Beyond* (London: Pan, 2001)

Leigh, Mike, 'Mike Leigh on *Abigail's Party* at 40', *Guardian* (24 February 2017)

Leitch, Vincent B., *et al.*, *The Norton Anthology of Theory and Criticism* (New York: W. W. Norton and Company, 2001)

Lem, Stanislaw, *Solaris* [1961] trans. Joanna Kilmartin and Steve Cox (London: Faber and Faber, 2003)

Lickorish, Leonard, and Victor T.C. Middleton, *British Tourism: The Remarkable Story of Growth* (Oxford: Elsevier: 2005)

Lilla, Mark, 'The Tyrant of the Commune', *The New York Review of Books* (7 August 2013)

Lilly, John C., *The Centre of the Cyclone: An Autobiography of Inner Space* [1972] (Great Britain: Paladin, 1972)

_____, *The Scientist: A Novel Autobiography* (Lippincott: Philadelphia, 1978)

_____, *The Deep Self: Profound Relaxation and the Tank Isolation Technique* (New York: Warner Books, 1978)

Lindahl, J.R., *et al.*, 'A Phenomenology of Meditation-Induced Light Experiences: Traditional Buddhist and Neurobiological Perspectives', *Frontiers in Psychology* 4. 973 (2014)

Lodge, David, *Changing Places: A Tale of Two Campuses* (London: Secker and Warburg, 1975)

Loomis, E.G., 'Meadowlark: A Healing and Growth Experience, *Reflections: Narratives of Professional Helping*, 3.1 (2014)

Lovelock, James, *Gaia: A New Look at Life on Earth* (Oxford: Oxford University Press, 2000)

Lucia, Amanda, 'Innovative Gurus: Tradition and Change in Contemporary Hinduism', *International Journal of Hindu Studies* 18.2 (August 2014)

Lyotard, Jean-François, *Libidinal Economy* [1974] trans. by Ian Hamilton Grant (Bloomington: University of Indiana Press, 1993)

_____, *The Postmodern Condition: A Report on Knowledge* [1979] trans. by Geoffrey Bennington and Brian Massumi (Manchester: Manchester University Press, 1984)

MacDonald, Ian, *Revolution in the Head: The Beatles' Records and the Sixties* (London: Pimlico, 1995)

Mack, Joanna and Stewart Lansley, *Poor Britain* (London: George Allen and Unwin, 1985)

Maher, E., 'An Outsider's View of Modern Ireland: Michel Houellebecq's *Atomised*', *Studies: An Irish Quarterly Review* 92.365 (Spring, 2003)

Mander, Anica Vesel and Annie Kent Rush, *Feminism as Therapy* (New York, Random House, 1974)

Manley, Marc *et al.*, 'Health Promotion Contrarians: Luther Terry, Halbert L. Dunn, Robert F. Allen, and Edward M. Kennedy', *The Art of Health Promotion* (November – December 2015)

Mann, Thomas, *The Magic Mountain* [1924] (Berlin: Woolf Haus, 2020)

Marcus, Josh, 'Amazon's new "AmaZen" booths are a spiritually dark solution for late capitalism', *The Independent* (27 May 2021)

Marcuse, Herbert, *One Dimensional Man* (New York: Beacon Press, 1964)

Marham, Patrick, *Trail of Havoc: In the Steps of Lord Lucan* (Harmondsworth: Penguin, 1988)

Marin, Peter, 'The New Narcissism', *Harper's* (October 1975)

Marks, John D., *The Search for the Manchurian Candidate* (New York: Dell, 1978)

Margolis, Jonathan, 'The Price of Free Love', *Guardian* (7 October 1999)

Marwick, Arthur, *British Society Since 1945* (London: Penguin, 1990)

Marx, Karl, *Capital: A Critique of Political Economy* [1867] trans. by Ben Fowkes (London: New Left Review, 1976)

_____, *Economic and Philosophic Manuscripts of 1844* trans. by Martin Milligan (New York: Prometheus Books, 2009)

Maslow, Abraham, 'A Theory of Human Motivation', *Psychological Review* 50 (1943)

_____, 'Eupsychia: The Good Society', *Journal of Humanistic Psychology*, 1.2 (1961)

_____, *Toward a Psychology of Being* (New York: D. Van Nostrand, 1962)

Maslow, *Eupsychian Management: A Journal* (USA: Irwin-Dorsey, 1965)

May, John, 'Sid Rawle Obituary', *Guardian* (15 September 2010)

McCormack, Win, 'Outside the Limits of the Human Imagination', *The New Republic* (March 27, 2018)

McFadden, Cyra, *The Serial: A Year in the Life of Marin County* [1976-77] (London: Prion Books, 2000)

McGuffin, John, *The Guineapigs* (Harmondsworth: Penguin, 1974)

McKay, Richard A., 'Patient Zero: The Absence of a Patient's View of the Early North American AIDS Epidemic', *Bulletin of the History of Medicine* 88.1 (2014)

McLaughlin, Neil, 'Origin Myths in the Social Sciences: Fromm, the Frankfurt School and the Emergence of Critical Theory', *The Canadian Journal of Sociology* 24.1 (1999)

McLellan, Vin and Paul Avery, *The Voices of the Guns* (New York: G.P. Putnam's, 1977)

McLuhan, Marshall, *The Gutenberg Galaxy* (Canada: University of Toronto Press, 1962)

McLuhan, Marshall and Quentin Fiore, *The Medium is the Massage: An Inventory of Effects* (Harmondsworth: Penguin, 1967)

Meadows, Donella H., *et al.*, *The Limits to Growth* (USA: Potomac Associates, 1972)

Meisler, Bernard, *There's Never Been a Better Time to Die* (USA: Sensitive Skin Books, 2019)

Mendes, Kaitlynn, '"Feminism rules! Now, where's my swimsuit?" Re-Evaluating Feminist Discourse in Print Media 1968–2008', *Media, Culture & Society* 34.5 (2012)

Meng-Tan, Chade, *Search Inside Yourself: The Secret to Unbreakable Concentration, Complete Relaxation and Effortless Self-Control* (London: Harper Collins, 2013)

Merriam, Ida C., 'Social Welfare in the United States, 1934-1954', *Social Security Bulletin* 51.6 (June 1988)

Miller, James, *The Passion of Michel Foucault* [1993] (London: Flamingo, 1994)

Miller, James William, 'Wellness: The History and Development of a Concept', *Spektrum Freizeit* 27.1 (2005)

Miller, Timothy, 'The Roots of the 1960s Communal Revival', *American Studies* 33.2 (1992)

Mole, Noelle J., *Labor Disorders in Neoliberal Italy: Mobbing, Well-Being and the Workplace* (Indiana: Indiana University Press, 2012)

Moriarty, Liane, *Nine Perfect Strangers* [2018] (Harmondsworth: Penguin, 2019)

More, Thomas, *Utopia and Selected Epigrams*, trans. by Gerald Malsbary (CTMS Publishers: University of Dallas, 2020)

Morrison, Patt, 'Cold War LA could have been a nuclear target. One response: the fallout shelter', *Los Angeles Times* (8 March 2022)

Moses, Robert, 'Asleep at the Fiscal Crisis', *New York Times* (16 September 1975)

Murphy, Walter F., 'The Political Philosophy of Gerrard Winstanley', *The Review of Politics* 19.2 (April 1957)

National Cancer Institute, *Changes in Cigarette Related Disease Risks and Their Implications for Prevention and Control* (USA: U.S. Department of Health and Human Services, 1997)

National Travel Survey, *1972 Census of Transportation* (USA: U.S. Government Printing Office, 1974)

Navarro, Espy M. and Robert Navarro, *Self-Realization: The Est and Forum Phenomena in America* (US: Xlibris, 2002)

Neill, A.S., *Summerhill: A Radical Approach to Child Rearing* (New York: Hart, 1960)

Nelson, Alondra, *Body and Soul: The Black Panther Party and the Fight Against Medical Discrimination* (Minneapolis: University of Minnesota Press, 2011)

Neville, Richard, *Play Power* (London: Jonathan Cape, 1970)

Nicholson, Ian, 'Bearing the Soul: Paul Bindrim, Abraham Maslow and "Nude Psychotherapy"', *Journal of the History of the Behavioural Sciences* 43.4 (2007)

Nittler, Alan H., *A New Breed of Doctor* (New York: Pyramid House, 1972)

Nobbs, David, *The Reginald Perrin Omnibus* (London: Arow, 1999)

'Oakland, California', *Impact of Antirecession Assistance On 52 Governments: An Update* (USA: US General Accounting Office, 1978)

Ofshe, Richard, 'The Social Development of the Synanon Cult: The Managerial Strategy of Organizational Transformation', *Sociological Analysis*, 41. 2 (Summer 1980)

Ogilvy, James, *Many Dimensional Man: Decentralizing Self, Society and the Sacred* (Oxford: Oxford University Press, 1977)

Oglesby, Carl (ed.), *The New Left Reader* (New York: Grove Press, 1969)

Oldfield, Mike, *Changeling: The Autobiography* (London: Virgin, 2007)

Oppenheimer, Mark, 'Queen of the New Age', *The New York Times Magazine* (4 May 2008)

Oransky, Ivan, 'Obituary: Henrik L. Blum', *The Lancet* 367 (February 2006)

Ortiz, Rafael Montañez, 'Destructivism: A Manifesto' [1962], *Theories and Documents of Contemporary Art: A Sourcebook of Artists' Writings*, ed. Kristine Stiles and Peter Selz (Berkeley: University of California Press, 1998)

Orwell, George, *Nineteen Eighty-Four* [1949] (London: Penguin, 2000)

Ostrander, Sheila, and Lynn Schroeder, *Psychic Discoveries Behind the Iron Curtain* (New York: Prentice-Hall, 1970)

Page, Stephen, *Tourism Management* (London: Routledge, 2000)

Palmer, Susan, J., 'Charisma and Abdication: A Study of the Leadership of Bhagwan Shree Rajneesh', *Sociological Analysis* 49.2 (Summer 1988)

Parfrey, Adam (ed.), *Apocalypse Culture* (USA: Feral House, 1990)

Parish, David, *The 1973 – 1975 Energy Crisis and Its Impact on Transport* (London: RAC, 2009)

Parks, James (ed.), *Cultural Icons* (London: Bloomsbury, 1991)

Patrick, Ted, *Let Our Children Go!* (New York: E.P. Dutton, 1976)

Payne, Les and Tim Findley, *The Life and Death of the SLA* (New York: Ballantine, 1976)

Pendleton, Don, *The Godmakers* (New York: Pinnacle Books, 1970)

Peplau, Letitia Anne, and Daniel Perlman (eds.) *Loneliness: A Sourcebook of Current Theory, Research and Therapy* (New York: Wiley, 1982)

Perry, Lee and Glenn Perry, *Floating in Quiet Darkness: How the Floatation Tank Has Changed our Lives and is Changing the World* (Nevada: Gateways Books and Tapes, 2021)

Peter, Karl, *et al.*, 'The Dynamics of Religious Defection among Hutterites', *Journal for the Scientific Study of Religion* 21.4 (1982)

Peters, Michael A., 'Neoliberalism, Education and the Crisis of Western Capitalism', *Policy Futures in Education* 10. 2 (2012)

Piesman, Marissa and Marilee Hartley, *The Yuppie Handbook: The State-of-the-Art Handbook for Young Urban Professionals* (New York: Pocket Books, 1984)

Pirsig, Robert, M., *Zen and the Art of Motorcycle Maintenance: An Inquiry into Values* [1974] (London: Vintage, 1999)

Price, Maeve, 'The Divine Light Mission as a Social Organization', *The Sociological Review* 27.2 (1979)

Polley, Martin, *Moving the Goalposts: A History of Sport and Society in Britain since 1945* (London: Routledge, 1998)

Power, Nina, *One Dimensional Woman* (Winchester: Zero, 2009)

Purser, Ronald E., *McMindfulness: How Mindfulness Became the New Capitalist Spirituality* (London: Repeater, 2018)

Puharich, Andrija, *Uri: A Journal of the Mystery of Uri Geller* (New York: Doubleday, 1974)

Quin, Ann, *et al.*, 'Ambit Drugs and Creative Writing Competition', *Ambit* 35 (1968)

Rabinow, Paul (ed.), *Ethics: Essential Works of Foucault 1954-1984 Volume 1* (Harmondsworth: Penguin, 2000)

Ramsey, Matthew, 'Alternative Medicine in Modern France', *Medical History* 43 (1999)

Rand, Ayn, *The Fountainhead* (Indiana: Bobs-Merrill, 1943)

_____, *Atlas Shrugged* (New York: Random House, 1957)

Randall, David, 'Faking It: How to do a Reggie Perrin and get away with it', *The Independent* (20 July 2008)

Ray, Carina, 'A Troubled Experiment's Forgotten Lesson in Racial Integration, *Point Reyes Light* (15 March 2012)

Reeve, John, *Floating World: Japan in the Edo Period* (London: British Museum Press, 2006)

_____, *The Book of est* (New York: Holt, Rinehart and Winston, 1976)

Reiterman, Tim, *Raven: The Untold Story of the Rev. Jim Jones and his People* [1982] (New York: Tarcher Penguin, 2008)

Repace, J., 'Flying the Smoky Skies: Secondhand Smoke Exposure of Flight Attendants', *Tobacco Control* 13 (2004)

Reynolds, Simon, *Rip it Up and Start Again: Postpunk, 1978-1984* (London: Faber, 2005)

Rhinehart, Luke, *The Dice Man* (Great Britain: Talmy, Franklin Ltd, 1971)

Rhomberg, Chris, 'White Nativism and Urban Politics: The 1920s Ku Klux Klan in Oakland, California', *Journal of American Ethnic History* 17.2 (Winter 1998)

Richert, Lucas, *Break On Through: Radical Psychiatry and the American Counterculture* (2019)

Riley, James, *The Bad Trip: Dark Omens, New Worlds and the End of the Sixties* (London: Icon, 2019)

_____, 'Terminal Data: J.G. Ballard, Michael Moorcock and the Fiction of the Decade's End', in *The 1960s: A Decade of Modern British Fiction* ed. by Philip Tew *et al.* (London: Bloomsbury, 2018)

Rigby, Andrew, *Communes in Britain* (London: Routledge & Kegan Paul, 1974)

Robbins, Lewis C., *How to Practice Prospective Medicine* (Indiana: Methodist Hospital of Indiana, 1970)

Robbins, Thomas, and Dick Anthony, 'Deprogramming, Brainwashing and the Medicalization of Deviant Religious Groups', *Social Problems* 29.3 (February 1982)

Rodley, Chris (ed.), *Cronenberg on Cronenberg* (London: Faber, 1993)

Rodriguez, Spain, *Trashman Lives!* (USA: Fantagraphics, 1985)

Robinson, R. P., 'Until the Revolution: Analyzing the Politics, Pedagogy, and Curriculum of the Oakland Community School', *Espacio, Tiempo y Educación* 7.1 (2020)

Rogers, Carl, *On Becoming a Person: A Therapist's View of Psychotherapy* (Boston: Houghton Mifflin, 1961)

_____, *A Way of Being* (New York: Houghton Mifflin, 1980)

Roszak, Theodore, 'Youth and the Great Refusal', *The Nation* (March 1968)

_____, *The Making of a Counterculture* (USA: Anchor / Doubleday, 1969)

Rothkoff, David J., *Superclass: The Global Power Elite* (2008)

Rowan, John, *The Transpersonal: Spirituality in Psychotherapy and Counselling* (Routledge: London, 1993)

Rubin, Jerry, *Growing (Up) At Thirty-Seven* (New York: M. Evans & Co, 1976)

Rubin, Theodore, *The Angry Book* (New York: Collier, 1969)

Rudling, Odeta, 'The Cult of the Balts: Mythological Impulses and Neo-Pagan Practices in the Touristic Clubs of the Lithuanian SSR of the 1960s and 1970s', *Region* 6.1 (2017)

Ruhlmann, William, *John Lennon* (New York: Smithmark, 1993)

Said, Edward, W., *Culture and Imperialism* [1993] (London: Vintage, 1994)

Sandbrook, Dominic, *State of Emergency. The Way We Were: Britain 1970-74* (Harmondsworth: Penguin, 2011)

Sargant, William, *Battle for the Mind: A Physiology of Conversion and Brain-Washing* [1957] (London: Pan, 1961)

Sassoon, Beverly and Vidal Sassoon, *A Year of Beauty and Health* [1976] (Harmondsworth: Penguin, 1977)

Sawyer, Miranda, 'A Temple to Athena', *Guardian* (15 November 2009)

Schulman, Bruce J., and Julian E. Zelizer, *Rightward Bound: Making America Conservative in the 1970s* (Cambridge: Harvard University Press, 2008)

Seale, Bobby, 'You Can't Drop Out of the System', *Ann Arbor Sun* (23 April 1973)

Seaman, Fred, *The Last Days of John Lennon: A Personal Memoir* (New York: Random House, 1992)

Segal, Erich, *Love Story* [1970] (London: Hodder & Stoughton, 2013)

Segreto, Luciano, *et al.*, (eds.), *Europe at the Seaside: The Economic History of Mass Tourism in the Mediterranean*, (New York: Berghan, 2009)

Seldon, Anthony and Alan Martin, *The Positive and Mindful University* (Oxford: HEPI, Occasional Paper 18)

Seltzer, David, *The Omen* (New York: Signet, 1976)

Senate Select Committee on Intelligence, *The Senate Intelligence Committee Report on Torture* (New York: Melville House, 2014)

Senk, Pascale, 'A l'Espace du possible: vacances en group avec soi-même', *Psychologies* (5 February 2009)

Seth, Vikas, *et al.*, 'Osho Dynamic Meditation's Effect on Serum Cortisol Level, *Journal of Clinical and Diagnostic Research* 10.11 (November 2016)

'Sgt. Pepper', 'SLA's Fahizah Just Naïve', *Berkely Barb* 19.3 (February 1974)

Shatz, Adam, 'Desire Was Everywhere', *London Review of Books* 32.4 (16 December 2010)

Shilts, Randy, *And the Band Played On: Politics, People and the Aids Epidemic* [1987] (London: Souvenir Press, 2011)

Shunyo, Ma Prem, *Diamond Days with Osho* (India: Rebel Publishing, 1992)

Siegel, Dan, 'Justice for Tyrone Guyton', *Crime and Social Justice* 2 (Fall – Winter 1974)

Sim, Stuart (ed.), *The Icon Critical Dictionary of Postmodern Thought* (Cambridge: Icon, 1998)

Singer, Loren, *The Parallax View* (New York: Doubleday, 1970)

Sismondo, Christine, 'Gurus Gone Bad: Is it time for reform in the self-help and wellness industry?', *Toronto Star* (21 September 2020)

Small, Melvin, *The Presidency of Richard Nixon* (USA: University of Kansas Press, 1999)

Smith, Glenn, *et al.*, 'Treatments of Homosexuality in Britain since the 1950s – An Oral History: The Experience of Patients', *The British Medical Journal* 429 (21 February 2004)

Southwell, David and Sean Twist, *Conspiracy Theories* (Great Britain: Carleton, 1999)

Spencer, John Palmer, *In the Crossfire: Marcus Foster and the Troubled History of American School Reform* (Philadelphia: University of Pennsylvania Press, 2012)

Spufford, Francis, 'Love that Bird', *London Review of Books* 24.11 (6 June 2002)

Stansill, Peter and David Zane Mariowitz, *BAMN (By Any Means Necessary): Outlaw Graphics and Ephemera* (Harmondsworth: Penguin, 1971)

Starks, Richard, *David Cronenberg's The Brood* (London: Granada, 1979)

Storey, John (ed.), *Cultural Theory and Popular Culture: A Reader*

Storr, Will, *Selfie: How We Became So Self-Obsessed and What It's Doing to Us* (USA: Overlook Press, 2018)

Strachan, Françoise (ed.), *Aquarian Guide to Occult, Mystical, Religious, Magical, London and Around* (Great Britain: Aquarian Press, 1970)

Steinem, Gloria, 'After Black Power, Women's Liberation', *New York* (April 1969)

Stiles, Kristine (ed.), *Correspondence Course: An Epistolary History of Carolee Schneemann and her Circle* (USA: Duke University Press, 2010)

Streitfeld, David, 'The Invisible Man', *The Washington Post* (13 February 1994)

Strombeck, Andrew, 'The Post-Fordist Motorcycle: Rachel Kushner's *The Flamethrowers* and the 1970s Crisis in Fordist Capitalism', *Contemporary Literature* 56.3 (Fall 2015)

Suri, Jeremi, 'The Rise and Fall of an International Counterculture, 1960-1975', *The American Historical Review* 114.1 (Feburary 2009)

Surís, Alina, 'The Evolution of the Classification of Psychiatric Disorders', *Behavioural Science*, 6.1 (January 2016)

Syman, Stefanie, *The Subtle Body: The Story of Yoga in America* (New York: Farrar, Straus and Giroux, 2010)

Tait, Theo, 'Gorilla with a Mobile Phone', *London Review of Books* 29.3 (9 February 2006)

Taylor, Michael, 'Forgotten Footnote: Before Hearst, SLA Killed Educator', *San Francisco Chronicle* (14 November 2002)

'Toko' *et al.*, 'Toko, Fahizah, Cinque Speak', *Berkeley Barb* 19.3 (April 1974)

Ten Great Birth Stories of the Buddha, The: The Mahanipata of the Jatakatthavanonoana trans. by Naomi Appleton and Sarah Shaw (USA: University of Washington Press, 2016)

Terry, Paul, E., 'The Wellness Movement', *The Art of Health Promotion* (May / June 2015)

Terry, Paul, E., and Donald B. Ardell, 'An Interview with Donald B. Ardell', *The Art of Health Promotion* (November / December 2015)

Tew, Philip, James Riley and Melanie Seddon (eds.), *The 1960s: A Decade of Modern British Fiction* (London: Bloomsbury, 2018)

Thomas, Kenn and David Hatcher Childress, *Inside the Gemstone File* (USA: Adventures Unlimited, 1999)

Thomas, Martin, *The Hand of Cain* (New York: Magnum, 1966)

Thompson, Jennifer, L., 'Eves Drop In: Out of Despair', *Berkeley Barb* 19.13 (April 1974)

_____, 'Reveal Esalen Sexism', *Berkeley Barb* 19.3 (Feburary 1974)

Toffler, Alvin, *Future Shock* (Great Britain: The Bodley Head, 1970)

Tomkins, Calvin, 'Profiles: New Paradigms', *The New Yorker* (January 1976)

Toobin, Jeffrey, *American Heiress: The Kidnapping, Crimes and Trial of Patty Hearst* (New York: Doubleday, 2017)

Townsend, Peter, *Poverty in the United Kingdom* (Berkeley: University of California Press, 1979)

Travis, John, *The Wellness Index* (Marin County: Wellness Resource Center, 1975)

_____, *The Wellness Workbook for Health Professionals* (Marin County: Wellness Resource Center, 1977)

Travis, John and Regina Sara Ryan, *The Wellness Workbook* [1981] (Berkeley: Ten Speed Press, 1988)

Turner, John, *et al.*, 'The History of Mental Health Services in Modern England: Practitioner Memories and the Direction of Future Research', *Medical History* 59.4 (2015)

Turner, Wallace, 'Jail Terms Deplete Ranks of Hell's Angels', *The New York Times* (18 March 1973)

Turk, Victoria, 'Goop on Psychedelics isn't bad, it's just boring' *Wired* (January 2020)

Tyler, Imogen, 'From "The Me Decade" to "The Me Millennium": The Cultural History of Narcissism', *International Journal of Cultural Studies* 10. 3 (2007)

Urban, Hugh B., *Zorba the Buddha: Sex, Spirituality and Capitalism in the Global Osho Movement* (Berkeley: University of California Press, 2016)

Urry, John, *The Tourist Gaze* (London: Sage, 2002)

Useem, Jerry, 'Bring Back the Nervous Breakdown', *The Atlantic* (March 2021)

Velikovsky, Immanuel, *Worlds in Collision* (New York: Macmillan, 1950)

Vernon, Jack, *Inside the Black Room: Studies in Sensory Deprivation* [1963] (Harmondsworth: Penguin, 1966)

Virgil, *The Aeneid*, trans. by W.F. Jackson Knight (Harmondsworth: Penguin, 1988)

Vittersø, Joar, (ed.), *Handbook of Eudaimonic Well-Being* (Switzerland: Springer, 2016)

Watts, Alan, *Out of Your Mind: Tricksters, Interdependence and the Cosmic Game of Hide-and-Seek* (USA: Souvenir Press, 2018)

Webster, Katharine, 'The Case Against Swami Rama of the Himalayas', *Yoga Journal* (November – December 1990)

Welch, Lew, 'A Moving Target is Hard to Hit' (San Francisco: Communication Company, 1967)

Wells, H.G., *The Time Machine: An Invention* (New York: Henry Holt, 1895)

Wheeler, Joanne, *et al.*, *Health and Wellbeing in Homes* (London: UK Green Building Council, 2016)

Whitmer Peter O., and Bruce VanWyngarden, *Aquarius Revisited* (New York: Citadel, 1991)

Wilcox, Deborah, A., and John Travis, 'How Culture Interacts with the Concept of Wellness: The Role Wellness Plays in a Global Environment', *The Art of Health Promotion* (May – June 2015)

Wilkinson, Amber, 'Retro Rainbow', *Eye For Film* (May 2011)

Wolfe, Tom, 'The "Me" Decade and the Third Great Awakening', *New York* (August 1976)

Women's Press Collective, The, *The Women's Gun Pamphlet: A Primer on Handguns* (Oakland: Women's Press Collective, 1975)

Wood, Linda Sargent, 'Contact, Encounter, and Exchange at Esalen: A Window onto Late Twentieth-Century American Spirituality', *Pacific Historical Review* 77.3 (August 2008)

Woolf, Virginia, *The Voyage Out* [1915] (New York: Dover, 2006)

Willetts, Paul, *Members Only: The Life and Times of Paul Raymond* (London: Serpent's Tail, 2010)

Williams, Charlie, 'On "Modified Human Agents": John Lilly and the Paranoid Style in American Neuroscience', *History of the Human Sciences* 32.5 (2019)

Williams, Roger J., *You Are Extraordinary* (New York: Random House, 1967)

Wilson, Bryan and Jamie Cresswell (eds.,), *New Religious Movements: Challenge and Response* (London: Routledge, 2012)

Wilson, Colin, *The Black Room* (London: Weidenfeld & Nicolson, 1971)

Wilson, Harold, *The New Britain: Labour's Plan. Selected Speeches 1964* (Harmondsworth: Penguin, 1964)

Wilson, Paul, *The Little Book of Calm* (Harmondsworth: Penguin, 1996)

Wiseman, Thomas, *The Romantic Englishwoman* [1971] (Great Britain: Granada, 1973)

Wright, Katie, 'Theorizing Therapeutic Culture: Past Influences, Future Directions', *Journal of Sociology* 44.4 (2008)

Wright, Patrick, *The Sea View Has Me Again: Uwe Johnson in Sheerness* (London: Repeater, 2020)

Wright, Pearce, 'Sir Douglas Black', *The Lancet* 360.9339 (5 October 2002)

Wylie, Timothy, *Dolphins, Extraterrestrials, Angels: Adventures Among Spiritual Intelligences* (USA: Bozon Enterprises, 1984)

Yeung, Ophelia and Katherine Johnston, *The Global Wellness Industry and its Implications for Asia's Development* (Philippines: ADB, 2018)

Young, Courtenay, 'The History and Development of Body-Psychotherapy: European Diversity', *Body Movement and Dance in Psychotherapy* (April 2010)

Young, David, C., 'Mens Sana in Corpore Sano? Body and Mind in Ancient Greece', *The International Journal of the History of Sport* 22.1 (January 2005)

Yonge, Charlotte, 'To Whom it May Concern', *International Times* 1.28 (April 1968)

Zelazny, Roger, *The Dream Master* [1966] (London: Panther, 1968)

Žižek, Slavoj, *Living in the End Times* (London: Verso, 2011)

_____, *Pandemic!: COVID-19 Shakes the World* (Cambridge: Polity, 2020)

II. Films and Television

2001: A Space Odyssey (Stanley Kubrick, UK / US, 1968)

60 Minutes (Don Hewitt, US, 1979)

Abigail's Party (Mike Leigh, UK, 1977)

A Bigger Splash (Jack Hazan, US, 1973)

Altered States (Ken Russell, US, 1980)

Alien (Ridley Scott, US, 1979)

Ashram (Wolfgang Dobrowolny, West Germany, 1979)

Astrologer, The (James Glickenhaus, US, 1975)

Asylum of Satan (William Girdler, US, 1972)

Bachelor Party (Neal Isreal, US, 1984)

Beyond the Black Rainbow (Panos Cosmatos, US, 2010)

Bikram: Yogi, Guru, Predator (Eva Orner, US, 2019)

Bob & Carol & Ted & Alice (Paul Mazursky, US, 1969)

Body Snatchers (Abel Ferrara, US, 1993)

Brainstorm (Douglas Trumbull, US, 1983)

Brood, The (David Cronenberg, Canada, 1979)

Century of the Self, The (Adam Curtis, UK, 2002)

Circle of Power (Bobby Roth, US, 1981)

Crimes of the Future (David Cronenberg, Canada, 1970)

Coma (Michael Crichton, USA, 1978)

Computer Networks (Peter Chvany, US, 1972)

Cult Explosion, The (Brian Barkley, US, 1980)

Diamonds Are Forever (Guy Hamilton, US, 1971)

Dreams (Giles Smith, UK, 2022)

Dreamscape (Joseph Ruben, US, 1984)

Fall and Rise of Reginald Perrin, The (Gareth Gwenlan, UK, 1976)

Good Life, The (John Howard Davies, UK, 1975-78)

Goop Lab, The (Yamit Shimonovitz, US, 2020)

Heavy Traffic (Ralph Bakshi, US, 1973)

Holiday on the Buses (Bryan Izzard, UK, 1973)

Holy Mountain, The (Alejandro Jodorowsky, Mexico/US, 1973)

Holy Smoke! (Jane Campion, Australia-US, 1999)

I Drink Your Blood (David Durston, US, 1970)

I Want It All Now (Joseph DeCola, US, 1978)

Interiors (Woody Allen, US, 1978)

Invasion, The (Oliver Hirschbiegel, US, 2007)

Invasion of the Body Snatchers (Don Siegel, US, 1956)

Invasion of the Body Snatchers (Philip Kaufman, US, 1978)

Ipcress File, The (Sidney J. Furie, UK, 1963)

Jane Fonda's Workout (Sid Galanty, US, 1982)

Long Good Friday, The (John Mackenzie, UK, 1980)

Love Story (Arthur Hiller, US, 1970)

Manchurian Candidate, The (John Frankenheimer, US, 1962)

Mad Max (George Miller, Australia, 1979)

Mad Men (Matthew Weiner, US, 2007- 15)

Magic of Oil Painting, The (Harry Ratner, US, 1974-1982)

Magnum Force (Ted Post, US, 1973)

Man Who Would Be King, The (John Huston, US/UK, 1975)

Mind Benders, The (Basil Dearden, UK, 1963)

Moonstone, The (Paddy Russell, UK, 1972)

Nine Perfect Strangers (Jonathan Levine, US, 2021)

Our Friends in the North (Simon Cellan Jones, Pedr James, Stuart Urban, UK, 1996)

Parallax View, The (Alan J. Pakula, US, 1974)

Persuaders!, The (Basil Dearden, UK, 1971)

Police Academy (Hugh Wilson, US, 1984)

Rabid (David Cronenberg, US/Canada, 1976)

Radio On (Chris Petit, UK/Germany, 1979)

Serial (Bill Persky, US, 1980)

Slaves in Paradise (Madonna Benjamin, UK, 1999)

Sleepwalker (Hylas Film, US, 2012)

Shampoo (Hal Ashby, US, 1975)

Shivers (David Cronenberg, Canada, 1975)

Solaris (Andrei Tarkovsky, Russia, 1972)

Spy Who Died Twice, The (Keely Winstone, UK, 2022)

Stepford Wives, The (Bryan Forbes, US, 1975)

Stereo (David Cronenberg, Canada, 1969)

Suspiria (Dario Argento, Italy, 1977)

Swimmer, The (Fred and Eleanor Perry, US, 1968)

Taxi Driver (Martin Scorsese, US, 1976)

This Old House (Russell Morash, 1979)

THX1138 (George Lucas, US, 1971)

Tribe of the Sun (Alan Sidi, UK, 1972)

To the Manor Born (Gareth Gwenlan, UK, 1979-81)

Velvet Goldmine (Todd Haynes, USA, 1998)

Wall Street (Oliver Stone, US, 1987)

What on Earth Is Wellness? (Posy Dixon, UK, 2016)

What We Do in the Shadows (Yana Gorskaya, US, 2021)
Wild Angels, The (Roger Corman, US, 1966)
Wild Wild Country (Maclain Way, Chapman Way, US, 2018)

III. Albums and Recordings

Beach Boys, The, *Summer Days (And Summer Nights!!)* (Capitol, 1965)
_____, *Pet Sounds* (Capitol, 1966)
Beatles, The, *The Beatles* (Apple, 1968)
Denver, John, *Rhymes & Reasons* (RCA, 1969)
_____, *Poems, Prayers & Promises* (RCA, 1971)
_____, *Windsong* (RCA, 1975)
Host, The, *Esalen Lectures* (Touch Sensitive, 2015)
John, Elton, 'Sick City' (MCA Records, 1974)
Konicov, Barrie, *Psychic Healing* (Potentials Unlimited, 1978)
Lennon, John and Yoko Ono, *Unfinished Music 1: Two Virgins* (Apple, 1968)
Lennon, John, *John Lennon/Plastic Ono Band* (Apple, 1970)
_____, *Mind Games* (Apple, 1973)
Stroud, Matt, *Guru: The Dark Side of Enlightenment* (US: Wondery, 2020)
Manson, Charles, *LIE: The Love and Terror Cult* (Awareness Records, 1970)
Moon Duo, *Circles* (Sacred Bones Records, 2012)
Ono, Yoko, *Yoko Ono/Plastic Ono Band* (Apple, 1970)
Primal Scream, *Screamadelica* (Creation Records, 1991)
Rundgren, Todd, *Todd Rundgren's Utopia* (Bearsville, 1974)
Watts, Alan, *Out of Your Mind: Essential Listening from the Alan Watts Audio Archives* (Sounds True, 2004)
Williams, Andy, '(Where Do I Begin?) Love Story' (Columbia Records, 1970)
William Penn Fyve, 'Swami' (Thunderbird, 1966)

IV. Online Sources

Aviary, The, *The Chambers Tape* (2015) http://youtube.com/watch?v=fsZZGwiXdSo
Alioto, Daisy, 'Infinity Jest: How the Infinity Pool Became a Social Media Status Symbol', *The Outline* (24 March 2018) https://theoutline.com/post/3872/infinity-pools?utm_source=contributor_pages
Baker, Rob, 'Extraordinary Pictures of "Hippiedilly" on Hyde Park Corner, 1969' (2019) https://flashbak.com/the-rise-and-fall-of-hippiedilly-in-1969-9044/
Bonnar, Myles and Steve Brocklehurst, 'The Scot Who Was the Sex Guru's Bodyguard', *BBC Scotland* (4 June 2018) hhtp://www.bbc.com/news/uk-scotland-44300915

Blei, Daniela, 'The False Promises of Wellness Culture', *JSTOR Daily* (January 2017) http://daily.jstor.org/the-false-promises-of-wellness-culture/

Caldwell, Stratton F., 'The Human Potential Movement: Body / Movement / Non-Verbal Experiencing' (1975) https://files.eric.ed.gov/fulltext/ED110423.pdf

Chapman, Adrian, 'R. D. Laing in the USA: His Message to the Smartphone-Obsessed 21st Century' (November 2019) https://universityofglasgowlibrary.wordpress.com/2019/11/08/r-d-laing-in-the-usa-1972-and-his-message-to-the-smartphone-obsessed-21st-century/

Choi, Connie H., 'Educate to Liberate: Black Panther Liberation Schools', The Studio Museum in Harlem http://studiomuseum.org/article/educate-liberate-black-panther-liberation-schools

Cumming, Gregory Garth, *The End of an Era: The Rise of the Symbionese Liberation Army and Fall of the New Left* (California: UC Riverside, 2010) https://escholarship.org/uc/item/8tw2935x

Flint, David, 'Dynamic Tension: The Charles Atlas Story', *The Reprobate* (18 June 2018) https://reprobatepress.com/2018/06/18/dynamic-tension-the-charles-atlas-story/

Gimson, Andrew, 'How Macmillan built 300,000 Houses a Year', *ConservativeHome* (17 October 2013) http://www.conservativehome.com/how-macmillan-built-300000-houses-a-year/

Göessl, Martin J., 'The Otto Mühl Commune: Self-Expression, Common Property and Free Sexuality' http://researchgate.net/publication/328686091_The_Otto_Mühl_Commune_self_expression_common_property_and_free_sexuality/

Harris, Aisha, 'The History of Self-Care', *Slate* (April 2017) http://slate.com/articles/arts/culturebox/2017/04/the_history_of_self-care.html

Hegberg, Ema, 'The Myth of Wellness', *Medium* (April 2019) http://medium.com/@emahegberg/the-myth-of-wellness-4eb60b43c5e2

Hettler, Bill, 'The Past of Wellness' (1998) https://hettler.com//History/hettler.htm

Holmes, Marcia, 'Edward Hunter and the Origins of Brainwashing', *Hidden Persuaders* (26 May 2017). http://www.bbk.ac.uk/hiddenpersuaders/blog/hunter-origins-of-brainwashing/

Hopkins, Kathryn, 'Goop Cruise is Cancelled Due to the Coronavirus', *WWD* (24 June 2020) https://wwd.com/feature/goop-cruise-is-cancelled-due-to-the-coronavirus-1203659759/

Lucia, Amanda, 'Hinduism in America', *Oxford Research Encyclopedia of Religion* (2017) https: //oxfordre.com/religion/view/10.1093/acrefore/9780199340378.001.0001/acrefore-9780199340378-e-436

Kevin Lyons, 'Altered States (1980)', The EOFFTV Review (September 2019) https://eofftvreview.wordpress.com/2019/09/08/altered-states-1980/

Malleret, Thierry, 'The "Wellness Divide" between Low and High-Income Countries Will Further Sharpen' (June 2022) https://globalwellnessinstitute.org/global-wellness-institute-blog/2022/06/14/the-wellness-divide-between-low-and-high-income-countries-will-further-sharpen/

Maxin, Tyler, 'Children of Synanon + The Child of the Future: How Might He Learn' (19 April 2022) http://screenslate.com/articles/children-synanon-child-future-how-might-he-learn

McFadden, Cyra and Debra Schwartz, 'The Mill Valley Oral History Programme' https://millvalley.pastperfectonline.com/archive/1DDF3 E40-ADCC-46FE-990F-711023561201

Naftulin, Julia, 'Goop threw a cruise and no Goopies came', The Insider (November 2021) www.insider.com/goop-at-sea-gwyneth-paltrow-first-cruise-2021-11

Nhất Hạnh, Thích, 'History of Engaged Buddhism', Mindfulness Bell 49 (October 2008) http://parallax.org/mindfulnessbell/article/dharma-tak-history-of-engaged-buddhism/

Offenhartz, Jake, 'How Bankers & Technocrats Used the 1975 Fiscal Crisis to Permanently Reshape NYC', Gothamist (21 April 2017) http://gothamist.com/arts-entertainment/how-bankers-technocrats-used-the-1975-fiscal-crisis-to-permanently-reshape-nyc

Orthofer, M.A., 'The Hospital Ship by Martin Bax' www.complete-review.com/reviews/gbx/baxm.htm

Parrott, James, 'Fiscal Purgatory in New York', The American Prospect (9 August 2017) http://prospect.org/labor/fiscal-purgatory-new-york/

Pendle, George, 'Shaved Heads, Snipped Tubes, Imperial Marines and Dope Fiends: The Fall and Rise and Fall of Chuck Dederich and Synanon', Cabinet 48 (Winter 2012-2013) https://www.cabinetmagazine.org/issues/48/pendle.php

Perry, Lee and Glenn Perry, 'In Pursuit of Nothing' https://www.youtube.com/watch?v=VdNjPZR2Edw

Phelan, John, 'The Return of the Misery Index', American Experiment (January 2022) https://www.americanexperiment.org/the-return-of-the-misery-index/

Rawle, Sid, Rick Mayes and Jeremy Sandford, King of the Hippies: Notes for an Alternative History of Britain, 1960-2000 (unpublished) http://www.jeremysandford.org.uk/jsarchive/sid-intro.html

Rawle, Sid, 'Interview with Sid Rawle (Part Three): Sid, John Lennon and Revolution' (2007) https://www.youtube.com/watch?v=azZm1P2FQ9E

Reft, Ryan, 'A Dive into the Deep End: The Importance of Swimming Pools in Southern California', *Tropics of Meta* (June 2014) https://tropicsofmeta.com/2014/06/30/a-dive-into-the-deep-end-the-importance-of-the-swimming-pool-in-southern-california/

Ryan, Michael and RTÉ, 'Westport Residents Reject Hippie Way of Life' https://www.rte.ie/archives/2016/0107/758290-hippies-in-county-mayo/

Storr, Will, 'The Birth of the Narcissism Revolution', *Quillette* (16 June 2018) https://quillette.com/2018/06/16/the-birth-of-the-narcissism-revolution/

Symes, Benjamin, 'Marshall McLuhan's 'Global Village'' (26 May 1995) https://aber.ac.uk/education/Undergrad/ED10510/ben-mcl.html

Thibert, Keshler, 'Remembering Marcus Foster: Role Model and Mentor to Philly's Broken Schools', *Hidden City* (23 June 2023) http://hiddencityphila.org/2023/06/remembering-marcus-foster-role-modle-and-mentor-to-phillys-broken-schools/

Travis, John, Donald Ardell and Peter Greenberg, 'A Keynote Interview with Jack Travis and Don Ardell' (2014) https://www.youtube.com/watch?v=Q1SqpFnoRtw

Travis, John, 'Dr. Jack Travis on Wellness' (2014) https://www.youtube.com/watch?v=7fTHygqEAeI

_____, 'How Has the Perception of Health and Wellness Changed?' (2017) https://www.youtube.com/watch?v=KXAPgz_OdRo

_____, 'Marin Valley Biography Night: Jack Travis' (2020) https://www.youtube.com/watch?v=v4Puj2azDCE

Thompson, Jessica, 'The Vagina Missing from Space', *Era Magazine* (December 2020) https://era-magazine.com/2020/12/21/the-vagina-missing-from-space/

Van Laarhoven, Kasper, 'How the Hare Krishna Movement Started 51 Years Ago in the East Village', *Bedford+Bowery* (17 June 2017) http://bedfordandbowery.com/2017/06/how-the-hare-krishna-movement-started-51-years-ago-in-the-east-village/

Vyas, Karishma, 'Gurus Gone Bad in India', *Al Jazeera* (27 August 2018) http://www.aljazeera.com/features/2018/8/27/gurus-gone-bad-in-india

Wenzell, Nicolette, 'City of Swimming Pools', *Palm Springs Life* (November 2014) https://www.palmspringslife.com/explore-palm-springs-city-of-swimming-pools/

Williams, Heathcote, 'The Inside Story of Ruff Tuff Creem Puff, The Only Estate Agency for Squatters' (1978). https://www.pasttense. co.uk/2021/02/23/the-squatters-estate-agency-ruff-tuff-creem-puff/

Worthington, Andy, 'RIP Sid Rawle, Land Reformer, Free Festival Pioneer, Stonehenge Stalwart' (September 2010) http://www. andyworthington.co.uk/2010/09/08/rip-sid-rawle-land-reformer-f ree-festival-pioneer-stonehenge-stalwart/

Other useful websites

www.aoghs.org
www.archives.gov
www.archivesmuehl.org
www.archives-nypl.org
www.artic.edu
www.atlasobscura.com
www.beatbooks.com
www.britishpoliticalspeech.org
www.celebritycruises.com
www.computerhistory.org
www.depts.washington.edu
www.dorinish.com
www.dropcitydoc.com
www.erhardseminarstraining.com
www.eutopism.co.uk
www.freedomarchive.org
www.globalwellnessinstitute.org
www.goodspaguide.co.uk
www.goop.com
www.headspace.com.
www.history.blog.gov.uk
www.johnlautner.org
www.lesbianpoetryarchive.org
www.marxists.org
www.nasa.gov
www.nationalarchives.gov.uk
www.newlanark.org
www.npg.org.uk
www.oaklandplanninghistory.weebly.com
www.OED.com
www.paulineroseclance.com
www.pfizer.com

www.potentialsunlimited.com
www.primaltherapy.net
www.rte.ie
www.samadhitank.com
www.sathyasaibaba.wordpress.com
www.scohealth.co.uk
www.sri.com
www.thepulp.net
www.thriveglobal.com
www.voicesofeastanglia.com
www.wellandgood.com
www.wellco.co.uk
www.who.int
www.whoownsengland.org
www.youtube.com

Acknowledgements

No one writes a book alone, no matter how hermetic the circumstances of its composition.

I'm enormously grateful to have had the support of a brilliant team for the duration of this retreat. First, I would like to thank Donald Winchester, agent extraordinaire, for his enthusiasm and guidance. Donald saw the potential of this project in its very early stages and did great work in bringing it into full actualisation. Second, many thanks are due to everyone at Icon Books. *Well Beings* would not have got this far were it not for Keira Jamieson, Sophie Lazar and Duncan Heath. Connor Stait has been a brilliant editor: enthusiastic, on-point and greatly knowledgeable. He is exactly the kind of editor an author needs, not least because of his patience and understanding. Alex Bennett did an outstanding job at the copy-editing stage and Anna Morrison once again worked her magic on the cover.

I have had the great pleasure of rehearsing some of the ideas in *Well Beings* with many friends and colleagues, among them Judith Noble, Ethan Pennell, Dominic Shepherd, Rod Mengham and Phil Tew. Very special thanks in this regard must go to Yvonne Salmon and Douglas Field. They saw this project in draft form and very generously offered the benefit of their enormous expertise in matters of literature, cultural studies and alternative health. My fellow travellers at the Inner Space Exploration Unit provided an extremely stimulating and productive forum for the discussion of 'work-in-progress'.

Girton College is a great place to work and write and I happily join the chorus of many other voices in thanking the staff of the College, Faculty and University Libraries for their professionalism, particularly during the strange and unprecedented days of lockdown. The Cambridge Centre for Teaching and Learning provided an invaluable insight into the operation of workplace mindfulness. A writing week at the Centre for Research in the Arts, Social Sciences and Humanities (CRASSH), University of Cambridge, offered some vital time away from it all at a crucial stage. My thanks to Joanna Page, Esther Lamb at all the team at CRASSH for being so hospitable.

On the home front, I would like to thank Charlotte, Simon, Jonny and Eden for their unfailing support. Mere thanks are simply not enough for Mum and Dad, who have always been there and to whom I owe everything and more. There could be no better training for a project like this than to grow up in a house where *Zen and the Art of Motorcycle Maintenance*, *A Year of Beauty and Health* and many others could be found on the bookshelves.

Finally, I would like to dedicate *Well Beings* to the memory of my grandmother, Vera Riley. There are many things I could say but, for now, one brief recall will suffice. She used to run an antique shop where, as children, my sister and I would go to sit out the afternoons. Hanging on the wall, high above all her other treasures, radiating with kitsch magnificence, was a copy of Stephen Pearson's 'Wings of Love'. Once seen, it was not easily forgotten, and no doubt some of the deeper seeds for *Well Beings* were planted at that point of first exposure. I'm glad that by writing about it now, the memory of the painting has remained fresh and vivid. I would not want it to fade because it's become a valuable link to the past. Back in time, sitting with my grandmother once again and talking with her about all kinds of weird and wonderful things – yes, that is the good place.

Index